"[The Russian people honor Ivan] as the celebrated source of our nation's strength . . .; they have . . . forgotten the name of torturer given him by his contemporaries, and among the dark rumors of Ivan's cruelty now only call him formidable."

— *N. M. Karamzin*

The Reign of
Ivan the Terrible

The Reign of
Ivan the Terrible

BY
N. M. Karamzin

Translated by
Geoff Baldwin

Nast, de Brutus & Shortt
Portola Valley, California

Copyright 2014 by Geoff Baldwin

All rights reserved. No part of this book may be reproduced or utilized in any form or by any means, electronic or mechanical, including photocopying, recording, or by any information storage and retrieval system, without permission in writing from the publisher.

Nast, de Brutus and Shortt
Portola Valley, California
www.nastdebrutusandshortt.com

Book Design and Production by

Day'sEye Press and Studios
PO Box 628
El Granada, CA 94018
www.dayseyepressandstudios.com

Cover design copyright 2014 by Diane Lee Moomey

ISBN: 978-0-9886986-1-1

Printed in the United States of America

GENERAL TABLE OF CONTENTS

Translator's Introduction . . . . *viii*
Genealogy . . . . *xi*
Illustrations . . . . *xii*
Karamzin's Table of Contents . . . . *xxix*
Chapter I *1*
   Regency of the Mother of Grand Prince and Tsar Ivan IV Vasilievich II, [Ivan the Terrible] 1533 - 1538
Chapter II *29*
   Young Ivan and the Boyar Duma, 1538 - 1547
Chapter III *57*
   Ivan Crowned Tsar, 1546 - 1552
Chapter IV *91*
   The Conquest of Kazan, 1552
Chapter V *135*
   Death of Ivan's First Wife, 1552 - 1560
Chapter VI *209*
   Ivan Changes For the Worse, 1560 - 1564
Chapter VII *241*
   Oprichnina Established, 1563 - 1569
Chapter VIII *297*
   Severe Opression, 1569 - 1572
Chapter IX *341*
   Oprichnina Abolished, 1572 - 1577
Chapter X *385*
   War with Poland, 1577 - 1582
Chapter XI *447*
   Death of Ivan, 1582 - 1584
Glossary *001*
Gazetteer *003*
Maps *011-015*
About the Author and Translator *016*
Index *017*

Translator's Introduction

The Reign of Ivan the Terrible (and the previously published *The Reign of Boris Godunov*) are spin-offs from a project now nearing completion: to translate and publish the entirety of N. M. Karamzin's classic 12-volume *History of the Russian State* into English, something that has not been done before. The intended reader is that endangered mythical beast, the intelligent layman. *The Reign* comprises a direct translation of volume VIII and of all but chapter 6 of volume IX of Karamzin's *History*.

Remarks on style:

Karamzin's lengthy paragraphs have been broken up, but his original structure has been indicated by a large initial capital to facilitate matching up the translation with the original Russian. I have also broken up his lengthy run-on sentences and have de-referenced pronouns, always striving for readability, clarity and accuracy.

His quotations are not usually verbatim. They are more often renderings of the original material into a style of Russian that would have seemed old-fashioned, but comprehensible, to an educated Russian two centuries back.

He occasionally interpolates a comment into the midst of a quotation. These I have enclosed in braces. My own comments and annotations are enclosed in brackets.

Karamzin only occasionally uses italics for emphasis: more often he is directly quoting a peculiar archaic locution found in his source.

He is very free in the use of exclamation points. Most of these I have suppressed, lest his prose sound like a teenage girl's diary.

Occasionally Karamzin will briefly switch to present tense in order to pontificate.

NOTES

The Illustrations, Karamzin's Table of Contents and the Chapters are from the original publication. All else is new material.

All dates are Old Style (Julian calendar).

REFERENCES:

There are many biographies of Ivan. Those mentioned here are by the same authors I cited in the introduction to **The Reign of Boris Godunov**: they provide a wide range of opinion. Each of them provides unique insights into Ivan and his reign.

There appears to be considerably disagreement as to just how crazy Ivan was, but this turns out to be more a question of how one chooses to define insanity, an issue that is still a matter of contention in our own day. There is more agreement about his deeds and motivations. Richard Hellie says, "From the available evidence it is reasonable to conclude that Ivan was a classic paranoid." Sergei F. Platonov, other the other hand, emphasizes his rational behavior: "However one judges his personal conduct, Ivan, as a statesman and politician, remains a distinguished figure."

Ivan the Terrible: Life of Ivan IV of Russia by Stephen Graham. Archon Books, Hamden CT, 1968. A vivid and imaginative depiction of Ivan and his times. Makes good use of English documents unavailable to Karamzin. First published in 1933.

Ivan the Terrible by Ian Grey. Lippincott, New York, 1964. A sympathetic and more modern biography.

Исторія Государства Россійскаго [by] **Н. М. Карамзинъ**. St. Petersburg, 1892. Karamzin's account is based on more original research and is certainly more entertaining than the others': he knows how to tell a story. Karamzin is much more condemnatory of Ivan's behavior than the other authors – this reflects his Russian Orthodox moral outlook.

Ivan the Terrible: First Tsar of Russia by Isabel de Madariaga. Yale University Press, New Haven, 2005. A very thorough, cautious academic biography. Has become the standard reference for Ivan.

Ivan the Terrible by Sergei F. Platonov. Leningrad, 1923. (English translation published by Academic International Press, Gulf Breeze FL, 1974.) Platonov's history deals less with Ivan's personality and more with governance. Excellent introductory essay by Richard Hellie. The endnotes give extensive and useful definitions of the administrative terminology of this period of Russian history.

introduction

IVAN'S LINEAGE

GRAND PRINCE IVAN III VASILIEVICH — SOFIYA PALEOLOG
(IVAN THE GREAT)
1440 1462 1505

GRAND PRINCE VASILII III IVANOVICH — ELENA GLINSKAYA
1479 1505 1533

TSAR IVAN IV VASILIEVICH — ANASTASIYA ROMANOVNA
(IVAN THE TERRIBLE)
1530 1533 1584

IVAN IVANOVICH
1554 1581

TSAR THEODOR I IVANOVICH
1557 1584 1598

NOTE: MIDDLE DATE IS THE DATE OF ACCESSION TO THE THRONE

The Reign of Ivan the Terrible

FIGURE 1

DRESS OF THE RUSSIAN BOYARS and their ladies in the 16th and 17th centuries. On the left: a young boyar in a rich caftan with a hat of sable throats. Next to him is a lady in a rich housedress, padded jacket and a tall kika with a veil around it. In the center: an elderly boyar, also with a tall hat, in a ferez with tall kozyr (high-standing collar); in his hand he holds a cane. On the right: two dignitaries (perhaps okolnichie or Duma boyars?) in caftans, above which they wear okhabni with slits and folding sleeves; fastened to the okhabni are kozyri with turn-down collars. Their headgear consists of the usual soft velvet caps trimmed with fur. One of the dignitaries holds a letter with a pendant seal in his hand.

The Reign of Ivan the Terrible

Figure 2

Emissaries' court in Moscow, the residence of foreign emissaries in the 16th and 17th centuries. This complex structure was erected in Kitaigorod to accommodate foreign embassies. This is our reproduction of a contemporary drawing by one of the foreign visitors to Russia in the time of Vasilii III. The buildings comprising this extensive complex surround a broad courtyard, on which foreigners were provided with a special place to play skittles and ball.

Figure 3

1) Cathedral of the Virgin's Veil, now named for Vasilii the Blessed [i.e., St. Basil's in Red Square]. This wonderful cathedral, erected by Tsar Ivan IV to commemorate the taking of Kazan, has been preserved in Moscow till the present day in all its magnificence. It stands on a rise in Red Square over the outlet to the Moscow River, near the Spasskie Gate. Its more recent popular appellation is due to the fact that next to the cathedral is the grave of the holy fool, Vasilii the Blessed, who is greatly esteemed by the people.

2) Wooden Church of the Ascension in Torzhok, built in the time of Tsar Ivan IV, which has also been preserved till our time. It was restored not long ago and the local residents celebrated its tercentenary.

The Reign of Ivan the Terrible

FIGURE 4-1

SCENE WITH DIFFERENT TYPES OF PEOPLE of the 16th and 17th centuries, from a sketch by foreign travelers.

1) **THIS OLD DRAWING** depicts a rural church, from which a religious procession is setting out.

FIGURE 4-2

2) THIS PICTURE shows old-fashioned Russian women's headgear. These same forms are still preserved in many of our museums and in many separate localities.

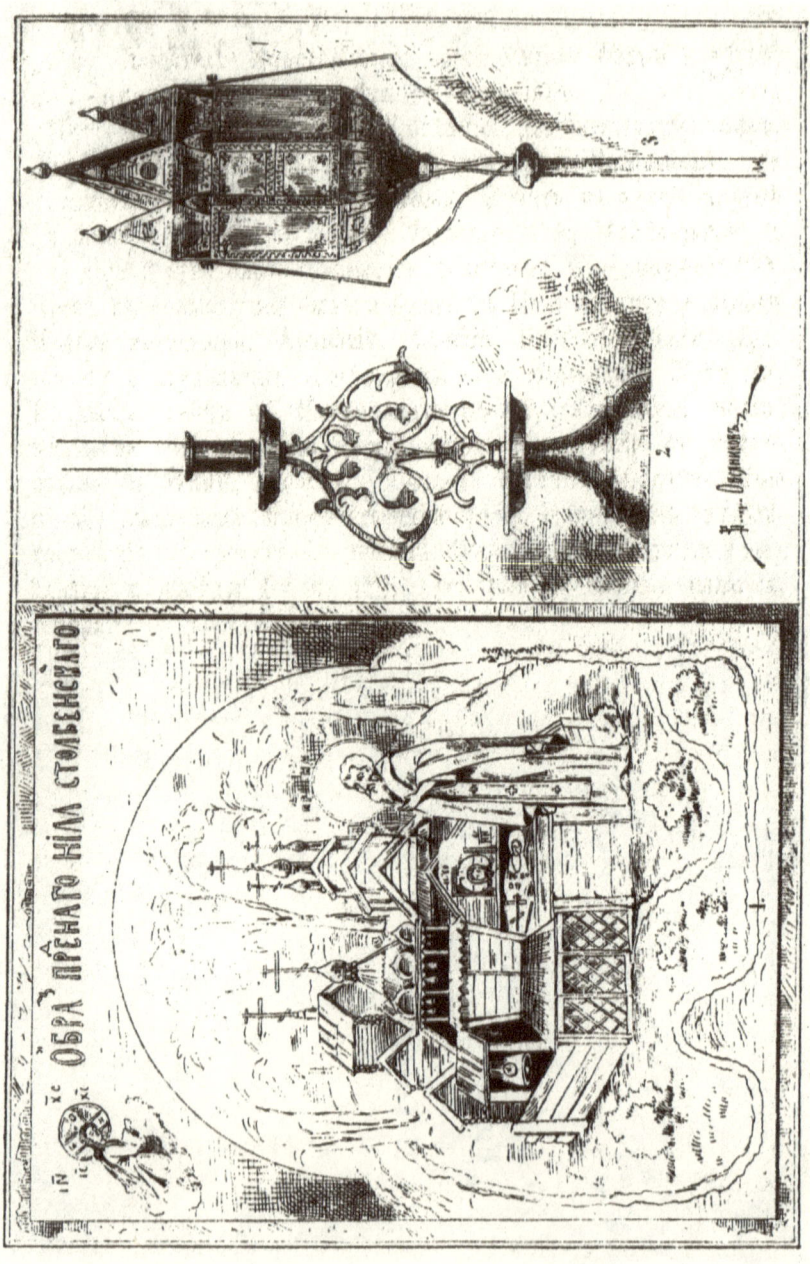

Figure 5

1) **Depiction of the Venerable Nil Stolbenskii church,** notable for the very exact representation of the Nilovskaya Cloister as it appeared at the beginning of the 16th century. All the cathedrals, cells and fences of the cloister are wooden. This icon is conserved at the Tver Museum.

2) **Church candlestick** of the 16th century.

3) **Incised lantern** of the same century, carried in church processions.

FIGURE 6

1) THE TSARITSA ON A PILGRIMAGE. The tsaritsa sits in a covered sleigh pulled by six paired horses. The windows are covered with lattice. On the front is the imperial coat-of-arms (double eagle). The coachmen ride on horseback, each one directing two pairs. Attendants follow – the tsaritsa's honorary retinue.

2) THE METROPOLITAN, TRAVELING FROM HIS PALACE TO CHURCH. The archprelate travels alone in the four-place sleigh, which is upholstered in carpeting. In front, an old soldier carries the metropolitan's crozier; behind is the metropolitan's boyar.

The Reign of Ivan the Terrible

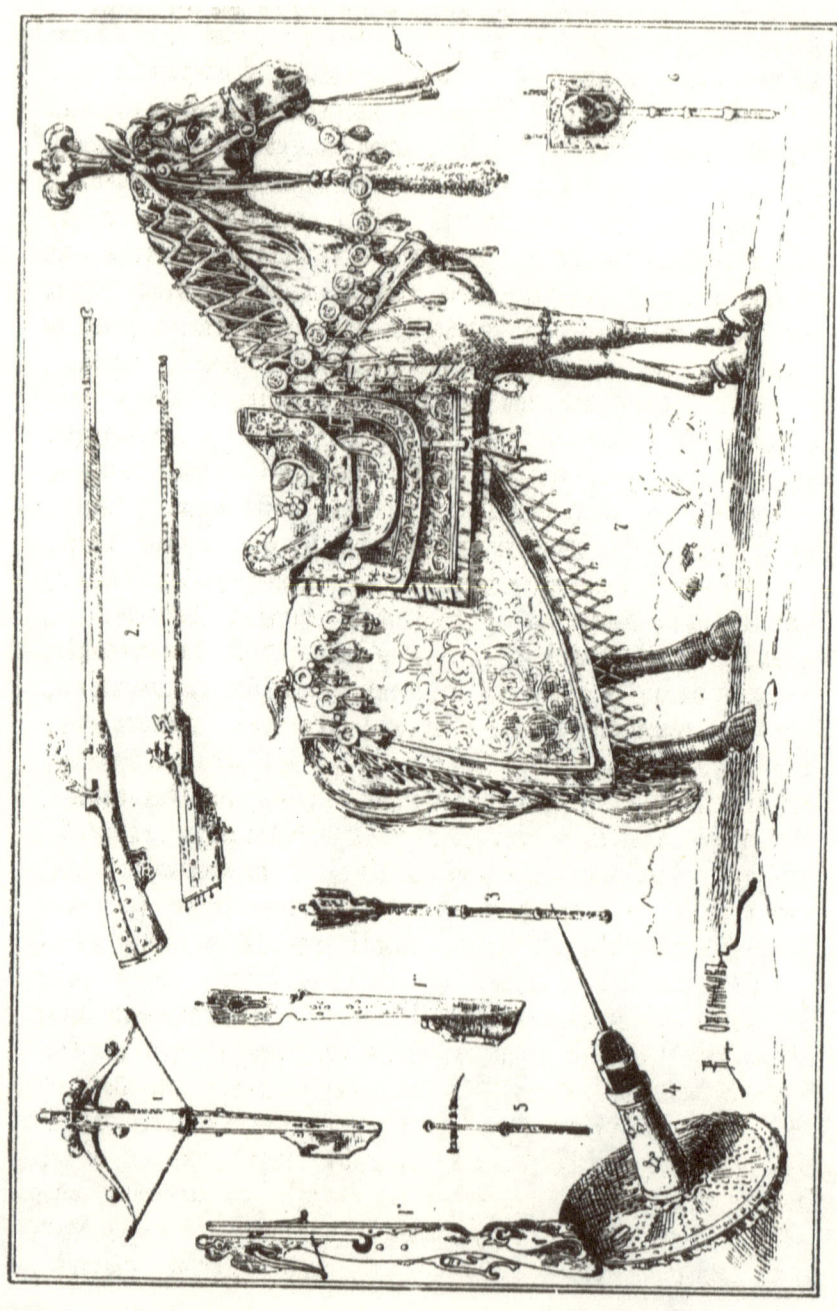

Figure 7

Warriors' armaments of the 16th century.

1, 1', 1'') Crossbow (arbalest) from different sides.

2) Arquebuses, one with match, the other with lock.

3) Six-pointed mace.

4) Tarch (combination of sword with shield and handle.

5) Hammer.

6) Mace on a holster.

7) Depiction of accouterments for a tsar's horse: above, a rich covering for the horse, and on it, the saddle. The entire harness is hung with jingling silver chains. The mane is covered with a net of pearls. The bridle is decorated with a feather plume.

introduction

KARAMZIN'S
TABLE OF CONTENTS

CHAPTER *I*
  Regency of the Mother of Grand Prince and Tsar Ivan IV Vasilievich II.
  [Ivan the Terrible] 1533-1538

Russians' discontent with Ivan's immaturity. Composition of the national Duma. The chief nobles Glinskii and Telepnev. Oath to Ivan. Imprisonment of Prince Yurii Ivanovich. General fear. Treachery of princes Simeon Belskii and Lyatskii. Imprisonment and death of Mikhail Glinskii. Death of Prince Yurii. The flight, conspiracy and imprisonment of Prince Andrei Ivanovich. Execution of boyars and boyar cadets. Death of Prince Andrei. Foreign affairs. Truce with Sweden and Livonia. Moldavia. A Turkish envoy. Astrakhan. Nogai affairs. Embassy to Charles V. Kazan takes oath of allegiance. Sigismund's proud reply. Attack by the Crimeans. War with Lithuania. Prince Islam rules in the Taurid. Fortress construction in Lithuania. Raid by the Crimeans. Lithuanians take Gomel and Starodub. Rebellion in Kazan. Shig-Alei in favor. War with Kazan. A victory over the Lithuanians. Fortresses on the Lithuanian border. Truce with Lithuania. Crimean affairs. Islam's death. The menace of Saip-Girei. Construction of Kitaigorod and new fortresses. Revaluation of the coinage. General dislike for Elena. Her death *1*

CHAPTER *II*
  Young Ivan and the Boyar Duma.
  1538-1547

Downfall and death of Prince Telepnev. Predominance of Prince Vasilii Shuiskii. Freeing of princes Ivan Belskii and Andrei Shuiskii. Discord among the boyars. Prince Ivan Belskii again imprisoned. Death of Prince Vasilii Shuiskii. His brother's supremacy. Overthrow of the metropolitan and the selection of Ioasaf. Character of Prince Ivan Shuiskii and pillage inside the country. Raids by external enemies. Embassies to Constantinople and

xxix

Stockholm. Treaty with the Hansa. Pact with Astrakhan. A Nogai delegation. Plot against Shuiskii. The freeing of Prince Ivan Belskii; his power. Pardon of Prince Vladimir Andreevich and his mother. A mitigated fate for Prince Dmitrii Uglitskii. Pardon of Prince Simeon Belskii. Ruler of Kazan attacks. Crimean khan invades. Courage of the people and the army. Flight of the enemy. Discord among the boyars: the downfall of Prince Ivan Belskii. Metropolitan exiled. Renewed preeminence of Prince Ivan Shuiskii. Ordination for Makarii. Truce with Lithuania. Raids by the Crimeans and the Nogai Tatars. Affairs in Kazan. Relations with Astrakhan and Moldavia. Change in administration. Insolence of the Shuiskiis. Ivan's poor upbringing. Plot against the chief nobles. Downfall of the Shuiskiis. Power of the Glinskiis. Governmental cruelty. A good agreement with Lithuania. Army to Kazan. Shig-Alei rules in Kazan, then flees. Expedition to the mouth of the Sviyaga. Travels of the grand prince and his people's discontent 29

CHAPTER III

Ivan Crowned Tsar.

1546-1552

Ivan crowned tsar. Marriage of the sovereign. Anastasiya's virtues. Ivan's vices and bad governance. Conflagrations in Moscow. Mutiny of the mob. Ivan's strange improvement. Silvestr and Adashev. The sovereign's speech at the place of execution. Changes at court and in powers. Mildness of the government. Code of laws. Restraints on the order of precedence. The Stoglav. Legal documents. Selection of jurors. Church institutions. Intention to enlighten Russia. Military activities. Expedition to Kazan. Truce with Lithuania. Crimean affairs. Death of the ruler of Kazan. Expedition to Kazan. Selection of site for a new fortification. Assault of the Nogai Tatars. Founding of Sviyazhsk. Subjugation of the High Bank. People of Kazan terrified. Conditions of the peace treaty with them. Syuyunbeka. Shig-Alei again accedes to the throne. Prisoners freed. Disloyalty in Kazan and the cruelty of its ruler. Negotiations with Alei. Ruler leaves Kazan. Final betrayal by citizens of Kazan 57

CHAPTER IV

The Conquest of Kazan.

1552

Preparation for the Kazan campaign. Russia's relations with western powers. Freeing of old Prince Bulgakov. Construction of new fortifications. Origins of the Don Cossacks. New khan in the Taurid. Affairs in Astrakhan. Sickness in Sviyazhsk. Ediger ruler of Kazan. Metropolitan's message to the Sviyazhsk troops. Council on Kazan. The sovereign's departure. Invasion of the Crimean

introduction

khan. Assault on Tula. The khan flees. Our trophies. Grumbling in the army. Campaign. Siege. First battle. Storm. Gabions deployed. A powerful sally. Effect of embrasures. Prince Yapancha, the raider. Exhaustion of the troops. Division of the legions. Destruction of Yapancha's army. Bitterness in Kazan. Destruction of a secret place. Dejection in Kazan. Ivan's energy. Town and stockade of Arsk captured. Attack of the lowland Cheremis. Imagined sorcery. Construction of a high tower. Proposal to Kazan. A bloody affair. Blowing up barricades. Capture of the turret of Arsk. Last offer to Kazan. Disposition of the army for assault. Detonation of mines and the assault. Heroism on both sides. Greed of many of the troops. Courage of Ivan and the boyars. Prince Kurbskii's valor. Capture of Kazan. Cross hoisted at royal gates. The sovereign enters Kazan. Liberation of Russian prisoners. Ivan's speech to the troops. Feast at the camp. Subjugation of the Arsk district and the lowland Cheremis. Triumphal entry into Kazan. The spectacle of Kazan. Establishing a government. Counsel of the nobles. Sovereign's return route to Moscow. Birth of a crown prince. Ivan's welcome. The sovereign's speech to the clergy. The metropolitan's reply. Feast at the court and Ivan's gifts *91*

CHAPTER V

Death of Ivan's First Wife.
1552-1560

Baptisms of Prince Dmitrii and two of Kazan's rulers. Plague. Rebellion in the Kazan lands. The tsar's Illness. Ivan's journey to Kirillov Monastery. Death of the crown prince. Ivan's important conversation with former bishop Vassian. Birth of Prince Ivan. Prince Rostovskii flees. Heresy. Rebellion in Kazan lands put down. Establishment of the Eparchate of Kazan. Astrakhan subjugated. The embassies of Khiva, Bukhara, Shavkal, Tyumen and Georgia. Submission of the Circassians. Amity with the Nogai Tatars. Siberian tribute. English ships visit Russia. Embassy to England. Crimean affairs. Suleiman's letter. The Crimeans attack. The Swedish war. Relations with Lithuania. The secretary Rzhevskii attacks Islam-Kirmen. Prince Vishnevetskii enters the tsar's service and takes Khortitsa. Conquest of Temryuk and Taman. Epidemic and famine in the Nogai and Crimean settlements. Vishnevetskii's zeal. Alliance with Lithuania proposed. Livonian affairs. An important plan, attributed to Ivan. The Livonian situation. Russia's new power. Army better-trained. Livonian war begins. Capture of Narva. Conquest of Neuschloss, Adezh and Neuhaus. Courage of burgomaster of Derpt. The [Livonian] master flees. A new head of the Order. Derpt and many other towns taken. Ketler takes Ringen. Russians lay waste to Livonia and Courland. Polish, Swedish and Danish kings intercede for Livonia. Ivan approves truce with Livonia. Crimeans attack. Russian assault on the Taurid. Livonia allied with Augustus. The master violates truce. Glorious defense of Lais. Threats from Augustus. Herald from the emperor. New devastation of Livonia. Capture of Marienburg. Prince Kurbskii's victories. Death of Tsaritsa Anastasiya *135*

xxxi

Chapter VI

Ivan Changes for the Worse.
1560-1564

Changes in Ivan. Slander against Adashev and Silvestr. Trial. Silvestr imprisoned. Death of Adashev. Beginnings of evil. New favorites. First executions. Livonian war. Bel's courage. Fellin taken. Words of the ruler of Kazan. End of the [German] Order. Negotiations with Sweden. War with Lithuania. Ivan's second marriage. Capture of Polotsk. Birth of Crown Prince Vasilii. Ivan's triumph. Death of the crown prince. Crimean affairs. The sultan's scheme. Events in Livonia. Truce with Sweden. Depravity of Ivan's wife. Death of Prince Yurii. Ivan's sister-in-law and Prince Vladimir's mother take vows. Death of Makarii. Composition of the Lives of the Saints and the Book of Degrees. Establishment of a printing house. Publication of Bible in Ostrog. Archiepiscopate of Polotsk. White klobuk [cylindrical head-gear] for the metropolitans. Athanasii ordained as metropolitan *209*

Chapter VII

Oprichnina Established.
1563-1569

Negotiations and war with Lithuania. Flight of Russians to Lithuania. Prince Andrei Kurbskii's betrayal. His correspondence with the tsar. Attack by Lithuania and the Crimeans. Embassy of the grand master of the German Order. Ivan's secret departure. Tsar's letter to the metropolitan and the people. Terror in Moscow. Establishment of the Oprichnina. Second round of executions. Aleksandrovskaya Sloboda. Ivan's monkish life. His foreign favorites. Courage of Metropolitan Filipp. Third episode of murders. Plague. Military actions and negotiations. Duma of the Land. Truce with Lithuania. Swedish affairs. The sultan's great undertaking. Calamity for the Turks. Relations with Persia. Siberian tribute. Trade. English embassy. Ivan's scheme to flee to England. Bomelius's villainy *241*

Chapter VIII

Severe Oppression.
1569-1572

Death of the tsaritsa. Fourth and most horrible period of torturing. Novgorod's desolation. Pskov saved. Executions in Moscow. Court jesters. Famine and pestilence. Relations with Lithuania. The Livonian kingship. Tsar's kindness towards Magnus. Embassy to Constantinople. Invasion by the khan. Conflagration in Moscow. Ivan married again. Fifth episode of murders. Death of the tsaritsa. Ivan journeys to Novgorod. Swedish affairs.

Ivan's fourth marriage. Alliance with Queen Elizabeth. Negotiations with Denmark and Lithuania. Ivan departs for Novgorod. The khan's invasion. Prince Vorotynskii's famous victory. Letter to the Swedish king *297*

CHAPTER *IX*

   Oprichnina Abolished.
   1572-1577

Abolition of the Oprichnina. Godunov. Crimean affairs. Relations with Lithuania. War in Estonia. Rebellion in the Kazan district. Marriage of Magnus. Truce with Sweden. Polish affairs. Alliance with Austria. Batory chosen as king. Livonian war. Perfidy of Magnus. Letter to Kurbskii. Sixth episode of executions. Struggles over precedence. An example of loyalty. Ivan's fifth and sixth marriages *341*

CHAPTER *X*

   War with Poland
   1577-1582

Negotiations with Austria. Treaty with Denmark. Crimean affairs. Negotiations and war with Batory. Amazing deed of the Muscovite cannoneers. Polotsk and Sokol captured. Kurbskii's letter. Conference in Moscow. Embassy to the emperor and the Pope. Conquest of Velikie Luki. Calamities for Russia. Ivan's seventh marriage. His unprecedented abasement. Letter to Batory and his reply. Embassy from the Pope. Glorious siege of Pskov. Swedes take Narva. Peace talks. Truce concluded. Filicide. Ivan considers renouncing the world. Stroganov the healer. Ivan's conversations with the emissary of the Roman Church. *385*

CHAPTER *XI*

   Death of Ivan.
   1582-1584

War and truce with the Swedes. Lithuanian affairs. Mutiny of the Cheremis. Relations with various powers, especially with England. Ivan's intention to marry an Englishwoman. Description of the prospective fiancé. Embassy to London. Elizabeth's envoy. Ivan's illness and death. The Russians' love for autocracy. Ivan compared to other torturers. Uses of history. Mixture of good and evil in Ivan. Ivan as developer of the nation and as legislator. His ministries. His secretaries. His clerks. Duma nobles. Nobles of the peerage and junior nobles. Service princes. Stewards. Military organization. Laws. Value of the ruble. Church institutions. A memorable church ceremony. Building towns. Situation in Moscow. Luxury and splendor. Ivan's renown *447*

CHAPTER I

REGENCY OF THE MOTHER OF GRAND PRINCE AND TSAR IVAN IV VASILIEVICH II.

[IVAN THE TERRIBLE]

1533-1538

Russians' discontent with Ivan's immaturity. Composition of the national Duma. The chief nobles Glinskii and Telepnev. Oath to Ivan. Imprisonment of Prince Yurii Ivanovich. General fear. Treachery of princes Simeon Belskii and Lyatskii. Imprisonment and death of Mikhail Glinskii. Death of Prince Yurii. The flight, conspiracy and imprisonment of Prince Andrei Ivanovich. Execution of boyars and boyar cadets. Death of Prince Andrei. Foreign affairs. Truce with Sweden and Livonia. Moldavia. A Turkish envoy. Astrakhan. Nogai affairs. Embassy to Charles V. Kazan takes oath of allegiance. Sigismund's proud reply. Attack by the Crimeans. War with Lithuania. Prince Islam rules in the Taurid. Fortress construction in Lithuania. Raid by the Crimeans. Lithuanians take Gomel and Starodub. Rebellion in Kazan. Shig-Alei in favor. War with Kazan. A victory over the Lithuanians. Fortresses on the Lithuanian border. Truce with Lithuania. Crimean affairs. Islam's death. The menace of Saip-Girei. Construction of Kitaigorod and new fortresses. Revaluation of the coinage. General dislike for Elena. Her death.

It was not just sincere love for Vasilii* that provoked general lamentation at his untimely death, but fear of what would happen to the country that also roiled men's hearts. Russia had never had such a young sovereign [as Ivan]. Never – if we exclude the almost

1533

RUSSIANS' DISCONTENT WITH IVAN'S IMMATURITY

---
* [Vasilii II Vasilievich, grand prince of Moscow from 1425-1462.]

legendary Olga of old – had it seen the helm of the nation in the hands of a young woman, a foreigner: Elena* was a Lithuanian, and detested as such. Traitors do not sit on thrones. The people feared Elena's inexperience, natural weakness, and her passion for the Glinskiis, whose name reminded them of treachery. Court flattery praised the virtues of the grand princess, her piety, kindness, fair-mindedness, courageous heart, penetrating mind, and clear resemblance to Igor's immortal wife,** yet the prudent could now and then distinguish the language of the court (and flattery) from the truth. They knew that the virtue of a ruler, which is difficult enough for a man with strong muscles, is much more difficult for a young, tender, sensitive woman, more susceptible to blind, flaming passions.

Elena was relying on the Boyar Duma: there sat experienced advisors to the throne, but a council without a sovereign is like a body without a head. Who is to direct its actions, weigh and resolve its opinions, and restrain the members' personal pride for the common good? The [late] sovereign's brothers and 20 distinguished boyars composed this supreme Duma: the princes Belskii, Shuiskii, Obolenskii, Odoevskii, Gorbatyi, Penkov, Kubenskii, Barbashin, Mikulinskii, Rostovskii, Buturlin, Vorontsov, Zakharin and Morozov. To be sure, some of them were district deputies and lived in other cities, and so did not attend its sessions. Two men seemed more important than the others because of their special influence on the princess's mind: One was the aging Mikhail Glinskii, her uncle, who was ambitious, audacious, and had been designated by Vasilii himself to be her chief advisor. The other was the equerry boyar Prince Ivan Thedorovich Ovchina-Telepnev-Obolenskii, who was young in years and was suspected of an intimate relationship with Elena. It was believed that these two noblemen, by mutual agreement, would be the legislators of the Duma, which would decide external affairs in Ivan's name and internal ones in the name of both the grand prince and his mother.

> COMPOSITION OF THE NATIONAL DUMA

> THE CHIEF NOBLES GLINSKII AND TELEPNEV

---

* [Elena Glinskaya, Ivan's mother.]
** [The aforementioned Olga.]

Chapter One

The first action of the new administration was a formal assembly of the priesthood, the nobles, and the people in the Cathedral of the Dormition,* where the metropolitan blessed the sovereign child to rule over Russia and to render account solely to God.

> OATH TO IVAN

The nobles brought Ivan gifts and sent officials to all corners of the country to inform the citizens of Vasilii's death and to obtain their sworn allegiance to Ivan.

Barely a week had passed – full of fear and hope provoked by the political changes – when the capital was shocked by the unhappy fate of Prince Yurii Ivanovich Dmitrovskii, the sovereign's eldest uncle, who was slandered (or was actually guilty) of secret schemes to gain illegitimate power. (The tales of the chroniclers do not agree.)

> IMPRISONMENT OF PRINCE YURII IVANOVITCH

It is written that Prince Andrei Shuiskii, who had been imprisoned for fleeing the sovereign to Dmitrov,** was graciously freed by the dowager grand princess, but planned to betray her and raise Yurii to the throne. He disclosed this intention to Prince Boris Gorbatyi, a diligent noble who angrily elucidated to him the full vileness of such a betrayal. Shuiskii realized his carelessness and, fearing denunciation, decided to resort to a shameful lie: he told Elena that Yurii had incited some distinguished officials, his own and those of Prince Boris, who were prepared to flee immediately to Dmitrov. Prince Boris exposed Shuiskii's slander and plot to disturb the peace of the nation; the former was thanked and the latter was imprisoned in a tower.

However, the excessively cautious boyars represented to the grand princess that if she wanted to rule peacefully with her son, she should also imprison Yurii as well, for he was power-hungry, cordial, quite popular and very dangerous to the sovereign child. Elena, who was still weeping for her husband, told them,

"You see my grief. Do what is necessary for the good of the nation."

---

* [The Uspenskii Cathedral.]
** [Sixty-five kilometers (40 miles) north of Moscow.]

Meanwhile, some of Yurii's faithful servitors, when they learned the intentions of the Moscow boyars, tried to convince their prince, who was completely innocent and at peace [with himself], to flee to Dmitrov.

"There," they told him, "no one will dare to look askance at you, but here you will not escape disaster." Yurii firmly replied, "I went to Moscow to close the eyes of my sovereign brother and to swear allegiance to my nephew. I have not violated my oath by the cross and am prepared to die for my innocence."

But another tradition indicts Yurii and vindicates the Boyar Duma. They assert that through his secretary, Tishkov, he did indeed try to get Prince Andrei Shuiskii to enter his service.

"Where is your conscience?" Shuiskii had responded. "Yesterday your prince kissed the cross to his sovereign, Ivan, but now he is enticing the sovereign's servitor."

The secretary argued that this oath was involuntary and illegitimate: the boyars extracted it from Yurii, but did not swear anything to him in return, in violation of the principle of mutual oath-giving. Shuiskii informed Prince Boris Gorbatyi, Prince Boris informed the Duma, and the Duma informed Elena, who ordered the boyars to do their duty.

We note that the *first* story is more probable, since Prince Andrei Shuiskii was imprisoned for the whole time she was in power. Be that as it may, on 11 December, Yurii was arrested, along with all his boyars, and was jailed in the same place in which young Grand Prince Dimitrii had died. It was a terrible portent, but one he was to fulfill!

Thus Ivan's reign began, bearing testament to its formidable decisiveness. People felt sorry for the unfortunate Yurii, and feared tyranny. Even though Ivan was sovereign in name only, and though Elena was acting on the advice of the Council, Russia saw itself under the rod of a rising oligarchy, whose torments were most threatening and most unbearable. It is easier to hide from

General Fear

one persecutor than from twenty. An angry autocrat is like an irritated deity before whom one can only submit, but in the eyes of the people, a system of many tyrants does not have even this advantage. The populace sees in them people like themselves, and detests the misuse of power all the more.

It was said that the boyars wanted to get rid of Yurii in hopes of working their own wills to the detriment of the country, and that the sovereign's other relatives should expect a similar fate. Naturally this idea powerfully affected the minds of Yurii's younger brother Andrei and even his nephews, the Belskii princes, who had been so tenderly entrusted by Vasilii to his boyars in the last moments of his life. Prince Simeon Thedorovich Belskii and the distinguished okolnichii* Ivan Lyatskii, who was a Prussian by birth and a man experienced in military affairs, were getting their legions ready in Serpukhov in case of a war with Lithuania. Displeased with the administration, they said to themselves that Russia was not their homeland, secretly corresponded with King Sigismund and fled to Lithuania.

> TREACHERY OF PRINCES SIMEON BELSKII AND LYATSKII

This unexpected treachery astounded the court, and new cruelties were the result. Prince Ivan Belskii, chief of the voivodes** and a member of the Supreme Council, was then in Kolomna setting up an army encampment. He and Prince Vorotynskii and his young sons were taken, clapped in chains and imprisoned as confederates of Simeon and Lyatskii without any evidence, or at any rate, without a formal trial, yet the oldest of the Belskiis, Prince Dimitrii, likewise a member of the Boyar Duma, was left in peace, like an innocent man.

> 1534

Up till now Mikhail Glinskii had been considered the soul and leader of the Duma; he was surprised to learn that he could neither condemn others nor save himself. This brave man's miserable end vindicated Vasilii's faith in him. He viewed with regret Elena's indiscreet weakness for Prince Ivan Telepnev-Obolenskii, who, having conquered her

> IMPRISONMENT AND DEATH OF MIKHAIL GLINSKII

---
* [A boyar was a member of the higher Russian nobility; an okolnichii was one rung down.]
** [A voivode was a senior military official, like a general, but sometimes a military governor as well.]

heart, also wanted to control the Duma and the country. It is written that Mikhail boldly and firmly lectured his niece on the shame of debauchery, which is always vile, but more so from the throne, to which people look for the virtues to justify autocratic power. He was ignored, came to be hated and was destroyed. Telepnev made the suggestion, Elena agreed and Glinskii was accused of an absurd plot to take over the country, along with his closest boyar and Vasilii's friend, Mikhail Semyonovich Vorontsov, who was no doubt likewise innocent.

Glinskii was deprived of his liberty and shortly thereafter his life in the same prison in which he had been previously confined. He was famous in Europe for his intellect and fiery passions, his good luck and misfortunes. He was a nobleman and a betrayer of two countries, pardoned by Vasilii because of Elena and also tortured by her. He was worthy of a traitor's death, but also worthy of praise for his courageous martyrdom in one and the same prison. Glinskii was buried without honor in the church of St. Nikita across the Neglinnaya River, but then, in a change of mind, his remains were exhumed and transferred to the Trinity Monastery, where a more fitting grave had been prepared for this grandfather of the sovereign. Vorontsov, however, was only dismissed from the court and outlived his persecutors, Elena and Prince Ivan Telepnev. He became a deputy of Novgorod and died in 1539 with the rank of Duma boyar.

The sovereign's young uncle, Prince Andrei Ivanovich, weak in character and possessing no shining qualities whatever, enjoyed the external tokens of respect at the court and in the Boyar Duma, which in relations with other powers gave him the title of First Guardian of the Nation. But in fact he took no part in government; he mourned the fate of his brother, feared for himself, and wavered irresolutely, sometimes desiring the court's favor, sometimes revealing himself to be its abusive critic, depending on the promptings of his favorites. For six weeks following the death of the grand prince he remained in Moscow, humbly petitioning Elena to add new districts to his appanage;* he was refused, but in accordance with ancient custom, he was given, in memory of the

---

* [An estate granted to male relatives of the sovereign.]

deceased, a large number of valuable vessels, fur coats and horses with expensive saddles.

Andrei then departed for Staritsa, complaining of the regent Elena. Gossips and informers were alert: some told this prince that there was a dungeon ready for him; others told Elena that Andrei was disparaging her. There were various issues to be argued, for which the boyar Prince Ivan Shuiskii rode to Staritsa, while Andrei traveled to Moscow. They assured each other of their mutual love, but neither side believed a word, even though the metropolitan vouched for their veracity. Elena wanted to know who was stirring up trouble between her and her brother-in-law, but Andrei would not name anyone, merely replying, "It seemed to me that someone was!" They departed amicably, but without a genuine reconciliation.

At this point – 26 August 1536 – Prince Yurii Ivanovich died in prison, *of hunger*, it is written. Andrei was in a funk. The regent summoned him to Moscow to consult on foreign affairs: he pled illness and requested a doctor. However, the well-known healer Theofil found nothing significant wrong with him. Elena was secretly informed that Andrei was afraid to come to the capital and was thinking of fleeing. Meanwhile, the unhappy man wrote to her,

1536

DEATH OF PRINCE YURII

"Due to sickness and torment I lost my senses. Warm my heart with kindness. Did the sovereign really order me carried out of here on a litter?"

Elena sent the senior priest Dosithei of the Krutitskoe Metokhion to relieve him of his groundless fears, or else, in case of evil intent, to pronounce anathema on him. But now Andrei's boyar, whom he had dispatched to Moscow, was arrested en route, and the princes Obolenskii, Nikita the Lame, and Telepnev's equerry entered Volok commanding a large contingent. They were to pursue the fugitive if Dosithei's admonition proved ineffective. When Andrei was told that the Obolenskiis

1537

THE FLIGHT, CONSPIRACY AND IMPRISONMENT OF PRINCE ANDREI IVANOVITCH

were coming to take him, he immediately departed Staritsa with his wife and young son, but stopped after 60 versts.* He thought things over and resolved to be the transgressor, to gather troops and to conquer Novgorod and all of Russia, if possible. He sent letters to the district boyar cadets,** writing to them,

"The grand prince is but a child, you are only serving the boyars. Come over to me; I am prepared to reward you."

Many of them indeed appeared before him, enthusiastic. Others presented the rebellious letters to the national Duma. It became necessary to take strong measures. Prince Nikita Obolenskii rushed to defend Novgorod, while Prince Ivan Telepnev and his contingent went after Andrei, who had left the main road and turned left towards Staraya Rusa. Prince Ivan caught up with him in Tyukhol. His troops were drawn up, banners unfurled, and he was prepared to commence fighting. Andrei likewise led out his force and drew his sword, but he wavered and began negotiations, asking for Telepnev's oath that the sovereign and Elena would not take vengeance on him. Telepnev gave the oath and arrived in Moscow with him, where the grand princess, according to the chronicler, expressed her wrath at her favorite, who apparently on his own and without his sovereign's knowledge, had assured the rebel of his safety.

> EXECUTION OF BOYARS AND BOYAR CADETS

She ordered Andrei shackled and shut up in a cramped chamber, while his princess and son were placed under guard. His boyars, advisors and loyal servitors were tortured, despite their distinguished princely rank; some died of the torture, others of imprisonment. The boyar cadets who had taken Andrei's side, thirty in all, were hanged as traitors along the Novgorod highway at great distances from each other. Andrei

> DEATH OF PRINCE ANDREI

suffered the fate of his brother: he met a violent death six months later, and, like him, was buried with honor in the Church of St. Michael the Archangel. He certainly deserved his punishment, for he had plotted rebellion, but secret executions always indicate a faint hearted malice and are always illegitimate. Elena's

---

* [A verst is approximately a kilometer, or 6/10ths of a mile.]
** [A junior boyar.]

pretended wrath at Prince Telepnev could not justify the breaking of the oath.

And so, in four years of Elena's rule in the name of the young grand prince, two of his father's brothers and the uncle of his mother were killed, and his second cousin thrown into prison. Many distinguished families were dishonored by the public execution of Andrei's boyars, among them the Obolenskii princes and the Princes Pronskii, Khovanskii, and Paletskii. Fearing the fatal effects of weakness during the minority of the sovereign-autocrat, Elena regarded ferocity as firmness. But as much as the latter, based on a pure fervor for the good, is necessary for the good of the country, so much is the former harmful to it and arouses hatred. There is no government that does not require popularity for its success. Elena surrendered herself simultaneously to the tender endearments of illicit love and to the savagery of bloodthirsty malice!

As for the foreign policy of the regent and the Duma, they did not veer from Vasilii's course: they loved peace but did not fear war.

| FOREIGH AFAIRS |

After they informed neighboring powers of Ivan's elevation to the throne, Elena and the boyars secured amicable relations with Sweden, Livonia, Moldavia, the Nogai princes and the ruler of Astrakhan. In 1535 and 1537, Gustav Vasa's emissaries came to Moscow with greetings, then set out for Novgorod and concluded a 60-year truce there. Gustav agreed not to aid Lithuania or the Livonian Order in the event we got into a war with them. They also agreed:

| 1534-1538 |

| TRUCE WITH SWEDEN AND LIVONIA |

1) to send emissaries to the Oksa River to re-establish the old borders between Sweden and Russia dating from the time of King Magnus;

2) to allow Russians in Sweden and Swedes in Russia to be able to trade freely under protection of the law;

3) to return fugitives from either side. Gustav entrusted Knut Anderson and Bjorn Klasson with this, while the Russians appointed Prince Boris Gorbatyi and Mikhailo Semyonovich Vorontsov. These were the Duma boyars and Novgorod deputies who in 1535 had established peace with Livonia for 17 years. The aged Plettenberg, most renowned of all the masters of the [Livonian] Order had died by this time; his successor was Herman von Brüggen.

The archbishop of Riga besought the grand prince for friendship and protection in the name of all the *Bearers of the Gold*, or Knights, German nobles and aldermen of Livonia. They determined that the Narova, as always, would serve as the border between Livonia and Russia; that no acts of violence would hinder mutual trade, and that even in the event of war itself, merchants and their property were not to be touched. Russians in Livonia were not to be punished, nor Livonians in Russia, without the knowledge of their own governments. Germans were to protect Russian churches and domiciles in their cities, and so on. In conclusion, the treaty stated,

"And if someone violates this oath, may God, anathema, plague, famine, fire and sword be upon him."

MOLDAVIA

The Moldavian voivode Peter Stefanovich likewise earnestly sought our protection. Although he still paid a light tribute to the sultan, he called himself a free sovereign: he had his own political regime, fought and made peace with whom he pleased, and ruled his land as an autocrat. Coreligionist Russia could support him in Constantinople and the Taurid, and help him to restrain Lithuania. The distinguished Moldavian voivode Sunzhar was in Moscow in 1535, and our emissary Zabolotskii travelled to Peter with assurances that the grand prince would not abandon him under any circumstances. In him Russia actually had a very eager ally against Sigismund, to whom he gave no peace, being ever ready to ravage the Polish lands.

However, Russia was unable to be his shield against the formidable Suleiman, who in 1537 laid waste to all of Moldavia with fire and sword, demanding a large, fixed tribute and complete subjection of all its inhabitants. They did not dare resist, although they did obtain from the sultan the right to choose their own rulers, a right which they continued to enjoy for about another 100 years. Turkey took their national treasury, a great deal of gold, some diadems, and rich icons and crosses that had belonged to Stefan the Great. The misfortune of this coreligionist power was regretted in Moscow, but they did not contrive a means to alleviate its fate. The regent and the boyars did not consider it beneficial to renew relations with Constantinople, but in 1538 Suleiman sent the Greek Andreyan [Russian transliteration] to Moscow for various purchases with a flattering letter for young Ivan, complaining about this chilling [of relations] and boasting of his friendship with Ivan's father.

> A TURKISH ENVOY

A boyar cadet was sent to the ruler of Astrakhan, Abdyl-Rakhman,* with a proposal for an alliance. Fearing both the Crimean khan and the Nogai, the ruler accepted gratefully, but lost his throne a few months later. The Nogai had taken Astrakhan, expelled Abdyl-Rakhman and declared a certain Derveshelei to be ruler in his place. Since they had a profitable trade with Russia, the princes of this populous steppe horde – Shidyak, Mamai, Koshum and others – wanted to be at peace with it, but complained that our Meshcherskii Cossacks** gave them no rest, driving off horses by the thousands and taking people captive. These princes demanded satisfaction, gifts (sable coats, cloth, and armor), respect and honor, e.g., that the grand prince call them *brothers* and *sovereigns* in his letters, as khans of no less esteem than that of the Crimea, and that he send them boyars and not low-ranking officials for negotiations. In the event of refusal, they threatened vengeance, reminding him that their fathers had looked upon Moscow and that their sons would likewise behold its walls. They boasted of 300,000 warriors, and that they flew like the birds.

> ASTRAKHAN

> NOGAI AFFAIRS

The boyars promised them satisfaction and made a free trade agreement with them that would enrich Russia with horses and

---
* [So Karamzin transliterates it. More conventionally, it would be Abdul.]
** [Cossacks were semi-independent cavalrymen inhabiting southern Russia.]

herds. For example, in 1534, the Nogai emissaries brought with them 5,000 merchants and 50,000 horses, in addition to other livestock. These princes also promised to inform our sovereign concerning the movements of the Crimean Horde and not to allow their brigands access to our territory. Shidyak considered himself chief of all the Nogai and wrote to Ivan to give him, as a khan, the scheduled memorial services. The boyars replied,

"Our sovereign rewards khans and princes according to their services, but does not set a schedule for anyone in advance."

The letters of Mamai, who called himself Shidyak's kalga,* were distinguished by eloquence and a kind of philosophy. Expressing condolences to the grand prince on the death of his father, he said,

"Beloved brother! It is not you or I who is responsible for death, but Adam and Eve. Fathers die and children inherit their property. I weep with you, but we must submit to necessity!"

These Nogai letters, written in the high-flown style of the East, show a mental development remarkable amongst nomadic peoples.

The regent and her boyars wished to renew amicable relations with the [Holy Roman] emperor, so in 1538 our emissaries Yurii Skobeltsyn and Dmitrii Vasiliev traveled to Charles V and to his brother, King Ferdinand of Hungary and Bohemia. We do not have their instructions or subsequent reports.

EMBASSY TO CHARLES V

However, the chief objects of our policy were the Taurid, Lithuania and Kazan. Young Ivan proposed an alliance to Khan Saip-Girei, peace to Sigismund and protection to Enalei. The ruler and the people of Kazan promised with new sworn documents to be completely subordinate to Russia, while King Sigismund replied proudly,

KAZAN TAKES OATH OF ALLEGIANCE

SIGISMUND'S PROUD REPLY

"I could agree to peace if the young grand prince were to respect my age and send his emissaries either to me or to our border."

---

* [A Crimean official second in rank after the khan.]

Hoping to take advantage of Ivan's minority, the king demanded all the cities Vasilii had taken from him, but expecting a refusal, he mobilized and persuaded the khan to make an alliance with Lithuania against Russia. Our herald had not yet returned from Saip-Girei when Moscow learned of the Azov and Crimean Tatars' attack on the Ryazan district. Our voivodes, the princes Punkov and Gatev, trounced them on the banks of the Pronya. For this first military success of Ivan's reign, these voivodes formally received the grand prince's favor.

ATTACK BY THE CRIMEANS

Convinced of the unavoidability of war with the king, however, the regent and the boyars hastened to prepare for it. Sigismund anticipated them, however. He had received our turncoats, the princes Simeon Belskii and Lyatskii, with especial kindness, giving them rich estates. The king listened to their stories of Elena's weakness, the boyars' tyranny and the people's dissatisfaction, and plotted to suddenly seize from us all the territory Ivan and Vasilii had obtained in Lithuania. The Kiev voivode Andrei Nemirov violated the borders of Novgorod Severskii, laid siege to Starodub and torched its suburbs.

1534

WAR WITH LITHUANIA

However, a bold sally by Russians under the command of the brave Andrei Levin so frightened the Lithuanians that they fled in disorder. The Starodub deputy Prince Aleksandr Kashin sent 40 enemy cannoneers with all their equipment to Moscow, along with the captive Sukhodolskii, a distinguished official. To make up for their first defeat, the Lithuanians burned down poorly fortified Radogoshch. The valiant Muscovite voivode Matvei Lykov was consumed in the flames. After taking many residents captive, they surrounded Chernigov and shelled the city with large cannons for several hours. The clever and hearty Prince Theodor Mezetskii was voivode there; by skillful employment of firearms and artillery he prevented the enemy from approaching the walls.

At night, when the barrage had quieted, he sent Chernigov troops to attack the Lithuanian camp, where the unexpected attack provoked panic. The somnolent Lithuanians were barely able to defend themselves, and in the darkness killed each other. They fled in all directions, leaving us their baggage train and cannons. By sunrise, there was no longer a single enemy left near the city and Sigismund's voivode had fled to Kiev in despair and shame. And so the king was disappointed in his hopes to conquer the Ukraine, which our turncoats Belskii and Lyatskii had told him was defenseless. Simultaneously, his other voivode, Prince Aleksandr Vishnevetskii, had appeared beneath the walls of Smolensk. The local voivode, Prince Nikita Obolenskii, prevented him from torching the trading quarter, defeated him and chased him for several versts.

> 13 September

When it learned of these enemy actions, our Boyar Duma, in the presence of the young grand prince and Elena, requested the metropolitan to bless the war with Lithuania, but the metropolitan turned to the sovereign child and said,

"Sovereign! Protect yourself and ourselves. You act, and we shall pray. Destruction to him who started this; verily God is our help!"

> 28 October

In deep autumn our legions set out from Moscow with two chief voivodes, Mikhail Gorbatyi and Nikita Obolenskii. Elena's favorite, Telepnev, desirous of glory for valor, led the van. Beyond the borders of the Smolensk region they torched Lithuanian villages and city suburbs: Dubrovno, Orsha, Drutsk, and Borisov. Without meeting the enemy in the field or bothering to besiege fortresses, the Muscovite voivodes brought fire and sword as far as Molodechno, where they linked up with troops from Novgorod and Pskov, and the deputy, Prince Boris Gorbatyi, laid waste all around Polotsk, Vitebsk and Bryaslavl [probably Bratislav]. Despite deep snow and cruel frosts, they approached Vilnius, where the king himself was anxious at the proximity of his enemy. He fussed and gave orders, but was unable to do anything to the Russians, who numbered around 150,000. Their light detachments burnt and pillaged to within 15 versts of the city. Our voivodes were pleased with the king's fear and with their destruction of Lithuania, where they had laid waste to dwellings and residents, livestock and grain as far as the Livonian border without losing a single man in battle. They returned to Russia through the Pskov district with prisoners and booty at the beginning of March.

Other voivodes, Prince Telepnev and the Trostenskii princes, had proceeded from Starodub to Mozyr, Turov and Mogilyov with the same kind of success, burning, killing and capturing everywhere, but nowhere fighting a battle. It was not the personal feebleness of the aged Sigismund, but the national debility of Lithuania that revealed to us the possibility of such destructive *military outings*. The country had no organized standing army: it took a long time to assemble troops and the Lithuanian government did not have our capability – that is, a strong, firm autocracy. Poland, on the other hand, with its pans* of the nobility, still constituted an independent kingdom, and was unwilling to take up arms for the defense of Lithuania. To the Russians' credit, the chronicler says that in their depredations they did not touch Orthodox churches and magnanimously freed many of their coreligionists from captivity.

The result of the Lithuanian alliance with the khan was that Prince Islam rebelled against Saip-Girei on the side of Russia, recalling, it is written, his old friendship with us. He got the nobles onto his side, overthrew the khan and began to rule, taking the title of khan for himself. Saip, however, ensconced himself in Kirkor, declared Islam a rebel and hoped to pacify him with the sultan's assistance. This change seemed fortunate for us: Islam, fearing the Turks, proposed a close alliance with the grand prince and wrote that 20,000 Crimeans were already fighting Lithuania. The Muscovite boyars were impatient to make use of the new khan's favorable disposition and ordered Prince Aleksandr Strigin to travel to the Taurid as our emissary. This official willfully remained in Novgorodok and wrote to the grand prince that Islam was deceiving us: he called himself khan, but was only the kalga, and in the presence of Lithuanian envoy Gornostaevich, had given his oath to Sigismund to be an enemy of Russia, in fulfillment of Saip-Girei's wishes.

PRINCE ISLAM RULES IN THE TAURID

This information was incorrect: Strigin incurred the sovereign's wrath and, instead of him, Prince Mezetskii was dispatched

---

* [A pan was a member of the Polish gentry.]

> 1535

to Islam to establish this important alliance as soon as possible. Nor did the khan tarry in sending to Moscow a sworn treaty document. However, in it, the boyars spotted the phrase "whoever is an enemy of the grand prince but a friend of mine, shall also be his friend."

They did not want to accept this. Finally, Islam agreed to exclude this offensive condition, swore his love for his *younger* brother Ivan and boasted of his magnanimous lack of greed, since he had scorned rich gifts from Sigismund: 10,000 gold coins and 200 measures of cloth, while requesting from us gratitude, cannons and 50,000 dengas.* He also complained that the grand prince was not in compliance with his father's will, in which the dying Vasilii had allegedly bequeathed him (Islam) half of his treasury as a token of friendship.

The khan also guaranteed the safety of our borders and informed the sovereign that Saip-Girei's nobleman, Prince Bulgak, had departed Perekop with a band of brigands, but would hardly dare to menace Russia. However, Bulgak, along with Ataman Dashkovich of the Dnieper Cossacks, contrary to Islam's assurance, had suddenly attacked our Severskii district and done no small injury to its inhabitants. In the name of the grand prince, the Muscovite boyars had complained to Islam about this, but they observed moderation in their reproaches; they did not threaten him with vengeance and showed that they believed his sincere friendship towards us.

Now Prince Belskii's and Prince Lyatskii's people fled from Vilnius to Moscow. They did not wish to serve traitors and had plundered their lords' treasuries. They told our boyars that Sigismund was sending a large army against Smolensk. It was necessary to thwart this enemy and our legions were ready. Prince Vasilii Shuiskii was the chief voivode and Elena's favorite, Telepnev, again took command of the vanguard. They hastened to meet the enemy, but finding them nowhere, burned the outskirts of Mstislavl, took the stockade, sent prisoners back to Moscow and proceeded further unhindered.

---

* [A denga was a coin worth 1/2 a kopek, or 1/200th of a ruble..]

Novgorod and Pskov were supposed to attack Lithuania from the other side. They were to establish a fortress on the shores of Sebezhskoe Lake and join up with Shuiskii, but their commanders, Prince Boris Gorbatyi and Mikhail Vorontsov, only partially obeyed the commands issued them. They detailed the voivode Buturlin with boyar cadets to Sebezh, but stayed in Opochka and did not care to join up with Shuiskii. Buturlin established Ivan-gorod at Sebezh, on Lithuanian territory just as if it were our own. He fortified it and filled it with all sorts of supplies, working for about a month. No one resisted him and there was no whisper of the enemy.

> FORTRESS CONSTRUCTION IN LITHUANIA

Sigismund, however, lost no time in inactivity: he gave the Russians free rein to rampage in the eastern part of Lithuania while sending 40,000 troops into our own southern possessions. Meanwhile, as Shuiskii was torching the outskirts of Krichev, Radoml and Mogilyov, the Lithuanian voivodes Pan Yurii Radziwill, Andrei Nemirov, Hetman Yan Tarnovskii, Prince Ilya Ostrozhskii, and our turncoat Simeon Belskii marched on Starodub. Informed of this, Moscow's boyars immediately sent new legions to defend the area, but suddenly they heard that 15,000 Crimeans were racing towards the banks of the Oka, that the villages of Ryazan were in flames and that the blood of their inhabitants was flowing like rivers – Islam had deceived us.

> 20 AUGUST RAID BY THE CRIMEANS

Enticed by Lithuanian gold, he was doing service to its king with these attacks, all the while maintaining that he considered himself Ivan's ally and shamelessly asserting that it was not he, but Saip-Girei who was fighting Russia. Islam's emissaries in Moscow were taken under guard; the army that had been sent to Starodub was immediately recalled and several thousand men were assembled in Kolomna. Princes Dimitrii Belskii and Mstislavskii cleared the brigands from the banks of the Oka and pursued them, forcing them to flee into the steppes.

> The Lithuanians, however, took advantage of the Crimeans' cooperation and the defenseless state of Little Russia* to assault Gomel, ruled by the cowardly Prince Obolenskii-Shchepin. He fled with all his military men, firearms and artillery to Moscow, where he was thrown in prison. Gomel surrendered. The Lithuanians also hoped to take Starodub, but it had a worthy commander, Prince Thedor Telepnev. A courageous daily defense cost them blood. Sigismund's voivodes decided to prolong the siege. They secretly dug a mine and blew up the wall. The terrible blast shook the city. Houses caught fire and the enemy burst through the smoke into the streets.

LITHUANIANS TAKE GOMEL AND STARODUB

29 AUGUST

Prince Telepnev and his troops displayed heroism: they crushed and pursued the Lithuanians and twice fought as far as their camp, but they were pressed by huge mobs of infantry and cavalry, overpowered and taken prisoner, along with Prince Sitskii. The distinguished Prince Pyotr Romodanovskii fell in battle, while Nikita Kolychev died of wounds two days later. 13,000 citizens of either sex died from fire or sword. Few were saved, and their tales produced horror over all the Severskii land. Poorly fortified Pochep was ruled by the hearty Muscovite Thedor Sukin. He ordered the residents to depart after burying anything they could not take with them and then torched the town. After conquering what was now only an ash heap the Lithuanians went home, while Shuiskii set out for Smolensk, having committed all the places around Knyazhichi, Shklov, Kopos, Orsha, and Dubrovno to the flames.

SEPTEMBER

> The number of our enemies was now increased due to a new betrayal by Kazan. They were dissatisfied, as always, with Russia lording it over them and were incited to rebellion by Saip-Girei. They scorned their young sovereign and, believing that Russia with its child-sovereign had also become weakened internally and their local nobility, under the command of Princess Gorshadna and Prince Bulat, deposed and murdered Enalei in the countryside by

REBELLION IN KAZAN

---

* [Roughly the same territory as the present Ukraine.]

Chapter One

the banks of the Kazanka. They summoned Safa-Girei once again from the Taurid to restore their liberty and independence. He was wed to Enalei's widow, the daughter of the Nogai Prince Yusuf.

Wishing to know the circumstances of this perfidy, the boyars sent a herald to Kazan with letters to the princess and to the uhlans.* He had not yet returned when Gorodetskii Tatars in our service brought the news that many Kazan dignitaries had secretly met with them on the banks of the Volga and that, displeased with the princess and Prince Bulat, and having upwards of 500 sympathizers, they wished to remain loyal to Russia and hoped to expel Safa-Girei if the grand prince would free Shig-Alei and formally declare him their ruler. The boyars advised Elena to immediately send for Shig-Alei, who was still imprisoned at Belo-ozero. He was told of the sovereign's favor and ordered to come to Moscow to appear at the palace. We shall here relate the memorable details of this audience.

SHIG-ALEI IN FAVOR

The 16-year-old grand prince was sitting on his throne. Alei,** overjoyed at the fortunate change in his fate, fell down before him, and then rose to his knees and made a speech about the favors Ivan's father had done him. He confessed to pride, craftiness and evil musings; he praised Ivan's magnanimity and wept. Alei was given a rich fur coat to wear. He had also wished an audience with the grand princess. Vasilii Shuiskii and the equerry Telepnev had met Alei at his sleigh. The sovereign was with his mother in the Palace of St. Lazarus and distinguished boyars were sitting next to Elena. Other boyars were further away, on both sides.

9 JANUARY 1536

Ivan himself received him in the vestibule and took him to Elena. Bowing to the ground, Alei once again cursed his own ingratitude, calling himself a slave. He said he envied his brother Enalei, who had been killed on behalf of the grand prince and desired the same fate for himself if it would atone for his transgression. The official Karpov replied instead of Elena, proudly but graciously,

---

* [Polish light cavalry.]
** [The Arabic form of this name is Ali.]

"Lord Shig-Alei! Vasilii Ivanovich put you in disgrace, but Ivan and Elena have forgiven you. You are worthy to behold their faces! We permit you to put the past behind you, but remember to honor your new promises!"

Alei was sent off with honors and gifts. His wife, Fatma-Saltan, was met by the boyars' wives at her sleigh and was taken to Elena's hall for dinner. Ivan greeted his guest in the Tatar language and sat at his own table with his nobles, while Alei's wife sat with the grand princess and her boyars. They were served by stewards and cupbearers. Prince Repnin served as Fatma's meat carver and at the end of the meal, Elena gave her a cup. According the chroniclers, there had never been such a sumptuous banquet in the Moscow court. The regent loved splendor and never missed a chance to show that the Russian state was in her hands.

WAR WITH KAZAN

Meanwhile, war with Kazan had commenced: the plot of some of its nobles against Safa-Girei had been ineffectual, and its ruler had replied rudely to Ivan's letter. Moscow's commanders, Prince Gundorov and Zamytskii, were supposed to march to the Kazan lands from Meshchera, but ran into Tatars near the Volga and fell back without even informing the sovereign of this enemy, which unexpectedly attacked the Nizhnyi-Novgorod district, rampaging at will. The residents of Balakhna took the field with more courage than skill, but were defeated. The Nizhnyi-Novgorod voivodes encountered the Tatars near Lyskovo. Neither side wanted a fight, and under cover of darkness the troops of Kazan and Russia fled in different directions. The pusillanimity of Moscow's voivodes demanded an example of strictness: Prince Gundorov and Zamytskii were imprisoned and replaced by Saburov and Karpov, who finally gained victory over the huge Kazan and Cheremis hordes at Koryakovo. The prisoners were sent to Moscow, where without exception they were all sentenced to death as perfidious rebels.

A VICTORY OVER THE LITHUANIANS

The Lithuanian war continued with some success for us: the establishment of our new fortress at Sebezh sealed a significant

CHAPTER ONE

victory. Sigismund could not with equanimity countenance it in his territory: he ordered the Kiev deputy Nemirov to take it no matter what the cost. His army, comprising 20,000 Lithuanians and Poles, surrounded the city. A terrible bombardment commenced. The earth shook, but the walls were unharmed – the mediocre Lithuanian cannoneers struck their own troops rather than their enemy's. Cannonballs flew left and right, but not one fell into the fortress.

27 FEBRUARY

The Russians, on the other hand, aimed skillfully and made a successful sally. The besiegers retreated to the lake, whose ice broke beneath them with a crash. The Sebezh voivodes, Prince Zasekin and Tushin, did not give them time to recover: they struck, crushed and drowned the unfortunate Lithuanians, seized their banners and cannons, and almost exterminated them. Nemirov escaped and galloped away on a fast steed to report to old Sigismund the demise of his army. There was as much lamentation in Kiev, Vilnius and Krakow as there was rejoicing in Moscow, where the people were shown the trophies and the valiant voivodes were honored and praised.

To commemorate this brilliant victory, Elena ordered the Church of the Life-giving Trinity to be erected in Sebezh. We gave Lithuania no peace: we restored Pochep and Starodub, and founded the towns of Zavoloche in the Rzhev district and also Velizh in the Toropets district. Princes Gorenskii and Barbashev torched the outskirts of Lyubech and Vitebsk, taking many prisoners and all sorts of booty.

In compliance with the principles of Ivan and Vasilii, the Duma did not care to take offensive action against the khan. His bands of brigands had appeared on the banks of the Bystraya Sosna but departed as soon as our troops showed up. In April 1536 they dared to attack Belev, but were trounced by our local voivode.

Islam, showered with the king's gifts, was about to reconcile himself with Saip-Girei so that together they could menace Russia with attacks, but although he yielded the title of ruler to him, he did not yield power. A new dispute broke out between them and the perfidious Islam sent courier after courier to Moscow with letters of friendship, expressing his enmity toward Saip- and Safa-Girei, ruler of Kazan.

> **TRUCE WITH LITHUANIA**

Sigismund now saw that Russia, even with its child-sovereign, was stronger than Lithuania and began to think of peace. He expressed his displeasure to our turncoats: he arrested Lyatskii and treated Prince Simeon Belskii so harshly that he, still burning with hatred towards Russia, departed in vexation for Constantinople, where he sought the protection and patronage of the sultan.

Back in February 1536 the king's noble, Pan Yurii Radziwill had written to Elena's favorite, Prince Telepnev (through his brother, who was a Lithuanian prisoner) of the advantages of peace for both powers. Telepnev replied that Ivan was no foe of tranquility, but they squabbled a long time over the site of the negotiations.

Sigismund had previously sent a dignitary to congratulate Ivan on his elevation to the throne, and desired that Ivan, since he was the younger, send his nobles to Lithuania out of respect for his greater age, to conclude a peace. However, Moscow's boyars considered this incompatible with our national prestige.

> **1537**

Sigismund was obliged to yield and at the beginning of 1537, the voivode of Polotsk, Yan Glebovich, along with 400 noted courtiers and servitors, arrived in Moscow.

Following custom, both sides demanded the impossible: the Lithuanians wanted Novgorod and Smolensk; we wanted Kiev and all of White Russia. They not only argued, but even became abusive. Tiring, they only concluded a truce for five years, with the condition that we control the new fortresses of Sebezh and Zavoloche, and they, of Gomel.

Consequently, the war ended with concessions and acquisitions by both parties, even though they were insignificant. The boyar Morozov and Prince Paletskii took the truce document to Sigismund, but they could not persuade him to free the Russian prisoners. The king permitted the grand prince's emissaries free passage through Lithuania to see the emperor and the Hungarian king, but would not allow a Moldavian official to come to us, saying that the voivode Peter was a rebel and a malefactor against Poland.

Just as the grand prince's policy did not tolerate concord between Lithuania and the Crimean khans, and tried in every way possible to foment enmity between them, so the Crimeans likewise did not care to see us at peace with Lithuania, since war gave them the opportunity to pillage both our territory and the king's. Islam was displeased when he heard of the truce negotiations and assured Ivan of his readiness to attack the king with all his forces. To demonstrate his desire for our friendship, he informed Ivan that Prince Simeon Belskii had arrived in the Crimea from Constantinople, boasting that he would conquer Russia with the sultan's help.

> CRIMEAN AFFAIRS

"Beware," Islam wrote. "I am familiar with Suleiman's cunning and love of power. He wishes to enslave the northern Christian lands, both yours and Lithuania's. He has ordered his pashas and Saip-Girei to assemble a large army so that your turncoat Belskii can march with him against Russia. I alone stand in friendship with you and I am interfering with his schemes."

Belskii indeed sought to destroy his homeland and, in order to work his evil more safely, he tried to shower the regent with assurances of his repentance. He wrote to her requesting safe conduct for himself, promising to come to Moscow immediately to atone for his flight with diligent service. How could such a criminal expect charity from Elena? His phony repentance was a new trickery and our government did not hesitate to resort to deceit as well in order to chastise this criminal. The boyars replied to him in Ivan's name that his transgression was excusable by his youth and would be permanently forgotten.

Even in ancient times, many distinguished people had left for foreign lands, then returned and were once again favored by the grand princes; Ivan would grace his relative, improved by years and experience, with love. A herald and gifts were now sent to Islam from Moscow, with a persuasive request that he hand the turncoat over to us or kill him. But Islam was no more: one of the Nogai

> ISLAM'S DEATH

princes, Bagyi, a friend of Saip-Girei, had killed him in a surprise raid and took many prisoners, among them Belskii, who was saved by fate for new criminal activities. Elena and the boyars tried to ransom him by sending money to the Nogai uluses* as if it came from Simeon's mother and brothers, but to please the khan, Prince Bagyi sent this important prisoner to him as a friend.

Islam's death and the restoration thereby of Saip-Girei's sole rule in the Taurid were extremely disagreeable to us. Islam had been perfidious, but as an enemy of the khan whom he had deposed and of the ruler of Kazan, he had found an alliance with Russia to his own advantage. Saip-Girei, however, under the tutelage of the sultan, had close ties to rebellious Kazan and had been irritated to see our friendship with Islam, even though we, while respecting the latter as more powerful, had from time to time also sent flattering letters to Saip. The khan lost no time in aggravating the grand prince: he robbed Moscow's emissary in the Taurid, but then, apparently satisfied with this vengeance, he informed us of the destruction of his malefactor and offered Ivan brotherhood. He wanted gifts and *forbade* him to menace Kazan.

THE MENACE OF SAIP-GIREI

1538

"I am prepared to live with you in friendship," he ordered the grand prince to be told, "and I will send one of my most distinguished nobles to Moscow if you send to me either Prince Vasilii Shuiskii or the equerry Telepnev. You will be reconciled with *my* Kazan and will refrain from demanding tribute from its people. But if you dare to fight, we do not wish to see your emissaries or your heralds. We shall then be enemies; we shall invade the Russian land and everything therein will be turned to ashes!"

At this point, our legions were getting ready to march on Kazan. Its brigands, scattered around the Volga by loyal Meshchera Cossacks, gained the upper hand over two Muscovite voivodes, Saburov and Prince Zasekin Pyostryi. The latter had been killed in a battle somewhere between Galich and Kostroma,

---

* [A Tatar encampment or settlement.]

while in January 1537 the ruler of Kazan unexpectedly attacked Murom. He burned the outskirts, but did not take the town, and fled when he saw our banners in the distance.

No longer afraid of Lithuania, Elena and the boyars planned a powerful operation against Kazan. They rejected all of Saip-Girei's peace proposals, but the khan's threats seemed so significant that our state council decided to postpone the war. They informed Saip-Girei and the ruler of Kazan that the grand prince was agreeable to peace on the condition that Safa-Girei retain his allegiance to Russia. In Ivan's name, the boyars responded to the ruler:

"You call Kazan *your own*, but look in the old chronicles: has it not always belonged to the country that conquered it? It would be possible to give it to another, but he would now be a subject of the former, like a high priest. You speak of your supposed rights, but are silent about Russia's actual rights. Kazan is ours because my grandfather conquered it, and it is only through deceit and trickery that you have gained temporary control of it. Let everything be as of old: we will be in brotherhood with you and forget about Safa-Girei's guilt. We will send you a distinguished emissary, but not Shuiskii or Telepnev, who are needed in the national Duma during my minority."

With this we conclude our account of the foreign affairs of Elena's regency, which was also distinguished by a number of beneficial internal innovations, especially the construction of new fortresses necessary for Russia's safety.

Grand Prince Vasilii, finding the Kremlin cramped by Moscow's large population and inadequate to defend itself in case of enemy attack, had wished to surround the capital with a new, more extensive wall. Elena realized his intention, and on May 20th, 1534, began to dig a deep ditch from the Neglinnaya River around the trading quarter (which contained all the merchants' shops and markets) to the Moscow River by way of Trinity Square (the site of judicial combats) and Vasilievskii Meadow. Servants of the court of the metropolitan,

> CONSTRUCTION OF KITAIGOROD AND NEW FORTRESSES

the boyars and all residents, with only officials and distinguished citizens excluded, worked on it and finished it in June.

On May 16th of the next year, after a religious procession and service led by the metropolitan, Petrok Maloi, a newly baptized Italian, laid the foundation of the wall next to the ditch. It had four towers with the Sretenskie (Nikolskie), Trinity (Ilyinskie), Vsesvyatskie (Varvarskie), and Kozmodemyanskie Gates on the main street. This [part of] town was named Kitai, or Middle, it was explained. In addition to two fortresses on the Lithuanian border, Elena founded

1) the town of Mokshan in the Meshchera district on the site long called Murunza,

2) Buigorod in the Kostroma uezd,*

3) the fortress of Balakhna at Sola on the former site of the trading quarter, and

4) Pronsk on [the site of] the old town.

Vladimir, Yaroslavl and Tver, which had been reduced to ashes, were rebuilt, while Teminkov was moved to a more convenient location. Ustyug and the Sofiya side of Novgorod were encircled by walls, and Vologda was fortified and extended. The regent, cognizant of the chief need of a realm so vast and so little settled, invited residents of Lithuania and gave them land, preferences and privileges, nor did she spare the treasury in ransoming the many Russians who had been taken into captivity by the Tatars. She requested the assistance of the priesthood and rich monasteries for this. For example, in 1534 Archbishop Makarii sent her 700 rubles from his eparchate, saying,

"The human soul is worth more than gold."

This wise Novgorod prelate enjoyed the respect of the court, and not only traveled to only to pray with the metropolitan for Russia's prosperity, but also aided the nation with his wise advice in the national Duma.

The chroniclers also credit Elena's regency with a revaluation of the country's coinage, which was necessitated by

---

* [A secondary geographic subdivision comprising *volosts*, which are low-level administrative units.]

CHAPTER ONE

circumstances. Formerly a funt* of silver usually made five rubles and two grivnas, but cupidity devised a ruse: people began to trim the edges of coins and to recast them with alloys, so that a funt now made 10 rubles. Many became rich at this craft, and it created chaos in the marketplace: prices rose. Sellers were afraid of being cheated, and weighed and tested the coinage, or demanded an oath from the purchaser that it was not counterfeit.

> REVALUATION OF THE COINAGE

Elena banned the circulation of trimmed, impure or old coins. She ordered them recast and minted, so that a funt now made six rubles without any alloying, and she ordered counterfeiters and trimmers to be executed (they had molten tin poured into their mouths and their hands were cut off). The depictions on the coinage remained as before: the grand prince on a steed, but with a lance in his hand, not a sword, as heretofore. Because of this, they began to be called *kopeks* [from *kopyo*: lance or spear].

But Elena was unable to please the people either by her prudence in foreign affairs or by her many praiseworthy deeds within her realm. Tyranny and lawlessness, and now her increasing love for Prince Telepnev-Obolenskii, evident to all, gave rise to hatred towards her and even contempt. Neither power nor sternness will save a ruler if his holy patron averts his face from him. The people were silent in the streets and the squares, but talked all the more in private of folly on the throne, for family circles and fellowships of the unfortunate are impenetrable to a tyrant.

> GENRAL DISLIKE FOR ELENA

The regent, wishing to deceive her people and her own conscience, frequently went on pilgrimages to monasteries with the grand prince. But hypocrisy and pusillanimous cunning earn not only hypocritical praise, but new accusations before the implacable court of morality. To the voice of outraged virtue was joined the voice of envy. Telepnev was the only real nobleman in the Duma and the nation; others, more senior, were boyars in name only, and none of them seemed to have any worth unless they were able to please the court favorite.

---

* [Obsolete Russian unit of mass: 409.5 grams, or a little less than a pound.]

| 3 April, Her Death | Change was wanted, and then – suddenly – young in years and in blooming health, the grand princess died. The contemporary, Baron Herberstein,* states positively in his memoirs that Elena was poisoned. He sees in this event only *justified vengeance*, but it is neither that of a child against a father nor of a subject against a sovereign. Elena had after all been the legitimate ruler of Russia during Ivan's minority. God, conscience and history punish bad rulers: they are hated in life and cursed when they die.

This is good enough for civilized society, without need of steel or poison; otherwise we should have to reject the essential principle of monarchy: that the person of the ruler is *inviolable*. Secret villainy does not diminish him. Although we abhor the crime, we agree that Herberstein's information is likely correct. The chronicles do not say a word about an illness of Elena. She died in the second hour of the day and was buried the same day in the Voskresenskii [Ascension] Monastery. Whether the metropolitan read the burial service over her body is not stated. The boyars and the people apparently did not manifest even a feigned grief. The young grand prince wept and fell into the embrace of Telepnev, who alone was in despair, for it was he alone who could be deprived of everything and gain nothing by Elena's death. With curiosity the people asked: who would rule the country?

---

* [German diplomat and historian, 1486-1566.]

CHAPTER II

YOUNG IVAN AND THE BOYAR DUMA

1538-1547

Downfall and death of Prince Telepnev. Predominance of Prince Vasilii Shuiskii. Freeing of princes Ivan Belskii and Andrei Shuiskii. Discord among the boyars. Prince Ivan Belskii again imprisoned. Death of Prince Vasilii Shuiskii. His brother's supremacy. Overthrow of the metropolitan and the selection of Ioasaf. Character of Prince Ivan Shuiskii and pillage inside the country. Raids by external enemies. Embassies to Constantinople and Stockholm. Treaty with the Hansa. Pact with Astrakhan. A Nogai delegation. Plot against Shuiskii. The freeing of Prince Ivan Belskii; his power. Pardon of Prince Vladimir Andreevich and his mother. A mitigated fate for Prince Dmitrii Uglitskii. Pardon of Prince Simeon Belskii. Ruler of Kazan attacks. Crimean khan invades. Courage of the people and the army. Flight of the enemy. Discord among the boyars: the downfall of Prince Ivan Belskii. Metropolitan exiled. Renewed preeminence of Prince Ivan Shuiskii. Ordination for Makarii. Truce with Lithuania. Raids by the Crimeans and the Nogai Tatars. Affairs in Kazan. Relations with Astrakhan and Moldavia. Change in administration. Insolence of the Shuiskiis. Ivan's poor upbringing. Plot against the chief nobles. Downfall of the Shuiskiis. Power of the Glinskiis. Governmental cruelty. A good agreement with Lithuania. Army to Kazan. Shig-Alei rules in Kazan, then flees. Expedition to the mouth of the Sviyaga. Travels of the grand prince and his people's discontent.

Several days passed with the people kept quietly ignorant, but with ambitious nobles meeting secretly and scheming. Up till now the regent had taken the sovereign's place, but now, with a seven-year-old sovereign, a period of total aristocracy – or boyar rule – commenced. A few of these boyars boldly craved supreme power over Russia; the rest merely got ready to take one side or the other to facilitate the best

> DOWNFALL AND
> DEATH OF
> PRINCE TELEPNEV

conditions for their own personal benefit. Elena's favorite, Prince Ivan Telepnev, was not idle: as the friend and brother of Ivan's governess, the boyarynya [boyar's wife] Agrippina Chelyadina, he thought to control the young monarch, to stay with him and fawn upon him, relying on the support of his former friends. However, in the changed circumstances, their numbers had diminished and their ardor had cooled.

Elena's sudden death – not by natural causes it was thought – presaged the appearance of new, more powerful rulers. In order to guess who might have secretly effected her death, the curious waited to see who might benefit from it. These true, or perhaps false, despite their likelihood (as is often the case), suspicions turned to the most senior boyar, Vasilii Vasilievich Shuiskii. He was descended from the Suzdal princes who had been expelled from their hereditary domain by Donskii's son.* Hating Moscow's sovereign, they had served Novgorod, and in the final days of its liberty, Prince Shuiskii-Grebenok had been its chief voivode.

After seeing the conclusive triumph of autocracy in Russia, these exiles, one after the other, entered Moscow's service and became its most distinguished nobles. Prince Vasilii Vasilievich had occupied the first seat on the Council in the time of Ivan's father and again in Elena's time, and all the more hated her favorite, who while outwardly deferring to him, had exclusive control over the Duma. The power-hungry Prince Shuiskii laid plans and attracted many boyars and officials to his side; in a cruel act of willfulness and violence, he declared himself head of the government.

On the seventh day after Elena's death, he ordered those dearest to young Ivan arrested: his governess, the boyarynya Agrippina, and her brother, Prince Telepnev. They were put in chains and imprisoned despite the tears and howls of the defenseless boy sovereign. The lot of the unhappy noble upon whom all the princes and boyars had fawned a week previously was to have neither trial nor righteous retribution, but an illegitimate and cruel execution. Telepnev died of starvation, just as the regent and he himself had had Glinskii and Ivan's uncles put to death. But evil does not justify evil, and the chroniclers condemn this personal vengeance,

---

* [Dmitrii Donskoi (which Karamzin renders as Dimitrii Donskii) was the hero of the Battle of Kulikovo in 1380. It is not clear which of his sons is referred to here.]

prompted by envy of Elena's former favorite, who had wished to be her son's favorite as well. Telepnev had intellect, energy and noble ambition; he was not afraid to leave the court to go to war. He was dissatisfied with power and wanted the glory that comes from deeds, not the favor of sovereigns. His sister, the boyarynya Agrippina, was exiled to Kargopol and ordained as a nun.

The Duma, the country and the sovereign himself came under the power of Vasilii Shuiskii and his brother, Prince Ivan, as well as a distinguished member of the Council, wherein only one boyar could dispute precedence with them. This was Prince Dimitrii Belskii, a relative of Ivan, whose friendship these members sought. Dimitrii's brother, Prince Ivan Theodorovich, and Andrei Mikhailovich Shuiskii had been imprisoned; they were released with honor, as innocent. The former resumed his previous seat in the Duma; the latter was promoted to boyar. Blinded by pride, Prince Vasilii Shuiskii wanted to establish himself at the highest level, by marriage into the royal family. A widower for 15 years or more, he married Ivan's young sister Anastasiya, daughter of Prince Pyotr of Kazan.

> PREDOMINANCE OF PRINCE VASILII SHUISKII

> FREEING OF PRINCES IVAN BELSKII AND ANDREI SHUISKII

Prince Shuiskii's absolute power lasted only about six months, however: Prince Ivan Belskii, whom he had freed, became his enemy and was in league with the metropolitan Daniil, the majordomo Mikhail Tuchkov and other important officials. It began when Belskii asked young Ivan to make Prince Yurii Bulakov-Golitsyn a boyar, and the son of the distinguished Khabar Simskii, an okolnichii, without saying a word to the Shuiskiis, who were enraged. Their enmity was multiplied by insults: one side spoke of base ingratitude and vile intrigues, the other, of despotism and tyranny.

> DISCORD AMONG THE BOYARS. PRINCE IVAN BELSKII AGAIN IMPRISONED.

Finally, the Shuiskiis demonstrated their power: they once again jailed Prince Ivan Belskii and exiled his advisors to various villages. The chief of them, the secretary Theodor Mishurin, was tortured by soldiers, stripped bare, and beheaded on the executioner's block in front of the city prison. All this was done in the name of the Shuiskiis and their boyar followers, and not in the name of the sovereign, that is, it was perpetrated brazenly and lawlessly. It is worth noting that Prince Dimitrii Belskii once again escaped the miserable fate of his younger brother; he was likely saved by his cautious and pacific character.

DEATH OF PRINCE VASILII SHUISKII

The despotic nobleman, Prince Vasilii, now considered himself to be the ruler of Russia. Word of his sudden illness and death, which may have been due to natural causes, doubtless served as the occasion for various speculations and inferences. His death showed the vanity of the love of power, but the lesson was lost on Moscow's boyars. Vasilii's brother, Prince Ivan Shuiskii, became their chief; he thought only to perfect his vengeance over their enemies, accomplishing that which his late brother had not been able or had not dared to do.

HIS BROTHER'S SUPREMACY

Neither the metropolitan Daniil's holy office nor his cunning mind saved him. He had plotted with Prince Ivan Belskii to overthrow the Shuiskiis, but he himself was now deposed from his metropolitan see by boyar edict and exiled to the Iosifov Monastery, where he had the means to atone for the sins of his ambition and sycophancy at court through the strict and austere life there. Fearing accusations of illegitimacy, the nobles had gotten a note from the former pastor in which he seemingly renounced his prelacy voluntarily in order to pray in silent solitude for the sovereign and the nation. The bishops replaced him with Ioasaf Skrypitsyn, abbot of the Trinity Monastery, *by the judgment of the devout and the grand princely* (i.e., the boyars), as it says in the chronicle.

OVERTHROW OF THE METROPOLITAN AND THE SELECTION OF IOASAF

CHARACTER OF PRINCE IVAN SHUISKII AND PILLAGE INSIDE THE COUNTRY

In the midst of such agitation and unrest, caused by boyars' personal love of power, how could the government have the requisite firmness, unity and vigilance for internal development and external security? In his deeds, the chief of the nobles (Prince Shuiskii) displayed neither a mind for policy nor a love of the good; he was but a crude despot. He wanted only henchmen and would not tolerate rivals.

In the Duma he gave orders like a despot, in the palace like a proprietor, and reveled in effrontery. For example, he never stood in young Ivan's presence: he sat in his bedchamber, leaned his elbow on the bed, and put his feet on the sovereign's chair. In short, he displayed all the base and cowardly arrogance of a slaveholder. Shuiskii was also reproached for his base cupidity. It is written that he stole from the treasury, forged a large number of vessels out of its gold and ordered the names of his ancestors be inscribed on them. In any case, his relatives, friends, minions and sycophants mercilessly plundered every district in which they had been given income property or governmental duties. Thus did the boyar Andrei Mikhailovich Shuiskii and Prince Vasilii Repnin-Obolenskii, deputies in Pskov, *rampage like lions,* as a contemporary expressed it. They not only oppressed farmers and townsmen with illegal imposts, concocted crimes, encouraged lying informers, dug up old matters, and demanded gifts from the rich and unpaid labor from the poor, but also sought loot in the holiest of monasteries with the rapacity of Mongol brigands.

Residents of the suburbs of Pskov did not dare to venture into town because it was like a den of thieves. Many people fled to other lands and the marketplaces and monasteries were deserted. Conjoined to this horrible misery of injustice and violence were the frequent devastating raids by foreign brigands. We were, say the chroniclers, the victims and laughing stock of the infidel. The khan of the Crimea made laws for us, while the ruler of Kazan cheated and plundered us. After the former had detained a grand princely official who had been dispatched to the sovereign of Moldavia, he wrote to Ivan:

| RAIDS BY EXTERNAL ENEMIES |

"I did what you have done repeatedly. Your father and mother, disregarding your country's laws, hunted down and vilely murdered my emissaries on the way to Kazan. I, too, have the right to interfere with your communications with my Moldavian enemies. You want good will from me: why do you express yourself so crudely? Did you know that I have more than 100,000 warriors? If each of them captures just one Russian, how much will be your loss and my gain? I do not hide, for I feel my strength. I am declaring everything ahead of time, for I shall do what I say. Where would you like to meet me? In Moscow, or on the banks of the Oka? Know that I am not coming alone, but with the great sultan, who has subdued the world from east to west. I will show him the way to your capital. But what would you do to me? You may rage as you wish, but you will not enter my territory."

Not just Ivan III and Vasilii, but also the regent Elena, had from time to time satisfied the greed of the khans, but our rulers had at least displayed a certain noble pride in their correspondence with them and did not forget themselves. The Shuiskiis' regime was marked by weakness and timidity with regard to Muscovite policy: the boyars did not even dare to respond to Saip-Girei's threats. A distinguished emissary was quickly dispatched to the Taurid to purchase a perfidious alliance with the barbarian with the promise not to fight Kazan, while the ruler of Kazan, assuring us of his love of peace, wanted us to send him annual gifts as tokens of our respect.

Moscow waited in vain for his plenipotentiaries: they did not come, and for two years Kazan incessantly violated our districts of Nizhnyi Novgorod, Balakhna, Murom, Meshchera, Gorokhovets, Vladimir, Shuya, Yurievets, Kostroma, Kineshma, Galich, Totma, Ustyug, Vologda, Vyatka, and Perm. They appeared only in large groups, burning, murdering and taking prisoners, so that one of the chroniclers compared the disasters of these times to Baty's invasion,* saying,

"Baty shot like lightning through the Russian land, but the men of Kazan never left, and Christian blood flowed like water. The defenseless hid in forests and in caves; sites of former settlements became overgrown with brush. Monasteries were reduced to ashes; the infidels lived and slept in the churches, drinking from the holy vessels. They stripped the icons to provide their wives with earrings and necklaces. They put glowing coals in the monks' boots and forced them to dance, and ravished the young nuns. They put out the eyes and cut off the nose and ears of those they did not take into captivity; they cut off arms and legs and, most horrible of all, they took many into their faith, and these unfortunates then pur-

---

* [The Mongol invasion of 1237-1240]

sued Christians as their fierce enemies. I write not from hearsay, but from what I myself have seen. I will never be able to forget it."

What were the administrators of the state doing, the boyars? They boasted of their patience with Khan Saip-Girei, explaining that Kazan was suffering due to the Russians and so to please the khan *we would not move a hair in the defense of our land*! The boyars only wanted peace, but did not get it. They had concluded an alliance with Saip-Girei but found it useless. The khan's emissaries were in Moscow while his son Imin pillaged the Kashira uezd with his gang of brigands. We were satisfied with the explanation that Imin had not heeded his father and had acted on his own.

Other external activities of Russia corresponded better to its national dignity. The official Adashev travelled with letters of friendship to the sultan and to the patriarch, while Zamytskii departed Novgorod to see the Swedish king. In both Constantinople and Stockholm our emissaries were shown great honors. The boyars ratified a commercial treaty with the Hansa and renewed an alliance with Astrakhan, where Abdyl-Rakhman was ruling once again. Nogai emissaries showed up in Moscow, one after another, offering their services and requesting only the favor of free trade in return. Lithuania observed the truce and did not threaten Russia: old Sigismund was living out his remaining time in peace.

> EMBASSIES TO CONSTANTINOPLE AND STOCKHOLM.
>
> TREATY WITH THE HANSA
>
> PACT WITH ASTRAKHAN
>
> A NOGAI DELEGATION

At this point there was an upheaval within our aristocracy. After deposing the metropolitan Daniil, Prince Ivan Shuiskii had figured the new archprelate would be his friend, but he was deceived. Ministering with perhaps a love of virtue and patriotism, and seeing Shuiskii's incapacity to govern the state, or perhaps for another, less praiseworthy reason, the metropolitan Ioasaf dared to stand up for Prince Ivan Belskii before the young sovereign and for Prince Ivan Belskii in

> 1540

> PLOT AGAINST SHUISKII

the Duma. Many boyars joined him. Some spoke only of mercy, others of justice.

> THE FREEING OF PRINCE IVAN BELSKII; HIS POWER

Suddenly, in Ivan's name, Belskii was formally released from prison and seated in the Duma, while Shuiskii, astounded by the effrontery of the metropolitan and the boyars, could not avert the blow. Trembling with malice, he swore to take vengeance on them for this treachery, and from that day did not care to participate in the affairs, much less attend the Duma, where Belskii's faction gained the upper hand and began to govern with moderation and prudence. There were no disgraces or persecutions. The government became more solicitous and diligent with regard to the public good, and the misuse of power diminished. Some bad deputies were replaced and Pskov was liberated from the violence of Prince Andrei Shuiskii, who was recalled to Moscow.

The Duma did for Pskov what Vasilii had done for Novgorod: it restored their judicial rights. Sworn jurors, chosen from the citizenry, began to try all criminal matters independently of the deputies, who were greatly vexed at thereby being deprived of the

> PARDON OF PRINCE VLADIMIR ANDREEVICH AND HIS MOTHER

means to act and gain things illegally. Pskov relaxed, praising the favors of the grand prince and the virtue of the boyars. The government earned still more praise by releasing Ivan's cousin, the young Prince Vladimir Andreevich and his mother, who had been imprisoned by Elena. The two removed to their home, where they lived in solitude.

A year later, on Christmas Day, mother and son were presented to Ivan. Andrei's rich estates were returned to them and they were permitted to have a court, boyars and princely servitors. But how can we call a favor the meager, pitiful boon that was then

> A MITIGATED FATE FOR PRINCE DMITRII UGLITSKII

shown to another of Ivan's relatives? Dimitrii, grandson of Vasilii the Dark and son of Andrei Uglitskii, was still among the living, forgotten by all. For 49 terrible years, from his tender youth to deep old age, he had been imprisoned in chains, alone with God and a quiet conscience, never having offended anyone or violated any human law in his life. He was there only on account of his father, for he had had the misfortune to be born the nephew of the despot who had been obliged to destroy the injurious appanage system in Russia, and who loved autocracy more than he did his blood relatives.

The rulers, while wishing to be merciful, did not resolve to return Dimitrii, like one from the grave, to a world strange to him. They merely ordered him freed from the weight of his chains and put in a prison more light and airy! Hardened by adversity, Dimitrii, perhaps for the first time, was now softened in his heart and wept tears of gratitude, no longer weighed down or cramped by fetters. He could see the sun and breathe more freely. He was being confined in Vologda, and there he died. His brother, Prince Ivan, had died some years before in a monastery. They lie side by side in Vologda's Church of the Savior at Priluki.

While easing the fate of the persecuted, the foremost noble, Prince Ivan Belskii, also wanted to return his accused brother Simeon to his homeland and [a life of] virtue. The metropolitan Ioasaf undertook to act as intermediary. The accused was exonerated as much as possible, excused by his youth and the unbearable tyranny and despotism of Elena's favorite. The sovereign pardoned him, one act for which history reproaches Prince Ivan Belskii! This turncoat and traitor, who had led foreign enemies into our land, would appear once again at the court and in the Duma, with honors based on his loyal, distinguished service to the country! But Simeon did not make use of this charity, which was so contrary to the principles of justice and public welfare. Moscow's herald did not find Belskii in the Taurid: the turncoat was in the field with the khan, scheming at Russia's destruction. Saip-Girei had sworn friendship with the grand prince solely to deceive us and open a path for himself into the heart of Muscovite territory with a sudden attack. The Duma, however, under the leadership of Prince Ivan Belskii, while concentrating on domestic development, still kept an eye on external dangers.

> 1540-1541
>
> PLOT AGAINST SHUISKII

Secretly preparing for war, the khan also invited the ruler of Kazan to march on Russia. Fortunately for us, it was inconvenient for them to go into action at the same time. The former was waiting for spring and pasturage on the steppes, while the latter did not have a strong force of boats and feared to have the Volga behind him in summer, where in case of his flight, the Russians might drown Kazan's troops.

> RULER OF KAZAN ATTACKS

Encouraged by our long-time patience and inaction, in December 1540 Safa-Girei skirted Nizhnyi Novgorod and managed to reach Murom unobstructed, but was not able to take a step further. The city's soldiers and citizens fought courageously on its walls and in sallies. Prince Dimitrii Belskii marched from Vladimir and Prince Alei came from Kasimov with his loyal Tatars. They destroyed the scattered enemy bands in the Meshcherskii lands and in the villages of Murom district. Safa-Girei fled home so fast that Moscow's voivodes did not pursue him. This rather unsuccessful campaign increased the numbers of dissatisfied people in Kazan.

The local princes and the most distinguished of them, Bulat, secretly wrote to Moscow to have the sovereign send them troops; they were prepared to assassinate or hand Safa-Girei over to us. Safa, having seized property from the nobles and the people, sent the treasury to the Taurid. Our boyars ordered the immediate consolidation of the legions from 17 towns in Vladimir under the command of Prince Ivan Vasilievich Shuiskii. They replied flatteringly to Bulat, promising him favor and amnesty, but they were awaiting further news from Kazan before sending troops there.

> 1541

Khan Saip-Girei was still concealing his intentions. Ivan's emissary, Prince Aleksandr Kashin, was in the Taurid and the khan's, one Tagaldyi, was in Moscow, but the boyars guessed that the ruler of Kazan was operating in concert with the Crimea and so, to cover any eventuality, they were gathering troops in Kolomna, where young Ivan personally inspected the camp. In the spring, Moscow learned (through prisoners who had escaped the Taurid) that the khan was moving on Russia with the entire

> CRIMEAN KHAN INVADES

horde, leaving no one at home except women, children and old people. With him he had a detachment from the sultan with gunpowder artillery and had been joined by bands from the Nogai uluses, from Astrakhan, Kaffa and Azov. They also learned that Prince Simeon Belskii had undertaken to be their guide.

The deputy of Putivl, Thedor Pleshcheev, was ordered to ascertain the truth of this information. Men he had sent into the steppes saw the traces of a marching army there, 100,000 or more. Prince Dimitrii Belskii, with the rank of commander-in-chief now arrived in Kolomna and took the army into the field. Prince Ivan Vasilievich Shuiskii remained in Vladimir with Prince Shig-Alei. Large units came to Serpukhov, Kaluga, Tula and Ryazan from all over. Our daring scouts encountered the khan near the Don; they observed his legions, but could not see the end of them in the open steppes. Saip-Girei was now on this side of the Don; he assaulted Zaraisk but could not take the fortress, repelled by the glorious valor of its voivode, Nazar Glebov.

| 28 July |

Meanwhile, as our legions were setting up camp near the Oka, Moscow was touched by a really moving sight: the 10 year old sovereign and his brother Yurii were praying to the Almighty at the Dormition Cathedral, before the icon of the Virgin of Vladimir and the grave of the metropolitan St. Pyotr, for the salvation of the nation. Ivan wept, and within earshot of the people, said,

"Lord! You protected my great-grandfather during the fierce Temir-Aksak's invasion. Protect us now, young and orphaned! We have neither father nor mother, nor the power of reason, nor strength in our right arms, yet the nation demands salvation from us!"

He ordered the metropolitan to the Duma, where the boyars were sitting, and told them,

"The enemy is coming. Decide whether I should stay here or go!" The boyars considered this quietly and calmly. Some said that in cases of enemy attack, the grand prince had never shut himself up in Moscow. Others responded as follows:

"When Edigei marched on the capital, Vasilii Dimitrievich left to gather troops from the Russian districts, but left Prince Vladimir Andreevich and his brothers in Moscow. Our sovereign now is a youth and his brother is even younger. Is it for children to gallop from place to place to assemble our legions? Will they not sooner fall into the hands of the infidels, who doubtless will scatter throughout the districts rather than come to Moscow?"

The metropolitan agreed with the latter argument and said,

"Where is safety to be sought for the grand prince? Novgorod and Pskov are next door to Lithuania and the Germans; Kostroma, Yaroslavl and Galich are subject to raids by Kazan; and who would be left in Moscow, where the saints are buried? Dimitrii Ivanovich left the city without a strong voivode and what happened then? May the Lord preserve us from such a catastrophe! There is no need to gather an army: one is stationed on the banks of the Oka, another is in Vladimir with Prince Shig-Alei and protects Moscow. We have the power; we have God and the saints, to whom Ivan's father entrusted his beloved son. Do not be disheartened!"

All the boyars unanimously exclaimed, "Sovereign, remain in Moscow!"

COURAGE OF THE PEOPLE AND THE ARMY

The grand prince thereupon verbally commanded the city bailiffs [*prikashchiki*] to prepare for a siege. The soldiers and the people were animated with enthusiasm and fervor. All swore to die for Ivan, to stand fast for their holy churches and their homes. The men were assigned to units for the defense of the walls, gates and towers; cannons were placed everywhere and the trading quarter was fortified with stakes. No one gave thought to flight and the chroniclers were amazed by the general inspiration of courage – as if by a supernatural action.

It was [later] likewise among the troops. The commanders generally ranked themselves on the basis of seniority or distinction in lineage and did not want to be subordinate to those of junior or equal ranking, despite their sovereign's orders. Vasilii and his father had been able to restrain the nobles' struggle for precedence, but young Ivan, while inspiring intrepidity and audacity in his chief officers, allowed this evil to proceed to extremes. Arguments and enmity ruled the walls. The grand prince dispatched his secretary Ivan Kuritsyn with a letter to Dimitrii Belskii and his distinguished comrades-in-arms trying to persuade them to set aside all personality issues, all dissent and disputes, to unite their hearts and minds for the homeland, for their faith and for their young sovereign, who was entrusting himself to God and their arms.

"Let the Oka be an invincible barrier against the khan!" Ivan wrote. "But if that does not hold back the enemy, I will block his road to Moscow with my breast. Fight mightily in the name of God the Almighty! I promise my love and favor not only to you, but also to your children. I order that anyone who falls in battle shall have his name entered for commemoration in churches and I will take care of his wife and children."

The commanders were filled with emotion as this letter was read to them.

"So!" they said. "We shall forget our enmity and even ourselves; we shall recall the favors of Grand Prince Vasilii; we shall obey Ivan, whose weak arm cannot yet command a weapon. We shall obey the young sovereign and gain glory from the grand prince! If we realize our fervent desire, if we are victorious, then we shall be famous not just in Russia, but also in distant, foreign lands. We are not immortal; we will die for our homeland! God and our sovereign will not forget us."

These hitherto quarrelsome and obstinate voivodes wept, embraced one another in joyous magnanimity, called each other brothers and swore be victorious or to leave their bones on the banks of Oka. They emerged from the tent and read Ivan's letter to the troops; they made speeches strong with deep, virtuous emotion. The effect was indescribable. The warriors shouted,

"What we want is to drink the cup of death with the Tatars for our young sovereign! If you, our fathers, are in concord with one another, then we shall march joyfully against the infidel foe!"

All the legions then moved forward, numerous, well formed up and hearty.

> **30 July**

The khan had now arrived at the Oka and stood on the heights. The other bank was occupied by the Muscovite vanguard under the command of princes Ivan Turuntyi-Pronskii and Vasilii Oklyabin-Yaroslavskii. Thinking that our army was no larger, the Tatars launched rafts into the river in an attempt to cross it. The Turks shot cannons and arquebuses to drive off the Russians, who were employing only arrows and at first were shaken and confused.

But princes Punkov-Mikulinskii and Serebryanyi-Obolenskii came rushing up with their legions and the Russians held firm. Soon new, dense groups of them appeared in limitless ranks: the princes Mikhailo Kubenskii, Ivan Mikhailovich Shuiskii and Dimitrii Belskii himself raised their banners on the riverbank. Troops kept coming from the left and right, and a huge reserve force could be seen in the distance. The khan saw this and was amazed; he wrathfully told our turncoat Simeon Belskii and the nobles,

"You have deceived me. You assured me that Russia did not have the strength to fight both Kazan and me at the same time. What an army! Neither I nor my experienced elders have seen the like."

Seized with terror, he tried to flee, but the mirzas* restrained him. Cannonballs, bullets and arrows flew from both sides. In the evening the Tatars departed for the heights while the Russians, animated by courage, shouted at them,

"Come back! We are waiting for you!"

> **Flight of the Enemy**

Night fell. Ivan's voivodes, according to the chroniclers, *feasted only in spirit* and prepared for a decisive battle on the following day. There was neither fear nor doubt; they did not want to rest: the sound of weapons and men shouting never quieted in the camp. New units arrived, one after the other, with heavy artillery. In the distance, the khan kept hearing happy shouting in our army. By firelight he saw how we had placed cannons on the hills on the shore. He did not wait till morning: riven by fear, malice

---

* [Mirzas were Tatar gentry.]

and shame, he galloped off in a cart. Behind him, after destroying part of their baggage train, fled his army. The remainder and some of the sultan's cannons were left as booty for us.

This was the first time Ottoman trophies had fallen into our hands! Dimitrii Belskii sent Prince Ivan Kashin to Moscow with the happy news, while Princes Mikulinskii and Serebryanyi were sent in pursuit of the khan. They captured stragglers, who informed us that Saip-Girei had gone to Pronsk. Having boasted that he would stand on the Sparrow Hills and lay waste to all of Moscow's districts, he thought to diminish his shame with the capture of this insignificant fortress, just as Tamerlan had conquered nothing in Russia except for Elets. Our chief voivode now sent new legions forward to more quickly expel the khan from Russian territory.

On 3 August Saip-Girei encircled Pronsk, where Vasilii Zhulebin was in charge. The latter had few troops but great audacity. He repulsed the enemy with cannons, stakes and stones. The mirzas wanted to talk to him, so he appeared on the walls.

"Surrender," they told him. "The ruler promises to favor you, or else he will stay here and take the town." The knight responded,

"This town was placed here by God's will and no one will take it without His will. Let your ruler stay: he will soon see Moscow's voivodes."

Saip-Girei ordered gabions* prepared for a new, more powerful assault while Zhulebin armed not only all the citizens, but the women as well. Rude stones and stakes lay on the wall; the kettles boiled with water and fuses burned over the loaded cannons. Then the besieged received word that the princes Mikulinskii and Serebryanyi were already nearby; happy cries resounded through the town. When the khan found out about this, he burned his gabions and on 6 August, withdrew from Pronsk, pursued by our voivodes all the way to the Don, while Prince Vorotynskii defeated Prince Imin, who had stopped to plunder Odoev uezd.

---

* [Wicker baskets filled with earth and stone to form portable fortifications.]

All Russia celebrated the fortunate expulsion of a powerful enemy from its innards and praised the sovereign and his commanders. Ivan's youth, which had touched the heart during the days of fear, was also especially charming during the popular celebrations, when the reigning youth gave thanks to Heaven in the Cathedral of the Most High for Russia's salvation, and also when he expressed his gratitude to the commanders in the name of the nation and they, touched by his favor, replied to him with tears of joy,

"Sovereign! We triumphed through your angelic prayers and through your *good fortune!*"

The people believed in this luck all the more, and Ivan's youthful years opened up an unbounded scope for hope. This is what contemporaries felt, who saw in Saip-Girei a new Mamai or Tamerlan and they praised his flight as a glorious event for Russia. They gave no thought to the future. [They did not consider the proverb:] What has happened might also happen again. Russia, while now really powerful, still remained subject to sudden raids. We wanted the enemy to give us enough time to prepare a defense. We had chased them off, but our villages were deserted and the state had been deprived of its most valuable resource – people! Only the experience of centuries brings a genuine measure of national security to a stable regime.

Prince Ivan Belskii, the soul of the administration, now stood on the highest rung of good fortune, supported by the personal favor of the reigning youth, whose mind was maturing, as well as by Ivan's close relation to him, his success at arms and his deeds of charity and justice. His conscience was at peace and the people were content . . . and yet malice secretly seethed and envy schemed untiringly in the world at large, but especially at court. Here our history shows the danger of magnanimity, which would otherwise seem to excuse the cruelty and vengefulness of the power-hungry, whose enemies find peace only in the grave. Prince Ivan Belskii, freed by the metropolitan and the boyars, might have exchanged his place in prison with Shuiskii, might have deprived him of life and liberty, but he scorned his impotent malice and did even more: he showed respect for Shuiskii's military abilities and made him a voivode.

This we might call an error of magnanimity: he had the goal of inner peace when he should have let his passions rule. Shuiskii had angrily yielded power to his incautious opponent. He thought only of revenge and the distinguished boyars, princes Mikhailo and Ivan Kubenskii, Dimitrii Paletskii and the treasurer Tretyakov entered into a conspiracy with him to destroy Belskii and the metropolitan, who were bound by friendship and probably a fervent patriotism. Apparently there was no plausible pretext: the plotters simply wanted to overthrow their master, take his place and demonstrate their power rather than the justice of their position.

> DISCORD AMONG THE BOYARS;
>
> DOWNFALL OF PRINCE IVAN BELSKII

They attracted many court nobles and boyar cadets, not only in Moscow, but in other districts as well, especially in Novgorod. Shuiskii was in Vladimir with his legions, intending to march on Kazan; with promises and flattery he multiplied the number of his confederates in the army. He extracted secret oaths from them and notified his minions in Moscow that the time had come for action. He sent to them 300 reliable knights from Vladimir with his son, Prince Pyotr. On the night of 3 January there was a terrible alarm in the Kremlin: the conspirators seized Prince Ivan Belskii in his home and imprisoned him. They did likewise to his loyal friends Prince Pyotr Shchenyatev and the distinguished official Khabarov: the former was taken out the rear doors of the sovereign's own apartments. They surrounded the metropolitan's cell, broke in the windows with rocks and nearly killed Ioasaf, who ran away from them to the Trinity residence house.

Only by invoking the name of St. Sergii could the monastery abbot and Prince Dimitrii Paletskii restrain the frenzied boyar cadets who had raised their hands against the arch-pastor. The metropolitan sought safety in the palace with young Ivan, but the sovereign, awakened by the fierce cries of the mutineers, himself trembled like an unhappy sacrificial victim. The boyars noisily entered the grand prince's chamber searching for Ioasaf. They seized the metropolitan and exiled him to the Kirillov

> METROPOLITAN EXILED

monastery at Belo-ozero. They then ordered the court priests to sing matins three hours before dawn. They shouted and made commands as if they had conquered the throne and the Church, without the least regard for propriety; acting like mutineers, they terrorized the capital. No one in Moscow was able to sleep a wink on this terrible night. Shuiskii galloped at dawn from Vladimir and once again became chief of the boyars. Prince Ivan Belskii was sent to confinement at Belo-ozero, Shchenyatev to Yaroslavl and Khabarov to Tver.

> RENEWED PREEMINENCE OF PRINCE IVAN SHUISKII

Peace and quiet were restored. But Shuiskii was still not content: he feared treachery as well as Prince Ivan Belskii's virtue and his widespread popularity. He ordered him killed, with the consent of the boyars, but without the knowledge of the sovereign. Three villains murdered the unfortunate prince in prison. Contemporaries write that he had been a genial nobleman, brave in war, and an enlightened Christian. Once suspected of secretly taking bribes because of the excessive love of peace he showed in the two wars against Kazan, he vindicated himself in public opinion by the renown of the last years of his life.

Russia already knew Shuiskii and could expect from his administration neither wisdom nor an unsullied fervor for the good of the nation, which could only hope that this man's power, clearly obtained illegitimately, would not be prolonged. The Duma remained as it had been, but some of its members, lost or gained power depending on their relationship to the chief noble. Prince Dimitrii Belskii mourned his brother and sat in the first place in the Council as the senior boyar. It was necessary to select a new metropolitan since Ivan's minority gave the arch-pastor of the Church still more importance. He would have free access to the sovereign, could counsel him, boldly contradict the boyars and influence the minds of the citizens with Christian exhortations.

> ORDINATION FOR MAKARII

Shuiskii and his friends did not want to make a second mistake in this choice. They tarried for about two months and then summoned Archbishop Makarii, who was brilliant, energetic and devout. He also loved worldly honors, and had perhaps rendered them service in Novgorod by inclining its citizens towards their side in hopes of taking Ioasaf's place. Seven days later Makarii was named archprelate and taken to the Metropolitan's Court, and 10 days later he was ordained. Thus had Prince Ivan Shuiskii willfully deposed two metropolitans solely out of personal animosity towards them and without any trial or legitimate pretext. The priesthood was silent and obeyed. All the former violence and injustice was renewed. Preferences and rights that had been given to district residents during the blessed rule of Prince Belskii were annulled by the machinations of the deputies. Russia again became booty for Shuiskii's minions, relatives, friends, and servitors, but meanwhile Ivan was growing up!

The most significant act of foreign policy of this time was a new truce with Lithuania for seven years, concluded in Moscow by the king's pans Yan Glebovich and Nikodim. A permanent peace was desired by both sides, but as before, they could not agree on the conditions. The boyars tried for an exchange of prisoners. The king requested Chernigov and six other towns in return, perhaps fearing that that the Lithuanian prisoners would return to him with changed hearts and that the Russian ones might disclose new ways for us to achieve victory. Finally they only agreed not to fight each other and to allow merchants to trade freely.

> TRUCE WITH LITHUANIA

Sigismund had now become enfeebled: the pans negotiated in the name of his son and heir, Augustus. The [treaty] documents were read in the presence of young Ivan; the grand prince kissed the cross and gave his hand to the emissaries, then the boyar Morozov rode to Lithuania to exchange the documents. His orders were to intercede on behalf of our prisoners, so that they would not be held in fetters and would be permitted to attend church – was this a final comfort for those unfortunates condemned to die in an enemy country? Meanwhile, they quarreled over the Sebezh and other lands; they tried, but were unable to fix boundaries. The official Sukin, sent to Lithuania for this purpose, was supposed to talk in secret with its nobles and tell them that Ivan was now looking for a bride and that Moscow's boyars wished to know their thoughts on the advantages of a marital union of the sovereigns of both powers. We find no reply to this proposal in Sukin's report, however.

Having tasted failure, Khan Saip-Girei agreed to friendship with us. He gave leave to Ivan's emissary, Prince Aleksandr Kashin to return to Moscow with a new sworn document, but the khan's son Imin and rapacious mirzas were raiding the Severskii district and Ryazan. Moscow's voivodes engaged the Crimeans and defeated them on the famous field of Kulikovo* and then pursued them to the Mecha. Kazan's men sued for peace, but Prince Bulat no longer wanted to overthrow Safa-Girei and wrote to this effect to the boyar Dimitrii Belskii, while Princess Gorshadna wrote to Ivan himself. The princess was renowned for her erudition and sorcery. The chroniclers assert that she formally foretold Kazan's doom and Russia's greatness.

Raids by the Crimeans and the Nogai Tatars

Affairs in Kazan

The Boyars' Duma did not reject a peace treaty, but Safa-Girei procrastinated and did not conclude one. Amicable relations with Astrakhan and Moldavia continued. Prince Ediger of Astrakhan came to Russia to enter our service. The voivode of Moldavia, Ivan Petrovich, Stefan's grandson, wrote to the grand prince that Suleiman had expelled him, but then had shown favor and returned him to Moldavia, and now demanded, in addition to annual tribute, about 300,000 gold coins, which were impossible to collect from a land laid waste. The Moldavian ruler appealed to Ivan for monetary assistance, which was indeed sent.

Relations with Astrakhan and Moldavia

However, the Duma was more concerned with court sedition and intrigue than the internal or external affairs of the nation. Prince Ivan Vasilievich Shuiskii had not enjoyed power for long when he was forced – by illness, we should think – to absent himself from the court. He lived for another two or three years, but did not take part in the government, which he

Change in Administration

---

* [The Russians scored a major victory over the Mongols there in 1380.]

handed over to his closest relatives, three Shuiskiis: Princes Ivan and Andrei Mikhailovich and Thedor Ivanovich Skopin, who possessed neither magnanimity nor elevated minds. They only loved to rule and gave no thought to earning the love of their fellow citizens, or the gratitude of the young ruler through sincere diligence on behalf of their homeland. The mastery of these oligarchs consisted in the fact that they did not tolerate contradiction in the Duma and allowed only their own adherents access to the sovereign, keeping away anyone who might be a danger to them by virtue of their audacity, intellect or nobility of heart. But Ivan, who had come to understand [the situation], now felt the burden of this illegitimate guardianship: he hated the Shuiskiis, especially Prince Andrei, who was brazen and ferocious: Ivan tended to be partial to those who secretly or openly wished them ill. Among these was the Duma councilor Theodor Semyonovich Vorontsov. The oligarchs wanted to get rid of him in a seemly manner but were unable to do so. They were full of malice, and seeing Ivan's growing fondness for him, they decided to resort to violence.

In the palace, at a formal session of the Duma in the presence of the sovereign and the metropolitan, the Shuiskiis and their confederates, the princes Kubenskii, Paletskii, Shkurlyatev, Pronskii and Aleksei Basmanov, after a noisy debate over the supposed culpability of Ivan's favorite, leapt up, apparently furious, and forcibly dragged him into another room, where they tortured him and intended to kill him. Horrified, the young sovereign implored the metropolitan to save the unfortunate man, and the archprelate and the boyars Morozov spoke [to them] in the name of the grand prince.

1543

INSOLENCE OF THE SHUISKIIS

The Shuiskiis, as if granting them a favor, gave their word to leave Vorontsov alive, but they hit, shoved him, took him out into the square and imprisoned him. Ivan once more sent the metropolitan and the boyars to persuade them to send Vorontsov for service in Kolomna if it was impossible for him to be at the court or in Moscow. The Shuiskiis did not consent [to the latter]; the sovereign was obliged to confirm their decision and Vorontsov and his son were taken to Kostroma. In depicting the arrogance of the nobles at this time, the chronicler says that in an argument with the metropolitan one of the minions, Thoma Golovin, trod on his cloak and ripped it as a sign of his disdain.

These extremes of illegitimate crude despotism and unbridled passions in the administration of the nation hastened a change that was desired by the people and by the Shuiskiis' enemies. Ivan was now 13. Born with a fiery spirit, a rare intelligence, and an especially strong will, he would have had all the qualities of a great monarch if his upbringing had developed or perfected his natural gifts. But he had lost his father and mother early and had been subject to the will of turbulent nobles who were blinded by a reckless love of personal power.

> IVAN'S POOR UPBRINGING

On the throne, he was the most unfortunate orphan in the Russian state, for his flaws were preparing an unhappy fate not just for himself, but for millions. Such flaws easily arise in the presence of the best natural qualities if the intellect, the governor of the passions, is mute within the young soul or a wise mentor does not elucidate the laws of morality for that soul. Prince Ivan Belskii alone might have been a teacher and example of virtue to the reigning youth, but the Shuiskiis had removed this worthy noble from the sovereign and the nation. They tried to attach Ivan to themselves by fulfilling all of his youthful desires, constantly amusing and entertaining him at court with noisy games and in the field with hunting; they nurtured in him a tendency towards the love of power and even cruelty, not foreseeing the consequences.

For example, while loving hunting, he also loved not only to kill wild animals, but to torment domestic ones, throwing them to the ground from a high roof, while the boyars said, "Let the child have fun!" They surrounded Ivan with a crowd of youngsters and laughed when he romped unseemly with them, or galloped through the streets trampling women and old people, enjoying their screams. They praised his daring, courage and agility!

They did not think of explaining to him the sacred duties of a monarch because they were not fulfilling their own. They did not care to educate his young mind because they figured that his ignorance would facilitate their fondness for power. They hardened his heart and scorned his tears over Prince Telepnev, Belskii and Vorontsov in hopes of compensating for their audacity by indulging his harmful whims and in hopes of furthering the youth's frivolity through continual amusing distractions. This crazy regime recoiled onto the heads of its perpetrators. The Shuiskiis wanted the grand prince to remember their indulgences and to forget their aggravations, but he remembered only the aggravations and forgot the indulgences, for he had come to realize that power was his, not theirs.

Every day as he became more and more mature the Kremlin palace intrigues multiplied, as did the complications for the ruling boyars and the numbers of their enemies, among whom the most powerful were the Glinskiis, the sovereign's uncles, the princes Yurii and Mikhailo Vasilievich, who were both vengeful and ambitious: the former sat in the Duma, the latter had the distinguished rank of equerry.

Despite the Shuiskiis' vigilance, they suggested to their 13-year-old, who was deeply hurt by Vorontsov's exile, that it was time for him to take real power as an autocrat and cast down the usurpers who were oppressing the people, tyrannizing the boyars and abusing the sovereign himself, by threatening death to everyone he loved. He only needed to arm himself with courage and give the command: Russia was awaiting his word. It is likely that the prudent metropolitan, displeased with the Shuiskiis' brazen violence, also took the Glinskiis' side and advised Ivan to do the same. They were able to conceal their main design – the court seemed utterly quiet. The sovereign, as was his wont, traveled in the fall to pray at the Sergiev Monastery and to hunt at Volok Lamskii* with his distinguished officials. He gaily celebrated Christmas in Moscow and then suddenly summoned the boyars.

> PLOT AGAINST THE CHIEF NOBLES

> 29 DECEMBER

For the first time he appeared commanding and formidable; he declared firmly that they had misused his youth, acted illegally, willfully murdered people and plundered the land; many of them were guilty but he would punish only

> DOWNFALL OF THE SHUISKIIS

---

* [I.e., the portage on the Lama River; now called Volokolamsk.]

the one most culpable: Prince Andrei Shuiskii, the chief councilor to the tyranny. He was taken and thrown to the dogs, which tore apart this distinguished noble in the streets, killing him. The Shuiskiis and their friends were silent, while the people expressed satisfaction. The crimes of the deceased were made public: it was written that with his insatiable greed he had seized lands belonging to the court, supposedly as purchases, and oppressed the peasants; and that even his servitors had ruled and tyrannized in Russia without fear of either courts or laws.

But was this barbaric execution, even though deserved by this unworthy noble, worthy of a real government and sovereign? It became apparent that the Shuiskiis' misfortune had made their successors none the wiser, that neither law nor justice had the upper hand. It was only one side against the other, and violence led to more violence. It was clear that young Ivan could not yet hold power on his own: the Glinskii princes and their friends issued orders in his name, although some chronicles also say that

| POWER OF THE GLINSKIIS |

"from this time on the boyars began to fear their sovereign."

The disgraces and cruelty of the new administration struck real fear into the heart. Thedor Shuiskii-Skopin, Prince Yurii Temkin, Thoma Golovin and many other officials were exiled to remote places, while the distinguished boyar Ivan Kubenskii, son of the sovereign's first cousin once removed, Princess Uglitskaya, was imprisoned: he had been found to have close ties to the Shuiskiis, but was distinguished by merit, intellect and a quiet disposition. He was imprisoned in Pereyaslavl together with his wife, in the same place where the ill-fated Prince Andrei Uglitskii and his children had been confined.

| GOVERNMENTAL CRUELTY |

| 1544-1546 |

A punishment invented by barbarians was the fate of the court official Athanasii Buturlin, who was convicted of insolent speech. His tongue was cut out in front of the prison, before the eyes of the people. Kubenskii was released five months later and the sovereign released him from disgrace, along with the princes Pyotr

Shuiskii, Gorbatyi, Dimitrii Paletskii and his favorite, the boyar Theodor Vorontsov. He pardoned them out of respect for the metropolitan's intercession, but not for long. A rumor spread that the khan of the Crimea was preparing to invade our territory. For several months his son Imin had been pillaging the appanages of Odoev and Belev at will (where our voivodes only squabbled over seniority and did not budge to repel the enemy).

Ivan, now a young man, commanded a large army himself. He traveled by water to the Ugreshskii monastery of St. Nikolai, then joined the army and stayed in Kolomna for about three months. The khan did not appear. The army camp became the court and the vilely ambitious engaged in intrigues. One time the sovereign, as was his custom, rode out to hunt and was stopped by 50 Novgorod arquebusiers, who wished to present him with some sort of complaint. Ivan would not hear it and ordered his courtiers to chase them off. The Novgorodians resisted and a fight commenced. Shots were fired and swords slashed, killing about 10 men from both sides. The sovereign returned to camp and ordered his privy secretary Vasilii Zakharov to find out who incited the Novgorodians to such impudence and mutiny. Zakharov, perhaps in collusion with the Glinskiis, reported to him that the boyars Prince Ivan Kubenskii and Thedor and Vasilii Vorontsov were the secretly to blame for the mutiny. This was sufficient: without any further investigation, the wrathful Ivan ordered them beheaded, declaring that they had also earned this punishment by their previous crimes during the reign of the boyars.

The chroniclers attest to their innocence, reproaching Thedor Vorontsov solely because he had wanted exclusive seniority among the boyars and was irritated when the sovereign conferred this favor on another. Having facilitated the downfall of the Shuiskiis and having been Kubenskii's enemy, this unfortunate favorite lost his head on the same block with them! Thus Ivan's new nobles, mentors and advisors tutored the young monarch in a terrible disregard of jurisprudence, and in cruelty and tyranny! Like the Shuiskiis, they effected their own downfall; like them, they did not restrain, but rather urged Ivan onto the path of debauchery. They did not take care to make the supreme power beneficial, but only to consolidate it in their own hands.

Nevertheless, we acted successfully and honorably in our relations with other powers. The Polish king abdicated in favor of his son, Sigismund II Augustus, who, when he informed the grand prince of this, assured Russia of his love of peace and of his firm intention to fulfill the treaty concluded with it.

A GOOD AGREEMENT WITH LITHUANIA

The deceits of the ruler and nobles of Kazan caused Ivan to lose patience, however. Two armies, one from Moscow and the other from Vyatka, met on the same day and hour beneath the walls of Kazan. They reduced the ruler's inns and the vicinity to ashes and killed a large number of people near the city. They took some distinguished prisoners on the banks of the Sviyaga and returned safely.

ARMY TO KAZAN

This sudden Russian invasion forced the ruler to consider that the Kazan nobles had secretly arranged it. He wanted vengeance: he killed a number of princes and expelled others, which produced widespread animosity, with the result that the men of Kazan, who had requested troops of Ivan, intended to hand over Girei and 30 Crimean officials to him. The sovereign promised to send an army, but first wanted them to depose and confine their ruler. The rebellion indeed broke out: Safa-Girei fled and many Crimeans were torn to pieces by the populace. The seits, uhlans,* princes and all Kazan's officials swore allegiance to Russia and once again accepted Shig-Alei as their ruler. He was formally elevated to the throne by princes Dimitrii Belskii and Paletskii.

1546

SHIG-ALEI RULES IN KAZAN, THEN FLEES

There was rejoicing and celebration, and a new betrayal. Apparently foreseeing the unavoidable and imminent demise of their state, they did not know what they wanted; they were roiled by passions and mental eclipse. They had accepted their ruler not to obey him, but to rule the country in his name. They held him like a prisoner and forbade him to leave the city or show himself to the people. They feasted in the palace and rattled their weapons; they drank from the ruler's golden vessels and took them for themselves. Alei's loyal servitors were imprisoned and some were

---

* [A seit is a very high Tatar official; an uhlan is a light cavalryman.]

even killed. They demanded that their ruler write letters to Ivan boasting of their fervor!

A chronicler tells us that Shig-Alei had foreseen his fate and had only agreed to come to Kazan out of obedience to the grand prince. He endured a month in silence because he trusted one of the most distinguished princes, named Chura, who was devoted to Russia. This fine noble was unsuccessful in appealing to the consciences of Kazan's rulers. In vain he threatened them with the consequences of their irrational inconstancy. Having exasperated Shig-Alei and fearing Ivan's vengeance, they thought to summon Safa-Girei once more – he was already on the Kama with a large group of Nogai. Prince Chura informed Alei of this plot, advised him to flee and got a boat ready.

Some sort of festival had begun: the nobles drank into the night, fell into a deep sleep and did not see their ruler as he left the palace; he successfully escaped to Russia via the Volga. For the third time, Safa-Girei took the throne of Kazan. He began a reign of terror: he killed Prince Chura and many other distinguished people. He surrounded himself with Crimeans and Nogai; he detested his subjects and only wanted to keep them terrified

Seventy-six princes and mirzas and Chura's brothers, as well as some of Safa-Girei's most frenzied villains, who had been deceived by him, sought refuge in Moscow. Emissaries of the highland Cheremis arrived in their wake with the assurance that all their men were ready to join with our army if it were to invade Kazan's territory.

It was now winter, and complete vengeance was deferred till summer, but Ivan wanted to verify the favorable disposition of the wild Cheremis towards us: he detailed several of their legions to the mouth of the Sviyaga.

> EXPEDITION TO THE MOUTH OF THE SVIYAGA

Prince Aleksandr Gorbatyi commanded them, but he did battle only with winter snow-storms and failed to find his opponents anywhere. He had not been ordered to lay siege to Kazan, but satisfied himself with booty and brought 100 Cheremis warriors to Moscow to serve as hostages for the loyalty of their people.

Travels of the Grand Prince and his Peoples' Discontent

Meanwhile the grand prince traveled around the various districts of his country, but only to see their famous monasteries and to engage in hunting in the untamed forests, but not to make a national inspection or to protect the people from the oppression of avaricious deputies. With his brothers Yurii Vasilievich and Vladimir Andreevich he visited Vladimir, Mozhaisk, Volok,* Rzhev, Tver, Novgorod, and Pskov, where, surrounded by a throng of boyars and officials, he could not see the sorrows of his people, nor, amidst the noise of amusing diversions, hear their groans of misery. He galloped about on fast hinnies** and left behind him tears, grievances and new miseries; the sovereign's journey, which provided not the slightest benefit to the nation, imposed costs on the people because the court demanded entertainment and gifts. In short, Russia did not yet see a father-monarch on the throne and could only comfort itself with the hope that years and maturity of mind would disclose to Ivan the sacred art of governing for the good of the people.

---

*   [Probably Volok Lamskii, now Volokolamsk.]
** [The offspring of a male horse and a female donkey.]

CHAPTER III

IVAN CROWNED TSAR

1546-1552

Ivan crowned tsar. Marriage of the sovereign. Anastasiya's virtues. Ivan's vices and bad governance. Conflagrations in Moscow. Mutiny of the mob. Ivan's strange improvement. Silvestr and Adashev. The sovereign's speech at the place of execution. Changes at court and in powers. Mildness of the government. Code of laws. Restraints on the order of precedence. The Stoglav. Legal documents. Selection of jurors. Church institutions. Intention to enlighten Russia. Military activities. Expedition to Kazan. Truce with Lithuania. Crimean affairs. Death of the ruler of Kazan. Expedition to Kazan. Selection of site for a new fortification. Assault of the Nogai Tatars. Founding of Sviyazhsk. Subjugation of the High Bank. People of Kazan terrified. Conditions of the peace treaty with them. Syuyunbeka. Shig-Alei again accedes to the throne. Prisoners freed. Disloyalty in Kazan and the cruelty of its ruler. Negotiations with Alei. Ruler leaves Kazan. Final betrayal by citizens of Kazan.

The grand prince was now 17. He summoned the metropolitan and talked with him alone for a long time. The metropolitan left with a happy expression, gave a service in the Cathedral of the Dormition and sent for the boyars, even those who were in disgrace, and went to the sovereign with them. The people did not yet know anything, but the boyars, like the metropolitan, expressed their joy. The curious guessed the reason and impatiently awaited the disclosure of the happy secret.

| 1546 |
| IVAN CROWNED TSAR |

Three days passed. Ordered to assemble at the court, the archprelate, the boyars

| 17 DECEMBER |

and all the important officials circled round Ivan, who remained silent for a while and then said to the metropolitan,

"Putting my trust in God's grace and in the holy protectors of the Russian land, I intend to marry. You, father, have blessed me. My first thought was to seek a bride in other lands, but after more thorough consideration, I have abandoned this idea. In my childhood I was deprived of my parents and was raised an orphan: I might not be agreeable to the customs of a foreigner. Would the marriage then be happy? I intend to find a bride in Russia in accordance with God's will and with your blessing."

The metropolitan replied with feeling,

"God himself suggested this plan to you, which is so desired by your subjects! I bless it in the name of the Heavenly Father."

The boyars wept for joy, according to the chronicler, and praised the ruler's wisdom with new delight when Ivan revealed to them another intention:

"to fulfill before his wedding the ancient rite of his ancestors and be *crowned before the nation.*"

He ordered the metropolitan and the boyars to prepare for this grand ceremony that would appear to confirm with the seal of religion the sacred bond between the sovereign and his people. This was no new thing for the Muscovite state: Ivan III crowned his grandson before the nation, but the grand prince's advisors – wishing either to impart more significance to this rite or else trying to avoid the sorrowful memory of Dimitrii Ivanovich's[*] fate – spoke only of the ancient example of Vladimir Monomakh, on whom the metropolitan of Ephesus had placed the crown, chain, and shoulder mantle of Constantine.

It was written and related that when Monomakh was dying, he gave this regalia to his sixth son, Georgii. He ordered him to protect it like the pupil of his eye and transmit it from generation to generation without using it until God was touched by Russia's misery and raised up a genuine autocrat over the nation who was worthy to adorn himself with these tokens of power. This tradition entered into a chronicle of the 16th century, when Russia indeed

---

[*] [Ivan III's grandson, 1483- 1509. Died in prison.]

CHAPTER THREE

saw an autocrat on the throne and Greece, expiring in misery, bequeathed to us the majesty of its rulers.

On the morning of January 16, Ivan entered the dining hall, where all the boyars were to be found, while the voivodes, princes and officials stood richly dressed in the vestibule. The sovereign's confessor, the Blagoveshchensk* archpriest, took from Ivan's hands a golden platter holding the life-giving cross, crown, and shoulder mantle and carried them to the Cathedral of the Dormition, accompanied by the equerry, Prince Mikhail Glinskii, the treasurers and secretaries. The grand prince soon followed, preceded by his confessor with a cross and holy water, aspersing people on either side and followed by Prince Yurii Vasilievich, the boyars, princes and the entire court.

1547

On entering the church the sovereign kissed the icons; the priestly assemblage wished him many years of life, the metropolitan blessed him and the service was performed. In the middle of the cathedral two places were made ready on the twelve-stepped ambo,** dressed with golden pillow-slips; at their feet lay velvet and damask coverings. Here the sovereign and metropolitan took their seats. In front of the ambo stood a richly-decorated lectern with the regalia. The archimandrites took them and gave them to Makarii, who was standing with Ivan; he placed the cross, shoulder mantle and crown on him and loudly prayed for the Most High to protect this Christian David with the power of the Holy Ghost, seat him on the throne of virtue, and provide him with terror for the recalcitrant and a favorable eye for the obedient.

The ceremony concluded with a new invocation for long life for the sovereign. After he had received congratulations from the priesthood, the nobility, and the citizenry, Ivan heard the liturgy and returned to the palace, stepping from velvet to damask and from damask to velvet. Prince Yurii Vasilievich showered him with gold coins at the cathedral doors and on the steps from a bowl that Mikhailo Glinskii carried after him. As soon as the sovereign departed the church, the people, who had been silent and

---

* [The Cathedral of the Annunciation, in the Kremlin.]
** [An elevated platform in front of the iconostasis.]

immobile up till now, rushed noisily to strip the royal seat; everyone wanted a scrap of the pillow-slip as a memento of this great day for Russia.

To summarize, this formal coronation was a repeat of Dimitrii's, with some change in the prayers and with the difference that Ivan III himself (and not the metropolitan) had placed the crown on the young monarch's head. Contemporary chroniclers do not mention a scepter, anointing with chrism or communion, nor do they say whether Makarii spoke a homily to the ruler. Even a very clever, elegant one could not have the same effect as a sincere and touching invocation to God, the Ruler of All, who gives sovereigns to the people and virtue to the sovereigns!

From this time on, Russia's monarchs began to call themselves *tsars*, not only in relations with other powers, but also inside the country, in all their dealings and papers. They also kept the title of *grand prince*, which had been sanctified by its antiquity: Moscow's scribes told the people that thereby the prophecy of Revelations was fulfilled concerning a *sixth kingdom*, which was the Russian one. Although this title did not increase [the ruler's] natural power, it affected the popular imagination, and the biblical title of *tsar* [king, in this context] recalled the Assyrian, Egyptian and Judean kings, and ultimately the Orthodox Greek emperors. In the eyes of the Russians, it magnified the dignity of their sovereigns.

The chroniclers say, "Our enemies submitted: infidel rulers and dishonorable kings. Ivan stood on the top rung of power amongst them!"

It is worth noting that in 1561 Patriarch Ioasaf of Constantinople, as a token of his keenness for the Russian monarch confirmed him in his rank of tsar in a consiliar letter, saying,

"Not just the tradition of reliable people, but the chronicles themselves attest that the present ruler in Moscow is descended from the unforgettable Princess Anna, sister of Emperor Porphyrogenitus, and that the metropolitan of Ephesus, duly accredited by a council of Byzantine clergy, crowned the Russian grand prince Vladimir." This letter was signed by 36 metropolitans and bishops.

Chapter Three

> **Marriage of the Sovereign**

Meanwhile, distinguished officials, okolnichie and secretaries rode all over Russia to see *all* the well-born unmarried women so they could present the best prospective brides to the sovereign. Of these, he chose young Anastasiya, daughter of the widow Zakharina, whose husband Roman Yurievich had been an okolnichii and whose father-in-law had been a boyar of Ivan III. Their line was descended from Andrei Kobyla, who had come to us from Prussia in the 14th century. However, it was not distinction, but personal merit which vindicated this selection and, in describing her qualities, contemporaries attributed to her all the feminine virtues for which they could find

> **Anastasiya's Virtues**

names in the Russian language: chastity, humility, piety, sensitivity and kindness, joined with a sound mind. They did not speak of beauty since that was considered a prerequisite for successful prospective brides for the tsar.

After performing the wedding ceremony in the Cathedral of the Virgin, the metropolitan told the newlyweds,

> **13 February**

"Today through the mysteries of the Church you have been joined forever. May you bow together before the Most High and live in virtue. Your virtue is truth and charity. Sovereign! Love and honor your wife, and you, Christ-loving tsaritsa, do obey him. As the holy cross is atop a church, so a husband is to his wife. Diligently fulfill all of God's commandments and behold the good of Jerusalem and peace in Israel."

The newlyweds appeared before the eyes of the people and blessings reverberated in the Kremlin streets and square. Both the court and Moscow celebrated for several days. The tsar showered favors on the rich while the tsaritsa fed the lowly. Raised fatherless in quiet solitude, Anastasiya saw herself as if thrust into the theater of worldly majesty and glory by a supernatural act, but she did not forget herself; she did not change in her soul with the new circumstances, but attributed everything to God, bowing to Him even in the royal halls just as fervently as in the humble, sad home of her widowed mother. Interrupting the court's joyous feasting, Ivan and his wife walked on foot, in winter, to the Trinity Sergiev

Monastery and spent the first week of Lent there, praying every day over the grave of Saint Sergii.

> IVAN'S VICES
> AND
> BAD GOVERNANCE

Neither Ivan's piety nor his sincere love for his virtuous wife was able to curb his fiery, restless soul, impetuous in bursts of anger and schooled in raucous idleness to crude and unseemly amusements. He loved to display himself as tsar, not in the business of wise administration, but in punishments and unrestrained whims. He toyed, so to speak, with favors and disgraces, multiplying the numbers of his favorites, but the numbers of outcasts even more so. He behaved willfully so as to show his independence, but he was still dependent on the nobles, for he did not work on organizing the country and did not know that a truly independent sovereign is simply a virtuous sovereign.

Russia had never been governed worse: the Glinskiis, like the Shuiskiis, did what they wanted in the name of the young sovereign, enjoying honors and riches, and viewed the malfeasance of local administrators with indifference, demanding servility from them, rather than justice. Whoever bowed down before the Glinskiis might dare to grind the people under foot, and being their servant meant to be a lord in Russia. The deputies knew no fear – and woe to those who bypassed the nobles to bring grievances to the throne!

Thus in the spring of 1547, the citizens of Pskov, who had been the last to join the autocracy and were more daring than the rest, complained to the new tsar about their deputy, Prince Turuntyi-Pronskii, a Glinskii toady. Ivan was then in the village of Ostrovka, where seventy petitioners stood before him with accusations and evidence, but the sovereign would not hear them out and began to seethe with anger. He shouted and stamped his feet, threw hot wine over them, burnt their beards and hair, and ordered them to disrobe and lie on the ground. They expected to die, but at that minute a report came to Ivan about the fall of a great bell in Moscow. He galloped off to the capital and the poor men of Pskov remained among the living. Honorable boyars remained silent in the court, with eyes cast down. Clowns and jesters amused the tsar, while flatterers praised his wisdom. The virtuous Anastasiya prayed along with Russia, and God was listening. A strong character requires a powerful shaking to cast off the yoke of evil passions and to be put on the fervent path of virtue. To correct Ivan, it was necessary that Moscow burn!

Conflagrations in Moscow

Every year this capital had grown in extent and in numbers of residents. The court was more and more cramped in the Kremlin and Kitaigorod; new streets joined old in the suburbs. Houses were constructed more pleasing to the eye, but no more safe than before. Decaying masses of buildings, here and there separated by gardens, awaited only a spark of fire to become ashes.

The Moscow chronicles often speak of conflagrations, calling them *great*, but fire had never raged there as terribly as in 1547. A fire on 12 April burned stores with rich wares in Kitaigorod, state merchant courts, the Epiphany Cloister and many homes from the Ilyinskii Gate to the Kremlin and the Moscow River. A tall tower where powder was stored blew up, along with part of the city wall; it fell into the river and dammed it up with bricks. On 20 August all streets on the far side of the Yauza, where potters and tanners lived, were reduced to ashes, and on 24 June, in a terrible storm around midday, a great fire started on the other side of the Neglinnaya, in the Church of the Exaltation of the Cross on the Arbat street. It spread along the river and soon broke out in the Kremlin, Kitaigorod and the Great Suburb.

All of Moscow presented a spectacle of a monstrous flaming bonfire beneath clouds of thick smoke. Wooden buildings vanished, stone ones collapsed, iron glowed red as if in a furnace and copper melted. The roar of the storm, crackling of the fire and the cries of people were from time to time drowned out by explosions of gunpowder that had been stored in the Kremlin and other parts of the city. Only lives were saved; riches, whether licit or illicit, were consumed. Royal palaces, the treasury, treasures, arms, icons, old manuscripts, books, and even the relics of saints were all ruined.

While praying in the Cathedral of the Dormition, the metropolitan began choking from the smoke. He was forcibly removed and they tried to lower him by a rope from a secret place to the Moscow River. He fell, was injured, and taken to the Novospasskii Monastery, barely alive. Only the image of Mary, painted by the metropolitan St. Pyotr, was saved from the cathedral, along with the *Church Regulations*, which had been brought from Constantinople by Kiprian. The famous icon of the Virgin of Vladimir was left behind, but fortunately the fire, which destroyed the roof and church-porch, did not penetrate the interior of the church. The storm died down towards evening and the flames were extinguished in the third hour of the night, but the ruins continued to smoke for several days, from the Arbat and Neglinnaya to the Yauza and the end of Great Street and Varvarskaya, Pokrovskaya, Myasnitskaya, Dmitrovskaya and Tverskaya streets.

Not a garden or yard remained intact; trees had been turned into charcoal and grass to ashes. 1,700 people were burned to death, not counting infants. According to contemporaries it was impossible to imagine or describe the catastrophe. People with singed hair and blackened faces wandered like shades amidst the horrors of an extensive, ashy wasteland. They were seeking children, parents and what was left of their possessions; not finding them, they howled like wild animals.

"Fortunate," says a chronicler "was he who was moved in his soul to weep and look to Heaven!"

There was no one to give comfort: the tsar and the nobles had gone to Vorobyevo Village, seemingly to avoid hearing and seeing the people's despair. The sovereign immediately ordered the reconstruction of the Kremlin palace and the rich likewise hastened to rebuild, but none of them thought of the poor. The Glinskiis' enemies made use of this: Ivan's confessor, the archpriest, Prince Theodor Skopin-Shuiskii, the boyar Ivan Petrovich Theodorov, Prince Yurii Temkin, Nagoi and Grigorii Yurievich Zakharin, uncle of the tsaritsa, formed a conspiracy, and the people were disposed by misfortune to a frenzy of malice and mutiny

MUTINY OF THE MOB	The next day the sovereign rode with his boyars to visit the metropolitan at the Novospasskii Monastery. There his confessor, Skopin-Shuiskii and their distinguished

confederates declared to Ivan that Moscow had burnt because of the witchcraft of certain malefactors. The sovereign was astounded and ordered an investigation of the matter. Two days later they rode to the Kremlin, gathered the citizens in the square and inquired as to who had burned the capital. Some voices answered them,

"The Glinskiis, the Glinskiis! Their mother, Princess Anna, removed the hearts from the dead, put them in water, and rode around Moscow aspersing the streets with the potion. There, that is why we burned!"

This fable was concocted and broadcast by the conspirators. The wise did not believe it, but remained silent, since the Glinskiis had earned this widespread hatred. Many, even boyars, incited the people. Princess Anna, the sovereign's grandmother, was then at her estate in Rzhev with her son Mikhail. Her other son, Prince Yurii, was standing in the Kremlin square in a circle of boyars.

Astonished by the absurdity of the accusation and seeing the fury of the mob, he sought safety in the Cathedral of the Dormition, but the people broke in after him. A crime heretofore unprecedented in Moscow then took place: the mutineers murdered the sovereign's blood uncle in a holy church, and then took his body from the Kremlin to the place of execution.* They plundered the Glinskiis' possessions and killed many of their servants and boyar cadets. No one tried to calm the lawlessness; it was as if there were no government.

At this terrible time, when the young tsar was trembling in his palace at Vorobyevo and virtuous Anastasiya was praying, an amazing man appeared, named Silvestr, of priestly rank and from a Novgorod family. He approached Ivan in the guise of a prophet, with a raised, menacing finger and proclaimed to him in a convincing voice that the judgment of God was thundering above the head of this tsar who was frivolous and subject to evil passions, that heavenly fire

> IVAN'S STRANGE IMPROVEMENT; SILVESTR AND ADASHEV

---

* [Lobnoe Mesto: a raised stone platform in Red Square, more often used to announce imperial edicts than for executions.]

had reduced Moscow to ashes and that a divine power had roiled the people and poured the phial of wrath into their hearts.

Opening the Holy Scripture, he showed Ivan the rules God had given earthly sovereigns and adjured him to diligently carry out these principles. He even showed him some sort of terrible vision, which shook his heart and soul, and took over the youth's imagination and his mind. This produced a miracle: Ivan became a different man. Weeping tears of repentance, he extended his right hand to this inspired preceptor. He asked him for the strength to become virtuous – and received it. The humble priest did not ask him for a lofty title, honors or riches, but stood by the throne to sanction and encourage the young monarch on the road to reform. He established a close alliance with one of Ivan's favorites, Aleksei Theodorovich Adashev, a handsome young man described as an earthly angel. He had a tender, pure soul, good morals, an attractive mind, and a fundamental and disinterested love of the good.

He sought Ivan's favor not for his own personal profit, but for the benefit of the nation, and the tsar found him to be a rare treasure and a friend, someone quite indispensable, so that the autocrat could better know people, the state of the country and its real needs, since from the lofty height of the throne an autocrat sees people and things at a remove, in a deceptive light, while a friend who is a subject stands at the same level as everyone else and looks directly into their hearts, viewing things up close. Silvestr excited a desire for good in the tsar, while Adashev facilitated his ability to accomplish it. So says the wise contemporary, Prince Andrei Kurbskii, who was then a distinguished court official. At any rate, the epoch of Ivan's glory now commenced: a new, fervent energy for governance, distinguished by successes and grand intentions fortunate for the country.

First of all, he restrained the mutinous mob that appeared in Vorobyevo on the third day after Glinskii's murder, which surrounded the palace and shouted for the sovereign to hand over his grandmother, Princess Anna and her son Mikhail. Ivan ordered the mutineers to be fired at and the mob dispersed. Some were seized and executed, others escaped, and some fell on their knees and confessed. Order was restored. The sovereign now displayed a father's care for the poor: he took measures that none of them remained without a roof and bread.

Secondly, the real culprits of the mutiny, those who instigated the mob – Prince Skopin-Shuiskii and his minions – had been deceived if they had hoped to overthrow the Glinskiis and seize the tsar. Ivan spared them, either out of respect for his confessor and his wife's uncle, or because of the lack of clear evidence, or perhaps because he consigned the matter to the sole judgment of God. Despite the mob's illegal means, it had satisfied the common and justified hatred of the Glinskiis. The rebellious reign of the boyars was utterly destroyed, replaced by the autocracy of the tsar, a stranger to tyranny and whim. The sovereign spent several days in solitude, in fasting and prayer, in order to sanctify with religion the blessed change in governance and in his heart. He summoned the prelates, touchingly repented his sins and, absolved by them and put at peace with his conscience, partook of the sacrament.

With his young, fiery heart, he wanted to show his face to Russia. He ordered select people of every rank and situation be sent to Moscow from every town for important national business. They assembled – and on Easter, after Mass, the tsar emerged from the Kremlin with the priesthood, crosses, boyars and a military guard and came to the place of execution, where the people were standing in profound silence. After public prayer, Ivan turned to the metropolitan and said,

> THE SOVEREIGN'S SPEECH AT THE PLACE OF EXECUTION 1547-1550

"Holy prelate! I know of your ardor for good and for our homeland. Be the champion of my intentions. Early on did God deprive me of my father and mother. The nobles were not concerned with me and wished only to be despots. In my name they hijacked titles and honors, grew rich through injustice and oppressed the people – and yet no one was upset by this. In my pitiable childhood I seemed deaf and dumb. I did not hear the groaning of the poor and there was no denunciation on my lips! You, those who did as you pleased, evil conspirators, corrupt judges! What response will you give us now? How many tears, how much blood has been shed because of you? I am innocent of this blood! You, however, await the judgment of Heaven! . . . At this point the sovereign bowed in all directions and continued,

"Has not God given me a pious people? I pray for your faith in Him and your love for me: be of good courage! I cannot correct *past* evils, I can only save you *in the future* from similar oppression and pillage. Forget that which is not and shall be no more! Put aside hatred and enmity; we shall all join in Christian love. Henceforth I shall be your judge and protector."

On this grand day, all of Russia, as personified by its representatives, was present at the place of execution to reverently receive the sincere promise of its young monarch to live for its happiness. Ivan, in a rapture of magnanimity, declared his sincere forgiveness of the guilty boyars. He wanted the metropolitan and the prelates likewise to forgive them in the name of the Heavenly Judge.

He wanted all Russians to embrace each other fraternally and he wanted all complaints and lawsuits to be peacefully suspended for a period designated by himself. This same day he entrusted Adashev with receiving petitions from the poor, orphans and aggrieved, and formally told him,

"Aleksei! You are neither well-known nor rich, but you are virtuous. I am placing you in a lofty position not in furtherance of your desires, but to assist my soul, which strives toward such people. May you soothe the grief of these unfortunates, whose fate has been entrusted to me by God! Do not fear the powerful or the famous when they steal honors and act illegally. Neither be deceived by the lying tears of a poor man when he hatefully slanders a rich one! Zealously investigate everything and report the truth to me, fearing only the judgment of God!"

The people wept with emotion, along with their young tsar.

| Changes at Court and in Powers |

The tsar spoke and acted, relying on the chosen pair Silvestr and Adashev, who took into their sacred circle not only the prudent metropolitan, but also all virtuous and experienced men who in their venerable age were still ardent about their country – they had previously been dismissed by the throne when this flighty youth could not abide their gloomy outlook. Flatterers and jesters became silent at the court: in the Duma the mouths of slanderers and intriguers were stopped, and the truth could emerge.

Despite the trust Ivan placed in the Council, he himself got involved in both national and in important judicial matters so as to fulfill his promise to God and Russia. People everywhere praised the government's diligence for the common good and everywhere unworthy administrators were replaced, to be punished by scorn or imprisonment.

But he was not excessively strict. He wanted to mark the happy change in governance not by the cruel punishment of bad senior officials, but by a better choice of new ones, as if thereby to declare to the people that misprision of local power is the common, unavoidable consequence of somnolence or corruption in the central authority: if it tolerates plunder, then the plunderers are almost blameless, since they were permitted to do so. In only a few autocratic states do we see an easy and rapid change from bad to good, since they are all subordinate to the will of the autocrat, who, like a skilled mechanic, sets the masses in motion, turns an immense machine around, and by its means takes millions to prosperity or misfortune.

In general, wise moderation, humanitarianism and a spirit of mildness and peace became the rule for tsarist power. Very few of the former palace courtiers – even the very worst – were sent away. It is written that the rest were curbed or corrected. Ivan's confessor, the archpriest Theodor, who had been one of the principal culprits of the mutiny, was torn by his conscience and shut himself up in a monastery.

MILDNESS OF THE GOVERNMENT

New boyars entered the Duma: the tsaritsa's uncle, Zakharin, Khabarov (a loyal friend of the unfortunate Ivan Belskii), the princes Kurakin, Bulgakov, Danilo Pronskii and Dimitrii Paletskii, whose daughter, Princess Yulianiya, was favored with the honor of becoming the wife of the sovereign's 16 year old brother, Prince Yurii Vasilievich. Although the hated Mikhail Glinskii's title of equerry was taken away from him, he remained a boyar, kept his estates and his freedom to live where he chose. Terrified by the fate of his brother, however, he fled towards Lithuania with his friend, Turuntyi-Pronskii. Prince Pyotr Shuiskii chased after them. Seeing that they could not escape, they returned to Moscow and were arrested. They swore that they were not headed for Lithuania, but rather were on a pilgrimage to Okovets. These unhappy ones were shown to be lying, but were graciously pardoned; their flight was excused as being due to fear.

Inside the sovereign's family itself, where formerly had dwelt coldness, mistrust, hatred and enmity, Russia saw the peace and tranquility of sincere love. Having recognized the happiness of virtue, Ivan learned to value his virtuous wife still more. The charming Anastasiya encouraged him in all his good thoughts and feelings, and he became both a good tsar and husband. After he married off Prince Yurii Vasilievich, he chose a wife for Prince Vladimir Andreevich: the young lady Evdokiya, of the Nagoi line. Ivan lived with the first brother in one of the palaces; he favored and honored them both, and adjoined their names to his in his decrees, writing,

"We decree with our brothers and the boyars."

Wishing to emulate the great Ivan III in all things, and wishing to be, in that sovereign's own words, a *tsar of truth* – he not only sharpened his sword against foreign enemies, but in the florescence of his youth also busied himself with that important governmental matter which even in the most enlightened times demands unusual mental effort, and for which some monarchs have obtained true, immortal fame: *legislation*. Surrounded by a throng of boyars and others knowledgeable in the civic arts, the tsar proposed that they examine and supplement Ivan III's *Code*, consistent with Russia's new experiences and new demands in its civic and governmental activities.

> CODE OF LAWS

The *Sudebnik* [Code of Laws], or the second *Russkaya Pravda*, came out in 1550, the second complete systematization of our ancient laws and worthy of detailed exposition in a special section* in which we shall speak of the general contemporary situation in Russia. Here we shall say only that Ivan and his worthy advisors

---

* [Apparently this intention never came to fruition.]

sought by their labors not a flashy, empty glory, but a true and clear benefit, with a fervent love of justice and civic development. They did not act merely with their imaginations, their minds did not ignore the existing order of things, they did not waste [their time] considering future possibilities, but looked around themselves and corrected malfeasance without betraying the principle ancient bases of legislation.

Everything was left as it was and the people were content with that; only that which caused known complaints was removed. They wanted something better, but were not seeking perfection. Without erudition, without theory, and knowing nothing but Russia, yet knowing it well, they wrote a tome that will always be of interest for as long as our country lasts, for it is a true mirror of the morals and the thinking of the age. In appendices to the *Sudebnik* there are also important contemporary decrees concerning precedence amongst the nobility [*mestnichestvo*]. The sovereign had not yet been able to eliminate this great evil, but he wanted to at least temper it: he forbade boyar cadets and descendants of appanage princes to consider themselves as a hereditary line of voivodes. He similarly decreed that the voivode of the main legion would be senior to all. The voivodes of the vanguard and reserve legions were to yield seniority to him alone and not reckon with the voivodes of the left and right wings [legions]. It would be the sovereign's duty to adjudicate lineage and distinction, and if someone was seconded to someone else, it was the former's duty to obey the latter.

> RESTRAINTS ON THE ORDER OF PRECEDENCE

After approving the *Sudebnik*, Ivan set the date of 23 February 1551 for a Council of Divines in Moscow. The Kremlin palace filled with distinguished men of the Russian state, both clerical and lay. The metropolitan, nine prelates, all the archimandrites, abbots, boyars and first-rank officials sat in silence, straining their gaze towards the young tsar, who spoke to them with intellectual power and eloquence concerning the rise and fall of the state from the wisdom or the riotous conduct of the authorities, and from good or evil popular customs. He described the utterly

> THE STOGLAV

unbearable *widowing* of Russia in the days of his orphanhood and youth, which was at first innocent, but later profligate. He reminded them of the lamentable deaths of his uncles and of the anarchy of the nobles, whose bad examples had corrupted his heart.

He repeated, however, that he had consigned everything in the past to oblivion. Ivan now depicted Moscow's misery, having been reduced to ashes, and the people's rebellion.

"Then," he said, "after my soul had been terrified and my bones had trembled within me, my soul was calmed and my heart was moved. Now I hate evil and love virtue. From you, pastors of Christians, mentors of tsars and nobles, worthy prelates of the Church, I request fervent exhortation! Do not spare me from my sins, boldly reproach my weaknesses. Thunder out the word of God, that my soul may live."

<blockquote>1547-1551</blockquote>

Later, after declaring his beneficent intention to arrange the fortunes of Russia with all the abilities God gave him, and demonstrating the necessity of correcting the laws to promote internal order, the tsar offered the prelates the *Sudebnik* for their perusal, as well as the

<blockquote>LEGAL DOCUMENTS
SELECTION OF JURORS</blockquote>

regulatory documents by which all towns and volosts would be required to choose elders and sworn jurors to adjudicate matters along with the deputies or with their tiuns,* as heretofore had been done only in Novgorod and Pskov. The captains of the hundreds [centurions] and fifties likewise would be chosen with general trust and would participate in the national reform, so that the tsarist officials would not be able to act despotically and so the people would not be without a voice. The council confirmed all of Ivan's wise new resolutions.

<blockquote>CHURCH INSTITUTIONS</blockquote>

Ivan's activities did not end with this, however. The sovereign, having put the state in order, proposed to the prelates to do the same for the Church, to correct not only its rites, but its books, which had been distorted by ignorant scribes, and also to improve its priests' morals to serve as an example for the laity. They would be educated to be worthy servants of the altar. Rules of decorum

---

* [A low-level official.]

would be established that should be observed in God's cathedrals. Error would be rooted out of monasteries; Russian Christianity would be cleansed of all remnants of ancient paganism, etc.

It was Ivan who indicated all the items, whether of greater or lesser importance, for the consideration by the council fathers. [The result] was called the *Stoglav* [Hundred Chapters] because of the number of articles it contained. One of its most beneficial effects was the establishment of schools in Moscow and other cities so that priests and deacons of good mental and moral character might teach children therein to read, write, and fear God. This institution was all the more necessary because many priests in Russia could barely distinguish the letters of the alphabet, having learned the church service by heart.

Desiring to instill the true faith in men's hearts, the council fathers took measures to curb superstition and false piety: they forbade the vainglorious construction of utterly unnecessary new churches and new cells in the forests and wastelands for wandering parasitical [priests]. In fulfillment of the tsar's wishes, they also forbade bishops and monasteries to purchase patrimonial estates without the tsar's knowledge and consent, for the sovereign had prudently foreseen that through such purchases they might ultimately come to own most of the real estate in Russia to the detriment of society and of their own morals. In brief, this memorable council, by the significance of its object, had greater distinction than any of the others that had ever taken place in Kiev, Vladimir or Moscow.

INTENTION TO ENLIGHTEN RUSSIA

To these great intentions of Ivan, it may be said, also should be added his plan to enrich Russia with the fruits of the arts of foreigners. In 1547, when the Saxon Schlitt was in Moscow, he learned our language, gained access to the tsar and conversed with him regarding advances in the arts and sciences in Germany that were unknown to Russians. Ivan listened to him, questioned him with interest, and suggested to him that he travel to the German lands as an emissary from us to bring to Moscow not only craftsmen, artists, healers, pharmacists, and printers, but also people skilled in ancient and modern languages – even theologians! Schlitt willingly undertook to serve the sovereign and Russia in this matter. He found the emperor, Charles V, at the Diet in Augsburg and handed over to him Ivan's letter concerning his mission. The emperor wished to know the sense of the Diet; they discussed it for a long time before agreeing to fulfill the tsar's wish, but on the condition that Schlitt swear in Ivan's name not to send scholars and artists from Russia to Turkey, and more generally, not to employ their skills to the detriment of the German Empire. Charles V gave our emissary a letter permitting him to seek people in Germany suitable for the tsar's service. Schlitt assembled more than 120 men and prepared to sail with them from Lübeck to Livonia.

But everything was ruined because of the base, envious policies of the Hansa and the Livonian Order. They feared our development and thought that Russia would thereby become still more powerful and dangerous to neighboring powers. With their cunning arguments they obliged the emperor to think likewise; as a result of which the senators of Lübeck illegally imprisoned Schlitt.

His many fellow travelers dispersed and for a long time Ivan did not know of the fate of his emissary, who finally escaped and returned to Moscow in 1557, alone and without money, in debt and with various hare-brained proposals, for instance, that the tsar assist the emperor with money and men in his Turkish war, give him hostages (25 princes and boyars) as a token of good faith, promise to unite our Church with the Roman, have a permanent emissary in Charles' court, found a military order for Russians and foreigners, hire 6,000 German mercenaries, establish a postal service from Moscow to Augsburg, and so on. Although the tsar's good intentions did not come to complete fruition due to the hostility of the Lübeckers and the Livonian administration (which he later punished severely), yet many of the German artists and artisans left in Lübeck, despite the prohibition by the emperor and the Livonian Master [of the German, or Teutonic Order], were able to travel on to Russia and were of benefit to it in the important task of civic development.

MILITARY ACTIVITIES

When it became necessary for Russia's prosperity, this truly royal undertaking was completed to the sound of arms and victories. The barbarians needed to be pacified, since they had been taking advantage of the sovereign's youth and the boyars' discord, and had long been rampaging within our borders, so that for 200 versts from Moscow, to the south and northeast, the land was scattered with ashes and the bones of Russians. Not a settlement or a family remained intact!

To begin with the nearest and most pernicious enemy, 17 year old Ivan, burning with fervor for glory, wished to lead an army to Kazan himself. He departed Moscow in the month of December, but fate trumped his resolve with defeat. Scorning comfort, he was prepared to endure the cold and snowstorms that were common at this time of year, but instead of snow, it rained without stop. Baggage trains and cannons sank into the mud. On 2 February, after the tsar had spent the night in Elna, fifteen versts from Nizhnyi-Novgorod he arrived on the isle of Robotka. The whole of the Volga was covered with water;* the ice cracked, the artillery fell through and many men lost their lives.

EXPEDITION TO KAZAN

The sovereign stayed three days on the island, waiting for passage [across] in vain. Finally, as if frightened by a bad omen, he returned sorrowfully to Moscow. However, he had ordered Prince Dimitrii Belskii to march on Kazan with his legions, not to conquer it, but to deal it a painful blow. Now Prince Shig-Alei and other voivodes marched from Meshchera to the mouth of the Tsivila and joined up there with Belskii. Safa-Girei was awaiting him on Arskoe Field, where Prince Simeon Mikulinskii, with just the vanguard, trounced him and *stomped* into the city, capturing the bogatyr** Azik and many distinguished people. The Tatars took vengeance on us by laying waste to villages in Galicia, but the Kostroma voivode, Yakovlev, destroyed the whole crowd of these brigands at Gusev Field on the banks of the stream Egovka and killed their commander, the bogatyr Arak.

Not satisfied with these minor actions by our forces, Ivan prepared for a decisive undertaking. For this, he wanted peace

TRUCE WITH LITHUANIA

---
* [Presumably the water was on top of the ice.]
** [Old term for knight.]

with Lithuania, where the aged Sigismund had ended his days and his young successor Augustus was more involved in affairs of the heart than in affairs of state and had not had any kind of relations with Moscow in the course of five years. Sigismund had died in 1548 and the truce had now expired, but the new king was silent and did not even inform Ivan of his father's death. Our boyars, Prince Dimitrii Belskii and Morozov, wrote to the Lithuanian nobles concerning this and let them know that we were awaiting their emissaries on the matter of peace.

In January 1549, the voivode of Vitebsk, Stanislav Kishka, and Marshalok* Komaevskii arrived in Moscow and entered into negotiations concerning a permanent peace. As usual, they demanded Novgorod, Pskov, Smolensk and the Severskii towns. To excuse this absurd proposal, they repeated to our boyars,

"An emissary is like fur: he brings whatever you stick to him. We are carrying out the orders given us by the king and Duma [Sejm, the Polish parliament]."

The boyars replied, "And so we will speak only of a truce."

One was concluded with the old conditions, but the Lithuanian pans would not agree to include the new title of tsar in the document. Both sides dug in, wherefore the emissaries apparently left Moscow, but were returned, and, while still observing the truce, squabbled over the title. Augustus would only recognize Ivan as grand prince. Irritated, we no longer called Augustus *King*. There were other dissatisfactions. The sovereign had offered 2,000 rubles ransom for our distinguished prisoners, the princes Thedor Obolenskii and Mikhail Golitsa, but was refused and in return, refused the king's request that the Lithuanian Jews might freely trade in Russia, in accord with previous treaties.

"No," Ivan replied. "These people have brought us corporal and spiritual poison. They sell lethal potions amongst us and defame Christ the savior. I do not want to hear of them."

Yet neither Russia nor Lithuania desired war.

---

* [Very senior Lithuanian official.]

Only Khan Saip-Girei was rattling his sword at Ivan. He was all the more haughty because he had now succeeded in conquering Astrakhan, rich in merchants, but poor in soldiers, and thus defenseless in spite of its impressive name of *kingdom* [tsarstvo]. After taking the city, the khan razed it to the foundations. He led off many of its residents to the Crimea and considered himself the legitimate ruler of the Nogai, who were kinsmen. He himself wrote to Ivan about this, saying that the Kabardians and the mountain Kaitaks were paying him tribute. He bragged of his power and said,

CRIMEAN AFFAIRS

"You are young, but have reached the age of reason. Declare what you wish – friendship or blood? If you wish friendship, then send not trifles, but significant gifts, like the king, who gives us 15,000 gold pieces a year. But if it pleases you to fight, then I am ready to march to Moscow and your lands will be beneath my horses' feet."

Aware that Saip-Girei was taking gifts but was not withdrawing from Kazan, and that a war with that city must be a war with the Crimea as well, the sovereign scorned the khan's wrath and jailed his emissaries, since he had learned that the khan was taking Muscovite merchants into his domestic service involuntarily and that our herald had been dishonored in the Taurid. In brief, we felt our strength, and hoped to deal with all of Baty's descendants.*

At this time (March 1549), Kazan lost its ruler: Safa-Girei had injured himself while drunk in his palace and died suddenly, leaving a two year old son, Utemish-Girei, whose mother, the beautiful Syuyunbeka, daughter of the Nogai prince Yusuf, he had loved more than any other women. The nobles elevated the infant Utemish-Girei to the throne, but sought a better ruler. They wanted the khan of the Crimea to give them his son to protect them from the Russians, and also sent a herald to Moscow with a letter from the young ruler asking for peace.

DEATH OF THE RULER OF KAZAN

Ivan replied that peace could only be discussed with emissaries and hastened to take

EXPEDITION TO KAZAN

---
* [I.e., the Tatars.]

advantage of the mutinous anarchy in Kazan. He ordered the legions assembled: the main in Suzdal, the van in Shuya and Murom, the reserve in Yuriev, the right in Kostroma and the left in Yaroslavl. On 24 November, the sovereign departed Moscow for Vladimir, where the metropolitan blessed him and exhorted the voivodes to bravely serve homeland and tsar in a spirit of love and fraternity and to forget pride and precedence, which was tolerable in peacetime, but criminal during a war. Prince Vladimir Andreevich was left in charge in Moscow, while Ivan took his younger brother, Prince Yurii, with him, as well as Prince Shig-Alei and all the distinguished Kazan refugees.

The winter was terrible: people were dropping dead on the roads from the unbearable cold. The sovereign endured everything and encouraged everybody, forgetting the comfort and luxury of the court and the charms of his lovely wife. The legions joined up in Nizhnyi-Novgorod and halted before Kazan on 14 February. Ivan and the court nobles were on the shores of Lake Kaban, Shig-Alei and Prince Dimitrii Belskii were on Arskoe Field with the main force, the other army contingents were across the River Kazanka, while artillery was at the mouth of the Bulak and at Pogano Lake. They prepared gabions* and assaulted the city.

Our sovereigns had never hitherto been beneath the walls of this rebellious capital: they had merely sent voivodes to punish its perfidious inhabitants. Now the beloved young and hearty monarch drew his sword. He saw and positioned everyone, and with his voice and courage summoned the troops to glory and easy victory. Kazan's ruler was in baby clothes, its distinguished nobles had either perished in plots or come over to us. They thronged around Ivan and through their secret friends they tried to persuade their compatriots to submit to his magnanimity. Sixty thousand Russians assaulted the wooden fortress, which was being destroyed by the terrible thunder of siege engines.

But Kazan's last hour was not yet at hand; they fought the whole day. The Russians killed many people in the city, including the Crimean prince Chelbak and the son of one of Safa-Girei's wives, but were unable to take the fortress. In the following days there was

| 25 February, 1550 |

---

* [Gabions are wicker cylinders filled with dirt or rocks to provide cover for cannoneers.]

a thaw, with heavy rains. The cannons would not fire, the ice on the river broke up and the roads were ruined: the army was without transport and feared famine. Bowing to necessity, it withdrew with great effort.

After sending the main legion ahead with the heavy artillery, the sovereign followed them with light cavalry to protect the cannons and to keep up pressure on the enemy. He showed firmness and did not become downcast, but kept a single thought in mind: to bring down this state that was pernicious and hateful to Russia, while attentively observing the lie of the land.

He halted at the mouth of the Sviyaga and beheld the lofty hill named Kruglaya. Taking Prince Shig-Alei, the Kazan princes, and the boyars, he rode to its summit. A boundless vista opened up in all directions: to Kazan, to Vyatka, to Nizhnyi-Novgorod and to the wastes of what is now Simbirsk Province. Amazed by the beauty of the site, Ivan said,

> SELECTION OF A SITE FOR A NEW FORTIFICATION

"Here there will be a Christian city and we shall put pressure on Kazan. God has placed it in our hands."

All praised his happy thought, and Shig-Alei and the Tatar nobles described to him the riches and fertility of the surrounding lands. The sovereign, hoping for future successes, returned to Moscow with a happy countenance.

> 23 MARCH

But all defeats seem culpable to the people. They excused the tsar's youth, but reproached the chief voivode, Prince Dimitrii Belskii, saying that the Belskii name had been unpropitious for the Kazan campaigns. They said that it seemed as if Kazan had clearly spared the estates of this boyar in its raids, out of gratitude for his spinelessness or his outright treason. He died this same year, being ultimately neither an enemy, nor a skilled general, nor a power-hungry noble. Otherwise the Shuiskiis would not have let him peacefully take the first seat in the Duma, after they had deposed and murdered his brother, the unforgettable Prince Ivan.

Neither the sovereign nor the army had managed to get a rest before news arrived in Moscow of Khan Saip-Girei's plan to invade Russia. Legions were immediately moved to the borders and Ivan himself inspected them in Kolomna and in Ryazan, but after a month he returned to Moscow, since autumn had begun and the enemy had not made an appearance. That winter, instead of the khan, other brigands appeared: Nogai mirzas in Meshchera and near Old Ryazan. Ivan's voivodes beat them everywhere they found them and pursued them to the Shatskie gates. Everywhere they took prisoners, among them the mirza Telyak. Cold weather eliminated the rest, and barely 50 of them survived. Accordingly the sovereign graciously entertained the voivodes in the Kremlin riverbank palace and greatly rewarded all the boyar cadets.

ASSAULT OF THE NOGAI TATARS

1551

Kazan still hoped to deceive Ivan and wrote to him concerning peace. Their intermediary was the Nogai Prince Yusuf, Safa-Girei's father-in-law, a ruler distinguished by intellect and power, to the extent that the Turkish sultan would write him flattering letters, calling him *Prince of Princes*. Yusuf wished to give his daughter, the widow Syuyunbeka, in marriage to Shig-Alei to harmonize Ivan's intent with the desires of the people of Kazan. He argued the vanity of the world and secular greatness, referring to the Koran and the Gospels, trying to persuade the sovereign not to spill blood and to be a true friend to him. Prince Yusuf accused his late father-in-law of faithlessness and being bloodthirsty, and the Kazan officials of having a mutinous spirit, but stood up for his daughter and grandson.

Ivan said that he would disclose peace terms if Kazan were to send five or six of its most distinguished nobles to Moscow. He wasted no time: at the very start of spring, after many conferences with the Duma boyars and after formal prayers in the churches, he received the metropolitan's blessing and dispatched Shig-Alei with 500 distinguished men of Kazan and a powerful army to the mouth of the Sviyaga, where they were supposed to build

FOUNDING OF SVIYAZHSK

a town in Ivan's name. [Timber for] the walls and churches had been hewn in the forests of Uglich and shipped on the Volga by boats.

The commanders of Moscow's army were Prince Yurii Mikhailovich Bulgakov and Simeon Ivanovich Mikulinskii, the major-domo Danilo Romanovich Yuriev (brother of the tsaritsa), the equerry Ivan Petrovich Fedorov, the boyars Morozov and Khabarov and the princes Paletskii and Nagaev. Prince Khilkov came from Meshchera, Prince Pyotr Serebryanyi-Obolenskii from Nizhnyi-Novgorod and Bakhteyar Zyuzin from Vyatka with musketeers and Cossacks. They seized from the enemy all the crossings of the Volga and Kama and all means of communication.

Prince Serebryanyi was the first to unfurl his banner on Kruglaya Hill on 16 May during a solar eclipse. They sang evening prayers and early on 18 May made a surprise attack on Kazan's trading quarter. They killed about a thousand sleeping people and more than a hundred princes, mirzas, and distinguished citizens. They freed many Russian prisoners and returned to the mouth of the Sviyaga to await the main army, which arrived by boat on 24 May. With joyous cries they greeted the land that was to become *New Russia* and triumphantly disembarked onto the bank where Prince Serebryanyi-Obolenskii's legions were drawn up, displaying their trophies to their brethren.

Dense forest shaded the hill, so, putting aside their swords, the warriors took up axes and after a few hours the summit was laid bare. They marked out and surveyed the site, then circumambulated it with crosses, blessed the water and began building its walls and a church in the name of the birth of the Virgin and St. Sergii. They completed the town of Sviyazhsk in four weeks, to the astonishment of the residents in the vicinity, who on seeing this threatening stronghold above the venerable country of Kazan, humbly asked Shig-Alei to take them under Ivan's power.

All the High Bank – the Chuvash, Mordvi and Cheremis – were idolaters of the Finnish race who had formerly been conquered by the Tatars, but were not bound to them by the same religion or language. They sent their dignitaries to Moscow, swore allegiance to Russia and received a grant document with a

SUBJUGATION OF THE HIGH BANK

gold seal from the tsar. They were registered at the new town of Sviyazhsk and exempted from *yasak*, or tribute, for three years. In order to be assured of their sincerity, Ivan ordered them to fight Kazan; they did not dare disobey. They assembled and were transported by boats to the lower bank of the river and in the presence of our officials did battle with Kazan's troops on Arskoe Field.

Although they were scattered by cannon fire and fled in cowardly disorder, they at least proved their loyalty. During the course of the year, their princes, mirzas, and lieutenants kept coming to Moscow, where they were feasted in the palace and awarded fur coats, cloth, armor, steeds and money; they praised the tsar's generosity and boasted of their new fatherland. The sovereign showered them with silver and gold, not stinting the treasury in order to realize his grand plan. Pleased with his voivodes' success, he sent a large number of gold medals to Shig-Alei to be distributed among the troops.

> PEOPLE OF KAZAN TERRIFIED

Meanwhile terror and mutiny reigned in Kazan, which did not even have 20,000 warriors. Its subjects betrayed it and its princes and mirzas secretly went over to Shig-Alei while the Russians laid waste to the neighboring villages and would not let anyone enter the city. Our units were stationed from the mouth of the Sura to the Kama and the Vyatka. An innocent infant devoid of speech played on the throne of Kazan. Its widowed Princess Syuyunbeka sometimes cried over him, sometimes frolicked with her lover, the Crimean uhlan Koshchak, who was hated by the people.

The citizens reproached the nobles, and the nobles reproached each other. Kazan's officials wanted to submit to Ivan, while the Crimeans abhorred their pusillanimity. They were waiting for troops from the Taurid, from Astrakhan and from the Nogai uluses, while the haughty Koshchak rattled his saber and promised victory to the princess. It is written that he planned to marry her, kill her son, and become the ruler, but there was a rebellion. The Crimeans saw that the people were prepared to hand them over to Moscow's voivodes and fled, numbering more than 300 princes and officials. They were unable to save themselves – they ran into the Russians and perished on the banks of the Vyatka, while proud Koshchak and 45 of his most distinguished compatriots were taken prisoner and executed in Moscow.

Kazan now concluded an immediate truce with our voivodes and sent emissaries to Ivan. They entreated him to once again give them Shig-Alei as ruler and pledged to send him the infant Utemish-Girei, Princess Syuyunbeka and the women and children left amongst them by the Crimeans. They also intended to free all the Russian prisoners. Ivan was agreeable, recalling the cautious policy of his grandfather, which was not to press the enemy to extremes, but to wear him down, to slowly but surely destroy him, to rely on chance as little as possible, to protect his men as much as possible and to vindicate reverses by their necessity.

> CONDITIONS OF A PEACE TREATY WITH THEM

Yet Ivan's grandfather, while observing moderation, also observed another rule: to *hold on to what has been taken*. Adashev was sent to the voivodes to execute the terms of the peace treaty and to pronounce Shig-Alei the ruler of Kazan. Ivan ordered that he be given only the lower side of the river, while the higher, conquered by the Russian sword, was assigned to Sviyazhsk. This scheme divided Kazan's territory and embittered its people, including even Shig-Alei.

"What will become of my country?" he asked. "How can I ask for my subjects' love when I have yielded the best part of their lands to Russia?"

The voivodes replied that this was Ivan's pleasure. In vain did Kazan consider cunning, rejecting the terms; it did not want to hand over the princess or the prisoners, but the voivodes told them decisively,

"Either they will be in our hands or this autumn the sovereign will come here with fire and sword to exterminate the perfidious."

They had to comply, and Kazan informed Shig-Alei that the princess and her son were already en route to Sviyazhsk.

| SYUYUNBEKA | Not only Syuyunbeka, but all of Kazan wept when it learned that this unfortunate woman was being handed over as a prisoner to the Muscovite sovereign. Reproaching neither the nobles nor the citizens, Syuyunbeka blamed only fate. In despair she kissed the grave of Safa-Girei and envied his peace. The people grieved in silence, while the nobles comforted her and said that Ivan was merciful, that many Moslem rulers served him, and that he would choose a worthy husband for her from among them and provide an estate.

The whole city followed her to the Kazanka River where there was a richly decorated boat. Syuyunbeka rode slowly in a chariot, while caregivers held her son. Pale and weak, she could barely step down onto the landing. She got into the boat and, full of emotion, bowed to the people, who fell on their knees and, weeping bitterly, wished their former princess good fortune. Prince Obolenskii met her on the banks of the Volga, greeted her in the name of the sovereign, and took her, Utemish-Girei and the families of distinguished Crimeans by boat to Moscow.

Thus the first condition of the treaty was carried out. The voivodes now demanded freedom for our prisoners and oaths of allegiance to Russia from all the people of Kazan. They designated the day and lined up near Kazan, from the Volga to Tsareva Meadow. Alei sent his nobles into the city to clean up the palace; he spent the night in a tent. The following morning all the officials and citizens gathered in the meadow and heard the oath that had been written for them. They thanked Ivan for the ruler he had given them, but for a long time did not want to yield the High Bank.

"But do you think," said the boyars, "that Ivan is as fickle as you are. Behold the mouth of the Sviyaga – there is a Christian town there! The residents of the surrounding territory have formally submitted to us and have fought against Kazan: how can they belong to it again? Forget the past – it will not return."

Finally the sworn document was formalized with the tsar's seal, and signed by all the dignitaries. The people gave their oaths over a period of three days, crowd after crowd. Shig-Alei entered the

CHAPTER THREE

capital and the boyars, Prince Yurii Bulgakov and Khabarov seated him on the throne. The royal court was filled with Russian prisoners; many of them had spent more than 12 years in captivity.

> SHIG-ALEI AGAIN ACCEDES TO THE THRONE PRISONERS FREED

When Alei announced their release, they could hardly believe their good fortune. Weeping, they lifted up their arms to Heaven and praised God.

"Ivan rules in Russia!" the boyars told them. "Go to your homeland and fear captivity no longer!"

In Sviyazhsk they were provided with all the necessities: clothing and edible provisions and sent up the Volga. There were 60,000 of them, not counting residents of Vyatka and Perm, who were sent by a different route.

"Never," contemporaries write, "had Russia seen such a pleasing sight: it was a new exodus from Israel!"

The liberation of so many people, the founding of Sviyazhsk, the taking of the best part of Kazan's territory and the enthronement of Shig-Alei had not cost Ivan a single man. The Russians had pursued and defeated their enemies everywhere in minor encounters on the banks of the Kama and Volga without spilling any of their own blood. Prince Bulgakov rode to his sovereign with the happy news. The boyar Danilo Romanovich and Prince Khilkov also returned. Khabarov remained with Shig-Alei with 500 musketeers, while Prince Simeon Mikulinskii, a man noted for wisdom and bravery, stayed in Sviyazhsk.

Had Kazan now remained tranquil and loyal to Russia, it might have prolonged its existence as a special Moslem realm, but fate was urging it on to destruction. In vain did Ivan show charity and favor to its ruler and nobles.

> DISLOYALTY IN KAZAN AND THE CRUELTY OF ITS RULER

He gave the former costly clothing, vessels and money and did the same for his wife, one of Safa-Girei's former wives. He also made gifts to all the distinguished citizens of Kazan and warned them against the fatal consequences of a new betrayal. Shig-Alei constantly pestered him about the High Bank [the territory Ivan had annexed], trying to get him to return even half or a fraction of it and, unhappy with determined refusals, was indifferent to the fact that many Russian prisoners were still being hidden, confined and in chains. He did not want to punish anyone for this and told our officials,

"I fear a rebellion!"

But when he learned that some of the nobles were reverting to their old habits by plotting sedition, corresponding with the Nogai and planning to kill him and all the Russians, Alei resolutely resorted to cruel measures. He gave a feast in the palace and ordered the guests cut down, whether guilty or only suspected of treachery. Some were killed in his dining hall, others in the royal courtyard, in all, 70 very distinguished men. Alei's princes and Muscovite musketeers served as the executioners. Blood ran for two days; the people were stunned and, guilty or not, fled in terror.

This horrifying event revealed to Ivan the necessity of finding another way to pacify Kazan. He sent Adashev there,

> NEGOTIATIONS WITH ALEI

who told Alei that the sovereign could no longer tolerate Kazan's criminal activities and the time had come to bring peace to this unfortunate realm and to Russia. Moscow's legions would come to his capital to protect its ruler and its people and establish safety for both them and us. [Shig-Alei replied:]

"I myself see that I cannot rule here. The princes and the people hate me, but who is at fault? Let Ivan give us back the High Bank. Then I will vouch for Kazan's loyalty. Otherwise I will abdicate voluntarily and come to the sovereign, for I have nowhere else in the world to go. However, I am a Moslem and will not bring Christians here. Otherwise, I can serve you, if the sovereign assures me of his favor. Before my departure from Kazan I shall kill the rest of the evil nobles, ruin all the cannons and prepare an easy victory for you."

Adashev returned to Moscow with this reply, where he found Kazan's emissaries, Prince Muralei, Kostrov and Alimerdin, all

> 1552

personal enemies of Shig-Alei. Guessing the sovereign's thoughts, they – either with the general consent of their compatriots, or on their own – reported to Ivan that their ruler was a bloodthirsty murderer and a brazen plunderer. Kazan wished only to escape from tyranny and was prepared to obey a Muscovite deputy.

"If you do not fulfill the wishes of the people," said the emissaries, "then rebellion will unavoidably break out, and soon. Avoid a catastrophe. Get rid of the hateful criminal. Let Russians occupy our capital; we will leave for the suburbs or the villages. We wish to be subordinate to your will in all things. We shall be your diligent servants, and if we deceive you, then let our heads fall in Moscow!"

Wasting no time, Ivan sent Adashev to Kazan once more to *depose its ruler to please its people.* He promised Alei charity and recompense, asking him to let our troops into the city without resistance. Alei once more showed noble resolve.

"I do not regret the throne," he told Adashev. "I am unable or do not know how to be happy on it. My very life is in danger here. I shall obey the sovereign, only do not command me to betray my religion. Take Kazan, but without me. Take it by force or by treaty, but not by my hands."

Neither flattery nor threats by Adashev could persuade him to hand over his realm to the sovereign's deputy. Secretly spiking some of the cannons and sending arquebuses with gunpowder to Sviyazhsk, Alei went fishing on the lake with a large number of uhlans and princes. He ordered the Muscovite musketeers to surround him and told the amazed officials,

Ruler Leaves Kazan

"You thought to kill me, abused me in Moscow and did not want to have a ruler. You requested deputies from Ivan. But we shall stand together before his court of law!"

Alei took them with him to Sviyazhsk.

Simeon Mikulinskii, who had been designated to administer Kazan, now gave notice to its inhabitants that their will had been fulfilled, that Alei had been dethroned and that they should swear allegiance to the Muscovite sovereign. The people of Kazan agreed, but wanted Mikulinskii to send them the two Sviyazhsk princes, Chapkun and Burnash, who, already being Russian subjects, might calm the people with a guarantee of Ivan's mercy.

The princes arrived in Kazan with our officials, and quiet reigned in Kazan. The nobles, citizens and even country folk swore allegiance and loyalty. The courts were tidied up for the deputy and the troops. Shig-Alei's wife was sent to him in Sviyazhsk and Prince Mikulinskii was summoned. They met him on the banks of the Volga and kowtowed* like diligent slaves of the sovereign. He was marching with his legions, and the voivodes had already sent light transport to Kazan and prepared to formally enter within its walls. Ivan had obtained this renowned realm without significant effort or bloodshed. It had been taken, so to speak, by a grab for its crown. But suddenly everything changed.

Three of the Kazan nobles, whom Mikulinskii had allowed to enter the city to go to their families, began to incite the people with the false news that the Russians were coming for them with the intent of exterminating every inhabitant. Terror spread and there was a general insurrection. The fortress was locked up and the people began to take up arms. Many princes tried to talk the people out of it, arguing that Ivan's boyars had formally sworn not to touch a person, neither in the city nor in the villages. They had promised to rule by law, without violence, to leave everything as it was.

> FINAL BETRAYAL BY CITIZENS OF KAZAN

But the people would not listen, and shouted that the boyar's oath was a deception, that Alei himself had secretly said so to those closest to him. When they learned of this disturbance, Prince Mikulinskii, Obolenskii and Adashev left the army by the Bulak and rode up to the city with a small contingent. The Royal Gates were closed and the walls were covered with armed men. Some officials came out, making excuses for the people and promised to calm them down, but they could not keep their word, for there was no way the citizens would let the Russians in.

They seized our baggage train and many boyar cadets, and spoke rudely to Moscow's voivodes. The voivodes learned that

---

* [From the Chinese kòutóu, literally meaning to bang the head. The Russian word literally means to beat the forehead. This was likely originally a Chinese custom.]

CHAPTER THREE

Prince Chapkun, who had been sent by them from Sviyazhsk to Kazan ostensibly as a diligent servant of the sovereign in order to calm the people, had deceived us and had become the leader of the rebels. Our voivodes spent the night in the suburbs. Seeing all persuasion was fruitless, they could have reduced the suburbs to ashes and laid siege to the city, but they [decided to] await their sovereign's orders. They peacefully withdrew to Sviyazhsk, jailed all the Kazan officials who were there, and immediately dispatched the boyar Sheremetev to Moscow with a report of this new and final treachery.

CHAPTER IV

THE CONQUEST OF KAZAN.

1552

Preparation for the Kazan campaign. Russia's relations with western powers. Freeing of old Prince Bulgakov. Construction of new fortifications. Origins of the Don Cossacks. New khan in the Taurid. Affairs in Astrakhan. Sickness in Sviyazhsk. Ediger ruler of Kazan. Metropolitan's message to the Sviyazhsk troops. Council on Kazan. The sovereign's departure. Invasion of the Crimean khan. Assault on Tula. The khan flees. Our trophies. Grumbling in the army. Campaign. Siege. First battle. Storm. Gabions deployed. A powerful sally. Effect of embrasures. Prince Yapancha, the raider. Exhaustion of the troops. Division of the legions. Destruction of Yapancha's army. Bitterness in Kazan. Destruction of a secret place. Dejection in Kazan. Ivan's energy. Town and stockade of Arsk captured. Attack of the lowland Cheremis. Imagined sorcery. Construction of a high tower. Proposal to Kazan. A bloody affair. Blowing up barricades. Capture of the turret of Arsk. Last offer to Kazan. Disposition of the army for assault. Detonation of mines and the assault. Heroism on both sides. Greed of many of the troops. Courage of Ivan and the boyars. Prince Kurbskii's valor. Capture of Kazan. Cross hoisted at royal gates. The sovereign enters Kazan. Liberation of Russian prisoners. Ivan's speech to the troops. Feast at the camp. Subjugation of the Arsk district and the lowland Cheremis. Triumphal entry into Kazan. The spectacle of Kazan. Establishing a government. Counsel of the nobles. Sovereign's return route to Moscow. Birth of a crown prince. Ivan's welcome. The sovereign's speech to the clergy. The metropolitan's reply. Feast at the court and Ivan's gifts.

On 24 March the sovereign learned of the events in Kazan. He ordered Shig-Alei to ride to Kasimov and his brother-in-law Danilo to march to Sviyazhsk with infantry. He announced in a formal session of the Duma that the time had come to decapitate Kazan.

> PREPARATION FOR THE KAZAN CAMPAIGN

"God sees my heart," he said. "I do not want worldly glory, but peace for Christians. How could I someday say to the Most High without trepidation, *'Here am I and the people Thou hast given me,'* if I do not save them from the ferocity of Russia's perpetual enemies, with whom neither peace nor respite is possible?"

The boyars praised Ivan's decisiveness, but advised him to stay in Moscow and send his voivodes against Kazan, since Russia did not have just one enemy:

"If the Crimeans or the Nogai attack our borders in the sovereign's absence, who will defend them?"

Ivan replied that he was taking measures for the defense of the country and would *go and attend to his own affairs.* He ordered troops to be assembled, from distant places in Kolomna and Koshira, and from nearer places in Murom. Prince Aleksandr Borisovich Gorbatyi and Pyotr Ivanovich Shuiskii were to take Moscow's legions to Nizhnyi-Novgorod; Mikhail Glinskii made camp on the banks of the Kama with boyar cadets, musketeers, Cossacks and troops from Ustyug and Vyatka, while the Sviyazhsk voivodes occupied the Volga crossings with their light detachments and awaited Ivan.

| RUSSIA'S RELATIONS WITH WESTERN POWERS |

In preparing for an outstanding exploit, the young tsar could be assured of the peacefulness of the neighboring powers to the west. Sweden and Livonia asked for nothing but free trade with us. We were squabbling with the Polish king over the [tsar's] title and the Sebezh lands; we berated each other with rude words, but both sides were a long way from making war. Augustus even did a favor for Ivan: without asking for money beforehand, he freed Prince Mikhail Bulgakov-Golitsa gratis. He sent him to Moscow with another official, Prince Selekhovskii, writing to the tsar,

| FREEING OF OLD PRINCE BULGAKOV |

"Thinking that we are obliged to respect loyalty not only in our own servitors, but also in others who die for their sovereign, I am giving your father's great voivode his freedom. All the other distinguished Muscovite prisoners taken by us in the famous Battle of Orshina are already in the grave."

The tsar informed Augustus of his sincere gratitude and received the aged Bulgakov, who had suffered 38 years of captivity, with animated affection. He sent him a rich fur coat, decorated his chest with a gold medal and embraced him as a friend. Worn out by protracted misfortune and exhausted by the long journey, the old man was unable to dine with the sovereign. He wept and blessed Vasilii's gracious, reigning son.

Fearing nothing from the developed European powers, Ivan busied himself all the more with the safety of our southeastern borders. Two newly-constructed fortresses – Mikhailov on the Pronya and Shatsk on the Tsna – served to guard Ryazan and Meshchera. But the most important intimidation for barbarians and defense for Russia between the Sea of Azov and the Caspian Sea was a new military republic. It was composed of people speaking our language and professing our faith, with a mixture of European and Asiatic features. Indefatigable in military affairs, its people were born cavalrymen and horsemen, sometimes obstinate, self-willed and predatory, but their diligent and valorous exploits atoned for their sins.

| CONSTRUCTION OF NEW FORTIFICATIONS |

| ORIGINS OF THE DON COSSACKS |

We are speaking of the famous Don Cossacks, who had now entered the theater of history. There is no doubt they were the ones who had formerly been called the *Azov* [Cossacks] and who, during the course of the 15th century, had terrified all travelers in the Kharkov and Voronezh wastes near the Don. They had robbed Muscovite merchants on the roads to Azov and Kaffa. They had also seized men sent into the steppes by our voivodes to gain intelligence concerning the Nogai or the Crimeans, and harassed the Ukraine with raids. Their origins were not particularly noble: they were considered Russian fugitives. They sought wild freedom and booty in the deserted uluses of Baty's horde and in unsettled but fertile places where the Volga approaches the Don, and where there has long been a trade route from Asia to northern Europe. They became firmly established in their present district and took the town of Akhas and called it, I believe, Cherkasskii or Kozachii (for both terms mean the same). They acquired wives, probably from the Circassian lands, and were thereby enabled to impart to their children a somewhat Asian appearance.

Ivan's father had complained about them to the sultan, who was the sovereign of the Azov lands, but the Cossacks abhorred being subject to the Mohammedan state and accepted Russia as the supreme power over them. In 1549, their leader Saryazman, calling himself Ivan's subject, constructed fortresses on the Don; they conquered this river all the way to its mouth and demanded tribute from Azov. They fought the Nogai, Astrakhan and the Taurid, nor did they spare the Turks. They pledged to serve as a distant, vigilant guard for Russia, their ancient homeland, and hoist the banners of the Cross on the borders of the Ottoman Empire. They extended the boundary of Ivan's territory to within sight of the sultan, who had hitherto been little concerned with us.

This, however, opened his eyes; he saw the danger and determined to be an active protector of the northern Mohammedan possessions. A new khan, Devlet-Girei, was ruling in the Taurid, a nephew of the dead or deposed Saip: he undertook to save Kazan. Suleiman's emissaries tried to convince the Nogai princes, Yusuf and others, to unite under the banner of Mohammed to curb our love of power.

<small>NEW KHAN IN THE TAURID</small>

"Distance," the sultan wrote to them, "hampers me in assisting Azov and Kazan. Closely ally yourselves with the khan of the Crimea. I have ordered him to send [back] all the former residents of Astrakhan to their homeland, which I am restoring to them. I will immediately send a ruler there; I will also give Kazan a ruler of the Girei line, but until then you are to be its defenders."

<small>AFFAIRS IN ASTRAKHAN</small>

However, these princes were finding profit in their trade with Russia and did not want war. Astrakhan, important and essential for western Asian commerce and ruled by Yamgurchei, was rising from its ruins. He offered to be a diligent servant of Ivan, and a Muscovite official traveled to him for negotiations. In Russia, the Astrakhan crown prince Kaibula, son of Akkubek, married Shig-Alei's niece in Russia; she was the daughter of Enalei, and received possession of the town of Yuriev. Fearing only the

Crimean khan, Ivan awaited news of his movements while gathering an army, and prepared to deal with two enemies: Kazan and the Taurid.

Meanwhile rebellious Kazan had sent to the Nogai uluses for a ruler and was agitating the High Bank. Unfortunately, in the spring a terrible sickness broke out in Sviyazhsk; it was scurvy, and was fatal to many. The voivodes were dejected and inert, while Kazan was all the more active. Partly by force, partly by persuasion they forced all their former subjects to secede from Russia. The sovereign ordered princes Gorbatyi and Shuiskii to hurry there with legions from Nizhnyi-Novgorod, but sad tidings, one after the other, kept arriving in Moscow: the illness had gotten worse in Sviyazhsk and the High Bank inhabitants, acting like enemies, had driven off our herds.

> SICKNESS IN SVIYAZHSK

Kazan was defeating the Russians in light skirmishes and killing all their boyar cadet and Cossack prisoners. The voivodes knew that the Astrakhan prince Ediger Mahmed was coming from the Nogai uluses with 500 warriors. They kept watch, but were unable to intercept him en route. He arrived in Kazan and took its throne, giving his oath to be Russia's implacable enemy.

> EDIGER RULER OF KAZAN

At the same time, Ivan, to his vexation, learned that not only a physical infection was reigning in Sviyazhsk, but also a spiritual one. It was full of military men who believed that they were outside of Russia and therefore outside its religious law. In the midst of the terrors of death, they surrendered themselves to vile, unbridled voluptuousness. Carrying out Ivan's will, the metropolitan dispatched the wise Arkhangel archpriest Timothei there with holy water and with admonitions both oral and written for the commanders and all the troops.

> METROPOITAN'S MESSAGE TO THE SVIYAZHSK TROOPS

"By the grace of God, the wisdom of our tsar and your valor," he wrote, "a Christian stronghold has been established in enemy territory.

> MAY 21

The Lord has also given us Kazan without bloodshed. We are famous and flourishing. Lithuania and Germany seek our friendship. How may we show our gratitude to the Most High? By fulfilling His commandments. But are you fulfilling them?

"Rumors among the people disturb both the sovereign and myself. They assert that some of us have forgotten the fear of God and are drowning in the sins of Sodom and Gomorrah; that many good-looking girls and women who are freed Kazan prisoners have been defiled by the debauchery amongst us; that to please them *you have taken razors to your beards* and in your disgraceful voluptuousness are ashamed to be men. I believe this is because the Lord has punished you, not only with illness, but also with shame.

"Where is your glory? Having been fearsome adversaries, you now serve as laughing-stock for your enemies. Your weapons are dulled when you have no virtue in your hearts and your strength is weakened by vice. Crime arises, treachery is manifest and you drop your shields against them! God, Ivan and the Church summon you to repentance. Mend your ways ere you see the tsar's wrath and hear the Church's anathema."

The sovereign was sometimes present in the Duma and sometimes busy inspecting the legions and the artillery; he was clearly impatient to take the field. The boyar Prince Ivan Thedorovich Mstislavskii and Prince Mikhailo Ivanovich Vorotynskii were now called, as a token of Ivan's special favor, *servitors of the sovereign.* They went with the main army to Kolomna, while the vanguard was commanded by princes Ivan Pronskii Turuntai and Dimitrii Khilkov.

The right wing was under the boyar Prince Pyotr Shchenyatev and Prince Andrei Mikhailovich Kurbskii, the left under Prince Dimitrii Mikulinskii and Pleshcheev, and the reserve was commanded by Prince Vasilii Obolenskii-Serebryanyi and Simeon Sheremetev, while the tsar's own guard was under Prince Vladimir Vorotynskii and the boyar Ivan Sheremetev.

Legions had been positioned from Koshira to Murom, while on the Oka and the Volga, boats with provisions and cannons were sailing for Nizhnyi-Novgorod. The tsar's Council, however, was not yet in agreement: many thought it better to march on Kazan in the winter than in summer; Shig-Alei in particular was of this opinion. Ivan had summoned him to Moscow from Kasimov; he had showered him with favors, given him villages in the Meshchera region and permitted him to marry Safa-Girei's widow, Syuyunbeka.

> COUNCIL ON KAZAN

Although he was not adept in military affairs, had a weak spirit and was exceptionally stout, Alei was renowned for his sound thinking.

"Kazan," he said, "is guarded by forests, lakes and swamps; winter will be your bridge." But Ivan did not want to wait, and said,

"The army is ready, provisions have been dispatched, and with God's help we shall find a way to our worthy goal." He decided to ride immediately to the camp at Kolomenskoe.

On 16 June the sovereign bade farewell to his wife. She was pregnant; she cried and fell into his embrace. He appeared stern; he comforted her and said that he was fulfilling the duties of a tsar and was not afraid to die for his country. He entrusted Anastasiya to God and all poor and unfortunate people to her, saying,

> THE SOVEREIGN'S DEPARTURE

"Dispense favors and do good in my absence; I will let you do as the tsar would. Open the dungeons and lift disgrace from the most culpable at your own discretion. The Most High will reward me for courage and you for goodness."

Anastasiya knelt and prayed aloud for her husband's health, victory and glory. She fortified her soul and in the last tender kiss gave an example of courage unusual in a young woman. The sovereign walked to the Cathedral of the Dormition and prayed for a long time. He asked the metropolitan and the bishops to be diligent intermediaries before God for Russia, comforters for Anastasiya and advisors for his brother Yurii, who would remain in charge in Moscow. The prelates, boyars and the people wept and embraced their sovereign. He left the church, mounted his steed, and rode with the tsar's guards to Kolomenskoe, where he supped with the boyars and voivodes. He was merry and kind, and intended to spend the night in his beloved village of Ostrov. On the way there, he encountered a herald with news from Putivl that the Crimeans were marching in dense hordes from the Malyi Don Severskii [Little Northern Don] towards our Ukraine. They did not know who was leading them, whether it was the khan or his son. The sovereign displayed not the slightest unease; he cheered up the officers who were with him by saying,

INVASION OF THE CRIMEAN KHAN

"We have not bothered the khan, but if he thinks to engulf Christianity, we shall stand up for our homeland. God is with us!"

Ivan hastened to Kolomna, taking with him Prince Vladimir Andreevich, whom he had been about to send back from Ostrov to Moscow.

JUNE 19

New tidings awaited the sovereign in Kolomna: the Crimeans were marching towards Kazan. Ivan immediately made dispositions: he ordered the main legion to take up positions at Kolychev, the vanguard at Mstislavl and the left legion near Golutvin. He consulted with Shig-Alei and sent him to Kasimov, then inspected the troops on the banks of the Oka with Prince Vladimir Andreevich. He gave a speech to the officers and the rank and file, boosting their morale, captivating them with his graciousness, and everywhere heard the men exclaim,

"We are prepared to die for our faith and for you, virtuous tsar!"

After he had chosen the battle site, he returned to Kolomna and wrote to Moscow, to the tsaritsa and the metropolitan, that he was awaiting the khan without fear, trusting in the goodness of the Most High and in their prayers and in the courage of the army. The churches in Moscow were to be open and their hearts to be at ease.

On 21 June news was received in Kolomna that the Crimeans had appeared near Tula. The voivodes, princes

Shchenyatev, Kurbskii, Turuntai, Khilkov and Vorotynskii sped to that city, but learned that the enemy was not there in force. It pillaged some villages and vanished. On 23 June as Ivan was sitting at dinner, a courier galloped up from Prince Grigorii Temkin, the Tula deputy, who had written the following for the tsar:

"The khan is here – besieging the city – with many cannons and the sultan's janissaries." Ivan immediately ordered the tsar's guards to set out from Kolomna, while the main army was to cross the Oka. He heard services in the Church of the Dormition and received Bishop Theodosiya's blessing, then rode his steed onto the field where the army was glittering in endless ranks.

> ASSAULT ON TULA

With clattering weapons it moved forward with a joyful cry and *marched into battle as if to a game.* The chroniclers do not state their numbers, saying only that all Russia seemed to be arrayed there, even though powerful units still remained in Sviyazhsk and Murom, while the Kolomenskoe [army] consisted solely of court nobles, and select boyar cadets from Novgorod, and other northern inhabitants.

Many legions had crossed the Oka by evening and Ivan himself was approaching Koshira. Now another courier from Prince Temkin reported to him that Tula was saved. On 22 June, in the first hour of the day, the khan had assaulted the city, shooting incendiary cannon balls. Houses were set ablaze and the janissaries rushed the walls. Tula had no troops for its defense, having sent them all to serve the sovereign, but it had a hearty chief and courageous citizens. Some put out fires while others fought valiantly; the janissaries were unable to take the fortress.

The khan postponed the assault until the following morning, but withdrew that night after he learned that powerful units were marching from Koshira. The citizens of Tula had stood on the walls the whole night; by the dawn's light they saw the Tatars' flight. In the other direction, they spotted a column of dust and exclaimed,

> THE KHAN FLEES

"The sovereign! The sovereign is hurrying to us!" They rushed after the enemy and captured his artillery. They killed many men, including the khan's brother-in-law, Prince Kambirdei. Even women and children were assisting them. The voivodes now arrived – the princes Shchenyatev and Kurbskii – and halted on the site where the khan's tents had been. Overjoyed with this victory, Ivan let his troops rest and spent the night by Koshira.

On the next day he received even more pleasant news: Shchenyatev and Kurbskii with only 15,000 troops had defeated 30,000 or more of the enemy who were rampaging in the vicinity of Tula. Unaware of the khan's flight, they thought they were coming to him, but ran into Russians instead. In this fierce battle, Prince Andrei Kurbskii, the young commander, was marked with glorious wounds: his head and shoulder were cut up. The voivodes pursued the Tatars and on the banks of Shevorona Creek gained a new victory over them and freed many Russians.

For booty, the khan left us his baggage train and whole herds of camels. Prisoners declared that he had been headed for Moscow, figuring our sovereign was at Kazan. When he learned of Ivan's powerful levies, he wanted to at least take Tula so he could flee homeward with less shame. Our light detachments kept running down Crimeans all the way to the steppes.

Ivan returned to Kolomna and informed the tsaritsa, his brother and the metropolitan of the glorious expulsion of the enemy. He sent the trophies to Moscow: enemy cannons, camels and prisoners to cheer the capital with evidence of our victories. He now organized an expedition against Kazan by two routes, announcing that the tsar's guards, the left wing and the reserve legion were to proceed with him to Vladimir and Murom, while the chief voivodes were to go to Ryazan and Meshchera in order to join up with their sovereign in the field beyond the Alatyr.

| OUR TROPHIES |

| GRUMBLING IN THE ARMY |

There was grumbling in the army: the Novgorodians and the boyar cadets complained that the tsar had not given them any rest. They had already been in service and in difficulties for several months, and it would be impossible for them to endure a distant campaign, for which they had neither the strength nor the money. Ivan was very distressed, but hid his vexation and ordered a list be made of ardent warriors who wished to serve their homeland, as well as those who, from sloth or disability, declined the glory of participating in a great exploit.

"The former," he said, "I shall love like my children; I want to know their needs and will share everything with them. But the latter may not remain: I do not need the faint of heart!"

These words had an amazing effect. All spoke with one voice,

"We shall go wherever it pleases our sovereign, and when he sees our service, he will not leave us poor."

Even the estate-less boyar cadets were mute with regard to their dissatisfactions in hopes of the sovereign's future favor.

On 3 July the entire army set out. Ivan prayed with notable fervor before the icon of the Virgin that had been with Dimitrii Donskii in the battle with Mamai* and now stood in the Kolomenskoe Cathedral of the Dormition. On the way he fervently kissed the tomb of the old-time Russian hero Aleksandr Nevskii and blessed the memory of Murom's saints, Prince Pyotr and Princess Fevroniya.

CAMPAIGN

In Vladimir, he received a report from Sviyazhsk that the illness there had abated, that the troops were animated with fervor and that the princes Mikulinskii and Serebryanyi and the boyar Danilo Romanovich were dealing with the rebels of the High Bank; they pacified many and had them make a new oath to be loyal subjects of Russia. In Murom the sovereign was informed from Moscow that his wife was steadfast and calm in her reliance on Providence, and that the priesthood and the people were constantly praying to the Most High for the wellbeing of the tsar and his host. The metropolitan wrote to Ivan with the tenderness of a friend and the fervor of a church preceptor.

"Be pure and chaste in your soul," he said. "Be humble in your glory and cheerful in disappointment. The tsar's virtues are the saviors of the realm."

---

* [At Kulikovo Field, where Donskii defeated the Tatars in 1380.]

Both the sovereign and the voivodes read this letter with affection.

"We thank you," Ivan replied to the metropolitan, "for your pastoral teaching, which is inscribed on my heart. Help us always with exhortations and prayer. We are proceeding further. May the Lord help us to return with peace for Christians!"

He did not waste even an hour in inactivity; on foot and on horseback he inspected the legions, both the men and their weapons. He ordered the boyar cadets be assigned to companies and chose a leader for each from the warriors of the most distinguished lineages. He sent off Shig-Alei in boats to Kazan with Prince Pyotr Bulgakov and musketeers, and dispatched the Yartolulnyi Guard to build bridges. On 20 July he followed the army across the Oka and spent the night in the Sakanskii Forest on the Veletema, 30 versts from Murom. A second camp was on the Shileksha and a third near the Sakanskii settlement. The Kasimov princes and Prince Temnikov joined the army with their own units, along with Tatars and Mordvi. On August 1st the sovereign blessed the waters of the river Myana. The next day the army crossed the Alatyr, and on 4 August they joyfully caught sight of the legions of the princes Mstislavskii, Shchenyatev, Kurbskii and Khilkov on the banks of the Sura. Both these large armies had marched through dense forests and wastelands, living off of game, berries and fruits.

"We had no provisions with us," eyewitnesses wrote. "Nature everywhere provided us with an abundant table until the start of Lent. Elk appeared in herds and fish crowded the streams; birds even fell from the skies before us."

Here, at the settlement of Boroncheevo, emissaries from Sviyazhsk and the Cheremis were waiting for the tsar with the report that the entire right bank of the Volga was obedient to him, peaceful and quiet. The rebels had repented, and the tsar, as a token of his mercy, dined with their elders. They swore to atone for their guilt and cleared the way through constricted places, built bridges over rivers and fervently wished to serve us with their swords at Kazan.

On 6 August by the stream of Kivat, Ivan heard the liturgy and partook of the sacrament. On 11 August the voivodes from

Chapter Four

Sviyazhsk met their sovereign with cavalry and infantry. They were marching in three legions. Prince Aleksandr Gorbatyi and the nobleman Danilo Romanovich were in the first, in the second were the princes Simeon Mikulinskii and Pyotr Serebryanyi-Obolenskii with boyar cadets, and in the third were Cossacks and inhabitants of the High Bank: Cheremis and Chuvash. The tsar welcomed both the voivodes and the troops, who numbered more than 20,000. He summoned them to kiss his hand, spoke to them, praising their discipline and courage and then entertained everyone on Beiskaya Meadow. The officers and the rank and file dined beneath the tent canopies.

The season and location were superb; on one side the eyes were treated to green plains, hills, groves and dark forests; on the other was the magnificent Volga with its wild cliffs and picturesque islands; and beyond them was a boundless meadow and oak forests. From time to time Chuvash settlements appeared on the steep slopes and in the gorges. The inhabitants gave us bread and mead. During the fasting period the tsar himself had no tastier fare. They drank plain water and nobody complained. Sobriety and gaiety ruled the camp.

Sviyazhsk appeared on August 13; the tsar viewed it with curiosity and lively pleasure. This young town, created by his command, was a symbol of the victory and triumph of Christians in the realm of the infidel. Priests with crosses, Prince Pyotr Shuiskii and the boyar Zabolotskii greeted Ivan with their military guard at the gates of the fortress. He walked to the main church; there the deacons sang, wishing him long life, and the boyars congratulated him as the conqueror and enlightener of the Sviyazhsk territory.

He inspected the fortress, its rich provisions, beautiful streets and houses, and then declared his gratitude to Prince Simeon Mikulinskii and the other commanders. He admired the picturesque views and told the nobles that there was no other site in Russia so favorable. A house had been prepared for him, but Ivan said,

"We are campaigning." He mounted his horse, left the town and stayed in the tents on the meadow by the Sviyaga.

The troops, tired from their journey, hoped to rest amidst the abundance and attractions of this new place, to which many merchants came from Moscow, Yaroslavl and Nizhnyi-Novgorod with all their goods. Boat after boat arrived at the landing stage and the river bank turned into a bazaar. The valuable items of European and Asiatic commerce were displayed on the sand and in cabins. Rich and distinguished people would find their provisions there, conveyed by the Volga. Everything was *just like home*: one could eat and drink delicious things, entertain friends and enjoy the luxury . . . . Ivan, however, had summoned Shig-Alei, Prince Vladimir Andreevich and all the Duma councilors; together they proposed to move immediately on Kazan.

Alei, being related to its new ruler, Ediger, undertook to write to him a persuasive letter, stating that he should not get carried away by pride, nor consider himself equipotent with this great Christian monarch, but to submit and come to Ivan in his camp, nor to have any fear. They also wrote to the Kazan nobles that the sovereign did not want their destruction, but their repentance: if they were to hand over to him those guilty of the rebellion, all else might be peaceful under his auspicious reign. This letter was sent with a Tatar on 15 August and on the next day the army began to cross the Volga.

In commencing the description of the memorable siege of Kazan, we note that it, along with the battle with Mamai, lives in the popular memory down to the present time as one of the most glorious exploits of bygone days; it is known to every Russian, be he in a mansion or a hovel. Two circumstances give it this extraordinary significance: it was our *first* proper experience in the art of taking fortified places. Its defenders showed surprising courage and rare, truly desperate valor, so that this victory cost us a very high price. These people had formerly been willing to submit to Ivan to avoid Shig-Alei's cruelties, but over the course of five months they had had time to consider the consequences.

Under Ivan's deputy, Kazan would continue to exist, but only as a Muscovite city. Its nobles and priesthood foresaw the ultimate downfall of its power and religion, and its people feared servitude. In their souls burned a noble love of independence, of the customs and laws of their forefathers. This was strengthened by recollections of bygone days and aggravated by hatred of Christians – formerly tributaries, but now oppressors of Baty's descendants. This overcame the people's natural predilection towards the peaceful enjoyment of life. It produced a rapture, a thirst for vengeance and blood, a zeal for danger and great deeds. In action, in an ardor for heroism, the people of Kazan did not perceive their own weakness. With this desperate resolve, hope still hid in their hearts when they considered that all of our prior assaults on their capital had been fruitless. They told each other,

"This is not the first time we have seen Muscovites beneath our walls; it will not be the first time they will flee homeward, and we shall laugh at them!"

Such were the feelings of the ruler and the people in Kazan, and yet Ivan proposed leniency, consistent with the policy of long-suffering patience of his father and grandfather.

On 19 August 1552, with 150,000 troops now on the lower side of the Volga, Shig-Alei set out in boats to occupy Gostinyi Island, while the boyar Mikhailo Yakovlevich Morozov was transporting artillery, wooden towers, and barricades in order to take action against the fortress.

It rained for several days; rivers overflowed their banks and turned the lower side into a swamp. Kazan had destroyed all the bridges and brushwood roads, making it necessary to construct a new route. On 20 August on the banks of the Kazanka Ivan received a letter in reply from Ediger: the ruler and nobles would not agree to peace. They reviled our sovereign, Russia and Christianity, calling Alei a traitor and criminal. They wrote,

"All is in readiness; we await you at the feast!"

This same day our army caught sight of Kazan and halted six versts from it in some flat, pleasant meadows, which extended *like a green cloth* between the Volga and the hill on which the fortress stood, with its stone mosques and palace, with high towers and wide, oaken walls (the insides of which were packed with silt and gravel). Two days were spent unloading cannons from the boats.

Then a fugitive from Kazan appeared, Mirza Kamai, and reported to the sovereign that he would have ridden to him with 200 comrades but that they were detained within the city. He said that the ruler Ediger, Kulsherif-Molna (the chief of the clergy), the princes Izenesh Nogaiskii, Chapkun, Atalyk, Islam, Alikei Narykov, Kebek Tyumenskii and Derbysh had been able to rouse the people with their malice towards Christians. No one was even thinking of peace; the fortress was full of grain and military provisions, with 30,000 troops and 2,700 Nogai within it. Prince Yapancha had been sent with a large detachment of cavalry to the Arsk* abattis** to arm and assemble the rural residents there in order to menace the Russian camp with incessant attacks.

Ivan received Kamai graciously, consulted with his boyars and ordered each soldier prepare a timber and every ten of them a gabion for fortification. The main force and the vanguard were to occupy Arskoe Field,*** the right wing the bank of the Kazanka, the reserve the mouth of the Bulak, the left wing to be above it, Alei across the Bulak in the cemetery, and the tsar's guards, commanded by him and Prince Vladimir Andreevich on Tsarskoe Meadow. Officers were strictly forbidden to commence hostilities on their own, without word from the tsar. At the dawn hour on 23 August the army moved forward. In front marched Prince Yurii Shemyakin-Pronskii and Thedor Troekurov with Cossack infantry and musketeers. Behind the voivodes were the atamans, the heads of the musketeers and company commanders, each according to rank and in his place, observing discipline and silence. The sun rose, lighting up Kazan for Ivan's eyes.

He gave the signal and the legions halted. Tambourines were struck and trumpets blared; banners were unfurled, as well as the sacred gonfalon**** on which Jesus was depicted. The life-giving cross was hoisted above: it had been at the Don with Grand Prince Dimitrii Ivanovich. The tsar and the voivodes dismounted and sang mass beneath the banners, and the sovereign made a speech to the troops: he encouraged them to perform great feats; he praised the heroes who would fall for the faith and swore in

---

* [Town 65 km northeast of Kazan.]
** [An abattis is a defensive obstacle made of felled trees.]
*** [To the east of Kazan.]
**** [A banner suspended from a horizontal crosspiece.]

Russia's name that their widows and orphans would be taken care of and comforted by their country. Finally, he consigned himself to death should that be necessary for victory and the triumph of Christians. Prince Vladimir Andreevich and the boyars tearfully replied to him,

"Hold fast, tsar! We are all of one mind, for God and for you." Ivan's confessor, the archpriest Andrei, blessed him and the army, which displayed a lively fervor. The tsar mounted his richly adorned argamak,* glanced at the image of the Savior on the sacred gonfalon, crossed himself and loudly called out,

"In Thy name we march!" He ordered them directly at the city, where everything seemed quiet and empty. There was no movement visible, nor were there people on the wall, and many of us rejoiced, thinking that the ruler of Kazan and his troops had fled into the forest from fear. But experienced voivodes told each other,

"We should be all the more cautious!"

The Russians were surrounding Kazan. 7,000 musketeers and Cossack infantry, using an improvised bridge, crossed the muddy Bulak, which flowed towards the city from Lake Kaban, and saw before them, no more than 200 sazhens away,** royal palaces and stone mosques soaring high as they marched in front of the fortress to Arskoe Field. Suddenly there was noise and a shout rang out: creaking, the gate opened and 15,000 Tatars, cavalry and infantry from the city charged at our musketeers, breaking up their formation and smashing into them.

| Siege |

| First Battle |

The young princes Shemyakin and Troekurov restrained those fleeing and closed up ranks. Some boyar cadets showed up and a fierce battle commenced. Not having any cavalry, the Russians stood their ground. They were victorious and chased the enemy all the way to his walls despite heavy fire from the city. They took prisoners and withdrew slowly in view of all our legions, which were calmly marching to their designated positions while admiring this first, glorious feat from a distance. The sovereign's orders

---
* [A central Asian breed of race horse.]
** [About 400 meters, or a quarter mile. A sazhen is 2.13 meters, or about 7 feet.]

were carried out precisely: no one rushed into battle without his word and military discipline was brilliantly exemplified.

The legions had Kazan surrounded. Tents were erected as well as three linen church tents, named after the militant Archangel Michael, St. Catherine the Martyr and St. Sergii. In the evening the sovereign assembled the voivodes and gave them all the necessary commands orally. The night was quiet. The next day there was an unusually powerful storm: it ripped many tents, including the tsar's. It swamped the boats loaded with provisions and frightened the troops. They thought it was the end of everything, that there would not be a siege, that without grain we would have to withdraw in shame. Ivan did not concur: he sent to Sviyazhsk and Moscow for provisions, for warm clothing for the troops, for money, and prepared to winter at Kazan.

> STORM

On 25 August the light detachment of princes Shemyakin and Troekurov moved from Arskoe Field to the Kazanka, upriver from the city, to cut it off from the lowland Cheremis, to join up with the right wing and to be closer to the walls. The Tatars made a sally and the valiant knight, Prince Shemyakin, was wounded, but Prince Dmitrii Khilkov, commander of all the forward elements, came to his aid with boyar cadets and drove the enemy back into the fortress. By night the reserve legion and the left wing positioned their gabions and cannons without a fight or any resistance. The musketeers dug a trench, while the Cossacks, right beneath the city wall, ensconced themselves in the so-called Dairova baths, which were made of stone. For these two days, Ivan did not dismount; he rode around the city to inspect the most favorable places for an assault.

> GABIONS DEPLOYED

On 26 August the main legion left camp towards evening. Prince Mikhail Vorotynskii marched with infantry and rolling gabions; Prince Ivan Mstislavskii led the cavalry to assist him in case of attack. The sovereign gave him crack boyar cadets from his own guards. Kazan's troops struck them with loud cries;

from the towers and walls they showered them with cannon shot and bullets. In the smoke and flame, the steadfast Russians drove off their cavalry and infantry by powerful cannon fire from their embrasures, with musket volleys, lances and swords. They coolly marched forward, pressed the Tatars into the city, and filled its bridges with enemy bodies. The arquebusiers and the Cossacks stood on the embankment and kept shooting until nightfall, giving time for Prince Vorotynskii to set up and fill gabions with dirt 50 sazhens* from the ditch, between Arskoe Field and the Bulak. Then he ordered them to withdraw to the gabions and dig in below them.

> A POWERFUL SALLY

Darkness did not halt the fighting, however: Kazan's troops kept emerging to slash at us until morning came. There was no rest; neither the troops nor their commanders got a wink of sleep. Ivan prayed in a church and could hear his most distinguished officers encourage the combatants hourly. Finally the enemy tired and the rising sun illuminated the Russian's decisive victory. The sovereign ordered a thanksgiving service to be held in the camp. Kazan lost many brave men in this action, including bold Prince Narykov and the bogatyr Syunchelei. Among the Muscovite dead was the fine knight Leontii Shusherin.

On 27 August the boyar Mikhailo Yakovlevich Morozov, covered by heavy fire from all our embrasures, rolled siege engines to the gabions, while the arquebusiers fired into the city from their entrenchments. The Kazan troops [mostly] hid behind their walls, but they wanted to get prisoners for information, and attacked men scattered across the field, near the place where Prince Mstislavskii was stationed with part of the main legion. This voivode managed to protect his own. He chased off the enemy, captured the renowned uhlan Karamysh and took him to the sovereign. He had displayed personal courage and was wounded by arrows in two places. The prisoner said that the people of Kazan were ready to die and would not hear of peace talks.

> EFFECT OF EMBRASURES

---

* [About 100 meters, or 110 yards.]

The next day, as the Russians awaited new sallies; the enemy appeared from the opposite direction. Dense crowds of them emerged from the forest onto Arskoe Field. They captured the sentries of the vanguard legion and charged towards its camp. The voivode Prince Khilkov resisted strenuously, but was in need of immediate assistance. The princes Ivan Pronskii, Mstislavskii and Yurii Obolenskii, one after the other, hurried to contain the enemy's charge. Ivan sent Khilkov part of the tsar's guards and got on a horse himself. Many of our officers were killed or wounded, but the number of Russians was growing by the minute. They drove the Tatars back into the forest and learned from prisoners that they had come with Prince Yapancha from fortifications Kazan had built on the road to the town of Arsk. He had been ordered to give us no rest and to do as much harm as possible with frequent raids.

> PRINCE YAPANCHA, THE RAIDER

On 29 August, the princes Shchenyatev and Kurbskii, voivodes of the right wing, moved out toward the city and began to reinforce the gabions along the Kazanka, protected by musketeers. Princes Shemyakin's and Troekurov's troops returned to Arskoe Field, where the enemy had again emerged from the forest and where Mstislavskii, Khilkov and Obolenskii stood in ranks, awaiting the Tatars. Meanwhile, other voivodes – Prince Dimitrii Paletskii, Aleksei Adashev and the officers of the tsar's guards – were setting up gabions from Arskoe Field to the Kazanka. Cannons, firearms and bows were shooting from both sides, but there were no sorties. The enemy saw the Russians were battle-ready, so they did not emerge from the forest. That evening it was reported to Ivan that the entire city was surrounded by our fortifications: gabions in the dry places and palisades in the wet ones. There was now no way either in or out of Kazan. Henceforth the boyar Morozov, who had positioned artillery everywhere, indefatigably thundered away at the walls with 150 heavy weapons.

> EXHAUSTION OF THE TROOPS

During the course of the week, however, our troops had become extremely exhausted. They were always standing at arms and had no time to rest. Because of insufficient provisions, they had only dry bread to eat. Our foragers did not dare leave the camp, since Prince Yapancha was watching for them in all directions and capturing them. Kazan was communicating with him by means of signals. They would set up a gonfalon on a tall tower and wave it to inform them that they should strike the besiegers. This dangerous raider kept the Russians in constant fear.

Ivan assembled a council and proposed to divide the army into two parts: one to fortify and to protect the tsar's person, the other, under the command of valiant and seasoned Prince Aleksandr Gorbatyi-Shuiskii, to take strong actions against Yapancha in order to screen the siege, clear the forest and bring relief to our camp. With 30,000 cavalry and 15,000 infantry troops, Prince Aleksandr deployed beyond the hills in order to keep his movements secret from the enemy; he also sent detachments into the forest of Arsk. Yapancha caught sight of them and his troops poured out onto the field. The Russians turned tail, as if terrified. The Tatars pursued them, squeezed into the baggage train and began to circle in front of our fortifications. They shot a rain of arrows, while other enemy cavalry and infantry marched in slow military order directly towards the camp of the Muscovite main legion.

| DIVISION OF THE LEGIONS |

With his alert troops, Prince Yurii Shemyakin now charged from ambush at the Tatars. They were surprised and since they were far from the forest, they were obliged to fight. Prince Aleksandr soon appeared with large cavalry units, while our infantry took the enemy in the rear from the left and right. The Tatars sought safety in flight: they were crushed and cut down over a distance of 10 or more versts, all the way to the Kilar, where Prince Aleksandr reigned in his exhausted horse and called the scattered victors together with the sound of trumpets. On the return journey, in the forest, they killed many more of the enemy, who were hiding in thickets and behind dense branches, and took several hundred prisoners. In short, they wiped out Yapancha. The sovereign embraced the commanders, who were covered with the dust of war and drenched with sweat and blood; he praised with lively delight

| DESTRUCTION OF YAPANCHA'S ARMY |

their intelligence and valor, and declared his gratitude to the rank and file. He ordered all the prisoners to be taken to pickets in front of our fortifications so that they could beseech Kazan to surrender. Simultaneously, the sovereign's officers rode up to the walls and said to the Tatars,

> BITTERNESS IN KAZAN

"Ivan promises them [the prisoners] life and liberty, and forgiveness and mercy to you if you submit to him."

The men of Kazan, who had quietly listened to their words, then loosed a multitude of arrows at their unfortunate captive fellow citizens, screaming,

"Better that you die by our unsullied hands than by the evil hands of the Christians!"

This outburst astounded the Russians and their sovereign.

Desiring to employ all possible means to take Kazan with the least bloodshed, he ordered the skilled German engineer serving in his army to construct a tunnel from the river Bulak between the Atalakovye and Tyumenskie gates. Mirza Kamai had informed the sovereign that the besieged were getting their water from a source near the Kazanka and they were walking there underground from the Muraleevye Gate. Our voivodes tried to discover this secret source, but were unable. The tsar ordered it to be undermined from the stone Daurovaya* baths which had been occupied by our Cossacks.

Our engineer assigned his experts to this scheme; they dug for 10 days under the supervision of Prince Vasilii Serebryanyi and Ivan's favorite, Aleksei Adashev. They could hear people's voices above them, going secretly for water. They rolled 11 kegs of powder into the tunnel and notified the sovereign. Early on 5 September, Ivan rode out to the fortifications. Suddenly, before his eyes, the ground exploded with a thunderous roar and a crash, destroying the secret water source, part of the city wall and a large number of people. Timbers and stones flew into the air, falling to crush residents, who were horror-struck and did

> DESTRUCTION OF A SECRET PLACE

---

* [Previously given as Dairova.]

not understand what had happened. At that moment, the Russians, seizing their banners, charged at the ruined wall. They broke into the city itself, but could not hold their ground within it. The residents of Kazan came to their senses and forced them out. The sovereign ordered them not to renew the assault. We took a respectable number of prisoners, killed many more, and awaited the aftermath.

Despite the resolve of the residents of Kazan, despondency was manifest in the city after this catastrophic event. Some of them thought that all was lost; that they no longer had the means to defend themselves. But those more bold encouraged them; they dug and found another water source, small and smelly, which would have to satisfy the whole city. They endured thirst and swelled up because of the bad water, but were silent and fought on.

> DEJECTION IN KAZAN

Ivan was amazingly energetic; no one knew when he was able to rest. Early and late he prayed in the church and rode around the fortifications. He would stop, talk to the troops and bolster their endurance. If Kazan menaced us with constant fire, then we did not give them any peace either; Russian cannons roared day and night, loaded with cannon balls and stones. The Arsk Gate was razed to its foundations; the besieged blocked it up with wooden barricades.

> IVAN'S ENERGY

On 6 September, Ivan charged Prince Aleksandr Gorbatyi-Shuiskii with taking the stockade that Kazan had built on the other side of Arskoe Field, 15 versts from the city on a steep height between two swamps: the remnants of Yapancha's beaten forces had regrouped there. Prince Simeon Mikulinskii marched forth; with him were the boyars Danilo Romanovich and Zakhariya Yakovlev, princes Bulgakov and Paletskii, the commanders of the tsar's guards, boyar cadets, musketeers, atamans with their Cossacks, and also Temnikovskie Mordvi and mountain Cheremis, who served as guides. With timbered barriers filled with dirt and fortified with abattises, the stronghold seemed

> **Town and Stockade of Arsk Captured**

unassailable. Our troops dismounted and followed their bold leaders across the swamp, through muddy thickets and copses, under a hail of arrows. Without pausing they climbed up from both sides, smashed the gate and took the fortification and 200 prisoners. Enemy bodies lay in heaps. The voivodes found excellent booty there, spent the night and then went on to the town of Arsk and to pleasant places, surprisingly fertile, where the Kazan nobles had their country estates, rich and beautiful.

The Russians were swimming in abundance; they took whatever they wanted: bread, mead, cattle, then burned the settlements and killed the residents, taking prisoner only the women and children. The citizens of Arsk had fled into the furthest forests, but there were still considerable valuables left in their homes and shops, especially all kinds of furs, such as marten and squirrel. Ten days after freeing many Christian compatriots who were there against their will, Prince Aleksandr returned victorious, with such an abundance that prices of edible provisions dropped, so that henceforth in the camp the price of a cow was 10 dengas, 20 for an ox. The tsar and the troops were overjoyed.

But dangers and difficulties had not diminished. Arrows were no longer shot at the Russians from the forest of Arsk, but the lowland Cheremis had driven off our herds and menaced our camp from the Galitskaya Road. The

> **Attack of the Lowland Cheremis**

voivodes of the right wing stationed there went after them and trounced them, but fear of new attacks and constant vigilance wearied their legion. In addition to that, they occupied the low plain along the Kazanka and were more than anyone else subject to fire from the fortress, foul weather, and the heavy rains customary at this time of year, but which the superstitious attributed to witchcraft.

Prince Kurbskii, an eyewitness valiant and prudent in equal measures, pays tribute to his age when he writes as fact that every

> **Imagined Sorcery**

day at sunrise, Kazan sorcerers would appear on the walls of the fortress and howl with terrifying voices, gesture, and wave clothing at the Russian camp, producing wind and clouds from which rain would pour in rivers. Dry places would turn into swamps, tents would be awash and the men would be soaked from morning till evening. With the advice of the boyars, the tsar ordered the royal life-giving cross be brought from Moscow to bless water and that it be sprinkled around the camp. We are assured that the power of sorcery vanished, beautiful weather commenced, and the troops took heart.

Desirous of taking stronger action against the interior of the city, two versts from their camp the Russians secretly constructed a tower six sazhens tall.* By night they moved it up to the walls, right to the Royal Gates. Inside it they placed 10 large weapons, 50 medium ones and a detachment of skilled gunners. They waited for dawn, which they announced with a thunderous volley. The gunners were positioned higher than the walls and fired at people in the streets and in the houses. The residents of Kazan took cover in pits; they excavated dugouts for themselves under the wooden barricades, from which, like snakes, they would crawl out to fight just as fiercely as before. They no longer could employ their heavy weapons, which had been destroyed by our barrages, but kept firing incessantly from muskets and small cannons, so that every day we lost a considerable number of fine warriors.

> CONSTRUCTION OF A HIGH TOWER

In vain did Ivan revive peace proposals, decreeing that if the besieged did not want to surrender, they would be allowed to go wherever they pleased, with their illegitimate ruler, with their possessions, and with their wives and children. We would demand only the city itself, founded on Bolgar lands in an ancient Russian possession.** The people of Kazan *did not even listen with the tips of their ears,* as the chronicler expresses it.

> PROPOSAL TO KAZAN

Meanwhile, the valiant Prince Mikhailo Vorotynskii was moving his gabions closer and closer to the turret at Arsk.

---

* [About 6 meters, or 40 feet.]
** [But in the associated endnote, Karamzin says that Bolgar territory had never belonged to Russia.]

A Bloody Affair

At last, only a ditch, three sazhens broad and seven deep, was between them and the wall. Musketeers, Cossacks and officers with boyars' men stood behind them, fought with all their might and then were relieved. But sometimes, despite the close proximity, the battle broke off due to exhaustion and warriors of both sides took a rest. One time Kazan's troops took advantage of this break: seeing that many of our troops had sat down for lunch and that our cannons were undermanned, upwards of 10,000 of them quietly crawled out of their burrows, and under the command of nobles (the chiefs of the ruler's advisers, called *karachi*), they charged at the gabions, crushed the Russians and seized their cannons. At this point Prince Vorotynskii himself, and behind him all the most distinguished officers, joined the fray.

"We shall not betray our fathers!" the Russians cried, and fought valiantly. The voivodes Pyotr Morozov and Prince Yurii Kashin fell in the press, gravely wounded, and were taken back to the camp. Prince Mikhailo Vorotynskii was wounded in the face but did not leave the battle, and his strong armor was sliced up by sabers. Many musketeer officers lay dead at their cannons, but the enemy had still not yielded up the trophies that he had captured from us.

But now Murom's men and the boyar cadets appeared, *of ancient stock and valorous*. They struck and smashed the enemy and squeezed them into the ditch. Victory was ours! Kazan's troops trampled each other pressing into the gates and crawling into their holes. This action was one of the most sanguinary. The enemy had also been simultaneously attacking the vanguard legion's gabions, but not very forcefully. The sovereign saw both actions with his own eyes: he favored Prince Mikhail Vorotynskii and the Murom knights especially, and called on the wounded voivodes, thanking them for their diligent service.

The Russians had now stood at [the gates of] Kazan for about five weeks. In sallies and inside the city they had killed no less than 10,000 of the enemy, not counting women and children. Approaching autumn frightened them more than the difficulties and actions of the siege; everyone wanted a quick conclusion. In order to facilitate the assault and inflict painful harm on the besieged, Ivan ordered the wooden barricades and dugouts near the Arskie Gates be mined – this is where people were taking cover from our fire. On 30 September, they exploded into the air. The terrible effects of gunpowder, albeit no longer a novelty to the people of Kazan, produced a stunned silence in the city for a few minutes.

> BLOWING UP BARRICADES

The Russians, however, lost no time in rolling their gabions up to the Arskie, Atalykovye* and Tyumenskie gates. Thinking that the decisive hour had arrived, the enemy poured out of the city to grapple with the legions ordered to protect the gabions. The battle was at full boil. Ivan hastened to encourage his troops; as soon as they saw him they exclaimed with a single voice,

"The tsar is with us!"

They charged at the walls, pursued and pressed the enemy on the bridges and at the gates. The combat was ghastly. The thunder of the cannons, the reports of the muskets and the cries of warriors resounded amidst the clouds of thick smoke that rose over the whole city. Despite the valiant and desperate resistance, many Russians were already atop the wall, in the turret by Arskoe Field and fighting fiercely with the Tatars in the streets. Prince Mikhailo Vorotynskii so informed the sovereign and requested that he order all the legions to the assault.

> CAPTURE OF THE TURRET OF ARSK

Success seemed most probable, but Ivan wanted certainty. The greater part of the army was still in camp and could not quickly be mustered, for excessive haste might produce anarchy and perhaps defeat, which would have the most deleterious effects for us. Disregarding the army's fervor, he ordered it to pull back. It obeyed unwillingly; the officers led it out of the fortress with difficulty and burned the bridges. But so that the blood shed on this hot day would not become futile, Prince Vorotynskii had our gunners occupy the turret of Arsk: they reinforced it with gabions and an array of stout shields and said to their voivodes,

"We will wait for you here."

---

* [Previously spelled Atalakovye.]

They kept their word. Kazan was unable to take it back from them. The bridges burned all night and part of the wall was burnt as well. The effects of our artillery had also destroyed it in many places. The enemy put up tall wooden barriers there and covered them with dirt.

Finally, on 1 October, Ivan announced to the army that it was ready *to drink from the common cup of blood*, that is, ready for the assault (for the mines were now in place), and ordered his warriors *to cleanse their souls* on the eve of the fateful day. At the same hour that some of them were humbly confessing their sins and [thus becoming] worthy of ardently partaking of the body of Christ, others, beneath the thunder of the embrasures, were hurling dirt and timbers into the ditch in order to extend a path to the walls. The sovereign still wished to test the efficacy of exhortation, and so Mirza Kamai and the gray elders of the High Bank approached the fortress, which was covered with people, holding a token of peace in their hands. They told them that Ivan was offering mercy to the city for the last time; it was already sorely pressed and half-destroyed. He asked only that they hand over the chief criminals; he would forgive its people. The people of Kazan replied with one voice,

LAST OFFER TO KAZAN

"We do not wish forgiveness! There are Russians in the turret and Russians on the walls, but we are not afraid. We will put up a new turret and a new wall. We all will either sit out the siege or die!"

The sovereign now began to form up his troops for *a great exploit.*

In order to screen his rear from the lowland Cheremis, from Tatars at large in the forest and from the Nogai uluses, and in order to cut off all escape routes from Kazan, Ivan ordered Prince Mstislavskii, with part of the main legion, and Shig-Alei with troops from Kasimov and inhabitants of the High Bank to occupy the Arsk and Chuvash roads, while Prince Yurii Obolenskii and Grigorii Meshcherskii with court nobles

DISPOSITION OF THE ARMY FOR ASSAULT

CHAPTER FOUR

of the tsar's guards were to take the Nogai road. Adjoining him, Prince Ivan Romodanovskii Galitskii with another detachment of court nobles were to be positioned above the Kazanka, at Staroe Gorodishche.

After dispatching these voivodes, Ivan made dispositions for the assault: he ordered the first therein to be the atamans with their Cossacks, the chiefs with the musketeers and house servants, divided into companies under the command of select boyar cadets. The voivodes' legions would follow them: Prince Mikhailo Vorotynskii and the okolnichii Aleksei Basmanov would strike at the fortress in the gap between the Bulak and Poganoe Lake; Prince Khilkov at the Kabatskie Gate, Princes Troekurov at the Zboilivye, Andrei Kurbskii at the Elbuginye, Semyon Sheremetev at the Muraleevye, and Dmitrii Pleshcheev at the Tyumenskie. A special voivode would assist each of them: for the first would be the sovereign himself, and for the others, princes Ivan Pronskii, Turuntai, Shemyakin, Shchenyatev, Vasilii Serebryanyi-Obolenskii, and Dmitrii Mikulinskii.

They were ordered to be prepared by the second hour of the following morning and to wait for the explosion of the mines. In the evening, Ivan retired alone with his spiritual father; he spent some time in an edifying conversation with him and then put on his armor. Prince Vorotynskii now sent to tell him that the engineer was ready: 48 kegs of powder were now in the mine. Kazan had noticed our labors and we should not wait a minute longer. The sovereign ordered the legions to move out, heard matins in the church, sent off the tsar's guards and prayed deep in his heart. On this important night, the precursor of a decisive day, neither the Russian camp nor Kazan gave thought to any rest. The unusual activity in our camp was seen from the city and both sides earnestly prepared for a fearsome battle.

Dawn lit up the sky, which was bright and clear. Kazan's troops stood on its walls, the Russians before them, under the protection of their fortifications and beneath their banners, in the silence, unmoving, with only the sounds of tambourines and trumpets, theirs and ours, not an arrow flew, not a cannon roared. The men looked at one another; everything was in expectation.

The camp was deserted, and in the silence the singing of the priests could be heard performing mass. The sovereign remained in the church with some of the people closest to him.

The sun was now up. The deacon recited the Gospels and had barely uttered the words *let there be one flock and one pastor!*

DETONATION OF MINES AND THE ASSAULT

when there was a tremendous roar, the earth shook and the church tent trembled. The sovereign came out onto the church porch and saw the terrible effects of the mine and the thick dark cloud over the entire city of Kazan. Clods of earth, pieces of towers, walls of houses, and people – all had been hurled upward into the clouds of smoke and then fell back onto the city. In the church the divine service was cut short, but Ivan calmly returned and wished to hear the rest of the liturgy. As the deacon was loudly praying before the Royal Gates for the Most High to uphold Ivan's authority and to cast down any enemy or adversary

HEROISM ON BOTH SIDES

before his feet, there was a new blast: another mine had exploded, this one larger than the last. And then, crying, *God is with us!* the Russian legions quickly moved in on the fortress.

The people of Kazan, steadfast and unwavering in the hour of their doom and destruction, cried *Allah! Allah!* invoking Mohammed, while awaiting our troops, shooting neither bows nor arquebuses. Then, measuring the range with their eyes, they suddenly let off a terrible volley. Shot, stones and arrows darkened the air . . . But the Russians, heartened by the example of their commanders, reached the walls. Kazan's troops crushed them with timbers and poured boiling water on them. Cautious no longer, they did not hide behind their cover, but stood in the open on the walls and scaffolding, scorning the heavy fire from our embrasures and gunners.

The slightest delay now could be fatal to the Russians. Their numbers lessened; many fell, dead or wounded, or simply out of fright. But the daring, with a heroic disregard of death, encouraged and saved the fearful. Some rushed into the gap; others clambered up the wall on ladders and timbers. They carried each other on their heads, on their shoulders, and struggled with the enemy in the gaps [in the wall]. Ivan had now heard the liturgy, taken communion, and received the blessing from his spiritual father; just as he entered the field on his war horse, Christian banners were being unfurled on top of the fortress! With a united cry, the reserve troops hailed their sovereign and victory.

This victory was not yet been completely decisive, however. The desperate Tatars, who had been crushed and cast down from the walls and towers, stood as a firm bulwark in the streets, slashing with their sabers, grappling with the Russians and slicing with knives in the fearsome melee. They fought at the barricades and on the rooftops; everywhere heads and bodies were trampled underfoot.

Prince Mikhailo Vorotynskii was the first to inform Ivan that we were inside the city, but that the battle was still raging and assistance was required. The sovereign detailed part of his own legion to the prince and also ordered other voivodes to march. Our troops were victorious [almost] everywhere and were pressing the Tatars at the fortified ruler's court. Ediger himself, with his most distinguished nobles, gradually withdrew from the breaches, halted in the middle of the city at the Merchants', or Tezitskii, Ditch and fought stubbornly.

He suddenly noticed that our crowds of troops had gotten smaller – after the Russians had conquered half of a city famed for its riches of Asiatic trade, they were enticed by its treasures. They left the fray and began to break into homes and shops. Even the officers, whom Ivan had ordered to follow the troops with drawn swords so that none of them would be able to pillage, rushed after loot. Now even fainthearted cowards came to life, they who had been lying on the ground as if dead or wounded, and from the baggage train, servants, cooks, even merchants came running. Everyone craved booty. They seized silver, furs, fabrics, took them back to the camp and then returned to the city with no thought of helping their comrades in the battle.

GREED OF MANY OF THE TROOPS

Kazan's troops took advantage of the exhaustion of our honorable and brave troops; they struck and sorely pressed them, to the horror of the pillagers, who all immediately turned and fled, hurling themselves through the wall and shouting,

"They are cutting us up! They are cutting us up!" The sovereign saw this general disarray and his expression changed as he came to believe that the enemy was chasing our whole army out of the city.

"With us were," writes Kurbskii, "the great senators, men of our fathers' time, men grown gray with virtue and in the arts of war."

COURAGE OF IVAN AND THE BOYARS They advised the sovereign, and the sovereign displayed courage: he took the sacred gonfalon and stood in front of the Royal Gates to halt the flight. Half of his select guard of 20,000 dismounted and rushed into the city; with them were the elders of the nobility and their young sons. These fresh, hearty troops, in shining armor and glittering helmets, descended on the Tatars like an unexpected storm. Unable to hold out for long, they closed up their ranks smartly and withdrew in good order to the tallest stone mosques, where all their priesthood – abyzi,* seits, mullahs and the archpriest Kulsherif – met the Russians not with gifts, not with prayers, but with weapons. In a frenzy of malice they rushed to certain death, and to the last man they fell beneath our swords. Ediger and the remaining Kazan troops ensconced themselves in the royal court and continued fighting for about an hour longer.

The Russians broke down the gates, whereupon the young wives and daughters of Kazan, in richly colored dresses, stood all together on one side, protected by their charms, while on the other side their fathers, brothers and husbands encircled their ruler, who was still battling forcefully. Numbering 10,000, they

PRINCE KURBSKII'S VALOR finally withdrew through the postern gate towards the lower part of the city. Prince Andrei Kurbskii and 200 warriors cut them off, confining them to narrow streets and steep slopes and impeding their every step. This made time for our troops to strike the enemy in the rear and to stop in the Zboilivye Gates, where they were joined by several hundred more Russians. Pursued and sorely pressed, the enemy climbed to the wall over bodies of their own people. They brought Ediger to a tower and shouted that they

---

* [Kazakh word for mullah. Mullahs are also mentioned explicitly – it is not clear what, if any, distinction there is.]

wanted to begin negotiations. The voivode nearest them, Prince Dimitrii Paletskii, stopped the fighting.

> CAPTURE OF KAZAN

"Listen," said the people of Kazan. "Up till now we had a country; we were dying for our ruler and our homeland. Now Kazan is yours. We are giving you our ruler, alive and uninjured. Take him to Ivan. We will go to the broad field and drink the last cup with you."

Along with Ediger, they handed over to Paletskii the chief senior noble, or *karach*, named Zaniesh and two *mamichei* [wet nurse's sons] who had been raised with the ruler. They then began to shoot once more, jumped down off the wall and tried to get to the camp of our right wing, but encountered heavy fire from our fortifications and turned to the left. Dropping their heavy weapons, they took off their shoes and crossed at a shallow place in the Kazanka River, in view of our troops, who were in the fortress, on the walls and the royal court, and also beyond the hills and precipices. Only the young Kurbskii princes, Andrei and Roman, and their small detachment managed to mount their horses, gallop after and overtake the enemy. They struck at the dense crowd, cut through to its center, trampling and slaughtering them.

But the Tatars still numbered 5,000 and the bravest at that. They stood their ground, for they did not fear death. They grappled with our heroes and cast them down, steaming with blood, dead on the ground, and continued unimpeded further across the flat meadow to a mucky swamp where cavalry could not pursue them, and then hurried into a dense, dark forest.

The remnant was small, but because of its frenzied courage, still dangerous to the Russians. The sovereign dispatched Princes Simeon Mikulinskii, Mikhail Vasilievich Glinskii and Sheremetev with a cavalry detachment to cross the Kazanka, overtake the fleeing Tatars and cut them off from the forest. The voivodes caught up with and trounced them; none surrendered and only a few of the wounded were saved.

The city had been taken. It was on fire in various places, and although the battle was over, blood still flowed. Our exasperated soldiers cut down everyone they found in the mosques, homes and holes, but took women, children and officials captive. The royal court, streets, walls, and deep ditches were filled with corpses. From the fortress to the Kazanka and further, in meadows and woods, more bodies lay or were carried along by the river. The shooting had ceased; in the smoke of the city, the only sounds were the clash of swords, the groans of the dying and the cries of the victors. The chief commander, Prince Mikhailo Vorotynskii sent to tell his sovereign:

"Rejoice, pious autocrat! Due to your courage and good fortune, victory is complete. Kazan is ours, its ruler is in your hands, its people either exterminated or in captivity and uncountable riches have been amassed. What is your command?"

> CROSS HOISTED AT ROYAL GATES

"Praise the Most High," Ivan replied, raising his hands to Heaven. He ordered a public prayer be performed beneath the sacred gonfalon and with his own hands raised the life-giving cross, designating this site for the first Christian church. Prince Paletskii presented Ediger to him: without any anger and with a mild expression, Ivan said,

"Unfortunate man! Did you really not know the might of Russia and the craftiness of the people of Kazan?" Encouraged by the sovereign's quiet demeanor, Ediger knelt, expressed repentance and asked for mercy. Ivan forgave him and then affectionately embraced his own brother, Prince Vladimir Andreevich, Shig-Alei and his nobles. He replied kindly and humbly to their enthusiastic congratulations, giving all the glory to God, to them, and to the troops. He sent his boyars and those closest to him to all units *with praise and gracious words*, and ordered that the city street from the Muraleevye Gates to the royal court be cleaned up. He then entered Kazan, preceded by his voivodes, court nobles and his confessor with a cross, while Prince Vladimir Andreevich and Shig-Alei followed him. A great number of liberated Russians who had been prisoners in Kazan were standing at the gate. When they caught sight of their sovereign they fell to the ground and with tears of joy called out,

> THE SOVEREIGN ENTERS KAZAN

> LIBERATION OF RUSSIAN PRISONERS

Chapter Four

"Liberator! You have delivered us from Hell! For us, poor and orphaned, you did not spare your lives."

The sovereign ordered them to be taken to the camp and fed from the tsar's table. He then rode past the heaps of bodies and wept. On seeing the corpses of Kazan's people, he said,

"They may not be Christians, but they are still people like us."

On viewing the fallen Russians, he prayed to the Most High on their behalf, as sacrifices for common salvation. On his entrance to the palace, the boyars, officers and troops again congratulated Ivan. They spoke to one another with feeling:

"Where the infidel has ruled, drinking Christian blood, we now see the life-giving cross and our sovereign in his glory!"

With hearts filled with emotion, with one voice and mind, everyone offered thanks to Heaven. Ivan ordered the fires to be put out in the city and that all booty, all the riches of Kazan and all the prisoners, except for Ediger, be turned over to his troops. For himself he took only the regalia: the crown, staff, the ruler's banner and the cannons, saying,

"My greed is for peace and the honor of Russia!"

He returned to the camp. He wanted to see the army, and with a radiant countenance went out to the legions. They were still steaming with infidel blood, as well as their own. Many knights, in the word of the chronicler, *were shining as if their wounds were gleaming like diamonds.* Ivan stood before the troops and loudly delivered a speech full of love and graciousness.

"Brave warriors!" he said. "Boyars, voivodes and officers! On this distinguished day of suffering in the name of God and for the faith, your homeland and tsar, you have at-

> IVAN'S SPEECH TO THE TROOPS

tained glory unheard of in our time. No one else has shown such bravery; no one else has achieved such a victory! You are the new Macedonians, worthy descendants of the knights with whom Grand Prince Dimitrii crushed Mamai! How can I reward you? As for Russia's dearest sons: you lie there on the field of honor; you now shine with heavenly crowns like the first Christian martyrs. This is God's work; ours is to glorify you through all the ages by entering your names on the commemorative roll in the main apostolic church. And you, incarnadine with your own blood, but still living, are to have our love and gratitude. All you brave men I see before me – heed and believe my promise to love and reward you till the end of my days . . . Now be at peace, victors!"

The army responded with joyous cries. Ivan now visited and comforted the wounded and immediately dispatched his brother-in-law, Danilo Romanovich with the happy news to Moscow – to his wife, to the metropolitan and to Prince Yurii. He then sat down to dine with his boyars and gave a feast for his troops. This splendid patriotic festival was embellished with memories of past evils, a feeling of present glory and hopes for future prosperity.

<small>FEAST AT THE CAMP</small>

That same day Ivan sent letters patent to all the places in the vicinity, announcing peace and safety for the residents.

"Come to us," he wrote, "without terror or fear. I shall forget the past, since the crime has already been punished. Pay to me what you paid to the rulers of Kazan."

Terrified by their capital's catastrophe, they had scattered throughout the forests, but calmed by Ivan's gracious words, they returned to their homes. The residents of Arsk were first, but later all the lowland Cheremis sent their elders to the sovereign in his camp and gave their oath of allegiance.

<small>SUBJUGATION OF THE ARSK DISTRICT AND THE LOWLAND CHEREMIS</small>

On 3 October the dead were buried and the city was completely cleaned up. The next day Ivan, the clergy, the councilors and the troops entered Kazan in triumph. They chose a site and founded the Cathedral of the Annunciation. They circumambulated the city with crosses and consecrated it to the *True God*. Priests aspersed the streets and walls with holy water, beseeching the Almighty to bless this new stronghold of Orthodoxy in order that wellbeing and valor flourish in it, that it forever be inaccessible to enemies, and that it forever be an

<small>TRIUMPHAL ENTRY INTO KAZAN</small>

inalienable possession and an honor for Russia!... After inspecting all of Kazan, designating where cathedrals were to be sited, and ordering the immediate reconstruction of the fortifications, walls and towers, the sovereign and the nobles rode to the palace, on top of which a Christian banner was fluttering.

Thus at Ivan's feet fell one of the most distinguished of the states founded by Chingis Khan's Mongols on the borders of present day Russia. After Kazan had risen from the ruins of Bolgaria and swallowed up its miserable remnants, it had both the predatory martial spirit of the Mongols as well as the feeling for commerce inherited from the ancient inhabitants of these lands, where merchants from Armenia, Khiva and Persia had long gathered (and where this spirit still is preserved, for the Kazan Tatars, remnants of the Golden Horde and the Bolgars, still have commercial ties with the East).

For about 115 years Kazan had been indefatigably at odds with us and we with them, from their first ruler, Makhmet, whose prisoner Ivan's great grandfather once was, to Ediger, whom Ivan took captive. His grandfather had called himself the sovereign of the Bolgars and had already considered Kazan to be our territory, but near the end of his life he had witnessed its terrible rebellion and had been unable to avenge the Russian blood spilled there.

New peace treaties served as the occasion for new betrayals, all of which were terrible for eastern Russia, where along the whole long line from Nizhnyi-Novgorod to Perm people were constantly on guard to protect themselves as if they were guarding a border. Even vengeance cost us dearly, and even the most successful campaigns sometimes resulted in the decimation of troops and horses from illness and from the difficulties of travel through wild places settled by ferocious peoples. Put simply, was it necessary to subjugate Kazan? This question was joined with another: was it necessary to ensure Russia's safe and peaceful existence?

Now a feeling of national wellbeing, strengthened by the fervor of religion, produced a general, vivid delight, and the chroniclers speak of this conquest with the passion of poets, summoning contemporaries and posterity to the *magnificent spectacle*

THE SPECTACLE OF KAZAN

of Kazan, restored in the name of Christ the Savior, shaded by religious banners, adorned with Orthodox churches, animated (after frightful bloodshed and the silence of death) by the presence of a huge, joyful army amidst fresh trophies, but now profoundly peaceful and quiet, rejoicing in the streets, squares and gardens, with the young tsar sitting on the gloriously conquered throne in a shining circle of nobles and commanders who had but one thought and one feeling: *we have earned the gratitude of our homeland!* The chroniclers say that Heaven favored this victorious triumph; that the weather stayed bright and warm, and when the Russians entered the city after besieging Kazan during a long, gloomy, rainy autumn, it was like springtime.

ESTABLISHING A GOVERNMENT

On 6 October, the sovereign's confessor and the Sviyazhsk priests consecrated the Cathedral of the Annunciation. The following day Ivan occupied himself with setting up an administration for the city and its districts. He announced that Prince Aleksandr Gorbatyi Shuiskii would be the deputy for Kazan and Prince Vasilii Serebryanyi would be his associate. He gave them written instructions, as well as 1,500 boyar cadets, 3,000 musketeers and a large number of Cossacks.

COUNSEL OF NOBLES

On 11 October he got ready to depart, even though prudent nobles counseled him to remain till spring with the whole army so as to complete the pacification of a territory inhabited by five peoples: Mordvi, Chuvash, Votyaks (in the Arsk district), Cheremis, and Bashkir (upstream along the Kama). Many of their uluses had not yet acknowledged our dominion and some of the worst people from Kazan had gone to them; it was easy to predict the dangerous consequences.

There were enough provisions in the camp and in Sviyazhsk to feed the troops, but Ivan was anxious to see his wife and show himself to Moscow in his glory. He rejected the advice of the wisest in order to fulfill the promptings of his heart. He was encouraged by the tsaritsa's brothers and other officials who were likewise interested in resting on their laurels as soon as possible. The tsar prayed at services in the Cathedral of the Annunciation and entrusted the

CHAPTER FOUR

protection of his new territory to Jesus, the Virgin Mary and the Russian saints. He departed Kazan, spent the night on the banks of the Volga opposite Gostinyi Island, and on 12 October, along with Prince Vladimir Andreevich, his boyars and an infantry guard, set off in boats for Sviyazhsk. Prince Mikhail Vorotynskii led the cavalry along the banks to the town of Vasilo, a route now safe, albeit difficult.

> SOVEREIGN'S RETURN ROUTE TO MOSCOW

Ivan spent only one day in Sviyazhsk, appointing Prince Pyotr Shuiskii administrator of the region. On 14 October, beneath the Vyazovye Hills, he embarked. He was met on the banks of the Volga at Nizhnyi Novgorod by all its citizens, with crosses. They knelt and wept tears of gratitude for their permanent deliverance from Kazan's terrible raids. He was loudly praised, with heartfelt admiration, so that this *grateful wailing* drowned out the priests' singing and obliged them to be silent. At this point emissaries from the tsaritsa, Prince Yurii and the metropolitan *congratulated the sovereign on the lands God had given him: the state of Kazan.*

He assembled all the troops in Nizhnyi Novgorod and again expressed his gratitude to his earnest comrades-in-arms, saying that he was parting from them until the next occasion to gloriously draw his sword for their homeland. He discharged them to go to their homes and proceeded by the land route through Balakhna to Vladimir. In Sudogda he met the boyar Vasilii Yurievich Trakhanyut, who had galloped to him from Anastasiya with news of the birth of his son, the tsarevich Dimitrii.

> BIRTH OF A CROWN PRINCE

The sovereign joyfully jumped off his horse and embraced and kissed Trakhanyut. He thanked Heaven, wept, and not knowing how to reward this fortunate courier, gave him his royal cloak and horse right there. Ivan already had had two daughters, Anna and Mariya, the first of whom had died at 11 months. The birth of an heir had been his heart's secret desire. He dispatched his brother-in-law, Nikita Romanovich, to Anastasiya with tender greetings and stopped in Vladimir and Suzdal only long enough to pray in their cathedrals and to show the depth of his love for their residents, who

> IVAN'S WELCOME

129

thronged from all around to see his face, shining with joy. He visited the famous Trinity Cloister of St. Sergii to pay his respects at his grave, took bread with the monks, and on 28 October spent the night in Taininskoe Village, where his brother Prince Yurii and several boyars were waiting to congratulate him.

Early the next morning as he was approaching his beloved capital, he caught sight such an uncountable throng of people on the banks of the Yauza River that for the distance of six versts, from the river to the trading quarter, there was only a very narrow passage left for him and his retinue. Ivan rode up this street amidst thousands of Moscow's citizens, bowing to each side while people kissed his hands and feet, constantly exclaiming,

"Long life to the pious tsar, conqueror of the barbarians, savior of Christians!"

There, where Muscovites had once received the image of the Virgin of Vladimir that had saved the city from Tamerlan's invasion – where the Sretenskii Monastery is now – there the metropolitan, the bishops, the priests with this icon, the elder boyars, Prince Mikhailo Ivanovich Bulgakov, Ivan Grigorievich Morozov, servitors of his father and grandfather, and all the officials were standing beneath the church gonfalons. Ivan dismounted, kissed the image, was blessed by the priests and said,

"Council of Orthodox clergy! Father Metropolitan and high priests! I beseech you to be diligent intermediaries before the Most High for tsar and country. May the sins of my youth be absolved, may I develop this country, and may I be its shield against barbarian attacks.

> SOVEREIGN'S SPEECH TO THE CLERGY

"I consulted with you concerning Kazan's perfidies and how to halt them, to extinguish the flames in our villages, to stanch the bleeding of Russians, to strike off the chains from Christian prisoners, to lead them out of their dungeons to return to their homeland and Church. My grandfather, my father and I all sent voivodes, but without success. Finally, acting on your advice, I myself took the field. Then another enemy appeared within Russia's borders, the khan of the Crimea, to eradicate Christianity in our absence. Remember the words of the apostle: *be vigilant and pray that you*

CHAPTER FOUR

do not come to disaster! You, worthy priests of the Church, did pray – and God heard you and helped us – and the khan, pursued only by the wrath of Heaven, fled in cowardice!

"Cheered by the clear efficacy of your prayers, we moved against Kazan, successfully achieved our goal, and by the grace of God, the valor of Prince Vladimir Andreevich, our voivodes and all our warriors, this populous metropolis fell before us. The Lord's judgment destroyed the infidel in a single hour, leaving no trace. Their ruler was taken captive, Mohammed's allure vanished and in its place the sacred cross was raised. The district of Arsk and the meadow district now pay tribute to Russia. Moscow's voivodes now administer their country, and we, hale and joyous have come to the icon of the Virgin here, to the relics of the saints, to our holy objects in our beloved patrimony. For this heavenly blessing, which you requested, to you, Father, and to all the holy council, I and Prince Vladimir Andreevich and all the troops do bow with overflowing hearts."

Then the sovereign, Prince Vladimir and all the troops bowed to the ground. Ivan continued,

"I now beseech you, by your fervent intercession at the throne of God and with your wise admonitions, to enable me to uphold the law, truth and morality within our realm. Let our homeland flourish in virtue, protected by peace; may Christianity flourish therein; let the infidels, our new subjects acknowledge the true God; and together with us glorify the holy trinity forever and ever, amen!" The metropolitan replied,

"Pious tsar! We who pray for you, who are amazed by the abundance of Heaven's favor to us, what should we say before the Lord? We can really only exclaim: *marvelous God, create a miracle!* ... What a victory! What glory for you and all your resplendent comrades-in-arms! What were we before? And what are we now? The perfidious and ferocious people of Kazan were terrifying Russia, eagerly drinking the blood of Christians, taking them away into slavery and defiling and destroying our holy churches. Torn by our homeland's misery, you, magnanimous tsar, placed unwavering hope in God, the ruler of all, and promised

> THE METROPOLITAN'S REPLY

to save us. You armed yourself with faith and marched into tribulation and death, you suffered deeply; you committed your body and soul for the Church, for our homeland – and heavenly grace shone upon you, as on the ancient rulers who pleased the Lord – on Constantine the Great, on St. Vladimir, on Dimitrii Donskii and on Aleksandr Nevskii.

"You were compared to them, but who surpassed you? This ruling city of Kazan, where a serpent nested as if in a deep hole, harming and poisoning us – this city, so renowned and so terrible, now lies inanimate at your feet. You have trampled the snake's head, freed thousands of Christian prisoners and purified Mohammed's pollution with the banners of the true Faith – you have set Russia at ease forever and ever! This was a divine act, but it was performed by you! For you remembered the word of the apostle: *Good servant! You have little faith, but I shall set you above the many!*

"Rejoice, O tsar, beloved by God and your country. Having given you victory, the Most High has also given you a longed-for firstborn son! Live in health with your virtuous tsaritsa Anastasiya, with your young tsarevich Dimitrii, with your brothers, with your boyars and with all your Orthodox warriors in this blessed sovereign city of Moscow and over all your territories in this year and for many years to come. We bow to you, pious tsar, along with all the prelates, with all Orthodox Christians, for your efforts and your great exploits."

The metropolitan, the priesthood, the officials and the people then fell face downward before Ivan; tears flowed from their eyes and benedictions resounded, long and incessant.

The sovereign now took off his military garb and put the purple on his shoulder, the life-giving cross on his neck and chest, the crown of Monomakh on his head, and walked behind the holy icons to the Kremlin. He heard services in the Cathedral of the Dormition and bowed with love and gratitude to the relics of the Russian saints and to the graves of his ancestors. He walked round to all the renowned cathedrals and finally hurried to the palace. The tsaritsa had been unable to meet him until now, for she was sick in bed, but when she saw her husband, she forgot her weakness and illness and fell with delight at the feet of the reigning hero, who, embracing Anastasiya and his son, tasted the full portion of happiness that is allotted to mankind.

Moscow and Russia were in an indescribable transport of joy. Heaven and the tsar were everywhere thanked in the churches, whose doors were thrown open, and enthusiastic subjects sped from all over to see Ivan's face. They spoke only of his great feat, of the difficulties overcome in the campaign, the efforts and subterfuges of the siege, of the evil cruelties of the people of Kazan, of the glittering valor of the Russians. With high hearts they kept repeating,

"We conquered a country – what sayeth the world?"

After several days that were blessed with familial happiness, Ivan gave a formal dinner on November 8th at the Great Faceted Palace for the metropolitan, the bishops, the archimandrites, the abbots, princes Yurii Vasilievich and Vladimir Andreevich, all the boyars and all the voivodes who had shown courage beneath the walls of Kazan.

> FEAST AT THE COURT AND IVAN'S GIFTS

"Never," say the chroniclers, "had we seen such splendor, such festivities and gaiety in a Moscow palace, nor such generosity."

Ivan presented gifts to all, from the metropolitan to the simple soldier marked by a glorious wound or enrolled in the list of the brave. He rewarded Prince Vladimir Andreevich with fur coats, golden French goblets and ladles; as well as the boyars, voivodes, court nobles, boyar cadets and each of the soldiers in accordance with his rank with clothing from his own shoulders, with velvets, sables, goblets, horses, armor or coins. He feasted with his most distinguished subjects for three days and for three days he showered gifts, which according to accounting by the treasury amounted to 48,000 rubles (about a million, currently), not counting rich patrimonies and service estates given military officers and court officials.

In order to mark for future centuries the taking of Kazan with a fitting memorial, the sovereign founded the splendid Cathedral of the Virgin's Veil at the Florovskie, or Spasskie Gate, with nine cupolas. To this day it is the finest product of so-called Gothic architecture in our ancient capital.*

This monarch, illuminated with glory and greatly beloved of his country, conqueror of a hostile state and bringer of peace to his own, magnanimous in all feelings and intentions, a wise ruler and legislator, was only 22, a phenomenon rare in the history of states! It seemed as if, in Ivan, God wanted to astound Russia and mankind with an example of perfection, majesty and good fortune on the throne... But at this point the first cloud appeared over the radiant head of the young monarch.

---

* [Now known as St. Basil's, in Red Square.]

CHAPTER V

DEATH OF IVAN'S FIRST WIFE.

1552-1560

Baptisms of Prince Dmitrii and two of Kazan's rulers. Plague. Rebellion in the Kazan lands. The tsar's illness. Ivan's journey to Kirillov Monastery. Death of the crown prince. Ivan's important conversation with former bishop Vassian. Birth of Prince Ivan. Prince Rostovskii flees. Heresy. Rebellion in Kazan lands put down. Establishment of the Eparchate of Kazan. Astrakhan subjugated. The embassies of Khiva, Bukhara, Shavkal, Tyumen and Georgia. Submission of the Circassians. Amity with the Nogai Tatars. Siberian tribute. English ships visit Russia. Embassy to England. Crimean affairs. Suleiman's letter. The Crimeans attack. The Swedish war. Relations with Lithuania. The secretary Rzhevskii attacks Islam-Kirmen. Prince Vishnevetskii enters the tsar's service and takes Khortitsa. Conquest of Temryuk and Taman. Epidemic and famine in the Nogai and Crimean settlements. Vishnevetskii's zeal. Alliance with Lithuania proposed. Livonian affairs. An important plan, attributed to Ivan. The Livonian situation. Russia's new power. Army better-trained. Livonian war begins. Capture of Narva. Conquest of Neuschloss, Adezh and Neuhaus. Courage of burgomaster of Derpt. The [Livonian] master flees. A new head of the Order. Derpt and many other towns taken. Ketler takes Ringen. Russians lay waste to Livonia and Courland. Polish, Swedish and Danish kings intercede for Livonia. Ivan approves truce with Livonia. Crimeans attack. Russian assault on the Taurid. Livonia allied with Augustus. The master violates truce. Glorious defense of Lais. Threats from Augustus. Herald from the emperor. New devastation of Livonia. Capture of Marienburg. Prince Kurbskii's victories. Death of Tsaritsa Anastasiya.

As soon as Anastasiya was able to rise from her bed, the sovereign set out with her and their son for the Trinity Cloister, where Archbishop Nikandr of Rostov baptized Dimitrii next to the relics of St. Sergii. Sated

1552, 1553 BAPTISMS OF PRINCE DMITRII AND TWO OF KAZAN'S RULERS

with worldly glory, Ivan concluded the national celebrations with a Christian one: two of Kazan's rulers, Utemish-Girei and Ediger, accepted the faith of the Savior. The former, still a boy, was baptized by the metropolitan in the Chudov Monastery and named Aleksandr. The sovereign took him into his palace and ordered him to be taught letters, Christian precepts and virtue. Ediger expressed the earnest desire to be illuminated by the light of truth, and to the metropolitan's questioning,

"Has compulsion, fear or worldly profit suggested this to you?" he decisively replied, "No! I love Jesus and hate Mohammed!"

| 26 February |

The holy ritual was performed on the banks of the Moscow River in the presence of the sovereign, the boyars and the people. The metropolitan was the godfather at the font. Ediger was named Simeon and retained the title of ruler; he lived in an exceptionally large house in the Kremlin and had a boyar, officials and many servants; he also married Mariya, the daughter of the noted official Andrei Kutuzov. He always enjoyed the sovereign's favor and showed a sincere love of Russia. He had forgotten, like a confused dream, his former realm and faith.

| Plague |

After many experiences of indescribable sweetness, Ivan now tasted sorrow. The lethal disease [the Black Death] that had so often laid waste to Russia in the course of the last two centuries broke out once again, in Pskov, where from October 1552 to the autumn of 1553, 25,000 were buried in cemeteries. This number does not include a great many buried secretly in the woods, or in ravines. When Novgorod learned of this, it immediately expelled Pskov's merchants and announced that if any one of them came back, he would be incinerated with his goods.

Neither caution nor severity saved Novgorod: in October the plague began to rage there as well, and in all its outlying areas. Its victims numbered half a million, among them Archbishop Serapion, who had not spared himself while comforting the unfortunate. In his perilous place the metropolitan appointed Pimen the Black, a monk from the Andreyanovskaya Hermitage; he joined the sovereign in formal prayer, blessing the waters, and on

Chapter Five

6 December he celebrated with feeling his first mass in the Sofiya Cathedral. This seemed to take the sting from the epidemic – it became less lethal, at least in Novgorod.

The sovereign was also much grieved by sad news from Kazan and saw that he was not yet done with bringing peace to Russia. The mountain and lowland inhabitants were killing Muscovite merchants and boyars' men on the Volga. The criminals were found and 74 were executed, but a rebellion soon broke out. The Votyaks and the lowland Cheremis did not want to pay tribute. They murdered our officials and kept to the high hills, amongst their abattises. They defeated the musketeers and Cossacks sent to pacify them, killing 800 Russians on the spot.

REBELLION IN THE KAZAN LANDS

Seventy versts from Kazan, on the Mesha, the rebels established an earthen fortress and incessantly harassed the High Bank with their raids. In the winter the voivode Boris Saltykov set out against them with a detachment of infantry and cavalry but became bogged down in the deep snow. The enemy, on skis, completely surrounded them. In a protracted and disorderly battle, the Russians fell from exhaustion, losing up to 500 men. The voivode himself was taken prisoner and murdered by the barbarians; few returned to Sviyazhsk. The rebels, boasting of their victories, believed that Russian domination of their land was now at an end.

Ivan now recalled the wise advice of the seasoned nobles not to leave Kazan until the complete subjugation of all these wild peoples. The despondency at the court was so great that some members of the Tsar's Duma proposed permanently forsaking this calamitous land and pulling our troops out of there. The sovereign expressed justified scorn at this pusillanimity, however. He wished to rectify his mistake but suddenly fell ill from a severe fever. The court, Moscow, and Russia all learned simultaneously of his illness and the uncertainty of his recovery. Everyone, from noble to peasant, was horrified, and earnestly tried to find their fault before God, saying,

THE TSAR'S ILLNESS

"Our sins must be immeasurable if Heaven is taking such an autocrat away from Russia!"

The people crowded into the Kremlin; they looked at one another but were afraid to ask. Pale, teary faces were everywhere, while at the court there was despair, indescribable confusion and secret whispering amongst the boyars that in such a terrible situation they should not groan or weep, but bravely attend to the fate of the nation.

> 11 March

It was a striking spectacle. Ivan was still conscious, and the tsar's secretary Mikhailov went to his sickbed and firmly told the patient that it was time to draw up his will. Despite being in the bloom of youth and full of life and health, Ivan had often spoken about this to those closest to him. Unafraid, he calmly ordered his will to be taken down. He declared his son, the young Dimitrii, to be his successor and sole sovereign of Russia. The document was written up and it was desired that it be sworn to by all the most distinguished officials, who were gathered into the tsar's dining hall. Now a noisy and rebellious dispute broke out: some made demands, others would not give their oaths, among the latter, Prince Vladimir Andreev, who angrily said to the nobleman Vorotynskii, who had reproached him for disobedience,

"Do you dare to quarrel with me?"

"I dare, and will fight," replied Vorotynskii, "as befits a diligent servant of my sovereigns and yours: Ivan and Dimitrii. It is not I, but they who order you to fulfill the obligation of a loyal Russian."

Ivan summoned the disobedient boyars and asked them,

"But whom do you think to choose as tsar, having refused to kiss the cross in the name of my son? Have you really forgotten the oath you gave to serve me and my sons? . . . I do not have the strength to say much," he added in a weak voice.

"Even in the cradle, Dimitrii is your legitimate autocrat, but if you are without conscience, you will answer to God."

[In reply] to this, the boyar, Prince Ivan Mikhailovich Shuiskii, told him that they had not kissed the cross because they had not seen their sovereign before them, while Thedor Adashev, the father of Ivan's favorite, with the rank of okolnichii, declared bluntly in these words,

"You, sovereign, and your son, we would diligently obey, but not the Zakharin-Yurievs, who would without doubt rule Russia in the name of a speechless infant. That is what we are afraid of! And we, before you came of age, drained the full cup of misery caused by boyar rule."

Ivan was silent from weakness: Russia's autocrat now felt himself to be a simple, weak mortal at the brink of the grave. The boyars and officials loved him and wept over him, but no longer obeyed him or spared his feelings. They had forgotten their sacred duty to comfort the dying; they were noisy, shouting right over the sickbed on which Ivan lay mute – and then they left.

But what did these impudent officials want, who were perhaps really animated by a love for the common good and really frightened by the thought of boyar discord, which would be ruinous to the country and which might again reestablish itself in the ruling Duma, to Russia's horror, during Dimitrii's minority? They wanted to place the crown on the head of Ivan's brother – not Yurii, for that unfortunate prince was ill-favored by nature and without common sense or sensibility – but Vladimir Andreevich had been endowed with many shining qualities: an inquiring mind, wit, energy, courage, and fortitude.

Presupposing the purest, noblest motives to be in the hearts of these boyars, the chroniclers justifiably censured their plot to willfully strike down the nation's law of succession, which from the time of Dimitrii Donskii had been affirmed by formal oath that was based on the common good and was a fruit of long-time experience and the reason for Russia's greatness.

All human laws have their dangers, inconveniences and occasional harmful consequences, but they are the soul of order, held sacred by prudent and moral people, and serve as the bulwark of the state. This premonition of disobedient boyars might not have been realized, but if the minority of the tsar were to produce a temporary catastrophe for Russia, it would be better to deal with it now. Otherwise the violation of a preeminent national law would precipitate the country into an abyss of perpetual disorder due to ignorance of that right of inheritance that is so important for monarchies.

Fortunately, the other boyars remained true to their consciences and the law. That very evening, the Princes Ivan Theodorovich Mstislavskii, Vladimir Ivanovich Vorotynskii, Dmitrii Paletskii, Ivan Vasilievich Sheremetev, Mikhail Yakovlevich Morozov, the Zaharin-Yurievs and the secretary Mikhailov all swore allegiance to the tsarevich, as did the sovereign's young friend Aleksei Adashev. Meanwhile, it was reported to Ivan that Princes Pyotr Shchenyatev, Ivan Pronskii, Simeon Rostovskii and Dmitrii Nemyi-Obolenskii were praising Prince Vladimir Andreevich at the court and in the squares, saying,

"Better to serve an older man than a young one and fawn on the Zakharins."

Exhausting the last of his strength, the sovereign wished to see Prince Vladimir and secure his loyalty with a sworn statement, but the prince formally renounced his oath. With surprising mildness, Ivan said to him,

"I see your intent. Fear the Most High!" To the boyars who had given their oath, he said,

"I am weakening. Leave me and act in accordance with honor and conscience."

With renewed earnestness they tried to get all the Duma councilors to carry out their sovereign's wishes. They were answered with:

"We know what you want: to be rulers, but we will not do as you wish."

They called each other perfidious and power-hungry. Wrath and malice seethed in their hearts and every word from either side was a threat.

During the hours of this terrible commotion, Prince Vladimir Andreevich and his mother Evfrosiniya gathered boyar cadets at their home and distributed money to them. The people

CHAPTER FIVE

expressed their displeasure. Prudent nobles told Prince Vladimir that he had recklessly mocked the common grief and it seemed as if he were celebrating the tsar's infirmity; it was no time to hand out awards when their homeland was in tears and afraid. The prince and his mother replied with biting words, with irritation, and so the boyars surrounding the sovereign no longer wished to let his brother see him, since Vladimir was clearly of evil intent.

It was at this point that that extraordinary man, Silvestr, stepped onto the stage. Up till now he had been Ivan's principal advisor, working for the good of Russia, but he also secretly displeased many who saw that a simple priest was directing the Church and the Duma. In the words of the chronicler, he lacked only the throne of a tsar or a prelate: he gave orders to the nobles and the metropolitan, to judges and voivodes; what he conceived, the tsar carried out. This power, which was not illegitimate, proceeded solely from the sovereign's justifiable trust in his sagacious advisor. However, it might pervert the purity of his original intentions and motives; it might produce in him a love of power and the desire to establish it permanently – a temptation perilous for virtue!

Respected by all, but not loved by all, Silvestr lost his political being with Ivan and confounded personal love of power with the nation's good. *Perhaps* he secretly sided with Prince Vladimir Andreevich, with whom he had ties of friendship. At any rate, when he saw the frenzied activity against this prince by those close to Ivan, he stood up for him and heatedly said,

"Who dares to keep brother from brother and speak ill of an innocent who wishes to weep over the sick man?"

The Zakharins and others replied that they were carrying out their oath to serve Ivan and Dimitrii, and would not tolerate traitors. Silvestr took offence and brought suspicion upon himself.

The next day the sovereign again summoned the nobles and told them,

"For the last time, I demand an oath from you. Kiss the cross in the presence of my closest boyars, the Princes Mstislavskii and Vorotynskii. I do not have the strength to be a witness. And you, who have already sworn to die for me and for my son, do you remember it when I am no longer. Do not allow the perfidious to destroy the tsarevich. Save him; flee with him to a foreign land. God will show you the way! . . . And you, Zakharins, what do you fear? You were tardy in sparing the rebellious boyars. They will not spare you; you will be *the first corpses*. So show courage: die bravely for my son and his mother. Do not let my wife be dishonored by traitors!"

These words strongly affected the boyars' hearts. They shuddered and silently went into the vestibule, where the secretary Ivan Mikhailov was holding the cross. Prince Vladimir Vorotynskii was standing next to him. Everyone gave their oaths in the silence and seemed touched. They prayed to the Most High to save Ivan or else that his son be like him for the happiness of Russia. But Prince Ivan Pronskii-Turuntai looked at Vorotynskii and said to him,

"Your father and you yourself were the first traitors at the death of Grand Prince Vasilii, and now you bring us to the holy cross!" Vorotynskii replied calmly, "Yes, I am a turncoat, but I ask you to give your oath to be loyal to our sovereign and his son. You are in the right, yet you do not want to give it!"

Turuntai was embarrassed and gave his oath.

But this holy rite did not assure everyone's loyalty. Prince Dmitrii Paletskii, father-in-law to the sovereign and to Yurii, now sent his brother-in-law Vasilii Borozdin to Prince Vladimir Andreevich and his mother to tell them that if they would give Yurii the appanage that had been designated for him in Grand Prince Vasilii's will, then he (Paletskii) was prepared, along with others, to assist him and raise him to the throne! Two more nobles remained under suspicion: Prince Dmitrii Kurlyatev, friend of Aleksei Adashev, and the treasurer Nikita Funikov. They were not at court because of illness, but according to the allegation of some informers, had secret relations with Prince Vladimir Andreevich.

Three days later, when all was quiet, Kurlyatev ordered himself taken to the palace to swear allegiance to Dimitrii; Funikov did likewise, but he was the last. Prince Vladimir Andreevich himself pledged in a sworn document *not to think of reigning* and in case of Ivan's death to obey Dimitrii as his legitimate sovereign. For a long time, Vladimir's mother did not want to place the royal seal on this document, but finally carried out the boyars' resolute command, asking,

"What meaning has an *involuntary* oath?"

These two days of commotion and threats brought Ivan's infirmity to the crisis stage. He seemed to be in a stupor that might presage his death. But the operations of nature are inexplicable: the severity of the disease sometimes waxed and sometimes waned in its extraordinary power. In what sort of turmoil was Ivan's soul? Life is sweet in one's youth: his life was still adorned with glory and flattering hopes for a virtuous rule. In the boiling of forces and feelings, he was touching the grave, falling from the throne to the tomb, and seeing the fearful treachery in people's face, the silence so far of his subjects, and the disobedience of his ardent favorites.

This autocratic sovereign was now dependent upon those whose fate had previously depended on him; he humbly implored them to save the life and honor of his family, even if in exile! However, although Ivan was terrified at such a time, the fire in his soul fortified his natural energies and he recovered, to the joy of all but a few. Although Prince Vladimir Andreevich and his confederates ultimately carried out Ivan's wish and swore to Dimitrii, how could the autocrat forget their mutiny and the torment in his soul, which they had lacerated as he struggled with the terrors of death?

But what did Ivan do now? He arose from his sickbed full of kindness towards all the boyars, full of goodwill and confidence in his former friends and advisors. He gave the rank of boyar to Adashev's father, who more daringly than most had rejected the tsar's will and testament He honored and treated Prince Vladimir Andreevich graciously; in short, he did not wish to remember what had happened during his illness and seemed simply grateful to God for his recovery!

This was on the outside – a dangerous wound remained in his heart. It was suggested to Ivan that not only Silvestr but also the young Adashev had secretly sided with Prince Vladimir. There was no doubting their earnestness for the good of Russia, but he began to doubt their personal gratitude towards him. While respecting both, his affection towards them had cooled. He was obliged to them for the signal successes of his reign and was afraid to seem ungrateful, but he merely adhered to decorum.

For six years he had earnestly served virtue and had tasted all of its sweetness; he did not want to betray it. He took no open vengeance on anyone, but this took an effort that may have weakened over time. Even worse, his wife, who up till now had, together with Adashev and Silvestr, nurtured his love for saintly morality, was alienated from them by a secret enmity. She thought that they intended to sacrifice her, her son and brothers to benefit their personal ambitions. Anastasiya probably abetted Ivan's coolness towards his friends. From this time on he chafed at his dependence on them, and was sometimes pleased to disagree with them, to do things his own way. It is written that the following circumstance confirmed the tsar in this even further.

IVAN'S VISIT TO KIRILLOV MONASTERY

To fulfill the promise he had given during his illness, Ivan announced his intention to travel to the monastery of St. Kirill of Beloozero together with the tsaritsa and their son. This distant journey seemed imprudent to some of his closest advisors. They suggested to him that he had not yet completely recovered his strength, that the trip might also be harmful to young Dimitrii, and that important affairs, especially the rebellion in Kazan, required his presence in the capital. Paying no heed to these representations, the sovereign rode first to the Cloister of St. Sergii.

MAY

The renowned Maksim the Greek was living there in his old age, in quietude and prayer. He had been exiled to Tver by Grand Prince Vasilii, but Ivan had freed him as an innocent martyr. The tsar visited the cell of this virtuous man, and while conversing with him, began to speak of his journey.

Chapter Five

"Sovereign!" said Maksim, probably at the suggestion of Ivan's advisors, "Is it proper for you to roam about to distant monasteries with your young wife and child? Are imprudent promises pleasing to God? It is not necessary to seek in desolate places Him who is Everywhere: the whole world is filled with Him. If you wish to express your fervent thanks for this heavenly blessing, then do good works on the throne. The conquest of Kazan, while happy for Russia, was fatal for many Christians. The widows, orphans and mothers of those killed are weeping; comfort them with your favor. That is the business of a tsar!"

But Ivan did not want to change his plans. Then Maksim, we are assured, ordered him to be told by Aleksei Adashev and Prince Kurbskii that the tsarevich Dimitrii would become a victim of his stubbornness. Ivan was not frightened by this prophecy; he proceeded to Dmitrov, to the Pesnoshskii Nikolaevskii Monastery, from which he traveled by boat by way of the Yakhroma, Dubna, Volga and Sheksna rivers to the Cloister of St. Kirill, and then returned through Yaroslavl and Rostov to Moscow, but without his son, for Maksim's prophecy had been fulfilled: Dimitrii had died while on the road. Yet the most important event of this so-called "Cyrillian" journey was Ivan's meeting with the former bishop of Kolomna, Vassian, in the Pesnoshskii Monastery on the banks of the Yakhroma.

> JUNE.
> DEATH OF THE
> CROWN PRINCE

> IVAN'S IMPORTANT
> VISIT WITH FORMER
> BISHOP VASSIAN

Vassian had once enjoyed the special favor of Grand Prince Vasilii, but during the rule of the boyars had been deprived of his eparchate because of his chicanery and cruel heart. Venerable old age had not softened it: approaching the grave, he still nurtured worldly passions in his breast, including malice and hatred towards the boyars. Ivan wished to get to know this man who had earned his father's trust. He spoke with him of Vasilii's times and requested his advice on how to better rule his realm. Vassian whispered in his ear,

"If you wish to be a true autocrat, then do not have advisors more clever than yourself; hold to the principle that you must be a teacher, not a student. Give orders, do not follow them. Then you will be firm in your rule and a terror to the nobles. A councilor wiser than his sovereign must inevitably master him."

These venomous words went to the depths of Ivan's heart. He seized Vassian's hand and kissed it, excitedly saying,

"My own father could never have given me better advice!"

"*No, sovereign!* "we might have retorted to him: "*No! The advice you have been given has the spirit of a lie, not the truth. A tsar must not just rule, but rule virtuously. His wisdom, being only human, has need of other minds, and the better the advisors he chooses, the more exalted he will be in the eyes of the people. Monarchs fearing wise advisors fall into the hands of the cunning, who, to please them, even pretend to be dullards. They do not attract his reason, but charm his passions, and thus lead him to their own goal. A ruler should not fear wise advisors, but rather crafty or foolish ones.*" With these or similar considerations, Prince Kurbskii describes the evil conversation with the elder, Vassian, which, he assures us, corrupted the soul of the young monarch.

But for a long time yet Ivan did not change overtly: he esteemed virtuous men and listened respectfully to Silvestr's admonitions; he was kind to Adashev, gave him the rank of okolnichii and employed him, instead of his secretary Mikhailov, for the most important matters of foreign affairs. Nine months later Ivan was comforted by the birth of a second son, [also] Ivan. In the new will he now drew up, the sovereign showed the greatest trust in his brother, Prince Vladimir Andreevich: he designated him, in case of his own death, not only to be the guardian of the young tsar, not only the regent, but also the successor to the throne in case the tsarevich Ivan died in his minority.

<blockquote>BIRTH OF PRINCE IVAN</blockquote>

Prince Vladimir gave his oath to be loyal to conscience and duty, and not to spare even his own mother, Princess Evfrosiniya, if she plotted some sort of evil against Anastasiya or her son, He also promised to eschew vengeance and partiality in the affairs of state, not to administer them without the knowledge or consent of the tsaritsa, the metropolitan, and the Duma councilors, and not to maintain more than 100 soldiers in his Moscow home.

Chapter Five

In the most justifiable punishments, the sovereign, as before, was prompted by mercy. For example, Prince Simeon Rostovskii, a noted noble, during the sovereign's illness had shown himself to be opposed to his wishes. He now had no peace of mind: he did not trust Ivan's outwardly calm manner and was tormented by fear. He was considering fleeing to Lithuania with his brothers and nephews; he corresponded with King Augustus and the pans of the Lithuanian Duma, disclosed state secrets to them, gave advice harmful to us and deprecated the tsar and Russia. He sent one of those closest to him, Prince Nikita Lobanov-Rostovskii, to the king. This prince was stopped in Toropets, interrogated, and acknowledged his treachery. Prince Simeon was arrested and admitted everything, pleading poverty and stupidity.

Prince Rostovskii Flees

The boyars unanimously sentenced the traitor to death, but the sovereign accepted the pleadings of the priesthood and ameliorated the sentence of the court: Prince Simeon was *put in disgrace* and confined at Belo-ozero. Ivan was just as merciful in matters of another sort. It was reported to the sovereign that a dangerous heresy had arisen in Moscow, that a certain Matvei Bashkin was preaching a totally un-Christian doctrine that rejected the mysteries of our faith, the divinity of Christ, the actions of the councils, and the holiness of the saints.

Heresy

He was taken for interrogation, but refused to talk, calling himself a true Christian, but after he was confined in prison he became despondent and revealed the heresy to the diligent monks of the Iosifovskii Monastery, Gerasim and Filothei. He described it, naming his confederates, Ivan and Grigorii Borisov, the monk Belobaev and others, saying that his corrupters were the Catholics, the apothecary Matvei Litvin and Andrei Khoteev, and that some sort of Zavolzhsk elders had explained this interpretation of Christ and the saints in a heart-to-heart conversation with him. Apparently Bishop Kassian of Ryazan had favored this error, and so on. The Council, the tsar and the metropolitan convicted the heretics, but did not want to impose cruel punishment. They were merely sentenced to prison so that they could not spread this error among the people; Bishop Kassian, stricken with palsy, was dismissed.

Ivan had shown that his illness and its sad consequences had not embittered his heart, that he could rise above ordinary human passions and that he could put aside painful personal insults. He now busied himself with matters of state with his former fervor. The most important of these matters was the pacification of the realm he had conquered. To the Kama River he dispatched Daniil Adashev, Aleksei's brother, with boyar cadets and troops from Vyatka, while the courageous voivodes, Prince Simeon Mikulinskii, Ivan Sheremetev and Prince Andrei Mikhailovich Kurbskii were sent to Kazan with many legions.

1553-1557

REBELLION IN KAZAN LANDS PUT DOWN

They set out in winter, in the cruelest frost, and fought for a whole month near the Kama and Mesha. There they destroyed a new fortress that had been built by the rebels; they crossed the Ashit and Urzhum and proceeded all the way to Vyatka and the Bashkir territories. Every day they did battle in the wild forests and snowy wastes; they killed 10,000 of the enemy and two of Russia's worst enemies, the Princes Yanchura Izmailtyanin and the Cheremis bogatyr Aleka. They captured 6,000 Tatars and 15,000 of their women and children.

The Princes Ivan Mstislavskii and Mikhailo Vasilievich Glinskii fought the lowland Cheremis, seizing 1,600 notables – princes, mirzas and Tatar officials – and killed them all. Voivodes and officers who acted diligently and tirelessly received golden medals from their sovereign – the flattering award of the time. Knights then decorated their chests with these instead of today's crosses of the orders.

The rebellion had still not been extinguished; fugitives from Kazan still hid in places near and far, agitating the people everywhere. They robbed and murdered our merchants and fishermen on the Volga and they built fortresses, trying to restore their state. One of their lowland lieutenants, Mamich Berdei, summoned some sort of Nogai prince and gave him the title of ruler, but then killed him for ineptness and cowardice. He chopped off his head, stuck it up in a tall tree and said,

"We acknowledged you as ruler for wars and victories, but all you and your retinue knew how to do was to feed off of us! Now let your head rule from its high throne!"

The highlanders lured this dangerous rebel into a trap: they amicably invited him to a feast, then seized him and sent him off to Moscow, and for this the sovereign reduced their taxes. The Arsk lands swore allegiance and then reneged several times, but the lowlanders prolonged their stubborn rebellion more than anyone else. For five years the Russians did not put away their swords; they burned and slashed. While destroying the oath-breakers without mercy, Ivan rewarded the loyal: many people of Kazan were willingly baptized; others, while not abandoning the faith of their fathers, served Russia along with the new Christians. They were given arable land and hayfields and all that was necessary for husbandry.

Finally the rebels' efforts slackened. All their leaders had perished without exception and their fortresses had been destroyed, others (Cheboksary and Laishev) were rebuilt and filled with our musketeers. Votyaks, Cheremis and even distant Bashkirs brought tribute and asked for mercy. In the spring of 1557, Ivan sent his steward, Semyon Yartsov, to this unhappy land full of ashes and graves to announce that the army's terror had passed and its people could now prosper quietly as loyal subjects of the White Tsar. The sovereign graciously received their elders in Moscow and granted them letters patent.

Kazan now became a peaceful Russian possession; the name of this realm was preserved in our monarchs' title. In 1553 in an ecclesiastical council, Ivan established an eparchate for its new Christians and gave it an archbishop, subordinate only to the Novgorod prelate, while Sviazhsk, Vasilgorod and Vyatka were in turn subordinated to his ecclesiastical administration. A tenth of Kazan's revenue was allocated for churchly expenses. Gurii, the abbot of the Selizharov Monastery was its first prelate. This virtuous man implanted the faith of the Savior in his flock, employing true Christian means, teachings of love and meekness, with such diligence that he was

> ESTABLISHMENT OF THE EPARCHATE OF KAZAN

ranked among the saints of our Church. It was with the same fervor that the sovereign's deputy, Prince Pyotr Ivanovich Shuiskii, established civil order in this new frontier, erasing the traces of devastation, bringing peace and animating trade and agriculture. Villages belonging to the tsar and princes were given to the archbishop, monasteries and boyar cadets.

> ASTRAKHAN
> SUBJUGATED

Another victory, less difficult, but no less glorious, was also achieved. From ancient times, even before the beginning of the Russian state, there had been a Khazar city at the mouth of the Volga, renowned for its commerce, named Atel or Balangiar [or Itil]. In the 13th century it had belonged to the Alans and was called Sumerkent; it became known in our chronicles as *Astrokan*, a possession of the Golden Horde. After the horde's fall it was the capital for its own khans, who were of the same stock as the Nogai princes. Pressed by the Circassians and Crimeans, these khans were weak, pacific, and always sought alliance with us.

The last of them, Yamgurchei, even wanted, as we have seen, to be Ivan's tributary, but, seduced by the sultan's protection, he deceived our sovereign and joined with Devlet-Girei and Iosuf. The latter was a Nogai prince, father of Syuyunbeka; he hated Russia for the captivity of his daughter and grandson, whom we had deposed from Kazan's throne. In Astrakhan Moscow's emissary was dishonorably treated and detained. In the opinion of contemporary bookmen, the sovereign used this opportunity to return this ancient possession to Russia, where St. Vladimir's son Mstislav is said to have ruled once. The bookmen considered Astrakhan to be ancient Tmutorokan, basing their reasoning on the similarity of the names.[*] Ismail and other Nogai mirzas, enemies of Yusuf, confirmed Ivan in his intention. They beseeched him to give Astrakhan to the exiled Derbysh; he was their kinsman, who had ruled there prior to Yamgurchei, and intended to help us with all his might.

In the spring of 1554, after summoning Derbysh from the Nogai uluses, the sovereign sent him off with troops in boats. These were not numerous, but they were select, comprising the

---

[*] [This is incorrect. Tmutorokan was on the Sea of Azov, not the Caspian.]

tsar's court nobles, servants, the best boyar cadets, musketeers, Cossacks and troops from Vyatka. Their commanders were Prince Yurii Ivanovich Pronskii-Shemyakin and the chamberlain Ignatii Veshnyakov, an exceptionally valorous man. On 29 June, after reaching Perevoloka, Shemyakin sent Prince Aleksandr Vyazemskii forward; near Chernyi Island he encountered and defeated several hundred troops from Astrakhan who had been sent to ascertain our strength. From prisoners, he learned that Yamgurchei was positioned five versts below the city, while the Tatars were distributed over the islands, in their uluses.

The Russians sailed past Baty's capital, Sarai, where for 200 years our sovereigns had abased themselves before the khans of the Golden Horde – but now there were only ruins there. In times of glory, viewing monuments to past shame is easier than looking at monuments to past glory in times of shame! In this once fearsome land *full of swords and lances*, there now was only pacific timidity: everyone had fled, both the citizens and their ruler. On 2 July Shemyakin entered a depopulated Astrakhan, while Prince Vyazemskii found a considerable number of abandoned cannons and arquebuses in Yamgurchei's camp. They pursued the fugitives in all directions, to Beloe Ozero and Tyumen.*

Some were killed and others were taken to the city in order to give some subjects to Derbysh, who had been declared ruler in the deserted capital. Yamgurchei galloped to Azov with 12 warriors; we only caught up with his wives and daughters. We also overtook many distinguished officials, who all wanted to serve Derbysh and to be subordinate to Russia; they asked only for their lives and personal liberty. When they were presented to the new ruler, he ordered them to live in the city; the common people he sent to the uluses. There were 500 princes and mirzas, and 10,000 commoners. Together with Derbysh they swore to obey Ivan as their supreme ruler, to send him 40,000 altyns** and 3,000 fish as annual tribute, and in case of Derbysh's death, not to seek a ruler anywhere else, but to wait until Ivan or his successor bestowed a leader on them.

---

* [Presumably not Belo-ozero (there are many "White Lakes" in Russia), nor the city Tyumen in Siberia, which had not yet been founded.]

** [An altyn was a small coin worth six Moscow dengas (*alty* is Tatar for "six"). The denga, in turn, was originally a silver Tatar coin, later replaced by the kopeck, which is 1/100th of a ruble. The plural, *dengi*, now simply means "money."]

In a sworn document fastened with seals it said that Russians and people from Astrakhan might freely fish from Kazan to the sea without taxes or reporting requirements. After they established order in the land and left Cossacks (along with the court noble Turgenev) with Derbysh both for his safety and to keep an eye on him, Prince Shemyakin and Veshnyakov returned to Moscow with five high-ranking captured princesses and a huge number of freed Russians, who had been involuntarily detained in Astrakhan uluses.

The sovereign received the news of this happy success on 29 August, his birthday, which was being celebrated in village of Kolomenskoe with the metropolitan and the whole court. He manifested the liveliest joy; he arranged for a church service, graciously rewarded his voivodes, met the captured princesses with great honor, and to please Derbysh, sent them back to Astrakhan, all except for the youngest one of them, who had given birth to a son on the way and was baptized in Moscow together with him. The son was named Crown Prince Pyotr, the mother, Iulianiya, and the sovereign married her to his distinguished courtier, Zakharii Pleshcheev.

Astrakhan did not remain a special state for long: Derbysh's perfidy soon demonstrated the necessity of setting up a Russian administration for it – there is no reliable middle ground between an independent and a completely subordinate state. The valor of our Cossacks repelled the exile Yamgurchei, who was trying to conquer Astrakhan with the assistance of the Crimeans and the sons of the Nogai prince Yusuf.

Derbysh plotted treachery, even though the sovereign had indulgently yielded to his people all the first year's tribute. He had secret relations with Khan Devlet-Girei and accepted Crimean prince Kazbulat in the position of *kalga*.* Ivan Cheremisinov, the head of the musketeers, was sent with a new military unit to unmask and punish the turncoat. Derbysh took off the mask himself and led all the residents out of the city to join with throngs of Crimeans and Nogai. Encouraged by the Russians' scant numbers, they daringly began a war.

---

* [In the Crimean khanate, the kalga was immediately subordinate to the khan.]

CHAPTER FIVE

We had a sincere and ardent friend, Prince Ismail of the Nogai, however, by whose intercession the throne had been given to this ingrate. He helped Cheremisinov, and Derbysh, soundly defeated (in 1557), fled in Yamgurchei's tracks to Azov. Now all the residents returned to the city and the surrounding uluses, after being assured of their safety. They gave their oath to Russia and stopped plotting treason; they were satisfied with their lot under the power of a great state, whose strength could defend them against the Crimeans and the Nogai. Cheremisinov confirmed them in their previous property on islands and arable land. He imposed a light tribute on everyone, upheld justice and gained general popularity and trust. In a word, he arranged everything in the best way for the benefit of the inhabitants and for Russia.

Henceforth, in his signature on documents the sovereign began to denote the years from the conquests of Kazan and Astrakhan;* this epoch was undoubtedly the most brilliant in our history during the middle ages. In the eyes of his Russian contemporaries the formidable title *protector of states* gave Ivan unexampled majesty, elevating their nation's dignity, stimulating ambition and feeding popular pride. This was surprising to foreigners, who did not understand its causes, since they saw only our national inadequacies in comparison to other European peoples and did not [think to] compare the Russia of Vasilii the Dark** with that of Ivan IV. The former had only 1,500 soldiers for its defense, while the latter took a foreign state with only a detachment of light troops, without drawing on his own main legions.

There was barely a century separating these two events and our people might naturally take pride in such rapid strides to greatness. Not only foreigners, but we ourselves will not properly evaluate the civic progress of ancient Russia if we do not look into the circumstances of those times. If we do not put ourselves in the place of our ancestors; we will not see events and deeds with their eyes, without deceptive comparisons with more recent times, after everything has changed. The seeds had been sown, and they

---

* [The endnote gives an example: *[in the year of] our reign over Russia 26, Kazan 20, Astrakhan 18.*]

** [Vasilii II, Grand Prince of Muscovy from 1435-1462. "Dark" presumably refers to his blindness.]

propagated. Great efforts yield greatness, and in national development, the beginning is scarcely less difficult than the completion.

After Russia extended its territory to the Caspian shores, in addition to glory and brilliance, it discovered new sources of wealth and power; its commercial and political influence had been magnified. The sound of arms had chased foreign merchants out of Astrakhan; peace and quiet returned them: they came from Shamakha, Derbent, Shavkal, Tyumen, Khiva and Saraichik with all sorts of goods and quite willingly paid the prescribed duties into the national treasury. The rulers of Khiva and Bukhara now sent their dignitaries to Moscow with gifts, hoping for Ivan's good will and for free trade in Russia. The Shavkal and Tyumen lands as well as Georgia wished to be our tributaries.

<small>THE EMBASSIES OF KHIVA, BUKHARA, SHAVKAL, TYUMEN AND GEORGIA</small>

<small>SUBMISSION OF THE CIRCASSIANS</small>

Circassian princes swore allegiance to our sovereign, requesting that he assist them in battling the sultan's possessions and the Taurid. Ivan replied that the sultan was at peace with Russia, but that we would defend them from Khan Devlet-Girei with all our strength. The faith of the Savior, which had been implanted between the Black Sea and the Caspian back in the old days of the Byzantine Empire, had not yet been completely extinguished in those lands; vague traditions and some of the rites remained.

Russia's fame and power revived memories of Christianity, and the love for it. Princes baptized their children in Moscow and handed them over to the tsar to be educated. Some of those fathers even became baptized themselves. Kudadek-Aleksandr, the son of Prince Sibok, and Temryukov and Saltanuk-Mikhail learned reading and writing at the Kremlin court along with Syuyunbeka's son. Grateful to our zealous Nogai allies, the sovereign permitted them during wintertime to roam in the vicinity of Astrakhan itself, where they peacefully engaged in trade. After killing his brother Yusuf, Prince Ismail wrote to Ivan from the town of Saraichik:

<small>AMITY WITH THE NOGAI TATARS</small>

"Your enemy is no longer in this world; my nephews and sons have unanimously given me *the reins to their bridles*. I now rule over all the uluses."

He advised the Russians to establish a fortress on the Perevoloka and another one on the Irgiz (in present-day Saratov Province), where some of the fugitive Nogai mirzas were roaming, not wishing to obey him and be our friends. While affirming amity with gifts and kindnesses, the sovereign did not permit Ismail to call himself either his father or his brother in sworn documents; he considered this would be demeaning to a Russian monarch.

Word of our conquests penetrated even to distant Siberia, whose name then denoted only the central portion of today's Tobolsk Province. It had long been known in Moscow through our Ugri and Perm tributaries. It was ruled by Mongol princes, descendants of Baty's brother Siban (or Shiban). It is likely that they had had previous relations with Russia, and even considered themselves to be somewhat subordinate to its powerful tsar. In 1554 Ivan had called himself Sovereign of Siberia in documents, but the chronicles say nothing of this before 1555, when Prince Ediger sent two officials to Moscow to congratulate the sovereign on his conquest of Kazan and Astrakhan.

SIBERIAN TRIBUTE

This was not just a matter of courtesy: Ediger volunteered to pay tribute to Russia on the condition that we assure the peace and safety of his land. The sovereign reassured the emissaries of his favor, took their oath of allegiance and granted them a letter patent.* They said that there were 30,700 inhabitants in Siberia. Ediger intended to give us a sable and a squirrel pelt for each person annually. The boyar cadet Dmitrii Kurov travelled to Siberia to receive the oaths of allegiance from the prince and his people. He returned at the end of 1556 with Ediger's emissary, bringing only 700 sables instead of the promised 30,000. Ediger wrote that his land had been laid waste by a Shiban crown prince and could not pay more, but Kurov demurred, and the tsar ordered the Siberian emissary locked up. Finally, in 1558, Ediger provided Moscow with the full tribute with the assurance that henceforth he would be a punctual

---

* [A sovereign's published written order granting a privilege to a person or organization.]

payer. It was in this manner that Russia opened the way to immeasurable acquisitions in northern Asia, heretofore unknown to the historians and geographers in the developed areas of Europe.

This memorable period of Ivan's reign was also renowned for Russia's close alliance with one of the most distinguished European powers, which had been beyond its political horizon. Russia barely knew of it from rumor and then suddenly and unexpectedly found access to these most remote and least known lands of Ivan's realm. With great profit to itself they gave us a new means of enrichment and new means of civic development.

ENGLISH SHIPS VISIT RUSSIA

England was not yet a first-rate sea power, but was already striving toward that goal, contending with Spain, Portugal, Venice and Genoa. It wished to establish a route to China and India via the Arctic Ocean, and in the spring of 1553, in the reign of young Edward VII, it sent three ships into the Northern Ocean. Its commanders were Hugh Willoughby and Captain [Richard] Chancellor. Separated by a storm, the ships were unable to reunite; two met their doom on the coast of Russian Lapland, at the harbor of Artsin, where Hugh Willoughby froze to death with all his men. In 1554 Lapp fishermen found him dead, sitting in a shelter before his journal.

Captain Chancellor, however, successfully reached the White Sea. On 24 August he entered the [Northern] Dvina estuary and put in to shore, where the Monastery of St. Nikolai had been established, and where later the city of Arkhangel was founded. The Englishmen caught sight of people, who were amazed by the appearance of a large ship. The sailors learned from them that this shore was Russian and they told the natives that they had a letter from the English king for the Russian tsar and wished to establish trade with the Russian state.

After giving them edible provisions, the leaders of the Dvina lands immediately send a courier to Ivan, who instantly grasped the significance of this event, which would be propitious for the development of our commerce. He ordered Chancellor to appear in Moscow and provided him all possible conveniences en route. On being presented to the sovereign, the Englishmen were astonished

CHAPTER FIVE

to see, in their words, the *unparalleled* splendor of his court: ranks of gorgeous officials, a circle of ranking boyars in golden raiment, a gleaming throne and on it a young sovereign with a glittering crown in silent majesty. Chancellor presented him with the following letter from Edward, written in different languages* *to all the northern and eastern* sovereigns:

"Edward VII to you, tsars, princes, rulers and judges of the lands, in all countries beneath the sun: he desires peace, tranquility and honor for you and your lands! The Lord Almighty has given man an amicable heart to benefit those closest to him, but especially travelers who come to us from remote places and clearly show thereby their surpassing love for fraternal fellowship. So thought our fathers, who were always hospitable, always kind to foreigners requesting protection.

"All men have the right to hospitality, but merchants even more, for they scorn danger and effort, putting behind them seas and wildernesses so that the blessed fruits of our land may enrich distant countries and in turn that we may be enriched by their products. For the Lord of the universe has spread the gifts of His goodness so that peoples may have need of each other and so that mutual service may establish amity between peoples. With this intention, a few of our subjects have undertaken a long sea voyage and requested our consent. To realize this desire, we have permitted a worthy man, Hugh Willoughby, and his comrades, our loyal servants all, to travel to lands hitherto unknown, and to exchange our abundance with them: to receive that which we have not, and to give of our abundance, for mutual benefit and friendship.

And so we beseech you, tsars, princes and rulers, to permit these people to travel freely through your lands, for they will touch nothing without your permission. Do not forget humanity. Magnanimously help them in need and accept from them that which may reward you. Treat them as you would wish us to treat your servants if any of them might come to visit us. And we swear by God, the Lord of all that is in the heavens, on earth and in the sea; we swear by the life and welfare of our realm that we shall greet each of your subjects as a compatriot and friend, out of

---

* [English and Latin, according to Karamzin's endnote 427.]

gratitude for the love which you shall have shown our [subjects]. To this end, we pray to God Almighty to give you long life on earth and eternal peace. Given in London, our capital, in the year 5,517 since the creation of the world and the 7th year of our reign."

The Englishmen, who had been graciously received, dined with the tsar in the Golden Palace, and viewed the regal splendor with renewed astonishment. More than 100 guests ate and drank from golden vessels, and the uniforms of 150 servants likewise glittered with gold. Afterwards Chancellor had very satisfactory parleys with the boyars. He was immediately sent home (in February 1554) with Ivan's reply.

The tsar wrote to Edward that he sincerely wished for his friendship and was ready to do anything to please him, consistent with Christian teachings, the principles of political science and his best understanding. Ivan had received Chancellor graciously and would receive Willoughby likewise should he happen to come to be amongst us. He said that friendship, protection, liberty and safety awaited English emissaries and merchants in Russia.

But Edward was no more, and Mary now ruled in England; Chancellor handed her Ivan's letter with a German translation. The news produced lively joy in London. Everyone spoke of Russia as a *newly discovered* land. They wished to know its interesting history and geography, and immediately formed a commercial society* to trade with it. In 1555 Chancellor once again set out for Russia in two ships with Graham and Killingworth, who were officers of this society, to conclude a commercial treaty with the tsar, to whom Mary and her husband Philip expressed their gratitude in writing in the strongest terms.

Ivan received Chancellor and his comrades in Moscow with renewed graciousness. When he dined with them, he usually seated them before himself; he spoke kindly and referred to Queen Mary as his most beloved sister. A special council, which included Muscovite merchants, was established to consider the rights and liberties the English had requested. It was proposed that the main exchange of goods would be in Kholmogory, in fall and winter; that prices would be arbitrary [i.e., not fixed], but that any deceit in

---

* [The Muscovy Company, chartered in 1555.]

the course of trade would be judged as a criminal offense. Ivan ultimately gave a commercial letter patent to the Englishmen, ruling therein that they might freely trade in all the cities of Russia without restrictions and without paying any sort of duty. They could live anywhere, own homes and shops, hire servants and workers and take oaths of loyalty from them. Only the accused would be answerable for an offense, and not the society as a whole. The sovereign, as legal judge, had the right to deprive a criminal of his honor and his life, but could not touch his property.

They were to choose an elder for sorting out disputes and suits amongst themselves. The sovereign's deputies were obligated to actively assist them in controlling the disobedient and were to provide the means of punishment. An Englishman could not be arrested if the elder declared himself his guarantor. The administration would immediately satisfy their complaints against Russians and strictly punish the offenders. Foremost among the goods that the English brought to Russia were cloth and sugar. Our merchants offered them 12 rubles (or guineas) for a "half" of cloth and 4 altyns (or shillings) for a funt* of sugar. These prices seemed low to us.

After this, the wharf at St. Nikolai – where, except for a poor, solitary monastery there were then only five or six huts – came to life and became an important trading place. The English built a large, beautiful house there and several extensive courts in Kholmogory for the storage of goods. Meanwhile, hoping to discover a passage through the Arctic Ocean, their captain, Stephan Borrow, reached Novaya Zemlya and Vaigach from the mouth of the Dvina, but, intimidated by storms and masses of ice, he returned to Kholmogory at the end of August.

In 1556 Chancellor sailed for England with four richly laden ships and the sovereign's emissary, Iosif Nepeya Vologzhanin. Fortune, which had always favored this skilled navigator, now betrayed him. A storm scattered his ships and only one made it to the London docks. Chancellor himself drowned near

EMBASSY TO ENGLAND

---

* [A Russian pound: 409.5 grams, or about 14.5 avoirdupois ounces.]

the Scottish coast; only Ivan's emissary was saved. He lost everything, but was showered with gifts and kindness in London. Distinguished state officials and 140 merchants, all on handsome horses and richly dressed, came out to meet him. He mounted a beautifully adorned horse and, surrounded by senior merchants, rode into the city. Curious Londoners crowded the streets, loudly welcoming the emissary. He was assigned to one of the best houses, where rich clothing matched the sumptuousness of the daily entertainments.

They guessed and anticipated all the desires of the guest, now inviting him to a banquet, now taking him to see all the sights of London: the palaces, St. Paul's Cathedral, Westminster, the fortress and city hall. He was received by Queen Mary with notable kindness. On the celebratory day of the Order of the Garter Nepeya sat in church on a raised seat near the Queen.

Nowhere had the Russian name been shown such honor. Ivan's undistinguished, but worthy personal representative was able to earn a very flattering recommendation from the English ministers, who reported to the Queen that his mind for affairs equaled his noble deportment. Along with the tsar's letter, Nepeya presented Mary and Philip with several sables, saying that Ivan's richer gifts had been stolen by the Scots at the time of Chancellor's shipwreck. The Queen sent the tsar the very finest produce of English textile factories, shining armor, and a lion and a lioness.

After the elders of the Muscovy Company had entertained Nepeya for the last time in the hall of the London cloth merchants, they announced that it was not the court, nor the treasury, but their corporation that had taken upon itself all the expenses necessitated by his sojourn in England, and that they did this with the greatest pleasure as a token of their good will, enthusiasm and *tender* friendship towards him and Russia. They presented him with a gold chain worth 100 pounds sterling and five valuable vessels. He returned home on an English ship in September 1557, bringing to Moscow craftsmen, miners and medical people, among whom was the skilled Doctor Standish. It was in this manner that Russia made use of every opportunity to acquire from foreigners that which was most necessary for its civic development.

CHAPTER FIVE

Ivan read with pleasure the letter from Queen Mary and Philip, which referred to him as a *great emperor*. When he heard from Nepeya how much honor and friendship the people and the court had shown him in London, Ivan treated Englishmen as Russia's dearest guests. He ordered them to be assigned houses in every commercial city, in Vologda and Moscow, and personally greeted them so kindly that they could not but write to their acquaintances in London concerning their feelings of great gratitude. In 1557 Anthony Jenkinson, the chief captain of the English ships, arrived at the mouth of the Dvina and then traveled from Moscow to Astrakhan to establish trade with Persia.

The sovereign expressed complete confidence in the plans of the English merchants and promised to provide them with every means for this distant transport of goods. In brief, our ties with Britain were based on mutual benefit without any perilous admixture of politics and had a rather special character of sincerity and amity that served to demonstrate the tsar's wisdom and added new luster to his reign. Other European merchants immediately took advantage of the English discovery. Ships from Holland and Brabant began to arrive on Russia's northern shores and to trade in the Korelskoe estuary. This continued from 1555 to 1557.

These memorable events were not the only subjects of Ivan's activity. While pacifying Kazan, subjugating Astrakhan, imposing tribute on Siberia, extending our power to Persia and our trade to Samarkand, the Scheldt and the Thames, Russia also battled with Khan Devlet-Girei, Sweden and Livonia – and kept a vigilant eye on Lithuania.

The utter downfall of the state of Kazan horrified the Taurid: Devlet-Girei, seething with malice, wished to swallow up Russia,

| CRIMEAN AFFAIRS |

but he perceived our strength and bided his time, enticing Ivan with peaceful promises while threatening attack. In 1553 the tsar was in Kolomna with his legions, awaiting the khan. The khan sent a sworn document to Moscow consenting to be our friend, but he wanted rich gifts and referred to Ivan merely as a grand prince. Our sovereign sent him a letter in reply that *we do not buy friends* and modestly informed of the conquest of Astrakhan. At this point some of the Duma councilors suggested to the sovereign that he perform a great deed for our glory, security and prosperity by conquering the last of Baty's realms – if he had taken their advice it would have anticipated by two centuries the celebrated feat of Ekaterina II [Catherine the Great], for it is unlikely that the Crimea could have resisted Russia's forces; it now stood with its heel on two states and was looking at a third as an attractive trophy. Two hundred thousand conquerors were ready to strike at this nest of brigands better suited for banditry than defensive warfare. There is a time for conquest, but it passes by and may not return for a long time.

SULEIMAN'S LETTER

The councilors' scheme seemed too audacious, however. The way to the Crimea was unfamiliar to the troops: the steppes, the distance, and the logistics were all intimidating. On top of that, Ivan feared to irritate the sultan, who held supreme power over the Taurid, and with whom we happened to have friendly relations. Although he had incited the Nogai princes against us, he hid his enmity and as a token of his esteem, wrote with *golden letters* to Ivan, calling him a *fortunate tsar and wise administrator.* He reminded him of their *old affection,* and sent merchants to Moscow to buy goods. But there was also another reason the sovereign spared the Taurid: like his grandfather, he hoped to employ its khans as instruments of our policy, to harm or threaten Lithuania. Experience had already proved the reliability of this instrument, but we needed more proof to assure ourselves of the necessity of exterminating the barbarians; consequently we left fire and sword against Russia in their hands!

THE CRIMEANS ATTACK

Having seen Devlet-Girei's lies and deceit, and having learned that he was marching to do battle in the land of our friends, the Pyatigorskie Circassians, in June 1555 the sovereign sent the voivode Ivan Sheremetev from Belyov via the Muravskaya Road into Mamai's Meadows toward Perekop with 13,000 boyar cadets, musketeers and Cossacks in order to drive off the khan's herds. Devlet-Girei, however, swung left from Izyumskii Kurgan and suddenly drove towards the Russian border with about 60,000 troops. Sheremetev, who was near Svyatyie Gory and the Donets, discovered the enemy movement, informed the sovereign, and struck out towards Tula after the khan.

Ivan immediately left Moscow with Prince Vladimir Andreevich, Simeon, the ruler of Kazan, and all the voivodes and boyar cadets. They no longer cared to wait for the Crimeans on the banks of the Oka, as they had in the past, but hastened to meet them in the field further on. Devlet-Girei was between two armies and did not know it. An indiscretion by the sovereign's secretaries saved him. They had written from Moscow to the Ukrainian deputies that the khan was in a trap, that he would be squeezed by the tsar from in front and Sheremetev from behind and would be destroyed. The deputies broadcast this happy news, which also reached the khan through inhabitants captured by the Crimeans. Terrified, he decided to flee.

In the meantime, the valorous and energetic Sheremetev seized Devlet-Girei's baggage train, 60,000 horses, 200 argamaks [a central Asian breed of race horse], and 180 camels. He sent these spoils to Mtsensk and Ryazan, leaving him with only 7,000 troops. Near Sudbishchi, 150 versts from Tula, he encountered the entire enemy force. He did not decline battle – he smashed their vanguard, captured the banner of the Shirinskie princes and camped that night on the battlefield. Two prisoners were brought to the khan, who tortured them. One remained silent, but the other could not take the pain and told him of the Russians' scant numbers.

Devlet-Girei feared our main army, but was ashamed to yield victory to a handful of valiant knights. Next morning he resumed his attack with all his legions. They fought for nearly eight hours and the Russians saw the enemy's rear on several occasions. Only the sultan's janissaries stood fast, protecting the khan and his artillery. Unfortunately, our hero Sheremetev had been wounded and the other voivodes did not have his spirit. Our efforts weakened, while the enemy redoubled his. The Russians were thrown into confusion and sought safety in flight. Then two brave officers, Aleksei Basmanov and Stefan Sidorov, struck tambourines and sounded trumpets. They halted the flight and sat tight in a gully with 2,000 troops. The khan attacked three times but could not overcome them. Fearing the loss of time, he withdrew into the steppes at sunset.

The sovereign was approaching Tula when it was reported to him that Sheremetev had been wounded and the khan was about to march on Moscow with an immense force. The timid advised the tsar to pull back across the Oka; the bold wanted to advance. He heeded the bold and went to Tula, where Sheremetev, Basmanov, Sidorov and the remnant of their troops were now to be found.

When he learned that the khan was hurrying towards the Crimean border and that it would be impossible to overtake him, Ivan returned to Moscow. He graciously rewarded all Sheremetev's doughty comrades-in-arms, who were not victors, but had been distinguished by glory in a desperate battle. Many of them died of wounds, among them the valiant voivode Sidorov, wounded by a musket ball and a lance; having served his tsar, he threw off his bloody armor and died [five weeks later] as a senior monk.

THE SWEDISH WAR

Ivan now needed to turn his attention to Sweden. Gustav Vasa viewed the rising power of Russia with unease and tried to secretly harm it: he had relations with the Polish king, Livonia, the Duke of Prussia and with Denmark, trying to make a common effort of the northern powers to counter Ivan's dangerous lust for power. Threatened by our profitable trade with England, he tried to persuade Mary to forbid it as incompatible with Sweden's welfare and providing its natural enemies new means for wealth and power. Despite this, neither Gustav nor the tsar wanted bloodshed; the former sensed his own weakness, the latter had no plans of making any conquests in Sweden at all.

Yet these disputes over unclear boundaries provoked a war. Referring to the old treaty of King Magnus with Novgorod, the Russians regarded the rivers Saya and Sestriya as the boundary between the two states. Sweden had transgressed this border: fishing, mowing hay, and plowing fields in our territory. They said the Sestriya was a completely different river and would not listen to any rebuttal. The Russians burned their grain fields and the Swedes burned our villages, killing several boyar cadets, one of whom they impaled. They captured several of our stockades in Lapland and tried to destroy the lonely monastery of St. Nikolai, on the Pechenga, across from Vardø.

The Novgorod deputy Prince Dimitrii Paletskii sent his official, Nikita Kuzmin to King Gustav, but he was detained in Stockholm as a spy because of false accusations by the Vyborg headman. Gustav gave no response to Prince Paletskii; he wanted to furnish a written explanation of his position to the tsar himself. Residents of the Novgorod district occupied several disputed places by force of arms, but the Swedes soundly defeated them.

Both sides still proposed to amicably investigate their mutual dissatisfactions. A time and place was designated for a session of the delegates, but the Swedes did not show up. The sovereign ordered Prince Nogtev and the Novgorod voivodes to defend the border. Gustav, fearing an attack, arrived in Finland, but solely for the purpose of defending it.

However, his admiral, Johann Bagte, who was burning to distinguish himself with a deed of glory, tried to persuade the king to forestall us. He informed him of his progress and reported that there were rumors of the tsar's sudden death, that Russia was in a state of confusion, and that he hoped to raise 20,000 troops and to penetrate to the middle of its territory. Old Gustav was seduced and agreed to go on the offensive. Bagte immediately laid siege to Nöteberg (Oreshek), with cavalry, infantry and many armed boats. He destroyed the walls with his cannons and torched our settlements.

The Russians took measures: the fortress was defended strongly; from one side Prince Nogtev and from the other the majordomo Simeon Sheremetev squeezed the enemy, broke up his formations, captured his foragers and seized his boats. Autumn had commenced and Bagte had lost a considerable number of men in the course of a month, so he returned to Finland, boasting only that the Russians had been unable to block his path and that he had bravely repulsed them everywhere.

That winter a large army was assembled in Novgorod, but the tsar still evinced a desire for peace. The Muscovite voivodes wrote to the king that he had violated the truce without conscience and would be to blame for a terrible bloodbath if within the course of two weeks he did not come out to them at the border or else send his nobles to consider their mutual dissatisfactions and to punish offenders.

Instead of Gustav, Vyborg officials replied, saying that Admiral Bagte had started the war without the king's permission and that the Swedes, having shown the Russians their valor, were ready to renew their old friendship with them.

But this reply seemed unsatisfactory, so the voivodes Prince Pyotr Shchenyatev, Dimitrii Paletskii and Prince Kaibula of Astrakhan invaded Finland. They took seven cannons from the abandoned Swedish town of Kiven and torched the place. Five versts from Vyborg they encountered the enemy, who crushed their leading units and took up positions on a hill. This site gave us an advantage: Ivan's skilled voivodes went around it and attacked from the rear, which decided the battle. Some of the king's most distinguished officials were taken prisoner and the rest of the Swedes shut themselves up in Vyborg.

In three days of bombarding the city the Russians were unable to break down its strong walls. They laid waste to the Voksa shore and destroyed Neishlot [Nyslott], taking a large number of prisoners. The chronicler says that they sold men for a grivna and women for five altyns. Ivan was pleased with his voivodes. He sent some sets of Swedish armor to the Nogai Prince Ismail, writing to him:

"Here are Russia's new trophies! The German [i.e., Swedish]** king offended us: we defeated his men, took a city and destroyed his settlements. Thus we punish our enemies – *do* be our friend!"

Right from his youth, Gustav had been an example of prudence among monarchs, for he knew how to be a hero without craving military glory. He courageously delivered his homeland from a foreign tyrant and always wished for peace, quiet and prosperity. In old age he might blame himself for the error

---

* [The Russians called all Germanic-speaking peoples *Germans*, particularly Scandinavians.]

of foolish thinking. He saw that without allies, Sweden did not have the strength to fight Russia, so he sent an official, Kanut, to Moscow. He respectfully and amicably wrote to Ivan requesting peace. He blamed the former Novgorod deputy, Prince Paletskii (who now had been replaced), and tried to demonstrate that it was not Sweden, but Russians, who had started the war.

Kanut presented Gustav's gifts: ten Swedish fox pelts. Although he was the emissary of an enemy, he had the honor to dine with the sovereign, for that enemy had now sued for peace. In replying to Gustav, the tsar disagreed with him about the causes of the war, but did agree with his desire to end it.

"Your men," he wrote, "committed terrible brutalities in our Karelian territory: not only did they burn and murder, but they also desecrated churches, taking crosses, bells, and icons. The residents of Novgorod requested large legions from me: Muscovite, Tatar, Cheremis, and others. My voivodes burned with impatience to march on Åbo and Stockholm. We restrained them because we do not love bloodshed.

"All this evil came about because you in your pride did not want to deal with Novgorod's deputies, who were distinguished boyars of a great country. If you do not know about Novgorod, then ask your merchants. They will tell you that its suburbs are larger than your Stockholm. Put aside your pride and we shall be friends."

Gustav put it aside: in February of 1557, his emissary, state councilor Sten Erikson, Archbishop Laurence of Uppsala, Bishop Michael Agricola of Åbo and the [keeper of the] king's seal, Olof Larson, arrived in Moscow in 150 carts. They were housed at the Lithuanian court almost like prisoners – they were unable to see anyone but the tsar's officials. They brought Ivan a silver goblet with a clock on it. They dined with him in the Faceted Palace and were obliged to accept all the conditions that he announced to them. They did not argue about the border, but restored the old one.

However, the emissaries persisted in demanding that we release all Swedish prisoners without payment and said that the king had business [to discuss] with the tsar alone. The boyars replied:

| 1557 |

"1) you, as the guilty party must free without ransom all the Russians – merchants and others – whom you seized, and we, as the injured party, will allow you to ransom the Swedish prisoners, wherever you find them, provided they have not accepted our religion.

2) It is not a dishonor, but an honor for the king to deal with the Novgorod deputies. Do you know who they are? Children or grandchildren of the sovereigns of Lithuania, Kazan and Russia. The current deputy, Prince Glinskii, is the nephew of Mikhail Lvovich Glinskii, who is so famous and renowned in the German lands. We shall likewise ask you, not as a reproach, but only from due consideration: who is your sovereign? He wears a crown, to be sure, but how long has it been since he traded in oxen? In a great monarch, humility is better than pride."

The emissaries yielded, and so the boyars, wishing to appear obliging, agreed not to call the king an oath-breaker in the agreement! They drew up a truce treaty for 40 years in Moscow and ordered the Novgorod deputies to affix their seals. Meanwhile, the emissaries were shown honor such as neither Ivan's father or grandfather had ever afforded the Swedes. In the palace they were greeted and accompanied by distinguished officials and they were served, lavishly and sumptuously, *on gold.*

Instead of a gift, the sovereign sent them 20 freed Finnish prisoners. A Swedish historian relates that Ivan wished to hear a theological debate between the archbishop of Uppsala and our metropolitan. The Greek language was chosen for this, but the interpreter did not understand the meaning of the most important terms, translating them so absurdly that the sovereign ordered that the debate be halted. As a token of good will, however, he affixed a gold chain to the archbishop's chest.

In this brief Swedish war, King Augustus and the Livonian master naturally favored Gustav; they also promised to help him, but in the event remained peaceful spectators. The former merely interceded for him in Moscow, trying to persuade Moscow not to press Sweden, which might cooperate with Poland against the infidel.

Chapter Five

"I am not pressing on anyone," he wrote in reply to Augustus. "I have an extensive realm, which has constantly expanded from Ryurik's time to my own. Conquests do not tempt me, but I do stand on my honor."

After he had renewed the truce with Lithuania till 1562, Ivan was agreeable to concluding a permanent peace with Sweden if Augustus would acknowledge him as tsar. But the king was obstinate, replying that he did not like novelties; that this sort of title belonged only to the German emperor and the sultan. Our boyars showed his emissaries letters from Pope Clement, Emperor Maximilian, sultans and the sovereigns of Spain, Sweden and Denmark that had even called Ivan's grandfather and father *tsar*; they also showed a recent letter from the Queen of England, but nothing would convince Augustus. It seemed he feared the title more than he did the Russian sovereign's strength. Ivan formally notified him of the conquest of Astrakhan; the king expressed to him his gratitude and wrote that he was overjoyed at his victory over the infidel! Such an assurance was only politeness, but Khan Devlet-Girei's brigandage, which did not spare even Lithuania, might incline these two countries towards a sincere alliance if they did not encounter new and significant clashes in their interests.

> RELATIONS WITH LITHUANIA

The khan's last assault on our territory had cost him dearly: he had lost not only his baggage train, but also the best part of his army in the battle with Sheremetev. But despite this, he boasted of victory and was once more taking up arms. Cossacks under the command of the secretary Rzhevskii were keeping an eye on him between the Dnieper and the Don. In May 1556 they informed the sovereign that the khan had encamped at Konskie Vody and was aiming at Tula or Kozelsk. Troops were gathered in a few days and the tsar inspected them at Serpukhov. He planned to meet the enemy beyond Tula, but then learned that the danger had passed.

The bold secretary Rzhevskii had taken 300 Little Russian Lithuanian Cossacks with the atamans Mlynskii and Eskovich and struck at Islam-Kirmen and Chekov. He battled the

> THE SECRETARY RZHEVSKII ATTACKS ISLAM-KIRMEN

khan's kalga for six days, killing a great number of Crimeans and Turks and driving off their herds. He came back with booty and obliged Devlet-Girei to hurry back to defend the Crimea, where, on top of everything else, a lethal epidemic was raging.

At this point, and to the sovereign's great satisfaction, one of the most distinguished Lithuanian princes, a descendant of St. Vladimir, Dmitrii Vishnevetskii, offered him his services; he was a man with a fiery mind who was courageous and skilled in military matters. He had been the popular leader of the Dnieper Cossacks and the chief of Kanev, and was bored with Augustus' peaceful regime. He wanted exploits and dangers, and, lured by the glory of our victories, was ardently seething to perform brave deeds under the banners of his ancient homeland, for whom Providence had clearly pointed the way to uncommon greatness.

Prince Vishnavetskii Enters the Tsar's Service and Takes Khortitsa

Vishnevetskii was ashamed to appear before Ivan in the guise of a fugitive, so he departed Lithuania with many enthusiastic Cossacks and occupied the island of Khortitsa near the mouth of the Dnieper, opposite Konskie Vody. He built a fortress there and wrote to our sovereign that he did not require troops from him, but merely wanted the honor of calling himself a Russian. He would confine the khan to the Taurid, as if to his burrow. Encouraged by Ivan's favor, this daredevil burned Islam-Kirmen and removed its cannons to his Khortitsa fortress. He gloriously repelled all the attacks of the khan, who assaulted his island for 24 days without success.

Conquest of Temryuk and Taman

From the other side, Circassian princes conquered two Azov towns, Temryuk and Taman, in Russia's name. This had been the site of our ancient principality of Tmutorokan. Devlet-Girei was frightened; he thought that Rzhevskii, Vishnevetskii and the Circassian princes were only the vanguard of our main army. Expecting Ivan himself, he sued him for peace and wrote the sultan that all would be lost if he did not save the Crimea. There had never, says a contemporary historian, been such an opportune chance to exterminate the remnants of the Mongols, who were clearly being punished by divine wrath.

The Nogai uluses, formerly populous and rich, were depopulated in the cruel winter of 1557; livestock and people perished in the steppes from the unbearable cold. Some of the mirzas sought shelter in the Taurid, but found disease and hunger there due to an extraordinary drought. The khan had barely 10,000 decent cavalry troops left, and there were even fewer among the Nogai. Internal strife was conjoined to these calamities: in the Nogai horde, ulus rose up against ulus. In the Taurid, the nobles wanted to assassinate Devlet-Girei and declare Tokhtamysh their ruler. The latter was an Astrakhan prince living among them, a brother of Shig-Alei. The plot was discovered and Tokhtamysh fled to Russia, where he managed to thoroughly inform the sovereign concerning the weakness of the Crimea.

> EPIDEMIC AND FAMINE IN THE NOGAI AND CRIMEAN SETTLEMENTS

In the opinion of a historian, the renowned Kurbskii, we did not follow where the divine finger pointed, but allowed the infidel to recover. Vishnevetskii did not stand his ground at Khortitsa when numerous units of Turks and Wallachians showed up, sent by the sultan to Devlet-Girei. Having exhausted his strength and provisions, he withdrew towards the Lithuanian border, occupying Cherkasy and Kanev, where he was popular with the residents. He wrote Ivan that he was again ready to march against the khan, and might show Russia even more significant service by subjugating all the southern Dnieper districts to its scepter.

> VISHNEVETSKII'S ZEAL

The proposal was attractive, but the sovereign did not want to violate the truce he had established with Lithuania. He commanded that Cherkasy and Kanev be returned to Augustus, summoned Vishnevetskii to Moscow and gave him the town of Belyov as an estate, along with many rich volosts so that he could threaten both the khan and the Polish king.

Meanwhile, Devlet-Girei was taking it easy. Although he kept expressing his desire to be at peace with Russia, and although he sent off our emissary Zagryazhskii with honor, he had detained him like a prisoner for five years.

> 1558

171

He furnished Ivan with a letter of alliance, promising to fight Lithuania as a sincere token of his friendship for us. However, he offered haughty conditions and demanded *tribute* of the kind Sigismund and Augustus sent to him.

"For you," Devlet-Girei said, "I am breaking my alliance with Lithuania. Consequently, you should reward me."

His sons were now energetically pillaging Volhynia and Podolia, to Augustus' consternation, since he had considered himself their friend. They were seeking easy plunder, and found it in these fertile districts, where the king's pans boasted of their courage at feasts and then cravenly fled from these brigands, being incompetent to guard even their own land. When he learned of this, our sovereign summoned his boyars: they all believed that the requests of the perfidious Devlet-Girei were unworthy of their consideration and that they should take advantage of the situation and propose an alliance against the khan to Augustus.

Prince Vishnevetskii was again dispatched to the Dnieper; he was given 5,000 resident guards,* boyar cadets, musketeers and Cossacks. He was ordered to join up with the Circassian princes and do battle with the Taurid. Ivan wrote the king that he had great sympathy for the calamity suffered by Lithuania from the lethal raid by the Crimeans: the time had come for both of them to consider the real welfare of their states and join forces to smash these miscreants, who lived on deceit and plunder. Russia was prepared to zealously assist him zealously with all the means God had given it. This proposal was such a happy surprise to the king, the nobles and the Lithuanian people, who were bound to us by ties of blood and religion, that they carried the Muscovite emissary in Lithuania in their arms as a herald of tranquility and prosperity for its citizens, who constantly feared war with Russia. He was honored at court and in the best homes, and Ivan's wisdom and magnanimity was praised.

> ALLIANCE WITH LITHUANIA PROPOSED

As a token of his sincere affection, Augustus released some old Muscovite prisoners and sent his Vilnius equerry, Yan Volchkov, to convey his great gratitude to our sovereign, and also promised to immediately send his most distinguished nobles to Moscow to

---

* [Zhiltsy: members of the lowest class of service people.]

CHAPTER FIVE

conclude a permanent peace and an alliance. Both sides spoke quite warmly of Christian brotherhood; they recalled the fate of Greece as a victim of discord among the European powers; they wanted to join in pacifying the khan and resisting the Turks. This mutual good mood vanished like a dream: affairs once again became entangled and the ancient animosity once again leapt up between us and Lithuania.

Livonia was to blame for this: since 1503 we had had neither a war nor a firm peace with it. We kept renewing the truce and were satisfied with commercial ties alone. Ivan had now undertaken to increase Russia's greatness not only through conquests, but also by internal civic development. Having given Russia new power, he viewed with irritation the enmity of the Livonian Order, which barred the way to Moscow not only to people skilled in the arts and in military affairs, but to all foreigners in general.

| LIVONIAN AFFAIRS |

"Russia is now so dangerous," wrote officials of the Order to the emperor, "that all the neighboring Christian sovereigns now bow their heads before its monarch, who is young, energetic, and power-hungry, and they beseech him for peace. Would it be prudent to increase the strength of our natural enemy by giving him access to military arts and ordnance? If we open a free path to Moscow for craftsmen and artists, then many people under these designations will rush there who belong to the evil sects of the anabaptists, sacramentists, and others who have been persecuted in Germany. They will become the tsar's most diligent servants. There is no doubt that he is scheming to make Livonia and the Baltic Sea his own in order to more conveniently subjugate the neighboring lands of Lithuania, Poland, Prussia, and Sweden."

| IMPORTANT PLAN, ATTRIBUTED TO IVAN |

In any event, Ivan did not wish to tolerate Livonian hindrance to his plans to benefit Russia, and he prepared to retaliate. In 1554, emissaries of Master Henrik von Galen – the archbishop of Riga and the bishop of Derpt – implored the tsar to renew the truce for 15 more years. He agreed, but on the condition that the Yuriev, or Derpt district pay him the long established annual

173

tribute. The Germans expressed astonishment, so they were shown Plettenberg's treaty document, written in 1503, where this tribute is actually mentioned, even though it had been forgotten in the course of 50 years. Their rebuttals went unheeded. In the name of the sovereign, Adashev said,

"It shall be thus, lest you have no truce!"

They yielded, and Derpt promised in a letter, guaranteed by the master, henceforth not only to give us annually one German mark for each person in his district, but also to make up within three years all the arrears for the past 50. The master swore not to enter into an alliance with the Polish king and to re-establish our old churches, along with those laid waste in Derpt, Revel* and Riga by Catholics and fanatics of the new Lutheran persuasion. Ivan's father had threatened vengeance on the Lithuanians for this, explaining,

"I am not the Pope or the emperor, who cannot defend their own cathedrals."

Trade was declared free, in accordance with Ivan's wishes. The Hansa complained that the administrations of Riga, Revel and Derpt had prohibited its merchants from importing metals, weapons and armor to us, and wanted the Germans to buy our tallow and wax in Livonia. The master held firm on only one point: he would not promise to allow foreigners passage to Russia. This circumstance made peace most unlikely.

With this document, written in Moscow with the seals of the Livonian emissaries affixed, Ivan's official, Kelar Terpigorev set out for Derpt, so that the bishop and the elders could ratify it with their oaths and seals in accordance with custom. But their bishop, burgomaster and councilors were horrified with the idea of becoming Russian tributaries. They entertained Terpigorev while secretly discussing the matter amongst themselves; they blamed their emissaries of negligence, of misusing the power given them; they did not know what to do.

Several days passed. Moscow's official demanded their oaths; he did not want to wait, and threatened to depart. Then the bishop's

---

* [Derpt was also known as Dorpat, Tartu and Yuriev; Revel as Reval and Tallinn.]

chancellor, a subtle politician, proposed that the Council deceive Ivan, saying,

"The tsar is strong in arms, but he is not cunning of mind. In order not to aggravate him, we shall ratify the treaty, but declare that we cannot enter into such an arrangement without the consent of the [Holy] Roman emperor, our lawful protector. We shall be pleasant to him, we shall wait, and we shall delay – and then it will be up to God!"

This idea gained the upper hand: they took the oath and returned the document to Ivan's emissary, with the proviso that it would not have full force without ratification by the emperor.

"My tsar has no dealings with the emperor!" he declared. "Just give me the paper – and give me silver, as well." He ordered his secretary to wrap the document in silk fabric, and said with a grin, "Be careful: it is a valuable thing! Terpigorev reported to his sovereign that the ceremony had been performed, but that the Germans were contemplating trickery.

Ivan kept quiet, but from this time on he signed documents as *Sovereign of Livonia*. In February of 1557 emissaries of the master and the bishop of Derpt again appeared in Moscow. Knowing that they had not come with money, but with empty words, and that they wanted to demonstrate to our boyars the injustice of our demands, the tsar ordered them to go home, with his reply:

"You freely gave your oath and are obliged to pay us the tribute. The matter is settled. If you do not wish to keep your promise, then we shall find the means to take [what is ours]."

He forbade merchants from Novgorod and Pskov to travel to Livonia, while declaring that the Germans could trade peacefully in Russia. He then sent the okolnichii, Prince Shastunov, to establish a town with a landing stage right at the mouth of the Narova, since he wished to have reliable and safe communications by sea with Germany. He began to prepare for a war, which in all likelihood promised us cheap victories and an easy conquest. In a better, more glorious time for the Order, in the days of the great Plettenberg,*

---

* [Walter von Plettenberg, 1450-1535, one of the greatest commanders of the German (or Teutonic) Order.]

The Livonian Situation

Livonia had already perceived the impossibility of successfully fighting Russia. Deprived of German support, the Order had become even weaker; the 50-year peace had enriched the land, increased the pleasures, the luxury and comforts of life, and had completely cut off the Order from any serious military activity. In their magnificent castles they lived only for sensual enjoyments and base passions (so contemporary chroniclers assure us).

They drank, made merry and forgot the ancient provenance of their brotherhood, its origin and its *raison d'etre*; they disdained not vice, but scarcity; they shamefully violated moral precepts. They were only abashed to be second to another in splendor, of not having costly clothing, numerous servants, richly caparisoned horses and beautiful mistresses. Sponging, feasting and hunting were now the chief business of the notables in their (in the expression of a historian) *earthly paradise.*

In the same manner that these officials of the Order and the Church lived, so, in their abundance, did the fashionable courtiers, the merchants and the lower middle class. Only the farmers lived by the sweat of their brow, burdened by insatiably greedy imposts. These were distinguished not by better morals, but by the crudest vices, by the thoughtlessness of their ignorance and by the fatal plague of their drunkenness. The complex and fragmented administration was weak in the extreme: five bishops, a master, a marshal of the Order, eight commanders and eight magistrates [*fokhty*, German: *Vögte*] ruled the land. Each had his own towns and volosts, regulations and rights; each was concerned with his own personal welfare and cared little for the common good.

The introduction of the Lutheran faith, which was accepted by the cities, lay courtiers, and even many Knights, made the situation in Livonia even more confused. The people, excited by fervor for the new faith, ravaged the Latin churches and monasteries. The local rulers, sometimes because of religion, sometimes because of greed, rose up against one another. Thus it was that Fürstenberg, the successor to Master von Galen, deposed and imprisoned the archbishop, the margrave Wilhelm of Riga (he was later freed by King Augustus's threats).

To preserve their own domestic tranquility, the peace-loving Order hired troops from Germany; they did not even consider means to resist a powerful external enemy: they had neither troops nor money. The master and the officials grew rich and the treasury ran low, depleted for their comfort and luxury. They regarded the Order's property as their own, but their own property as not belonging to the Order. In brief, the abundance of the land, the weakness of its government and the languor of its citizenry attracted a conqueror.

But Russia was more powerful than before. Aside from the glory of our famous conquests, we had obtained substantial new forces: the pacification of Kazan was giving us new troops as Circassian princes arrived with their large cavalry units to serve the tsar. But most important of all was the new and better training of our troops, which almost doubled their effectiveness. This notable achievement of Ivan's reign was completed in 1556 while blood was still running on the banks of the Volga: we were fighting Sweden and awaiting a Crimean attack. This was a development equally noteworthy for both military and civil legislation in Russia.

>RUSSIA'S NEW POWER

>ARMY BETTER TRAINED

Since the time of Ivan III, many of the grand prince's officials and boyar cadets had been awarded land. Others were given legal rights in towns and volosts, so that, with the title of deputies, they lived off judicial quit-rents and duties while preserving the social system, justice and public safety. Many performed their duties honorably, but many also thought only of personal gain, oppressing and robbing the residents. The sovereign received constant complaints; he replaced the deputies and they were tried, with the result that even the innocent were ruined from lawsuits and slander.

To eradicate this evil, Ivan eliminated judicial fees, and commanded that lawsuits be decided by select elders and centurions[*] and instead of duties, he imposed a general tax on towns and volosts, businesses and land, to be collected for the treasury by the

---

[*] [A commander of 100 men. That number should not be taken too literally.]

tsar's secretaries, while officials and boyar cadets without exception were to be treated equally, either with monetary remuneration or with service estates in accordance with their merit and service. He took personal land away from some and gave it to the landless. He established service not only with estates, but also with boyar patrimonies, so that an owner with 100 chetverts* of favorable land would have to go campaigning on horseback and in armor, or send someone else instead of himself, or to remit the specified amount to the treasury.

In order to attract men to his service, Ivan designated a monetary salary for *everyone* during campaigns, and double for boyar cadets who provided personal troops in excess of the legally required number. In this manner, military strength could be deduced by measuring land; military people could have the means to live without want in peacetime and support themselves on campaign. He could demand better performance from them and strictly punish the lazy who avoided service. After that, according to the chroniclers, the number of our troops was vastly multiplied. Ivan had 150,000 at Kazan; several years later he could field up to 300,000 cavalry and infantry.

The latter, called musketeers [*streltsy*] armed with arquebuses, were chosen from rural men in the volosts and constituted a standing army. They were usually quartered in the towns and cities and were primarily employed in sieges of fortresses. This was an arrangement some ascribed to Ivan, but in any case, he perfected it. Although we could not yet quickly replace our old, Asiatic form of warfare, we were now converging on the European style. It gave greater stability and more organization to the militias.

We may add to this the indefatigability of the Russians, their physical stamina in difficult situations, their experience in enduring want and cold in winter campaigns, and more generally, their military experience. In conclusion, we may also add: the immense moral force of an autocratic state, its ability to be mobilized by a single thought, a single word from a young and hearty monarch who, according to our own and foreign contemporaries, *lived only for exploits of arms and faith.* What might the Livonians expect in dealing with such an enemy? Doom!

---

* [By one computation, this would be 56 hectares, or 270 acres.]

CHAPTER FIVE

Each struggle of the weak against the strong arouses a natural sympathy in our hearts and inclines us to seek justice on the side of the former. Yet both Russian and Livonian historians blame the Order because it exasperated Ivan with trickery, deceptions and a clear lack of good will. Although it acted out of an excusable animosity towards a dangerous neighbor, it acted imprudently. Realistic policy demands that one be a friend if one has not the strength to be an enemy. Straightforwardness may sometimes appeal to the conscience of even a power-lover, depriving him of a pretext for legitimate vengeance, since it is not easy to brazenly trample moral principles, and the most cunning or audacious policy must cover itself with a mask.

Ivan, in starting a war with Livonia, might secretly act in accordance with his love of power, which is born and nurtured by glittering successes. However, he could sincerely assure himself and others of the justice of his cause, for which advantage he was indebted to the miscalculation of the Livonian rulers, who, knowing the physical strength of the Russians, hoped to fool them with cunning, with embassies, respectful words and deceitful promises. Thereby they brought on themselves a 25-year catastrophe in which the antiquated Order fell like a rotten tree in the midst of ruins and graves.

When he learned we were taking up arms, Master Fürstenberg and the bishop of Derpt requested letters of safe conduct from the tsar so that their new emissaries could travel to Moscow. Ivan issued them, but the German couriers could see our frightening preparations for war everywhere: wagon trains with military provisions were moving towards the Livonian border; everywhere bridges were being built, camps established, and posts and lodgings built along the highway. By the end of autumn 1557, 40,000 troops were stationed on the border, under the command of Shig-Alei, the boyars Glinskii, Danilo Romanovich and Ivan Sheremetev, as well as the Serebryanyi princes, Andrei Kurbskii and other noted officers. In addition to Russians, this army contained Tatars, Cheremis, Mordvi and Pyatigorsk Circassians.

They were just waiting for the sovereign's word, while the sovereign was awaiting the Livonian emissaries. They arrived with rich gifts and eloquent words, but Ivan did not care for either. Aleksei Adashev and the secretary Ivan Mikhailov showed them the treaty document and demanded the tribute. They ultimately agreed that instead of a yearly head tax, Derpt would send us 1,000 Hungarian gold coins and that Livonia would pay 45,000 thalers for military expenses.

The treaty was written up; it remained to fulfill its terms, but the emissaries declared they had no money with them. It is recorded that the sovereign then invited them to dinner at the palace, but ordered them to be given only *empty* plates. They got up from the table hungry and returned home with nothing but our army following them in the middle of a cold, snowy winter. On 22 February we invaded Livonia with fire and sword. Despite the fact that Ivan's threats had been clear and his preparations for war long known, Livonia's rulers were surprised, feasting as they were at the sumptuous wedding of some sort of Revel official. The Russians did as they wished to the countryside while leaving the Germans sitting peacefully inside their fortified cities.

LIVONIAN WAR BEGINS

The Princes Barbashin and Repnin, and Danilo Fedorovich Adashev terrorized southern Livonia over an extent of 200 versts; they torched the suburbs of Neuhaus, Kirempe, Marienburg, Kurslav and Ultsen. Near Derpt they joined up with the principal voivodes, who had taken Altenturn and had also reduced everything on their route to ashes. The Germans ventured to make a sally from Derpt with 500 cavalry and infantry, but were wiped out. After remaining before this important fortress for three days, some of our voivodes departed for the Gulf of Finland, while others headed for the Aa River. They defeated more Germans near Wesenberg and torched the outskirts of Falkenau, Kongot, Lais and Pirkel. They were only 50 versts from Riga and 30 from Revel at the end of February when they headed back to Ivan-gorod with masses of prisoners and wagon trains full of rich booty, having killed a large number of people.

German historians speak with horror of the ferocity of the Russians, especially complaining of the gangs of so-called hunters [*okhotniki*] from Novgorod and Pskov who, on finding Livonia defenseless, everywhere laid waste to its settlements with a ferocity exceeding even that of the Tatars and Circassians in their army. The Russians, who had been sent not to conquer, but to lay waste to the country, thought that they were doing their duty by doing as much damage as much as possible. The commander, Mikhail Glinskii, was so enamored of loot that he pillaged even in our Pskov districts. He was counting on the sovereign's favor since he was a relative, but he was mistaken. After expressing his gratitude towards all the other voivodes, Ivan, in a righteous rage, ordered that all he had taken illegally in the campaign be confiscated.

Having completed this *punishment*, the Muscovite voivodes wrote the master that the Germans had only themselves to blame for daring to make a plaything of a sacred treaty; if they wanted to turn over a new leaf, they could still gain Ivan's favor through submission. Shig-Alei and his boyars were ready to intercede for them out of pity for their poor country, which was steaming with blood.

Livonia was indeed in a pitiable situation. The unfortunate farmers who had avoided the sword and captivity were unable to find room in the cities and died of exhaustion and cold in the forests and in cemeteries. Everywhere the peoples cries demanded protection or peace from their rulers, who, in discussions in the Sejm at Wenden, considered at length the best measures for their salvation, now bragging of the glory and courage of their forbears, but then terrified, imagining the puissance of the tsar, and finally deciding to dispatch yet another embassy to Moscow. Shig-Alei, whom some of the Livonian historians call ferociously bloodthirsty, but others call a very wise and discreet man, had tried to sway Ivan towards peace, but finally acted on the instructions his sovereign had given him. Fate wished the Order to be a victim of the imprudence of its officials, so that the powerful Ivan would seem justified in lacerating weak Livonia.

While awaiting the master's emissaries, the sovereign ordered all military operations halted until 24 April. Lent had begun and devout Russians were peacefully fasting and praying in Novgorod, separated by the river from Narva, where the Germans, new Lutherans, scorned the rules of their old religion and did not consider it a sin to feast during this period. Suddenly, flushed with wine, they began to shoot at Ivan-gorod. The local voivodes, Kurakin and Buturlin, informed the sovereign of this; he ordered them to defend themselves and sent Prince Temkin, who was stationed in Izborsk, to do battle on the closest Livonian territory in order to punish the Germans for breaking their oath.

Temkin torched villages in the vicinity of Walk, defeating an enemy detachment and capturing four cannons before returning. Moscow's main army still had not budged, but shot kept flying at Ivan-gorod from Narva, hitting its residents. The Germans of Narva derisively informed Ivan's voivodes:

"It is not we, but the Order's magistrate who is shooting; we cannot stop him."

At this point, the voivodes opened up with a powerful barrage. Cannonballs, both incendiary and stone, showered Narva for a week. People were killed, homes were burned and destroyed. In horror, the Germans forgot their hauteur and asked for mercy. The burgomasters and councilors came out to our voivodes and declared that they would not resist Ivan's will in any way. They implored them to stop the barrage. They gave hostages and sent the deputies Joakim Krumhausen and Arnt von Deden to Moscow. When these deputies appeared in the Kremlin palace, the okolnichii Adashev and the secretary Mikhailov came out to them from the sovereign and asked what they wanted.

"To be as we were," replied the wise Krumhausen. "Not to change our laws; to remain a Livonian city; to satisfy all the other demands of the gracious tsar."

"No!" exclaimed Adashev. "We do not dare inform him of such conditions. You rashly violated the truce by firing on Russians and now that you see destruction visited upon you, you declare that you are prepared to carry out the tsar's wishes. However, the tsar will be pleased if you send to Moscow the chief of your Order (the magistrate Schnellenberg) and surrender the city to us. To that end, Ivan graciously promises not to take you from your homes and not to touch your persons, your property, or your ancient customs. He will preserve general prosperity and freedom of trade. In a word, he will rule Narva as the officials of the Order have ruled it. It shall be thus, and not otherwise!"

Chapter Five

Weeping, the deputies swore allegiance to Russia for themselves and all their fellow citizens; they were presented to the sovereign and received from him a letter patent. After ordering the government of Narva informed of this, Ivan wrote to his voivodes that they were to protect this city, as a Russian one, from the master.

But everything had changed in Narva: its flighty citizens had learned that the master was sending them 1,000 troops with the Revel commander. Taking heart, they forgot their terror and sent to tell our chief voivode that their deputies did not have the power to hand over their homeland to Moscow's tsar. The commander planned to take advantage of surprise and catch the Russian guard on the other side of the Narova. He struck, but fled at the first volley. News of this new German perfidy reached Moscow almost at the same time as some other, happier news that was completely unexpected: the Russians had captured Narva!

This event was celebrated as a miracle. It is said that drunken Narva Germans spotted the icon of the Virgin in a house in which merchants from Pskov were living. They threw

> CAPTURE OF NARVA

it into the fire, which suddenly turned into a conflagration (on 11 May) coupled with a terrible storm. The Russians across the river saw the general confusion in the city; ignoring their voivodes, they rushed across, some in boats, some on logs or planks. They leapt onto the riverbank and assaulted Narva all at once.

The voivodes could no longer remain idle observers; they brought the remaining troops with them. It was all over in a few minutes: the commanders of the musketeers with the boyar Aleksei Basmanov and Danilo Adashev (a courageous okolnichii, brother of the sovereign's favorite) broke down the Russian Gate, while Ivan Buturlin smashed through the Kolyvanskii Gate. In the smoke and flame they cut down the terrified Germans and chased them into the strong castle called Vyshegorod [*Upper Town*] and did not give them time to collect their wits. They fired on it with all the cannons, their own and those taken in Narva. They broke down the walls and got ladders ready.

Meanwhile, two commanders from Fellin and Revel, Ketler and Segehafen with a powerful detachment of infantry, cavalry and artillery was three miles from the city. They saw the fire and heard the barrage, but did not move from the spot, figuring that the fortress had stone walls and iron gates and should be able to repel the enemy without their help. But the castle surrendered towards evening, on the condition that the victors allow the magistrate Schnellenberg, the German troops and all residents who so desired, to leave.

The prominent departed, but only with their wives and children, leaving all their property to us as booty. Others sent off their families, but they themselves, along with the people, swore to be faithful to the tsar. The Russians captured 230 cannons and great wealth, yet in extinguishing the fire, they energetically and unselfishly saved the property of those residents who had just become our subjects.

This significant conquest, which gave Russia a renowned commercial port, so overjoyed Ivan that he celebrated with great splendor in Moscow and throughout the country. He rewarded the voivodes and the troops, and graciously confirmed the letter patent given to Krumhausen and von Deden, despite the change in circumstances. He freed all the Narva prisoners, ordered everyone's property be returned to them, and allowed all those residents of Narva who had left, to return. The archbishop of Novgorod was obliged to immediately send the archimandrite of the Yuriev Monastery and the archpriest of the Sofiya Cathedral there to sanctify the place in the name of the Savior. With a religious procession and services they *purified it from the Latin and Lutheran faiths.* They erected a church in the castle and another in the city and placed in it the icon of the Virgin that had caused Narva to burn, which they had found intact in the ashes.

The Livonian emissaries had now at last arrived in Moscow: Theodor, the brother of Master Fürstenberg, and other officials. They did not bring tribute, but rather the prayer that the sovereign turn it over to their stricken land.

"All the Derpt territory," they said to the boyars, "groan in misery, and have not seen a happy day in a long time. From whom do you demand tribute? You have already taken it with your arms, and ten times more, at that. Let us remedy this in the future, and then we will pay you in accordance with the treaty." The sovereign replied through Adashev,

"After all that has happened, how can we even listen to you? Who believes oath-breakers? All that remains to me is to seek satisfaction with the sword. I have conquered Narva and shall enjoy my good fortune. However, I do not like bloodshed and now suggest a means to stop it. Let the master, the archbishop of Riga and the bishop of Derpt personally bow before me and pay the tribute *from all of Livonia* and henceforth obey me as do the rulers of Kazan and Astrakhan, as well as other renowned rulers. Otherwise I shall take Livonia by force." The emissaries were horrified and said,

"We see that we have no business here." They requested leave to depart, which was immediately given. Although the master and the bishop of Derpt, staggered by the fate of Narva, had been prepared to pay us 60,000 thalers, and although they had gathered this sum with considerable effort, it was too late. The sovereign was no longer demanding the Yuriev tribute, but rather the subjection of the entire country. Another war began. The Russians invaded Livonia; no longer satisfied with its devastation, they now wanted its cities and permanent dominion.

On 25 May, Prince Thedor Troekurov and Danilo Adashev laid siege to Neuschloss [Nyslott] and on 6 June entered into negotiations. The local magistrate and a few others emerged from their fortress with empty hands, having already handed over all weapons and possessions to the conquerors. The residents of the city and the whole uezd (60 versts long and 40 or 50 wide), as well as the Latvians and even the Germans acknowledged themselves to be Russian subjects, so that the shores of Lake Chud* and the banks of the Narova from its upper reaches to the sea was now under our dominion.

<blockquote>CONQUEST OF NEUSCHLOSS, ADEZH AND NEUHAUS</blockquote>

After sending gold medals to the voivodes, the sovereign ordered the fortifications there repaired and a church erected in

---

* [The northern part of Lake Peipus.]

the name of St. Ilarion, for it was on his remembrance day that Neuschloss surrendered. The inhabitants of the uezd and town of Adezh voluntarily swore allegiance to Ivan, along with some neighboring Wesenberg volosts, and handed over to the Russians all state property, cannons and provisions.

Our main force, under the command of many renowned voivodes and the Princes Pyotr Shuiskii, Vasilii Serebryanyi and Andrei Kurbskii, now marched on Derpt. First it was necessary to take Neuhaus, a very strong town where there were not even 200 warriors, but which had a knight of the Order named Uxkil von Padenorm, who armed both citizens and farmers and bravely held out against this very large army for about a month. With this hero, as our chronicler puts it, the Germans *fought to the bitter end.* They fought desperately and indefatigably, astonishing the Muscovite commanders.

After knocking down the walls and towers, the Russians entered the city. Uxkil retired to the castle with a handful of men, intending to die in the last of its ruins, but his comrades-in-arms told him that they had no more strength. Out of respect for their bravery, our voivodes permitted them to depart *with honor.* This example showed that Livonia, bordered with many fortresses and having a wealth of artillery, might severely impede the progress of Ivan's arms if its other defenders, although small in numbers, had Uxkil's spirit and if its citizens had the virtues of Tile. He was one of the burgomasters of Derpt, who in an assembly of the officials of the land, powerfully and touchingly depicted their homeland's misery, saying,

> 30 June

> Courage of the Burgomaster of Derpt

"The time has come to sacrifice or die. Even if we lose everything, let us save our honor and liberty. We shall take our gold and silver to the treasury, leaving nothing precious for ourselves, neither vessels nor adornments. We shall give our government the means to hire troops and buy the friendship and protection of neighboring powers!"

This brave man's persuasion and tears had utterly no effect, however: they listened to him but remained silent.

Chapter Five

During the siege of Neuhaus, the Master Fürstenberg, the commanders and even the bishop of Derpt remained motionless with 8,000 troops, thirty versts away in an inaccessible place on the other side of the Dvina and mucky swamps, doing nothing to save the fortress. But when they learned that it had surrendered, they torched their own camp and the town of Kirempe, where there was a great quantity of provisions of all kinds.

Fleeing night and day, they hastened away: the master to Walk, the bishop to Derpt, pursued by our voivodes. They caught up with the bishop 30 versts from Derpt and defeated him, capturing his officers and all his baggage train and artillery. After choosing a strong-point near Walk, the master halted. Our voivodes ordered the vanguard to commence battle with him, while they encircled him and forced him to flee further towards Wenden with such speed and heat that his men and horses were dying of exhaustion. The Russians destroyed Fürstenberg's rear guard and almost captured his most distinguished commander, Gothard Ketler, when his horse collapsed beneath him. We took the master's baggage train as booty, and after informing the sovereign that the enemy had quit the field, our voivodes returned to Derpt.

> THE [LIVONIAN] MASTER FLEES

In these circumstances, terrifying for the Order, the aging Fürstenberg laid aside his title of master and young Ketler, in obedience to the officials, tearfully accepted it. Renowned for his outstanding intellect and firmness of character, he inspired hope in others, but had little himself. It was only out of magnanimity that he agreed to become the last master of the expiring order.

> A NEW HEAD OF THE ORDER

In order to employ all possible means of salvation, Ketler diligently tried to fire cold hearts with love of country, exhorting his officials to work together, sparing neither their property nor their lives for the good of all. He gathered money and men and requested protection from the emperor and the kings of Denmark, Sweden and Poland. He also wrote to the tsar, beseeching him for peace, but did not realize the success he wished for: the dissension and mutual suspicion of the Livonian rulers stymied all the new master's good intentions.

They wished for salvation without sacrifice, ceremoniously pointing out that rich people should not have to ruin themselves for it. Ketler could only fill the Order's empty treasury with loans for unavoidable military expenses. Of outside help there was none.

Emperor Charles V, having encompassed all of Europe in his view, now put aside crown and throne, and like a second Diocletian, retired from the world that his love of power had agitated for so long. In the wilderness he wished to surprise people with a special kind of renown that was rare, but no less vain; a renown that seemed higher than earthly greatness. The new emperor Ferdinand quarreled with the Pope, reconciled with Germany, feared the Turks, and merely felt sorry for poor Livonia. Other sovereigns were satisfied with trying to persuade Ivan towards peace. The tsar replied to Ketler,

"I await you in Moscow, and seeing your petition, I shall be gracious." This graciousness seemed to the master to be the ultimate catastrophe for the reigning Livonian Knights: he wished rather to die with honor than in humiliation and futility.

> DERPT AND
> MANY OTHER TOWNS
> TAKEN

Ivan's voivodes lost no time: they took Kirempe, Kurslav and the strong castle of Verbek on the Embach. With all their forces they assaulted Derpt, renowned for the wealth of its inhabitants and for its many public and beneficial institutions. Aside from its armed citizenry, who were prepared to stand up for honor and liberty, 2,000 German mercenaries were defending this significant and skillfully fortified site under the overall command of Bishop Herman Weiland, who boasted more of his military prowess than of the humble piety of a Christian pastor.

The fighting continued for six days, ferocious and worthy of *knightly men,* as the voivode Kurbskii writes, an eyewitness and truthful judge of military affairs. Overwhelming force won the day, however: sallies cost the besieged dearly, and the Russians, taking advantage of dense mist, blockaded the city on all sides with gabions. They dug mines and made embrasures. They destroyed the walls with cannon fire while suggesting very advantageous conditions to the residents should they surrender.

At first the bishop did not want to hear of negotiations, but the master reported to him that the city did not have the strength to hold out for long, that many of its troops and citizens had fallen in sallies, or were ill, or could barely wield their weapons due to exhaustion. The enemy cannons, in destroying the walls, were also killing people in the streets. Secret messengers were sent to the master; they returned safely: the master wrote that the Order was hiring troops and praying that Derpt be saved!

According to a contemporary Livonian historian, Ivan's chief voivode, Prince Pyotr Ivanovich Shuiskii, was a man with a virtuous, honorable and noble soul. After the mines had been dug and the gabions rolled right up to the walls, he ordered it be announced to the residents, to the beating of drums, that he would give them two days to consider the matter; on the third he would take the city by assault; Ivan formally promised them mercy, freedom of religion and the integrity of their ancient rights and laws. Everyone would be able to safely leave the city and safely return. The master and the citizens now unanimously told the bishop,

"So long as we have *a plate on the table and a spoon in our hand*,* we are prepared to die to defend our city if our resistance should be praiseworthy courage and not thoughtless audacity. But is it prudent to reject the tsar's magnanimous proposal when indeed we do not have the strength to resist him?"

Now the German troops also spoke up, requesting leave and an attestation as to their loyalty. Likewise did the priests of the Roman faith, fearing that stubbornness would aggravate the enemy. The bishop agreed. They wrote out the following conditions:

"1) the sovereign is to turn overgive to the bishop the monastery of Falkenau with the volosts belonging to it, and the house and garden in Derpt;

2) the Latin clergy and churches, with their properties, will be under his administration;

---

* [I.e., they would fight by all means available.]

3) court nobles who wish to be Russian subjects will peacefully manage their own castles and lands;

4) German soldiers will depart the city with their weapons and belongings;

5) for 12 days residents of Derpt will be free to go where they wish;

6) the Augsburg Confession will remain primary and without change;

7) the *German* master will direct all as before, retaining his rights and incomes;

8) merchants will be free to trade with Germany and Russia without duties;

9) no one is to be removed from the Derpt district to the Muscovite districts;

10) anyone wishing to move to another land may take his possessions or sell them;

11) citizens are to be exempt from billeting soldiers;

12) all crimes, even state crimes and those offending the majesty of the tsar, are to be adjudicated by the master's officials; and

13) new citizens are to swear allegiance to both the tsar and the master."

The prudent Shuiskii, having been granted full powers by Ivan, did not reject a single item. He was guided not only by humanitarianism, but also by politics, since charity, indulgence and a spirit of humility were needed to lessen the hatred of the Livonians towards Russia; thereby facilitating our conquest of their land.

When all these conditions had been approved by the victor and when all that remained was to affix the seals, the elder, Anton Tile, the virtuous burgomaster of Derpt, stepped forth from the silent circle of despondent officials,

"Prince and sovereign! Your Highness!" he said to the bishop. "If anyone thinks that Derpt can be saved by arms and battle, let him show himself! I shall join him and we shall die together for our homeland!"

The speech, manner, and voice of this elder produced a deep impression. The bishop responded,

"Worthy sir! None of us deserve to be called faint-hearted: we are yielding to necessity."

Derpt surrendered on 18 July. Wishing to do as much as possible for the unfortunates, Prince Shuiskii posted guards at the gates and ordered no Russians to be let into the city, so that its residents could pack up and leave peacefully. He also guarded them on the road and gave them guides to safe havens. He sent the bishop off to Falkenau with 200 crack Muscovite knights.

When everything had quieted down in the city, the master's deputies handed over the keys to the fortress to Shuiskii. He mounted his horse and formally entered the city. A young voivode rode in front holding a flag of peace; behind him came Shuiskii, surrounded by deputies and church canons. The sovereign's boyar cadets stood in the streets in two rows. The people were no longer afraid of the conquerors and looked on curiously at their peaceful, orderly progress; not even the women tried to hide.

The master brought Shuiskii a golden cup. After expressing his thanks, this wise prince said that his house and ear were open to all and that he had come to punish the bad and benefit the good. He kindly invited the Derpt officials and elders to dine with him, gave them a sumptuous feast in the castle and through this courteous treatment gained general popularity. The Russians acquired 552 cannons in Derpt as well as considerable wealth, both public and private, that had been left behind by those residents who had departed for Riga, Revel and Fellin.

The sovereign ratified the treaty concluded by his voivodes, but ordered Bishop Herman and the most distinguished Derpt officials to appear in Moscow. This formerly reigning bishop, now cursed in his homeland for imagined treachery, never returned from Russia and ended his days in sorrow after hearing that his friends and servants, accused of secret collaboration with the enemy, had been tortured and executed in Livonia. The rulers of the Order were attempting thereby to cover up their weakness and assure the people that a single act of treason was the cause of our success.

However, this cruelty did not hinder the progress of prudent power. The example of Derpt proved that Ivan could spare the vanquished. Shuiskii now wrote to all the Livonian municipal leaders demanding submission, using promises and threats; the fortresses of Wesenberg, Pirkel, Lais, Oberpahlen, Ringen (or Tushin), and Atsel surrendered to our voivodes, who everywhere let the Order's rulers go peacefully; they were content with residents' oaths of allegiance and did not touch their property.

They committed, however, everything in nonsubmissive districts to fire and sword, including Fellin, Revel, Wenden and Schwanenburg; they torched the outskirts of Wittenstein, ruled by the brave young knight Kaspar von Oldenbock. The Germans were defeated in the field near Wenden and Schwanenburg and two noted officials were captured.

In all the Russians took 20 towns, leaving necessary provisions and guard troops in each, and at the end of September they rode to their sovereign. He was in the Trinity Monastery and met them graciously and joyfully; he embraced them and praised them for their diligent service. He prayed with them, thanking God, and then rode to the town of Aleksandrovskaya, where he personally rewarded them with fur coats, goblets, and armor. He commanded them to choose any of the tsar's steeds, and also gave them rich estates. To the boyar cadets he gave land and real property in conquered Livonia so that they would more diligently guard it.

Prince Dmitrii Kurlyatev and Mikhailo Repnin, the new governors sent there from Moscow, were less fortunate: although they conquered the town of Kavelekht, torched Verpol [possibly Werpel] and defeated the Germans right in the suburbs of Revel, the master and the Riga archbishop's voivode Felkersam managed to gather more than 10,000 troops.

KETLER TAKES RINGEN

They laid siege to Ringen in the sight of our legions and captured its citadel despite the valor of its defender, the chief of the musketeers Rusin-Ignatiev, who with only 200 or 300 warriors held out for nearly five weeks, repelled two assaults and ultimately ran out of gunpowder.

Chapter Five

Ivan's voivodes excused themselves, citing the strength of the German camp and the exhaustion of their own troops, but boasted of the victory they achieved over the master's brother, Johann Ketler, whom they captured between Ringen and Derpt along with 260 Germans. But the master himself fell upon them, trampling Prince Repnin's unit and could have seized Derpt from us, where we had left few troops and whose notables had secretly summoned him. Fortunately for us, the exhausted Germans needed a rest. Their numbers had decreased to 6,000. Knowing that Moscow's commanders were expecting assistance and liked to fight in winter, the master pulled out at the end of October, inhumanely killing all the Russians he had captured in Ringen, and we occupied the city once more. The enemy was simultaneously harassing the Pskov district with raids from Luzha, Rezitsa and Walk: they torched the outskirts of Krasnyi, the monastery of St. Nikolai near Sebezh, and many villages.

In December, against Kurlyatev's and Repnin's desires, the sovereign sent to Livonia the valiant voivodes, the Princes Simeon Mikulinskii, Vasilii and Pyotr Serebryanyi, Ivan Sheremetev, Mikhail Morozov, Crown Prince Tokhtamysh, the Circassian princes, and a powerful army to march directly towards Riga, lay waste to the land and destroy the enemy in the field. When they were prepared to commence the bloodbath, they wrote to the master that the question of war or peace depended on him, that Ivan could still forgive them if the Germans would announce their submission.

There was no reply. On 17 February the Russians invaded Livonia. Starting from the town of Krasnyi they took an extent of 200 versts or more. They marched on Marienburg and met the Germans commanded by Felkersam near Tirsen. Only Prince Vasilii Serebryanyi and his unit were there. The enemy showed courage: the distinguished knights of the Order and officers of the archbishop of Riga stood in ranks. The valiant Felkersam and 400 Germans fell in this battle. The archbishop's chancellor and 13 of the best court nobles were among those captured, while the remainder were scattered.

> RUSSIANS LAY WASTE TO LIVONIA AND COURLAND

Prince Serebryanyi opened a safe route for our troops all the way to the sea. The winter was cruel. Since they were not busy laying siege to the large fortresses of Wenden and Riga, our voivodes attacked only the smaller towns. The Germans had pulled out of these. Only Schmilten did not surrender, so our Cossacks broke down its stone walls with crowbars and fought for a long time in the streets with the desperate enemy.

The Russians seized the cannons, bells and provisions, and incinerated everything they could not take with them. They laid waste to 11 towns in this manner. They stood three days beneath Riga, torched a large number of ships at the mouth of the Dvina, laid waste to its riverbanks, the coastal lands, and Courland as far as Prussia and Lithuania. Rich with booty and with an uncountable number of prisoners, they departed on 17 February for Opochka. They informed Ivan that his army was intact, but Livonia was in ashes.

POLISH, SWEDISH AND DANISH KINGS INTERCEDE FOR LIVONIA

Finally an intercessor appeared on behalf of this unhappy land. We had left King Augustus with a firm peace and an alliance with Russia against the khan. Because of this Lithuanian emissaries arrived in Moscow in March 1559 and began to talk of peace. Ivan desired that both powers rule uncontested that which they already controlled, but Augustus demanded Smolensk right off. Not only that: he told us not to fight Livonia, since it had supposedly been given him by the emperor and the German officials! Ivan ordered the emissaries to return, saying,

"I see that the king has changed his mind. Well, let it be as he wishes! The Livonians are Russia's ancient tributaries, not yours. I am punishing them for disloyalty, deceit, commercial crimes and the destruction of churches."

The emissaries departed. The sovereign did not even agree to conclude a new treaty with Livonia; he only promised not to violate the old one (in effect till 1562) if the king would give better justice to Russians who had been harmed by his subjects. In brief, it was clear that the Livonian war had resulted in a Lithuanian one. Augustus was not concerned with magnanimously saving the old, weak Order, but with seeing that its rich possessions were not handed over to Ivan, and if possible, to acquire them for himself.

This was a very natural desire, given the current states of the Order, Lithuania and Russia, and quite in accord with prudent policy, which would accuse this monarch of negligence if he did not employ all means possible to wrest Livonia from the tsar's hands. All that was required was resolve and firmness, qualities that Augustus lacked. He would go to war, and then want out; he would daringly conceive it beforehand, but then be afraid to swiftly draw his sword.

Another defender of the Order was much more indifferent, much less enthusiastic: old Gustav Vasa. He had tried in vain to resist power-hungry Russia through a union of the northern powers' forces. He had seen that Augustus and the master had not considered helping him in his war with Ivan, limiting themselves to empty assurances of their good will. Gustav now wrote to the tsar:

"I am not instructing you in your own affairs and I make no demand. But just to please Emperor Ferdinand, I implore you as a magnanimous neighbor, out of humanitarian compassion and for the general good of Christendom, to give peace to Livonia. I myself am unable to praise the sincere friendship and integrity of the Livonians: I know them from experience! If you wish, I will write to them that they should fall down at your feet with repentance and humility. Whether you stop the bloodshed or not, in any case I shall hold sacred our treaty with Russia and greatly esteem your friendship."

Ivan thanked Gustav for his kind intentions, explained the cause of the war, and said,

"If you have no particular desire to become involved in Lithuania's affairs, there is no need for you to write to the master. I myself will find a way to bring him to reason."

A third intermediary was King Frederik II of Denmark. It is known that Estonia was once one of his territories. Pressed by Ivan, and seeing that the Order could not save it, this land had sought the protection of Frederik's father, Christian III. Revel, all of Garriya and Virland [Wierland] expressed the desire to be his subjects once again. However, Christian, who was now old and near death, answered indifferently,

"I am having trouble ruling my own lands. How would it be prudent to seek new lands and do battle for them?"

However, he gave Estonia several thousand guldens, some cannons and appointed an embassy to go to Moscow, but then he died. His son was more power-hungry and more energetic and wished to restore this not insignificant district to Denmark. He wrote to the master, the bishop of Revel and the Estonian nobility, promising them not only intermediation, but also troops in the case of need. He gave his emissaries their instructions and ordered them to hasten to Moscow. For more than 40 years we had had no relations of any sort with this kingdom: Frederik I and Christian III considered an alliance with Russia as useless, although it had been highly valued by Christian II, who was a friend to Vasilii Ivanovich. Even commercial ties had been broken between Copenhagen and Novgorod.

Frederik informed Ivan, as a *kind and courteous neighbor*, of his accession to the throne and declared his fervent desire to be his friend and restore trade with us, which had been destroyed *by the confused situation of former times*. Frederik persuasively asked that Ivan not menace Estonia, which had formerly been a Danish district, *only temporarily entrusted to the master*, and that he graciously respect his (Frederik's) disinterested intercession and give peace to the Order. In the name of the tsar, Adashev told the emissaries,

"We have listened attentively to your speech. We have read the documents sent by the Russian sovereigns to Denmark, and those sent by Denmark's to Russia. We have seen their mutual affection, and we have seen that the subjects of both powers traded freely and profitably with each other. If the king wishes to renew this happy friendship, then we, too, are genuinely in favor of it. Yet we are surprised that he finds Danish territory in this land, which for 600 years now has belonged to Russia. Grand Prince Georgii Vladimirovich, called Yaroslav, conquered Livonia, founded

> IVAN APPROVES TRUCE WITH LIVONIA

Chapter Five

the city of Yuriev,* built a Greek [Orthodox] church there and imposed a tribute on the whole land, and since that time it has not been the possession of any other sovereigns. I know that its inhabitants, without Russia's consent, had been about to acknowledge two Danish kings, but my ancestors punished them with fire and sword for this and expelled the king's sons. They were punished a second time when we found out that the Livonians had secretly acknowledged the fictitious power of the Roman Kaiser** over them. If Frederik is unaware of this, then we shall command that you be shown the Order's old agreements with the Novgorod deputies: read them and consider the truth of what we have told you!

"There was a time when we were orphaned in our childhood and were unable to protect our rights: our enemies rejoiced, oppressing and harming Russia. The master and the Livonian bishops did not then want to pay us tribute. Even though they took it from the farmers and from the cities, they kept it for themselves." After describing their guilt, our sovereign continued,

"And so let not Frederik encroach on Estonia. Denmark and Norway are his lands; we know of no others. If he wishes to benefit Livonia, let him advise its master and bishops to appear in person before us in Moscow. Then, out of our special respect for the king, we will give them peace in accord with the honor and welfare of Russia. We are setting a period of time: Livonia may have peace for six months!"

The emissaries were handed letters of safe conduct addressed to the Livonian rulers in which it was stated that the tsar was *awarding* the Order a truce from May to November of 1559 and that the master would either come to Moscow to kowtow, or instead of himself, send high dignitaries to establish a permanent peace. For this respite, Livonia was in fact obliged not to King Frederik, but to the servitors of another, unsought-for benefactor: Khan Devlet-Girei. Ivan needed to pacify the Crimeans, and so as not to divide his forces, gave the Order peace for the time being, confident that Russia could always deal with this weak enemy.

---

* [Derpt, or Tartu.]
** [I.e., the Holy Roman Emperor.]

In 1558, Prince Vishnevetskii was dispatched to do battle with the Taurid. He reached the mouth of the Dnieper without encountering a single Tatar in the field: Devlet-Girei and all his uluses were sitting on their peninsula waiting for the Russians. Vishnevetskii left the valiant secretary Rzhevskii behind with the Cossacks and returned to Moscow.

Meanwhile, the khan wished to find out what was happening in the Kazan lands and sent some light detachments to the banks of the Volga; it was wiped out by the highland inhabitants and Cossacks. For a long time he did not dare to do anything significant, but then he heard of the Livonian war and believed the false information that all our forces were engaged there – that Russia was defenseless and that Ivan himself was wrestling with a terrible enemy on the distant shores of the Baltic. Devlet-Girei took heart and enticed many Nogai to join him, gathering, it is written, up to 100,000 cavalry. That winter (December 1558) he ordered his son Mahmet-Girei to proceed to Ryazan, the uhlan Mahmet to Tula and the Nogai and the Shirinskie princes to Koshira.

> CRIMEANS ATTACK

These troops had reached the river Mecha when the crown prince heard from prisoners that Ivan was in Moscow and that only a small part of our army was in Livonia. He was amazed and inquired as to the whereabouts of bold Prince Vishnevetskii and brave Ivan Sheremetev. Mahmet-Girei learned that the former was in Belyov, the latter in Ryazan and that Prince Mikhailo Vorotynskii was stationed in Tula with powerful legions.

Mahmet-Girei did not dare to proceed further: pursued by fear alone, he fled homewards, losing horses and even riders from exhaustion. Prince Vorotynskii pursued him to Oskol past their dead bodies, but was unable to overtake him. Meanwhile the Don Cossacks, taking advantage of the absence of the Crimean army, defeated near Perekop the Nogai uluses that had left their Khan Islam for Devlet-Girei. The Cossacks captured 15,000 men, as well as horses.

So that the khan would not have time to come to his senses, Ivan ordered Prince Vishnevetskii to go to the Don with 5,000 light troops, build boats, sail to Azov, and threaten the

Taurid with attacks from that direction. Now the okolnichii Danilo Adashev, known for his valor, departed Moscow for the Dnieper with a unit of boyar cadets, Cossacks and musketeers to deliver a painful blow to the enemy, the nature of which would depend on circumstances.

Vishnevetskii had some insignificant successes: he wiped out several hundred Crimeans who were once again trying to force their way to Kazan, but Danilo Adashev, the young, worthy brother of the sovereign's favorite, astonished his contemporaries with his skill and daring. Near Kremenchug with 8,000 troops he boarded boats which he had built in these then unpopulated places and laid waste to the land as far as the mouth of the Dnieper. He also seized two ships on the sea and began harassing the Taurid. He created indescribable terror in all the uluses, where they cried,

> RUSSIAN ASSAULT ON THE TAURID

"Russians! Russians! And the tsar is with them!"

These people fled to the mountains and hid in the bush. Quaking with fear, the khan summoned his warriors, but saw only fugitives. For more than two weeks, Adashev was free to terrorize the western part of the peninsula, burning yurts, seizing herds, capturing people and freeing Russian and Lithuanian prisoners. After filling his boats with loot, he triumphantly returned to Ochakov. There were Turks among the prisoners taken from the ships and the uluses, whom Adashev sent to the pashas of Ochakov after ordering them to say that the tsar was fighting the land of his malefactor, Devlet-Girei, and not the sultan, with whom he wished always to be a friend. The pashas came out to him with gifts, praising his valor and Ivan's good will towards the sultan.

Meanwhile, the khan had come to his senses: he learned of his enemy's scant forces and chased along the shore after Adashev, who slowly sailed up the Dnieper, shooting at the Tatars. He got past the rapids and halted on Monastery Island, prepared for battle. But Devlet-Girei, fearing new humiliations, turned back, full of pusillanimous malice.

News of the young knight's happy exploit was delivered to Moscow by his comrade-in-arms, Prince Thedor

Khvorostin. Not just the sovereign, but the whole populace was greatly pleased and the metropolitan held a service of thanksgiving. Adashev's report was read triumphantly, and there was rejoicing that he had opened a path for us into the bowels of this *dark* realm where *Russian sabers had not hitherto tasted infidel blood.* They recalled that Christianity had once flourished there, and that in fact it was there that St. Vladimir had acknowledged the True God.

It was believed that Ivan intended to remain in the Taurid and that the Cross would once again shine on the banks of the Salgir.* The tsar now wished to reform our old, timid method of warfare against these indefatigable brigands and go on the offensive. He sent gold medals to Adashev and his comrades and ordered him to come consult with him. But the Livonian war now flared up worse than before and saved the Taurid. Ivan left only the Nogai and the Cossacks to threaten the khan and in response to the khan's new peace proposal wrote to him,

"You see now that war with Russia is no longer a matter of pure profit. We know the way to your land both by steppe and by sea. Stop talking nonsense and show your genuine love of peace by your actions. Then we will be friends."

The tsar had eager servitors in the south: the Circassian princes, in addition to the Nogai serving Prince Islam, a loyal ally of Russia, and the Don Cossacks. They requested a commander from us in order to fight the Taurid, and church pastors to enlighten their whole land with the teachings of the gospel. Both wishes were immediately fulfilled. The sovereign sent hearty Vishnevetskii to them and a great number of priests, who in the bush and on the mountain slopes of the Caucasus, reinvigorated the ancient Christianity there.

Since he had given the Order a truce out of charity, as it were, the sovereign did not think that the Livonians would break it. He had pulled the greater part of his army out of Estonia and was waiting for word from the master. But Ketler was silent, convinced that one must either beat the Russians or belong to them, and so he resolved to travel not to Moscow, but Krakow to

---

* [A river on the Crimean peninsula that flows to the northeast.]

persuade Augustus to take an active and ardent role in the war on whatever conditions he could get, even though they might be dangerous to the very independence of the Order, for in its extremity, Livonia would rather be subordinate to Poland than Russia, which had always been hostile to it.

The general opinion of the prestige of the Order's master was still intact. Young Ketler, who had been endowed with good looks, intelligence, eloquence, and noble personal qualities, appeared before Augustus with a humble majesty, surrounded by many noted officials. He powerfully depicted Livonia's predicament, the danger to Poland itself and Ivan's frightening schemes. He showed the king the inevitability of war as well as the likelihood of success. He did not deprecate the Russian's huge numbers, but rather spoke scornfully of our military skill.

Augustus wanted to know the opinion of the Sejm: the Polish nobles, touched by the master's eloquence, wanted to draw the sword at once, but the Lithuanians had a better appreciation of Russia's strength, and advised first using all other means to protect the Order, such as persuasive intercession, insistent demands and threats, backed up by a military buildup. Finally they signed a treaty. As an earnest, the master and the archbishop of Riga gave the king the fortresses of Marienhausen, Luban, Asherat [probably Ascheraden], Düneburg, Rositten and Lutsen with the stipulation that they pay the king 700,000 guldens at the conclusion of the war. The king promised to support Livonia with all his forces, to restore its national integrity and to fraternally share future conquests in Russia with the Order.

> LIVONIA ALLIED WITH AUGUSTUS

Ketler returned to Livonia with this document as with a trophy; he heartened the officials and the citizens; he vouched for the king's reliability and guaranteed success. He demanded only ardor and courage from genuine sons of the homeland. Hope shone in their hearts. They convinced themselves of Lithuania's puissance and recalled its glorious battle of Dnieprovsk. They sought new *Konstantin Ostrozhskiis*[*] from amongst Augustus' renowned voivodes.

---

[*] [Konstantin Ivanovich Ostrozhskii, 1460-1530, was hetman (highest ranking military officer) of Lithuania.]

"We must show them the path to victory," said Ketler. "He who requests collaboration, must himself act, be first to draw the sword and induce his friends to take the field with him."

Duke Christof of Mecklenburg, the bishop of Riga's coadjutor, brought a new contingent of mercenaries from Germany. The imperial Sejm promised Ketler 100,000 gold pieces. The Duke of Prussia, the Revel master and several ardent citizens loaned him a considerable sum: a Rigan shopkeeper loaned him 30,000 marks on account. Rich emigrants from Derpt wished to flee to Germany with their possessions: gold and silver was taken from them for the Order's treasury.

THE MASTER VIOLATES TRUCE

In this manner the master doubled the number of his troops. Knowing that there were few Russians in Livonia, he departed Wenden in autumn and in terrible mud a month before the truce period designated in the treaty document was due to expire. Suddenly appearing near Derpt, he trounced the careless voivode, Zakharii Pleshcheev, killing more than 1,000 Russians on the spot. Ivan seemed justified in considering this to be new perfidy.

He entrusted vengeance to his most distinguished voivodes: the Princes Ivan Mstislavskii, Pyotr Shuiskii and Vasilii Serebryanyi, who hastened with the best boyar cadets from Moscow and Novgorod to save that part of Livonia that we had conquered. Bad roads prevented a speedy march, and the enemy might have had significant success in this land where all the inhabitants were on his side and prepared to cast off the Russian yoke, had not the valor and intelligence of two of our officials nullified the master's victory.

Ketler immediately headed for Derpt. The local voivode, the boyar Prince Andrei Kavtyrev-Rostovskii, managed to take measures: he locked up the dangerous citizens in the city hall, greeted the Germans with a powerful barrage, and made a successful sally. The master stood off a verst from the city for 10 days, firing his cannons, but doing no harm to the besieged. Frosts, snow storms, and bad food caused grumbling in his camp: the German mercenaries were not fond of such hardships.

Ketler had to decide between a prolonged winter siege and an assault – neither seemed prudent to him. The strong walls had many embrasures and enclosed a powerful complement of troops and a skilled voivode, and the [confined] citizens were unable to communicate with the besiegers or help them towards victory. The Russians' numbers in the field were increasing daily; they took the Germans in the rear and appeared to be trying to encircle them. The master was obliged to withdraw from Derpt, but wished to at least take Lais, where we had 400 troops under Koshkarov, the intrepid chief of musketeers. The Germans set up gabions and broke down the walls, but could not break into the citadel.

GLORIOUS DEFENSE OF LAIS

The Russians so astounded them with their desperate resistance, that Ketler, after making heated assaults for two days, pulled back to Wenden as if vanquished, with significant casualties and his troops so despondent that for a long time he lacked the means to do anything consequential. When one considers that it was not the numbers of participants, but their valor, which determined the outcome, this amazing defense of Lais was one of the most brilliant military operations of ancient or modern times. Prince Andrei Rostovskii sent Koshkarov himself to report on the Germans' flight. The sovereign expressed extreme gratitude to him and the others for saving our honor, military reputation and the city entrusted to them.

1560

It is probable that the master, who had renewed the bloodshed with such haste and effort, was expecting Augustus, in accordance with their agreement, to make some sort of move against Russia. The king indeed got his army ready, but that is all. He sent his secretary, Volodkovich, to Moscow with a letter in which he firmly demanded that Ivan pull his troops out of Livonia and return all the cities he had taken.

"Otherwise," he wrote, "I shall be obliged to defend my possession with armed force, since the master has formally sworn allegiance to the Grand Duchy of Lithuania. Russia's supposed

THREATS FROM AUGUSTUS

right to Livonia is a new invention: neither your father, nor your grandfather, nor you yourself have ever claimed this before now."

Volodkovich tried orally to convince Moscow's boyars to facilitate peace, imparting to them the secret that the Polish nobles were ready to depose their king if he failed to stand up for Livonia. Ivan ordered Volodkovich to be shown the treaty with the master regarding Derpt's tribute, saying,

"There is our right!" On the advice of his boyars, he replied to Augustus,

"To whom Livonia belongs is known not only to God and every sovereign, but also to its own people,. While choosing its German masters and clergymen with our knowledge and consent, it has always paid tribute to Russia. Your demands are ridiculous and improper. I know that the master rode to Lithuania and illegally handed over some fortresses to you. If you want peace, then remove all your governors and stop supporting these traitors, whose fate must depend on our mercy. Remember that honor obliges sovereigns to act and speak truthfully. I have genuinely wanted an alliance with you against the infidel and even now I am not refusing to conclude one. I *expect* emissaries and more reasonable proposals from you."

But Ivan *expected* war. It only remained to discover who would start it.

> HERALD FROM
> THE EMPEROR

But now a herald arrived in Moscow from Vienna, from Kaiser Ferdinand, who up till now had had no relations with Russia. The Kaiser wrote to Ivan that he desired his friendship and requested he not do battle with Livonia, an imperial district. The letter was respectful and flattering, but the sovereign dryly replied to Ferdinand that if he, like Maximilian and Charles V, really wanted Russia's friendship, then it would be necessary to communicate with him through emissaries, distinguished people, since important matters cannot be arbitrated by heralds. He said not another word, although the emperor, as the legitimate protector of Livonia, had more right than Lithuania or Denmark to stand up for it.

Chapter Five

Meanwhile, Livonia was ablaze. With fire and sword, the Russians charged out of Derpt after the fleeing Ketler to punish his perfidy. They came up to Tarvastu, where old Master Fürstenberg was to be found, crushed him in a sally he made, burned the suburbs and defeated the Germans at Fellin as well. Moscow's chief voivodes, the Princes Mstislavskii, Shuiskii and Serebryanyi, laid waste to the whole country from Lake Pskov to the Gulf of Riga. In the uezds of Wenden and Wolmar, many places had remained intact until this new attack, which their miserable inhabitants had not expected.

> NEW DEVASTATION OF LIVONIA

After seeking the master and battles in the field in vain, our voivodes arrived at Marienburg. This town was then one of the most beautiful in Livonia; it was on an island in the middle of a large lake and seemed inaccessible in summertime, but winter opened the way to it, and the Russians rolled up their heavy artillery under the command of the boyar Mikhailo Morozov, who had gained fame in the siege of Kazan. In a few hours, they had smashed its walls to their foundations. The Germans prudently surrendered, but because of this, their chief, Commander Siburg perished in prison in Kirchholm, since the master wanted the Order's officials to defend their fortresses, as Uxkil and Koshkarov had done.

> CAPTURE OF MARIENBURG

Our voivodes repaired the walls and left a strong force in Marienburg, then returned to Pskov and received gold medals from their sovereign. In the spring, the Russians once more marched out of Derpt and into Estonia. They lured the Germans out of Werpel and wiped them out to the last man in an ambush. Freebooters from Pskov, finding nothing in the villages, looked for farmers in the woods. They chased them down in droves, in order to sell them in Russia.

Ivan, however, foreseeing inevitable war with Lithuania, wished to deal with the Order as quickly as possible. At the end of winter, he sent another army under Prince Andrei Kurbskii to Derpt. Wishing to express

> PRINCE KURBSKII'S VICTORIES

his special faith in him, Ivan summoned him to his bedchamber, where he enumerated all the distinguished deeds of this courageous man, saying,

"I must either ride to Livonia myself, or instead send a seasoned voivode, bold and hearty, but also prudent. I choose you, my favorite! Go forth and conquer!"

Ivan knew how to charm his eager servitors: Kurbskii delightedly kissed his sovereign's hand. The young sovereign promised his lasting favor; the young boyar lifelong diligence. Neither kept his word, which was unfortunate for both of them and for Russia. Kurbskii's assistant was the renowned Danilo Adashev.

At the end of May they left Derpt for White Rock, or Wittenstein, and took the bishop of Revel's strong castle, Fegefeer. They laid waste to the very wealthy district of Koskul, where there were a great number of knights' beautiful country estates, and captured a detachment of Germans close by Wittenstein. From prisoners they learned that former master Fürstenberg, with nine legions of cavalry and infantry was positioned eight miles from the city on the other side of a mucky swamp.

After sending a baggage train to Derpt loaded with booty, they decided to march against him with 5,000 crack, light troops. The Russians spent a whole day stuck in the swamp, and if Fürstenberg had attacked them during this period, he could have utterly wiped them out with a small number of troops, but he happened to be awaiting the enemy on a flat, broad field 10 versts from there. The sun set; the Russians let their horses rest and proceeded silently in the bright, very clear night such as occur in summer only in coastal areas. They caught sight of the Germans prepared for battle and engaged them at midnight. The powerful barrage lasted about two hours; we had the advantage in that we were facing the enemy's fires and could aim better. Kurbskii had left his reserve troops behind.

The time was ripe: the Russians charged forward, smashing the Germans and pursuing them about six versts to a deep river, where the bridge collapsed beneath the fugitives. Fürstenberg saved himself, along with a few others; some drowned, the rest fell from our swords or surrendered. At sunrise, Kurbskii returned to the master's camp, where he captured his entire baggage train and took 170 ranking prisoners to Derpt. In the next two months this voivode gained another six or seven victories, the most important being Fellin. Fürstenberg was guarding this fortress when he saw several hundred Tatar horsemen beneath its walls. He emerged with some troops, but fell into a trap and barely managed to gallop away on a fast steed, leaving many knights dead on the battlefield.

At this time, however, as Ivan's strong hand was throttling weak Livonia, Heaven was preparing a terrible change of fate for him and for Russia.

For 13 years he had enjoyed complete family happiness based on love for his tender and virtuous wife. Anastasiya had given birth to another son, Theodor, and a daughter, Evdokiya. The mother was in the bloom of youth and health when in July 1560 she contracted a severe illness that was amplified by fear. In dry weather during a strong wind, the Arbat* caught fire. Thick smoke and burning embers were carried to the Kremlin.

> DEATH OF
> TSARITA ANASTASIYA

The tsar took the sick Anastasiya to the village of Kolomenskoe. While putting out the fire, he was exposed to great danger: while standing against a wind filled with sparks, his intrepidity provoked such great fervor among the dignitaries that the court nobles and boyars rushed into the flames, broke down buildings, brought water and climbed up on roofs.

The fire revived several times and required a costly battle: many people lost their lives or were severely injured. Distraught by fear, the tsaritsa grew worse. Skilled doctors had no success, and, to the despair of her husband, Anastasiya passed away on 7 August in the fifth hour of the day. Never had common grief been expressed so touchingly and powerfully! Not just the court, but all Moscow came to bury this *first*, beloved tsaritsa. When her body was brought to the Devichii Voznesenskii Monastery, the people would not make way either for the clergy or the nobility as they crowded the streets leading to the grave.

---

* [Old Moscow street, originally home to numerous craftsmen.]

Everyone wept, and all the inconsolable poor and lowly called her *mother*. An attempt was made to distribute the alms customary in these circumstances, but people would not accept them, and turned down all other comfort on this sad day. Ivan walked behind the casket; his brothers – the Princes Yurii and Vladimir Andreevich – and Aleksandr, the young ruler of Kazan, led him by the hand. He groaned and broke down. Only the metropolitan, who was weeping himself, dared remind him of a Christian's fortitude. They were as yet unaware that Anastasiya was taking their good years with her to the grave.

This marked the end of happy days for Ivan and for Russia, for he lost not only his wife, but his virtue as well, as we shall see in the next chapter.

CHAPTER VI

IVAN CHANGES FOR THE WORSE.

1560-1564

Changes in Ivan. Slander against Adashev and Silvestr. Trial. Silvestr imprisoned. Death of Adashev. Beginnings of evil. New favorites. First executions. Livonian war. Bel's courage. Fellin taken. Words of the ruler of Kazan. End of the [German] Order. Negotiations with Sweden. War with Lithuania. Ivan's second marriage. Capture of Polotsk. Birth of Crown Prince Vasilii. Ivan's triumph. Death of the crown prince. Crimean affairs. The sultan's scheme. Events in Livonia. Truce with Sweden. Depravity of Ivan's wife. Death of Prince Yurii. Ivan's sister-in-law and Prince Vladimir's mother take vows. Death of Makarii. Composition of the Lives of the Saints and the Book of Degrees. Establishment of a printing house. Publication of Bible in Ostrog. Archiepiscopate of Polotsk. White klobuk [cylindrical head-gear] for the metropolitans. Athanasii ordained as metropolitan.

We now embark on a description of a terrible change in the tsar's soul and in the fate of the realm.

<small>CHANGES IN IVAN
1560-1561</small>

Both his Russian contemporaries and foreigners then in Moscow portray the young, 30-year-old monarch as an example of a devout and wise ruler, eager for his country's glory and good fortune. They expressed this as follows:

"It is Ivan's custom to keep himself pure before God. In the cathedral or in solitary prayers, in the boyars' council or among the people, he has but one sentiment: *may I rule as the Most High has instructed his anointed sovereign!* Ever on his mind were honest judgment, security for all, the general integrity of the realm entrusted to him, the triumph of the Faith and liberty for Christians.

Burdened by affairs, he knew no other solace than a peaceful conscience and the satisfaction of performing his duty. He did not care for the customary aloofness of monarchs; he was kind to the nobles and the people. He rewarded each according to his merit and eradicated poverty through generosity and evil by good example. On the Day of Judgment this tsar, when summoned forth by God, wished to hear the voice of grace: *you are a just tsar!* and to reply with feeling,

'It is I and the people whom you gave to me!'"*

Praising him no less were foreign observers, Englishmen who had come to Russia for trade.

"Ivan," they write, "eclipsed his forebears both in power and virtue. He has many enemies, but he pacifies them. Lithuania, Poland, Sweden, Denmark, Livonia, the Crimea and the Nogai all fear the Russian name. In his relations with his subjects he is surprisingly indulgent and courteous. He loves to talk with them and often gives them dinners at the palace, but he also knows how to be imperious. He says to a boyar: go! and the boyar runs; he expresses his irritation to a boyar and the boyar is in despair and hides himself in miserable solitude, letting his hair grow until the tsar shows him forgiveness. In brief, there is no people in Europe more devoted than the Russians to their sovereign, whom they fear and love equally. Constantly ready to hear complaints and to render assistance, Ivan is involved in everything and decides everything. Affairs do not bore him, nor does he delight in hunting or music; he is only concerned with two questions: how to serve God and how to destroy Russia's enemies!"

How is it possible that a sovereign so beloved and revered could plummet from the heights of goodness, happiness and glory into the abyss of monstrous tyranny? Yet the evidence of good and evil are equally convincing and incontrovertible. It remains for us to show the surprising phenomena accompanying his gradual change.

---

* [The Russian Orthodox priest Fr. Hermogen Holste has been kind enough to supply some much-needed context here. He writes that this passage is a slightly-altered reference to Hebrews 2:13: "Behold I and the children which God hath given me", which is itself a reference to Isaiah 8:18. The idea being conveyed is the profound sense of boldness with which the speaker takes responsibility before God for those whom He has entrusted to his care.]

Chapter Six

History does not resolve the question of man's moral freedom, but it alludes to it in its judgment of deeds and personalities, illuminating one and the other firstly through people's natural qualities and secondly through the operation of circumstances and influences on the soul. Ivan was born with fiery passions, a powerful imagination and with an intellect more acute than firm or well-founded. A bad upbringing spoiled his natural tendencies, leaving to religion alone the ability to improve him, since even the most audacious of the tsar's corrupters did not dare to interfere with this sense of the sacred. In these extraordinary circumstances, friends of virtue, patriots, were able to touch, to strike his heart with salutary terror; they tore the youth away from the snares of voluptuousness and, with the help of the gentle and devout Anastasiya, enticed him onto the path of virtue.

The unfortunate aftermath of Ivan's illness destroyed this excellent alliance, enfeebled the power of friendship and set the stage for change. The sovereign had come of age, when passions ripen along with the mind, and in one's mature years false pride operates even more powerfully. Although Ivan's trust in his mentors' intellects did not lessen, his confidence in himself kept growing. Grateful to them for their sage advice, he stopped feeling the necessity of [their] further guidance and felt the burden of restraint even more when they failed to change their old habits and spoke boldly and decisively on all occasions without giving any thought to indulging his human weaknesses. Such frankness seemed to him to be improper rudeness, and offensive to a monarch. For example, Adashev and Silvestr did not approve the Lithuanian war, insisting that they must first eradicate the infidel and evil foes of Russia and Christ; that although not of the Greek persuasion, Lithuanians were still Christians and no danger to us; and that God only blesses those just wars that are necessary for the integrity and liberty of a nation.

The court was full of men devoted to these two favorites, but Anastasiya's brother did not like them, nor did the many usual envious people who could not bear someone higher than themselves. These were not napping; they assessed Ivan's disposition and insinuated to him that Silvestr and Adashev were cunning hypocrites preaching heavenly virtue while desirous of worldly gain. These two loomed large before the throne and did not let the people see the tsar. They seemingly wanted to make the successes and glory of his reign their own, but at the same time they hindered these by counseling the tsar to be temperate in good fortune. Supposedly they inwardly feared these successes, believing that an abundance of praise might give him a justified feeling of majesty that would imperil their ambitions. It was asked,

"Who are these people, who dare to prescribe rules for our great and wise tsar, not only in matters of state, but also in domestic and family affairs, even in his way of life? They dare to instruct him in how to treat his wife, and even in how much to eat and drink."

Silvestr, the preceptor of Ivan's conscience, always demanded of him restraint and moderation in physical pleasures, for which the young monarch had a strong propensity. Ivan did not restrain this malignant gossip, for he had tired of his favorites' excessively severe moral teachings and wanted freedom. He did not contemplate abandoning virtue – he only wanted to escape these instructors and show that he could manage without them. There were moments when his fiery temperament overflowed with immoderate words and threats. It is written that soon after the conquest of Kazan, he was angry at a particular voivode and told the nobles,

"I no longer fear you now!"

Yet the magnanimity he evinced after his illness put hearts at ease. He spent 13 flourishing years in the diligent fulfillment of his sacred monarchical duties, which seemed to testify to his immutable love of the good. Although the sovereign's feelings towards his favorites had now changed, his principles had not noticeably altered. Decorum ruled in the Kremlin palace, diligence and frank candor in the Duma. It was only in ambiguous matters, where truth or goodness are not obvious, that Ivan liked to contradict his advisors. This situation obtained until the spring of 1560.

At this point the tsar's coolness towards Adashev and Silvestr became so obvious that they perceived they must leave the court. Up till now the former had occupied the most important position in the Duma, and was always employed in negotiations with the European powers. He wished to continue to serve the tsar in another capacity: he received the rank of voivode and proceeded to Livonia, while Silvestr, out of the pureness of his heart, gave the sovereign his blessing and retired to a wilderness monastery. Their friends felt abandoned, while their enemies triumphed, praising the tsar and saying,

"Now you are a true autocrat, anointed by God. You alone rule the land. You have opened your eyes and now masterfully behold your entire realm!"

His deposed favorites, however, still seemed intimidating to him. Despite his sovereign's evident lack of favor, Adashev was honored in the army; even the citizens of Livonia manifested marked respect for him. Everyone deferred to his intellect and virtue. Not to be outdone, Silvestr, now a humble monk, radiated Christian virtues in the wilderness. The monks were amazed to see in him an example of piety, love and meekness. Since the tsar might learn about this, repent and restore the exiles, it would be necessary [for the slanderers] to deliver a blow that would make the sovereign so unjust, so at fault with respect to these men that he would not then be able to even consider a genuine reconciliation with them. The death of the tsaritsa provided the opportunity.

Ivan was torn up by grief. Everyone around him wept – either out of genuine compassion or to ingratiate themselves with the sorrowing tsar. In some of those tears vile calumny was hidden behind a mask of concern and love, supposedly caused by the discovery of an unheard of evil.

SLANDER AGAINST ADASHEV AND SILVESTR

"Sovereign!" they said to Ivan. "You are in despair, and so is Russia while these two miscreants triumph. Silvestr and Adashev destroyed your virtuous princess. They were her secret enemies and *sorcerers*, for without sorcery they would not have been able to control your mind for so long."

These people presented evidence that did not convince even the most gullible, but the sovereign knew that at the time of her illness she had not liked either Silvestr or Adashev, and he believed they had not liked her either. He swallowed the slander, perhaps wishing to vindicate his disfavor towards them. Even if there were no reliable evidence of their maleficence, there was at least the suspicion. Informed of this denunciation, the exiles wrote the tsar requested a trial with the opportunity to confront their accusers. Their enemies did not want this and argued before the tsar that the two were like venomous basilisks who might again enchant him with a single glance and that these favorites of the people, the army and the citizenry would incite a mutiny, and fear would seal the lips of their accusers. The sovereign ordered the accused to be tried in absentia. Accordingly, the metropolitan, the bishops, the boyars and many other ecclesiastical and lay officials assembled at the palace. Numbered among the judges were the cunning monks Vassian Beskii and Misail Sukin, Silvestr's chief enemies. They reckoned not just one, but many offenses, which were expounded by Ivan himself in a letter to Prince Kurbskii.

TRIAL

"For the salvation of my soul," wrote the tsar, "I became close to the priest Silvestr in hopes that by his rank and reason he might help me towards the Good, but this sly hypocrite seduced me with sweet words while thinking only of worldly power. He befriended Adashev in order to rule the realm without the tsar, whom they despised. They once again instilled a spirit of willfulness in the boyars; they distributed towns and volosts to their confederates. They seated whomever they wished in the Duma; they filled every position with their toadies.

"I became a slave on the throne. How can I describe what I endured in these days of shame and abasement? With a handful of warriors they dragged their tsar across the perilous territory of the enemy (Kazan), careless of his health and life. They concocted childish terrors to frighten my soul; they ordered me to rise above human nature. They forbade me to travel to holy monasteries or to punish Germans . . . To these illegitimacies they conjoined treachery: when I was suffering from a serious illness, they forgot their loyalty and their oath. In a rapture of despotism they intended to bypass my son and get themselves a different tsar.

"Neither touched nor rectified by our magnanimity, in the cruelty of their hearts, how were they going to make up for this? It would be by new outrages: they hated and disparaged Princess

Chapter Six

Anastasiya and favored Prince Vladimir Andreevich in all things. Is it so surprising that I, now in my majority, decided at last to cease being a child and to cast down the yoke imposed on my reign by this sly priest and this ungrateful lackey of Aleksii? {etc.}"

We note that Ivan does not blame them for Anastasiya's death and thereby gives the lie to this ridiculous accusation. The rest of the charges are either dubious or imprudent coming from the lips of this 30 year old autocrat. By his admission that he had been a slave, he discloses the secret of his pitiable weakness. Adashev and Silvestr may have been blinded as people by their ambition, but by these intemperate accusations, the sovereign must yield to them a more favorable reputation in the history of his reign. We are surprised how he could now rule without them, and if it was not Ivan, but his favorites who governed Russia from 1547 to 1560, then the happiness of the tsar and his subjects would have required these virtuous men not to abandon the helm of state – it is better to involuntarily do good than to willfully do evil.

In wishing to blame them, Ivan slanders himself. It is far more likely that he sincerely loved good and recognized its attraction, but that, finally, lured by passions merely restrained but not eradicated, he betrayed those principles of magnanimity that had been imparted to him by these wise preceptors. It would have been easier to change [for the worse] than to restrain himself for such a long time, but who else would do this? An autocratic sovereign is always able to break such an imaginary chain of servitude with a single word. As an advisor, Adashev had not approved of the Lithuanian war, but served Ivan as a subject, as a minister and as a warrior, i.e., as a diligent instrument for the war's success. Therefore the sovereign *was in command* and, contrary to his complaint, was not a slave of his favorites.

After hearing the indictment against Adashev and Silvestr, some of the judges declared that the malefactors were guilty and deserving of punishment. Others, lowering their eyes, were silent. The aged metropolitan Makarii, approaching death and holding the rank of archpriest, now resolved to speak the truth. He told the tsar that he must summon and hear the defendants. All the nobles of good conscience concurred in this opinion, but the *throng of assassins*, as Kurbskii expresses it, cried out against this, maintaining that people convicted in the opinion of a wise and gracious sovereign could not present any sort of legitimate justification, that their presence and machinations would be dangerous and that the tranquility of the tsar and the country demanded the immediate resolution of this important matter. And so the court decided the defendants were guilty. All that remained was to determine the punishment, and the tsar, still wishing to appear merciful, tempered it.

SILVESTR IMPRISONED	Silvestr was sent to a wilderness island in the White Sea, to the secluded Solovetskaya Cloister, while Adashev was ordered to live in recently pacified Fellin, whose capture he had facilitated with his wits and with the measures he had taken. But his firmness and calmness irritated his malicious persecutors. He was confined in Derpt, where he died of a fever two
DEATH OF ADASHEV	

months later, to the delight of his enemies, who told the tsar that *the convicted traitor died of his own venom*.

He was a man unforgettable in our history, an ornament to the age and to humanity, according to the credible tales of his friends, for this distinguished favorite had arisen with the tsar's virtue and also perished with it. He was a surprising phenomenon in the circumstances in Russia at that time, explainable only by his boundless sincere love of the good, the divine inspiration of which illuminates natural intelligence in [times] of darkest ignorance and guides people to greatness better than science or learned wisdom. Indebted to Ivan's favor for some of his wealth, he knew only the luxury of good deeds; he fed the lowly and maintained 10 lepers in his household. He bathed them with his own hands, diligently fulfilling his Christian duty and was ever mindful of human misery.

BEGINNINGS OF EVIL	And so began the evil. The two chief agents of the blessed period of Ivan's reign were no longer present, but their thought, principles

and friends remained. Having gotten rid of Adashev, it was necessary for the slanderers to destroy his spirit and his virtues, which were perilous for them and troublesome for the sovereign in these new circumstances. Oaths were demanded of all the boyars and distinguished people that they not take the part of these exiled and punished *traitors* and be loyal to the sovereign. They swore, some joyfully, others sorrowfully, guessing the consequences, which immediately became apparent. All that previously had seemed meritorious and able to please the sovereign now became reprehensible and reminiscent of Adashev and Silvestr. These courtiers asked Ivan,

"Must you always weep for your wife? You will find another, equally charming. But you will injure your priceless health with this intemperate grief. God and the people demand that you seek temporal comfort for your temporal grief."

Ivan had sincerely loved his wife, but he had a lightness of temperament that did not square with his profound grief. Without anger, he heeded his comforters and eight days after Anastasiya's death the metropolitan, the prelates and the boyars formally proposed that he seek another bride: the laws of decorum were not strict at this time. In memory of the deceased, Ivan distributed several thousand rubles to churches and for the poor, and sent rich alms to Jerusalem and Greece. Then on 18 August he announced that he intended to marry the Polish king's sister.

The weeping in the palace now ceased. The tsar began to be amused, first with pleasant conversation and jokes, soon with happy feasting. People reminded one another that wine brings joy to the heart; they laughed at the old habit of moderation and called fasting hypocritical. The palace now seemed too confining for these noisy gatherings, so the young princes, Ivan's brother Yurii and Aleksandr, the ruler of Kazan were now invited to private homes. New amusements were invented daily, festivities in which sobriety and even dignity and decency were considered improper.

Many boyars and officials were unable to quickly change their habits: they would sit at the merry tables with clouded faces, avoiding their cups, not drinking, and sighing. They were ridiculed and belittled, and wine was poured over their heads. Distinguished among the sovereign's new favorites were the boyars Aleksei Basmanov, his

| NEW FAVORITES |

son, the royal carver Thedor, Prince Athanasii Vyazemskii, Vasilii Gryaznoi and Malyuta Skuratov-Belskii, who were ready to do anything to satisfy their own ambitions. Formerly they had been lost behind a mask of morality amongst the palace regulars, but now they came forward and through their sympathy for evil stole into Ivan's soul.

He found them pleasant due to their frivolity, artificial gaiety and a boastful eagerness to fulfill and even anticipate his desires as if they were divine, without any consideration of those other principles that restrain both good rulers and their good servitors, the former in their desires, the latter in the fulfillment thereof. Ivan's old friends had loved their sovereign and virtue, too; the new ones only loved the sovereign, and therefore seemed more obliging to him.

They made an arrangement with two or three monks who had earned Ivan's trust. These were sly and cunning men who reassured the tsar's fearful conscience with indulgent teachings and seemed by their presence to vindicate his noisy and scandalous feasts. Here Kurbskii names in particular Levkii, archimandrite of the Chudovskii Monastery, as the principal court sycophant. Vice leads to more vice, and the philandering Ivan, inflamed by wine, forgot his virtue and, while awaiting eternal and exclusive love with a new bride, sought temporary objects to satisfy his coarse lusts. An imaginary, transparent curtain of secrecy could not hide the monarch's weakness: people spoke to one another in amazement. What sort of destructive impulse might cause their sovereign, till now an example of restraint and spiritual purity, to stoop to such debauchery?

This truly great evil gave rise to something even more terrible. The libertines would point out the despondent faces of important boyars to the tsar and whisper,

"These are men who wish you ill! Despite the oath they gave, they live with Adashev's habits, sowing injurious rumors, agitating minds. They hope regain their former willfulness."

These venomous calumnies vexed Ivan's heart, already agitated by his vices. His gaze would darken and coarse words burst from his mouth. He accused the boyars of evil intentions, of disloyalty, of stubborn devotion to the supposed traitors. He resolved to be harsh, and became a torturer the like of which can hardly be found in Tacitus' Annals! Of course his soul, which had once loved virtue, did not become savage all at once, for the progress of good or evil is gradual. The chroniclers were unable to peer into it, unable to view the struggle of his conscience with mutinous passions, and called Ivan's tyranny *a strange tempest*, seemingly sent from the bowels of Hell to torment and cripple Russia.

It began with the persecution of all those who had been close to Adashev: their property was confiscated and they were exiled to distant places. The people felt sorry for these innocents and cursed the tsar's fawning new advisors, while the tsar became embittered and tried to suppress this effrontery with cruel measures.

FIRST EXECUTIONS

There was a woman named Mariya who was renowned in Moscow for her Christian virtues and her friendship with Adashev; it was said that she hated the tsar and was planning to use sorcery to destroy him. She was executed along with her five sons; soon many others were as well, accused of the same thing, such as the okolnichii Danil Adashev, Aleksii's brother, famed for his military exploits. He was executed along with his 12 year old son, as well as the three Satin brothers, whose sister was married to Aleksii, and also the latter's relative, Ivan Shishkin, with his wife and children. Prince Dmitrii Obolenskii-Ovchinin, the son of a voivode who had died in Lithuania, perished due to an indiscreet word. Offended by the arrogance of Thedor Basmanov, a young favorite of the sovereign, Prince Dmitrii had said to him,

"We serve the tsar with our beneficial labors, you with your vile sodomitical deeds!"

Basmanov brought his complaint to Ivan, who in a fit of rage at dinner thrust a knife into the unfortunate prince's heart. But others write that he ordered him to be strangled. The boyar Prince Mikhail Repnin was likewise a victim of his courageous boldness. On seeing indecent games in the palace, where the tsar, drunk on strong mead, was dancing with his favorites in masks, this noble wept with sorrow. Ivan tried to put a mask on him, but Repnin tore it off, stamped it under foot and said,

"Is our sovereign to be a clown? At least I, a boyar and counselor of the Duma, can keep from acting like a madman."

The tsar chased him out and a few days later ordered him killed. Repnin was standing at prayers in a sacred cathedral [when they came for him], and the blood of this virtuous man stained the church podium. A host of informers appeared to oblige Ivan's unfortunate disposition. Quiet conversations within families and among friends were overheard, faces were scrutinized and secret thoughts guessed at; nor did these vile slanderers fear to invent crimes, since these denunciations pleased the sovereign, and judges did not require reliable evidence. Thus without guilt and without trial Prince Yurii Kashin, a member of the Duma was killed, along with his brother. Prince Dmitrii Kurlyatev, a friend of the Adashevs, was involuntarily tonsured and soon murdered with all his family. The ranking noble, distinguished *Servitor of the Sovereign* and conqueror of Kazan, Prince Mikhail Vorotynskii, was exiled to Belo-ozero with his wife, son and daughter. That terror of the Crimeans, voivode boyar Ivan Sheremetev, was thrown into a stifling prison, mutilated and placed in heavy chains. The tsar came to him and coldly asked,

"Where is your treasury? You are said to be rich." The half-dead martyr replied,

"Sovereign! With my unworthy hands I sent it to Christ my Savior!"

Released from prison, he attended the Duma for several more years. Finally he retired from the world to the Belo-ozero wilderness, but he could not escape persecution. Ivan wrote to the monks there that they were honoring this former noble excessively, as if to irritate their tsar. His brother, Nikita Sheremetev, also a Duma counselor and voivode who had been wounded in battles for his country, was strangled.

Moscow was numb with fear. Blood flowed and victims groaned in prisons and monasteries. But the tyranny was still maturing: the present portended a terrifying future! There was no improvement in our torturer, who became ever more suspicious and ever more savage; his thirst for blood became more and more unquenchable. It became the fiercest of his passions, inexplicable since it was madness – a scourge of the people and even the tyrant himself.

It is curious to note how this sovereign, to the end of his life was an ardent respecter of the Christian religion and tried to reconcile its divine teachings with his unspeakable cruelty. Sometimes he rationalized this as justice, insisting that all he tormented were traitors, *sorcerers*, enemies of God and Russia; other times he humbly admitted his guilt before God and the people, calling himself *a vile murderer of the innocent*, and ordering that they be prayed for in the holy cathedrals, but comforting himself with the hope that sincere repentance would be his salvation and that he, after putting aside his worldly majesty, would in time become a model monk at the peaceful cloister of St. Kirill at Belo-ozero! Thus did Ivan write to Prince Andrei Kurbskii and to the heads of his favorite monasteries, showing that the voice of his unquiet conscience menaced the turbid dreams of his soul, preparing it for a sudden terrible awakening in the grave!

We shall for a time leave this terrible tyranny to follow the course of national affairs, in which Ivan's natural intellect still was seen as a ray of light amidst dark clouds.

Our successes in the Livonian war were crowned with a powerful and decisive blow. In 1560, the sovereign sent a new army to Derpt: 60,000 cavalry and infantry, 40 siege cannons and 50 field cannons with the distinguished voivodes, Princes Ivan Mstislavskii and Pyotr Shuiskii, to take Fellin without fail. This city was Livonia's chief defense, where Fürstenberg, the former master, had shut himself up. Moscow's legions moved slowly along the banks of the river Embach while the heavy artillery was transported by boat. The voivode Prince Barbashin with 12,000 light cavalry hastened to gain control of the road to the sea since there was a rumor that Fürstenberg was sending a rich treasury to Hapsal for safekeeping.

| LIVONIAN WAR |

After exhausting his horses, Barbashin was taking a rest about five versts from Ermis. In the hot noontime, as his troops were sleeping in the shade, there was an alarm: 500 German cavalry and as many infantry under command of the valiant Landmarshal Philip Bel charged from the woods with shouts and cries towards our quiet encampment, which was protected by only a small number of guards.

Although the Russians had known of the enemy's proximity, they did not think he would join battle with their overwhelmingly superior numbers. Surprise gave the enemy only a brief advantage: after the initial confusion, the Russians stopped the Germans, pressed in on them and accounted for all of them to the last man. They captured 11 commanders and 120 knights, including their chief commander. The loss of so many officers, especially the landmarshal, who was called their last ardent defender and Livonia's last hope, was the worst possible catastrophe for the Order. Presented to Moscow's voivodes, this distinguished man was unwaveringly steadfast. He did not conceal his inner chagrin, but gazed on them with a proud majesty; he replied to all their questions sincerely, calmly and boldly. Kurbskii, praising his character, intellect and eloquence, relates the following:

> BEL'S COURAGE

"We tried to ameliorate the cruel lot of this exceptional man with courtesy, and at dinner conversed amicably with him about the history of the Livonian Order.

'When,' he said, 'fervor for the True Faith, virtue and piety abided in our hearts, then the Lord clearly helped us: we feared neither Russians nor Lithuanian princes. You have heard of that glorious, memorable battle with the formidable Vitovt, in which six masters of the Order, chosen for excellence, were killed, one after the other. Such were the knights of old and such were the later ones with whom Ivan the Great,* the grandfather of the present Muscovite tsar, made war, and so were those who so valiantly did battle with your renowned voivode Daniil.

'But when we abandoned God and cast aside the canons of the True Faith and accepted new ones, which had been devised by human ingenuity to indulge the passions, then we forgot true morality and gave ourselves over to vile voluptuousness and rushed

---

* [Ivan III, 1440-1505.]

unbridled along the broad road of depravity; God then committed our Order into your hands. Beautiful cities, lofty fortresses, glittering palaces and courts created by our forebears; gardens and vineyards planted by them – all fell to you effortlessly. But what should I say about the Russians? At least you got it by the sword. Others {Poles} never drew a sword, but got it by cunningly promising us friendship, protection and assistance. Here is their friendship: we stand before you in shackles and our beloved homeland is lost! . . . No, do not think you conquered us with valor. God is employing you to punish us sinners.' At this point he wept, then dried his tears and continued more cheerfully:

'But even in fetters I give thanks to the Most High. It is sweet to suffer for my country and I do not fear death!'

"The Russian voivodes listened to him with interest and heartfelt emotion. Then they sent him to Moscow with all of the other prisoners, persuasively writing to the sovereign that he should be charitable towards this virtuous knight, who, since he was so respected in Livonia, might render us a great service by persuading the master to submit. But Ivan was now fond of cruelty. He summoned the landmarshal and began to speak angrily to him. His courageous prisoner replied that Livonia stood for honor and liberty and abhorred servitude and that we had waged war like ferocious, bloodthirsty barbarians. Ivan ordered him beheaded."

This was for his *offensive* words, says the chronicler, and for perfidiously violating the truce. Inadvertently amazed by Bel's bold resolve, Ivan later sent to halt the execution, but it had already been carried out.

Our commanders laid siege to Fellin and destroyed its walls with cannon fire; in a single night they set fire to the city in various places. At this point, the German troops declared to Fürstenberg that they must enter into negotiations. In vain did the renowned old man try to convince them not to betray their honor and duty, offering them all of his treasure, gold and silver, as a reward for courage. The mercenaries did not care for the prospect of certain death, since there was nowhere from which they could expect assistance.

| FELLIN TAKEN |

Fürstenberg asked that the Russians let him depart with his treasury. The boyar's council rejected this condition, replying that for reasons of honor, their sovereign wanted to have the master as a prisoner, but it magnanimously promised him mercy. They let only the German troops leave on 21 August, but when Prince Mstislavskii learned that they had broken into Fürstenberg's baggage and stolen many valuables that the Livonian nobility had brought to Fellin, he ordered the confiscation of everything they had illegally seized, and even their own belongings. These unfortunates were sent, stripped, to Riga, where Ketler hanged them as traitors. After the Russians occupied the city, they were amazed at the faintheartedness of the Germans, who along with the great forces of the besieged could have held out for a long time: there were three stone fortresses with deep ditches inside the city, 450 cannons and a great deal of provisions of all kinds.

"Such timidity on the part of the enemy," they said, "is a grace from God to our Orthodox tsar."

| WORDS OF THE RULER OF KAZAN |

When the prisoners from Fellin arrived in Moscow, Ivan ordered them to be shown to the people and led from street to street. It is written that the ruler of Kazan, who was among a number of curious spectators of this triumph, spat on one of the German officials, saying,

"This is your doing, madman! You taught the Russians to master weapons: this led to disaster for us and yourselves!"

The sovereign received Fürstenberg very favorably; he fulfilled all his voivodes' promises and gave him the small town of Lyubim in Kostroma as an estate, where he ended his days complaining about his fate but sincerely praising Ivan's charity.

The fall of Fellin presaged the complete collapse of the Order. The towns of Tarvastu, Ruya, Werpol and many fortified castles surrendered. Prince Andrei Kurbskii defeated the new landmarshal of the Order at Wolmar and, when he learned that a light detachment of Lithuanians was approaching Wenden, met them as hostiles, put them to flight and chased them out of Livonian territory.

Chapter Six

The voivode Yakovlev laid waste to coastal Estonia, seizing a great deal of cattle and riches, since the most distinguished residents of Garriya had concealed themselves there with their possessions. As he was marching past Revel, its audacious citizens, numbering less than 1,000, made a sally, but became victims of our superior forces: those not killed on the spot were taken off into captivity. It is probable that the Russians might then have conquered Revel as well, but on the way there their head voivode, Prince Mstislavskii, without orders from the sovereign, tried to take the stronghold of Weissenstein, which was surrounded by a mucky, musty marsh. He invested it for six weeks, not daring to make an assault. After exhausting all his provisions he was obliged to return to Russia in the fall.

Meanwhile, Livonia had ceased scheming to preserve its independence. Exhausted by futile efforts, it sought only a better ruler so as to save its miserable remnants from captivity and the Russian sword. King Frederik of Denmark wanted Estonia and purchased the bishopric of Ösel for his brother Magnus. This young prince had been condemned to be a surprising plaything of fate. In the spring of 1560 he arrived in Hapsal with flattering promises for the Knights.

The Swedish king had not manifested power-hungry designs on the Order's territory, but he did fear the Russian successes. He let the master know that he was prepared to provide Revel with military provisions, that in case of siege, its residents could send their women and children to Finland, and that Sweden, forgetting the Order's infidelity, sincerely favored it and would never agree to its annihilation. This is what old Gustav Vasa thought: he died at the end of 1560.

The new king Erik acted decisively. He presented the Estonian officials with the choice of unavoidable doom on the one hand, on the other, protection and salvation. He convinced them without much effort to declare themselves Swedish subjects, to the master's irritation, since he was then in secret negotiations with Sigismund. This important event hastened the resolution of the drama. Seeing that the Order's [headquarters] building had been destroyed, Ketler, the archbishop of Riga and the Livonian deputies

> **END OF THE [GERMAN] ORDER**

hurried to Vilnius, where on 28 November 1561 in the presence of the king and the Lithuanian nobles they permanently abolished the famed *brotherhood of sword-bearers* on the strength of a formal, sworn treaty by which Sigismund-Augustus was acknowledged as the sovereign of Livonia – on condition that he not change their religion, their laws or their civic rights. Ketler would become the hereditary duke of Courland and a vassal or subordinate of the king. In this memorable document it says that,

"Livonia, lacerated by the most ferocious of enemies, cannot save itself without a close union with the kingdom of Poland. Sigismund is obligated to stand up for the Christians oppressed by the barbarians. He will drive out the Russians and bring war to their own land, for it is better to drink the enemies' blood than to have him drink yours."

On his return to Riga, Ketler publically put aside the title of master, as well as his cross and robe. Weeping, the knights did likewise. After swearing loyalty to the king, he handed over the seal of the Order, the documents from the emperor and the keys to the cities to the royal deputy, Prince Radziwill. In the name of the king, Radziwill gave him the rank of Livonian ruler.

In this manner, the lands of the Order were divided into five parts: Narva, Derpt, Allentaken, and some uezds in Erven, Virland [Wierland] and all the lands neighboring Russia that had been conquered by Ivan. Sweden got Garriya, Revel and half of Virland; Magnus ruled Ösel; Gothard Ketler, Courland and Semigallia; and Sigismund, southern Livonia. Each of these new rulers attempted to gain popularity with his subjects, since Ivan, who was terrible as an enemy, was declaring mercy for the people and the nobles in the districts he had conquered. But the end of the Order would not be the end of misery for oppressed Livonia, where four northern powers found themselves in perilous proximity to each other; each of them wishing to expand its dominion.

> **NEGOTIATIONS WITH SWEDEN**

Meanwhile, after Swedish troops entered Revel, Erik offered peace and friendship to us, but on condition that he deal directly with the tsar in all things, and not with the Novgorod deputies, and the important article of the former treaty whereby Gustav Vasa promised to help neither Lithuania nor the Order be excluded. In the negotiations with the Muscovite boyars, the Swedish officials threatened them as follows:

"The emperor, King Sigismund and Frederik of Denmark have persuaded our sovereign to fight Russia with them. Their emissaries are in Stockholm. Erik has not given them a definitive reply, for he awaits your own."

The boyars replied that for seven centuries Russia had pursued a single political system and was not about to change its old customs.

"In Sweden," they said, "there were many rulers before Erik, but who of them did not have relations with Novgorod? Gustav Vasa did not want any, but then he saw the terrible destruction of his lands and submitted. Gustav was renowned for wisdom, while Erik remains an unknown quantity. Bad actions are easily begun, but hard to correct. Ivan wished for, and took two countries.

"What has your new king done? Either reaffirm his father's treaty document before you return to Stockholm or the flame of war will break out; it will not easily be extinguished. You threaten us with Lithuania, the Kaiser and Denmark, but even if you are friends with every ruler and king, we shall not be frightened."

This firmness forced the Swedes to renew the old treaty. Although Ivan could not but be irritated when he heard of the doings in Estonia; although Novgorod officials sent to Stockholm with a peace treaty document complained to the tsar that Erik had treated them very rudely (they were even served meat on fast days); and although they let the king know that we would not be indifferent spectators to his love of power, yet peace was made, for the tsar did not want to multiply his enemies while he was dealing with his chiefest, i.e., Lithuania.

We have spoken of Ivan's matchmaking: although he had no doubt as to its ultimate success, he was quite mistaken, to the detriment of his self-esteem. Our emissaries who had been sent to Vilnius formally told Sigismund of the peace, and secretly, of the tsar's desire to be his brother-in-law. Our emissaries were to choose either the queen's older sister Anna, or her younger, Katarina, depending on their *beauty, health and fertility*. They chose Katarina. Sigismund responded that for this they would need the consent of the emperor, the prince of Braunschweig and the king of Hungary, her relatives and protectors, and that her dowry, kept in the Polish treasury, consisted of chains, buttons, dresses and gold, worth 100,000 chervontsy* in all. Also, although a younger sister should not be married off before the elder, he would not object to the marriage, provided that Katarina remained in the Roman faith.

The emissaries wanted to be introduced to the prospective bride: they were permitted to see her in church and were presented with portraits of both sisters. But Sigismund, convinced of the inevitability of a war for Livonia, reckoned that a relation by marriage with Ivan would present no advantage. The marshalok** Shimkovich was sent to Moscow, ostensibly for a peace agreement and matchmaking; he demanded Novgorod, Pskov, the Severskie lands and Smolensk!

The emissary departed and hostilities began when the Lithuanian hetman, Radziwill, invaded Livonia with his troops and took the town of Tarvastu. The siege had lasted five weeks, but Moscow's voivodes had not managed to provide any support. They had assembled and prepared, but would not listen to one another, wrangling over seniority.

Ivan's new severity was unable to mitigate this harmful [struggle over] precedence. The sovereign, although he would punish nobles for a single indiscreet word, a reproachful glance or courageous boldness, still indulged this old custom. The exploits of our huge army consisted solely of the renewed devastation of some Livonian settlements. Prince Vasilii Glinskii and Pyotr Serebryanyi followed in the tracks of Radziwill and defeated his detachment near Pernau. The Lithuanians did not remain in Tarvastu after occupying more important fortresses. Ivan ordered the town be razed to its foundations!

---

* [This term was used for various foreign coins circulating in Russia.]
** [Marshalok: a high ranking official in the Grand Principality of Lithuania and the Polish Republic in the 15th century.]

Chapter Six

Sigismund now wrote to the tsar that after a long and futile attempt to persuade him to leave Livonia in peace, he was forced to resort to arms. After taking Tarvastu, Radziwill had allowed the Russians to leave it. The one guilty of the bloodshed would answer to God. He said that we could still avert war if we pulled out of the territories of the former Order and paid for all damages; otherwise Europe would see on whose side were truth and courageous vengeance, and on whose side were ferocity and shame. To the bearer of this letter, the court noble Korsak, our coreligionist, the boyars explained that he would not be shown the honors due an emissary, for the king's letter was full of unseemly expressions. The tsar replied to Sigismund:

> WAR WITH LITHUANIA

"You know how to lay your guilt on others. We have always respected your *justified* demands, but you have forgotten your forebears' provisos and your own oath. You are encroaching on an old Russian possession, for Livonia is, has been and will be ours. You reproach me for pride and hunger for power, but my conscience is at peace. I battle only to give liberty to Christians and punish the infidels and oath-breakers.

Are you not inducing the Swedish king to violate the peace he concluded with Novgorod? While speaking to me of friendship and matchmaking, are you not summoning the Crimeans to do battle against my country? Your letter to the khan is in my hands; I enclose a copy so that you may be ashamed... And thus we know all about you; there is nothing else to learn. We place our hopes in Heavenly judgment, which will give you your due for your evil cunning and falsehood."

Now that Ivan had decisively abandoned the idea of becoming Sigismund's brother-in-law, he began to search for another bride for himself in the lands of Asia, following the example of our ancient princes. He was told that one of the most renowned of the Circassian rulers, Temgryuk, had a charming daughter. The tsar wanted to see her in Moscow; he fell in love with her and ordered her to be instructed in the Orthodox religion. The metropolitan was her godfather at the baptismal font and gave

> IVAN'S SECOND MARRIAGE

her the Christian name Mariya. The marriage was performed on 21 August 1561, but Ivan had not ceased pining for Katarina. In any case, he was still irritated and prepared to avenge himself on the king both for Livonia and for his refusal of the match, which was insulting to his pride.

1562

However, despite mutual threats, the military operations by either side were half-hearted. Ivan feared the khan and kept his legions in southern Russian, where they were commanded by Prince Vladimir Andreevich. Sigismund had posted his troops in the fortresses in Livonia and had only small detachments in the field. These set out for Opochka and Nevel. Prince Pyotr Serebryanyi defeated the Lithuanians near Mstislavl, Kurbskii torched the suburbs of Vitebsk and other voivodes from Smolensk marched on Dubrovno, Orsha, Kopys and Shklov. They did more plundering than fighting. The pan Khodkevich, commander of Sigismund's troops in Livonia, tried to persuade our voivodes not to waste men in futile skirmishes. Peace talks were about to commence: the Livonian nobles wrote to the metropolitan and the Muscovite boyars to get them to intercede to stop the bloodshed. The aged Makarii ordered them to be told,

"I know only of ecclesiastical affairs; do not involve me in affairs of state." The boyars replied that Ivan would be agreeable to a peace if Sigismund would stop quarreling with us over Livonia and the title of tsar.

"Remember," they added, "that Lithuania itself is also the patrimony of the Muscovite sovereign! To promote peace between both powers, Ivan desired to wed your princess. Sigismund turned down this offer. And why? No doubt to please the khan! It is still possible to correct this: seize the hour!"

But 1563 had begun and the king's emissaries, who were awaited in Moscow, had not shown up. Ivan no longer feared the khan, who had attacked southern Russia but had fled from the city of Mtsensk. Accordingly, Ivan was planning a significant strike on Lithuania.

CHAPTER SIX

At the beginning of winter, our legions gathered in Mozhaisk. The sovereign himself set out for there on December 23rd.

1563

With him were Prince Vladimir Andreevich, the rulers Aleksandr and Simeon of Kazan, and the crown princes Ibak, Tokhtamysh, Bekbulat and Kaibula in addition to distinguished voivodes, 12 Duma boyars, five okolnichie and 16 secretaries. The numbers of troops, we are assured, were 280,000; with 80,900 transport personnel and 200 cannons. This huge and unusual levy invaded Lithuania so suddenly that the king, who was in Poland at the time, at first did not want to believe the news.

Ivan laid siege to Polotsk on 31 January and captured its external fortifications on 7 February. While there, he learned that 40,000 Lithuanians were marching from Minsk with 20 cannons, under the command of Hetman Radziwill, who had given his word to the king to save the besieged city. However, when he encountered the Muscovite voivodes, the princes Yurii Repnin and Simeon Palitskii, he did not dare to do battle. He wished only to threaten the Russians and did not succeed in accomplishing anything at all, since the city was already in Ivan's hands on 15 February.

Dovoina, the local chief, served the tsar by his imprudence. He had allowed 20,000 peasants into the fortress, but expelled them after a few days, giving Ivan the opportunity to show a magnanimity dangerous in this sort of situation. These unfortunates were walking toward [what they thought was] certain death, but were received in the Muscovite camp as brothers. Out of gratitude they showed us a large amount of grain that they had buried in deep pits; they then secretly informed the city's inhabitants that the tsar was the father of all his coreligionists; he conquered but also showed mercy.

Meanwhile cannon fire was raining down on the city and the walls fell. To please the inhabitants, the pusillanimous voivode hastened to conclude an advantageous treaty with an [apparently] indulgent enemy who promised personal liberty and integrity of personal property, but did not keep his word. Polotsk was renowned for commerce, industry and abundance, and after

CAPTURE OF POLOTSK

231

seizing the national treasury, Ivan also took the property of the distinguished and rich, of courtiers and merchants: gold, silver and precious things. He dispatched the bishop, and the voivode of Polotsk and many royal officials, gentry and citizens to Moscow. He also ordered the Latin churches razed and Jews baptized, with the disobedient to be drowned in the [Western] Dvina.

Only the king's foreign troops could praise the victor's magnanimity: they were given stylish fur coats and magnanimous, written passes, in which Ivan was pleased to call himself Grand Prince of *Polotsk* and commanded his boyars and Russian, Circassian, Tatar and German officials to render them protection and aid en route. For several days he celebrated the easy, brilliant conquest of this ancient Russian principality, which was the legacy of the memorable Gorislav, famous in the history of our civil strife; he had avoided the Mongol yoke by taking Lithuanian citizenship early on. Ivan sent couriers everywhere so that Russians would show their gratitude to Heaven for his glorious new victory. He also wrote to the archprelate Makarii:

"This now fulfills the prophecy of the extraordinary metropolitan Pyotr, that Moscow would place its hands on the shoulders of its enemies!"

Sigismund and his pans were frightened: populous and well-fortified Polotsk had been considered Lithuania's primary citadel. Moscow's voivodes were wasting no time, marching toward Vilnius, Mstislavl and Samogitia, freely laying waste to the land, since the hetman had fled back to Minsk. In these circumstances, the king's nobles wrote to our boyars that their emissaries were ready to go to Moscow if we would cease hostilities. The tsar ordered the reply to be,

"One does not flog emissaries, nor execute them"; he gave Lithuania a truce for 6 months. He ordered Polotsk's walls repaired, held services at its Sofiya Cathedral and entrusted the city's defense to valiant Prince Pyotr Shuiskii. On 26 February, the sovereign left with his entire army. He dismissed it at Velikie Luki and hastened towards his capital. On the way he met some boyars who had been sent to him from Moscow with congratulations from his wife and sons. Evfrosiniya, the mother of Aleksandr Andreevich,

CHAPTER SIX

lavishly entertained him at her son's appanage in Staritsa. Crown Prince Ivan was waiting for his father at St. Iosif's Cloister, as was Theodor in the village of Krylatskoe.

There was another feast there and on the next day, 21 March, while the sovereign was riding on Krylatskoe Field, the boyar Trakhanyutov appeared with the news that the tsaritsa had given birth to a son, Vasilii. At the Church of Boris and Gleb in the Arbat, the priesthood was standing by with gonfalons and crosses as Ivan thanked the metropolitan and the prelates for their fervent prayers, and the prelates thanked the tsar for his valor and his victory.

> BIRTH OF CROWN PRINCE VASILII

He proceeded in triumph from the Arbat to the cathedrals, amidst greetings and exclamations, amidst the nobles and the people, just as after the capture of Kazan . . . The only things missing were the people's love for their sovereign, and the sovereign's happiness, since there is no happiness for tyrants! The newborn prince only lived five weeks.

> IVAN'S TRIUMPH

> DEATH OF THE CROWN PRINCE

Ivan had no hesitation about continuing the war against Lithuania and hoped for favorable results from his outstanding victory. He wrote to the khan concerning this with pride and flattery, reminding him of Mengli-Girei's sincere friendship with Grand Prince Ivan, which had been so propitious for both powers, and of the poor success of Crimean attacks, which although harmful to Russia, were even more damaging to the Taurid itself, which now lacked men, arms and horses. He pointed to the Christian churches in Kazan and Astrakhan; he boasted of the ardor of the loyal Circassian and Nogai princes and deplored the impotent malice of Sigismund, who had been chastised by shame and the destruction of his land, saying,

> CRIMEAN AFFAIRS

"All the king's pans kowtowed to our boyars [in hopes of] putting an end to their misery. The boyars beseeched Prince Vladimir Aleksandrovich, and together with him fell at my feet, declaring,

'Sovereign! You have the same religion – why continue this bloodshed? Your hands are filled with prisoners and riches; you have taken Sigismund's best cities. The enemy is in tears and wishes to submit to you.'

"I did not wish to offend my beloved brother and good nobles, and so we turned back! ... Is it your pleasure to be my friend?"

We had had the perfidious Devlet-Girei's emissaries in close confinement for several years: they were now released as a token of our sovereign's favorable disposition towards him, but Ivan did not wish to call him *brother* in his letter, and ordered that instead of the old kowtow, the khan be merely bowed to. That notwithstanding, Moscow's emissary Athanasii Nagoi was ordered to secretly inform the Crimean nobles that the tsar had dismissed Adashev's [adherents], the voivode Sheremetev and the secretary Ivan Mikhailov, ostensibly for their hatred of Devlet-Girei!

Our emissary's wisdom, cunning and rich gifts had an effect: the khan was inclined towards peace and for about two years did not menace us. As a token of good will, he disclosed to us an important secret. We have seen that the puissant Suleiman did not view with equanimity Ivan's progress towards greatness and the downfall of Moslem states. However, he was busy with other, more proximate perils and enterprises important to his love of glory, and he tarried.

THE SULTAN'S SCHEME

Finally, at the suggestion of the noted Astrakhan refugee, Prince Yarlygash, he planned a great undertaking: to join the Don and the Volga with a canal. He established a fortress at Perevolok, where these rivers approach one another, a second on the Volga where Tsaritsyn is now and a third near the Caspian Sea, initially to assure the safety of his Azov possessions but later to take Astrakhan and Kazan, thereby pressing on and weakening Russia. His primary instrument or agent was to be the khan. The sultan ordered the latter to proceed to Astrakhan, promising to send via the Don cannons and men skilled in constructing fortresses.

However, fortunately for Russia, Devlet-Girei feared Turkish domination even more than Russia's power. He did not want to yield Baty's realms to the sultan and tried to convince him of the project's impossibility. He informed Ivan of this enterprise, which would imperil us, but was then incomplete. Despite amicable relations with the Crimea, the sovereign was buttering up Devlet-Girei's perpetual enemy, Ismail, chief of the Nogai rulers, who guarded Astrakhan. He informed us about the perfidious schemes of its princes, who were secret friends of the Crimea. Regrettably for the Russians, he died in 1563, leaving a son, Tin-Akhmat, to be the new chief of the Nogai horde. Nevertheless, like his father, this prince ardently sought Ivan's favor.

Poland, Denmark and Sweden were now fighting over Livonia. The first two wished to join forces to restrain Erik's love of power, since Sweden had taken Pernau and Weissenstein from Sigismund, and Leal and Hapsal from the Danes. King Frederik of Denmark wanted an alliance with Ivan. The tsar made peace with him and yielded him Ösel and Vik, ostensibly out of magnanimity, but proudly rejected his intermediation in our affairs with Lithuania, saying,

| EVENTS IN LIVONIA |

"We can stand up for ourselves and desire no other assistance than God's."

He ordered that merchant courts be set aside for the Danes in Novgorod and Narva, on the condition that the same be done for our merchants in Copenhagen and Visby, where Russians had long traded. Frederik's steward, Eller Gardenberg, and other officials were in Moscow for talks, while Prince Romodanovskii was on his way to Denmark to exchange documents. Meanwhile, Sweden was trying everything to cajole the dangerous tsar: Erik apologized for the disrespect shown our emissaries and sent six distinguished officials to Moscow to conclude negotiations concerning Livonia with the tsar himself, and not just with his voivodes. The response was coarse mockery. Ivan ordered Erik be told,

"When I and my court move to Sweden, then you can issue commands and puff yourself up, but not now! I am as far from you as the sky from the earth."

The Swedes gave in. The sovereign ordered the boyar Morozov, his deputy for Livonia, to give the king a special truce for seven years for

| TRUCE WITH SWEDEN |

Livonian matters and *permitted* Erik to rule Revel and all the towns he had occupied in Estonia, but reserved to himself the right, on the expiration of the designated period, to eject the Swedes like brigands. In other words, Ivan was not interfering with the mutually hostile powers fighting over Livonia: he would instead take advantage of their fatigue to annex it to Russia. We shall see the unanticipated consequences of this cunning policy . . . But now we shall speak of internal events during this time.

Ivan's second marriage did not have the happy effects of his first. Mariya, who had captivated her husband solely by her beauty, was no substitute for Anastasiya, either in his heart, or in the country's, which could no longer associate the tsaritsa with the idea of royal virtue. Contemporaries write that the Circassian princess, with her wild manners and cruel heart, further reinforced Ivan's evil propensities. She could not hold his love, which soon cooled. He had now tasted the perilous charms of inconstancy and no longer knew its shame.

DEPRAVITY OF IVAN'S WIFE

DEATH OF PRINCE YURII

Indifferent to Mariya, he recalled Anastasiya, and for seven more years distributed rich alms to the holy monasteries of [Mount] Athos in her honor. In a similar manner he honored the memory of his brother Yurii, who had died at the end of 1563. This prince of meager mind had enjoyed the outward tokens of respect: incompetent both in military and national affairs, he governed Moscow in name only whenever the sovereign left the capital.

IVAN'S SISTER-IN-LAW AND PRINCE VLADIMIR'S MOTHER TAKE VOWS

His widow Iulianiya, considered a second Anastasiya for her uncommon merits, decided to renounce the world. Ivan, the tsaritsa Mariya, Prince Vladimir Andreevich, the boyars and the people followed her in deep silence, walking behind her as she proceeded from the Kremlin to the Novodevichii Monastery, where she was named Aleksandra amongst the nuns. She wished to end her days in peace, not foreseeing that the tsar, touched by her fervent, angelic piety, and seemingly filled with love and brotherly tenderness for her, would in an outburst of insane rage become her ferocious murderer! He wanted his sister-in-law, now a humble nun, to have royal honors. He built her a splendid court amongst the cells, gave her officials to serve her, and rich estates as property, seemingly wishing to bind her to the vanities of the world!

Even earlier than Iulianiya, Prince Aleksandr Andreevich's mother, the ambitious Evfrosiniya, willingly or not, had taken the veil along with her son. They had incurred the tsar's wrath because of the accusations of their secretary, who was imprisoned for his wrongful deeds. The sovereign had summoned the accused, the metropolitan and the bishops. He *exposed the lies*, as it says in the chronicle, of the mother and son, but due to the supplication of the priesthood, absolved them of guilt.

Evfrosiniya then renounced the world and secluded herself in the Voskresenskii Monastery at Belo-ozero. She was accompanied there by distinguished court officials. Ivan gave Prince Vladimir *new* boyars, stewards and secretaries, taking the old ones into his own service. That is, he surrounded the prince with overseers. At the same time, he treated him kindly, rode with him to visit Staritsa, Vereya and the village Vyshegorod so that they could feast and make merry. Yet inner malice remained hidden behind the mask of amity.

On the last day of 1563 the distinguished metropolitan Makarii died at a great age. He had been accused by contemporaries of both ambition and timidity of spirit, but was praised for good conduct. He was not a bold denouncer of the tsar's vices, but he was not a base flatterer either. Several days before his death he bared his soul before God and the people in a valedictory letter.

> DEATH OF MAKARII

Makarii wrote that, exhausted by many sorrows, he several times had wished to retire from affairs and lead a life of silence, i.e., an anchoritic existence, but each time the tsar and the prelates had been relentless in persuading him to stay. This pastor of the Church had apparently not been a calm observer of Ivan's depravity and had preferred the quiet of the wilderness to his glorious priestly rank.

> **COMPOSITION OF THE LIVES OF THE SAINTS AND THE BOOK OF DEGREES**

A diligent promoter of Christian enlightenment, he had ordered the Greek Menology to be translated,* and appended to it a Lives of the Russian Saints, both ancient and modern, for whom in the council of 26 February 1547 he had established services and festivals. These saints included Archbishop Ivan of Novgorod, Aleksandr Nevskii, Savvatii and Zosima of Solovetskii. Makarii also ordered composed the well-known Book of Degrees [*Stepennaya Kniga*], [a history] running from the time of Ryurik to the year 1559, and promoted the establishment of the first printing press in Moscow.

Europe had already been using this happy discovery of Guttenberg, Faust and Scheffer for about a century. Moscow's sovereigns had heard of it and wished to obtain its benefits, so important for the advancement of education, which they favored. Grand Prince Ivan III had provided a salary to the famous Lübeck printer Bartholomew, and tsar Ivan in 1547 had sought artisans in Germany for the making of books and probably engaged them to train our own, since in 1553 he ordered the construction of a special house for printing under the management of two masters:

> **ESTABLISHMENT OF A PRINTING HOUSE**

Ivan Thedorov, deacon of the Church of St. Nikolai Gostunskii, and Pyotr Timofeev Mstislavets. In 1564 they published the *Acts* and *Epistles* of the apostles, the earliest books printed in Russian, noteworthy for their beautiful type faces and paper.

It is also said that Makarii blessed the tsar for the good deed he had done Christians: instead of unreliable manuscripts we had printed corrected books containing God's law and the Church services. To do this it was necessary to compare the oldest and best manuscripts so as not to err either in word or meaning. This important enterprise, prompted by fervor for Christian education, provoked the displeasure of many scribes who made their living copying ecclesiastical books. These people combined superstition with bafflement at novelty. There began to be rumors and the artisan Ivan Thedorov, who had lost an ardent protector with Makarii's death, was obliged, along with his comrade Pyotr Mstislavets to escape from his persecutors to Lithuania as a supposed heretic.

---

* [A menology is a compilation of saints' biographies.]

CHAPTER SIX

Although the Moscow printing house, now moved to Aleksandrovskaya Sloboda, still printed the Gospels, the tsar yielded the honor of publishing the entire Bible to the Volhynian prince Konstantin Konstantinovich, a descendant of St. Vladimir. This prince, an ardent son of our Church, received the exiled Ivan Theodorov very amicably and founded a printing house in his city of Ostrog.

> PUBLICATION OF BIBLE IN OSTROG

In Moscow he obtained (through the royal Lithuanian secretary Garaburda) a complete copy of the Old and New Testaments. He had it checked by philologists against a Greek Bible sent to him by Patriarch Jeremy of Constantinople and then printed it in 1581, thereby earning the gratitude of all his coreligionists. Among the memorable ecclesiastical deeds of Makarii's time we also note the establishment of the archiepiscopacy of Polotsk in honor of that ancient principality and the famous Sofiya Cathedral there. The former prelate of Suzdal, Trifon Stupishin, who was ordained by St. Iosif Volotskii, was a virtuous man, but even though old and ill, he accepted the title of archbishop of Polotsk to please the tsar.

> ARCHIEPISCOPATE OF POLOTSK

On Makarii's death, all the bishops travelled to Moscow to choose a new Church pastor, but even before this, to carry out their sovereign's will, they had established by a letter of the Council that henceforth Russian metropolitans should wear white klobuks* and cassocks with cherubs such as are depicted on icons of the metropolitans Pyotr and Aleksii, Archbishop Ivan of Novgorod and the wonderworkers of Rostov Leontii, Ignatii and Isaiya.

> 1564

> WHITE KLOBUK [CYLINDRICAL HEADGEAR] FOR THE METROPOLITANS

"Because," it says in the letter, "because some Novgorod prelates now wear white klobuks, we have searched in the scriptures but have not found this in them. Let us return to the metropolitans their ancient distinction! Likewise, also let them, like the

---

* [A type of clerical headgear, comprising a *kamilavka* (a flat-topped cylindrical hat) with a veil.]

239

archbishops of Novgorod and Kazan, seal all their letters with *red wax*. They were to be sealed on one side of the page with an image of the Virgin and Child, and on the other a hand *blessed* with the name of the metropolitan."

> ATHANASII ORDAINED AS METROPOLITAN

A few days later, Athanasii, a monk of the Chudov Monastery was chosen to be archprelate. He had formerly been archpriest of Blagoveshchensk and the sovereign's confessor. At the end of the liturgy, the high priests removed the metropolitan's official clothing and dressed him with *a pendant golden icon*, a cloak with ribbons and a white klobuk. Athanasii stood in the prelate's spot, listened to the tsar's welcoming speech, gave him his blessing and in a loud voice prayed to the Most High to grant Ivan health and victories. It seems he no longer dared to speak of virtue!

CHAPTER VII

*OPRICHNINA ESTABLISHED**

1563-1569

Negotiations and war with Lithuania. Flight of Russians to Lithuania. Prince Andrei Kurbskii's betrayal. His correspondence with the tsar. Attack by Lithuania and the Crimeans. Embassy of the grand master of the German Order. Ivan's secret departure. Tsar's letter to the metropolitan and the people. Terror in Moscow. Establishment of the Oprichnina. Second round of executions. Aleksandrovskaya Sloboda. Ivan's monkish life. His foreign favorites. Courage of Metropolitan Filipp. Third episode of murders. Plague. Military actions and negotiations. Duma of the Land. Truce with Lithuania. Swedish affairs. The sultan's great undertaking. Calamity for the Turks. Relations with Persia. Siberian tribute. Trade. English embassy. Ivan's scheme to flee to England. Bomelius's villainy.

The truce that Ivan had given Sigmund did not interfere with Russians and Lithuanians attacking each other. The former completed their conquest of the Polotsk district with small detachments, while Sigismund's servitor, Prince Mikhail Vishnevetskii, laid waste to the uezds of Chernigov and Starodub with hordes of Cossacks and Belgorod Tatars. Prince Ivan Shcherbatyi, the Severskii voivode, defeated him soundly. Sigismund's emissaries, long awaited in Moscow, finally arrived on 5 December 1563 and, following custom, demanded Novgorod and Pskov of us in addition to all the conquests of Ivan's grandfather, father and himself. Our boyars, also following custom, replied that for a firm peace, we should have to

NEGOTIATIONS AND WAR WITH LITHUANIA

---

* [Ivan the Terrible's secret police, as well as the system it operated under.]

take from Lithuania not only Kiev, Volhynia and Podolia, but also Vilnius, which had anciently belonged to Russia.

They spoke of the king's injustices, craftiness and arrogance in not wanting to call Ivan *Tsar* and in scheming to become Livonia's sovereign, where even in the 9th century Yaroslav the Great had founded the city of Yuriev [Derpt] and where Aleksandr Nevskii had punished his subjects, the Germans, with fire and sword for their rebellion and disobedience.

"So it was," the boyars concluded with their sovereign's words, "so it was until the time of that great avenger of injustice, his grandfather; until his glorious father, a resident of our ancient patrimony; and until himself, the pacifier."

Both sides moderated their demands and we agreed not to speak any more of Vilnius, Podolia and Volhynia. We would also amicably yield Courland to Sigismund while wishing to keep only the Polotsk lands in order to facilitate a truce of 10 or 15 years, but still the emissaries would not accept our conditions. Ivan personally told them,

"If the king does not want to give me the title of tsar, let it be as he wishes! I have no need of the title, since everyone knows my line is descended from Caesar Augustus and what has been given by God man cannot take away."

This pedigree must have astounded the emissaries – but no doubt it was explained to them. One must understand that the Muscovite bookmen of this age, perhaps to indulge Ivan's ambitions, derived the first prince of Novgorod, Ryurik, from the fictitious Pruss, [Caesar] Augustus's brother, who supposedly became the ruler of Prussia after leaving Rome. The emissaries did not argue over Ryurik's forebears, but they remained unwilling to concede to us either the Polotsk district or Livonia. They departed Moscow on 9 January.

| 1564 |

Moscow's voivodes now immediately began to move out in order to take action against Lithuania: Shuiskii from Polotsk and the Serebryanie-Obolenskii princes from Vyazma. The sovereign ordered them to join up by Orsha and proceed to Minsk and

Lithuanian Novgorodok; he designated all their camps and prescribed all their movements. But Prince Pyotr Shuiskii, who had conquered Derpt and was renowned for both valor and compassion, displayed a surprising lack of caution, as if fate had blinded him. His troops marched without any discipline in unarmed bunches. Their armor was carried in sleighs; there was no vanguard and no one was giving any thought to the enemy.

The voivode Trotskii and Nikolai Radziwill, with the king's court and the best Lithuanian legions, were stationed near Vitebsk. They had reliable spies and knew everything. In dense woods near Orsha they suddenly fell upon the Russians, who were unable to form ranks or arm themselves; both voivodes and troops ran off in cowardly flight. The unfortunate Shuiskii paid for his lack of caution with his life. Some write that he was shot in the head and found dead in a well; others that a Lithuanian peasant hacked him to pieces with an ax.

Of the men of distinction, two brothers, the princes Simeon and Thedor Palitskii, also fell in combat. The Lithuanians captured the voivode Zakharii Pleshcheev-Ochin, Prince Ivan Okhlyabinin and several boyar cadets. We lost less than 200 warriors out of 20,000; all the rest fled to Polotsk, leaving the baggage trains and cannons as booty for the enemy. Shuiskii's body was taken triumphantly to Vilnius and the prisoners were presented to the sick king in Warsaw: he ordered services held and his joy was such that he recovered from his illness.

Despite this victory, there were no further happy outcomes for Sigismund. The Obolenskii princes were stationed by Orsha: Radziwill did not want to fight them; he only wanted them to depart from the king's territories. To this end a Lithuanian courier with news of Shuiskii's catastrophe was purposely sent to Dubrovno through places where he was bound to run into Russians. He was seized and brought to our voivodes, who, when they found out what had happened, nimbly retreated to Smolensk, but took vengeance on the enemy with fire and sword: they torched settlements from Dubrovno to Krichev and took a large number of farmers captive.

9 February

About five months now elapsed with no action by either side. In July Ivan's commander, Prince Yurii Tokmakov, with a small number of infantry and cavalry, marched from Nevel to Ozerishche in hopes of capturing that town. When our voivode, who was known for his courage, learned that 12,000 Lithuanians were proceeding from Vitebsk to save the besieged town, he sent his artillery and infantry back to Nevel on boats and then, with cavalry alone, he met the enemy and defeated their vanguard. But when the main Lithuanian army arrived, he had to withdraw, after inhumanely killing the prisoners he had taken.

> 22 July

The Smolensk voivode Buturlin, commanding boyar cadets, Tatars and Mordvi, once again laid waste to the right bank of the Dnieper and took away 4,800 prisoners of either sex. Meanwhile, the Lithuanians were threatening the Derpt district with attack, while Sigismund's Cossacks were robbing merchants and Ivan's envoys en route from Moscow to the Taurid. The war soon heated up – at any rate, it became more perilous for us, due to the unexpected defection of one of Ivan's most renowned voivodes.

> Flight of Russians to Lithuania

The terror brought about by the tsar's cruelties against all Russians induced many of them to flee to other lands. Prince Dimitrii Vyshnevetskii served as an example: he was anxious for our country's glory and loved Ivan when he was virtuous, but he did not want to subject himself to a malicious and capricious tyrant. He went over to Sigismund from his military encampment in southern Russia. Dimitrii was graciously received as an enemy of Ivan and the king provided his own doctor to cure this warrior of a serious illness produced by poison.

However, Vyshnevetskii would not think of spilling the blood of his Russian coreligionists. He was clandestinely convinced by some Moldavian nobles to try to expel their unworthy sovereign Stefan. He hastened there with a detachment of loyal Cossacks in search of new glory, but became the victim of a ruse. No one flocked to the banners of this hero: Stefan took Vyshnevetskii prisoner and sent him to Constantinople, where the sultan ordered him killed. Two brothers, the distinguished officials Aleksei and Gavrilo Cherkasskii, doubtless threatened with disgrace, followed after Vyshnevetskii to Lithuania.

Flight is not always treason: civil laws cannot be more powerful than the natural one: *to save oneself from a tormentor*, but it is grievous for a citizen to take vengeance on his homeland because of a tyrant! A young, vigorous voivode, distinguished by glorious wounds in the tender bloom of youth, a man of battle and council, participator in all of Ivan's glittering conquests, a hero at Tula, at Kazan, in the Bashkir steppes and in the fields of Livonia, and once a favorite and friend of the tsar, placed the seal of shame upon himself, and upon the historian the duty to enroll such a distinguished citizen in the list of state criminals.

> PRINCE ANDREI KURBSKII'S BETRAYAL

This man was Andrei Kurbskii. Up till now, in the eyes of posterity, he would have had the glory of his spotless service, but Ivan was no longer fond of him, since he had been a friend of Adashev – the tsar was only looking for a chance to accuse this innocent man. While governing Derpt, this proud voivode endured reprimands and various insults; he heard threats and finally realized that his doom was being prepared.

He did not fear death in battle, but was terrified of execution. He asked his wife which she would prefer: to see him dead before her, or to separate from him forever with him still alive. The brave lady firmly replied that her husband's life was more precious than her happiness. Weeping, he took his leave from her and blessed his 11 year old son.

He secretly left his home by night, climbed over the city wall, where he found the two saddled horses his faithful servant had made ready and safely made it to Wolmar, which was held by the Lithuanians. Sigismund's voivode there received him as a friend, and in the name of the king promised him a high rank and wealth.

The first thing Kurbskii did was to explain himself to Ivan, baring his soul, which was full of grief and indignation. In an outburst of powerful feelings he wrote a letter to the tsar. His

> HIS CORRESPONDENCE WITH THE TSAR

loyal servant, his sole companion, undertook to deliver it and did so faithfully: he gave the sealed letter to the sovereign himself in Moscow at the Red Porch, saying,

"From my lord, your exile, Prince Andrei Mikhailov."

The enraged tsar struck him on the leg with his staff. Blood poured from the wound while the servant stood immobile, silent. Ivan leaned on his staff and ordered the contents of Kurbskii's letter to be read aloud:

"To the tsar, once radiant and glorified by God, but now, through our sins, benighted with hellish malice in his heart and possessing a leprous conscience, a tyrant unexampled amongst the most faithless rulers of the land. Take heed! Due to the sorrowful consternation of my heart, I have little to say, but I speak the truth.

"For what reason did you torture the strong in Israel[*] with diverse torments, distinguished leaders given you by the Almighty, and spill their sacred, victorious blood in God's cathedrals? Did these men indeed not burn with fervor for their tsar and country? Inventing calumnies, you called your loyal men traitors, Christians sorcerers, the light dark and the sweet bitter! What incurred your wrath against these defenders of our homeland? Did they not destroy Baty's realm, where our forebears languished in arduous servitude? Did they not take the German fortresses to honor your name? But with what did you repay us miserable ones? Ruin!

"Are you really immortal? Is there indeed no God or higher justice for the tsar? ... I am not going to describe all that I suffered from your cruelty, for my soul is still in disarray. I shall say only that you have deprived me of holy Russia! My blood, spilled for you, cries out to God! He sees into my heart. I sought my guilt, both in deed and in secret thought; I inquired of my conscience, heeded its answers, but I do not know how I have wronged you. I led your legions and we never turned our backs on the enemy: my glory was your glory. I served you not for one year, nor for two, but for many years, in difficulties and military exploits, enduring

---

[*] [Cf. Judges 5:2. A rather obscure passage in the Hebrew, with various disparate translations. The sense here seems to be "your loyal and patriotic commanders."]

want and sickness, not seeing my mother nor knowing my wife, far from my beloved homeland.

"Count my battles, reckon my wounds! I am not boasting, for this is all known to God. I entrust myself to Him, in hopes of succor from the saints and my forefather, Prince Theodor Yaroslavskii. We have now parted forever; you shall not see my face until the Day of Judgment. The tears of innocent victims are preparing an agonizing punishment [for you].

"Fear the dead: those you murdered are still living yet with the Most High: at His throne they demand vengeance! Armies will not save you; flatterers will not make you immortal, nor unseemly boyars, comrades at your feasts and revels, nor the destroyers of your soul who bring you their children as sacrificial victims! [A copy of] this letter, dampened with my tears, I have ordered placed in the grave with me and I shall appear with it before the judgment of God. Amen. Written in the city of Wolmar in the territory of King Sigismund, *my* sovereign, from whom with God's help I hope for favor and comfort in my grief."

Ivan finished listening to the reading of the letter and then ordered the bearer tortured to learn all the circumstances of Kurbskii's flight, all his secret contacts and all his confederates in Moscow. The virtuous servant, named Vasilii Shibanov (a name that belongs to history), did not reveal anything. Under terrible torments he praised his lord and was cheered by the thought that he was dying for him. Such valiant resolve, dutifulness and love amazed everyone, even Ivan himself, and he speaks of this in a letter to the exile, for the tsar, agitated by rage and inner unease of conscience, immediately replied to Kurbskii:

"In the name of God Almighty," wrote Ivan, "He by whom I live and move and by whom tsars rule and the powerful do speak, a humble Christian reply to the former Russian boyar, our councilor and voivode, Prince Andrei Mikhailovich Kurbskii, *who wanted to be lord of Yaroslavl*... Why, unhappy man, do you endanger your soul with treason, seeking to save your transitory body with flight? If you are just and virtuous, then why do you not wish to die at my hands, your obdurate lord, and inherit a martyr's crown? What is life? What are the riches and glory of this world? Vanity and darkness. Blessed is he who at death obtains spiritual salvation!

"You have been shamed by your servant Shibanov: he maintained his piety before both tsar and people; having promised loyalty to his lord, he did not betray him even at the gates of death. But you, because of my single word of anger, burden yourself with a traitor's oath. This involves not just your own soul, but also those of your forebears, for they swore to my great grandfather to serve us loyally through all their descendants. I have read and considered your missive. The mouth of a traitor has the poison of an asp; his words are like arrows. You complain of the persecution you suffered, but if I had not been too gracious to you, unworthy man, you would not have gone over to our enemy! I sometimes punished you for your faults, but always lightly, and with love; and I rewarded you most excellently.

"You were a voivode in your youth and an advisor to the tsar; you had all kinds of honors and wealth. Recall your father: he served with Prince Mikhail Kubenskii's boyars! You boast of the blood you expended in combat, but you were only paying the debt due your country. And is the glory of your exploits so great? When the khan was fleeing from Tula, you were feasting with Prince Grigorii Temkin and gave the enemy time to return home. You were at Nevel with 15,000 men but were unable to defeat 4,000 Lithuanians. You speak of Baty's dominions as if you had conquered them; you mention Kazan (since your grace never saw Astrakhan), but what did it cost us to lead you to this victory? You yourself did not want to go, and with irrational words chilled the ardor of others for martial glory.

"When a storm destroyed our supply boats at Kazan, you wanted to flee in a cowardly manner. And you prematurely demanded a decisive battle so as to return home, victorious or defeated, but quickly in any case. When God bestowed that city on us, what did you do? You plundered it! And how can you boast of Livonia? You were taking it easy in Pskov and we wrote to you seven times, and also to Prince Pyotr Shuiskii: *march on the Germans!* With a small number of men you then took 50 more towns, but was this due to your brilliance or bravery? No, you were only carrying out our orders, albeit in a leisurely manner. But what did you later accomplish with your wise chief, Aleksei Adashev, who had a large army with him? You were barely able to take Fellin, and withdrew from Paide (Weissenstein)!

"Were it not for your obduracy, all of Livonia would long since have belonged to Russia. You conquered unwillingly, like a serf, acting only when compelled by necessity. You say you bled for us, but we sweated and wept because of your disobedience. What was our country like during your rule and our minority? A wasteland from east to west. But we, taking control from you, built villages and towns where the wild beasts had roamed. Woe to the home that is ruled by the wife; woe to the realm that is ruled by many men!

"Caesar Augustus ruled the world because he did not share power with anyone. Byzantium fell when its emperors began to heed eparchs, councils and priests, the brothers of our Silvestr."

Here Ivan describes the crimes, already known to the reader, of his former favorites; then he continues:

"Shameless liar that you speak of our imagined cruelties! We do not destroy *the strong in Israel*. We do not stain God's churches with their blood: the *strong* and virtuous prosper and serve us. We only punish traitors – and where are *they* ever shown mercy? Constantine the Great did not even spare his son, and your forefather, the sainted Prince Theodor Rostislavich – how many Christians did he kill in Smolensk? Many fell, grieving my heart, but even more, there was vile treachery, which is known everywhere to everyone.

"Ask foreign merchants who come to our realm: they will tell you that your *defenders* are known miscreants whom the Russian land cannot abide. And what sort of *defenders of the homeland* are they? Are they holy? Are they gods, like Apollo and Jupiter? Up till now Russian rulers have been free and independent: they rewarded and punished their subjects without having to give account. Thus it was and thus it shall be! I am no longer a child. I have need of God's grace: the pure Virgin Mary's and the holy saints', but I do not require instruction from men.

"Praise be to the Most High, Russia prospers; my boyars live in love and harmony while a few of your friends and advisors still scheme in the darkness. You threaten me with the judgment of Christ in the next world, but really, is not this world in God's hands? This is the Manichaean heresy! You think that God rules only in Heaven and the Devil in Hell, while men rule on earth. No, no! God's power is everywhere, both in this and the future life. You write that I do not see the face of your Ethiopian: woe is me! What a catastrophe!

"You surround the throne of the Most High with those I killed: this is another heresy! According to the apostles, no one may see God. Put your letter in the grave with you; by this you will prove that the last spark of Christianity has been extinguished in you, for a Christian dies with love and forgiveness, not malice. To complete your treason, you call the Livonian city of Wolmar one of Sigismund's districts and hope for his favor, having abandoned your legitimate ruler whom God gave you.

"You have chosen a better lord for yourself! Your great king is the slave of slaves: is it surprising that slaves praise him? But I shall be silent: Solomon does not command one to converse with the insane, for such you certainly are. Written in the capital city of Moscow of our Great Russia, in the year 7072 from the creation of the world, on the fifth day of the month of July."

This letter, filled with aphorisms from the Old and New Testaments, historical citations, theological explanations and crude gibes, takes up a whole book in the original. Kurbskii replied to it with scorn, reproaching Ivan for forgetting a ruler's dignity since his letter is debased by abusive language, pathetic irrelevancies and an indecent mixture of scripture, lies and slander.

"I am innocent," he says, "and miserable in my exile. Good men take pity on me, but evidently you do not! We have not long to wait: the truth is nigh."

So far we may criticize this exile only for the mordancy of his complaint, in that he enjoys his vengeance and takes satisfaction in lacerating his tormentor with bold words, although to the detriment of his good and diligent service. At any rate, we no longer see Kurbskii as a state criminal, and cannot countenance the accusation that he allegedly wanted to call himself *Lord of Yaroslavl*.

But carried away by passion, this ill-starred man deprived himself of the advantage of being in the right, as well as that important consolation in the midst of calamities: an inner sense of virtue.

He might without remorse of conscience have sought refuge from his pursuers in Lithuania, but he did more – he became an enemy of his homeland. Sigismund treated him with great kindness, awarding him the rich estate of Kovel and he went over to the king with both his honor and his soul. He advised the king on how to harm Russia, reproached him for weakness in war and tried to persuade him to act more boldly, not sparing the treasury to arouse the khan against us.

> ATTACK BY LITHUANIA AND THE CRIMEANS

Moscow soon learned that 70,000 Lithuanians, Poles, Prussians, Germans, Hungarians and Wallachians were marching on Polotsk with Kurbskii, and that Devlet-Girei had invaded the Ryazan district with 60,000 brigands.

This last bit of news astounded the tsar. He had gone on a pilgrimage to Suzdal and spent the whole day awaiting a new sworn document from the khan promising him both peace and an alliance. The document had in fact been written and Ivan's emissary Athanasii Nagoi was preparing to depart the Taurid; Sigismund's gold changed everything: Devlet-Girei took it and invaded Russia, which was defenseless, as he had expected, since the king had written him that Ivan was on the Livonian border with all his legions.

Deceived by the khan's friendly assurances, the tsar had actually disbanded our Ukrainian legions, so that (except for the residents) there were no troops at all in Ryazan, which was besieged by Devlet-Girei. The city was saved by the heroic spirit of the sovereign's favorites, the boyar Aleksei Basmanov and his son Thedor, who had been at their rich estate on the banks of the Oka and had been first to inform the tsar of the enemy and the first to arm their people. They defeated several of the khan's detachments and consolidated in Ryazan, where the old walls were falling down, but where the fervor and intrepidity of the Basmanovs' knights and the exhortations of bishop Filothei inspired the citizens to rare bravery.

The Crimeans attacked day and night without success: their corpses lay in heaps beneath the walls. Our artillery gave them no rest, even in their camp. When Devlet-Girei learned that Ivan was in Moscow, that the voivodes Thedor and Yakovlev were already positioned on the banks of the Oka with the tsar's guard, that an army was coming at them from Mikhailovo and Dedilovo, and that the bold Russian cavalry was striking the Crimeans everywhere and was even approaching their camp, he withdrew even more rapidly than he had arrived, without waiting for those of his detachments that had been torching the banks of the Oka and Vozha.

No one was chasing him, but his Shirinskii prince Mamai, who had wanted to keep on pillaging the villages around Pronsk, was defeated and taken prisoner, along with 500 Crimeans. More than 3,000 of their troops were left dead on the battleground. Six days later all was quiet, however, and there was not even a rumor of the Crimeans. Leaving the tsaritsa and their children behind in Aleksandrovskaya Sloboda, Ivan was departing Moscow for the army when the Basmanovs reported the enemy's flight to him. The personal valor and glory of these two favorites cheered him further, and he gave them gold medals.

The sovereign's attention now turned to Polotsk, and there we were winning, to the shame of our traitor [Kurbskii] and the proud pan Radziwill, Sigismund's chief voivode. They had placed their camp two versts from the city, between the Dvina and the Polota, in hopes of taking it by intimidation or treachery alone, but our Polotsk voivode, Prince Pyotr Shchenyatev, replied to their proposals with cannonades, while Simeon, erstwhile ruler of Kazan, Prince Ivan Pronskii, and Pyotr and Vasilii Obolenskii-Serebryanyi rushed from Velikie Luki to take the enemy in the rear – the tsar had guessed the effect of Kurbskii's counsel and had reinforced his legions on this border in a timely manner.

Radziwill had not trusted Kurbskii (such is the lot of a traitor!), and despite the latter's views, had feared a battle in which he might be between two fires. For 17 days he stood idle, losing men to artillery fire from the fortress, and on 4 October he crossed over to the Lithuanian side of the Dvina. That was not all: after chasing

> 6 NOVEMBER

off the Lithuanians, Moscow's voivodes took Ozerishche by storm while Shuiskii's renowned vanquisher made not the slightest move to save this important fortress. That same fall, Prince Vasilii Prozorovskii repelled the Lithuanians from Chernigov and captured Pan Sapega's banner, thereby earning the tsar's favor. During the winter Kurbskii invaded the district of Velikie Luki with 15,000 of the king's troops, but only managed to torch villages and some monasteries.

"That happened against my will," he wrote to Ivan. "It was impossible to restrain the predatory troops. I fought my homeland the same way as David fought Israel when he was pursued by Saul."

The king's voivodes operating in Livonia were also under his general command: to facilitate the success of the khan and Radziwill, Sigismund ordered Prince Aleksandr Polubenskii and other voivodes of his to march on Marienburg and Derpt in the Pskov district. There were a number of fairly important actions: in one Ivan's brave knight Vasilii Veshnyakov defeated the enemy, in another, Prince Ivan Shuiskii and Menshii Sheremetev ceded the field of battle to the Lithuanians.

The latter were unable to conquer Krasnyi, nor defend the outskirts of Schmilten, Wenden, Wolmar or Ronneburg, from which the valiant noble Buturlin took 3,200 prisoners – the sovereign sent him a gold medal. The Lithuanians forces were divided: they were fighting both us and the Swedes, with the latter on land, but on the sea with the Danes over the matter of Livonia. This pleased Ivan: he laughed inwardly at their efforts, since he considered himself to be their sole legitimate ruler.

Ivan hoped to spread the flame of the Livonian war yet further and to find in the German Grand Master Wolfgang a new, eager comrade in arms against King Sigismund. The ancient Order no longer existed in Prussia, but had re-established itself in Germany, more in name and ceremony than in spirit and character. Wolfgang wrote to the tsar that he was planning to conquer Prussia with the help of the emperor

> EMBASSY OF THE GRAND MASTER OF THE GERMAN ORDER

and wanted an alliance with Russia so that they could join forces to attack Sigismund. He sent emissaries to Moscow who arrived in September 1564 with letters from Emperor Ferdinand and the master, but only to intercede for the release of the aged prisoner Fürstenberg – there was not a word about an alliance or a war.

Irritated, the sovereign replied that the master would say one thing today and another tomorrow; that if Wolfgang took Riga and Wenden from Sigismund, then the tsar would grant them Fürstenberg, and that there would be no reply to the emperor, since he had communicated with the tsar not through his own emissaries, but through another's .

And so Kurbskii's betrayal and Sigismund's plan to intimidate Russia produced only brief trepidation in Moscow. But Ivan's heart was still uneasy; more and more it seethed with wrath and was roiled by suspicions. All the good nobles seemed to him to be secret malefactors, partisans of Kurbskii: he saw betrayal in their sorrowful glances and sensed reproach or threats in their silence. He demanded denunciations and complained that they were too few; even the most shameless slanderers could not satisfy his thirst for torture.

A kind of invisible hand still seemed to restrain the tyrant: his victims were at his feet and yet would not expire, to his amazement and anguish. Ivan sought pretexts for new horrors, and then, suddenly, at the beginning of winter 1564, Moscow learned that the tsar was travelling, no one knew where, with those closest to him, as well as courtiers, clerks and soldiers summoned by name from the most distant cities with their wives and children.

| IVAN'S SECRET DEPARTURE |

Early on 3 December a great number of sleighs appeared in the Kremlin square. In them were gold and silver taken from the palace, sacred icons, crosses, precious vessels, clothing and money. The priesthood and the boyars were awaiting the sovereign at the Cathedral of the Dormition.

He arrived and ordered the metropolitan to perform the service; he made fervent prayers, received Athanasii's blessing and graciously gave his hand to the boyars, officials and merchants to kiss. Then he got into his sleigh with the tsaritsa and his two sons. Along with Aleksei Basmanov, Mikhail Saltykov, Prince Athanasii Vyazemskii, Ivan Chebotov and other favorites, and accompanied by a whole legion of armed cavalry, he left for the village of Kolomenskoe where he remained for two weeks due to impassable roads – there had been unseasonable thaw; rains had come and the ice had broken up on the river.

On 17 December he crossed over with his baggage train to the village of Taininskoe, thence to the Trinity Monastery and on to the Aleksandrovskaya Sloboda for Christmas. In addition to the metropolitan there were then many prelates in Moscow. Along with the boyars and the people, they did not know what to make of their sovereign's strange secret journey. They were upset and downhearted, fearful of something extraordinary and no doubt infelicitous. A month passed.

On 3 January the metropolitan received a letter from Ivan carried by the official Konstantin Polivanov. In it, the sovereign described all the rebellions, the anarchy and lawlessness of the boyar's reign during his minority. He argued that both the nobles and the clerks had raided the treasury and stolen land and estates belonging to the sovereign.

> TSAR'S LETTER TO THE METROPOLITAN AND THE PEOPLE

They had concerned themselves with their own wealth and had forgotten their country. Nor had they changed in this respect: they had not ceased doing evil: the voivodes did not want to protect Christians, had avoided service and had let the khan, Lithuania and the Germans lacerate Russia.

Further: if the sovereign, moved by justice, were to declare his anger at these unseemly boyars and officials, then the metropolitan and the priesthood would stand up for the guilty, harassing and insulting its tsar.

"Therefore, as a consequence," wrote Ivan, "not wishing to put up with your treacheries, and with heartfelt sorrow, we have retired from the state and will go now wherever God shows us the way." He sent another letter to visitors, merchants and tradesmen, which the secretaries Putilo Mikhailov and Andrei Vasiliev read loudly at a public meeting. The tsar assured good Muscovites of his favor, writing that his wrath and disfavor would not touch the people.

> **TERROR IN MOSCOW**

The capital was horrified: everyone thought anarchy to be even more frightening than tyranny.

"Our sovereign has abandoned us!" the people cried. "We are doomed! Who will be our defender in wars with the foreigners? How can there be a flock with no shepherd?" The priesthood, boyars, officials and clerks wept and asked the metropolitan to propitiate Ivan, who spared no one and was afraid of nothing. They all spoke as one:

"Let the tsar punish his evildoers. In life and death, let his will [be done]. But do not leave the nation without a head! He is our ruler, given by God: we know no other. We shall follow you to personally petition the sovereign and to weep." The merchants and tradesmen said the same thing, adding,

"Let the tsar point out his betrayers to us. We will exterminate them ourselves!"

The metropolitan wanted to go see the tsar immediately, but it was proposed in a general council that the archpastor remain to watch over the capital, which was in indescribable confusion. All business had been curtailed; courts, government offices, shops and guardhouses were deserted.

The Novgorod prelate Pimen and the Chudovskii archimandrite Levkii were chosen as the principal emissaries, but all the other bishops set off after them as well: Nikandr of Rostov, Elevtherii of Suzdal, Filothei of Ryazan, Matthei Krutitskii, the archimandrites of the Trinity, Simonovskii, Spasskii and Andronikovskii monasteries, and behind the priests, the nobles: the princes Ivan Dmitrievich Belskii and Ivan Thedorovich Mstislavskii, all the boyars, okolnichie, court nobles and clerks, straight from the metropolitan's palace, without first going home; likewise many traders, merchants and tradesmen, all went to kowtow* before their sovereign and weep.

---
* [From the Chinese kòutóu, literally meaning to knock the head. The Russian word literally means to beat the forehead. This is an old Chinese custom.]

Chapter Seven

The prelates stopped in Slotin and sent to announce themselves to Ivan. He ordered them to come to Aleksandrovskaya Sloboda with his constables, and on 5 February admitted them to the palace. After the bishops pronounced the metropolitan's blessing upon the tsar, they plaintively implored him to lift his disfavor from the priesthood, the nobles, the courtiers and the clerks; they begged him not to abandon the nation, but to rule and act according to his pleasure. Finally, they entreated him to let the boyars see him. Ivan now admitted the boyars: with the same great emotion and power, they tried to persuade the tsar to take pity on Russia, which had been raised to greatness by his victories and wise statutes, the glorious valor of its large population, by its rich natural treasures and even more by its glorious, true religion.

"If," said the clergy and state officials, "if you do not value worldly greatness and glory, then remember that in leaving Moscow, you are leaving its holy cathedrals where wonders of divine grace were performed for you and where lie the curative relics of Christ's saints. Remember that you are the guardian not only of the state, but also of the Church. You are the first and only monarch of Orthodoxy! If you withdraw, who will save the truth and purity of our faith? Who will save millions of souls from eternal damnation?"

The tsar replied with his customary loquacity: he reiterated all his well-known reproaches to the boyars with regard to their willfulness, negligence and obduracy. He cited history, showing that they had long been guilty of bloodshed and internal strife in Russia and had long been enemies of the reigning heirs of Monomakh. They wanted (a new accusation!) to get rid of the tsar, his wife and sons . . . The boyars stood in silence.

"But," continued the tsar, "for my father, the metropolitan Athanasii, for you our pilgrims, archbishops and bishops, I agree to take up my reign once again, and on such conditions as you will learn."

These conditions were that Ivan would be free to punish traitors with death, disgrace and loss of property without any restriction, without any bothersome meddling on the part of the priesthood. With these brief words, Ivan pronounced the doom of many of the boyars who stood before him. It appeared that none of them was thinking of his own life; they only wanted the tsar to return to his duties, and they all, both the nobility and the clergy, with tears in their eyes, thanked and praised Ivan's graciousness. The sovereign had just deprived them of the ancient, sacred right to intercede not only on behalf of the innocent, but also on behalf of the guilty who were yet deserving of mercy! This formidable ruler, as if mollified by the humility of his doomed victims, ordered the prelates to celebrate Epiphany with him. He kept princes Belskii and Shchenyatev in Sloboda, but sent the rest of boyars and clerks back to Moscow so that the ministries would not cease in their labors.

Moscow had long been waiting impatiently for the tsar. It was said that he was occupied with some secret business with those closest to him and there was fearful speculation. Finally, on 2 February, Ivan formally entered the capital and on the next day summoned the priesthood, boyars and distinguished officials. His appearance amazed everyone. Here we shall describe Ivan's former appearance. He was tall in stature and well-built. He had high shoulders, strong musculature, a broad chest, good-looking hair, a thin mustache, a Roman nose, normal-size eyes that were grey, but bright, piercing and filled with fire, and a face that had once been handsome.

But now he had changed so much that it was impossible to recognize him: his face expressed a dark ferocity. All his features were distorted, his glance was dulled and on his head and in his beard there was almost no hair left due to the inexplicable action of the fury that seethed in his soul. After once more enumerating the sins of the boyars and confirming his willingness to remain tsar, Ivan carefully discussed the duties of a monarch to preserve the peace of the state and to take all necessary measures for this. He spoke of the brevity of life and the necessity to see beyond the grave, and proposed the law of *Oprichnina* – a word heretofore unknown!

ESTABLISHMENT OF
THE OPRICHNINA

Ivan said that he was establishing a special bodyguard both for his own safety and the state's. This sort of thinking surprised no one: they knew of his distrustfulness and fearfulness

– both qualities of an impure conscience. But the circumstances were disconcerting and led to new terror in Russia.

1) The tsar declared as his own the cities of Mozhaisk, Vyazma, Kozelsk, Peremyshl, Belyov, Likhvin, Yaroslavets, Sukhodrovya, Medyn, Suzdal, Shuya, Galich, Yurievets, Balakhna, Vologda, Ustyug, Staraya Rusa, Kargopol and Vaga as well as Muscovite volosts and others with their revenues;

2) he chose 1,000 bodyguards from the princes, court nobles and boyar cadets and gave them estates in these cities while moving the local big landowners and proprietors to other places;

3) In Moscow he took for himself the streets of Chertolskaya and Arbatskaya with Sivtsovyi Vrag and half of Nikitskaya with various towns from which it was necessary to expel all court nobles and clerks not on the list of 1,000;

4) he designated *special* officials for his service: a major domo, treasurers, stewards and even cooks, bakers and craftsmen;

5) and finally, as if he hated the glorious memory of the Kremlin and the sacred graves of his ancestors, he did not want to live in Ivan III's sumptuous palace, and instead ordered a new one constructed across the Neglinnaya, between the Arbat and Nikitskaya Street – it was like a fortress, surrounded by high walls.

These parts of Russia and Moscow, this 1,000-man bodyguard and the new court were all under his direct supervision and called the Oprichnina. All the rest, i.e., the rest of the country, was called the Zemshchina, which Ivan entrusted to the Zemskii boyars, the princes Belskii, Mstislavskii and others.

He ordered the senior state officials – the equerry, major domo, treasurers and secretaries – to sit in their offices and resolve all state matters, and for the most important of them to deal with the boyars, who were permitted to report to the sovereign only in extraordinary circumstances, particularly those to do with military matters.

In other words, Ivan apparently wanted to withdraw from the state and surround himself with a small ruling circle, and to prove that *sovereign's* and *state* no longer meant the same thing in Russia. He also demanded 100,000 rubles from the Zemskii treasury for the expenses of his travel from Moscow to Aleksandrovskaya Sloboda! No one uttered a protest, for the tsar's will was law. The new measures were promulgated.

SECOND ROUND OF EXECUTIONS

On 4 February Moscow was astonished by the realization of the *conditions* the tsar had announced to the priesthood and the boyars at Aleksandrovskaya Sloboda. Executions began of the supposed traitors, who were alleged to have plotted with Kurbskii against the lives of Ivan, the late tsaritsa Anastasiya and his children.

The first victim was the renowned voivode Prince Aleksandr Borisovich Gorbatyi-Shuiskii, a descendant of St. Vladimir, Vsevolod the Great and the ancient Suzdal princes, a distinguished participant in the conquest of Kazan, a man of profound intellect who was skilled in military affairs and an ardent friend of the nation and Christians. He was to be put to death together with his son Pyotr, a 17-year-old youth. Both went to the place of execution without fear, calmly, arm in arm. The son did not want to see his father executed and so was first to bow his head beneath the sword, but his father pulled him from the block, exclaiming,

"Do not let me see you dead!" The youth yielded to him, then took his father's severed head and kissed it, looked up to the sky, and with a happy face gave himself into the hands of the executioner. Gorbatyi's brother-in-law, Pyotr Khovrin (of Greek extraction), the okolnichii Golovin, Prince Ivan Sukhoi-Kashin and the royal carver, Prince Pyotr Ivanovich Gorenskii were also executed that same day. Prince Dmitrii Sheryev was impaled: it is written that this unfortunate man suffered for a whole day, but fortified by faith forgot his torment and sang the canon to Jesus.

Two boyars, the princes Ivan Kurakin and Dmitrii Nemoi, were tonsured; many court nobles and boyar cadets had their property confiscated and others were exiled to Kazan with their families. One of the most distinguished nobles, a close relative of the virtuous tsaritsa Anastasiya, the boyar and voivode Ivan Petrovich Yakovlev, had also brought disfavor upon himself, but Ivan even at his most callous still liked to boast of his mercy. He forgave Yakovlev, took a written oath from him undersigned by the prelates wherein he promised not to depart Russia for Lithuania, the Pope, the emperor, the sultan or *Prince Vladimir Andreevich*, and to have no secret ties with them.

We have mentioned the exile of a first-rank boyar, the renowned voivode Prince Mikhail Vorotynskii. Deprived of his property, he spent nearly four years at Belo-ozero, where he received about 100 rubles per annum from the state treasury, in addition to provisions: wine, foreign fruits, clothing and linens. Ivan finally restored this distinguished exile to the court and the Duma; he was made deputy of Kazan and *holder* of Novosil after promising his loyalty in the same sort of letter as Yakovlev, with the addition that the metropolitan and the bishops were his intercessors. Since the tsar had forbidden the clergy to stand up for the disgraced, he favored Yakovlev with this phrasing – but in fact there were no longer any intercessors! The priesthood could only dampen their altars with their tears and direct fervent prayers to God for the salvation of the unfortunate!

Other boyars – Lev Andreevich Saltykov and the princes Vasilii Serebryanyi, Ivan Okhlyabinin and Zakharii Ochin-Pleshcheev – were obliged to present guarantors for their devoted service to the sovereign. In the event of their flight, the guarantors (not only eminent officials, but merchants as well) would be obliged to pay a hefty sum of money to the treasury, for example, 25,000 rubles for Prince Serebryanyi (about half a million present-day rubles). This was a useless and shameful precaution for a sovereign to take, but this sovereign was a tyrant!

After the executions, Ivan busied himself with training his new guard. His advisors were Aleksei Basmanov, Malyuta Skuratov, Prince Afanasii Vyazemskii and other favorites. Young boyar cadets were brought to him, distinguished not by merit, but by a so-called audacity, dissoluteness and readiness for anything. Ivan questioned them about their lineage, their friends and protectors. He required that they have no kind of ties with eminent boyars, and he made a virtue of obscure or lowly birth. Instead of 1,000, Ivan selected 6,000.

He took oaths from them to be loyal and true to him, to inform on traitors, not to make friends with the Zemskie (i.e., with anyone not enrolled in the Oprichnina), not to bring them bread and salt [i.e., be inhospitable to them] and not to acknowledge their father or mother, but only their sovereign.

In return, the tsar gave them not only the land, but also the houses and furniture of all the displaced big landholders (numbering 12,000). They had been expelled from Oprichnina territory with empty hands, so that many of them, honored men who had been wounded in battle were obliged to travel on foot in winter with their wives and children to other distant and deserted estates. Even farmers were victims of this unjust institution. New court nobles, who had risen from nothing to become great lords, wanted to embellish their baseness with luxury; they needed money and burdened the peasants with imposts and labor so that their towns fell into ruin. Yet this evil seemed insignificant compared to others.

It soon became apparent that Ivan had made all of Russia a victim of his oprichniki:* they always prevailed in the courts and there were no judgments against them, nor any justice. The oprichniki, or *infernals* [kromeshniki], as they came to be called, were like brutes from the infernal darkness. They could safely oppress and rob their neighbors and in case of complaint, extract a fine from them for the slur. In addition to many other crimes, the following became commonplace, to the horror of the peaceful citizen: the servant of an oprichnik, obeying his master's will, would hide with several items in the home of a merchant or court noble. The master would disclose his pretended flight and alleged theft, request an officer of the law, catch his fugitive red-handed and get 500, 1,000 or more rubles from the innocent homeowner.

There was no leniency: the debtor had to pay up immediately or go for *pravezh*, whereby an unsatisfied claimant had the right to take a debtor to the square and publically whip him until he paid up. Sometimes the oprichnik himself would drop something in an upscale shop, leave and return with a constable and on the basis of this supposedly stolen item he would bring the merchant to ruin. Sometimes the oprichnik would seize a man in the street and take him to court, complaining of an imaginary insult or curse, since to say something disrespectful to an *infernal* was tantamount to

---

* [Agents of the Oprichnina. They have been likened to a cross between secret police and a motorcycle gang.]

offending the tsar himself. In such a case the innocent man could save himself from severe corporal punishment by paying a stiff fine.

In brief, the Zemskie people, from court noble to lower middle class, were without a say and had no recourse against the oprichniki. The former were the prey, the latter the predators, and this was all so that Ivan could rely on the diligence of his brigand bodyguards in the further murders he was plotting. The more the nation hated the oprichniki, the more faith the sovereign had in them: this widespread hatred served him as an earnest of his men's loyalty. Ivan's ingenious mind devised a fitting symbol for his diligent servants: they would always ride with dogs' heads and brooms attached to their saddles, denoting thereby that they would gnaw at the tsar's malefactors and sweep out Russia!

Although the new palace was becoming an inaccessible fortress, Ivan still did not feel safe in it. In any case, he did not like Moscow and henceforth spent most of his time at Aleksandrovskaya Sloboda, which became a city ornamented by stone churches, houses and shops. The glorious local Cathedral of the Virgin shone on the outside with various colors and with silver and gold; every brick had a representation of the cross. The tsar lived in a great palace, surrounded by a rampart and a ditch; the court, state and military officials lived in their own houses. The oprichniki had their own street, likewise for the merchants. No one dared enter or leave without Ivan's knowledge; for this reason the land up to three versts from the city was called *The Forbidden* and was usually under military guard.

> ALEKSANDROVSKAYA SLOBODA

In this formidable pleasure palace, surrounded by a dark forest, Ivan devoted the greater part of his time to church service so as to quiet his soul with incessant pious activities. He even wanted to turn the palace into a monastery, and his favorites into monks: he chose 300 of the oprichniki, the very worst, and named them *brothers* and himself *abbot*. Prince Athanasii Vyazemskii was the cellarer and Malyuta Skuratov the paraclesiarch [sacristan]. He gave them skullcaps and black cassocks,

> IVAN'S MONKISH LIFE

beneath which they wore rich caftans, shining with gold, and with sable trimming. He composed monastic regulations for them and served as an example of obedience to them.

Ivan's monastic life has been described thusly: at the fourth hour of the morning he would walk to the bell tower with the tsaritsa and Malyuta Skuratov to ring for matins; the brothers would hasten into the church and if anyone did not show up, he was punished with eight days' confinement. The service continued to the sixth or seventh hour. The tsar would sing, recite and pray so vehemently that there were always marks on his forehead from his strenuous bowing to the ground. At the eighth hour they would again gather for mass and at the tenth hour meet at the refectory table, where everyone would take a seat except Ivan, who would remain standing, reciting edifying precepts.

Meanwhile the brothers would eat and drink their fill; every day was like a holiday: they did not lack for wine or mead. The leftovers would be taken from the palace to the square for the poor. The abbot – i.e., Ivan – would eat later; he would then converse with his favorites about Church principles, and then nap or go to the prison to feed some unfortunate. It seems this terrible spectacle amused him: he would return with a look of heartfelt satisfaction. He would then make jokes and converse more merrily than usual. At the eighth hour of the evening he would go to vespers and at the tenth hour he would retire to his sleeping chamber, where three blind men, one after another, would tell him stories. After listening, he would fall asleep, but not for long. At midnight he would get up and his day would begin with prayer! Sometimes reports on governmental matters would be given to him while in church, and sometimes he would issue his cruelest commands while at matins or mass!

To break the monotony of his life he would go on so-called *excursions*: he would visit monasteries both near and far, inspect fortifications on the frontier and go hunting in the forests and wildernesses. He especially liked to hunt bears. Nevertheless, he was always and everywhere occupied with affairs, since the Zemskii boyars, supposedly fully empowered to rule the country, did not dare to do anything without his say-so.

Whenever distinguished foreign emissaries would come to us, Ivan would show up in Moscow to receive them formally with all the usual splendor in the new Kremlin palace, near the Church of St. John. He would also appear there on other important occasions, but not very often. oprichniki, gleaming in their golden garments, would fill the palace but would not block the way to the throne or to senior boyars: these guards would just look at them haughtily, puffing themselves up like lowly serfs at some undeserved honor.

Aside from his favorites, Ivan honored some Lithuanian prisoners in a surprising manner. In June 1565, accusing citizens of Derpt of secret relations with the former master, he deported all the Germans there and sent them to Vladimir, Uglich, Kostroma and Nizhnyi Novgorod with their wives and children, but he gave them proper financial support and a Christian preceptor, the Derpt pastor Wetterman, who was able to travel freely from city to city to comfort them in their sad exile. The tsar especially respected this virtuous man and ordered him to examine his library, in which Wetterman found a large number of rare books which had been brought from Rome, probably by Princess Sofiya.

> HIS FOREIGN FAVORITES

The Germans Eberfeld, Kalb, Taube and Kruse entered our service and with cunning flattery were able to insinuate themselves into Ivan's confidence. It is even asserted that Eberfeld persuaded him to accept the Augsburg Confession,* demonstrating its purity to him orally and in writing! In any case, the tsar permitted the Lutherans to have a church in Moscow and extracted a significant fine from the metropolitan for some sort of offense he had done to one of these Protestants. Ivan praised their customs, gloried in his German heritage and wanted marry a son to a German princess and a daughter to a German prince in order to cement friendly ties with the Empire.

In heart-to-heart conversations with foreign favorites he complained about the boyars and the priesthood; he did not hide his thoughts of eradicating the former so that he could rule more freely

---

* [The primary confession of faith of the Lutheran Church.]

and safely with a renewed nobility, or with the Oprichnina, which was devoted to him since it saw him as its father and benefactor. The boyars yearned for Adashev's time, when they were free and the tsar was not (so said Ivan)! These foreigners naturally had no love for Russia, which was frightening to neighboring power; they wished only to please the tsar. They doubtless had no intention of leading him out of his dark folly or angering him with frank talk of the truth. They might even have taken secret pleasure in watching the storm that was destroying the chief pillars of this great monarchy, since the tsar was eliminating his best voivodes and best state councilors.

The foreigners kept silent, or against their conscience, praised the tyrant. Distinguished Russians were denied free access to their sovereign, since they were stigmatized by the rather suspicious term *Zemskie*, brazenly insulted by the violent *infernals*, threatened with disgrace and punished without guilt. They likewise maintained their silence, along with the priesthood. Yet when the aged metropolitan Athanasii, exhausted by a serious illness and perhaps by spiritual sorrow as well, retired in 1566, a bold and virtuous man appeared, fervent in his love of country, who undertook to correct the tsar. But, less fortunately than Silvestr, all he could do was die for his country while wearing the crown of a martyr.

Displaying fervor for the good of the Church, Ivan wanted to give it a pastor of outstanding Christian merit. The choice fell at first on Archbishop German of Kazan, who had long avoided such a dangerous title, given the circumstances in Russia and under such a tsar, but he was obliged to obey Ivan's resolute will and to consent. The bishops all met in Moscow and wrote a letter of election. German stayed for a few days in the metropolitan's palace getting ready for his ordination.

Now, in conversing with Ivan alone, German wanted to test his heart: he began to speak with him, as an archprelate should, of sin and Christian repentance, quietly, discreetly, but with some force. He reminded him of death, the Day of Judgment and eternal torment for evildoers.

Ivan thought this over, and then left with a dark countenance. He relayed to his favorites what the archbishop had said and asked them what they thought. Aleksei Basmanov replied,

"We think, Sovereign, that German wants to be a second Silvestr: he frightens your imagination and acts hypocritically in hope of gaining power over you. Save us and yourself from such an archpastor!" German was expelled from the palace and the tsar sought another archprelate.

Amidst the cold waves of the White Sea is the island of Solovetskii in the wild wastes, but renowned in Russia due to the sanctity of the first toilers there, Savvatii and Zosima; it shone with the virtues of its abbot Filipp, son of the boyar Kolychev, who in the very bloom of youth came to hate the vanity of this world and served as an example of the rigorous life for the anchorite monks. The sovereign heard of Filipp and gave his monastery precious vessels, pearls, rich fabrics, land and villages. He helped him with money to build stone churches, wharfs, inns and dikes.

> COURAGE OF THE METROPOLITAN FILIPP

The abbot was not only a wise preceptor for the brothers, but also an energetic proprietor of this heretofore wild and inaccessible island. He cleared forests, built roads, drained the swamp with channels, introduced reindeer and domestic cattle, fishing and a salt works. As much as possible he made the wasteland beautiful; he ameliorated the severe climate and made it more salubrious.

The immortal Silvestr, loved and respected by Filipp, had ended his days here at the Solovetskii Monastery. It is likely that they both lamented the change in Ivan's disposition; it is probable that the former unburdened his soul to the abbot – a soul that had once been blessedly happy reforming the young sovereign and developing the prosperity of the realm. These conversations might have prepared Filipp for greatness, but he was a diligent toiler at the remote edge of the world and could not expect such glory. Doubtless no one paid him any mind, except Ivan. After the tsar had rejected German, he thought to make Filipp the metropolitan, bypassing all the prelates and archimandrites. He wished to demonstrate thereby his special respect for Christian virtues and show that they were not concealed from his eyes even in the most remote wildernesses.

The abbot was summoned to Moscow by the tsar's gracious letter, for spiritual advice. Before leaving, he performed the liturgy once more, served communion to all the brothers and departed his beloved cloister with tears in his eyes, as if foreseeing that only his dead body would ever return there. The humble Solovetskii abbot was met three versts from Novgorod by all the residents of that ancient capital, with greetings, gifts and the plea that he intercede for them before the throne, for there was a rumor that Ivan was threatening them with his wrath.

The tsar received Filipp with special honors, dined, and conversed amicably with him, finally told him that he would be the new metropolitan. This monk of the wilderness was astounded, wept, and did not want this glittering burden. He tried to convince Ivan not *to place so great a load in such a small boat*, but the tsar was adamant. Filipp now suggested a condition: he told the tsar,

"I shall obey, but it will kill my conscience. Let there be no Oprichnina! Let there be only one Russia! In the words of the Most High, all divided kingdoms come to ruin. Seeing the grief of the nation, I cannot in sincerity bless you."

Ivan kept his self-control; he kept the wrath from rising in his heart and responded quietly,

"Do you really not know that my people want to devour me, that those closest to me are preparing my doom?"

He tried to show why this institution was necessary, but soon lost his patience at the old man's frank objections and ordered him to be silent. Everyone thought that Filipp, like German, would be sent away in dishonor. They saw the opposite occur. This time Ivan did not want to give the abbot the glory of being persecuted for his virtue. He wanted to convince him to keep silent and appear weak in the eyes of Russia, to become a sort of accomplice in the new regulations of his regime. The principal pastors of the Church served as an instrument for this.

Obeying Ivan's will, they tried to convince Filipp to accept the title of metropolitan unconditionally, to think only of the good of the Church and not to anger the sovereign with boldness, but rather to soothe his wrath through his meekness and change it into benevolence. They attempted to show Filipp that his supposed firmness in this case was due to pride and was inconsistent with the spirit of a true servant of Christ, and that the duty of a prelate was to pray for and to exhort the tsar solely for the salvation of his soul, not for affairs of state.

Some of the prelates secretly approved of Filipp's boldness, but did not possess it themselves. Others – namely Pimen of Novgorod and Filothei of Ryazan – sought worldly honors and fawned on Ivan's passions. Their suasion caused Filipp to waver. He was not afraid of the tsar's wrath, nor was he blinded by the glitter of the archpastorship, as will be shown in the sequel, but he was perhaps troubled by the thought that his intention to turn down this supreme title might really be due to secret pride, obduracy and a lack of faith in Providence, which rules over tsars and does not allow them to step outside the limits set by Its highest laws, which are no doubt wise, but inexplicable to the human mind. Filipp replied,

"Let it be as the sovereign and the pastors of the Church wish!"

A letter was written in which it said that the newly chosen metropolitan had given his word to the archbishops and the bishops not to interfere with the sovereign's Oprichnina and not to abandon his position of metropolitan on the pretext that the tsar had not acceded to his requests and had forbidden him to involve himself in the affairs of the world. The prelates countersigned this manuscript and Filipp, a declared enemy of the Oprichnina, was immediately elevated to the metropolitanate, to the general satisfaction of the public and the irritation of Ivan's depraved favorites.

It seemed as if the sovereign had gained a happy victory over himself and had paid honor to virtue. The metropolitan had yielded, but had disclosed something important: Russians now knew what he wanted and might have hope for the future with such an archprelate. All good people listened with delight to the new metropolitan's inaugural speech to Ivan, which was genuinely worthy of a pastor. He spoke of the duty of rulers to be fathers to their subjects, to guard justice and respect merit. He spoke of vile flatterers who cluster around the throne, blinding the sovereign's mind and serving his passions and not the nation. These people praise those worthy of abuse and rebuke those worthy of praise.

Filipp spoke of the transitory character of worldly greatness, of the victories of *unarmed love*, which are achieved by the state's good deeds and are more glorious than military victories. It seemed that Ivan himself was moved by the voice of this preceptor, a voice that had been long silent in this cathedral, and that this voice that had once been pleasant for him reminded him of a happy time and gave him a taste of a sweetness he had forgotten. The first days and months passed peaceably in the hopeful capital. Complaints against the infernals were fewer: the monster was napping. The tsar was kind to the metropolitan, and this virtuous man, seemingly afraid of forgetting the Solovetskii wilderness and the strict vows of his youth, began to build a church in Moscow named for its saints Zosima and Savvatii.

But this quiet interlude, whether due to Ivan's gnawing conscience or his dissimulation, was the precursor of a new storm. From his lair in Aleksandrovskaya, the tyrant turned his ferocious gaze on Moscow. Ivan had hoped to astound Russia with the choice of a metropolitan no one had considered, but soon came to see him as an instrument of the hated boyars: he convinced himself that they had given him the idea of requesting the elimination of the Oprichnina and arousing the people against this corps of royal bodyguards. The infernals sent to the capital to keep an eye on things reported that on the streets and in the squares the citizens were fleeing them like the plague; everyone would go silent when an oprichnik appeared.

Plots and conspiracies were forming in Ivan's imagination and he felt it necessary to expose and verify them. The following event served as a pretext for new murders. Secret letters signed by King Sigismund and the Lithuanian hetman Khotkevich were given to the chief boyars of Moscow, to the princes Belskii, Mstislavskii and Vorotynskii, and to the equerry Ivan Petrovich Thedorov. The king and hetman tried to convince them to leave their cruel tsar and come over to them, promising these notables appanages and reminding the first two princes that they

THIRD EPISODE OF MURDERS

were of Lithuanian ancestry, the third that he had once been a sovereign prince, and the equerry Thedorov that he had felt the tsar's wrath on numerous occasions.

The boyars gave these letters to Ivan and replied to the king that it was dishonorable to try to persuade loyal subjects to commit treason; that they would die for their good tsar, who was terrible only to malefactors. If the king wanted to call them forth from Russia, he could give them all of Lithuania, Galicia, Prussia, Samogitia, Belorussia and the territory of Volhynia and Podolia. Thedor wrote to Sigismund:

"How could you imagine that I, with one foot in the grave, would consider dooming my soul with vile treachery? What would you have me do? It is beyond my strength to command your legions, I do not like feasting, I do not know how to amuse you and I have not learned your dances." In his letter to Hetman Khotkevich, he added,

"With what would you tempt me? I am rich and renowned. You threaten me with the tsar's wrath, but from him I see only favor."

Ivan himself probably undertook to provide the king with these replies, written in the same style, but it is not known whether he followed through. At any rate, although he always liked to upbraid Sigismund for his intrigues, in his correspondence with Lithuania there is no mention of such a dishonorable and reckless invitation to our nobles. If the sovereign had composed phony letters from the king to test the loyalty of his boyars, then that loyalty had been proven in his eyes by this instance.

But not in the eyes of Russia: a citizen who had given enemies the hope of persuading him to defect was now under a shadow of suspicion. This time princes Belskii, Mstislavskii and Vorotynskii were left alone, but Thedorov, a man of old customs, adorned with martial glory and gray with service to the state, who had held the distinguished rank of equerry for 19 years and was chief of the treasury, a generous and splendid nobleman, now became the subject of slander. He was still serving the tsar diligently, living out his days with his saintly wife, but without children, preparing to make his report to the court on high when a worldly court declared him a principal conspirator, believing or fabricating that this decrepit old man was planning to dethrone the tsar and rule Russia in his place. Ivan hastened to destroy this frightening imaginary conspiracy. It is written that in the presence of the entire court he dressed Thedor in the tsar's garments, placed the crown on his head, sat him on the throne and placed an orb in his hand. The tsar then removed his hat, bowed low and said,

"Health to you, great tsar of the Russian land! I have given you the honor you desire! But since I have the power to make you tsar, I can also dethrone you!"

So saying, he struck him in the heart with a dagger. The oprichniki finished him off, dragged his mutilated body from of the palace and threw it out for the dogs to eat. They also murdered the equerry's aged wife Mariya. Then they executed all the imagined confederates of this innocent man: the princes Ivan Andreevich Kurakin-Bulgakov, Dmitrii Ryapolovskii (a valiant warrior who had obtained many victories over the Crimeans) and three Rostovskii princes. One of these was then ruling in Nizhnyi-Novgorod: the 30 infernals dispatched from Moscow found him standing in a church there and said to him,

"Prince Rostovskii! By order of the sovereign, you are our prisoner."

The voivode threw his mace of power onto the ground and calmly surrendered to them. They stripped him and carted him naked to a place 20 versts away on the banks of the Volga, where they stopped. He coolly asked why. They answered,

"To water the horses." "It is not for the horses," said the unfortunate man, "but for me. You will have me drink this water and not stop!"

In an instant they cut off his head and threw his body into the river. They placed the head at Ivan's feet; he shoved it away and laughed nastily that this prince who liked to cover himself with blood of his enemies had finally done the same to himself. The distinguished commander Prince Pyotr Shchenyatev thought to hide from death in a monastery. He renounced the world, his possessions, his wife and his children, but the murderers found him in his cell and tortured him. They burned him in a large frying pan (so says

1567-1568

Kurbskii) and drove needles under his fingernails. Prince Ivan Turuntai Pronskii, gray with age, had also served Ivan's father and took part in all of the campaigns, all of the battles that were so glorious for Russia. He, likewise desiring at last to become a monk, was trampled to death.

The sovereign's treasurer, Khozyain Yurievich Tyutin, renowned for his wealth, was cut to pieces along with his wife, two infant sons and two young daughters. This execution was carried out by Prince Mikhailo Temgryukovich Cherkasskii, the tsaritsa's brother! The keeper of the seal, or Duma secretary Kazarin Dubrovskii was likewise torn to pieces. Many other eminent people were murdered as they unsuspectingly entered a church or their offices. The oprichniki, armed with long knives and poleaxes, ran around the city searching for victims; they would openly murder 10 or 12 people a day; the bodies would lie in the streets and in the squares: no one dared bury them. Citizens feared to leave their homes. In Moscow the cries of the tsar's executioners resounded all the more terribly.

The virtuous metropolitan was also silent before the desperate citizens and boyars, but God saw into his heart, while the tsar heard his secret admonitions and the fiercest reproaches, which were unfortunately futile. The tsar fled, not wishing to see the archprelate. The good nobles went to Filipp, weeping, to point out to him the bloodstained bodies in the streets and squares. He comforted the bereaved in the name of the Heavenly Father; he gave them his word he would not spare his own life to save the people, and he kept it.

However, at the hour of mass on Easter Sunday, Ivan, accompanied by several boyars and a large number of oprichniki, entered the main Church of the Dormition. The tsar and all his retinue were in black chasubles and tall hats. The metropolitan was standing in his place within the church; Ivan approached him, awaiting his blessing. The metropolitan looked at the icon of the Savior without saying a word. Finally the boyars said,

1568

"Holy prelate, this is your sovereign: bless him!" Filipp looked at Ivan and then answered,

"In this guise, in this strange clothing I do not recognize the Orthodox tsar. Nor do I recognize him in the workings of affairs of state... O sovereign! We are making an offering to God here, but innocent Christian blood is running past the altar. As long as the sun has shone in the heavens, it has never been seen or heard that a pious tsar has troubled his own realm so terribly! Even in the most infidel and pagan countries there is law and justice, and compassion towards the people, but in Russia there is none!

"The citizens have no protection for their lives and property. There is plundering and murder everywhere, and it is being done in the name of the tsar. You sit high on the throne, but there is a higher judge for us and for you. How will you stand before Him? Covered in the blood of innocents, deafened by the cries of their torment? The very stones beneath your feet cry out for vengeance. Sovereign! I tell you this as the pastor of your soul. I fear only the Lord!"

Ivan shook with anger; he hit the stone with his staff and said in a terrible voice,

"Monk! Ere now I have been merciful with you, you renegade; from now on I shall be just what you call me!"

With this threat, he departed. The next day there were new executions, notable among them Prince Vasilii Pronskii's. All of the metropolitan's chief officials were arrested, tortured and questioned about Filipp's secret schemes, but nothing was learned. Ivan did not yet dare to lay hands on the archprelate himself, who was now loved and honored by the people more than ever. The tsar prepared to strike him, but was patient – and in the meantime, what did he do?

Eyewitnesses write that one midnight in the month of July 1568, Ivan's favorites Prince Athanasii Vyazemskii, Malyuta Skuratov, Vasilii Gryaznoi and the tsar's guard broke into many homes of eminent people, secretaries and merchants. They took such of their wives as were noted for beauty and removed them from the city. At sunrise Ivan followed after them, surrounded by thousands of infernals. On the first night of his stay the women were presented to him. He chose some for himself, gave the rest to his favorites, and rode around Moscow with them. He burned the homesteads of the disgraced boyars, executed their loyal servants and even killed the cattle, especially in the Kolomenskoe villages of the murdered equerry Thedor. When he returned to Moscow, he ordered the women to be taken to their various homes by night. Some of them died of shame and sorrow.

While avoiding the metropolitan, the tsar still saw him in church. On the day of the holy apostles Prokhor and Nikanor, 28 July, Filipp held services at the Novodevichii Monastery and walked along the wall with crosses. The tsar was also there, with his oprichniki, one of whom followed the archprelate in a skullcap. The metropolitan saw this disrespect, stopped and indignantly spoke to the sovereign about it, but the oprichnik had already hidden his skullcap.

The tsar was convinced Filipp had made up this story to arouse the people against the sovereign's favorites. Ivan forgot all propriety: he formally cursed the metropolitan, calling him a liar, renegade and malefactor. He swore that he would prove all this, and embarked on this course with the advice of his cunning confessor, the archpriest Evstafii of the Blagoveshchensk Monastery, who secretly hated Filipp. Bishop Pafnutii of Suzdal, the archimandrite Theodosii of the Andronikovskii Monastery and Prince Vasilii Temkin, formerly a renowned warrior, but now a diligent servant of tyranny like Basmanov and others, set out at once for Solovki.*

Was it necessary to seek so far for vile slanderers? But the tsar wanted to darken virtue right at its radiant source. He wished to uncover Filipp's fancied hypocrisy and spiritual impurity right where he was praised for it. To Ivan, this idea seemed like skillful cunning. The tsar's emissaries now flattered, now terrorized the Solovetskii monks, demanding that they bear shameless false witness against their former abbot. But everyone said that Filipp was saintly in his heart and in his deeds. Nevertheless, they found one who dared to assert the opposite: their chief, Abbot Paisii, who hoped to become a bishop. Denunciations and evidence

---

* [The monastery complex in the White Sea.]

were concocted and presented to Ivan; and the metropolitan was ordered to appear in court. The tsar, prelates and boyars sat in silence. Abbot Pansii stood and slandered the holy man with unheard of audacity. Instead of futile justification, the metropolitan quietly told Pansii that the evil he had sown would not bear him the desired fruits. He told the tsar,

"Sovereign! Grand Prince! You think that I fear either you or death. It is not so! I have achieved ripe old age blamelessly. In the wilderness I knew neither mutinous passions nor worldly intrigues, so I wish to devote my soul to the Most High, who is my Lord and yours. It is better to die as a blameless martyr than to quietly endure the terror and lawlessness of this unhappy age as a metropolitan. Do as you wish. Here is the pastor's staff; here is the white klobuk and the mantle with which you wished to exalt me. And you, prelates, archimandrites, abbots and all who serve the altars: tend Christ's flock faithfully and prepare to render account – and fear your heavenly ruler more than your earthly one."

He started to leave, but the tsar stopped him, saying that he must await judgment: he could not judge himself. Ivan forced him to take back the ritual implements and hold mass on the day of Archangel Michael (8 November). However, when Filipp, in full sacerdotal robes, stood before the altar in the Cathedral of the Dormition, the boyar Aleksii Basmanov appeared with a bunch of armed oprichniki, holding a scroll in his hand.

The people were astonished. Basmanov ordered the scroll to be read: they heard that Filipp had been relieved of his pastoral rank by the ecclesiastical council. The soldiers came up to the altar and tore off the metropolitan's, tore off his priestly garments and clothed him in a poor priest's chasuble, chased him out of the church with brooms and drove him in a wooden sledge to the Epiphany Cloister. The people ran weeping after the metropolitan: with a bright expression, Filipp lovingly blessed the people and told them,

"Pray!" The next day he was brought to the Palace of Justice. Ivan himself was there to hear the judgment. Filipp was alleged to be guilty of serious crimes and witchcraft and would have to spend the rest of his days in confinement. He bid farewell to the world magnanimously, movingly; he did not reproach the court, but for the last time implored Ivan to have compassion on Russia and not lacerate his subjects. The tsar should recall how his forbears ruled, how he himself had ruled in his youth, for the people's good and his own. The sovereign did not say a word in reply but gestured for the soldiers to take him. He was imprisoned in irons for perhaps eight days, and then transported to the Cloister of St. Nikolai the Elder on the banks of the Moscow River, where he endured hunger, but was sustained by prayer. Meanwhile, Ivan was exterminating the renowned Kolychev line. He sent Filipp the severed head of his nephew Ivan Borisovich, and ordered that he be told,

"Here is your beloved kinsman; your sorcery was no help to him!" Filipp got up, took the head, blessed it and returned it to the bearer. The tsar feared the people's love for the deposed metropolitan; he heard that they were crowding around Nikolai's Cloister from morning till evening, staring into the prisoner's cell and telling each other about the miracles of his holiness. He ordered the martyr taken away to the Otroch Monastery in Tver and immediately chose a new metropolitan: the Trinity archimandrite Kirill. This vexed Pimen, who had nurtured hopes of taking Filipp's place.

After freeing himself from this strict and unbending archpastor and giving this important position to a good, but weak-willed and taciturn monk, Ivan could rampage more boldly and freely. Up till now he had destroyed people; henceforth he destroyed whole cities. He began with Torzhok, where the violent oprichniki picked a fight with the residents on the day of the fair. The tsar declared the citizens rebels and ordered them to be tortured and drowned in the river. The same thing happened in Kolomna and with the same consequences. That city had some estates that had belonged to the unfortunate Thedor. The people had loved him and thus to Ivan seemed to be rebels.

In a word, the tyranny had matured, but its end was still far off! Nothing was able to disarm the rampaging tsar – neither submission, nor courageous sacrifice, nor even the natural catastrophes of this age. Russia, darkened by the terror of torture, was

> **PLAGUE**

now scourged by a plague that came to us from Estonia or Sweden. In July 1566, a pestilent epidemic broke out in Shelonskaya Pyatina in the Novgorod district; a month later it had spread to Novgorod, Polotsk, Ozerishche, Nevel, Velikie Luki, Toropets and Smolensk. People were dying suddenly with *signs*, as it says in the chronicle – probably blotches or boils.

Many villages were left empty and in the cities many homes were closed up. There were no hymns sung in the churches, which had lost their priests, who had not taken precautions during the diligent performance of their duties. Priests were sent from other towns to replace them. More clerics and citizens died than military people. The plague even reached Mozhaisk, where the tsar established pickets and ordered no one from infected places be let into the capital. Communications were severed between many towns and cities. People suffered from fear and endured want and high prices. Some districts had bad harvests: in Kazan and neighboring districts an indescribable number of mice appeared, emerging from the forests in swarms to eat grain down to the roots and attack ricks and granaries so that farmers were unable to protect themselves from these animals. The epidemic died down at the beginning of spring, but then flared up again several times.

> **1565-1569**
>
> **MILITARY ACTIONS AND NEGOTIATIONS**

During these internal calamities, with the nobles and the people in low spirits, the sovereign did not slacken from military affairs and external politics. He still appeared glittering and majestic when dealing with other powers. The Lithuanians were utterly unsuccessful in their attacks on Russia: from Smolensk the boyar Morozov, and from Polotsk Prince Andrei Nogtev wrote to the sovereign that our light detachments were hitting the enemy everywhere.

We wanted peace with the Taurid, but the Kazan refugees, the princes Spat and Yamgurchei-Azi, and the uhlan Akhmamet, who were influential in the khan's court, convinced their ruler that Ivan was tricking him, talking of peace but ordering the Cossacks to build a town on the Don and readying boats on the Psla and

Dnieper with the intention of taking Azov and opening a route to Taurid. They said that this tsar was cleverer and luckier, and hence more dangerous than all the previous Muscovite sovereigns; that while making war on the khan he had been able to conquer Kazan, Astrakhan, Livonia and Polotsk. He had taken the Circassian lands and had the Nogai at his disposal; if Devlet-Girei were to betray King Sigismund, then the latter could lose Poland within a year. After destroying the king, Ivan could eliminate Baty's last outpost at leisure. These arguments were effective, and Sigismund's gifts were even more so: he had quickly sent 30,000 gold coins to the greedy Taurid. The khan drew his sword once more, writing to Ivan:

"Remember that your forefathers were happy with their own lands, and did not disturb the Moslems; if you wish peace, hand over Astrakhan and Kazan to me!"

But the sovereign was on guard. The Cossacks coursed over the Don steppes as soon as the first enemy movement was discovered. Troops were stationed in the towns, while the main army, under the command of the distinguished boyars, the princes Belskii and Mstislavskii, were on the banks of the Oka.

In September 1565, the khan crossed the Donets with his heavy cannons in carts and by 7 October had reached Bolkhov, from which the voivode princes Ivan Zolotoi and Vasilii Kashin made a sally. They fought valiantly, preventing the Crimeans from torching the environs and took prisoners as well. Belskii and Mstislavskii were approaching, so the khan fled by night, complaining about Lithuania, since the king had persuaded him to fight Russia and had sworn to act against us from the other direction with all his forces, but had not kept his promise.

Meanwhile, our emissary Athanasii Nagoi, who had stayed in the Crimea, was indefatigably active in bribing Jews and the khan's officials, and he had spies everywhere. He energetically refuted lying rumors spread by the enemy that Ivan had died. Nagoi knew all and wrote to the sovereign that Devlet-Girei had relations with the Kazan Tatars, the Mordvi and the Cheremis: secret emissaries from these turncoats had assured the khan that on entering their lands he would find 70,000 eager comrades-in-arms and that not one Russian would be left alive either in Sviazhsk or Kazan. When the khan tried to expel Athanasii from the Taurid, Ivan's diligent servant replied,

"I shall die here: I shall not depart until I have finished my business."

That is, he would not leave without a peace, for which he still had hopes. Sometimes the Lithuanians, at other times our side gained the upper hand in the khan's council, so that in 1567 with the sultan's permission, Devlet-Girei laid waste to part of the king's territory for defaulting on payment of *tribute*. But neither did the khan make peace with us: he demanded such rich gifts of Ivan as had been sent from Moscow to Mahmet-Girei, and he also forbade Russia entry into the Circassian lands.

The sovereign consulted several times with his boyars, then turned down the khan's demands, suggesting that he marry a son or grandson to a daughter of Shig-Alei and take as her dowry her father's city of Kasimov. (This noted exile had died by this time, almost at the same time as the other former rulers of Kazan, Simeon and Aleksandr.) However, after thinking it over and vacillating, he once more demanded the impossible: Astrakhan and Kazan.

We were also in negotiations with Lithuania. It seemed that Sigismund sincerely wanted an end to the war, which was burdensome for him. The tsar also seemed to want a respite. Both sides showed rare flexibility. Solely to observe the old custom, the king's grand emissaries came to Moscow to demand Smolensk, while our boyars insisted on Kiev, Belorussia and Volhynia. In fact neither we nor they even dreamt of such an impossible restitution. Sigismund went so far as to offer us Polotsk, and the sovereign ordered his emissaries to be told,

"Since I love tranquility for Christians, I now no longer demand the title of tsar from the king: it is enough that all other monarchs give it to me."

The difficulty lay with Livonia. Sigismund proposed that we and he each rule our own territories within it, that we join forces to drive Sweden out of Estonia, and then divide it between Poland

and Russia. Were this to happen, he would be obliged to be Ivan's friend and call him tsar. The tsar, however, wanted Riga, Wenden, Wolmar, Ronneburg and Kokenhusen [Koknese]; in return, he would yield Ozerishche, Lukoml, Drissa, Courland and 12 towns in Livonia to the king, free all the king's prisoners *gratis*, and ransom his own. The emissaries balked at Riga and Wenden and finally told our boyars that the fastest way to conclude a genuine, sincere peace treaty between their sovereigns would be for them to meet face-to-face on the border.

This idea immediately appealed to Ivan. A site was chosen. The tsar was to go to Smolensk, the king to Orsha, each with 5,000 troops of the nobility. But the emissaries did not take it upon themselves to arrange the protocol of the meeting. For example, Ivan wanted to entertain Sigismund in his tent the first day, but this seemed to the emissaries to be unbefitting the dignity of their sovereign. About two months were expended on these negotiations.

Then, in July 1566, Ivan showed Russia an unusual sight: he summoned to the Duma of the Land [*Zemskaya Duma*] not only the most eminent ecclesiastics, boyars, okolnichie, other officials, treasurers, secretaries and court nobles of the first and second ranks, but also commercial travelers, merchants and landed gentry from other cities to have them consider our negotiations with Lithuania and to ask them what should be done: to make peace with the king or to do battle with him?

DUMA OF THE LAND

There were 339 delegates at the meeting. All of them answered – the priesthood for themselves, the boyars, officials and citizens likewise, but unanimously – that the sovereign could not possibly be more indulgent without doing harm to Russia; that we must have Riga and Wenden to ensure the safety of Yuriev (Derpt), and indeed Pskov and Novgorod, whose commerce would [otherwise] be constricted and curtailed if these Livonian cities were to remain in the king's possession. The sovereign should be willing to meet with him on the border to promote tranquility among Christians, but Sigismund apparently only intended to buy time so as to arrange complicated affairs within his country, to reconcile with the Kaiser and to reinforce his troops in Livonia. The clergy added,

"Sovereign! You have the authority to act as God intends; our duty is to pray for the tsar – it is improper for us to advise you."

The military officials expressed their readiness to shed their blood in battle; the citizenry offered their last possessions for the war if haughty Sigismund were to reject the peace conditions offered him. But was there freedom in these opinions; was there sincerity in the responses of these dumas of the land and state? Yet this assembly had a solemn aspect and the people reverently viewed Ivan not as surrounded by the hated oprichniki, but in the true majesty of a sovereign heeding the voice of the country from the mouths of eminent Russians – a phenomenon worthy of the best times of Ivan's reign!

The Duma confirmed this judgment in a letter. They told the king's pans that the sovereign would explain his views to the king via his emissaries, and in the meantime would cease military operations and exchange prisoners. With this the matter was concluded.

In 1567 following the Lithuanian emissaries we sent our own, the boyar Umnoi-Kolychev and the major-domo Grigorii Nagoi, to Sigismund with full powers to sign a peace treaty. This was a novelty: previous treaties with Lithuania had been executed only in Moscow. Sigismund met our boyars in Grodno; when they went in to see him, all the Lithuanian nobles stood up, but our emissaries caught sight of Andrei Kurbskii and scornfully turned away: they had been ordered to demand the head of this turncoat!

They met nine times with the king's pans, but were unable to agree on anything. Ivan firmly wanted to expel the Swedes and the Danes and take control of all of Livonia while yielding Courland to Sigismund. The king, despite his sincere desire for peace, turned down this proposal. He would not agree to hand over Kurbskii, either. It was decided to continue the war.

"I see," wrote Sigismund to Ivan, "that you hanker for bloodletting; you speak of peace, but set your legions in motion. I hope the Lord will bless my arms in defense of what is necessary and just."

Chapter Seven

Our legions moved out vigorously from Vyazma, Dorogobuzh and Smolensk to Velikie Luki. The goal was Livonia. Having founded the new fortresses of Usvyat, Ula, Sokol and Kopie on the border, the sovereign and Prince Ivan departed Moscow and headed for the army. On 5 October in the field near Medno, the king's emissary Yurii Bykovskii, with Sigismund's aforementioned letter, was presented to the tsar. Ivan was sitting in his tent, armed and in full armor amidst his boyars and a large number of officers likewise armed from head to foot; he said,

"Yurii! We sent our eminent boyars to our brother Sigismund Augustus with a very moderate proposal. En route they were detained, insulted and dishonorably treated. So it is no wonder that we are sitting here in full armor, for you have come to us from our brother with poison arrows."

He asked Yurii about the king's health, bade him be seated, but did not give him his hand. Ivan sent all the military officials out of the tent except for his advisors, principal court nobles and secretaries. He heard out the emissary's speech, ordered that he be given hospitality at another headquarters and immediately sent him on his way – to prison in Moscow! This violation of *jus gentium*[*] was hardly excused by the coarse expressions in the king's letter or the fact that our boyars Kolychev and Nagoi had arrived at Ivan's camp complaining to him of their bad treatment in Lithuania.

In addition to a large number of officials and bodyguards, the tsar was accompanied to Novgorod by Bishop Pafnutii of Suzdal, the archimandrite Theodosii and Abbot Nikon. He stayed there eight days, fervently praying at the ancient Sofiya Cathedral and busying himself with the disposition of his legions for the march on the Livonian cities of Luzha and Rezitsa [Rezekne]. However, Ivan's martial ardor suddenly cooled when his troops encountered difficulties and perils that he had not foreseen; accordingly, he summoned all his chief voivodes for advice.

They met in the settlement of Orshanskii near Krasnyi on 12 November and discussed with the tsar whether to begin the siege of the enemy cities or to postpone the campaign. Because of bad roads, the baggage trains with the heavy artillery were making

---

[*] [The law of nations: an early concept of international law]

slow progress towards the border; horses were collapsing and men were deserting. This necessitated long waits and camping in places with scant grain. It was also learned that the king was assembling an army in Borisov, intending a winter march on Polotsk and Velikie Luki. The voivodes feared exhausting the troops besieging fortresses when the enemy might appear in our own territory from the opposite direction. Most of all they feared to find an epidemic in Livonia, where, according to rumor, many people were dying from contagious diseases. It was decided that the sovereign would return to Moscow, while the voivodes would stay in Velikie Luki and Toropets to keep an eye on the enemy.

And so Ivan returned to his capital, not without inner vexation. But the king did likewise, which salved our sovereign's pride. In 1568 Sigismund assembled 60,000 or more troops, boasting that he would drive towards Moscow in Olgerd's footsteps, but after actually taking the field with his glittering court, Sigismund stood idle in the Minsk district for several weeks and then disbanded his main army. He departed for Grodno and sent only small units into western Russia.

The Lithuanians suffered heavy casualties by Ula, but also had some successes. Princes Pyotr Serebryanyi and Vasilii Palitskii were sent to build a new fortress named Kopie, but the Lithuanians killed Palitskii in a sudden attack and Prince Serebryanyi barely managed to gallop off to Polotsk. After capturing the renowned officer Pyotr Golovin near Velizh, the Lithuanians destroyed several villages in Smolensk district. In the beginning of 1569 they took Izborsk by some sort of ruse, but the Russians quickly expelled them. Menacing Polish Livonia, they torched the greater part of Vitebsk.

Meanwhile, prisoners were exchanged on the border: Ivan released the king's voivode Dovoina and Sigismund freed Prince Temkin. Since Dovoina's wife had died in Moscow, the tsar consented to send her remains back to Lithuania on condition that the king send the corpse of Prince Pyotr Shuiskii to Moscow – the loyal sons of this unfortunate voivode had requested this.

CHAPTER SEVEN

Heeding the advice of his boyars not to disrupt peaceful relations with Lithuania, the sovereign freed Sigismund's emissary, who had languished in prison for seven months. He received him personally and spoke kindly with him, saying,

"Yurii! You handed us a letter so coarse that you should not have been allowed to live. However, we do not like blood. Go in peace to your sovereign, who forgot you in your misfortune. We are ready to meet with him and are prepared to put an end to the calamities of this war. Give our regards to our brother, Sigismund Augustus." Negotiations were resumed and couriers rode from country to country. In talks with our boyars, Sigismund's called Ivan *Tsar*, and when questioned as to the significance of this novelty, they answered,

"The Lithuanian nobles have ordered us to do so." Moscow's couriers were likewise exhorted to be peaceable, and the following instruction is worthy of note:

"If in Lithuania you happen to speak to Andrei Kurbskii or a similar eminent Russian fugitive, tell him,

'Your vile treachery is not harming either the glory or the fortunes of the great tsar: God gives him victories, but punishes you with shame and despair.'

"But with an ordinary fugitive, do not say a word; just spit in his eye and turn away... If they ask you what the Moscow Oprichnina is, say,

'We do not know of any Oprichnina. Whomever the sovereign orders to live close to him, does so, and whomever he wants to live far away does likewise. All the people are both God's and the sovereign's.'"

Ivan and Sigismund finally agreed to cease hostilities. Lithuanian emissaries were to come to Moscow to conclude the peace treaty, which both sides sincerely wanted due to the circumstances of the times. Sigismund had no children and, motivated by a sincere love of his country, desired an indissoluble union of Lithuania with Poland to consolidate their power. He feared that one or the other power would choose independence on his death. His intention was praiseworthy and would be beneficial,

TRUCE WITH LITHUANIA

but difficult to implement since the Polish and Lithuanian nobles lived in permanent mutual animosity and only the king's power could restrain their passions.

Sigismund desired peace abroad in order to succeed at this important task at home, which he was now proposing to the Lyublin Sejm. On the other hand, the tsar wanted Sigismund's crown, for there was a rumor going about that the pans were thinking of choosing the king's son Ivan to be king. Our heralds in Lithuania were ordered to investigate this matter and to butter up the nobility. The tsar was eschewing bloodshed so as to suppress hostile Lithuanian feelings towards us.

| SWEDISH AFFAIRS |

A change in Sweden's relations with Russia also considerably enhanced Ivan's desire for peace in relations with Sigismund. In order to gain Estonia for himself in defiance of Denmark and Poland, King Erik needed not only peace with the tsar, but also an alliance.* He used all possible means towards this and even contemplated base and vile acts. Sigismund's charming and warm-hearted sister Katarina, whom the tsar had wanted to marry (and might thereby have saved Russia and himself from great misfortunes), had in 1562 married Gustav Vasa's beloved son, Duke Johann of Finland.

The envious and imprudent Erik had long been unable to stand this brother and hated him even more for his alliance with the Polish king against him; he invented a calumny and imprisoned Johann. Katarina's courage was now revealed: she was given the choice to either leave her husband or the world. By way of an answer, she displayed her ring, with the inscription *nothing except death*.

For four years she was a nursing angel to the ill-fated Johann in the Gripsholm prison, unaware that two tyrants were preparing a much more terrible fate for her. The tsar proposed, and the king consented to give him Katarina, either as an object of his strange love or of his malice for the dishonor caused by the previous rejection. The matter began with a secret correspondence and ended with a formal agreement. In February 1567 Chancellor Nils Gyllenstierna and other Swedish state officials travelled directly to

---

* [Erik XIV, king of Sweden 1560-1568.]

Aleksandrovskaya Sloboda, where they were sumptuously entertained and signed a treaty of alliance between Sweden and Russia.

The tsar called Erik a friend and brother, permanently ceded Estonia to him, promised to help him in war against Sigismund and to make peace with Denmark and the Hanseatic cities. In return, Erik promised to send the bride to Moscow. The Duma councilor Vorontsov and the court noble Naumov travelled to Stockholm with the treaty document while the boyars Morozov, Chebotov and Sukin were to receive Katarina at the border.

But Providence did not allow Ivan to triumph. Our emissaries were received in Stockholm with great honor, but remained there a whole year without any progress in their mission. When Erik had them dine with him, he fell into a swoon and could not get up from the table. Our emissaries did not see the king after that; they were told either that he was ill or fighting with the Danes.

Only the king's councilors showed up for talks with Vorontsov and he was told that to hand over Katarina, to take a wife from her husband and a mother from her children, was contrary to God and the law, that the tsar would forever dishonor himself with such an unchristian act. They said Sigismund had another sister, unmarried, whom Erik might *provide* for the tsar, and that Sweden's emissaries [to Moscow] had concluded the agreement concerning Katarina without the king's knowledge. In response, Moscow's boyar spared neither the councilors nor their sovereign; he argued that they were liars and oath-breakers, and demanded a meeting with Erik.

The unhappy king was in a regrettable position: his many cruelties and rash acts had earned him general hatred. He feared both his people and his court; he was tormented by his conscience and divided in his mind. He first freed, and then thought to reincarcerate his brother; in his mental confusion and pusillanimous fright he would now announce to our emissaries that he himself was going to Moscow, and then decide once more to send Katarina to the tsar.

Finally a blow was struck: on 29 September 1568, Moscow's emissaries witnessed a terrible commotion in the capital and did not remain peaceful onlookers for long. Soldiers with guns and drawn swords broke into their house, broke the locks and took everything – silver and furs. They even separated the emissaries and threatened them with death.

At that moment, Prince Karl, Erik's younger brother, appeared. The boyar Vorontsov, clad only in a shirt stood before him and firmly told him that such behavior was suited to a den of thieves, not a Christian power. Karl expelled the frenzied soldiers and explained to our boyar that Erik had been deposed as an insane tyrant and that the new king, his brother Johann, wished friendship with Moscow's tsar. The offenses done to the emissaries would not go unpunished, but were only the consequences of the disorder, combined with the change in supreme power.

The emissaries asked leave to depart; they left Stockholm, but were involuntarily detained in Åbo for eight months and only returned to Moscow in July of 1569. They reported to the tsar the fate of his *friend and brother*, the unfortunate Erik, who had been formally condemned to die in prison by government officials for various crimes, as it stated in the sentence of the court, and for the dishonorable, *unchristian* conditions of his proposed alliance with Russia.

It is easy to imagine Ivan's irritation, but he hid his feelings and gave permission for the Swedish emissaries, the bishop of Åbo, Paul Just, and other eminent officials to come to Moscow. However, he ordered them robbed and detained in Novgorod, exactly as had been done to the boyar Vorontsov and Naumov in Sweden. This action seemed justified vengeance to him, but he wanted something even more significant: he wanted to expel the Swedes from Estonia at once, and to this end made a temporary reconciliation with Sigismund so he would not have to deal with two enemies at once.

It was necessary to ward off another peril that now faced Russia. However, it did not threaten Ivan for long and gave his reign new martial glory without a victory. That which Suleiman the Magnificent had schemed against us, his pusillanimous son Selim wanted to implement: the restoration of a Moslem state on the banks of the Akhtuba. The sultan had been persuaded on this course by some Nogai princes of Khiva and

THE SULTAN'S
GREAT UNDERTAKING

Bukhara, who argued that the Russian sovereign was destroying the Mohammedan religion and had cut their communications with Mecca. They said that Astrakhan was a major port on the Black Sea, filled with ships of all the Asiatic peoples and that the tsar's treasury received nearly 1,000 gold coins daily from there. The Lithuanian emissaries in Constantinople also said this.

But Khan Devlet-Girei maintained that it was impossible to march on Astrakhan either in winter or summer: in winter because of the cold, which was unbearable for the Turks, and in summer because of the lack of water; it would be much better to do battle against the Muscovite Ukraine. Selim paid no heed to the khan's objections: in the spring of 1569 sent 15,000 spagis* and 2,000 janisseries to Kaffa and ordered its pasha Kasim to march to Perevoloka and unite the Don with Volga, the Caspian Sea with the Azov and take Astrakhan or at least establish a fortress there to mark the sultan's reach.

The pasha embarked upon this campaign on 31 May; so did the khan with upwards of 50,000 cavalry. They joined up in present-day Kachalinskaya Stanitsa and waited for boats to arrive from Azov via the Don with heavy artillery and a rich treasury, but with only about 500 troops for its defense and 2,500 oarsmen, for the most part Christian captives in chains. The Turks offloaded the cannons on sandbars and dragged them along the banks with indescribable difficulty. About 2,000 Russians might have captured the artillery and treasury without bloodshed.

The captives were awaiting them hopefully, and the Turks fearfully – but no one showed up! The Don Cossacks, frightened by rumors of the sultan's march, hid in the distant steppes, and on 15 August the boats reached Perevoloka safely. Now they undertook a task both pathetic and ridiculous: Kasim ordered a canal be dug from the Don to the Volga, but on realizing its impracticability, ordered the boats be dragged overland.

The Turks did not want to obey, saying that the pasha had been crazy to undertake a task that would have taken all the workers in the Ottoman Empire centuries to complete. The khan advised going back, but to Kasim's delight, emissaries from Astrakhan appeared, asking,

---

* [Light cavalry.]

"What are the boats for? We will give you some – as many as you wish. Just go and protect us against the Russians."

The pasha calmed his army; on 2 September he sent his cannons back to Azov and proceeded towards Astrakhan with 12 light cannons. Although the people there were prepared to receive him as a deliverer, their hopes were to be disappointed.

Ivan's emissary Athanasii Nagoi wrote to the sovereign from the Taurid concerning the sultan's scheme; the letter reached him after some delay. A war with Turkey would present Ivan with nothing but perils. He assembled a large army in Nizhnyi-Novgorod and immediately dispatched the valiant Prince Pyotr Serebryanyi with a light detachment to occupy Astrakhan. At the same time he also sent gifts to the pasha of Kaffa to incline him towards peace. The pasha took the gifts, kissed Ivan's letter, honored Moscow's heralds for three days and imprisoned them on the fourth. But the sovereign was relieved to learn of the Turks' small numbers and Devlet-Girei's lack of enthusiasm for this campaign; he surmised the consequences, nor was he deceived.

On 16 September the pasha and the khan halted below Astrakhan, at Gorodishche, where the ancient capital of the Khazars had likely been located. There they awaited our Astrakhan turncoats with their boats and the Nogai with friendly assurances. Kasim, who had ordered the Nogai to migrate towards the Volga, began to construct a new fortress at Gorodishche and the Turks learned, to their amazement, that the pasha intended to winter below Astrakhan, where a handful of plucky Russians were suppressing the residents' mutiny and seemed so frightening to the sultan that he did not dare to venture an assault. Indeed, nothing could have been more imprudent than his plan: the pasha was giving the Russians time to prepare a defense while his own men were becoming exhausted from hardships and hunger, since the people of Astrakhan were unable to provide them with enough grain.

Grumbling turned into mutiny when the Turks heard that the khan was to return to the Taurid upon completion of the fortress. They firmly declared that none of them would overwinter in hostile territory. Kasim maintained his obstinacy, but suddenly, on 26 September, torched the wooden fortifications he had built and together with the khan withdrew from Astrakhan. The reason was that Prince Pyotr Serebryanyi and his troops had entered the city, and behind him, it was said, was a still more powerful force.

The Turks and the Crimeans were fleeing night and day. Sixty versts away they were met at White Lake by couriers from the sultan and the Lithuanians. Selim had written to the pasha that he must by all means hold out near Astrakhan until spring. A new army would come to him from Constantinople: that summer Russia would see Ottoman banners deep in its territories. The khan would be obliged to follow them to Moscow after establishing an alliance and friendship with the Lithuanians.

But Kasim continued his flight. His guide Devlet-Girei intentionally led the Turks through arid lands and barren wastes where horses and men died of exhaustion, and where Circassians watched them from ambushes, taking the exhausted and half-dead into captivity. The Russians could have utterly exterminated this pitiable army had they not adhered to the principle of letting a fleeing enemy get away free. The Turks were in despair, cursing the pasha and not even sparing the sultan, who had sent them into an unknown land, into horrible Russia, not for victory, but for famine and a dishonorable death. Kasim reached Azov a month later with a throng of pale shades and paid them off with gold to avoid being hanged. He ascribed his misfortune solely to the fact that he had been unable to start the campaign earlier, but Devlet-Girei stressed to the sultan the impossibility of taking or holding Astrakhan: it was too far from Turkish territory. He told our Crimean emissary,

> CALAMITY
> FOR THE TURKS

"Your sovereign should thank me: I destroyed the sultan's army. I did not want to assault Astrakhan nor build a fortress there on the site of old Gorodishche, firstly, because I wanted to please him [Ivan] and secondly, because I did not wish to see Turkish lords in the ancient Tatar uluses."

We blew up the Azov fortress with all its gunpowder stores to assure our safety from this quarter. It is thought that the Russians not only burned a large part of the city, but also reduced the wharves and military boats to ashes.

This unhappy expedition of Selim's army has been described for us in the tales of an eyewitness, Semyon Maltsov, one of the tsar's officials, and should be made known to posterity. He had ridden from the Nogai uluses and had encountered the enemy on the banks of the Volga. Surrounded by them, he hid the tsar's orders, like an inviolable sacred object, in a tree on Tsaritsyn Island. Half dead from wounds, he surrendered and was chained to a cannon.

Tormented by pain, thirst and hunger and hourly threatened with death, he never stopped serving his tsar diligently. He frightened the Turks with his tales: he assured them that Astrakhan and the Nogai were luring them into a trap, that the Persian shah was an ally of Russia and that we had sent him 100 cannons and 500 arquebuses to attack Kasim. He said that Prince Serebryanyi was sailing to Astrakhan with 30,000 men and that Prince Ivan Belskii was taking the field with an uncountable number of troops. Maltsov also instructed the other Russian prisoners to say the same and persuaded Greeks and Wallachians with Kasim to come over to our side if there was a battle. He invited Devlet-Girei's sons into our service, telling them,

"Your father has many of you. He distributes you among the peoples. You are neither sated nor hungry, and migrate from place to place. But in Moscow you will find honor and wealth. Even your father will envy you,"

Without any hope of seeing holy Russia again, without any thought of reward or glory, on the brink of death this diligent citizen still tried to be of use to his sovereign, to his country. That Ivan the Terrible had such servitors as he was feasting on the blood of his subjects! Maltsov was saved by Providence. He was ransomed in Azov by our Crimean emissary, Athanasii Nagoi, and returned to Moscow, reporting to the tsar that the Russians need not fear the Ottomans.

And so Russia's external operations and relations with foreign powers were rather successful. We were expecting peace with Lithuania and had gained new and important conquests; weak Sweden was scorned, and we had seen the backs of the sultan's army and its doom. We had learned of the khan's enmity toward the Turks and so had less fear of his attacks and more hope of making peace with him. We had a large army and fortified borders; in farthest Terek, Ivan had founded a town as much to protect his father-in-law, the Circassian Prince Temgryuk, as to establish our power on this frontier.

Shah Tamas of Persia wanted to be a friend to Ivan. The tsar desired a close alliance with him against the sultan and sent his official, Aleksei Khoznikov, to Persia in May 1569. Siberia was now paying us tribute: around 1563, its new ruler, the Shiban crown prince Ediger, had killed our tribute collector there. The sovereign accordingly detained the Siberian emissary in Moscow but soon released him out of respect for the intercession of Ismail, the Nogai ruler.

RELATIONS WITH PERSIA

In 1569 a formal treaty with the new Siberian ruler, Kuchyum, established this land as a Russian tributary. Ivan took Kuchyum under his hand in tutelage, with the condition that he give him 1,000 sable pelts annually, while the tsar's envoy who came to collect the tribute would get 1,000 squirrel pelts.

SIBERIAN TRIBUTE

In 1571, the boyar cadet Tretyak Chabukov took Ivan's patent, adorned with a golden seal, to Siberia. Internally, Russia was in dire straits, from plague, hunger and tyranny, but its commerce was flourishing. The rulers Abdula Shamakhanskii, Abdula Bukharskii and the seit of Samarkand,* Azim Zhivinskii, sent gifts to Ivan in Moscow to induce him to permit their subjects to trade not only in Astrakhan and Kazan, but also in our other cities.

Despite the sultan's open hostility, Russians still traded in Kaffa and Azov, and the Turks in Moscow, along with Armenians. The sovereign himself sent valuable furs from the treasury across the Caspian and dispatched Muscovite merchants to Antwerp, London and even Hormuz. The Hansa did not cease from seeking Ivan's favor, exchanging goods with us in Narva. They envied the English, who enjoyed the tsar's good will and had exclusive rights in Russia, especially after Elizabeth's succession to the throne, for that

TRADE

---

* [An official second only to the khan.]

renowned queen, who was gifted with a great intellect and obliging qualities, had won his friendship.

ENGLISH EMBASSIES

The London Muscovy Company gifted the tsar with diamonds and Elizabeth wrote him flattering letters. Her envoy Jenkinson came to Moscow three times, and travelled on to Persia, diligently carrying out his sovereign's secret orders with regard to the shah. As a result, in 1567 and again in 1569 Ivan gave new privileges to the Englishmen: he permitted them to travel to Persia, to found a settlement on the Vychegda, to prospect for iron ore and smelt it (with the condition that they teach Russians this art) and pay one denga per funt to export it to England*.

The Englishmen were obliged to show all precious things to the sovereign's treasurer and also to sell the tsar's goods in England and Persia. On the other hand, the English could trade freely without duties, build dwellings and stores anywhere, and mint thalers for themselves everywhere. They could be judged only by the Oprichnina courts and their compound in Moscow, in St. Maksim's Church, was under their own administration. The Hanseatic merchants tried in vain to poison Ivan's mind against the English, and the kings of Poland and Sweden tried in vain to convince Elizabeth not to facilitate Russia's dangerous might through trade. There were mutual dissatisfactions, but they were settled amicably. For example, in 1568 Elizabeth's envoy Thomas Randolph resided in Moscow for about four months without seeing the tsar. Ivan was vexed at the queen's merchants because they annually raised the price of their goods.

Finally he ordered Randolph to come see him, but did not provide horses. The Londoners went to the palace on foot, and none of the tsar's officials bowed to the queen's representative. The proud Englishman was offended by this rudeness and put on his hat inside the palace. Wrath and disfavor were expected, but instead, Ivan received Randolph quite kindly, assured him of his friendship towards his *beloved sister* Elizabeth and returned the English merchants to favor. He had another meeting with Randolph alone, at night, in which they talked for three hours. He then dispatched his court noble Andrei Savin on secret business,

---

* [Karamzin's endnote here asks if this is not *per pood* (about 16.4 kg or 36.1 lbs).]

about which we know solely from Elizabeth's reply, which is preserved in our national archive: it is quite interesting and shows Ivan's pusillanimity. This monarch, who was still victorious, still a threat to neighboring powers, who met with not the slightest protest from his miserable subjects, whom he destroyed even though they were blameless – this monarch trembled within his heart, expected punishment and dreamt of rebellions, of exile, and was not ashamed to write of this to Elizabeth and ask her for asylum in her land in such a case.

> IVAN'S SCHEME TO FLEE TO ENGLAND

This was an abasement appropriate for a torturer! The prudent queen replied that she wanted him to rule in glory in Russia, but was prepared to receive him along with his wife and children if as a consequence of a secret conspiracy internal rebels or external enemies exiled him from his homeland. She told him he might live wherever he liked in England, observe all the rites of the Greek faith at mass, have his own servants and always be free to go back to Russia or on to another land. To confirm these promises, Elizabeth gave him *the word of a Christian monarch* and a letter, signed by herself in the presence of all her state councilors, Grand Chancellor Nicolas Bacon, the lords North, Russell and Arundel, and others, with the addendum that England and Russia would always unite their forces against a common enemy. Although he was very well treated in London, Savin's report was not very favorable to the English: he told the tsar that Elizabeth was solely concerned with the profits of the English merchant class. Ivan was also displeased with the fact that in an affair so important she had replied to him through his envoy, and had not sent her own, but he stayed friends with her, since he genuinely wished to be able to flee overseas in extremity.

We are assured that the Dutch doctor, Eliseus Bomelius,* implanted this idea in Ivan's mind. He was a vagabond and a rogue who had been exiled from Germany and gained access to the tsar. He caught the tsar's fancy by means of his machinations: he nourished his fears and suspicions, denigrated the boyars and the people and predicted rebellions and mutinies so as to cater to the unhappy disposition

> BOMELIUS'S VILLIANLY

---

* [A Dutch-German physician and astrologer.]

of Ivan's troubled soul. The tsar always had earnest assistants for good or evil: Bomelius earned seniority among Ivan's servitors, i.e., among Russia's malefactors. Divine punishment was being prepared for them, but the tyrant's bloody banquet was only half over. The curtain now rises on a new scene of horrors.

CHAPTER VIII

SEVERE OPPRESSION.

1569-1572

Death of the tsaritsa. Fourth and most horrible period of torturing. Novgorod's desolation. Pskov saved. Executions in Moscow. Court jesters. Famine and pestilence. Relations with Lithuania. The Livonian kingship. Tsar's kindness towards Magnus. Embassy to Constantinople. Invasion by the khan. Conflagration in Moscow. Ivan married again. Fifth episode of murders. Death of the tsaritsa. Ivan journeys to Novgorod. Swedish affairs. Ivan's fourth marriage. Alliance with Queen Elizabeth. Negotiations with Denmark and Lithuania. Ivan departs for Novgorod. The khan's invasion. Prince Vorotynskii's famous victory. Letter to the Swedish king.

On 1 September 1569, Ivan's wife Mariya passed away, hardly mourned sincerely even by the tsar himself, although to preserve decorum, all of Russia was obliged to make a show of profound sorrow. Commerce came to a halt and the boyars, court nobles and clerks put on mourning clothes (velvet and damask coats without gold). The office for the dead was performed in all the cities and towns; alms were given to the lowly and endowments were made to monasteries and churches. False sorrow was manifested, hiding the true, common feelings produced by Ivan's ferocity.

1569
DEATH OF THE TSARITSA

Ten days later he was already able to calmly receive foreign emissaries in the Moscow palace, but he hastened to leave the capital in order to conceive new betrayals and executions in the strange solitude of Aleksandrovskaya Sloboda. The deaths of his two wives, with such dissimilar spiritual qualities, had equally unfortunate consequences. Anastasiya had taken Ivan's virtues with her; but it seemed that Mariya bequeathed him the ability to exceed himself in malevolent homicide. A rumor spread that Mariya, like Anastasiya, had been poisoned by secret malefactors, and served to prepare Russia for more frenzied outbursts of his terrible rage.

> FOURTH
> AND MOST HORRIBLE
> PERIOD OF
> TORTURING

Ivan punished the innocent, but there was one who was guilty, really guilty, who remained before the tyrant: he who in violation of the law had wished to take the throne, who had not obeyed the ailing tsar, who had rejoiced in thoughts of his impending death, and who had won over nobles and warriors to his treason – Prince Vladimir Andreevich! Sixteen years had passed, but Ivan, as we have seen, did not forget old crimes and had always been a threat to the prince. None of the boyars dared to have friendly relations with him, but some spies got close to him in order to use any indiscreet words in a denunciation.

What was saving this unhappy man? Was it the natural horror of staining one's hands with the blood of a close relative? This is possible, since there are difficulties and restraints for even the cruelest tyrant. Ivan had once been a human being, but no longer loved the good, and was subject to extremes of evil. With a troubled conscience, he comforted himself with the thought that there were some crimes he still resisted committing! Yet this was an unreliable safeguard for Prince Vladimir, since evildoing leads to more of the same. He could foresee his ineluctable fate, despite the gracious pardon given him in 1563 and despite Ivan's hypocrisy, for he always honored and showed the prince kindnesses.

As a token of his favor, the tsar had given him a large lot inside the Kremlin for a sumptuous new palace, as well as the towns of Dmitrov, Borovsk and Zvenigorod, which the tsar had given in exchange for Vereya, Aleksin and Staritsa, no doubt because the prince seemed less dangerous with new estates, rather than the hereditary ones that still preserved the spirit of the old appanage system. Ivan, in gathering troops in Nizhnyi Novgorod for the defense of Astrakhan in the spring of 1569, had no hesitation in

CHAPTER EIGHT

entrusting them to his courageous brother, but this illusory trust led to the latter's disgrace and doom. Prince Vladimir had ridden to Nizhnyi by way of Kostroma, where the citizens and the clergy met him with crosses, with bread and salt,* with great honor and expressions of love.

When the tsar learned of this, he ordered the local chiefs brought to Moscow and had them executed, but gave his brother a flattering invitation to come see him. Vladimir, with his wife and children, had stopped about three versts from Aleksandrovskaya Sloboda, in the village of Slotin. They had notified the tsar of their arrival and were awaiting his reply. Suddenly Vladimir spotted a cavalry legion at full gallop, with drawn swords as if charging into battle. They surrounded the village; Ivan was with them, but dismounted and hid in a farmer's house.

Vasilii Gryaznoi and Malyuta Skuratov announced to Prince Vladimir that he had been plotting against the sovereign's life. They presented his accuser, the tsar's cook, to whom Vladimir had allegedly given money and poison to assassinate Ivan. It had all been fabricated and prepared in advance. The unfortunate prince, with his wife and two young sons, was taken to the sovereign. They fell on their knees before him, swore their innocence and requested to be tonsured. The tsar replied,

"You wanted to kill me with poison: take it yourself!" They were given the poison. Prince Vladimir was prepared to die but did not want to poison himself by his own hands. His wife Evdokiya (née Princess Odoevskaya), a wise and virtuous woman, saw that there was no way out; that there was no mercy in their executioner's heart. She turned her face away from Ivan, dried her tears and resolutely told her husband,

"It is not we, but our tormentor who is poisoning us. Better to accept death from the tsar than from an executioner." Vladimir bade farewell to his wife, blessed his sons and drank down the poison, followed by Evdokiya and their sons. They prayed together. The poison began to take effect, while Ivan witnessed their agony and death. He summoned Evdokiya's boyars' wives and maidservants and said,

---

* [This was a hospitality offering.]

"There are the bodies of my malefactors! You served them, but I shall be merciful and give you your lives." Trembling, they viewed the corpses of their masters and replied with a single voice,

"We do not wish your mercy, you bloodthirsty beast! Do your worst to us, may it shame you. We scorn life and torture!"

These young women, inspired by loathing towards their malefactor, feared neither death nor shame: Ivan ordered them stripped and shot. Vladimir's mother Evfrosiniya had at once time been ambitious, but now led a humble life in a monastery, concerned only with her own salvation. Ivan, having killed her son, now murdered his mother as well. She was drowned in the Sheksna, along with another nun, the virtuous Aleksandra, his sister-in-law, guilty perhaps of weeping over the victims of the tsar's wrath.

The fate of the unfortunate Vladimir provoked widespread pity. People put aside their fears and wept in their homes and in churches. Doubtless no one believed this prince's supposed design on the sovereign's life: they saw only a vile fratricide, prompted more by malice than suspicion. Although Vladimir did not have great qualities, those he had were praiseworthy. If only he had ruled Russia – he would not have been a tyrant! The prince had long borne his public disgrace with resolve, awaiting his inescapable fate with a sort of Christian calm and led the good-hearted to affection and a tender, growing love for him.

Ivan heard, if not bold reproach, then at least the sighs of brave Russians, and tried, through the disclosure of a supposedly important plot to show the necessity for cruelty in order to curb his enemies, who were allegedly Prince Vladimir's confederates. Was this new calumny upon the living and the dead only an invention of Ivan's addled mind, or was it a hellish scheme of his accomplices in murder to thereby demonstrate their ardor and to nurture his enthusiasm for torture?

Did Ivan hope to deceive contemporaries and posterity with crude lies, or to deceive himself through his own credulity? The chroniclers assert the latter: that Ivan thereby lightened the burden of his terrible deeds. But does not that gullibility itself cry out to Heaven? Does it not strengthen our disgust for his unprecedented murders?

CHAPTER EIGHT

Novgorod and Pskov, once independent states, had been humbled by autocracy, deprived of their ancient rights and their most distinguished citizens, and had been partially settled by outsiders. The public spirit had changed, but still preserved a certain majesty based on memories of times gone by and some relics of their civil life. Novgorod had called itself *Great*, had concluded treaties with Swedish kings, and had chosen, like Pskov, its own tax collectors.

Children inherited a secret dislike of Moscow from their parents; in Novgorod they still related the Battle of the Shelon,* and in Pskov eyewitnesses to the last public assembly [*veche*] might still be alive. The calamities of liberty had been forgotten, but its benefits had not. These attitudes of their powerless citizenries, now no longer dangerous to a mighty autocracy, nevertheless upset and angered the tsar. Accordingly, in the spring of 1569, he moved 500 families from Pskov and 150 from Novgorod to Moscow, following the examples of his father and grandfather. Those deprived of their patrimonies wept, those left in theirs, shuddered. This was only the beginning; they awaited future consequences.

Now at this time, we are told, a certain Volhynian vagabond named Pyotr, punished in Novgorod for bad dealings, thought to avenge himself on its residents. Aware of Ivan's indisposition towards them, he fabricated a letter from the archbishop and the local citizens to the Polish king and hid it behind the icon of the Virgin in the St. Sofiya's Cathedral, and then sped to Moscow to report to the tsar that Novgorod was betraying Russia. It was necessary to produce the evidence. The tsar gave him a loyal servitor, who rode with him to Novgorod and removed the phony letter of the archbishop from behind the icon. In this letter, it stated that the prelate, the clergy, the officials and all the people were going to submit to Lithuania. No further evidence was required. Taking this absurdity for the truth, the tsar condemned Novgorod and all of its people, whom he suspected or hated.

In December 1569 the tsar set out from Aleksandrovskaya Sloboda with Prince Ivan and all the court, along with his

---

* [The Novgorod Republic suffered a major defeat at the hands of the Grand Principality of Moscow in 1471, which led to the loss of its independence. It was absorbed into Muscovy in 1478.]

favorite guards unit, bypassing Moscow and arriving at Klin, the first city of the former Grand Principality of Tver. He likely believed that all of the inhabitants of this district, which had been subdued by his grandfather, were secret enemies of the Muscovite autocracy. Accordingly, he ordered his lethal legion to commence warfare, murder and pillage where no one imagined an enemy, no one knew of any guilt of their own, and the peaceful subjects had greeted their sovereign as their father and protector.

The houses and streets were filled with corpses; women and infants were not spared. From Klin to Gorodna and further the despoilers ranged with their drawn swords stained with the blood of the miserable inhabitants, and on to Tver itself. There in a close, solitary cell of the Otroch Monastery, sainted old Filipp still breathed, praying (without being heard!) to the Lord to mollify Ivan's heart. The tyrant had not forgotten the metropolitan he had deposed; he sent his favorite, Malyuta Skuratov, to him, supposedly to get his blessing. The old man replied that he blessed only good people and goodness. Guessing the evil purpose of Skuratov's mission, he meekly added,

"I have long awaited death: let the sovereign's will be done!"

It was carried out: the vile Skuratov strangled the holy man, but wishing to conceal the murder, announced to the abbot and the brothers that Filipp had died from the unbearable heat in his cell. The frightened monks opened up a grave behind the altar and, in the presence of the murderer, buried this great hierarch of the Russian Church, crowned with martyrdom and glory: for to die for virtue is a superhuman virtue and neither ancient nor later histories show us a more distinguished hero. Some years later, in 1584, his holy relics were translated to the Solovetskii Monastery, and later, in 1562, to the Cathedral of the Dormition of the Virgin, where we, touched by emotion, now bow to them.

This secret crime was followed by overt ones. Ivan did not want to enter Tver and for five days stayed by himself in one of the nearby monasteries. Meanwhile, a throng of frenzied troops plundered the city, beginning with the priesthood and leaving no house intact. They took what was valuable or easy to take with them and burned what they could not. They tortured, murdered and hanged people for their own amusement. In brief, it reminded the unfortunate residents of Tver of the horrible year of 1327 when Khan Uzbek's vengeance was accomplished upon their ancestors. Many Lithuanian prisoners confined in the local prisons were hacked to pieces or drowned in ice holes in the Volga while Ivan watched!

At last he left Tver, which was steaming with blood, and rampaged similarly in Medno and Torzhok, where there were Crimean prisoners in one tower and Livonians in another, in fetters. He killed them, but Malyuta Skuratov was severely wounded as the Crimeans defended themselves, and Ivan himself barely escaped injury. With fire and sword they laid waste to Vyshnyi Volochok and all other places as far as Lake Ilmen. They also killed everyone they met on the road, because Ivan's campaign was supposed to be a secret from Russia!

On 2 January the sovereign's large vanguard entered Novgorod after surrounding it on all side with fortified outposts so that no one could escape. They sealed the churches and monasteries in the city and its environs; they tied up the monks and priests and extracted 20 rubles from each. Whoever was unable to pay this fine was publicly beaten with cudgels and the floggings continued from morning till evening. They also sealed the courts of the rich citizens. Merchants, commercial travelers and clerks were put in chains, while women and children were confined to their homes. Quiet terror reigned. No one knew what he was blamed for or the pretext for this disfavor. They awaited their sovereign's arrival.

1570

Towards evening on 6 January, Epiphany, Ivan and his troops halted at Gorodishche, two versts from the trading quarter. The next day all the monks who had been unable to pay the fine were beaten to death with cudgels and each corpse was carted back to his own monastery for burial. On January 8th, the tsar entered Novgorod with his son and guards unit, where Archbishop Pimen met them on the Great Bridge with wonder-working icons. They did not receive the prelate's blessing and Ivan menacingly said,

"You dishonorable man! That is not the life-giving cross you hold in your hand, but a lethal weapon, with which you want to pierce us through the heart. I know of your schemes and those of all the vile residents here. I know that you are about to go over to Sigismund Augustus. As of now, you are no longer a pastor, but an enemy of the Church and St. Sofiya – a predatory wolf, a destroyer who hates the crown of Monomakh!"

Having said this, the sovereign ordered him to go to the Sofiya Cathedral with his icons and crosses. There Ivan heard the liturgy, prayed fervently, and went to the archbishop's palace. He sat down at the table there with all the boyars and began to dine. Suddenly he cried out in a terrible voice . . . Troops appeared and seized the archbishop and his officials and servants; they plundered the palace and the cells, while his major domo Lev Saltykov and the sovereign's confessor Evstafii did the same to the Sofiya Cathedral: they took the vestments, vessels, icons and bells. They also denuded other churches and rich monasteries.

Immediately afterward they convened a court in Gorodishche. Ivan and his son presided in the following manner: every day they would be presented with 500, 1,000 or more residents of Novgorod, who were beaten, tortured and burned with some sort of fiery substance. Then they would be bound by the head or foot to sleighs and dragged to the banks of the Volkhov, to places that had not yet frozen over. There they were hurled from the bridge into the water, whole families, wives and their husbands, and women with babes at the breast. The Muscovite troops sailed in boats along the Volkhov with poles, boathooks and poleaxes. Anyone who had been thrown in and managed to swim to the surface, they hacked and cut to pieces.

This massacre continued for five weeks and ended in general pillaging. Ivan and his guards rode around to all the cloisters on the outskirts of the city; they took all the church and monastery treasuries, ordered all the courtyards and cells emptied and destroyed grain, horses and cattle. He also committed all of Novgorod to plunder – stores, homes and churches.

He himself rode from street to street, observing his predacious troops breaking into houses and storerooms, breaking down the doors, climbing in through the windows, dividing furs and silken fabrics amongst themselves. They burned skins and furs and threw wax and lard into the river. Gangs of these miscreants were also dispatched to the five Novgorod quarters to destroy property and life without oversight or accountability to anyone. As a chronicler puts it,

"This unfathomable disturbance, assault and destruction of Great Novgorod continued for about six weeks."

At dawn on February 12th, the second Monday of Lent, the sovereign summoned the remaining eminent men of Novgorod, one from each street. They seemed like shades: pale, exhausted by the terror, awaiting death. But the tsar *looked on them with kind and gentle eyes:* the wrath and fury, which had till now flamed in his eyes like a terrible meteor, were extinguished. Ivan quietly told them,

"Men of Novgorod, all of you who are still living! Pray to the Lord for our pious autocracy, for our Christian army, so that we may vanquish all enemies, visible and invisible! May God judge my traitor, your Archbishop Pimen and his evil counselors! It is they – they are responsible for the blood-shed here! Let the weeping and wailing be stilled; let sorrow and grief be calmed. Live and prosper in this city! In place of myself I am leaving you my governor, boyar and voivode Prince Pyotr Daniilovich Pronskii. Go to your homes in peace."

The archbishop's fate was still undecided: he was seated on a white mare, in tattered clothing, with bagpipes and tambourines in his hands, like a clown or jester, led from street to street and then transported under heavy guard to Moscow.

After sending an uncountable amount of sacrilegious booty and plunder to the capital, Ivan quickly departed Novgorod via the Pskov road. No one complained about the stolen loot: anyone still alive was thanking God, and beside himself with relief! We are assured that no less than 60,000 citizens and rural residents perished. For a long time the bloody Volkhov, blocked by the bodies and limbs of cut-up people, could not convey them into Lake Ladoga.

Famine and disease completed Ivan's punishment, so that the priests in the course of six or seven months were unable to bury all of the bodies – they just threw them into a pit without any rites. At last, Novgorod seemed to awaken from its deathly stupor.

On 8 September those still living, clergy and laymen, gathered in a field by the Church of the Nativity of Christ and held a requiem service for the dead at the local cemetery in which 10,000 bodies had been unceremoniously buried! (At the fore stood the aged pauper, Ivan Zhgaltso, who had single-handedly committed the bodies to the earth with a prayer during these terrible times.) Great Novgorod was deserted. The richest part of the trading quarter, once populous, had been turned into vacant lot where all the remaining uninhabitable homes were demolished and foundations laid for the sovereign's palace.

Novgorod's Desolation

Ivan was preparing Novgorod's fate for Pskov, believing that its residents also wished to betray Russia. The good Prince Yurii Tokmakov governed there, and the famous pious holy fool and hermit Nikola lived there also. They saved the city: one by fortunate counsel, the other by fortunate audacity.

On Saturday of the second week of Lent, the tsar spent the night at the Monastery of St. Nikolai on the Lyubatova, in view of Pskov, where, in expectation of the approaching threat, no one slept a wink and everyone was milling about. They either encouraged one another or bid farewell to life: parents to children, wives to husbands. At midnight the tsar heard the sound of church bells ringing in Pskov.

His heart, contemporaries write, was miraculously softened. He could vividly imagine with what feeling the citizens were going to matins for the last time to pray to the Most High for salvation from the tsar's wrath, with what fervor they were prostrating themselves, weeping, before the icons. The thought that the Lord was acknowledging the voices of their grieving hearts touched his cruel soul! In some kind of inexplicable outburst of pity, he told his voivodes,

Pskov Saved

"Blunt your swords against stone! Let the murders stop!" The next day, on entering the city, he was amazed to see on every street, and in front of every house, tables with prepared viands (this had been done on the advice of Prince Yurii Tokmakov.) The citizens, their wives and children held bread and salt, knelt before the tsar, blessed him and greeted him, saying,

"Great Sovereign Prince! We, your loyal subjects, eagerly and lovingly offer you bread and salt. Do as you will with us and our lives, for we ourselves and all that we have are yours, Great Autocrat!"

This unexpected submissiveness pleased Ivan. The abbot of the Pecherskii Monastery and the clergy greeted him in the square next to the churches of St. Barlaam and the Savior. The tsar attended the service at the Trinity Cathedral, knelt at the grave of St. Vsevolod-Gavriil, viewed with amazement that ancient prince's heavy sword and visited the cell of the aging holy fool Nikola, who, protected by his mental condition, did not fear to accuse the tyrant of bloodthirstiness and sacrilege. It is written that he offered Ivan a piece of raw meat and that Ivan told him,

"I am a Christian and do not eat meat during Lent." The hermit replied,

"You do worse: you feed on human flesh and blood, forgetting not only Lent, but God as well!"

He threatened Ivan, prophesying misfortune, and Ivan was so frightened that he immediately departed from the city. He remained a few days in the suburbs, however, permitting his troops to plunder the property of rich people, but not to touch monks or priests. He took only monastery treasuries, some icons, vessels and books, and as if involuntarily sparing Olga's homeland, hastened back to Moscow to slake his unquenchable thirst for torture with new blood.

Archbishop Pimen and several eminent Novgorod prisoners who had been sent with him to Aleksandrovskaya Sloboda were awaiting their end. About five months passed, but not in inactivity. There were important consequences: denunciations and evidence

EXECUTIONS IN MOSCOW

were gathered; Pimen's secret associates were sought in Moscow: they had escaped the sovereign's wrath so far. They were in the chief government ministries and even in the tsar's council, enjoying Ivan's special trust and favor. The keeper of the seal, or chancellor, Ivan Mikhailovich Viskovatyi, a man very experienced in governmental affairs; the treasurer Nikita Funikov, likewise a loyal servant of the tsar and the nation from his youth till his declining years; the boyar Semyon Vasilievich Yakovlev; and the prudent secretaries Vasilii Stepanov and Andrei Vasiliev all were taken under guard.

Arrested along with them, to general amazement, were Ivan's foremost favorites: the nobleman Aleksei Basmanov, a valorous voivode, but a shameless toady of tyranny; his son, the royal carver Theodor, of handsome face and vile soul, without whom Ivan would be unable to enjoy himself at feasts nor indulge in murderous rampages; and finally, the one closest to his heart, the wicked Prince Athanasii Basmanov, who was accused of planning with Archbishop Pimen to give Novgorod and Pskov to Lithuania, depose the tsar and put Prince Vladimir Andreevich on the throne.

While taking pity on these fine and honored servitors, Russians could look with secret satisfaction at God's punishment of the torturer's minions, who were doubtless innocent before the tsar, but guilty before the nation and humanity. These cruel courtiers learned too late that a tyrant's favor is as dangerous as his hatred, that he cannot put his trust for long in people whose baseness is known to him. The tiniest suspicion, a word, a single thought is sufficient for their downfall, and a devastator who punishes his minions enjoys a feeling of justice done – a rare satisfaction for a bloodthirsty heart sunk in evil, yet gnawed on by its conscience for its evildoing! Having long been slanderers, these men were destroyed by slander.

It is written that the tsar had had unbounded trust in Athanasii Basmanov: it was only from the hands of this favored armorer that he would take the medicine of his doctor, Arnolf Lenze, and it was only with him that he would talk over all his secret intentions in his bedchamber in the deep stillness of the night. The boyar cadet Thedor Lovchikov, who had been much favored by Prince Athanasii, denounced him, saying that he had supposedly informed Novgorod of the tsar's anger, apparently having been one of their confederates. Ivan did not doubt it: for a while he said nothing and then suddenly summoned Prince Vyazemskii and spoke to him in his usual trusting manner about important government affairs. Meanwhile, the tsar had ordered the prince's best servants murdered. When the prince returned home and saw their bodies, he showed neither surprise nor regret, but just walked on past them in hopes of thereby disarming the sovereign with his devotion.

However, he was thrown into the same prison as the Basmanovs, who, like him, had been accused of treachery. All the accused were tortured: anyone who could not stand the torment would slander himself and others, who were likewise tortured in order to find out things that the former did not know. The testimony of the tortured victims was written down and compiled into a serious charge that was then presented to the sovereign and his son, the tsarevich Ivan. The traitors would be informed of the punishment, which would have to take place in Moscow before the eyes of the whole people, so that the capital, already inured to the terror, might be further astounded.

On 25 July, in the great commercial square in Kitaigorod, eighteen gibbets were erected and a large number of instruments of torture were laid out. A great bonfire was lit and a giant cauldron of water was suspended over it. Seeing these fearsome preparations, the unhappy residents imagined that Moscow's final day had commenced, that Ivan intended to utterly exterminate them all. In blind panic, they hastened to hide: the square was deserted; in the open shops, goods and money lay out in the open. There was not a soul, except for the oprichniki gangs by the gibbets and the flaming bonfire.

The silence was now broken by the sound of tambourines. The tsar appeared on a steed with his beloved eldest son, boyars and princes, and a legion of the infernals, marching in formation. Behind them came the condemned, 300 or more of them, like dead men, lacerated, bloodied, and barely able to walk. Ivan stood by the gibbets, watching, and seeing no people, ordered the oprichniki to seek them out and drive them into the square from all around.

Lacking the patience to wait, he followed them and summoned Muscovites to witness his justice, promising them safety and mercy. The residents did not dare disobey: they emerged from pits and cellars, trembling, but they came, and filled the entire square; the onlookers stood on walls and roofs. Ivan now raised his voice, saying,

"People, you will see torture and death, but I am punishing traitors! Answer me: is my judgment just?" They loudly replied,

"Long live our great sovereign! Let the traitors die!"

He ordered 180 men removed from the crowd of the condemned and granted them their lives, as less guilty. The sovereign's Duma secretary now unrolled a scroll and pronounced the names of the condemned. He summoned Viskovatyi and read the following,

"Ivan Mikhailov, formerly the sovereign's privy counselor! You falsely served his majesty and wrote a letter to King Sigismund with the intention of handing Novgorod over to him. This is your first crime!" So saying, he struck Viskovatyi on the head and continued,

"Your second crime is less grave: you, a treacherous ingrate, wrote to the Turkish sultan that he should take Astrakhan and Kazan." The secretary struck him again, and a third time, and added,

"You also called on the Crimean khan to lay waste to Russia. This is your third evil deed!" Vyskovatyi now submissively, but bravely, raised his eyes to Heaven and replied,

"I testify before the Lord God, who knows men's hearts and minds, that I always served my tsar and country loyally. I hear bald-faced slander, but I will not justify myself further, for my earthly judge does not wish to hear the truth. Our Heavenly judge, however, perceives my innocence. And you, O sovereign! You will see this truth before the face of the Most High!"

The infernals put a gag in his mouth, hoisted him up by his feet, stripped him and cut him to pieces. Malyuta Skuratov had previously dismounted and cut off the unfortunate man's ears. The second victim was the treasurer, Funikov-Kartsov, a friend of Viskovatyi, just as absurdly convicted of the same treachery. He told the tsar,

"I greet you for the last time on this earth, praying to God that in Eternity you will receive just recompense for your deeds!" Both boiling and cold water was poured over him and he died in terrible agony. The rest were stabbed, hanged and cut to pieces. Ivan himself, seated on his horse, ran his lance through one old man. About 200 people were killed in the course of four hours. Finally the deed was completed and the murderers, dripping with blood, stood before the tsar with steaming swords, exclaiming,

"Let's go! Let's go!" and praising his justice. Ivan rode around the square and looked over the heaps of bodies, satisfied with his murders, but not yet content with his people's despair. He wanted to see Funikov's and Viskovatyi's wives, so he went to their homes to laugh at their tears. He tortured the former, demanding her valuables. He also wished to torture her 15 year old daughter, who was moaning and wailing, but turned her over to his son, the tsarevich Ivan. Later he locked her up in a nunnery, along with her mother and Viskovatyi's widow, where they all died of grief.

The citizens of Moscow who witnessed this terrible day did not see Prince Vyazemskii or Aleksei Basmanov among his victims. The former expired during torture, the [manner of death of the] latter – despite all the unparalleled crimes we have described – seems unlikely. This terrible account will have been an impious fabrication due to natural hatred of the tyrant, but nonetheless a calumny: contemporaries write that Ivan allegedly compelled young Thedor Basmanov to kill his father at the same time, or prior to, forcing Prince Nikita Prozorovskii to murder his brother, Prince Vasilii!

In any case, the son, who was a monster of cruelty, hardly saved himself by his [alleged] patricide: he was executed along with the others. The victims' property was confiscated by the sovereign. Many eminent people were exiled to Belo-ozero and the prelate Pimen, deprived of his rank of archbishop, was sent to the Monastery of St. Nikolai in Tula. Many gave guarantees and were released from prison; some even gained the tsar's clemency.

Ivan now rested for three days – the bodies had to be buried! But on the fourth day a number of condemned men were again brought to the square and executed. Malyuta Skuratov, who commanded the executioners, cut up the corpses with axes and the parts were left unburied for a whole week to be torn at by dogs. (There, on top of the bones and the blood, near the Kremlin moat, a church stood in later times, as a meek Christian memorial of this atrocity.) The wives of the executed court nobles, numbering 80, were drowned in the river.

In brief, Ivan had finally reached the apex of his insane tyranny: he could still murder, but he could no longer astound Russians with any novel savageries. Hardening our hearts, we shall reluctantly describe just a few of the numberless crimes of these times.

There was no safety for anyone, least of all for those known for their merits or their wealth, since the tyrant hated virtue and loved acquisition. The renowned voivode from whom Selim's huge army had fled, who had not dismounted his horse in 20 years, who had conquered Tatars, Lithuanians and Germans – Prince Pyotr Semenovich Obolenskii-Serebryanyi – was summoned to Moscow, where he heard and saw nothing but kindness from the tsar.

But suddenly an oprichnik legion rushed his Kremlin house, breaking down the gates and doors. Before Ivan's face – at his feet – they beheaded this voivode, who had been accused of nothing. Also executed at this time were the Duma councilor Zakhariya Ivanovich Ochin-Pleshcheev; Khabarov-Dobrinskii, one of the richest officials; Ivan Vorontsov, Thedor's son and a favorite in Ivan's youth; Vasilii Razladin, a descendant of the boyar Kvashin, famous in the 14th century; the voivode Kirik-Tyrkov, equally renowned for the angelic purity of his morals and his brilliant administrative mind – he was an example of martial prowess and had been wounded in many battles; the heroic defender of Lais, Andrei Kashkarov; the Narva voivode Mikhailo Matveevich Lykov, whose father in 1534 incinerated himself rather than surrender the town to the enemy and who, having been a prisoner in Lithuania in his youth, had learned Latin, had knowledge of the sciences and who was distinguished by a noble soul and pleasant manner; and a close relative of this voivode, also a Lykov, a handsome youth who had been sent by the tsar to study in Germany – he had just returned to eagerly serve his country with his fiery spirit and enlightened mind! The Mikhailov voivode Nikita Kozarinov-Golokhvastov, awaiting death, had left the capital and took vows in some monastery on the banks of the Oka. When he found out that the tsar had sent oprichniki after him, he went out to them and said,

"I am the one you are looking for." The tsar ordered him to be blown up on a powder keg and joked that such monks were angels and should fly to Heaven. The official Myasoed Visloi had a charming wife: she was taken, dishonored, and was hanged before her husband's eyes and then his head was cut off.

The tyrant's wrath fell on whole families. He killed not only children with their fathers, and wives with their husbands, but often all the relatives of the alleged criminal. Thus, in addition to 10 Kolychyovs, many Yaroslavskii princes died (one of them, Prince Ivan Shakovskii, the tsar killed with his own hands, with a mace); likewise many Prozorovskii and Ushatyi princes, and many Zabotskiis and Buturlins. Eminent Russians sometimes escaped execution by a glorious end. The two brothers, the princes Andrei and Nikita Meshcherskii, fell in battle with the Crimeans while bravely defending the new fortress on the Don.

The bodies of these knights, damp from the tears of their comrades in arms, were laid out yet unburied when Ivan's executioners showed up to kill both brothers; they were shown their bodies. Something similar happened to Prince Andrei Olenkin; the killers who had been sent found him dead on the field of honor. Not affected in the least by this, Ivan exacted cruel vengeance on the brave prince's children, who died in prison.

But death now seemed easy: the victims often requested it as a favor. It is not possible to read without shuddering the notes of contemporaries about the hellish inventions of this tyranny – of all the ways to harm people. We have mentioned big frying pans; in addition, special ovens were made for torture, and iron tongs, sharp nails and long pins. They cut people to pieces, cut them in two with fine cords, flayed their skin and tore it in strips from their backs.

COURT JESTERS

And as Russia became numb from the horror of these killings, the palace rang with exultant cries. Ivan amused himself with his executioners and gleemen, or jesters, who had been sent from Novgorod and other districts along with bears! He used the latter to chase down people, out of anger or for amusement. Sometimes he would espy a crowd of people, always peaceful and quiet, near the palace; he would order two or three bears loosed on them and laugh uproariously as they ran away, at their terrified cries as they were pursued by them and even torn up. He would always reward those mutilated, however, with a gold denga apiece, or more.

One of his principal amusements was a large number of jesters, who made him laugh before and after his murders, but who sometimes paid with their lives for a sharp word. Famous among them was Prince Osip Gvozdev, who had a distinguished court rank. Once, when the tsar was dissatisfied with one of his tricks, he poured a bowl of hot soup on him. The poor comedian yelled and tried to get away. Ivan kicked him, drawing blood, and Gvozdev fell unconscious. Doctor Arnolf was immediately summoned.

"Heal my good servant," the tsar said. "I was playing carelessly with him."

"So carelessly," replied Arnolf, "that perhaps God and your royal majesty might raise the dead, for he no longer has any breath in him."

Waving his hand, the tsar consigned the dead jester to the dogs and continued to make merry. Another time, while he was having dinner, the Staritskii voivode Boris Titov came to him. He bowed to the ground and did his sovereign the customary honors. The tsar said,

"Good health to you, my beloved voivode: you deserve our reward," and cut off his ear. Titov showed no reaction at all to the pain and with a calm expression thanked Ivan for his gracious punishment and wished him a fortunate reign! Sometimes the pleasure-seeking tyrant, putting aside his hunger and thirst, would suddenly turn down meat and drink and leave the table. He would shout loudly to summon his guards, mount his horse and gallop off to wade in blood.

Thus he once rushed off from a sumptuous dinner to cut up some Lithuanian prisoners in a Moscow jail. It is written that one of them, the nobleman Bykovskii, tore a lance from his tormentor's hands and tried to run him through, but fell at the hand of the tsarevich Ivan, who eagerly participated in these affairs, as if to deprive Russia of any hope in a subsequent reign! After killing more than 100 men, the tyrant would return triumphantly to his palace to the usual cries of *Let's go! Let's go!* from his guards and once again sit down at his table. But sometimes at these murderous feasts, a human voice with words of courageous audacity would be heard. The brave Molchan Mitkov, forced by Ivan to drink down a cup of strong mead, exclaimed in grief,

"O Tsar! You command us to join you in drinking mead mixed with the blood of our brothers, Orthodox Christians!" Ivan thrust his sharp staff into him. Mitkov crossed himself and died with a prayer.

Such was the tsar, and such were his subjects! Should we be more astounded at him, or at them? Even if he did not exceed all others in torture, they exceeded all others in forbearance, since they considered a tsar's power to be divine and any resistance to be unlawful. They ascribed Ivan's tyranny to the wrath of Heaven and repented of their sins in faith and hope of propitiation. They did not fear death, but comforted themselves with the thought that there is another world for the felicity of virtue, that this one serves only as a taste thereof. They perished, but preserved Russia's might for us, for the strength of the people's obedience is the strength of the state.

We now complete our portrait of the terrors of the times: hunger and disease helped the tyrant to devastate Russia. It seemed as if the land had lost its fertility: grain was planted, but there was none to gather – cold and drought ruined the harvest. There were unheard of rises in prices: the price of a chetvert* of rye in Moscow was 60 altyns, or about nine of today's silver rubles. The poor gathered at the markets, asking about the price of grain, and crying out in despair. Alms were scarce – they were requested even by those who up till now had fed the poor.

> FAMINE AND PESTILENCE

---

* [About 210 liters, or approximately 6 U.S. bushels.]

People wandered around like shades, dying in the streets and on the roads. There were no overt disturbances, but there were terrible crimes: starving people murdered and ate each other! Weakness due to starvation and unnatural foods gave rise to contagious, lethal illnesses in various places. The tsar ordered many highways closed and mounted guards hunted down all travelers on unauthorized roads who did not have written passes; they had orders to incinerate them along with all their goods and horses. This calamity continued until 1572.

However, neither fate nor the tyrant had yet had their fill of victims. Although we are not finished, we will interrupt our description of these evils so that we may marvel at Ivan, apparently indifferent and calm in the midst of his tireless political activities.

RELATIONS WITH LITHUANIA

In the spring of 1570 Sigismund's emissaries arrived in Moscow to conclude a peace treaty; they wanted one with the Swedish king as well, but Ivan did not want to hear of the latter. In a secret conversation they told the tsar that their nobles were thinking, in the case of Sigismund's likely impending demise, of offering him the king's crown as a sovereign of the Slavic race, a Christian and a powerful ruler. Ivan showed neither pleasure nor firm agreement, coolly replying,

"By the grace of God and the prayers of our forefathers of great Russia, why [do you want to give] me Lithuania and Poland? If you are really considering this, then you should not keep harassing us with regard to the sacred matter of Christian peace."

Although they spoke of peace, they only concluded a truce for three years. This was ratified by Sigismund in Warsaw in the presence of our emissaries, who then reported to the tsar that the Lithuanian nobles wanted to give him Sigismund's sister Sofiya in marriage, and that they now saw him as their future ruler. They did not want to submit to the Kaiser, who was a poor protector of even his own lands, or to other sovereigns who were fairly weak in comparison with the Muscovite ruler, who was dangerous as an enemy, but also a most reliable protector. The ambitious Ivan believed them, and in his mind he was already reaching out his bloody right hand for the Jagellonian crown!

Meanwhile, he was actively occupied with Livonia. His favorites, Taube and Kruse, whom he had promoted to the Duma, suggested that he make a special kingdom out of the Order's lands, under ultimate Russian authority. They assured him that in such a circumstance, all the inhabitants would come over to him heart and soul, chase out the Swedes and Lithuanians, and become, along with their king, completely loyal subjects of the great Muscovite sovereign.

> THE LIVONIAN KINGSHIP

It is written that back in 1565 Ivan had suggested in the most gracious terms that his renowned prisoner Fürstenberg become ruler of Livonia and a vassal to the tsar. The courageous old man replied, however, that it would be better for him to die in captivity than betray his conscience and his sacred oath to the Knights. In 1569 Taube and Kruse, who enjoyed Ivan's trust, had contact with the citizens of Revel, trying to persuade them to come over to the tsar. These Duma councilors promised them a *golden age*, liberty and tranquility, telling them,

"What does Livonia show over the course of 12 years? A picture of terrible calamity, bloodshed and destruction. No one is confident of his life or property. We serve the great Muscovite tsar, but we have not betrayed our first, true homeland, for which we wish both good things and deliverance. We know that he intends to strike Livonia with all his forces to expel the Swedes, Poles and Danes.

"Where are your defenders? Germany does not care about you: you know of the emperor's incaution and weakness. The Danish king does not dare to say a rude word to the tsar. The decrepit Sigismund is failing, and seeks peace with Moscow, but he only oppresses his Livonian subjects. Sweden awaits vengeance and punishment. You would now be under siege if not for the fierce plague that is raging in Russia and is preventing the tsar from contemplating any military operations. He is fond of the Germans: he himself is descended from the house of Bavaria and promises you that under his rule there will be no happier city than Revel.

"Choose your own ruler from among the German princes. It will not be yourselves, but just this ruler who will be subordinate to Ivan, just as the German princes are subordinate to the emperor – nothing more. Enjoy peace, liberty and all the benefits of commerce without paying tribute or knowing the hardship of military service. The tsar only wishes to be your benefactor!"

At the same time they offered Duke Gothard of Courland the title of king in Ivan's name. However, as hated servants of the Muscovite ruler, a tyrant now known everywhere, they were not believed. Revel did not want to betray Sweden, nor Gothard to betray Sigismund. Ivan's confidants now turned to Prince Magnus of Denmark, the ruler of Ösel. Beguiled by them, the gullible youth consented to become an instrument of Ivan's policy, unknown to his brother, the Danish king.

As a sign of his confidence in the great favors promised him, Magnus traveled to see the tsar. In Derpt he learned the fate of Novgorod. He halted, tarried, and fearfully considered retracing his route, but ambition gained the upper hand. He arrived in Moscow in great pomp with a large number of servants and officials on 200 horses. He was received with great favor, entertained at feasts, and a few days later concluded his important business. The tsar designated Magnus *King of Livonia*, while Magnus acknowledged the tsar as his supreme ruler and father, and was awarded the honor of marrying Ivan's niece Evfimiya, daughter of the unfortunate Prince Vladimir Andreevich.

TSAR'S KINDNESS TOWARD MAGNUS

The wedding was postponed until a more propitious time, however. Ivan promised the bride five casks of gold, released the Derpt prisoners on behalf of his future son-in-law and gave him troops to expel the Swedes from Estonia. Accompanied by a great number of Germans and some Russian legions, Magnus entered Livonia and announced to the inhabitants his kingship, Ivan's favor, the union of all the Order's lands and the beginning of peace and prosperity.

Fully empowered by the tsar, Taube and Kruse vouched for Ivan's sincerity and good will. They said and wrote that Livonia would remain free and pay only a light tribute to the Muscovite

Chapter Eight

sovereign, that all our officials would leave, and that only Germans would govern the land, in the name of their king and the law. Many believed this and rejoiced, but not for long. Magnus, a victim of his ambition and gullibility would be to blame for the new calamities to befall unhappy Livonia.

Heeding Taube and Kruse in all things, on 23 August he entered Revel with 25,000 Russians and a large German guard, hoping to take control without bloodshed, but the citizens responded to his proposal by saying that they were aware of Ivan's cunning, that it was impossible that a tyrant over his own people could be a benefactor of a foreign one and that the young and inexperienced Magnus had advisors who were either ill-intentioned or imprudent. They said that the same fate as Prince Mikhail Glinskii was being prepared for him in Russia and that Revel did not want to become like Smolensk.

A siege and sallies commenced, as well as a lethal epidemic, both in the city and in the Russian camp, in which more patience was displayed than skill or courage. The besiegers were uselessly exhausted building earthworks and their artillery had but slight effect. They occupied the heights right in front of the Revel gates and erected wooden towers from which they launched grenades and red-hot cannonballs into the fortress, but without doing significant damage to the enemy.

Autumn began, and then winter. Moscow's voivodes, the boyar Ivan Petrovich Yakovlev and the princes Lykov and Kropotkin, could not figure out how to take Revel and merely pillaged Estonian villages. In February they sent off 2,000 sleighs loaded with booty to Russia. They were waiting until hunger forced the besieged to surrender, but the Swedish fleet was successful in providing them with an abundance of both edible and military provisions. Finally, the troops began to express their discontent.

Magnus was in despair; he blamed the tsar's advisors, Taube and Kruse. He did not know what to do and sent his confessor Schraffer with new arguments to win over Revel's citizens. This eloquent pastor shamelessly assured them that Ivan was a real Christian sovereign and preferred the Latin Church to the Greek – he might easily subscribe to the Augsburg Confession. It was out of necessity that he was severe with the Russians, but Germans were his true friends and that by their futile resistance Revel was delaying the golden age offered by this young king. The citizens ordered him to return without a reply.

On 16 March, after investing Revel for 30 weeks, Magnus raised the siege, burned his camp and withdrew to Oberpahlen with his German guard, which had been given him by the tsar as an earnest of his future kingship, while our troops took up positions in eastern Livonia.

This initial defeat must have incensed the tsar. At this same time, he learned that the Danish king had made peace with the Swedes. He expressed his liveliest displeasure to Magnus, blaming his brother of violating his treaty with Russia and in befriending its malefactors. Another unexpected event disturbed the tsar and Magnus even more. Ivan had promised Kruse and Taube freedom, distinction and wealth. Following the unsuccessful siege of Revel, they had lost the trust of the new king of Livonia and feared losing the sovereign's, as well.

Forgetting their oaths and their honor, they entered into secret negotiations with the Swedes and the Poles and took it into their heads to gain control of Derpt in order to give it to one or the other of them. It seemed easy: they had the guard's German troops at their disposal. Since these were serving the tsar for money, they would not scruple to betray him. The eminent residents of Derpt who had long been prisoners in Russia hated its rule more than did other Livonians. Consequently it should have been possible to rely on their enthusiastic cooperation.

With this thought in mind, the conspirators broke into the city. They killed the guards, summoned their friends and brothers and shouted that the hour of liberty and vengeance was at hand. But the astounded citizens remained mere spectators. No one joined these traitors, whom the Russians dealt with in a few minutes: some were cut down, others chased off. In their fury a great number of innocents were killed because the Russians considered them to be traitors.

Taube and Kruse escaped: cast out by Revel's citizens, who did not want to hear or see them, they sought refuge in Polish territory, where the king and especially the ruler of Courland received these foolhardy men with great honor, in hopes of learning important Russian state secrets from them, but all they learned about were the horrors of Ivan's tyranny! A year before this, Taube and Kruse had written to Emperor Maximilian that only Ivan could drive the Turks from Europe, since he had an army that was experienced, invincible and innumerable.

After these two had betrayed Russia, they assured Maximilian and other European sovereigns of its impotence and the possibility of conquering it or at least pressuring it! Although blameless, Magnus feared to become a victim of their treachery and Ivan's wrath; he hastened to depart Oberpahlen for the island of Ösel.

But the tsar knew how to hold firm in his intentions, to hide his irritation, to seem cool in the greatest adversity. He attempted to calm Magnus with new assurances of his favor and sorrowfully informed him of the sudden death of his bride-to-be, the young Evfimiya, offering him the hand of her still younger sister, Mariya, with the same conditions and the same rich dowry, and once again promised to conquer Estonia for him.

Magnus was consoled and once again gratefully became the fiancé of a niece of the tsar. He waited with her for his kingdom and wrote to his brother, to the emperor and to the German princes that it was not vain ambition, but a real passion for the general welfare of Christians that obliged him to seek an alliance with Russia in order to become an intermediary between the Empire and this great power – one that might join with other European monarchs to restrain Turkey. The emperor and all of Germany had this same hope, for they were frightened by the sultan's lust for power.

But as we shall see, Ivan was not thinking of the glory of defending Christian Europe from Mohammedan arms. He was concerned only with facilitating his own policies, i.e., with the surest way to gain control all of Livonia and humble the pride of Revel, which dared to formally declare him a tyrant and magnified the victory it had gained over the Russians by establishing an annual holiday in its memory, on 16 March. He was preparing his vengeance, which had been delayed by the terrible calamity in Moscow and all of southeastern Russia.

EMBASSY TO CONSTANTINOPLE

Following the principle of not multiplying Russia's enemies, Ivan intended to avert another futile war with the sultan, whose good will towards us might restrain the khan. To this end, the court noble Novosiltsov traveled to Constantinople in 1570 to congratulate Selim on his accession to the throne. In a flattering letter to him, Ivan enumerated all the friendly relations Russia had had with Turkey since the time of Bayazet. He was shocked at Selim's army's invasion of our territory without a declaration of war, and offered him peace and friendship.

"My sovereign," Novosiltsov was charged to tell the sultan's nobles, "is not an enemy of the Moslem faith. His servitor Sain-Bulat rules in Kasimov, Prince Kaibula in Yuriev, Ibak in Surozhik and the Nogai princes in Romanovo. All of them freely and reverently praise Mohammed in their own mosques, for among us, all foreigners live by their own religion. In Kadom and Meshchera, many of the sovereign's officials are men of the Moslem faith. If Simeon, the late ruler of Kazan, or if Prince Murtoza became Christians, this was because they themselves wanted to, they themselves requested to be baptized."

1571

Novosiltsov was pleased with his favorable reception, noting only that the sultan did not inquire as to Ivan's health, and contrary to our own custom, did not invite him to dine with him. Yet this embassy and another one in 1571 did not have the desired results, even though the tsar, to please Selim, agreed to dismantle our fortress in Kabarda. The proud sultan wanted Astrakhan and Kazan, or else that Ivan in ruling them acknowledge himself as a tributary of the Ottoman Empire. This proposal was so absurd that it went without a reply.

At this same time, the tsar learned that Selim had requested Kiev from Sigismund to facilitate an invasion of Russia; that he had ordered bridges be built over the Danube and grain be stored in Moldavia; that the khan, at the instigation of the Turks, was preparing to go to war with us; and that a Crimean prince had crushed our sovereign's father-in-law Temgryuk and taken two of his sons captive.

Devlet-Girei, who now had direct ties with Moscow, was again starting to threaten, to demand tribute and the restoration of Baty's dominions of Kazan and Astrakhan.

The sovereign had been informed from Donkov and Putivl of the movements of the khan's troops. Our mounted patrols in the steppes had seen unusual clouds of dust, fires by night and tracks of numerous horsemen; in the distance they had heard the snorting and the neighing of large numbers of horses. Moscow's commanders were stationed on the Oka. Ivan came out with his son twice to see the troops, who were in Kolomna and Serpukhov. There had already been light skirmishes near Ryazan and Koshira, but everywhere the Crimeans would appear in small numbers and then vanish, with the result that the sovereign was ultimately reassured; he declared the reports by the Ataman's sentries groundless and disbanded most of his army that winter.

He was all the more alarmed at the onset of spring, when the khan, having mustered all of his uluses, 100,000 or more men, crossed the southern borders of Russia with unusual speed. Here he encountered some refugees: our boyar cadets, who had fled their homeland due to the terror of the Moscow executions. These turncoats told Devlet-Girei that hunger, disease and constant denunciations had in the course of two years destroyed most of Ivan's army and that the remainder was in Livonia or in garrisons. They said that Ivan would take the field with his few oprichniki only for glory, only for show; they would not hesitate to flee into the northern wastes. The turncoats swore on their lives that this was true and that they would be faithful guides for the Crimeans.

> INVASION BY THE KHAN

Unfortunately, the turncoats were telling the truth: we now had far fewer valiant voivodes and regular troops. The princes Belskii, Mstislavskii, Vorotynskii and the boyars Morozov and Sheremetev hastened, as usual, to occupy the banks of the Oka, but they were unsuccessful. The khan bypassed them, approaching Serpukhov by another route. This is where Ivan and the oprichniki were. Resolve and courage were required, but the tsar fled! He first went to Kolomna, then to Sloboda, then past unfortunate Moscow. From

Sloboda he went to Yaroslavl to save himself from the enemy, from traitors, since it seemed to him that both Russia and the voivodes were going to hand him over to the Tatars!

Moscow was without troops, without commanders, without any sort of organization, and the khan was now 30 versts away! But the tsar's voivodes on the banks of the Oka were not just sitting there; they were coming to the city's defense – but what did they do then? Instead of meeting and defeating the khan in the field, they occupied Moscow's suburbs, which were filled with a vast number of refugees from the surrounding villages. The voivodes were trying to mount a defense amongst close-packed, vulnerable buildings.

Prince Ivan Belskii and Morozov were stationed in Varlaamovskaya Street with the main legion; Mstislavskii and Sheremetev were in Yakimovskaya Street with the right wing; Vorotynskii and Tatev were on Taganskii Meadow, opposite Krutitsy, while Temkin and the oprichnik guard were on the other side of the Neglinnaya. The next day, May 24th – on Ascension Day – the khan reached Moscow, and that happened which one would have had to expect: the khan ordered the suburbs torched.

CONFLAGRATION IN MOSCOW

The morning was calm and clear. The Russians bravely prepared for battle, but found themselves surrounded by flames. Wooden houses and huts burst into flame in 10 different places. The sky was darkened by the smoke; a whirlwind arose and in a few minutes a stormy sea of fire spread from one end of the city to the other with a terrible howling noise. It was beyond human strength to halt the destruction and no one tried. The people and the soldiers frenziedly sought safety and perished beneath the ruins of flaming buildings or stifled each other in the crush, trying to reach the city or to go to Kitaigorod.

But pursued everywhere by the flames, they threw themselves in the river and drowned. The commanders no longer gave orders, or else they were not obeyed. They barely managed to shut the Kremlin gates and did not let anyone into this last refuge of safety, which was surrounded by high walls. People were scorched and fell dead in the stone churches from the heat and smoke. The

Tatars tried, but were unable, to pillage the suburbs; the flame chased them out and the khan, frightened by the inferno, withdrew to the village of Kolomenskoe.

Within three hours Moscow was no more: neither the suburbs nor Kitaigorod existed any more. Only the Kremlin remained intact, where the metropolitan Kirill sat in the Church of the Dormition of the Virgin amongst his sacred objects and his treasury. Ivan's beloved palace in the Arbat was destroyed. People perished in incredible numbers, more than 120,000 soldiers and citizens, not counting women, children and rural residents who had fled from the enemy into Moscow – about 800,000 in all.

The chief voivode, Prince Belskii, was asphyxiated in the cellar of his court, likewise the boyar Mikhailo Ivanovich Voronoi and Ivan's primary doctor, Arnolf Lenze, and 25 London merchants. In the ashes, where there had been buildings, there were heaps of burned corpses, both human and equine.

"Whoever saw this spectacle," eyewitnesses write, "will always recall it with new horror and pray never to see its like again."

Devlet-Girei had completed his exploit. He had no desire to lay siege to the Kremlin, and from the Sparrow Hills he surveyed his triumph: heaps of smoldering ashes over an extent of 30 versts. He decided to withdraw immediately, frightened, we are assured, by false rumors that Duke (or King) Magnus was approaching with a large army. Ivan was in Rostov when he received news of the enemy withdrawal. He ordered Prince Vorotynskii to go after the khan, who nevertheless managed to lay waste to the greater portion of Moscow's southeast districts.

He took more than 100,000 prisoners back to the Taurid. The tsar lacked the magnanimity to comfort his subjects in this terrible calamity and was afraid to view this theater of terror and tears. He did not want to go to the ashes of the capital and returned to Sloboda, where he gave orders to clear the decaying corpses from the ruins of Moscow.

Few were buried: only the eminent or the richest were interred with Christian rites; the bodies of the rest filled the Moscow River, cutting off its flow. They lay in heaps, infecting both air and water with the poison of their decay. The wells were either dry or filled in and the remaining residents were faint with thirst. Ultimately, people were gathered from the outlying towns. They dragged the bodies out of the river and committed them to the earth. Thus was the vial of Heaven's wrath poured out over Russia. What miseries were lacking after hunger, disease, fire, sword, captivity and a tyrant?

Now we shall see how cowardly this tyrant was in the first really important decision of his reign. On 15 June he was nearing Moscow and stayed in Bratovshchina, where two heralds from Devlet-Girei were presented to him. The khan was departing Russia as a majestic victor and wanted to make himself clearly understood. The tsar was simply dressed, as were the boyars and court nobles in token either of their grief or lack of respect for the khan. To Ivan's inquiry about the health of his brother Devlet-Girei, the khan's official replied,

"Our ruler says the following to you:

'We called ourselves friends, but now we have become enemies. Brothers fight and then make peace. Hand over Kazan and Astrakhan and I will eagerly march against your enemies.'"

Having said this, the herald displayed the khan's gifts, including a knife of forged gold, and continued,

"Devlet-Girei wears it on his thigh; do you the same. My sovereign also wanted to send you a steed, but our horses were worn out in your land." Ivan rejected this gift as *improper* and ordered Devlet-Girei's letter be read.

"I have burnt and laid waste to Russia," wrote the khan, "solely because of Kazan and Astrakhan. I have turned your wealth and money to dust. I sought you everywhere, in Serpukhov and in Moscow itself; I wanted your crown and your head. But you ran away from Serpukhov and fled Moscow, and yet you dare to boast of your royal majesty, while you have neither courage nor shame! I now know the way to your realm: I shall come to you again if you do not release my emissary, who is futilely languishing in Russia, and if you do not do that which I ask, which is to give me a sworn letter binding on yourself, your sons and grandsons."

How did Ivan behave, who was so haughty before the distinguished Christian crowned heads of Europe? He *kowtowed* to the khan and promised to yield Kazan to him on the formal ratification of a peace treaty, while entreating him not to menace Russia before then. He made no reply to the khan's abusive and sarcastic words; he agreed to release Crimea's emissary if the khan would release Athanasii Nagoi and send a noble to Moscow for further negotiation. Genuinely prepared in this extremity to relinquish his brilliant conquest, Ivan wrote to Nagoi in the Crimea that we should at least enthrone future rulers of Astrakhan in collaboration with the khan.

That is, he wished to preserve a shadow of control over this state. Betraying our national honor and welfare, he no doubt betrayed the precepts of our Church as well: to ingratiate himself with Devlet-Girei, he now gave him an eminent Crimean prisoner, the son of a prince, who had freely accepted the Christian faith in Moscow. He handed him over to be tortured or reconverted, an unheard of offense against Orthodoxy.

After abasing himself before his enemy, Ivan seemed happy with a new pretext to work evil on his own poor country. While Moscow was still smoking and the Tatars were still rampaging within our borders, the tsar was executing and torturing his subjects! We have seen that Russian turncoats led Devlet-Girei to our capital. Ivan used this treachery to explain away the enemy's success. As before, he justified the frenzy of his rage and malice.

He also found something else to blame, no less important. Tired of being a widower, although hardly chaste, he had been seeking a third wife for a long time now. The khan's invasion had interrupted this, but when the danger had passed, the tsar once again took it up. From towns and cities everywhere, young women were brought to Sloboda, whether distinguished or not, numbering over 2,000; each was presented to him personally. At first he selected 24, later 12, whom his doctor and some old women were to examine.

For a long time he compared them as to beauty, charm and intelligence. Ultimately he preferred Martha Vasilievna Sobakina most

> IVAN MARRIED AGAIN

of all; she was the daughter of a Novgorod merchant. At the same time, a bride was chosen for his elder son, one Evdokiya Boldanovna Saburova. The fathers of the fortunate beauties were elevated to boyars from nothing; their uncles, future royal okolnichie and a brother, to royal carver. After these promotions, they divided wealth, loot that had belonged to those disgraced, and possessions taken from the ancient lines of princes and boyars.

But the tsar's bride became ill, began to lose weight and waste away. It was said that she had been *ruined* by miscreants and haters of Ivan's family, and suspicion turned to the close relatives of the deceased tsaritsas, Anastasiya and Mariya. There was an investigation, probably using both fear and cajolery to elicit either truth or calumnies. We do not know all the circumstances; we know only who they were and how they died in this fifth episode of murders. Ivan's brother-in-law, Prince Mikhailo Temgryukovich, was a stern Asiatic – sometimes a distinguished voivode and sometimes a vile executioner – who was showered with both favors and curses, often enriched and often deprived of everything jist to amuse the tsar. He was supposed to go after Devlet-Girei with a legion of oprichniki.

FIFTH EPISODE OF MURDERS

He set out, but was suddenly disgraced and impaled! The nobleman Ivan Petrovich Yakovlev (pardoned in 1566), his brother Vasilii, former tutor the elder tsarevich, and the voivode Zamyatnya Saburov, nephew of the unfortunate Solomonida, first wife of Ivan's father, were all flogged to death. The boyar Lev Andreevich Saltykov took vows as a monk at the Trinity Monastery and was murdered there.

Another form of execution came to light: the evil slanderer, Doctor Eliseus Bomelius, whom we have already mentioned, suggested the tsar eradicate evildoers with poison. He concocted a lethal potion, we are assured, and with such infernal skill that a person poisoned would expire in the very minute designated by the tyrant. Ivan poisoned one of his favorites in this way, Grigorii Gryaznoi, as well as Prince Ivan Gvozdev-Rostovskii and many others who were avowed to have been participants in the poisoning of the tsar's bride or of the treason that had disclosed the route from Kazan to Moscow.

Meanwhile, on 28 October, the tsar married the ailing Martha, hoping, in his own words, to save her by this act of love and his trust in the grace of God. Six days later, his son married Evdokiya, but the wedding feasts concluded with funerals. Martha passed away on 13 November, either an actual victim of human malice or only the unfortunate cause of the murder of innocent people. At any event, her royal grave lies next to those of Ivan's two other wives at the Devichii Monastery of the Ascension, where it is an object of the sorrowful thoughts and emotions of posterity.

> DEATH OF THE TSARITA

Solaced by this vengeance, Ivan sought further diversion in the affairs of state. Fearing a second invasion by the khan and wishing to take measures for Moscow's safety, he got rid of Moscow's suburbs. He moved all the merchants and workers there into the city and forbade them to build tall wooden houses, which would be dangerous in case of fire. He inspected and deployed his troops and ordered the ruler of Kasimov, Sain Bulat, to march against the Swedes with his vanguard, to Oreshek, while he himself set off for Novgorod.

It seems it had not been easy for him to view the site of these shameful, ferocious executions, these terrible tokens of his wrath – where, in the fearful silence of the people, the very stones cried out against this murderer. It was a place of grief, dejection and destitution, as well as the diseases that still raged there. The Novgorod deputies ordered all the residents to gather in front of the empty and uninhabited Archbishop's Court and read out Ivan's letter to them.

> IVAN JOURNEYS TO NOVGOROD

The tsar wrote that they should remain calm and prepare, according to ancient custom, provisions for his visit. They cleaned out a court and garden for him on Nikitskaya Street, set up a new royal place for him in the Sofiya Cathedral, with a golden dove over it, as if to symbolize their submission and lack of ill will. They also restored the prelate's place in the cathedral, now orphaned without its chief.

Stern measures were taken to protect the tsar's health: no burials were allowed in the city for those who had died from contagious disease; their remains were taken to a cemetery on the banks of the Volkhov near the Khutynskii Monastery. Guards walked the streets from morning until night, keeping an eye on the homes and closing up those in which illness was discovered. Nor were priests allowed to see the sick; both were threatened with incineration on a bonfire if they disobeyed.

This cruel strictness had, however, a beneficial effect: at the beginning of winter, the priesthood formally announced to the sovereign's envoys that the epidemic was over in Novgorod, and on 23 December, to the residents' delight, their new archbishop, Leonid, arrived. He had been chosen from among the archmandrites of the Chudovskii Monastery. On the following day the sovereign himself arrived, with his sons and eminent officials. Ivan's court, despite the slaughter of so many nobles, still appeared splendid and brilliant; and there were still men near the throne who were gray-haired with service.

His campaign or military council now comprised boyars and the princes Mstislavskii, Vorotynskii, Pronskii, Trubetskii, Odoevskii, Sitskii, Sheremetev and the most eminent of them, Pyotr Tutaevich Shiidyakov Nogaiskii. There was the okolnichii Vasilii Sobakin and the Duma nobles Malyuta Skuratov and Cheremisinov, the keeper of the seal Olferiev and the secretaries Andrei and Vasilii Yakovlev Shchelkalov, who were the principal perpetrators of the death of the ill-fated Ivan Mikhailovich Viskovatyi. The legions were gathered at Oreshek and Derpt to join in battle against Finland and Estonia in order to take vengeance on the Swedish king for failing to fulfill Erik's crazy agreement and also for Magnus' defeat at Revel.

SWEDISH AFFAIRS

But the ashes of Moscow, the impoverishment of Russia and a new threat from the khan inclined Ivan towards peace: he simply wanted an honorable one. Swedish emissaries had been sent to Murom and were taken to Novgorod, where they were informed of the conditions of the tsar's favor. Ivan demanded 100,000 thalers from the king for the insults done to Vorontsov and Naumov in Stockholm, the cession of all of Estonia and the silver mines in Finland, an alliance with the tsar against Lithuania and Denmark, and in case of war, that he be given 1,000 cavalry and 500 infantry.

Finally, he wanted the king to call him *Ruler of Sweden* and send his coat of arms to Moscow so that it could be incorporated into the tsar's seal!

The emissaries, who were exhausted from their cruel confinement, were afraid to irritate Ivan, as much for their own sake as for weak Sweden, which was threatened with attack by a powerful army. They implored the tsareviches and the boyars to convince their sovereign to stay his sword, send them back to their king, and agree to peacefully await a reply. They said there was no silver ore in Finland and that Sweden was a poor country and it was not within its power to help us with troops. When they were presented to Ivan, they fell to the ground. The tsar ordered them to get up and said,

"I am a Christian ruler and do not want earthly worship." He enumerated the king's offenses, repeated his demands and then added,

"Our will be done lest we see whose sword is sharper."

Later he declared to them that when he had asked Erik for Katerina that he had thought her to be a childless widow and consequently had not violated divine law. He had only wanted a reliable guarantee of Sigismund's pacification. The emissaries assured him that the king would straighten everything out and bow to him with regard to his offenses.

They dined with Ivan and signed a letter in which it stated that the great Russian sovereign had exchanged wrath for mercy with regard to Sweden and agreed not to make war on its territories before Whitsunday, on condition that the king now send other emissaries to Novgorod with 10,000 thalers for the offenses done Vorontsov and Naumov, and 200 cavalry troops equipped in the German manner to serve Moscow, as well as some skilled metallurgists. He also required that the king freely allow the export to Russia of copper, tin, lead, petroleum and sulfur; and likewise for medical people, artists and artisans, and military men.

In a cordial conversation with the bishop of Åbo [Turku], his boyars inquired about the age, intellect and fertility of the king's younger sister. They expressed a desire for her portrait and intimated that the tsar might want to marry her. Finally, Ivan sent the emissaries off with honors to Stockholm and with a letter to the king, writing,

"You will get nothing from me if you do not relinquish Livonia. Your hopes in the Kaiser are vain. Say what you will, but you cannot protect your land with words."

The tsar then declared war, but postponed hostilities out of respect for the Swedish petition. He did no harm to anyone during 26 days in Novgorod, and to the residents' pleasure, he restored the ancient custom of judicial single combat and also gave them as deputies Pronskii and the first-rank boyar Prince Mstislavskii. He departed on 18 February and was sent off with the people's blessings.

1572

IVAN'S FOURTH MARRIAGE

His first order of business on returning to Moscow or Aleksandrovskaya Sloboda was an ecclesiastical illegitimacy heretofore unheard of: he married *for the fourth time* – to a quite undistinguished young woman, one Anna Alekseyevna Koltovskaya, without considering the advantages of asking for a prelate's blessing.

He soon had second thoughts, however; he summoned the bishops and implored them to affirm the marriage. The metropolitan Kirill had passed away by this time and Archbishop Leonid of Novgorod had seniority at the council. He was avaricious and eager for secular power. Ivan accordingly told the prelates (formally, at the Cathedral of the Dormition),

"Evildoers carried off my first wife, Anastasiya, by sorcery. My second, the Circassian princess, was also poisoned and went to meet the Lord in agony and torment. After waiting for a considerable time, I decided on a third marriage, partly for my own bodily needs, partly for my children, who are not yet fully grown. Their youth prevented me from leaving the world [i.e., to become a monk], but to live in this world without a wife is wrong.

"Blessed by the metropolitan Kirill, I long sought a bride for myself; I investigated and finally chose. But envy and animosity killed Martha, who was tsaritsa in name only. While yet a bride, she lost her health and two weeks after the wedding died a virgin.

Chapter Eight

"In despair and sorrow I wished to devote my life to becoming a monk, but again, in view of the pitiable youth of my sons and the calamities of my country, I ventured to undertake a fourth marriage. Now, kneeling, with tears in my eyes, I beseech you prelates for your permission and blessing."

Such humility on the part of the great tsar, as it says in the Acts of this cathedral, profoundly moved the archbishops and the bishops, who wept and were compassionate with regard to the sinner and the sin. They read the ordinances of the ecumenical council, debated and proposed to ratify the marriage because of the sovereign's ardent and touching repentance. However, they forbade him to enter a church before Easter and then only to partake of the holy sacrament.

For a year he would have to stand in church with others who knelt in prayer, for [another] year with the faithful, and only partake of the blessed bread on holidays. In the event of war they would release him from this penance and take it upon themselves. Meanwhile, they promised to pray for the tsaritsa Anna, and so that the tsar's crime would not lead people into error, they threatened terrible anathema on anyone who, like Ivan, might dare to take a fourth wife. In addition to Leonid, the letter of dispensation was signed by the archbishops Kornilii of Rostov and Antonii of Polotsk, seven bishops and a number of archimandrites and eminent abbots. Having put Ivan's conscience at peace, they busied themselves with another important matter: they chose a metropolitan. This honor was awarded to Archbishop Antonii.

> 29 April

> May

Meanwhile, desirous of peace, but preparing for war, he ordered all the boyar cadets into service and fortified the southern cities of Volkhov and Oryol, which had been founded in the steppes not long before. Ivan undertook negotiations with various powers. He renewed his alliance with Queen Elizabeth, although he had been unhappy at her coolness towards his declared intention to seek refuge in England, and he had almost expelled the London merchants from Russia after they

> Alliance with Queen Elizabeth

had been accused of illegal avarice. To mollify the tsar, Elizabeth sent Jenkinson for a fourth time with assurances of friendship sincere and everlasting.

"But why did the queen," said Ivan, "concern herself solely with profits of English commerce and not show an active interest in matters that would determine my fate? I know that trade is important for a country, but the personal affairs of rulers are more important than commercial ones."

Jenkinson vindicated Elizabeth, blaming bad interpreters, who did not know how to render her words, which were animated by love for the tsar. Jenkinson inquired about the crimes of the London merchants. He enumerated their services, showing that, in accordance with the queen's will, they had cooperated in the success of our arms in Livonia by not allowing the northern powers to block the sea lane to Narva, which would have deprived Russia of the benefits of the Baltic trade. Ivan was mollified and declared his favor towards all Englishmen. He did not wish to speak of their guilt and said,

"He whom I forgive is no longer at fault. We shall be friends, as before. Formerly secret matters will remain secret. Circumstances are different now, and in case of need, I will confide with total trust in my beloved sister Elizabeth."

In other words, after getting rid of imagined internal enemies, he was no longer thinking of fleeing to London! Having again obtained for his merchants the tsar's gracious permission to trade in Russia, Jenkinson proposed to open an office in Astrakhan for trade with Persia, and a merchant's court in Kholmogory. He also requested

1) that English artists and artisans be free to return to London from Moscow,

2) payment for wares taken from the English for the debts of certain disgraced and executed courtiers of the tsar, and

3) payment for everything belonging to these merchants that had been burnt up during the Moscow conflagration. It seems these requests displeased Ivan. He said that foreigners were free to live among us, or not; that he had ordered these debts taken care of and did not want to hear anything more about them; and that the

sovereign was not responsible for the fire or the wrath of God that had reduced Moscow to ashes. Jenkinson was sent off with honors and with a flattering letter for Elizabeth.

In his new relations with Denmark and Lithuania, Ivan followed the old principle of proud intransigence. King Frederik had not informed him about his peace with Sweden, nor had he manifested the slightest sympathy about the fate of Magnus, but he assured the tsar of his undying friendship. He complained that Russians had taken land and fisheries from the Norwegians and requested safe conduct for the emperor's emissaries to come to Moscow on important business. The tsar said,

> NEGOTIATIONS WITH DENMARK AND LITHUANIA

"Frederik does well when he wishes to be our loyal friend for life, but he does wrong to make peace with an enemy of Russia without our authorization. Let him make amends. Let him stand together with us. Let him persuade the Swedes to obey my will! As for the Norwegian matter, we shall investigate and do prompt justice. We await the emissaries of our brother Maximilian. The way is open to them, both coming and going."

Sigismund's emissary Garaburda informed Ivan that abusive letters in his name were circulating in many German cities; they were very offensive to the king and full of lies and absurdities.

The tsar should formally renounce the spreading of this malicious slander. The emissary also said that Duke Magnus had made war on the royal house with Russian help, that we had occupied Tarvastu in violation of the treaty and that Sigismund might voluntarily relinquish to us some of the Livonian towns beyond Polotsk.

The tsar's secretary Andrei Shchelkalov replied that the offensive letters about the king were composed by the Germans Taube and Kruse, as they had reported to Ivan, to refute Sigismund's malicious gossip and that these two scoundrels had since fled to Livonia. The king should send them to Moscow for punishment, and then the sovereign would at once inform all the sovereigns of Europe about these forgeries that had slandered Sigismund. We had occupied Tarvastu because it was ours. Magnus was not fighting the Poles, but the Swedes. If the king were to cede all of Livonia to us, then we were prepared to yield him Polotsk and

Ivan Departs for Novgorod

Courland. For a matter of such importance Ivan would await the royal emissaries in Pskov, since the tsar had once again gone to Novgorod to either conclude a peace with, or fight with the despicable Swedes.

Ivan had had no recent news from the Crimea, but he could guess the khan's evil intentions. There were already rumors that he might soon invade. The safety of Moscow and Russia demanded the tsar's presence in Moscow, which was now emerging from the ashes and was weak and fearful due to its memories of the recent catastrophe. Ivan seemed concerned only for his personal safety in this distant land: he sent 450 carts with a treasury to Novgorod and took with him his wife, both sons, Crown Prince Mikhail (Kaibula's son), the sons of the Moldavian and Wallachian voivodes, Stefan and Radul, the brothers of the tsaritsa, Grigorii and Aleksandr Koltovskii, several boyars, all his favorites, his best secretaries and his crack troops.

In the event of a siege (evidently he had foreseen this), he had entrusted Moscow to the princes Yurii Tokmakov and Timothei Dolgorukii. The army was left in the field, however. The renowned Prince Mikhailo Vorotynskii, his worthy comrades, the boyar Sheremetev and the princes Nikita Odoevskii and Andrei Khovanskii were stationed on the Oka to await and repel the khan. The sovereign also gave them his 7,000-strong contingent of Germans under the command of Georg Fahrensbach, but he himself was already long gone!

After arriving in Novgorod, Ivan reinforced the troops in Derpt, Fellin and Lais. He was waiting for news from the Swedish king and wrote to Sigismund that success in the affairs of state depends on the choice of men. The castellan Trotskii, Evstafii Volovich and the clerk Mikhailo Garaburda might sooner than any other Lithuanian pans provide their country with a reliable peace with Russia. The king apparently did not care to do what Ivan wished, and replied that his emissaries would be officials of equal distinction as Volovich and Garaburda. This letter was Sigismund's last word to the tsar: he died on 18 July after advising his nobles to offer the Jagellonian crown to the

Chapter Eight

Russian sovereign. At any rate, they hastened to inform the tsar of Sigismund's demise and promised to enter into important negotiations with him immediately. A new and propitious prospect for Ivan's ambitions had been opened, but he was now concerned more with saving his own realm than acquiring another one.

Devlet-Girei was still not satisfied with either the destruction of the Moscow districts or the humbling of Ivan's pride. In hopes of further enriching himself with prisoners without a fight, killing only unarmed men, reaching our capital unhindered and even overthrowing and expelling the tsar, the barbarian khan had remained quiet, resting *without unsaddling his horses.* He suddenly told his uhlans, princes and nobles that it would be better not to waste time in deceitful correspondence, but to resolve the matter of Astrakhan and Kazan with the Muscovite sovereign personally, face-to-face.

THE KHAN'S INVASION

He hastened along his old familiar route to the Don, to the Ugra, across the safe (for him) steppes, past burned towns, through the ashes of destroyed villages with an army such as had not been assembled since the days of Mamai, Tokhtamysh and Akhmet. He was coming with the Nogai, with the sultan's janissaries and with artillery. The outnumbered Russians remained immobile inside their fortresses; their knights rarely appeared in the field, and then not to fight, but to scout. The khan now saw the Oka before him, and there he saw the Muscovite army at last. It was stationed on the left bank, three versts from Serpukhov, in trenches protected by many cannons. This place was considered the most convenient for a crossing, but the khan, while keeping the Russians busy with a fierce barrage, sought another, less defended place, and on the following day was already on the left bank of the Oka and on the road to Moscow.

Ivan learned of this on 31 July, in Novgorod. Concealing his inner unease, he feasted with his boyars at various monasteries, celebrated the wedding of his brother-in-law Grigorii Koltovskii and drowned some boyar cadets in the Volkhov. He still had his legions but did not have enough time left to defend the capital with them, so he idly awaited further news, while Moscow trembled, having heard that the khan had already chosen homes within its walls for his Crimean nobles. The wrathful sovereign had always accused the Russian commanders of cowardice, negligence and indifference to the good, and to the glory, of the country. The hour had come to see if he was justified.

On 1 August, at Voskreseniya v Molodyakh [Molodi], 50 versts from the capital, Vorotynskii abandoned his useless fortifications and charged after the enemy. Hot on their heels, he caught up with them, halted them and forced them to fight. The khan had 120,000 troops; we had far fewer. The former needed to win so that they could take Astrakhan and Kazan and thereby open a free passage for themselves to decamp back to their distant uluses, while the Russians stood fast for everything they might love in life: their faith, their homeland, their parents, wives and children.

Without Ivan, Moscow touched hearts to pity it all the more; it seemed to have arisen from its ashes only to face new destruction. Both sides entered into a battle to the death. The banks of the Lopasnya and Rozhai streamed with blood. Men fired their weapons, but mostly slashed with their swords and throttled one another in desperate hand-to-hand combat. They tried to win through audacity and steadfastness.

Prince Vorotynskii both fought and observed; he positioned his men and encouraged them. He used cunning to lure the Tatars into places where they fell in heaps from the effects of cannons he had hidden. When both armies, surging back and forth, became tired and began to weaken, unwillingly expecting an end to the fray, this voivode, covered in blood and sweat, caught the enemy in the rear by way of a narrow ravine.

PRINCE VOROTYNSKII'S FAMOUS VICTORY

The battle was decided: the Russians had won. The khan left them his baggage trains, tents and his own banner, as booty. He fled by night into the steppes, and, we are assured, he returned to the Taurid with no more than 20,000 cavalry. His best princes had fallen in battle and the infidels' most distinguish hero, a scourge and destroyer of Christians, Divii Mirza of the Nogai, had surrendered to the Suzdal knight Alalykin.

Chapter Eight

This day belongs in the list of our great days of martial glory: the Russians had saved Moscow and their own honor. They had secured Astrakhan and Kazan for us, avenged Moscow's ashes and had suppressed the Crimeans, if not permanently, then at least for a long time. They had filled the land between the Lopasnya and the Rozhai with enemy corpses where lofty kurgans still stand as monuments to this famous victory and to the glory of Prince Vorotynskii.

The joyful news reached Novgorod on 6 August. The senior officer Davydov and Prince Nogtev, eyewitnesses and participants in the battle, with beaming faces such as Ivan had not seen for a long time, presented him with trophies: two bows and two sabers that had belonged to Devlet-Girei. They humbly bowed before him on behalf of the valorous voivodes, who attributed all the glory to God and to their sovereign.

Although unaccustomed to feelings of gratitude, Ivan was happy to be freed from his tormenting fear: he showered the messengers and the voivodes with favors. He ordered bells be rung and church services to be held day and night for three days in a row. He then hastened to return to the capital with his wife, the tsareviches and his whole court to receive the people's thanks for saving the nation! This revealed his cowardice and proved that it was not Livonia or Sweden, but fear of the khan's invasion that had caused him to leave Moscow,

Prior to departing Novgorod, Ivan wrote a threatening letter to the king of Sweden.

LETTER TO THE SWEDISH KING

"Believing," he said, "that you and your land, having been chastised by our wrath, had come to your senses, I awaited your emissaries. They did not arrive, and you spread rumors that I had *asked* you for peace! ... You are not sorry for Sweden – you hope for your own enrichment! . . . Ask what my voivodes have done to the khan! We are going to Moscow now, but will return again to Great Novgorod by December. Then you shall see how a Russian tsar and his army *request peace* from Sweden."

CHAPTER IX

OPRICHNINA ABOLISHED

1572-1577

Abolition of the Oprichnina. Godunov. Crimean affairs. Relations with Lithuania. War in Estonia. Rebellion in the Kazan district. Marriage of Magnus. Truce with Sweden. Polish affairs. Alliance with Austria. Batory chosen as king. Livonian war. Perfidy of Magnus. Letter to Kurbskii. Sixth episode of executions. Struggles over precedence. An example of loyalty. Ivan's fifth and sixth marriages.

Ivan entered Moscow in triumph and glory. Everyone was well disposed towards him. The disasters, dangers and enemies had vanished away. The lethal epidemics and the famine had ended in Russia. The khan had been pacified. The sultan was no longer contemplating war with us. Lithuania and Poland, orphaned without a king, unhypocritically sought Ivan's friendship. Sweden was impotent and disorganized, while the tsar, after leaving a large army in Livonia, found that he had 70,000 victors in Moscow prepared for new conquests.

1572

And yet he was able to accomplish a great feat: to carry out without arms or bloodshed his father's plan to return that which we had lost in Baty's unfortunate era and reunite Russia with this ancient possession of the Piast dynasty,* i.e., as a consequence of his being peacefully and voluntarily chosen to be the Polish king. Only the internal rebellion of his evil heart could interfere with his enjoyment of this ambitious vision, but as it turned out, Heaven, which had delivered Russia from plague and famine, now even wanted to soften the tsar's heart.

---

* [The Piasts ruled Poland from the 10th through the 14th centuries.]

The unprecedented horrors of his tyranny had tested the people's steadfast loyalty. His tortures had elicited not a shadow of protest or jeopardy. He had exterminated Adashev's *proud and despotic* friends, who had been his chief comrades-in-arms during his earlier, beneficial reign. He conferred their titles and wealth to new officials who were silently eager to please him. But now Ivan, to the sudden delight of his people, suddenly abolished the hated Oprichnina, which had served for seven years as his arm of doom, tearing at the innards of his realm.

> ABOLITION OF
> THE OPRICHNINA

At any rate, its fearful name and vile emblem had vanished, and its crazy division of districts, cities, courts, ministries and the military. The disgraced Zemshchina was once again called Russia. The infernals lost their uniforms and now stood in the ranks of the ordinary court nobles, government officials and troops. They no longer had an ataman, but a tsar, one for all Russians, who might hope that the times of murder and pillage had passed, that the measure of evil had been fulfilled and that their sorrowing homeland might find shelter under the power of law.

Some of Ivan's judicial activities at this time doubtless nurtured good men's hopes. He declared the enemies of the courageous hierarch Filipp to be blatant calumniators and imprisoned the Solovetskii abbot, the cunning Pansii, to the wild island of Valam*. The shameless Filothei, archbishop of Ryazan, lost his prelacy; Filipp's cruel and crude enforcer, Stefan Kobylin, was exiled to the monastery of Kamennyi Ostrov, and many other evil accomplices were wrathfully banished from his sight. This comforted the people, who in their misery saw this as evidence that God had not consigned Russia to be the victim of blind fate, that is, that there is a Supreme Avenger as well as Heavenly law and truth!

One man yet remained, but he was the chief calumniator of this tyranny: Malyuta Grigorii Lukyanovich Skuratov-Belskii, who remained Ivan's confidant to the grave. He survived, along with the tsar and his friends, for judgment in the hereafter.

---

* [Probably the island of Valaam in Lake Ladoga.]

Chapter Nine

The sovereign's love for him (if tyrants could love!) now began to elevate another youth of the nobility, his son-in-law and a relative by marriage of the first wife of Ivan's father. This was Boris Thedorovich Godunov, in whom a great talent for administration and a criminal love of power were already ripening.

GODUNOV

In these times of terror, young Boris, adorned with the rarest natural gifts, distinguished, grand and perspicacious, stood next to the bloody throne, but remained untainted. With a fine cunning, he avoided participation in these vile murders while awaiting better times. In the midst of the beastly Oprichnina, he shone not only with handsomeness, but with a quiet morality as well. Outwardly courteous, inside he was undeviating in his far-reaching schemes. More a courtier than a warrior, Godunov was the only one to appear beneath our nation's banners next to the person of the monarch, among his foremost armor bearers. In 1571, before he had any significant rank, he attended Ivan's wedding to the tsaritsa Martha as her best man, with his wife as matchmaker; this was evidence of his unusual favor with the tsar.

It is possible the cunning power seeker Godunov, who wished to gain his country's due gratitude, participated in the abolition of the Oprichnina, not in the name of disfavored virtue, but for the sake of a policy that was indulgent and agreeable to tyrants. This allowed him to do much that was condemned by religion and morality, but which seemed necessary for his own personal advantage, while he rejected only the evil that was of no use to his scheme – for as we shall see, the tsar was unreformed, and [although he had] destroyed what had up till now been his favorite instrument of torture – he remained a torturer!

Pleased by the mood of a grateful people and liberated from shame and fear, on his return to the capital, Ivan received the khan's herald in a grand manner. Devlet-Girei wrote that he had absolutely no intention of making war on Russia, but was coming to Moscow solely to conclude a peace. He stated that our voivodes were boasting of an imaginary and fabricated victory – that the Nogai had exhausted their horses and had tearfully convinced him

CRIMEAN AFFAIRS

to withdraw, and that the insignificant skirmishes that had taken place proved the superiority of the Crimeans, not the Russians.

"How long," said the khan, "are we to be at loggerheads over Astrakhan and Kazan? Hand them over and we shall be friends forever. This would save me from a sin, for according to our scriptures, we may not leave a Moslem territory in the hands of the infidel. We do not demand your treasury. On one side of us is Lithuania, on the other, Circassia. We shall fight these neighbors and shall not go hungry." Although Devlet-Girei had *requested* only Astrakhan, Ivan now replied to him as a victor,

"Eschewing bloodshed, we have up till now *entertained* our brother Devlet-Girei, but have in no way *coddled* him. His requests are absurd. At present we see before us a single *saber*: the Crimea. And if we hand over our conquest to the khan, then Kazan will become *another saber*, Astrakhan a third and the Nogai a fourth."

Devlet-Girei at long last released the distinguished Russian emissary Athanasii Nagoi to return to Moscow. He now wanted the sovereign to release the Crimean Yan-Boldy. He had languished as a prisoner among us for 17 years. However, this khan's nobleman, after gaining his freedom, was unable to make use of it, for he died in Dorogobuzh. One of Ivan's favorites, Vasilii Gryaznoi, had been taken by the Crimeans on the way to Molochnie Vody: the khan now proposed to the tsar to exchange this prisoner for Mirza Divii. Ivan would not agree, although he regretted Gryaznoi's fate and wrote him a *friendly letter*, in which, as was his character, he gently mocked his services, saying,

"You thought fighting the Crimeans would be as easy as joking at my table. They are not [like] you: they do not doze in enemy lands, nor do they keep insisting *it's time to go home!* How did you think to call yourself a man of distinction? It is true that we, surrounded by boyar traitors, had to get rid of them and to elevate you lowly slaves before us, but do not forget your father and grandfather! Can you compare yourself to Divii? Freedom will restore you to a soft bed, but him to a sword against Christians! It is enough that we, while pitying our diligent slaves, are prepared to ransom you with our treasure."

"No, sovereign," Vasilii Gryaznoi wrote in reply – a slave in mind and soul, boastful and base – "I was not napping in enemy territory. I was carrying out your orders, acquiring pagans for Russia's safety. I did not put my faith in others, but remained alert day and night. They captured me when I was wounded and half dead, abandoned by my timid comrades. In battle I destroyed the enemies of Christendom and also in my captivity: of those who betrayed you, none were left alive here – they all fell secretly at my hands . . .

"I made jokes at my sovereign's table to amuse my sovereign. But now I shall die for God and for you. I breathe still, but only by the exceptional grace of God and my eagerness to serve you. May I return to comfort my tsar! I am in the Crimea in body, but my soul is with God and with you. I am not afraid to die: I fear only disgrace."

Ivan had need of such men for his amusement and (as he thought) his safety, and so ransomed Gryaznoi for 2,000 rubles. Divii, however, died in captivity in Novgorod, to the tsar's regret, since the khan had been ready to swear to an alliance with us in return for releasing this important prisoner – the khan was no longer demanding Astrakhan. Meanwhile, Moscow's couriers were riding to the Crimea with letters of friendship, not so much to conclude a peace, but as it turned out, for news that was most favorable for the security of Russia.

A terrible famine was ravaging the Taurid, and the Don and Dnieper Cossacks were laying waste to the uluses with their constant raids. The former had even taken Azov, and although they were unable to hold it, their audacity astonished Constantinople. The khan was living in constant dread: he feared both the wrath of the sultan and internal rebellion. He had also heard of the Lithuanian nobles' intention to elevate Ivan to the throne of their country, and feared Russia's new strength.

These circumstances improved the security of our southeastern borders and left the tsar free to attend to other important matters of foreign policy. Polish and Lithuanian nobles tried to convince Ivan to have pity on their orphaned land and not to menace it, nor

RELATIONS WITH LITHUANIA

Livonia itself, with any sort of military action before a permanent peace [could be established]. He received the Lithuanian emissary Voropai and formally declared to him his desire to become Sigismund's successor. He boasted of his power and wealth, sincerely confessed his cruelty, but excused it by blaming, as usual, perfidious boyars. This curious speech, marked by a sort of *artificial* artlessness, condescension and moderation, is a memorable portrayal of Ivan's mentality. The tsar told the emissary:

"Theodor! You have informed me in the name of the pans of the death of my brother, Sigismund Augustus. Although I had heard of this earlier, I had not believed it, since we Christian sovereigns are often declared to be dead, even while we, in accordance with God's will, still remain alive and in good health. I believe it now and regret all the more that Sigismund did not leave a brother or a son who could attend to his soul and good memory. He did leave two sisters: one married (unfortunately everyone knows what sort of life she has in Sweden). The other is a spinster, without an intercessor or a defender – but God is her protector!

"The noble pans currently are without a chief. Although you have many *heads,* none are preeminent; there is no one in whom all governmental minds and thoughts would be united like the currents in the sea . . . A fair amount of the time we were in contention with our brother Sigismund, but the animosity died down and there came to be a friendship between us, but it was not yet steadfast – and now Sigismund is no more! Impiety is on the rise and Christianity is in decline.

"Were you to acknowledge me as your sovereign, you would see whether I could be a sovereign-defender! Impiety would cease to rejoice; neither Constantinople nor great Rome itself would belittle us! In your homeland I am defamed by those who are malicious and quick to anger: I do not deny this, but ask me: against whom do *I* bear malice? Against malicious men – but for the good man I would not hesitate to give him this golden chain and this clothing that I wear..." At this point, the nobleman Malyuta Skuratov broke in and said,

"Autocratic Tsar! Your treasury is not impoverished! It is that by which you reward your loyal servants!" The sovereign continued,

CHAPTER NINE

"In Vilnius and Warsaw they know of the wealth of my father and grandfather: I possess twice as much wealth and power. I mention this only in passing. Is it surprising that your kings love their subjects, who love them in return? But mine wanted to hand me over to the khan, and although they were at the front, would not fight. Although they might not have gained victory, they would have given their tsar time to prepare for another battle. I would have gratefully accepted from them, as a token of their zeal, just one Tatar whip, just one scourge! Although I had no more than 6,000 troops with me, I did not fear the numerous enemy; it was only when I saw my troops' treachery that I withdrew.

"Just a thousand men could have saved Moscow, but its eminent men did not want to put up a defense: what was to be done with this army and these people? The khan burned the capital and I was not told. This was the doing of my boyars! I punished the traitors, nor was I merciful even in Vilnius, where the criminal Viktorin was executed: he was convicted of trying to get rid of my brother Sigismund, and a rumor was spread that I was a party to this scheme – a vile and absurd calumny!" This Viktorin was quartered* in Vilnius around 1563 for secret relations with the Muscovite tsar. Ivan continued:

"Who are saying spiteful things about me in your country? Those who hate me, turncoats: Kurbskii and his like... Kurbskii! ... This man took his mother from him. {here he pointed to the tsarevich Ivan.}... and took my dear wife away from me. I only intended to deprive him of his boyar rank for a while, and the property awarded to him – I had no thought of capital punishment. I testify to this before God! In brief, if you want to know of my nature, good or bad, send your sons to serve me faithfully... once showered with the tsar's favors, they will see the truth!

"If it please the Most High that I rule over you, then I promise to keep intact all your laws, rights and liberties, and even to extend them where necessary. If the pans are thinking of choosing my tsarevich as king, then know that I have two sons as I have two eyes: they shall not be separated from each other.

"If you have no desire to acknowledge me as your sovereign, then you may send grand emissaries to arrange a peace with me.

---

* [The head and the limbs are cut off. Messy.]

"I will not fight over Polotsk; I shall also agree to give your future sovereign some of my hereditary possessions if you will yield me all of Livonia along the Dvina. Then we shall bind ourselves by oath, I and my sons, not to make war on Lithuania as long as our house rules in Orthodox Russia. I will not violate the truce prematurely. I am giving you letters of safe conduct for your emissaries, and I shall expect them. Time is precious."

>WAR IN ESTONIA

After this, Ivan left Moscow in late autumn with both his sons to review his troops in Novgorod and to keep the promise he had given to the Swedish king. The legions stood ready to move on Narva. The tsar himself commanded them; with him were all his most eminent boyars, the ruler Sain-Bulat and King Magnus, weapon in hand. He had been captured at Arensburg and had been presented to Ivan more as a prisoner than as a future son-in-law. On a single day, 80,000 Russians invaded Estonia, where no one had expected them and where the pacific nobles were celebrating Yuletide in their castles – our forward elements encountered feasting, music and dancing everywhere.

The tsar ordered no one be spared: homes were looted, residents murdered and maidens dishonored. There was no opposition until the fortress of Wittenstein where 50 Swedes along with citizens and rural residents had resolved to rebuff Ivan's whole army. The Russians took Wittenstein by storm, but the tsar lost a friend: Malyuta Skuratov died the honorable death of a warrior.

> 1573

He died atop the wall, as if to prove that his evil deeds were beyond earthly punishment. His body was sent along with a rich donation to the Monastery of St. Iosif Volotskii, where his mother and son were buried. Ivan now showed no compassion, but rather wrath and malice. He had all the prisoners, both Swedes and Germans, incinerated on a pyre – a sacrifice worthy of the deceased, who had lived on evil deeds!

After conquering this important fortress, Ivan wrote a new, abusive letter to the Swedish king.

Chapter Nine

"We have punished you and the Swedes," he said, "Right always triumphs! Deceived by lying rumors about Katerina's widowhood, we wanted her in our hands only so we could hand her over to the Polish king in order to gain Livonia without bloodshed. That is the truth, despite the slanders against us. What is your woman to me? Is she worth a war? Polish queens were also for the stablemen. Ask knowledgeable people, who was Voidilo* in Yagailo's time? Nor is King Erik dear to me: it is ridiculous to think that I planned to return him to a throne neither he nor you were born to.

"Tell me, whose son was your father? What was your grandfather called? Send us your pedigree and expose our error, for we have heretofore been convinced that you are of peasant blood. Of which *ancient Swedish kings* did you write in your letter to us? You had a King Magnus, and that was self-styled, for he should have been called a *prince*. We also wished to award you the title of *Swedish sovereign*, not vainly, but for the honor you requested of us, the honor of dealing directly with me, bypassing the Novgorod deputies.

"Choose whichever you wish: either deal with them as always before or submit to us. From time immemorial, your people have served my ancestors. The old chronicles mention the Varangians who were in the army of the autocrat Yaroslav-Gyorgii – these Varangians were Swedes, and evidently his subjects. You write that we employ the seal of the Roman Empire. No, it is our own and ancestral. But neither are Romans foreign to us, for we are descendants of Caesar Augustus. We are not bragging, nor are we disparaging you. We speak the truth, so be reasonable: do you want peace? Then have your emissaries appear before us!"

Ivan returned to Novgorod, leaving the ruler Sain-Bulat and Magnus with the legions, in order to make war on Estonia. They took Neuhof and Karkus, but the Swedish general Akeson defeated one of our detachments near Lode, taking our baggage train, cannons and banners. Livonian historians write that there were fewer than 2,000 Swedes, but 16,000 Russians, and that this glorious victory demonstrated the skill of the former and inclined Ivan to peace. At any rate, after our tsar had heard his voivodes'

---

* [Counselor and son-in-law of Lithuanian grand prince Yagailo (Jagiello, c. 1362-1434). He began his career as a baker.]

reports and the consensus of his boyar council, he wrote a new letter to the Swedish king, no longer abusive, but peaceable, informing him that our voivodes had been ordered to cease all hostilities prior to the arrival of the king's emissaries in Novgorod, where they were anxiously awaited, to establish true friendship between both nations.

This change in Ivan's mood is explained not so much by General Akeson's success as by another important, unexpected circumstance that now threatened both the tsar and Moscow. This was a powerful rebellion in the Kazan district, where the fierce and wild Cheremis, both lowland and highland, had secret ties with Khan Devlet-Girei and were clearly seceding from Russia. Our sovereign was accordingly immediately obliged to send a large army to the banks of the Volga. Fortunately the rebels quickly perceived their imprudence: the khan was unable to provide them with troops and Russians were already stationed in Murom, prepared to chastise them with fire and sword. The rebels submitted.

Rebellion in the Kazan District

Marriage of Magnus
12 April

After calling off the war in Livonia, Ivan now celebrated the marriage in Novgorod of Magnus and young Princess Mariya Vladimirovna; he feasted and made merry with his favorite German guests. He himself made the arrangements for dancing and sang hymns with the monks. Magnus, who had been honored and favored, hoped now to become a real king. He imagined that, in addition to the promised rich dowry, the tsar would give him all the Livonian towns and cities taken by the Russians. But instead of the five *casks of gold*, just a few trunks were brought to his house, containing linens and fine clothing for the young queen, and instead of the entirety of Livonia, the sovereign awarded his son-in-law the town of Karkus, with the following oral and written instructions:

"King Magnus! Proceed with your wife to the appanage assigned to you. I now wish to entrust to you dominion over other Livonian towns, along with a rich monetary dowry. Yet I recall the treachery of Taube and Kruse, who were showered with our

Chapter Nine

favors . . . You are the son of a monarch; hence I may have more faith in you than in lowly servants. But: you are still a man! Were you to betray me, then with the gold from my treasury you could find soldiers to collaborate with our enemies, and we should again be obliged to recover Livonia with our own blood. Earn my favor with loyalty, which will be constantly tested!"

And so, with a heavy heart, Magnus left for Karkus, and thence to Oberpahlen, where, in expectation of his dominion, he lived very penuriously, *not having more than three plates for his table* (as his brother, King Frederik of Denmark wrote to his father-in-law, the ruler of Mecklenburg), *amusing his 13-year-old wife with children's toys, feeding her sweets, and, to the Russians' displeasure, dressing her in German clothing.*

The duke, Johann Albrecht, who was then in contact with the tsar, sent the Mecklenburg official, Doctor Feling, to Novgorod, desiring that Russia affirm his (Albrecht's) son's right to Riga, which had been promised him by King Sigismund Augustus of Poland. In the name of the duke, Feling presented Ivan with the gift of a golden lion, adorned with diamonds and gems, with the explanation that *the lion terrifies all other beasts, and the sovereign of Moscow terrifies all his enemies.* The tsar replied,

"I thank you for your humility and kindness, but I cannot cede that which I do not have, even though Livonia along with Riga is my patrimony and not the king's. I intend to dispatch an embassy to the German emperor to conclude an alliance with him against the infidel and to deal with Livonian matters. I counsel the ruler to arm himself with patience: I will be able to give him Riga when I obtain it, whether by treaty or saber."

Meantime, Ivan observed with some irritation that the Swedish king, whom he despised, was becoming haughty. For a long time there was no news at all from Stockholm, but at last a report came that his emissaries had never been in such a country, where people's rights were unknown – where they were robbed and imprisoned. They said that the tsar could send the king's emissaries back to him if he really desired peace, or at least as far as the border, to which Swedish plenipotentiaries would also come,

> 1573-1575

and that he should have discussed a truce three years earlier, not now when the Swedish army had taken the field. Moreover, our herald in Stockholm endured abuse unheard of amongst developed countries.

"The king's nobles," he reported to the tsar, "wished to know the contents of your letter in advance. I demonstrated to them the absurdity of this request, whereupon one of them struck me in the chest and reviled me with indecent language.

'If,' your slave answered this insolent Swede. 'If I were armed and mounted on a horse, you would not dare dishonor me, nor raise a hand, nor open your vile mouth. But we are not here to do battle . . .'

"Another noble tried to detain me as I was approaching the royal throne, saying, 'Hand over the letter and do not step on the carpet before the throne.'

"I stepped onto the carpet and handed the letter to the king. The next morning, the Swedish official, Christopher Fleming, told me,

'You should know that you did not see our sovereign yesterday: I was sitting in his place, whilst he was standing amongst his nobles, since he did not want to receive your tsar's letter, thinking that there might be more abuse in it such as would be impossible to read aloud even to a simple tradesman . . . Dismissing me, the king said *the tsar has become desirous of peace, but I do not want to make peace with him, nor do I fear him.*'"

Briefly, Sweden was encouraged, having hired 3,000 Scots and 2,000 English, while the tsar, who had more than 100,000 troops in Livonia and Novgorod, showed mildness, did not mention the offenses against his herald, but rather bore the gibes and tried to be pleasant to the king. That is, he sent his boyar, Prince Sitskii, with some comrades to the river Sestra, which served as the border between Finland and Russia, for peace negotiations with Admiral Klas Fleming and other royal officials.

TRUCE WITH SWEDEN

They spent a long time arguing over where to meet. Fleming demanded that it be on the bridge, in tents, but Prince Sitskii obliged the Swedes to cross over to the Russian side of the river. They could agree on nothing further. The tsar wanted Estonia, in which case he would give the king the privilege of dealing with him directly, but the king wanted that privilege without any conditions and showed Ivan the long genealogy of the exalted house of Vasa to convince of its ancient distinction. They concluded only a truce, from Ilya's Day [2 August] 1575 to 1577, between Finland and our northern territories. We were not to do battle with the former, nor were the Swedes to make war on our Novgorod territories: Korela, Oreshek and other places. There was no word about Livonia, which remained a theater of war.

1575

Ivan was pleased with the promise that he would soon be visited by Swedish emissaries for new peace negotiations, and formally promised to receive them honorably and not to deprive them of their liberty or possessions – nor to offend them by word or deed! Henceforth the Swedish kings no longer dealt with Novgorod – this had always seemed demeaning to them, as really stemming from the Muscovite sovereigns' lack of respect for their monarchs – but this had heretofore been an inviolable principle of our prideful policy.

If the tsar's indulgence seemed not to benefit himself, it also failed to provide the king with any essential advantage: the hostilities in Livonia continued. The Swedes and their Scottish mercenaries fruitlessly assaulted Wesenberg, while the Russians laid waste all around Revel and took the city of Pernau, which cost them 7,000 troops killed in its fortifications. Ivan's commander, Nikita Romanovich Zakharin-Yuriev, was amazed at the valor of its inhabitants and left it up to each of them whether to swear allegiance to the tsar or leave with his possessions.

The result of such a humane and sensible policy was that the castles Gelmet, Ermis, Ruen, Purgel, Leal, Lode and Fikkel submitted without resistance, and the important fortress of Hapsal soon did likewise. It was full of all kinds of provisions and many troops and nobles who always had boasted of their valor. It is written that these peaceable heroes, who had been convinced by the tsar's voivode of their utter safety, were amusing themselves and making merry

1576

12 February

at the very time that the Russians entered the city, and that one of our young princes, seeing them at play, asked a German friend,

"If we Russians had been alive to surrender such a fortress to the enemy, what would the tsar have done to us? Who of us would have dared to look a good Christian in the eye? But you Germans are celebrating your shame!"

They partied on amidst the graves and ashes. It seemed that Livonia, torn by all the catastrophes of a protracted war and a victim and spoil for all its neighboring peoples, was no longer sensitive to any of these evils. Famine and destitution were rampant, not only in hovels, but in castles as well. Thus a chronicler reports that the wife of the eminent knight von Tedwen, who had formerly had a sumptuous home, glittering with splendor that surprised even the very rich, now expired in Hapsal on the straw and was placed naked in the earth!

But fate was preparing yet more horrors for this unhappy land and Ivan still held his hand high, armed with sword and flame, to subjugate or destroy it. On his guard, but no longer afraid of Devlet-Girei, he was obliged to threaten him from time to time by mustering troops on the banks of the Oka. He himself departed Novgorod in the summer of 1574 to inspect his large army in Serpukhov. He would also send detachments into the steppes, where the khan's bands or bandits would occasionally appear. But most of all, Ivan followed events in Warsaw, where the Poles flattered his love of power. This had consequences that were humiliating for our tsar and injurious for Russia.

1573-1577

The Sejm convened in Warsaw at the beginning of 1573 to choose a new king. The primary candidates were

1) young Ernest, son of Emperor Maximilian,
2) the duke of Anjou, brother of Charles IX,
3) the Swedish king, or his son Sigismund, and
4) the Russian sovereign.

Emissaries of Spain and Maximilian lobbied for the first, French emissaries for the second, and Swedish for the third; we had none.

Chapter Nine

The tsar was expecting emissaries of the Sejm to come to him, figuring,

"They need me, but I do not need them!"

Despite this hauteur, many of the king's men, especially the Lithuanian nobles, were thinking of choosing Ivan to obtain thereby a permanent and happy alliance with dangerous and powerful Russia. This was a consideration suggested by a sound and farseeing policy. No doubt aware of all his cruelties, they hoped that the laws of their republic would restrain the tyrant, but in this they might be deceived. Yet fate obviated this ordeal. The conditions proposed by either side were equally intemperate and equally offensive to the other party. After listening to the Lithuanian emissary Mikhail Garaburda in Novgorod on 28 February 1573, Ivan gave him the following reply:

"I was surprised by the protracted silence of your pans in a matter of such importance, since a nation without a sovereign fares but poorly. You are excused by the catastrophe of the pestilence that was raging in your country. I sympathize; it was God's will. Now you inquire whether I myself wish to reign over Lithuania and Poland, or to give you the tsarevich Theodor as king, and you request of us an oath to faithfully observe your laws. You wish further, after sending my son to you, that Smolensk, Polotsk, Usvyat and Ozerishche be returned to the Principality of Lithuania, and to award Theodor some particular towns from ancient Russian possessions. One proposal is natural, the other is improper.

"It is natural that each country preserve its own customs, precepts and laws, and we of course would be able to confirm your rights by oath. But is it reasonable to demand of us Smolensk, Polotsk and even Moscow's hereditary towns as a *dowry* for Theodor? Is he really a maiden or bride? Glory lies in increasing one's realm, not diminishing it. Poland and Lithuania do not lack cities; there is room for your king to live there. And it is not you, but we, who must demand requital. Hear me: if you want to have Theodor as your king, then

"1) write my full title, as ordained by God; call me *Tsar*, for I inherited this distinction from my forebears and will not accept another.

"2) When God takes my son from this world, then let his sons rule over you by right of *inheritance*, and not by *election;* if he leaves no sons, then let Lithuania and Poland be *inseparable* from Russia, as the patrimony of my descendants in perpetuity, but without any change to the people's rights and liberties, with the particular terms *Polish Kingdom* and *Grand Principality of Lithuania* to be in the Russian sovereigns' title.

"Is it proper that the son of a king not succeed to his throne? For the general welfare of these three powers, they should have a single ruler. I know that Austria and France are quite indulgent in negotiations with you, but they are no example for Russia: for we know for a fact that except for the sultan and ourselves, Europe has no line of sovereigns who have now ruled for 200 years. Some are descended from princes, some from foreigners, and therefore attracted to the honor of kingship; but we are tsars *anciently* and descend from Caesar Augustus (as is known to all).

"3) If any of my descendants dies in your land, let his remains be conveyed to Moscow for interment.

"4) The city of Kiev, Russia's most ancient possession, should be joined to its territory; to that end, out of love for tranquility and Christian harmony, I will no longer seek our ancient possessions along the river Bereza in Lithuania.

"5) All of Livonia shall be Russian! These are the conditions under which I can send you my beloved son. However, he is still too young and does not have the strength to resist his enemies and ours. Besides, I know that many of the pans want me, not the tsarevich, as king. If they tell you otherwise, they are being hypocritical. I also hear that you are thinking of getting my son from me by a ruse, with the intention of handing him over to the Turks in order to make peace with them. Whether this is the truth or a lie, I do not know; but I cannot conceal this from you in a sincere correspondence."

Seeing that Ivan wanted the kingship more for himself than for his son, the wise emissary said,

"Sovereign! We would wish to have such a powerful and wise ruler as yourself, but Moscow is far from Warsaw and the king's presence is necessary for our external safety and our internal justice and order. We have no custom that the king may leave his realm and leave a deputy behind. *In addition, you cannot be crowned without accepting the Roman faith.*" Ivan ordered the emissary to depart.

The next day, the tsar again summoned Garaburda, and said, "We have thought it over, and find that we are able to rule three states together, traveling from one to another, and that the obstructions of which you told us are easily removed. I only ask for Kiev, without any other towns or volosts. I shall give Polotsk and Courland to Lithuania.

"I shall take Livonia up to the Dvina. Our title shall be: *By the Grace of God Tsar and Grand Prince of all Russia, Kiev, Vladimir, Moscow, King of Poland and Grand Prince of Lithuania.* The names of all other territories we shall write according to their eminence. Poland and Lithuania are to be permanently Russian. I ask for respect for the Greek faith; I request authority to construct Orthodox churches in all my lands. *Let me be crowned not by a Latin archbishop, but the Russian metropolitan!*" ...

"However, I shall make no change to your rights and liberties. I shall distribute property and award ranks with the consent of the Polish and Lithuanian Dumas. When, however, my spiritual and physical strength is exhausted by the years, I shall renounce the world and my throne and take up a life of prayer in a secluded cloister. Then you may choose whomever of my sons you wish, but no one else, nor a foreign prince.

"The pans say that Lithuania and Poland are inseparable: that is their will. But I say I would rather be merely the grand prince of the former. Then after I had confirmed all its laws by kissing the cross, I would take for Russia only Kiev, and return to Lithuania, by force or treaty, all its ancient territories taken by the Poles, and I would include in my title *Grand Prince of Moscow and Lithuania.*

"Hear me further: I could, although not without difficulty, travel from country to country, for I am approaching old age. However, a sovereign must see everything with his own eyes. So might it not be better for you to choose a son of the Kaiser as king after concluding a peace treaty and alliance with us with the following conditions:

"1) Kiev and Livonia go to Russia; Polotsk and Courland to Lithuania;

"2) if I, as well as the Kaiser and his son were to help each other against our common enemies with troops or money, then I would desire good things for Lithuania and Poland as much as for my Russia – and whom should we fear with such a close alliance? Do not all the other sovereigns of Europe desire to join as one against the enemies of Christendom? What glory, and what benefit! ... Finally, I instruct you to tell your pans not to choose a French prince, since these princes are friends of the wicked Turks and not of Christians. But should you so choose, then know that I would not remain a peaceful spectator of your imprudence. Also tell your pans that many of them have written secret letters to us advising me to march with my army into Lithuania to acquire the kingdom through intimidation. Others ask gold and sable furs of me for them to choose my son. Let your state council be aware of this!"

Garaburda took this reply back to Warsaw with him. It is likely that the Lithuanian pans were demanding Smolensk and the Russian cities only to keep up appearances and observe decorum, and that they themselves did not expect such pliancy from the tsar and might have retracted this demand without further obstinacy. Hoever, the tsar was so unbending that his conditions were unanimously rejected by the Sejm; this immediately eliminated him as a candidate.

Had Ivan's thinking changed? Was he convinced of the impossibility of ruling over Poland and Lithuania as he would have wished? Did he fear the example their willful nobles would make for mute Russia? Did he figure that this close alliance would have advantages for the other two powers, but none for our homeland? That we would be obliged to aid them, not they us, with men and treasure in the case of war with Turkey, Austria or the Taurid? Or that the title of king with its limited and unreliable powers would not be worth the increased danger and expense for a hereditary sovereign over a great power that Heaven had predestined to become strong, not through outside influences, but through its own natural powers?

Or did the tsar think that the Sejm might actually agree to such strict proposals, to nullify the fundamental laws of its republic, voluntarily abolish their choosing their own kings, set up a supreme, hereditary rule, cede us Kiev and entrust the Jagellonian crown to a prelate of another faith to perform Ivan's coronation? It is hard to imagine that pride blinded him to imprudence of this magnitude. It is much more likely that he initially had had a sincere desire to replace Sigismund Augustus, but on deeper consideration of all the circumstances had become lukewarm to such an idea.

On the other hand, would not the selection of the archduke, which he had approved, threaten us all the more with the dangerous proximity of Austria, a powerful state, since its emissary, interceding on behalf of Ernest, had formally promised the pans the assiduous assistance of the emperor in any wars with Russia? Should Ivan not more quickly facilitate the quests of distant France, which was consequently less threatening to us? We cannot condemn his policies: he was aware of the friendly ties between Paris and Constantinople and thought that Henri d'Anjou* would set Turkey's forces against our homeland, while the sultans, in addition to their false religion, would threaten the emperors with their renowned army and many victories

To the irritation of the tsar and Maximilian, the Warsaw Sejm chose Henri, encouraged by the stratagems of the French emissary [Jean de] Montluc, who in his overblown speeches shamelessly praised the Polish and Lithuanian nobles, comparing them to the ancient Romans and calling them the terror of tyrants and heroes of virtue. The emissary also promised them a million florins and a powerful army to drive the Russians out of Livonia, as well complete independence of the king from the Supreme Council.

Such *disobedience* of the Sejm, as Ivan put it, aligned our policies with Austria. The emperor hastened to make use of the tsar's favorable disposition by writing him a flattering letter.

---

* [A.k.a. Henry of Valois, later king of France.]

He complained of the "crimes of Charles IX, who exterminated more than 100,000 loyal subjects on St. Bartholomew's Day solely because they had a different faith."

He spoke indignantly of the friendship of the French with the sultan, whose earnest assistance had provided Henri with the Jagellonian crown. He tried to persuade Ivan to stand up for Christians; he proposed that he take Lithuania, but leave Poland to Austria, and conclude a close alliance with the emperor against the Turks. The tsar immediately sent a courier to Maximilian advising him to employ every means to impede Henri on the way to Warsaw. He would rather see the emperor's emissaries in Moscow so as to establish a permanent alliance of Austria with Russia, and wrote:

"We all will try to prevent the Polish Kingdom and Lithuania from *seceding from* our realm. We are as one regardless of whether my son or yours sits on that throne . . . You, our beloved brother, lament the terrible extermination of innocent people and children on St. Bartholomew's day: all Christian sovereigns must be outraged by the inhuman cruelty of the French king, who insanely spilled so much blood!"

But Ivan, following his peaceable principles, did not want to declare himself an enemy of the new Polish king prematurely. On the contrary, when he learned of the king's presence and triumphal coronation in the ancient capital of the Piast dynasty, he was just about to send an eminent official with his salutations. But Henri thwarted the tsar: he informed him of his elevation to the throne and tried to persuade him not to violate the truce with the republic, good till 1576. He wrote that he was in mourning: the French king had died and he must travel to Paris, and that this temporary absence would not interfere with tsar's discussing affairs with the Polish pans. Ivan replied,

"Our brother Henri! We are delighted at your accession to the throne and sympathize with your grief. The death of Christian sovereigns is a calamity for Christians and a cause of joy for the infidels. We wish to live in amity with you. My emissaries will travel to Warsaw when you return; we expect yours in Moscow, but it is improper for me to deal with the pans without you. We

CHAPTER NINE

have given orders to our voivodes concerning the preservation of the truce."

However, Henri was now a fugitive king! He had sought the Polish crown solely to please his mother, the ambitious Catherine de' Medici, who was acting in this instance on the suggestion of the cunning dwarf and vagabond, Ivan Krasovskii. Henri was indolent and pleasure-loving: for three months he was active not in administration, but in feasting, voluptuousness and hunting, and came to hate his kingdom and his limited powers. He secretly prepared to make a getaway, and galloped by night from one throne to another. He sped to inherit the power and ill fortune of his brother, ruling like him, amongst rebels, treachery and crime. He showed himself to be faint-hearted and perfidious, but would die with a beautiful quote on his lips, one which will remain forever in history as worthy of the best of rulers*.

Stunned by the flight of their king, the pans were obliged to seek another. At this point many of them – the archbishop of Gnezno, the castellan of Minsk, Yan Glebovich, and others – again turned to the tsar. They advised him to once again send wise boyars to Warsaw, with the same conditions as those under which Henri was chosen. He corresponded with the clergy, the knights and especially with each of the nobles to ask about his (Ivan's) selection as king.

He said in the letter that he was not a heretic, but a Christian, and had indeed been baptized in the name of the Trinity; he said that Poles and Russians, being of one tribe, Slavonic or Sarmatian, should, like brothers, have but one father-sovereign.** Ivan wrote to them very amicably, thanking them for their good intentions; he promised to send his boyars to the Sejm, but did not say anything decisive with regard to the conditions, since he was awaiting the Kaiser's emissaries, who had already set out for Moscow.

In August 1574 our courier, Skobeltsyn, returned from Vienna without a reply, saying that the emperor wished to send a

---
* [Translated from the Russian, from endnote 436: "Lord! If my life is of use, let me live. If it is harmful or futile, end it!"]
** [The Scythians or Sarmatians spoke an Iranic language, not Slavic. However, the ancient Greeks were wont to call any people north of the Black Sea *Scythians*, which would tend to include the Slavs. In Russian poetry *Scythia* is sometimes used to denote Russia.]

letter to the tsar using his own man. This oddity was clarified as follows: Maximilian's new courier brought Ivan the complaint that Skobeltsyn had not accepted the letter of reply, apparently because it had been written without the tsar's full title; he had then willfully departed. Aside from that, he had behaved without decorum and had maligned the emperor.

Maximilian assured the tsar of his sincere friendship and gratitude, while the tsar informed him that he had placed Skobeltsyn in disgrace. Other Austrian officials came to Moscow after this with the excuse that Maximilian had delayed agreeing with Ivan about Polish affairs because he had been quite ill. As a sign of their eagerness, one of the couriers reported to the boyars that the pans were trying to get Magnus to betray Russia, promising him the city of Riga.

> ALLIANCE WITH AUSTRIA

Finally, in January 1576, the eminent Austrian officials Jan Kobenzel and Daniel Prinz came to see us. The sovereign received them splendidly and sumptuously in Mozhaisk. He sat on the throne in a traditional Russian inlaid robe, wearing a crown and diadem, and holding a scepter in his hand. The throne was surrounded by all the boyars and nobles in golden raiment. Ivan and the tsarevich stood up, inquiring about the health of the emperor, who had sent *to his brother* and *ally* the gift of a golden chain adorned with precious stones and a representation of Maximilian's name, valued at 8,000 thalers. The emperor *entreated* Ivan to assist him in word and deed, by letters and by sword, to elevate Ernest to the Polish throne and not to make war on Livonia, whose territory had *of old belonged to the Roman Empire*.

"Then," said Maximilian's emissaries to Ivan, "all Christian Europe will conclude an alliance with you to cast down the lofty Ottoman state at one blow, [to be delivered] both by land and by sea. That will be an exploit that will enable you to forever glorify yourself and Russia! We shall chase the Turks out of Constantinople and into Arabia, eradicate the Mohammedan faith and again raise the banner of the cross over Thrace and Hellas, and may all the ancient realm of Greece *to the sunset* be yours, O great Tsar!"

Thus promised the emperor, the Holy Father Pope and the king of Spain. Ivan listened coolly, unenticed by the thought of ruling as far as the shores of the Bosporus and the Hellespont. He said that his word was firm and immutable; that he had not changed his thinking in regard to the Polish kingship: he would give it to Ernest and again write to the king's nobles about this. However, Lithuania and Kiev would have to be permanently united with Russia. He said that Livonia was, is and will be ours; that previously no one had given this matter any thought, and when Russia took it, only then did the emperor, Denmark, Sweden and Poland think to declare their fictitious rights to this land. In order to conclude an alliance against the infidel, emissaries must come to Moscow from the kings of Spain and Denmark, from the German princes and other sovereigns.

The fate of Ludwig of Hungary was known in Russia: believing the emperor's promises, he had taken the field, but lost his life after being abandoned by everyone in uneven battle with the Turks. The tsar said that after the Kaiser's emissaries had agreed to cede us Livonia and Kiev, they had argued the impossibility of separating Lithuania from Poland: the Poles wished to have but one ruler.

"Do you know," they told Moscow's boyars, "of the secret plot by some rebellious Poles to take as their king the Ottoman vassal, the prince of Sedmigrad [Stefan Batory], in order to please the sultan and harm Christendom?"

"That will not happen," the tsar replied, demanding that the emissaries confirm the Livonian agreement by oath. Kobenzel and Daniel Prinz, however, announced that their sovereign, as a token of special respect for Ivan, was sending others to Moscow for this purpose: *great men, sovereign princes*. Nonetheless, they asserted that all would be accomplished to the tsar's satisfaction, and gave their word that the emperor would persuade the Swedish king to comply. This satisfied Ivan; he had dinner with them in the palace, where they were dazzled by the splendor.

He sat with his son at a special table in crimson velvet raiment that was covered in precious stones and pearls, wearing a pointed hat on which a gem of unusually large size glittered. Two crowns (belonging to the tsar and tsarevich) lay to the side, with large, glittering diamonds, rubies and emeralds; there were also heaps of silver and gold in the chambers . . .

"Any palace," wrote Kobenzel to the Austrian ministers, "has special storerooms filled with such bowls and dishes, but the Kremlin palace surpasses all others . . . To sum up, I have seen the treasures of his imperial majesty, of the kings of Spain, France, Hungary, Bohemia, and the duke of Tuscany, but I have never seen the likes of Ivan's . . . While we were travelling to Russia, the Polish nobles frightened us with tales of the unbearable rudeness of the Moscow court, but what in fact happened? We would never have found a better reception: neither in Rome nor in Spain – the tsar knows how to treat people: he snubs the Poles and the Swedes, but honors those whom he respects and likes."

Ivan made a present to Maximilian of black sable furs worth 700 rubles and sent them in a sleigh with the "lightweight emissaries" Prince Sugorskii and the secretary Artsybashev with convincing arguments that it was necessary to conclude a clear, formal treaty between Austria and Russia quickly. To the royal nobles, he wrote that they should choose Ernest if they wished friendship with the puissant Muscovite state, and that they should not accept a ruler from the sultan's hands if they did not want to answer to God for a terrible bloodbath. Yet in a letter to the Lithuanian pans, he now expressed the desire to be their grand prince, or else he might give them the tsarevich Theodor as their sovereign, adding

"But if you do not think it would be good to have an extraordinary ruler, then together with Poland, choose Maximilian's son."

There is no doubt that Ivan and the Kaiser could have prescribed laws for the Sejm had they decisively declared their demands to it and backed it up by troop movements by both sides, for that is what Lithuanian nobles favoring us wrote to the tsar – they knew the thinking in Vilnius and in Warsaw. But Maximilian, now weak in body and spirit, tarried. He honored our emissaries in Regensburg, but did not send his own to Moscow, and in unproductive dealings with Ivan, carried on by means of couriers, he irritated Ivan, firstly, because he found it difficult to call him

Emperor or *Tsar of Russia*, employing only *Tsar of Kazan and Astrakhan*, and secondly, because he never stopped interceding for *pitiable* and *wretched* Livonia, insisting that it was a German territory.

In replying to Maximilian, although the tsar was always courteous and amicable, his enthusiasm for obtaining the Polish crown for Ernest had cooled, and he was not angry to hear that the knights and the gentry opposed the nobles in this choice. The Sejm now announced the candidates:

1) Ernest;

2) Ferdinand, brother of Maximilian;

3) the Swedish king, or prince; and

4) Alfonso, Duke of Modena. There was no mention of the tsar, since he had not formally retracted the offer he had made in 1574 that was so incompatible with the laws of the republic, and had not considered it worthwhile to send distinguished, plenipotentiary officials to Warsaw again – he was content with threats and secret communications with some of the pans.

In the meantime, our couriers kept him informed of all the actions of the Sejm. From his palace in Sloboda, Ivan saw all the politicking and struggle of passions in its noisy theater, where cleverness and eloquence earned applause, but gold and power were decisive – where they not only argued and shouted, but where swords were drawn and lances flashed, and where they rejected all the candidates, choosing at last two kings: instead of Ernest, the emperor himself, and Stefan Batory, whose name had been little known heretofore, but which must be glorified in Russian history, to the dishonor of Ivan's!

Back in 1574, when Sultan Selim had learned of Henri's flight, he made known to the pans of the nobility that if their king were to be the Austrian prince, who had been brought up to hate the Ottoman Empire, then war and bloodshed were unavoidable for either power. He said that the Russian prince was also dangerous, and that they could crown the most virtuous of the nobles, the voivode of Sandomir, or the Swedish king – or if they wanted the best – Prince Batory of Sedmigrad, a man of eminent intellect and valor, who would bring them good fortune and honor, since he was a loyal friend of the powerful Porte.*

This proposal was ineffective, for the sultan was the most dangerous of the Polish kingdom's enemies. In Warsaw and Krakow, they were talking of Stefan, who owed his princely honor and power not to his forebears, but to his own mind and character – he had been the choice of the nobles and people of Sedmigrad.** In this semibarbarous and undeveloped country, inhabited by coarse people with rebellious spirits and different origins and faiths, he had established tranquility, safety and religious tolerance. He was of the Roman confession, but gained the love of both Lutherans and Calvinists; he gained the sultan's trust and at the same time rendered significant service to the emperor. He was distinguished by valor, learning and eloquence, but also by a very majestic appearance: at 42 he was still a handsome man. In a word, due to his zeal for the national welfare of the Poles, they could scarcely desire a more worthy monarch.

His faction was strengthened by the intercession of the nobleman Samuil Zborovskii, who had been an exile in Transylvania, where he had been done much favor by Stefan. Love of country and Batory's gold were also operative, still more so the inveterate popular hatred towards the house of Austria. The senate exerted efforts in favor of the emperor and Ernest, but at the critical hour, a voice rang out,

"We want Batory! He will give us peace with the Turks and victory over all other enemies!" The gentry shouted,

"Batory!"

BATORY CHOSEN AS KING

In vain many nobles argued that he was a tributary of the infidels, that it was shameful for a Christian republic to have the sultan's slave as its head. The royal hetman Yan Zamoiskii, the bishop of Krakow and the wealthier portion of the nobility named the Sedmigrad prince as king, while the primate and the Polish senators named old and ailing Maximilian, apparently employing the likelihood of an impending new choice to please the rebellious gentry, who liked to legislate through the

---
*   [The Ottoman court.]
**   [Transylvania.]

Sejm. Both parties informed their candidate of this honor, and Maximilian, already on his deathbed, wrote to Moscow that he was now the Polish king.

"I rejoice," replied the tsar, "But Batory is already in Krakow!"

He had indeed arrived there with the sultan's gonfalon and the title of king, to the sincere chagrin of many Lithuanian nobles, who ardently wished to have Theodor as their sovereign, in hopes that the young tsarevich, who was innocent of his father's cruelties, would live permanently in Lithuania, accept their customs and morals, and come to love this coreligionist country as a second homeland, assure its integrity by peace with the Russians and return to it not only Polotsk, but perhaps even Smolensk and all of the Severskie lands.

"Why," they asked Ivan's official, Bastanov, in Vilnius, "why would Ivan not want happiness for us and glory for himself? Why did his emissaries not come to the Sejm with conditions consonant with the welfare of both states? We do not like the Kaiser and will not tolerate Batory as Selim's vassal."

Some of them even thought that there was still time to act, that it would be possible to rescind the illegitimate choice of two kings if Ivan would deal with the chief Polish nobles with flattery and gifts, and if our troops were to invade Lithuania immediately. But Maximilian died on 12 October 1576 and Batory was seated on the throne in Krakow after giving a formal promise to religiously observe Henri's agreement and all the laws of the republic, as well as marry Sigismund Augustus' 50 year old sister Anna.

In addition, he was to conclude an alliance with the Ottoman Empire, pacify the khan, free all the prisoners in the Taurid by sword or through ransom, guard the safety of the country with fortresses, and if the Senate and the people wanted war with Russia, to always personally command the army and reunite with Lithuania those lands conquered by the Muscovite tsars.

"Let craven fear begone!" he said. "I have seasoned comrades in arms, power in my hand and valor in my heart!" Dissension was at an end and those who were dissatisfied fell silent. Poland and Lithuania shouted with one voice,

"Long live King Batory!"

Ivan appeared calm and indifferent. When he learned that Stefan's emissaries were coming to see him, he ordered them accorded the necessary honors. The boyars asked them about Batory's pedigree and they wanted to know which title the sultan, the emperor and other sovereign's gave him in their letters. The emissaries replied,

"The tsar will see Stefan's title in his letter."

These were presented to the tsar, who sat on his throne, wearing a crown, with the elder tsarevich next to him. The boyars sat on benches in the throne room, court nobles and secretaries were in the vestibule and boyar cadets stood on the porch and in the passageways to the Shoreline Palace. Next to this palace, at the banisters and as far as the Church of the Annunciation there were guests and ministry clerks, all without exception in golden costumes, and the streltsy were on the square with their muskets. After receiving Batory's letter, the tsar inquired as to the king's health, but did not invite the envoys to dine. In his letter, which was respectful and unassuming, Stefan promised to observe *neighborly amity for the full term [of the truce]*; he requested a visa or letter of safe conduct permitting free travel for the Lithuanian grand emissaries to Moscow and assured him of his sincere love of peace.

Batory complained of Maximilian, who in vexation and enmity, had maligned him by calling him a Turkish tributary, and who himself paid the sultan ten times as much and was actually more servile toward him than the Sedmigrad princes. In the name of their sovereign, the boyars told the emissaries that King Stefan was clearly headed for a bloodbath because:

1) in his letter he had not given Ivan the title of *Tsar*, nor of *Prince of Smolensk* or *Polotsk*, which everyone acknowledged except for the silly Poles, who called Gustav of Sweden a king although he had no crown;

2) he dared to call the tsar his *brother*, although he was only the voivode of Sedmigrad and a tributary of the Hungarian king, and consequently no loftier than the Ostrozhskii, Belskii or Mstislavskii princes; and

3) he exalted himself as the sovereign of Livonia. The emissaries were dismissed with the instruction,

CHAPTER NINE

"If the king wishes brotherhood with Ivan, he must not invade Livonia, and must in his letters title Ivan *Tsar and Grand Prince of Smolensk and Polotsk.*" They were, however, given safe conduct for his emissaries.

This took place in November 1576. Ivan had discerned the character of his opponent Stefan, his firmness and inflexibility, and that he had no hope of achieving his goals either by threats or by persuading him to voluntarily cede us Livonia. Accordingly, Ivan decided to attack the Swedish and Polish possessions in this land with all his strength. The time seemed opportune to him: the Swedish king, to please his wife, had surrounded himself with Jesuits and reintroduced the Latin faith into his kingdom. This damaged his popularity and produced rebellions and schisms, so that the king could not now even think of mounting a strong resistance to the Russians in Livonia. Meanwhile Stefan was fighting in Prussia and was obliged to undertake a bloody siege of mutinous Danzig.

In 1576, Khan Devlet-Girei, fearing that protracted inactivity would earn the scorn of the Russians, ventured to take the field with 50,000 cavalry, but he pulled back from Molochnie Vody when he learned that Russian legions were stationed on the banks of the Oka, that Ivan himself was in Kaluga, and that the Don Cossacks had seized Islam-Kirmen in a daring raid. Ivan was taking all necessary provisions for the safety of his country, including putting more troops into the fortresses in southeast and western Russia so as to repel the khan and the Lithuanians. In addition to that, he also raised a notable water-borne force on the Volga composed of residents of the Dvina, Perm and Suzdal districts in order to restrain the rebellious Cheremis, Nogai and inhabitants of Astrakhan, and to act in concert with the Don Cossacks against the Taurid itself. Ivan was now prepared to decide the fate of Livonia.

The year 1577 began even more terribly for this unhappy land. It had been presaged (as the people believed) by frightful autumn winds and unheard of winter snowstorms so that the Baltic was covered with remnants of shipwrecks, while the

1577

| LIVONIAN WAR | shore and roads were full of corpses that had been drowned in the stormy deep or buried in the snow. 50,000 Russians now set out from Novgorod for Revel, whose citizens waited in vain for help by sea from Finland, Sweden and Lübeck. The ships carrying provisions and troops either sank or turned back after encountering strong headwinds. Everyone was anxious and fearful, but the Swedish king, apparently in jest, wrote Ivan that they had no reason to fight each other, that Sweden had sold Revel to the German emperor and if the tsar wanted this city, he should request it of Maximilian's successor.

But the people of Revel cheered themselves with the recollection of 1571, when Magnus fled from their walls and, when under the leadership of Swedish General Horn, they had met the Russians with cool courage. The tsar's chief voivodes were young Theodor Ivanovich Mstislavskii and the ranking Muscovite commander, Ivan Vasilievich Menshii Sheremetev, who had given his word to his sovereign to take Revel or die. Prince Nikita Priimkov-Rostovskii, who had numerous German and Scottish cannoneers, was in charge of the heavy artillery.

The siege began on 23 January and, barrages from all our fortifications on the 27th; it lasted about six weeks, but had no decisive effect. Churches and houses caught fire, but the citizens put out the blazes, and answered the barrage with one of their own. Their frequent sallies sometimes gained the upper hand and the Russians' numbers were significantly diminished due to combat, cold and illness. Sheremetev kept his word: he did not take Revel, but he laid down his life there, killed by a cannonball. The body of this brave voivode was transported to Moscow, along with booty and prisoners, both Estonian and *Finnish:* despite the two-year truce concluded with Finland, Prince Mstislavskii had sent Tatar cavalry across the ice of the Gulf to lay waste to their land.

In order to terrorize Revel's troops and to encourage his own, the Muscovite voivodes spread the rumor that the tsar himself was coming to see them, but the former knew (through the turncoat Mirza Bulat, who had defected from the camp to the fortress) that the sovereign was in Moscow, our commanders had poor morale and their troops had no faith in them. Accordingly, Revel proudly rejected all of Mstislavskii's peace offers. On 13 March the Russians torched their camp, which was full of bodies. They were ordered to tell the citizens that they were leaving, but not for long.

The aftermath of Revel's second triumph was the devastation of all of Ivan's possessions in Livonia. Not just the Swedes and the Germans, but even the Estonian peasants attacked the numerous Russians everywhere. A knight appeared, the son of a Revel coiner, one Iv Schenkenberg, nicknamed Hannibal for his audacity. Commanding a band of armed farmers, he took Wittenstein, burned Pernau, pillaged several towns and castles in Erven and Virland [Wierland] near Derpt, and villainously tortured and killed our prisoners. Thereby he provoked the cruel vengeance that soon fell on Livonia, since those of our troops who had been so unsuccessful at Derpt were now just the vanguard of our main forces.

That spring Ivan came to Novgorod with both his sons. There and in Pskov he assembled all the military forces of his vast realm: from all territories and cities, from south and north, Christian and infidel, from the shores of the Caspian to the North Sea, Circassian and Nogai, Mordvi and Tatars, princes, mirzas and atamans, ultimately all the voivodes except those left to guard the border from the Dnieper to Voronezh. Under Ivan's command was the ruler of Kasimov, Sain-Bulat, who was now a Christian known as *Simeon, Grand Prince of Tver*. The princes Ivan Shuiskii, Vasilii Sitskii, Sheidyakov, Thedor Mstislavskii and the boyar Nikita Romanovich Zakharin-Yuriev commanded special legions. Russia had not seen such a powerful army in a long time. Everyone thought that it would attack Revel.

"Take heart once more," he [Stefan] wrote to his citizens in Riga, after sending them boats loaded with grain and military equipment. "Prepare yourselves for a third terrible storm, and may the Lord save you a third time from a dishonorable tyrant!"

After leaving Novgorod on 15 June, the tsar remained for about a month in Pskov, where Magnus came to see him, now apprehensive and perfidious, as we shall see, but the tsar did not yet know of his secret treachery and ordered him to proceed to Wenden with his German troops. As for Ivan, he invaded southern Livonia on 25 July, to the astonishment of the Poles ruling there – they had believed themselves to be at peace with Russia. Thus commenced the war between Ivan and Batory, which had such significant consequences!

Stefan's chief voivode Khotkevich, not in the least prepared for defense, fled, followed by the rest. In a few days the tsar took Marienhausen, Luitsen, Rositten, Düneburg, Kreutzburg and Laudon. Their defenders, Poles and Germans, did not draw their swords, and asked for mercy. Those who had surrendered without taking time to think it over were free to go; those who had tarried were taken prisoner. Laudon was razed to its foundations and the other fortresses were taken by Moscow's units. Ivan detailed the voivode Thoma Buturlin to the town of Sesswegen, governed by the brother of the traitor Taube. The Russians took the trading quarter, but Buturlin informed the tsar that the Germans had rejected their mercy and were holding out in the fortress until death. The sovereign himself arrived and ordered the cannons to fire. The walls came down and the Germans fell at his feet. There was now no mercy: the most eminent of them were impaled, the rest sold to the Tatars as slaves. Berson and Kaltsenau surrendered unconditionally and Ivan sent all the Germans there to Courland with their wives and children. From the other side, Magnus likewise took cities, not by force, but voluntarily.

"Would you like to save your lives, liberty and property?" he wrote to the Livonians. "Surrender to me or you will know the swords and shackles of the Muscovites."

All gladly acknowledged him as king on conditions favorable to their safety and in hopes of thereby avoiding the menace from Ivan. Without informing our sovereign, Magnus took Kokenhusen, Ascheraden, Lenward, Ronneburg and many other fortresses, and ultimately Wenden and Wolmar, where the citizens handed over Stefan's voivode, Prince Aleksandr Polubenskii, to him. With thoughtless pride he informed the tsar of his successes and asked that the Russians not harm these Livonians, who were now loyal to their own king. Among the cities now in his power, he even named Yuriev, or Derpt. Ivan was astounded!

Chapter Nine

We have seen that the tsar, having chosen Magnus as an instrument of our policy, was not blinded by excessive faith in him. He remembered the treachery of Taube and Kruse, and knew that a familial alliance is no reliable guarantee of the loyalty of someone who loves power. He of course continued to pay attention, nor did he forget rumors of Magnus' secret relations with the pans, but he had heretofore kept his silence and concealed his suspicions. Now, seething with wrath, he assaulted Kokenhusen. He ordered 50 of Magnus' German guard killed there and sold all the residents into servitude. He wrote the following to his son-in-law:

"To our *vassal*, King Magnus. I saw you off from Pskov with permission to take Wenden only . . . However, you, following the suggestions of evildoers or your own imprudence wanted it all! Know that we are not distant from one another. This matter is easily put to rights: I have troops and biscuits – I need nothing more. Either obey, or if you are not content with the towns I have given you, return across the sea to your own land. I can even send you to Kazan, and clean up Livonia without your assistance."

The tsar sent his voivodes to Ascheraden, Schwanenburg, Lenvard, Tirsen and Pebalge. He then rested for two days in Kokenhusen, where, fond of theological debate, he peacefully conversed with the chief pastor concerning the evangelical faith, but almost put him to death for his indiscreet comparison of Luther with the apostle Paul.

When he learned that the fortresses of southern Livonia were not resisting our troops, he departed for Erl, where he took all its residents prisoner because they had not surrendered immediately; he then hastened to Wenden. At the same time, Bogdan Belskii and his Muscovite musketeers encircled Wolmar, which was governed by Magnus' official, Georg Wilke. This fortress was considered to be one of the most important. Wilke did not want to admit the Russians, replying that it *had been taken by the king's saber*. However, when he saw our preparations for assault, he rode out to our voivode and said,

"I know that my king is the tsar's vassal. I am refraining from bloodshed. Take the city; I shall ride to Magnus."

Wilke was sent to Ivan along with 20 Germans and 70 other of Magnus' men, where they were hacked to pieces. Merchants and all the residents were put in fetters and their homes and property were put under seal. As a token of his special gratitude, the tsar awarded Belskii a golden chain and gave gold medals to the court nobles with him.

> 31 August
> Perfidy of Magnus

Magnus was in Wenden himself, but he did not want to come out to meet with the tsar. However, to comply with his will, he sent him Stefan's voivode, Prince Polubenskii and two eminent officials with his excuses. It is written that Ivan extracted an important secret by flattering the former. He learned of his vassal's perfidy, that Magnus had been dealing with the tsar of Courland and was considering submitting to Batory with the Livonian cities, since he inwardly hated the Russians or at least their tsar. What compelled Stefan's voivode to betray Magnus' trust? The desire to take vengeance on him for the rebellion of the residents of Wolmar? Craven fear? Ivan's unexpected graciousness?

Whatever it was, Ivan could now legitimately execute the traitor and might indulge himself in a natural, legitimate wrath. However, since he could occasionally control himself, he coolly ordered Magnus' two emissaries birched, telling them that their lord was to appear at our camp immediately. Magnus was shaken, but dared not disobey. With 25 officials he rode to meet his doom. When he caught sight of Ivan, he dismounted and fell at the tsar's feet. Ivan raised him up and told him the following, with more contempt than anger,

"Moron! You dared to dream of a Livonian kingdom? You, a base vagabond, received into my family, wed to my beloved niece, clothed and shod by me, given a treasury and towns – you betrayed me, your sovereign, father and benefactor? Answer me! How many times did I hear of your vile scheming? But I did not believe it, and kept my silence. Now it is all in the open. You wanted to take Livonia by deceit and serve the Poles. But the gracious Lord has preserved me and delivered you into my hands. And so you will become a victim of my justice: return what is mine and

CHAPTER NINE

crawl back into insignificance!" Magnus and all his officials were locked in an empty old house where they spent several days on the straw. Meanwhile, what was happening in Wenden?

The Russians had entered the city without opposition. The voivodes, Prince Golitsyn and Saltykov, ordered them not to disturb the residents. They posted strong guards everywhere and cleaned out some houses for the sovereign and the boyars. All appeared peaceful and quiet. But Magnus' Germans, fearing Ivan's ferocity, took shelter in the castle with their wives, children and valuable possessions and would not open the gates to him. The Russians wanted to use force. The Germans began shooting; they killed many boyar cadets and wounded the voivode Saltykov. They would not even obey Magnus, who ordered them to surrender. When he learned of this, the angry tsar ordered his eminent prisoner, Georg Wilke, to be impaled, cannons to destroy the castle and all the Germans killed. They pounded the walls for three days, but then they fell. There was no salvation for the besieged. One of them now said,

"We shall die, if such is pleasing to God, but we shall not surrender to the tyrant to be tortured. We shall blow up the castle!"

Everyone agreed, even the pastors who were with them. They filled the vaults of the Master's old house with powder, partook of the holy sacrament, knelt next to one another, by families, both husbands and wives, mothers and children, and prayed fervently. When they saw the Russians charging at them, the sign was given and Magnus' official, Henrik Boisman, threw a burning fuse through a window and onto a heap of powder . . . and with a terrible blast, the building flew into the air.

Everyone perished, except for Boisman, who was found among the ruins, deafened by the blast and maimed, but still alive. He expired a few minutes later, but even though dead, was impaled. A terrible vengeance also descended on the peaceful residents, who were tortured and executed, flogged and burnt, while the women and girls were dishonored in the streets. Their corpses lay unburied around the city. In brief, this *chastisement of Wenden* is among the most terrible deeds of Ivan's tyranny: it redoubled the Livonians hatred of the Russians.

From there, the tsar went to Ronneburg, Trikat and Schmilten. These fortresses were occupied by Lithuanians and did not resist him. The governors met peaceably with him, glad to have the liberty to return to their homeland, albeit without arms or property. The Germans, however, were taken into captivity with their wives and children. Only Riga remained to be taken, but Ivan foresaw a bloody siege. He hastened to Wolmar to celebrate his victories, giving a sumptuous feast for the Russian voivodes and the eminent Lithuanians who had been freed from captivity. He was especially kind to Prince Aleksandr Polubenskii; he presented him with fur coats and goblets and proudly told him,

> 12 September

"Go to King Stefan. Persuade him to conclude a peace on conditions pleasing to me, for my arms are long! You have seen for yourself – let him know."

Wolmar reminded Ivan of the fugitive Kurbskii; he wrote him a letter with the following contents (and entrusted its delivery to Prince Polubenskii):

> Letter to Kurbskii

"We, the Great Sovereign of all Russia, to the former Muscovite boyar . . . Let there be humility in my heart and on my tongue. I know of your lawlessness, which is alleviated only through the grace of God. This is my salvation, and as the apostle says, that the Lord rejoices more over the repentance of a single sinner than over ten righteous men. This deep sea of goodness drowns the sins of the torturer and the prostitute! . . . No, I do not boast of honor: the honor is not mine, but God's . . .

"Behold, O Prince, the providence of the Most High. You, the friends of Adashev and Silvestr, wanted to rule the country . . . but where are you now? You are cast down by justice; seething with rage, you cry out that there are no men left in Russia, that it is now impotent and defenseless without you. But even though you are not here, German resolve collapses before the might of the life-giving cross!

"We are in a place you have never been. No, you were here, but not in the pride of victory, but in the shame of flight, thinking that you were now far from Russia, in a safe refuge for your treachery, inaccessible of its avengers. Here you have been spewing abuse at your tsar, but here your tsar is, and it is now Russian! . . .

"What is my guilt before you? Was it not you [and your associates], who by taking my dear wife from me, became those truly responsible for my human weaknesses? You speak of the tsar's ferocity, you who wanted to deprive him of his throne and his life! Was it not through war and blood that I obtained my realm, I, who became the sovereign while still in the cradle? And Prince Vladimir, who was obliging to you traitors, did he have the right to power by virtue of his birth and personal merits?

"He was a prince as foolish as he was ungrateful, who had been cast into prison by your fathers and freed by me? I defended myself: criminal frenzy demands implacable judgment. But I am not fond of verbosity; I have said enough. Marvel at the workings of Heaven; get control of yourself; consider your deeds! It is not pride that compels me to write to you, but Christian love. May remembrance reform you, may your soul be saved."

This bogus *humility* did not, of course, reform or deceive the turncoat, but it may have aggravated the poison in his heart, to the pleasure of the vengeful tsar. Kurbskii, just as vengeful, was waiting for an opportune time to reply, and that time was approaching.

Up till now, Ivan had gotten what he wanted; he ravaged and chastised Livonia without cease; he laughed at the weakness of his enemies; he haughtily imagined the fear and desperation of the kings of Sweden and Poland. He believed his arms had now decided everything, that all that remained was a treaty of the strong with the weak.

After detailing part of his cavalry to Revel for renewed devastation of Swedish territories, distributing the rest of his army throughout the cities and towns, and entrusting it to Grand Prince Simeon of Tver and the princes Ivan Shuiskii and Vasilii Sitskii, the tsar rode to Derpt. The traitorous Magnus and his important courtiers were transported after him, expecting death at any hour, but Ivan, who did not respect the principles of governmental morality or of implacable governmental jurisprudence, was able overlook this treachery for political advantage. Thus, since he was in Düneburg, he *graciously* began communicating with the fugitives Kruse and Taube, since these perfidious men, having seen his success, had once again dared to offer him their services, whether sincerely or slyly, employing promises to assist us in further conquests.

Thus, to general amazement, Ivan pardoned Magnus in Derpt, after getting his oath of loyalty along with the obligation to pay Russia 40,000 Hungarian guldens. He restored to him his liberty and the possessions of Oberpahlen and Karkus and included Gelmet, Zigevalde [Siegewalde?], Rosenberg and other towns and cities. He left Magnus with the title of king, and himself with that of supreme commander of Livonia, and ordered that the churches there receive the following inscription consisting of bad German verses which, we are assured, he composed himself:

"I am Ivan, sovereign of the many lands enumerated in my title. I profess the true Christian faith of my forefathers in accordance with the teachings of St. Paul the Apostle, along with other good Muscovites. I am their natural tsar: I did not beg or buy my title, and my own tsar is Jesus Christ."

Ivan rode from Derpt to Pskov, seeing all the Livonian prisoners. Some he released, others he sent to Moscow in fetters, and then, seemingly wearied by his great exploits, sped to rest in the solitude of Aleksandrovskaya Sloboda.

This was the end of our martial successes in Livonia, which, although not very significant for posterity, were notable and brilliant in the eyes of contemporary Russians, who glorified the capture of 27 towns and cities in two or three months. We shall see the cruel turn of fate, ill-starred for Russia and shameful for the tsar, and we shall see new proof of the tyrant's cowardice. Disasters are a punishment for a tyrant, not an incentive, and faith in Providence was as far from his fearful heart as was his trust in his people's zeal. But before our description of the war, the likes of which Russia had not seen, we shall for the last time show Ivan as a destroying angel of darkness for Russians, covered with the sacred blood of the innocent.

Chapter Nine

> Sixth Episode of Executions

The term *oprichniki* was no more, yet victims still died, but not as often, nor in such numbers. The tyranny seemed to be drowsy and nodding, only reawakening from time to time. There was still another great name to be inscribed in the huge book of murders of Ivan's lethal reign. The foremost of the Russian voivodes, the sovereign's *first servant*, he who at the most glorious moment of Ivan's life sent to tell him: *Kazan is ours;* he who, already persecuted, already designated for disgrace, dishonor, exile and imprisonment, shattered the khan's forces on the banks of the Lopasnya and obliged the tsar to show him the nation's gratitude for saving Moscow – this was Prince Mikhail Vorotynskii, who ten months after his triumph was put to death by torture, accused by a slave of sorcery, of secret meetings with evil witches and conspiring to remove the tsar.

The charge was absurd, although commonplace in these times and, as always, worked to the tyrant's benefit. This man of glory and valor was brought before the tsar in fetters. After hearing the charges and seeing his accuser, Vorotynskii said quietly,

"Tsar! My grandfather and father taught me to diligently serve God and my tsar, not a devil, and when in heartfelt grief to resort to the altars of the Most High, not to witches. This calumniator is my fugitive slave, who was exposed as a thief: do not believe this criminal."

But Ivan wanted to believe him: heretofore he had spared the life of this last of Adashev's loyal friends, with seeming reluctance, apparently in order to have a single victorious voivode in case of unexpected peril. The danger had now passed, and the 60-year old hero was chained to a tree between two fires: he burned, he suffered. We are assured that Ivan himself raked glowing coals with his bloody staff towards the victim. The badly burned and barely breathing Vorotynskii was taken to Belo-ozero; he died on the way. His distinguished remains lie at St. Kirill's Cloister.

"Oh great man!" writes the unhappy Kurbskii. "Man of powerful spirit and reason! Your hallowed memory will not be forgotten by the world! You served your country without thanks, where virtue perishes and praise is silent, but it is posterity and Europe, too, who shall hear of you. They know how with your bravery and brilliance you destroyed the infidels' army on the fields before Moscow, thereby comforting Christians and shaming the prideful sultan! Accept here resounding praise for your great deeds, and there, among Christ and God, eternal beatitude for your innocent sufferings!"

The distinguished line of Vorotynskii princes, descendants of St. Mikhail of Chernigov, has long been broken off in Russia, but the name of Prince Mikhail Vorotynskii has become our history's heritage and glory.

Tortured along with him were the boyar and voivode Prince Nikita Romanovich Odoevskii, brother of the ill-fated Evdokiya, Ivan's bride. He had long been foreordained to die for the fictitious crimes of his brother-in-law and sister, but the tyrant sometimes liked to delay punishment, while boasting of his patience or enjoying the protracted fear and trembling of these unfortunates.

Next to be killed was the old boyar Mikhail Yakovlevich Morozov, with his two sons and wife Evdokiya, who was the daughter of Prince Dimitrii Belskii and praised for her piety and the sanctity of her life. This man had passed unharmed through all the storms of the Moscow court; he had withstood all the vicissitudes of the mutinous rule of the boyars; he had been a favorite of the Shuiskiis, the Belskiis and the Glinskiis. At Ivan's first wedding in 1547, he had been his best man and clearly close to the tsar. For a time he had risen above Adashev, by virtue of his talents. He had served in embassies and wars, and had directed artillery at the siege of Kazan. He had not been assigned to the Oprichnina and had not attended the bloody feasts with the Basmanovs and Malyuta, but had instead, with his mind and his efforts, worked for the good of the country. He finally fell in his own turn, as an annoying relict, a hateful reminder of better times.

Another old boyar fell in 1575, Prince Pyotr Andreevich Kurakin, over a course of 35 years one of the most energetic voivodes, along with the boyar Ivan Andreevich Buturlin, who had survived his numerous kinsmen and was even able to earn Ivan's special favor, but did not escape disgrace, neither by his services nor by his skill at court. In this year and the next two the following okolnichie were executed: Pyotr Zaitsev, a zealous oprichnik; Grigorii Sobakin, uncle of the late Tsaritsa Martha; Prince Tulupov, a house voivode and evidently a favorite of the sovereign; and Nikita Borisov. Also: the royal carver Kalist Vasilievich Sobakin, Martha's brother and Ivan's brother-in-law; and the armorer Prince Ivan Devetelevich.

We do not know with what they were charged with, or, to put it better, what the pretext was for their executions. All we see is that Ivan had not abandoned the *principle of confusion* in his destructive policy; having completed the downfall of the old nobles, who were condemned by his policies, he dispassionately destroyed the new as well, and while punishing the virtuous, he also punished the evil ones.

And so, at the same time, he ordered the Pskov abbot Kornilii, a holy man, and his humble pupil Vassian Muromets, killed, along with archbishop Leonid of Novgorod, an unworthy, greedy and cupidinous pastor. The former were cut up by some sort of implement of torture; the latter was sewn in a bear hide and set upon by dogs! Nothing could amaze Russians now – their feelings had been numbed by tyranny. It is written that Kornelii left for posterity a history of his times that depicted the country's catastrophes, rebellions, the splitting of the realm and the destruction of its people through Ivan's wrath, famine, pestilence and foreign invasions.

Kurbskii now tells of the liquidation of the virtuous archimandrite Theodorit. This man had been a monk of the Solovetskii Cloister, a friend of St. Aleksandr Svirskii and the renowned elder Porfirii; he had been persecuted by Ivan's father for his bold intercession on behalf of the unfortunate Prince Shemyakin. He was renowned for having baptized many primitive Lapps. He did not fear the snowy wastes – he penetrated the depths of the dark, cold forests and proclaimed Christ the Savior on the banks of the Tuloma. He learned the inhabitants' language, explained the Gospel to them, invented an alphabet for them and founded a monastery near the mouth of the Kola. He taught and performed good works, similar to St. Stefan of Perm, and witnessed with heartfelt emotion the ardor of this peaceful, simple-hearted people for the true faith.

In 1560, in obedience to Ivan's will, he traveled to Constantinople and brought back to him from the local Greek clergy a blessing on the tsars' estate and an old book on the coronations of the Byzantine emperors. After this he lived in the Monastery of St. Dimitrii Prilutskii in Vologda, and despite his age, often visited his beloved Kola monastery amongst the new Christian Laplanders. He traveled from wilderness to wasteland, in the summer by river and sea, in the winter by reindeer.

Everywhere he found that people loved him personally and heeded his teachings. Respected by all, even the tsar, Theodorit aroused Ivan's wrath through his friendship with Prince Kurbskii, who had been an ardent spiritual son of this diligent Christian pastor. He dared to remind the sovereign of the pitiable fate of this distinguished fugitive who was as unfortunate as he was guilty, and dared to speak of forgiveness. Some say Theodorit was drowned in a river, others assure us that although he was disgraced, he died peacefully in seclusion.

STRUGGLES OVER PRECEDENCE

Sparing neither virtue nor sanctity, and demanding silent obedience in everything, Ivan at the same time nevertheless sanguinely tolerated the constant struggle for precedence among our voivodes, who on this issue did not fear to manifest the most audacious recalcitrance. They watched silently those closest to them executed or silently lay their own heads on the executioner's block, but were quite insubordinate if the tsar assigned their ranks in the army not in accordance with their time-honored seniority.

For example, someone whose father or grandfather had commanded the main legion did not now want to be subordinate to a voivode whose father or grandfather had only commanded the vanguard or flank, the left or right legion. The unwilling would send the sovereign's orders back with their complaints, demanding justice. The tsar would consult the Book of Degrees to decide suits over seniority, or, in the case of important personages, reply, telling them

CHAPTER NINE

"to deal with their voivodes without regard to precedence; everyone will keep his own rank pending investigation."

But to the harm of the nation, the time to deal properly with this had already passed, and the guilty were in no danger of punishment. This problem of seniority also afflicted the court. In 1578, Ivan's favorite, Boris Godunov, the new royal carver, went to law with the boyar Prince Vasilii Sitskii, whose son had not wanted to serve with him at the tsar's table.

Despite Prince Vasilii's rank as a boyar, a letter from the tsar declared that Godunov was many levels higher than he because Boris's grandfather was ranked higher than the Sitskiis in the old books of ranks. While allowing voivodes to squabble over precedence, Ivan did not permit negligence in military affairs. For instance, the renowned officer, Prince Mikhail Nozdrovatyi was *flogged at the stables* for making poor dispositions at the siege of Schmilten.

"But these men," writes a Livonian historian, "did not decrease their ardor for their monarch because of punishment or dishonor. We shall here present a memorable event: in 1576, one of Ivan's officials, Prince Sugorskii, was dispatched to Emperor Maximilian. He became ill in Courland. The tsar, out of respect for the tsar, several times had one of his ministers call on him. The latter always heard these words from him,

'My life is nothing. Just let my sovereign be of good health.' The minister expressed his amazement to him.

'How can you' he asked, 'serve a tyrant so diligently?' Prince Sugorskii replied,

'We Russians are devoted to our tsars, whether gracious or cruel.' As evidence, the sick man told him that not long before, Ivan had ordered one of his eminent men impaled for a small infraction. The unfortunate man survived a whole day and night in incredible torment, then said to his wife and children,

| An Example of Loyalty |

'God! Have mercy on the tsar!'" That is to say, the Russians boasted of that for which foreigners reproached them: blind,

383

unbounded devotion to their monarchs' will, even should it irrationally deviate from national and human law.

In these years, Ivan's lack of restraint showed a new tendency to violate the holy laws of the Church with unheard of shamelessness. The tsaritsa soon lost her husband's affection, either because of her infertility or just because of his carnal passions, which, betraying conscience and the law, kept seeking new objects of enjoyment. The unfortunate woman, like Solomoniya before her, was obliged to renounce the world, seclude herself in the Tikhvin Monastery and, as a nun or schematic* with the name of Dariya, lived there until 1626.

The tsar, who no longer observed even the smallest proprieties, no longer requested a blessing from the bishops and without any dispensation from the Church, married again, for the fifth time, to Anna Vasilchikova in about 1575. However, we do not know if he gave her the title of tsaritsa, or formally crowned her, since in the descriptions of his weddings there is not this *stain*, nor do we see any of her relatives at court or ranked among those closest to the tsar. She was buried in the Suzdal nunnery, where Solomoniya also lies. Ivan's *sixth* wife, or as it is written, *concubine*, was the beautiful widow Vasilissa Melenteva. Without any church ceremony he made only a prayer to bless their living together. We shall see that this was not the last of the tsar's illegitimate marriages, for he was an insatiable murderer and voluptuary!

IVAN'S FIFTH AND SIXTH MARRIAGES

---

* [The highest rank of Orthodox monasticism.]

CHAPTER X

WAR WITH POLAND

1577-1582

Negotiations with Austria. Treaty with Denmark. Crimean affairs. Negotiations and war with Batory. Amazing deed of the Muscovite cannoneers. Polotsk and Sokol captured. Kurbskii's letter. Conference in Moscow. Embassy to the emperor and the Pope. Conquest of Velikie Luki. Calamities for Russia. Ivan's seventh marriage. His unprecedented abasement. Letter to Batory and his reply. Embassy from the Pope. Glorious siege of Pskov. Swedes take Narva. Peace talks. Truce concluded. Filicide. Ivan considers renouncing the world. Stroganov the healer. Ivan's conversations with the emissary of the Roman Church.

It seems that while Ivan was celebrating his Livonian conquests in Moscow and scorning Batory and Sweden, he did not see or even guess what great danger he was in. He still sought allies, however. He wrote to the new emperor, Rudolf, in reply to his notification of the death of Maximilian, expressing his readiness to conclude a treaty of *love* and brotherhood with him. He also sent his courtier, Zhdan Kvashnin, to Vienna in hopes of persuading the Kaiser to make war on their common enemy, to expel Stefan, divide up Poland and Lithuania and at last take up arms with all of Europe against the sultan.

| 1577-1578 |
| NEGOTIATIONS |
| WITH AUSTRIA |

This was the great idea of the age, urged on the emperors by the popes. Living in Vienna at this time was the eminent refugee, the Siradskii voivode Albrekht Lasko, an enemy of Stefan, who was in secret contact with Ivan. Our sovereign tried to convince him with his intellect and enthusiasm to invigorate the slow and overly deliberate Austrian politics. We note that while in Germany Kvashnin was supposed to find out whether the Pope was on friendly terms with the emperor, the kings of Spain, France and Scotland, as well as Elizabeth of England; whether the internal rebellions in France had been put down; how the Kaiser's negotiations with it and other powers were proceeding and how much revenue and how many troops he had.

Our tsars had not shunned Europe since the time of Ivan III, the founder of the Russian state and its administrative system. We wished to know about the mutual relations of sovereign states, partly out of curiosity (the sign of an active intellect) and partly to seek direct or indirect advantages for our own policies in their alliances and enmities.

18 June, 1578

However, Kvashnin returned with nothing but the promise that the emperor would not delay sending one of his foremost nobles to Moscow, since he wished to establish friendship with us. Also, to Ivan's displeasure, Rudolf complained to him of the catastrophic devastation of Livonia, which was incompatible with their *brotherhood*, humanity and justice. Kvashnin also brought a letter from the Hungarian voivode Robert, praising the intellect of the tsar's emissary and imploring him, as a *second* Christian monarch, to become the savior of Europe. He promised him gold and men for a war with the Turks and tried to persuade him to take Moldavia, *bequeathed to Russia,* by the hospodar [*lord*] Bogdan, who had died in Moscow.

This was a secret letter, since the Austrian cabinet, which had long been apprehensive, would doubtless not have permitted a Hungarian baron to communicate in the name of his people with a foreign sovereign in a matter so important.

Robert knew the emperor, who was a skilled chemist, astronomer and equestrian, but a very bad monarch; he foresaw the threat to Hungary from the power-hungry sultans and wished to use newly power-hungry Russia, whose strength was now renowned, to counter them. (Maximilian's emissaries who had come to us in 1576 had spread the rumor in Europe of Ivan's uncountably immense army.) But Maximilian's pusillanimous successor, even though he hated Batory and feared the sultan, would not consider employing an alliance with the tsar to take Poland and save Hungary.

King Frederik of Denmark could have been another natural ally for us. Despite his peace with Sweden, he put no faith in its friendship, and sought Ivan's: in 1578 he sent his eminent officials Jakob Ulfeld and Gregory Ulstand to Moscow to complain that Russians were occupying some Danish possessions in Livonia: Hapsal, Leal and Lode. They brought a proposal for permanent peace on conditions favorable to both powers. Frederik wanted to have part of Estonia and to help us expel the Swedes, boasting that he in no way accepted the lying promises of our mutual enemy Stefan.

TREATY WITH DENMARK

But as Ulfeld writes, the proud and inflexible Muscovite boyars would only consider that which would aid their own love of power. They showed not the slightest accommodation and would listen neither to request nor counterargument. They rejected a genuine alliance with Denmark and a permanent peace, merely concluding a truce for 15 years, whose conditions were the following:

1) the king acknowledges all of Livonia and Courland as the tsar's own, while the tsar confirms the island of Ösel with all its territory and towns as theirs;

2) the former is to give neither men nor money to Batory, nor to the Swedes in their war with Russia, which likewise will not aid Denmark's enemies;

3) the ancient boundaries between Russian and Danish possessions in Norway are to be restored;

4) both sides declare full liberties for merchants and safety for travelers; and

5) Frederik is not to detain German artists and artisans on their way to Moscow. Ulfeld lost Frederik's favor because of this [proposed] treaty, which was clearly of advantage only to the tsar. In his description of his journey, Ulfeld vilifies the Russians, cursing their obstreperousness, deceitfulness and unexampled immoderation.

| CRIMEAN AFFAIRS | Ivan desired, if not an alliance, then at least peace with Devlet-Girei, who was now weak and dying. The tsar did not cease from communicating with the khan through couriers – Ivan did not yield him anything, but neither did he request anything of him, except a sworn document and peaceful inactivity. Devlet-Girei died on 29 June 1577 and on succeeding his father, his son Mahmet-Girei very amicably informed Ivan of this fact and did something further: he attacked Lithuania and devastated and burned no small part of the Volhynian lands. He was following the advice of his nobles, who said that a new khan should mark his accession to the throne with conflagrations and bloodbaths in neighboring lands!

Ivan hastened to send him his distinguished official, Prince Mosalskii, with greetings and rich gifts, the like of which the Taurid heretofore had not seen. Ivan also gave the prince very solicitous instructions, for example, he was

"to *kowtow* to the khan; to promise *annual* gifts in case of an alliance, but not to include this in a sworn document; to request, but not insist that Mahmet-Girei call the grand prince *Tsar*; to generally conduct himself *humbly*, avoiding sharp remarks, and not to show anger if the khan or his nobles recalled the days of Kalita and Khan Uzbek, but to reply softly: *I know not of bygone days; they are known but to God and yourself, Sovereign.*"

In this manner Ivan was able to make a comrade-in-arms of the new khan and instill fear in Stefan of the Crimeans and their lethal raids on Lithuania. But this had only been a successful policy back in the reign of Ivan III; his son and grandson had had no success with it. Mahmet-Girei wanted Astrakhan in exchange for his friendship, promising to give us Lithuania and Poland! He also wanted the tsar to remove the Cossacks from the Dnieper and Don regions.

These demands were announced by the khan's emissaries in Moscow. They were told that the Dnieper and Don Cossacks were not subordinate to us; the former served Batory and the latter were Russian and Lithuanian fugitives who had been ordered executed should they appear within our borders. They were also told that arms and religion had permanently established Astrakhan as Russian; that Christian churches had been erected there, monasteries founded and indigenous Christians now lived there. The khan reiterated to the tsar,

"You were going to yield the city to us: fulfill your *promise!* Then your widows and orphans may walk safely with their silver and gold: none of my warriors will touch them even on the most deserted highways."

Meanwhile, he asked for 4,000 rubles. The sovereign sent him 1,000, but did not stint gifts for his wives and nobles, yet he did not achieve his goal: Stefan forestalled us and purchased a shameful friendship with this ataman of bandits, and was able to operate against Russia with all his forces.

Fond of great deeds and glory, but knowing how to bide his time, Batory, who was busy with the siege of Danzig, seemed to view Ivan's successes in Livonia with indifference. He no doubt knew that it would not be negotiations, but the sword that would resolve the matter. Even so, he wrote to the tsar that he was surprised at his hostility and proposed that they not shed blood if it was still possible to combine peace with advantages, honor and security for both Russia and Poland.

> NEGOTIATIONS AND WAR WITH BATORY

"Your irritation is unfounded," Ivan replied to him. "After I took my towns in Livonia, I sent your people away without any kind of *punishment.* You are a king, but not of Livonia."

Stefan's emissaries, the voivodes of Mazovia and Minsk, arrived in Moscow in January 1578 and formally announced to the boyars that the king was thinking only of peace between the Christian powers and wished to live in amity with all of them, especially Russia. They said that the truce had been violated by the tsar's hostile activities in Livonia and that Stefan had empowered them (the emissaries) to permanently reestablish tranquility.

In response, the boyars demanded that the king call Ivan *Tsar and Grand Prince of Smolensk and Polotsk,* not encroach on Livonia, nor on Courland, which was inseparable from it, and also hand over Kiev, Kanev, Vitebsk and other cities to Russia. The king's pans demanded not only all of Livonia, but also *all* of the ancient Russian districts, from Kaluga to Chernigov and the

Dvina. Realizing the impossibility of a peace treaty, they agreed only to restore the truce for three years, but the Russian document includes the phrase *the king will not encroach on Livonia*, which is not in the Polish version. In confirming this agreement with the customary oath, the sovereign said,

"I kiss the cross for my *neighbor*, King Stefan: I will fulfill its conditions, but I shall not withdraw from the lands of Livonia and Courland."

The officials Karpov and Golovin journeyed to Stefan to witness his oath and to exchange documents, but the agreement had no effect, and did not diminish the bloodshed.

To Ivan's irritation and to Russia's detriment, circumstances now began to change. Back in 1577 the Swedish admiral Gillenanker had appeared with armed ships before Narva; he burned its wooden fortifications and killed or captured a number of Russians. Another gang of Swedes laid waste to part of the Kexholm uezd. Men of Revel as well as those belonging to Schenkenberg-Hannibal likewise menaced Russian Estonia with their incessant attacks, while Ivan's voivodes took their ease peaceably in the cities, scorning their weak enemies, whose audacity was magnified by our own inactivity.

It is written that Lithuanian officers, wishing to take Düneburg from us, employed a ruse. Seemingly as a token of friendship, they sent the local Muscovite troops a cask of wine. That night they broke into the fortress and killed all our drunken soldiers. Just as suddenly and easily did Germans in Batory's service take the extremely important city of Wenden, famed for the courageous obliteration of Magnus' guards and for the tsar's cruel vengeance. Our bungling voivodes did not see or hear anything as the Germans entered Wenden with copies of the keys to the city gates and cut up the sleeping Russians.

At the same time, Ivan learned that the shadow of his phony Kingdom of Livonia, an invention of his cunning policy, had at last vanished with the flight of its supposed king. The treachery that had long been contemplated was now accomplished. Magnus, a victim of ambition and fear, who had once again sworn allegiance to Ivan, once again turned to Batory and concluded an agreement with him. He secretly departed Oberpahlen for the town of Pilten in Courland with his young wife, who had sorrowfully sacrificed her homeland for him, even though she had no love for her uncle, the murderer of her unfortunate parents.

As gullibility was not in Ivan's character, he was of course hardly surprised by Magnus' flight; he had only wanted him temporarily as an instrument of his policy; and yet he seemed surprised and blamed himself for excessive kindness to the oathbreaker. He sent his most distinguished voivodes to Wenden: Prince Ivan Thedorovich Mstislavskii and his son, the boyar Morozov and others, so that the land there, wet with Russian blood, might be dampened further with that of the Germans.

But the voivodes were unable to take the fortresses; after firing their cannons and breaching the walls, they withdrew – they had learned that Batory's voivodes Dembinskii, Büring and Khotkevich were marching towards them. The tsar's junior officers made up for this defeat: Prince Ivan Mikhailovich Eletskii and the court noble Leontii Grigorievich Voluev with a handful of men were besieged in Lenwarden by Germans from Riga with a Lithuanian voivode.

They had no grain, just iron and powder, but fought like heroes for a month. They subsisted on horsemeat and leather, and with their bravery and endurance defeated the enemy, who withdrew leaving many corpses beneath the walls. Meanwhile, the Swedes with the indefatigable Schenkenberg-Hannibal incinerated the suburbs of Derpt, killing all the Russians they captured along with their wives and children. There was no mercy or humanity: both sides justified their horrible cruelties by the law of vengeance.

At the end of the year, the Muscovite voivodes, the princes Ivan Yurievich Golitsyn, Vasilii Agishevich Tyumenskii, Khvorostinin and Tyufyakin, assaulted Oberpahlen, which, with the consent of the local Germans, had been occupied by the Swedes following Magnus' flight. After taking this fortress and 200 prisoners, our voivodes sent them to Moscow for punishment and death. They now urgently needed to march on Wenden, but they quarreled amongst themselves over the command and failed to carry out the tsar's orders. Ivan angrily dispatched his eminent secretary Andrei Shchelkalov and his court favorite Danilo Saltykov to Derpt with orders to replace the voivodes in the event of further disobedience.

The voivodes finally set out, only after giving the enemy time to prepare and time for the Lithuanians to join up with the Swedes. They laid siege to Wenden, but saw the enemy behind them a few days later, on 21 October. Sapega with his Lithuanians and Germans, and General Boe with his Swedes attacked 18,000 Russians, who had barely managed to form up outside their trenches. They fought long and bravely, but our unreliable Tatar cavalry betrayed our infantry by fleeing at the crucial hour. The Russians faltered, became confused and fell back to their fortifications, whence a heavy barrage was still checking the enemy's impetus.

Nightfall put an end to the battle. Boe and Sapega intended to renew the battle in the morning, but the Muscovite commander Golitsyn, along with the okolnichii Thedor Sheremetev, Prince Andrei Palitskii and the secretary Shchelkalov, as intelligent as they were cowardly, galloped in mad fear on fast steeds to Derpt, leaving their army in terror in the night – the result was a general rout. A few still spoke of duty and honor, but they were not heeded. Yet they had said what they believed, and had shown an example worthy of the best of Roman times. These voivodes: the boyar Prince Vasilii Andreevich Sitskii, the okolnichii Vasilii Thedorovich Vorontsov (commander of the artillery), Danilo Borisovich Saltykov and Prince Mikhailo Vasilievich Tyufyakin did not budge from their spot, inviting death.

They found it the next morning when the enemy, seeing only a handful of brave men in the camp, assaulted them with all their forces. The okolnichii Tatev, the princes Khvorostinin and Semyon Tyufyakin, and the secretary Klobukov were taken prisoner. The enemy had charged at the artillery and was astounded to see a rare action of martial dedication: the Muscovite cannoneers, horrified at the thought of surrendering them to the enemy, hanged themselves from their weapons. These men were not dreaming of glory and

> AMAZING DEED OF THE MUSCOVITE CANNONEERS

their names remain unknown. Posterity would not have heard of their deed had not the sagacious royal secretary Heidenstein put it in his history. He was amazed at their noble spirit and appreciative of its greatness, even in his enemies.

The victor's spoils were 17 cannons, the entire baggage train and a large number of Tatar horses. Russian fatalities were greater than 6,000 men. Thus began a series of victories for Batory and defeats for Ivan in this ill-starred war. It was, however, not without glory for Russia, which still had the power and valor needed for victory, but lacked a courageous father-sovereign.

Up till now Ivan had not really considered peace. No doubt he thought not even a truce would be ratified by the king because of the concomitant obligation not to encroach on Livonia. From one direction he awaited news from Moscow's emissaries in Krakow, from the other, tidings from his voivodes concerning the long hoped-for easy conquest of Wenden, so he did not want to meet with Stefan's courier, who had been sent to persuade him to conclude a special agreement regarding the Livonian towns and cities.

Anxious about the fate of our troops outside Wenden, he immediately replied to Batory's letter that he was agreeable to an amicable resolution of Livonia's fate and to that end would wait for new royal emissaries in Moscow. He wrote that he was surprised that ours had not returned from Krakow, and ardently desired an honorable peace. However, Batory had now subdued Danzig and was ready for war.

> 11 January, 1579

This dangerous foe had expressed his love of peace to us while at the same time proposing to the Warsaw Sejm the necessity of securing the safety of his realm through arms.

"We have two dangerous enemies," he said. "The Crimeans burn and the Russians seize our territory. Shall we march on both at once? Otherwise whom shall we begin with?"

The presence of this great man had inspired the nobles and the gentry with beneficial fervor for their homeland. Batory spoke their language but poorly, but knew the history of Lithuania and Poland by heart. He enumerated the lands taken from them by Russia; he blamed the weakness of their kings and flattered the people's self-esteem. He pointed to his sword and listened to the Sejm's debate.

"The Taurid," said the pans, "is a dependency of the sultan. An offensive war with it might provoke him. While we are in the Taurid, the Ottomans will be in Poland; and what will be the profit? These primitive foes are always plundering and always impoverished. It would be better to seek a temporary peace with the khan. The Muscovite state is strong and powerful. Victory over it will be more glorious! It flourishes because of its natural abundance and its commerce. Our booty will be that much greater!"

They unanimously decided to make war on Russia and the order went out to gather a great army. Proprietors and citizens were burdened by taxes heretofore unheard of, but no one protested. They took up arms and paid their taxes with enthusiasm, or at least the semblance of it. Batory did not deceive himself by excessive reliance on his own strength and requested help from other powers – from the sultan and the Pope! He especially wished to gain the favor of the former and did not hesitate to violate the sacred obligations of honor, for he believed that conscience should remain silent in politics and that for a sovereign the good of the nation is the highest law.

At the same time, Stefan was looking for peace and alliances everywhere, so as to operate forcefully against us. This indigent Dnieper Cossack of Wallachian provenance, a renowned equestrian and strongman (he had broken a horseshoe in two with one hand and for that he was nicknamed *Horseshoe*), had been able, with a band of vagabonds, to suddenly conquer Wallachia, where the hospodar Peter, a vassal of the sultan and a friend of Batory, had been ruling.

Sorely vexed by such a triumph of audacity, Stefan sent his troops to expel the bandits. The brave Cossack believed the voivodes and Batory's word concerning his personal safety and voluntarily surrendered to them. What did the king do? To please the sultan, he ordered Peter beheaded, and in the presence of the sultan's emissary and told his nobles,

Chapter Ten

"I will not irritate the powerful to the detriment of my realm for the sake of the popular justice!" This perfidy gained only flattery from Mahmet's wise vizier Murad, who told Stefan's emissaries in Constantinople,

"We desire glory and victories for your king. It is possible to defeat the Muscovite tsar, but it will not be easy: only the sultan is more formidable than he."

The Pope promised Batory to intercede for him in all the cabinets of Europe and sent him a sword with a blessing, while the Brandenburg elector sent him some cannons. The Danish king, who secretly favored our enemies, was wavering while awaiting the outcome, but the Swedes immediately concluded a defensive and offensive alliance with Stefan.

The khan demanded gifts of Lithuania, and received them, on condition that he help them in war with Russia. Stefan's old, seasoned guard unit came to him from Transylvania, and from Germany, a mercenary army. The country's revenues were still not sufficient to cover all the military expenditures, so he trimmed court expenses, poured his own gold and silver into the treasury and borrowed more wherever he could. He inspected and drilled his troops and prepared their provisions, and as if he had time to spare, established new law courts, introduced new national laws, flattered the nobility and consolidated his royal power.

It was under these circumstances that Ivan's emissaries Karpov and Golovin came to him with a letter of peace. The king's officials had detained them for a long time while en route and quarreled with them over the titles of both sovereigns. The vacuous name of *neighbor*, which the tsar had given Batory, was rejected: they wanted parity, and made no secret of the fact that the agreement forged in Moscow had gone unimplemented.

The emissaries were received honorably, but Batory, sitting on his grand throne, did not care to rise for them, nor inquire as to the tsar's health. Indifferent to their displeasure he ordered that they be told they could leave the palace and return home, and that a Lithuanian courier would furnish Ivan with the king's reply. Our emissaries departed, and after dispatching the official Lopatinskii with a letter for Moscow, the king set out after them with his army.

But Ivan was no longer in the capital. He knew what had happened at the Warsaw Sejm, although he had not heard from Karpov and Golovin in a long time. He had heard of the powerful, unexampled arming of Lithuania and Poland and did not waste any time. In a general council with the boyars and the priesthood he declared that *a year of great bloodshed* had begun and that, after requesting divine favor, for the nation and for himself, he had embarked on this venture into German and Lithuanian lands.

He had moved all his legions to the west and assigned them routes and locations, while leaving troops in 80 towns and cities for their defense, as well as on the banks of the Volga, Don, Oka, Dnieper and Dvina. He ordered these units, both European and Asiatic, to join up with his main forces at Novgorod and Pskov. In addition to the Russians, there were Circassian and Shevkal princes, princes of the Mordvi and the Nogai, princes and mirzas of the ancient Golden Horde and of Astrakhan and Kazan.

Day and night they marched towards Lakes Ilmen and Peipus. The roads were jammed with infantry and cavalry. These troop movements continued during winter, spring and part of summer. Finally, after entrusting Moscow to Prince Andrei Petrovich Kurakin, the tsar took all his boyars, Duma nobles and a multitude of secretaries with him for military and civilian tasks. He departed the capital in July for Novgorod, where all the voivodes were waiting for further orders.

Our emissaries now came to him from Lithuania to report that Batory had rejected the truce document and was marching on Russia. They said that the king had 40,000 troops, but that this number was being augmented by suitable troops from Transylvania, from the German lands and by Lithuanian freemen. This was the force that planned to trample Russia! Yet the tsar had 40,000 men in just his own special legion alone: court nobles, boyar cadets, musketeers and Cossacks, in addition to the main Novgorod and Pskov units, commanded by Grand Prince Semyon Bekbulatovich, the princes Ivan Mstislavskii, the Shuiskiis, Nogtev, Trubetskii, and many other voivodes.

A single word from Ivan could send this mass of men striking into Lithuania, where the people and the nobility were not very

Chapter Ten

favorably inclined towards Stefan's martial schemes. Inwardly they desired peace with Russia, and cries of horror resounded from the Dvina to the Bug.

But the shades of Shuiskii, Serebryanyi and Vorotynskii haunted Ivan's dreams, amongst the graves of Novgorod filled with victims of his wrath: he doubted the zeal of his voivodes and his own populace. Trust is a characteristic of pure consciences only. Having destroyed all his heroes, the tsar now spared his unworthy voivodes: the princes Ivan Golitsyn, Palitskii and Thedor Sheremetev, who were marked with the shame of their flight from Wenden, were once again put in command of the troops.

Ivan saw a perilous war ahead of him and did not dare punish them, lest others likewise betray him and flee to Batory. With this lack of faith in his legions' commanders, Ivan considered delay and irresolution to be prudent. He wished to frighten the enemy solely by the numbers of troops he had assembled. The tsar still hoped for peace but expected he might have to use the sword.

The latter contingency came to pass. When he found out that Batory's official, Lopatinskii, was traveling to Moscow, the tsar ordered him halted at Dorogobuzh. This courier had brought Stefan's letter to him, which was very much to the point: terse and dry, but sagacious. Stefan had written from Vilnius on 26 June that our letter of truce was deceitful, that the Muscovite boyars had deceptively included an article concerning Livonia, that Ivan, was making war in the king's lands while talking of peace and that he had concocted the fable of his descent from the Roman caesars.

The king said that Russia had illegitimately taken Novgorod and the Severskii region from Lithuania, as well as Smolensk and Polotsk, that Karpov and Golovin had not done or said anything before they departed Krakow; that further embassies would be futile and that he (Stefan), with God's help, had resolved to seek justice through arms. Simultaneously the tsar was informed that Batory had already transgressed Russian borders.

After he honorably declared war on us, Stefan had consulted with his nobles and commanders in the settlement of Svir as to where and how to begin it. Many of them counseled invading

Livonia, expelling the Russians and laying siege to Pskov, an important, wealthy city, and, they believed, poorly fortified. The king was of a different opinion: he argued that it would be difficult to carry the war into Livonia, which had been laid waste, imprudent to leave it in their rear and dangerous to withdraw from its border.

It would be better to take Polotsk, the key to Livonia and Lithuania itself. Such a conquest would be a dependable shield for their rear, expose Russia to them, provide secure communications with Riga via the Dvina, and also furnish benefits for both military operations and commerce. It would be necessary to conquer Livonia from the outside. Polotsk was strong, but taking it would be all the more glorious and desirable; it would encourage their troops and frighten their enemies.

The great man spoke, and they took heed. Stefan's army was like Hannibal's: composed of men whose languages, customs and religions were different from one another. They came from Germany, Hungary, Poland, ancient Slavic Galicia, Volhynia and the Dnieper region; there were also Krivskie and indigenous Lithuanians. Batory knew how to give them unity and a challenge.

Setting out from Svir, he published a manifest to the Russian people. He declared that he was drawing his sword on the Muscovite tsar, not on Russia's peaceful inhabitants, who would be spared and favored in any event. He said that he loved valor but hated barbarism. He desired victory, not destruction and futile bloodshed. He did as he said: never had war been less disruptive and more humane for farmers and citizens than Batory's campaign. He spoke like a Christian, but acted like a politician; he wanted to get the inhabitants on his side, for he wanted lasting victories. At the end of August, Batory laid siege to Polotsk.

POLOTSK AND SOKOL CAPTURED

There were few troops there, since the tsar had not expected a powerful attack across the Lithuanian frontier; he believed that Livonia would be the significant theater of military operations. However, Polotsk had long been renowned for its fortifications, which had been improved and extended since 1561. Two fortifications, the Musketeers' and the so-called Stockade, around which flowed the Dvina and Polota were joined by a bridge. They had been erected on precipitous heights and served as protection for the main city, in addition to its deep ditches, wooden walls and towers. Prince Vasilii Ivanovich Telyatevskii was in charge of the city, Pyotr Volynskii commanded the Stockade, and Prince Dmitrii Shcherbatyi and the secretary Rzhevskii were in the [other] fortress.

They had sufficient provisions and munitions, great zeal and valor, but very little skill, according to our books of ranks. In order to frighten the enemy and leave themselves no choice but victory or death, they took some Lithuanians prisoner and ordered them killed, tied to logs and thrown in the Dvina for the king's army to see.

The battle started from the city; the outnumbered Russians torched it themselves and retreated into the citadel, where they bravely held out for more than three weeks. The times were propitious for them: the rains poured down. The besiegers' artillery was ineffective, their baggage trains loaded with grain sank into the mud, horses collapsed, the troops suffered from hunger and their assaults on the citadel were ineffectual. Could the tsar take advantage of this situation?

Ivan was in Pskov. On 1 August, he detailed his voivodes, the princes Khilkov and Beznin, to cross the Dvina into Courland with 20,000 Asiatic cavalry, tasked only with risk-free devastation. He then sent more troops to defend Karelia and the Izherskie lands, which was being laid waste by the Swedes. Next he reinforced his garrisons in Livonia, yet still had so many troops that he could have boldly marched on Vilnius and Warsaw.

Alarmed by news of Batory's unexpected siege of Polotsk, he ordered Shein and the princes Lykov, Palitskii and Krivoborskii to hasten to the city with units of boyar cadets and Don Cossacks and to enter it either by ruse or force. If this were impossible, they were to occupy the fortress of Sokol in order to harass the enemy and interfere with his communications with Lithuania while we awaited our main army. Shein approached Batory's camp. He did not dare to do battle, but occupied Sokol after spreading the rumor that Ivan himself would soon be there with a powerful army.

But the king was unperturbed: he perceived merely the necessity of resolving the outcome of the siege more quickly. He realized the ineffectiveness of his artillery batteries and proposed to some Hungarian daredevils that they climb the heights to the citadel and set fire to its walls, promising them glory and gold. The weather was clear and dry, as if it were trying to augment their audacity. They charged at the walls with flaming torches. Many fell dead, but some reached their goal, and within five minutes the fortress was in flames.

Now, crying victory, all the Hungarians joined the assault, disobeying their officers and the king. Showered by cannonballs, bullets and firebrands, they broke into the fortress through its flaming, falling walls, but the Russians unexpectedly stood to face their enemy, tearing into them and forcing them out. The Hungarians attacked once more, reinforced by throngs of Germans and Poles, but once again yielded to our fury.

Forgetting his personal safety, the king himself was in the midst of this bloody battle, trying to reestablish order and to restrain and reunite his fleeing troops. The hour of decision was at hand. If Shein and the princes Lykov and Palitskii were to strike into Lithuania, then they might save both the fortress and Russia's honor. They could see the conflagration and from afar they could see the battle itself and hear the loud cries of the besieged, at the moment victorious, summoning their brothers in Sokol.

However, the perspicacious Batory held the road. He sent out fresh troops to Drissa to check the Russians if they moved on Polotsk. Now the Don Cossacks betrayed our voivodes in Sokol. They selfishly departed for home, leaving Shein and his comrades to apologize for them. Stefan, who had anticipated their attack for a whole day and night, was much relieved and hastened to remedy his lack of success.

After beating off the assault, the Russians extinguished the fire in the fortress, while the enemy made new gun emplacements, new trenches approaching the partially destroyed walls and once again set fire to the towers with red-hot cannonballs. The besieged continued to hold out stubbornly for several days. They could scarcely breathe due to the smoke and heat.

They were laid low by Lithuanian cannon balls and from exhaustion due to continually putting out fires. They were waiting for assistance and relief, but finally, completely dispirited, the troops asked for negotiations. At first our voivodes and the worthy Archbishop Kiprian did not want to hear of it, saying,

"We do not fear Stefan's malice, but the tsar's wrath!"

With the desperation of the brave they considered blowing up the fortress so as to bury themselves in its ruins, but the pusillanimous Pyotr Volynskii and the musketeers did not let them carry this out and proposed conditions to Stefan. Either out of respect for the valor they had shown or fearing to lose time, Batory agreed to let the officers and men in the stockade and the fortress return to Russia with their families and possessions; he promised great favors for those wishing to join him.

The voivodes did not want to participate in this agreement; together with the archbishop, they locked themselves up in the old Sofiya Church, from which they were forcibly extracted and presented to Batory, subdued, but not abased. A historian and eyewitness writes that the Russians, while vividly perceiving the king's magnanimity and humanity, in no way wished to serve him, that almost all of them, expecting inevitable execution by an angry tsar, marched steadfastly back to him and did not pay attention to Stefan's promised blandishments:

"proof of their surprising patriotism," this historian writes.

But despite the conditions, Stefan was in no hurry to release these prisoners, as if afraid to return such loyal and valiant warriors to his enemy. After the fortress, full of bodies, had been ordered cleaned up, the king entered it triumphantly: he declared Polotsk to be the domain of a Lithuanian voivode. He ordered a splendid church of the Roman faith to be constructed there, while leaving the Sofiya Cathedral Greek. He gave them a former prelate of Vitebsk as bishop and provided a document confirming freedom for our faith. He had further conquests in Russia in mind and wanted to please its populace through this prudent toleration, in spite of his Jesuit favorites. He gave the latter rich estates and lands in Belorussia, with the obligation to improve the morals of the people by instruction and example.

From this time on, our ancient Polotsk, appanage of Vladimir and Rogneda, which had been easily taken and ingloriously lost by Ivan, for 18 years a district of the Muscovite state, became once again a Lithuanian possession and remained so until the time of the immortal Ekaterina [Catherine the Great].

Stefan dispatched troops to Sokol, and light cavalry to Pskov itself, to observe the movements of Ivan's army. On 19 September, the Lithuanians laid siege to Sokol and on the 25th they set fire to its towers and assaulted its walls to the blaring of trumpets. The Russians tried to put out the fires, but a great number of flimsy buildings quickly ignited, so that no safe place remained for the five or six thousand troops there. They made a sally, fighting for a long time, but at last yielded to superior force and turned back, pressed into the fortress with the Germans.

A desperate slaughter commenced – desperate for both sides, since the Russians closed the gates and dropped the iron portcullis, leaving no hope of escape for the enemy or themselves. They did battle amidst the flames and were choked and burned, until the Lithuanians and the Poles broke into the city and virtually wiped out our troops, some 4,000. Only Sheremetev and a small number of boyar cadets were taken prisoner. In a frenzy of malice the Germans cut up our dead, butchering the corpse of Shein and many other Russians. The Lithuanians captured Krasnyi, Kozyan, Sitna, Turovl and Neshcherda; laid waste to the Severskie lands as far as Starodub, and burned 2,000 settlements in the Smolensk district, while the tsar remained motionless in Pskov!

KURBSKII'S LETTER

At this time, as good Russians were perishing, consigned as sacrifices to the enemy by Ivan's fearfulness, and as our homeland was grieving in undeserved humiliation, one Russian, once his country's favorite, was celebrating, to his eternal shame: Andrei Kurbskii. Having lost the name of Russian for his crime, he maliciously sought new consolation in vengeance and found it, together with another Muscovite fugitive, Vladimir Zabolotskii, under Batory's banners. He energetically facilitated the success of the king's arms, and from the fresh ashes of the conquered fortress of

Polotsk, steaming with Russian blood, he wrote a reply to Ivan's letter to him from Wolmar.

"Where are your victories?" he wrote, "They are in the graves of the heroes, the real voivodes of Holy Rus, whom you destroyed. The king, with a few thousand men, solely by the valor of his forces, is taking the districts and strongholds in your realm that we once seized and fortified, while you, with your huge army, just sit, hiding in the forests, or flee, pursued by nothing but your conscience, which condemns you for your lawlessness.

"These are the fruits of the precepts given you by the false prelate Vassian! You rule alone, without wise advisors; you fight alone, without proud voivodes. And why is that?

"Instead of the people's love and blessings that were once sweet to your heart, you have won hatred and universal malediction; instead of martial glory, you are intoxicated with shame. There is no good realm that lacks good nobles, and without skilled commanders, a huge army is just a herd of sheep, scattered by the sound of the wind and the falling of leaves. Flatterers are not councilors, and dwarves with crippled souls are not commanders.

"Is it not clear that the judgment of God is already upon the tyrant? Behold famine and plague, the sword of the barbarian, the ashes of the capital and – worst of all – ignominy, ignominy for the monarch, who was once so renowned! Is this what we wanted, what we have prepared, through our fervor and sanguinary service, for our ancient homeland? . . ."

The letter concludes with praise for Stefan's valor, a prediction of the impending doom of the tsar's entire house, and these words:

"I place my finger to my mouth, I wonder and weep!"

Moved by hatred for Ivan, Kurbskii could justify himself in his own mind but not in his conscience, which troubled him until the end of his life. He ruled towns and villages in Volhynia, but found peace neither in wealth nor fame; he married a Dubrovitskaya princess, but did not love her. He sought consolation in friendship and in study; knowing Latin, he translated Cicero; he wrote about the glorious conquest of Kazan, the Livonian war and the tortures of Ivan, whom he outlived.

In his old age, he still missed Russia, calling it, with feeling, his *beloved homeland.* The gloom of ignorance covers his last days, as well as the grave of this man, who was distinguished by military glory, intellect, eloquence – and inglorious criminality!

Ivan did not reply to Kurbskii at this time, for he had nothing to boast about, nor anything with which to threaten him under the circumstances, with the disarray of his soul. He wrote to his secretary Andrei Shchelkalov in Moscow that he should announce the enemy's successes coolly and calmly to its residents. Summoning the citizens, the wise secretary told them,

"Good people! Know that the king has taken Polotsk and torched Sokol – sad tidings, but prudence demands firmness of us. Nothing is permanent in this world – fortune betrays even great sovereigns. Polotsk is in Stefan's hands, but all of Livonia is in ours. Some Russians have fallen, but many more Lithuanians have died. We shall comfort ourselves in this minor setback by recalling all the victories and conquests of our Orthodox tsar!"

Assured of peace and quiet in Moscow, Ivan ordered his boyars to write to the Lithuanian Duma that he was thinking of marching against the king at once, but his councilors, regretting Christian tears, had entreated him, although not without great effort, to cease all hostilities, and that Stefan would show true humanity and love of justice if he were to stop the bloodshed and enter into negotiations with the tsar concerning a permanent peace, kinship and true friendship.

A courier was sent to Vilnius with such a letter of peace. Batory likewise sent an officer to Ivan, but with a very rude letter, declaring that he was battling for Livonia and to restrain Ivan's impetuous love of power. He demanded that Lopatinskii, who had not been allowed home from Dorogobuzh, be freed in accordance with the Law of Nations. This enemy courier was dining with the tsar in Novgorod and treated like a nobleman from a friendly power, which heretofore had not been the case.

"I do not care," Ivan replied to the king, "to respond to your obloquy, for I wish to be in brotherhood with you. I am giving a letter of safe conduct for your emissaries, whom I await with good will. Meanwhile, let there be peace in Livonia and on all the borders! And as a token of peace, release the Russian prisoners, for exchange or ransom."

This is what Ivan wrote, and it was sent to the king with a new courier and also with Lopatinskii, who had been quickly released. The tsar was then occupied for several months with his voivodes' quarrels over precedence. He did not consider marching against Stefan, since he was satisfied with the partial success of our defensive scheme in Livonia, where the Russians, in a heated engagement had finally captured the notorious brigand Hannibal (who was later executed in Pskov). They also bravely repulsed the Swedes from Narva and chased them as far as Revel. Thus ended 1579. The tsar was now in Moscow, and he was not idle.

In January 1580, he summoned the most eminent churchmen to the capitol: Archbishop Aleksandr of Novgorod, Ieremii of Kazan, David of Rostov, and all the bishops, archimandrites and abbots, as well as those monks who were most renowned for intellect or piety. The tsar formally declared to them that the Church and Orthodoxy itself were in peril, that countless enemies were rising up against Russia – unbelieving Turks, Nogai and the khan from one side and Lithuania, Poland, Hungary, Germany and Sweden from the other, who, like wild animals, were opening their jaws to swallow us up.

> 1580 CONFERENCE IN MOSCOW

He said that he, his son, his nobles and his voivodes were working day and night to save the nation, but that the clergy were also obliged to assist him in this great task – we had people, but not a sufficiently large treasury; our troops were meager and in want, while the monasteries were growing rich. The sovereign was asking a sacrifice from the priesthood, and that the Most High would bless their ardent patriotism. This proposal was both important and fraught with difficulties.

Ivan's eminent grandfather had wanted to get his hands on churchly wealth, but stayed the thought when he encountered powerful objections from the prelates. The grandson moderated his request, and the council agreed on a document whereby *princely* lands and villages that had at any time been bequeathed to metropolitans, bishops, monasteries or churches, or had been purchased by them, would henceforth belong to the state, but all the rest would remain the inalienable property of the Church in perpetuity. In the future they should no longer acquire real property, whether by donation or purchase, and lands mortgaged by them would likewise be surrendered to the treasury.

By so easily increasing the property and revenue of the state, Ivan was able to keep increasing the size of the army. Officers rode from district to district with lists of boyar cadets, seeking out and inflicting corporal punishment all those who were hiding or avoiding service. These would be sent under bond to Pskov or Novgorod, where the main army was stationed. This shortened the time available for offensive operations – for Russians always like to take the field when others are leaving it to go home because of bad weather or frosts.

Although Batory had not considered giving us a truce, fall and winter put an end to his glittering successes. The mercenaries demanded their pay and the king's own troops wanted leave. After stationing troops in the open spaces near the border, Stefan hastened to Vilnius and the Sejm in Warsaw to prepare new means for victory, to enjoy his glory, to test and put the delegates to shame for their ingratitude, and to overcome all obstacles to achieve his goals.

The citizens and the nobility in Vilnius greeted him with loud blessings, but in Warsaw many of the pans did so with somber faces, and the displeased grumbling of those who loved their own legitimate and illegitimate power more than they loved their country, which their willfulness, self-satisfaction and greed had weakened. Great men are both praised and maligned.

Frightened by the king's powerful will and strong measures, the pans complained of his absolute rule and trust in foreigners. They spread rumors that he was fighting only so he could impose taxes on the land and that he was secretly scheming to leave for Transylvania with the rich royal treasury. The effect of these calumnies might have been the rejection of the state grants necessary for the war, but when Batory appeared before the Sejm, slander ceased. He said what he had done and would do: all of his proposals were unanimously approved and new troops were ordered recruited.

The tsar, however, was soliciting peace. Our heralds returned with the reply that the king did not even want to hear of an embassy to Moscow, although he was condescendingly prepared to receive Ivan in his [Stefan's] capital if we were really disposed towards moderation and honorable negotiations. He also said that prisoners would not be released during a time of war, that they were in a Christian land and therefore safe and unoppressed. Ivan once more wrote a friendly letter to Stefan:

"In Moscow's truce documents," he said, "there are *different* words, inserted with the knowledge and consent of your emissaries. You could have rejected this agreement, but why do you accuse us of deceit? Why did you so rudely send our emissaries back from Krakow empty-handed and write to us with such caustic expressions? We shall forget these words of anger and your enmity and malice. It is not in Lithuania and not in Poland, but in Moscow that we have of old concluded agreements between these powers and Russia. Do not demand something new! It is here that my boyars and your plenipotentiaries have resolved all difficulties to the mutual satisfaction of both our countries."

But in case of Batory's recalcitrance or open preparation to resume hostilities, Moscow's herald was to tell him secretly that the tsar had agreed to send his boyars to Vilnius or Warsaw. This abasement was futile. The king replied that he was giving Ivan five weeks and would await our emissaries in peaceful inactivity, even though his army was prepared to invade Russia and was burning with impatient valor. The tsar's eminent officials – the steward Prince Ivan Sitskii, the Duma courtier Pivov and the secretary Petelin were on their way to Vilnius when Moscow learned that Batory and his army had transgressed Russia's borders.

"The designated period has expired," he wrote to the tsar. "You must hand over to Lithuania Novgorod, Pskov, [Velikie] Luki and all the Vitebsk and Polotsk districts, as well as all of Livonia if you want peace."

| AUGUST |

> EMBASSY TO THE
> EMPEROR AND THE POPE

This attack seemed perfidious to Ivan, at any rate, he had not expected it at the end of the year. He consulted with his boyars and hastened to send his herald Shevrigin to the emperor and even to the Pope to convince them to support us. In the letter to the former, he tries to show that Stefan was making war on Russia because of its close friendship with Maximilian, and requested that Rudolf keep his promise and send plenipotentiaries to Moscow to reestablish the alliance against common enemies.

He then complained to the Pope about Batory's malice and perfidy; he proposed that the Pope exhort the king to break his hateful ties with the Turks. Our emissaary tried to persuade him that Ivan ardently wished to join with the other European sovereigns to mobilize against the sultan, and to this end wished to have permanent, amicable relations with Rome.

Having strength in his arms, but faintheartedness in his soul, Ivan abased himself by seeking aid from afar, which would be both unnecessary and unreliable. He did not dare to take the field himself, and positioned troops solely for defense. Not knowing where Batory might strike, the tsar sent his legions to Novgorod, Pskov, Kokenhusen and Smolensk. He occupied the banks of the Oka near Serpukhov because he feared the khan. This state of ignorance continued two or three weeks, and then Batory again showed up where he was not expected.

Stefan's historian describes in lavish eloquence the organization and morale of the king's troops, inspired by the genius of its commander. His cavalry was led by senators and the best voivodes; many eminent officers, both citizens and courtiers, served in it alongside simple cavalrymen. The greater part of the infantry were new levies who had not yet seen combat, while seasoned German and Sedmigrad warriors formed its firm foundation. Among them, distinguished by his heartiness, was our turncoat, the Danish commander Georg Fahrensbach, who knew the Russians' strengths and weaknesses, having commanded Ivan's Livonian guards.

The enemy marched through swamps and wild forests that had not seen an army in 150 years. Only Vitovt, in 1458, had been able to open a route here to the Novgorod districts, and some places still bore his name. Batory, like Vitovt, cut through the forests, building corduroy roads, bridges and rafts, struggling with difficulties and putting up with insufficiencies. He emerged to take the fortresses of both Velizh and Usvyat, and another filled with provisions.

After defeating one of our light cavalry detachments, he set out for Velikie Luki at the end of August. This city, beautifully situated, wealthy and commercial, was the key to the old southern possessions of the state of Novgorod. It promised rich booty to the greedy troops, and with its proximity to Vitebsk and other Lithuanian fortresses, was convenient to besiege. There were only six or seven thousand Russians there, but the voivode Prince Zhilkov and his sufficiently numerous legions were in Toropets.

There were bold sallies, some even successful; in one of them the besieged captured the royal banner, but Zhilkov avoided a general battle. He was everywhere on the lookout for Lithuanians. He seized them on patrols and destroyed them in whole groups, while he waited for the other voivodes, from Smolensk, Pskov and Novgorod.

At this point, when it was essential for Russia to rise up and throttle Batory's audacity, Ivan's plenipotentiaries, Prince Sitskii and Pivov, hastened to Stefan's camp for a humiliating treaty. The king, majestic and proud, received them in his tent; he remained seated with his hat on when they presented the tsar's greetings and did not deign to speak a courteous word to them.

Our emissaries requested that the king raise the siege at once: instead of replying, the Lithuanian cannons opened fire. Our emissaries showed forbearance: they said that this was the first time a Muscovite sovereign had entered into negotiations with Lithuania outside of Moscow, and that he would call Stefan *brother* if he would return Polotsk to us.

However, then they agreed not ask even for Polotsk and offered up Courland and 24 towns and cities in Livonia proper. But Stefan wanted all the districts of Livonia, and even Velikie Luki, Smolensk, Pskov and Novgorod.

Conquest of Velikie Luki

Sitskii and Pivov declared they could not yield anything more and requested leave to go, or permission to write to Ivan. A courier was dispatched to Moscow that same day, September 5th. Part of the fortress blew up due to the explosion of a tower filled with gunpowder. Fire completed the destruction of the walls and the enemy's swords doomed the Russians. The king took possession of the site, damp with their blood and covered with torn bodies and limbs. He ordered that the fortifications of this important place be restored immediately, then fell on Zhilkov near Toropets and defeated him.

The following tsarist officials were captured in this heated engagement: Grigorii Nashchokin, who was employed as an emissary; the Duma noble Cheremisinov, one of Ivan's favorites; and 200 boyar cadets. Meanwhile, the Lithuanian noble Filon Kmita was nearing Smolensk with 9,000 cavalry, hoping to torch its suburbs.

He was met in the field, however, by the brave local deputies Danilo Nogtev and Prince Thedor Mosalskii. Kmita fled, abandoning his banners, baggage train and 60 light cannons. These, our only trophies, were sent to Moscow along with 380 prisoners, and Ivan accordingly rewarded the voivodes with gold medals.

Although it was deep autumn, Batory still vigorously continued the war. Nevel and Ozerishche surrendered to him. Zavoloche, fortified by its location and the bravery of its voivode Saburov, held out and cost the enemy dearly. Finally, it too, surrendered; Batory let the Russians leave it with honor. With this he concluded his campaign. His troops were weak from their labors and from illness; the king himself lay sick in Polotsk, but all the same, appeared, wan and pale, at the Warsaw Sejm to give account of his exploits.

"Rejoice in victory," he told the pans. "But this is not enough; you must be able to take advantage of it. It seems fate is handing us all of Muscovy: audacity and hope lead to greatness. Do you wish to be moderate? At least take Livonia, which is the main goal of this war. Joined permanently to the Polish empire, it will remain for posterity as a notable monument to our valor. We have had no peace up till now."

In requesting new assistance in men and money, the king complained to the pans that they had not given him the means to carry on the war continuously; time was being wasted in his traveling back and forth and in the Sejm's noisy debates; the troops were losing their morale in idleness while the Russians were taking it easy. Batory had indeed lost time, but his Lithuanian voivodes still menaced the Russians in winter: in a sudden raid they had taken Kholm and torched Staraya Rusa after enriching themselves with its booty. In Livonia, they had taken Schmilten and, together with the renegade Magnus, some of the possessions of Derpt and even Pskov.

> CALAMITIES FOR RUSSIA

The Swedes showed up from another direction: they took Kexholm and laid siege to Padis, where there were a small number of Russians were weak with hunger, eating dogs and cats, and even the corpses of dead infants, and yet they shot down a Swedish officer who proposed they surrender the fortress to them. The aged voivode Danilo Chikhachev was holding out there with a handful of desperate men.

When the Swedes took the castle they found not men, but wraiths within. They killed everyone except for the young officer, Prince Mikhailo Sitskii. Over the course of the winter, they also acquired Wesenberg through negotiation. There were about a thousand Muscovite musketeers there, who departed with only some wooden icons.

Russia appeared weak, almost disarmed, yet it had upwards of 80 military camps or fortresses full of troops and equipment, and a large number of field troops in addition, ready to charge into battle. It was an amazing spectacle, worthy of note by the most distant posterity and by the peoples and rulers of the land, striking evidence of how much tyranny lays low the spirit, blinds the mind with fearful visions and destroys the power of a sovereign and his realm. The Russians were not disloyal – their tsar betrayed *them*!

Hiding out in Aleksandrovskaya Sloboda, he wrote to the chief voivodes in Rzhev and Vyazma, to Grand Prince Simeon Bekbulatovich of Tver, and to Prince Ivan Mstislavskii:

"Busy yourselves with the affairs of the realm and the land, as the Most High gives you to understand, to make Russia more secure. I am placing all my hope in God and in your zeal."

However, the voivodes had been disconcerted by the tsar's irresolution and were afraid to act decisively on their own. They sent out detachments to observe and to defend the border, but only occasionally ventured into enemy territory. Princes Mikhailo Katyrev Rostovskii, Dmitrii Khvorostinin, Shcherbatoi, Turenin and Buturlin joined up in Mozhaisk and moved on Dubrovno, Orsha, Shklov, Mogilyov and Radoml. They burned the uezds and outskirts of those cities, defeated the Lithuanians beneath the walls of Shklov (where the valiant Buturlin fell at its very gates) and took a large number of prisoners to Smolensk. Ivan gave them gold medals, but failed to take heart, as we shall see.

> IVAN'S SEVENTH MARRIAGE

At this moment, in which, in an excess of pride the hero Batory was promising all of Russia to the noble pans, the tsar was celebrating weddings: he married off his second son, Theodor, to Irina, sister of the noted Boris Godunov, while he himself married for the sixth or seventh time, without any churchly dispensation, a young woman, Mariya, the daughter of Thedor Thedorovich Nagoi.

These two marriages had unexpected and horrible consequences for Russia that were the cause of protracted evil. Godunov, promoted now to the rank of boyar, could perhaps now espy dimly in the distance the bold goal of his thirst for power, hitherto unexampled in our history. As a favorite of the sovereign, he had only one man to envy: Bogdan Yakovlevich Belskii, the tsar's armorer and personal servant, who was day and night the constant guardian of Ivan's person.

As brother-in-law of the heir apparent, Godunov shared respect and honor with the tsar's relatives by marriage: with Prince Ivan Mikhailovich Glinskii and with the Nagois, who had quickly filled Ivan's palace. As Duma councilor, he saw still more senior boyars: Mstislavskiis, Shuiskiis, Trubetskiis, Golitsyns, Yurievs and Saburovs, but not one of them with an administrative mind equal to his own. These two fateful weddings were celebrated in

Chapter Ten

Aleksandrovskaya Sloboda by Ivan with only those closest to him – these were days of sorrow for our country.

Two future tsars and a vile traitor of Russia hid in the guise of diligent servants and flatterers. Godunov was Mariya's best man, Prince Vasilii Ivanovich Shuiskii was Ivan's, and Prince Mikhailo Mikhailovich Krivoi Saltykov led the wedding procession. Also feasting with them was another, less important, but equally contemptible traitor, a relative by marriage of Malyuta Skuratov, one David Belskii, who defected to Stefan a few months later.

Except for one man whose downfall was noteworthy and approved by all, we do not know who was disgraced or executed in these times. We refer to the physician Bomelius, hated advisor in the tsar's murders. Not long before Ivan's marriage to Mariya Nagoya, he had been accused of secret relations with Batory and was publicly incinerated in Moscow. Others write that some Russians lost patience with the evils of this calumniator; they had sought and found a way to destroy him. They say that he, whose calumnies had doomed so many innocents, himself became a victim of calumny, to the glory of divine justice.

Perhaps informers' reports, whether true or false, now touched even Belskii; perhaps, like Kurbskii, he departed an innocent, but became a criminal when he began to provide Batory with counsel detrimental to Russia.

From unhappy Aleksandrovskaya Sloboda (where the tyrant usually rampaged or feasted, terrifying his loyal subjects or trembling before his country's enemies), the tsar, after learning of the attack on Velikie Luki, gave new orders to Sitskii and Pivov, who followed Batory from place to place as humble and pitiable witnesses of his triumphs. In Warsaw they yielded him a few more Livonian districts in exchange for Russian towns Stefan had taken, and tried to persuade the king to send emissaries to Moscow for a peace treaty and to stop the war, but the king ordered them to return to the tsar with his response:

1581

"There will be no embassy, no peace, no truce until the Russian army clears out of Livonia!"

More and more obsequious, Ivan, in a flattering letter, called Stefan *brother* and complained that the Lithuanians had not ceased to menace Russia with their attacks. The tsar implored him not to gather troops for the summer, not to exhaust his national treasury. He quickly sent the Duma courtiers Pushkin and Pisemskii to the king: he had ordered them to not only be humble and meek in negotiations, but even (an unheard of humiliation) endure beatings!

> HIS UNPRECEDENTED ABASEMENT

Thus Ivan drank the cup of shame, which he, not Russia, had earned! Our new tractability produced new demands. Batory, in addition to Livonia, wanted the cities of Severskii, Smolensk, Pskov and Novgorod, or at least Sebezh. He also wanted 400,000 Hungarian gold pieces from Russia, and sent a herald to Moscow for a definite reply. Finally, Ivan expressed irritation. On receiving the Lithuanian herald, he did not get up or inquire as to the king's health. He wrote to Stefan,

> LETTER TO BATORY AND HIS REPLY

"We, the humble sovereign of all Russia, *by the will of God, and not by the will of rebellious men* . . . If Poland and Lithuania had hereditary monarchs like us, they would be horrified at this bloodshed: you have no Christianity in you! Neither Olgerd nor Vitovt violated truces, but you – after you concluded one in Moscow, you and others of our malefactors (Kurbskii, et al.) attacked Russia. You took Polotsk by treachery and in a formal manifesto, tempted my people to betray their tsar, their conscience and God!

"You wage war not with the sword, but with treachery, and with such savage brutality! Your troops mutilate the dead . . . Our emissaries come to you with peaceable words and you set [Velikie] Luki afire with red-hot cannonballs (a new and inhumane invention); they speak to you of friendship and love and you destroy and exterminate!

"As a Christian, I could give you Livonia, but would you be satisfied with it? I hear that you have sworn to your nobles to annex all the conquests of my father and grandfather to Lithuania. How could we agree to that? I want peace, you want slaughter; I yield something, you want more, and what is unheard of – you illegally and without conscience laid waste to my land and now you demand gold of me! . . . Man of blood, remember God!"

But Ivan, despite his vexation, still ceded to Lithuania all the Russian fortresses that Batory had conquered. He only wanted to keep eastern Estonia and Livonia, Narva, Weissenstein and Derpt, and to conclude a seven-year truce on these conditions. Batory's response was to take the field a third time and send a letter filled with caustic reproaches, as voluminous as it was improper for a monarch.

"You boast of your hereditary monarchy," wrote Stefan. "I do not envy you, for I think it better to obtain a crown by merit rather than to be born to the crown through a Glinskaya, the daughter of Sigismund's enemy. You reproach me for mutilating the *dead*, which I did not do.

"But you torture the *living*: which is worse? You condemn me for imagined perfidy, you, the composer of counterfeit agreements, perverting the meaning through deceit and secret additions that favor only your insane love of power! You call traitors those of your voivodes, honorable prisoners whom we were obliged to release to you because they are loyal to their homeland!

"We take lands by martial valor and have no need of the services of your imagined enemies. But where are you, *god* of the Russian land, as you order your unhappy slaves to call you? We have not yet seen your face, or your gonfalon with the cross by which you boast. You do not frighten your enemies with your crosses, only miserable Russians. Do you regret the spilling of Christian blood? Name the time and place and appear there on your horse to fight me in single combat, and may God crown the righteous man with victory!"

Batory would not agree to leave an inch of land in Livonia for Russia. He did not wish to converse further with our emissaries and expelled them from his army camp. He mockingly sent Ivan a German publication in the Latin language concerning Russian princes and his own reign, to prove, as he explained, that Moscow's ancient sovereigns had been tributaries of the khans of Perekop [in the Crimea], and not descendants of Caesar Augustus. Stefan also advised him to read the 50th psalm of David, and as a Christian, recognize himself. A Lithuanian courier gave Stefan's abusive letter to Ivan. After hearing it read, the tsar softly told him,

"We will answer our *brother*, King Stefan." He then stood up and added respectfully, "Convey our salutations to your sovereign!"

That is, Ivan had been freshly scared by Lithuanian troop movements and again wished to seek peace, placing his hopes in an important intermediary who had now come between him and Batory.

Moscow's herald Shevrigin, who had been sent to Vienna and Rome, had now returned. Weak and happy-go-lucky Rudolf had responded that he could do nothing without informing the imperial princes, and that his nobles who were supposed to go to Moscow to conclude an alliance were either dead or ailing. But Pope Gregory XIII, who was renowned for his fervor to extend the Roman faith – who had illuminated Rome with sportive lights when he learned of the atrocities of St. Bartholomew's Day in France – expressed great pleasure [at Shevrigin's proposal], seeing, as he believed, a chance to annex Russia to his extensive flock.

Back in 1576 he had wanted to send the priest Rudolf Klenchen, who knew Russian customs and speech, to Moscow with very astute and cunning written instructions according to which he was to announce to the tsar's nobles that the Pope had heard of Ivan's power, victories, heroism, wisdom, piety and all of his other great qualities, amazing and obliging in equal measure – he was now fulfilling at last his long-held fervent desire to show such an unusual monarch his heartfelt friendship and hope that he would be pleased to pacify those bitter enemies of Christendom, the Ottomans, and restore the integrity of the Holy Faith on earth.

It is probable that the emperor's emissary Kobenzel had suggested this idea to Gregory, for he praised in Europe not only the Russians' power, but their alleged goodwill towards the Latin Church; in his report to the Viennese ministry, he said,

"They are unjustifiably considered to be enemies of our faith. This may have been the case in the past, but Russians now love to talk about Rome and want to see it. They know that the great martyrs of Christendom, whom the Russians revere even more than we, suffered and are buried in this city; they know better than many Germans and Frenchmen the sanctity of Loretta, and when they heard that I was of the old faith and not that of Luther, whom they hate, they had no misgivings about taking me to see the icon of Nikolai the Wonderworker, which is this people's most important sacred object."

However, it seems that Klenchen was never in Moscow and the instructions he was given are found only in the Roman archives. The Pope received Shevrigin warmly, giving him golden chains and long velvet robes. He ordered the renowned Jesuit theologian Antonio Possevino to travel to Batory and on to Moscow to make peace between these warring states. Antonio found the king in Vilnius:

> EMBASSY FROM THE POPE

"The Muscovite sovereign," Batory said to the Jesuit, "wishes to deceive the Holy Father. He sees the threat looming over him and is happy to promise anything – to unite the faiths, to make war on the Turks – but he will not fool me. Go there and do what you have to. I will not protest. I only know that it is necessary to fight for an advantageous and just peace, and we shall have it. I give you my word."

After the peacemaker Antonio blessed the king for deeds worthy of a hero and a Christian, he traveled on to see the tsar; following him in August, Batory quickly moved on Pskov.

This time the attack was not unexpected: Ivan was waiting for it and entrusted Pskov's defense to reliable voivodes: the boyar princes Shuiskii, Ivan Petrovich and Vasilii Thedorovich (Skopin), Nikita Ivanovich, Ochin-Pleshcheev, Prince Andrei Khvorostinin, Bakhteyarov and Rostovskii-Lobanov. The tsar gave them written orders, and in the Cathedral of the Dormition before the icon of the Virgin of Vladimir, they formally swore not to surrender the city to Batory while they yet lived. The voivodes in turn took the same oaths from the boyar cadets, musketeers and senior and junior citizens of Pskov. Everyone kissed the cross in a rapture of love for their homeland, crying,

> GLORIOUS SEIGE OF PSKOV

"We may die, but we shall not surrender!"

They were 30,000 strong. The old fortifications were repaired; cannons, bombards and arquebuses were positioned; places were designated for each voivode with his unit for the defense of the citadel, the city center and city proper, the outskirts and the outer fortifications over a distance of seven or eight versts. The tsar wrote constantly to the officers and men, reminding them of their oath and their duty. The Novgorod lord Aleksandr also wrote to them. The Pecherskii abbot, the virtuous Tikhon, left his cloister and appeared in the theater of coming bloodshed to serve his country with exhortations and prayers.

Everyone was prepared to receive Batory with that bravery that he did not love in Russians, but could respect. In Novgorod there were 40,000 troops with Prince Yurii Golitsyn, and about 15,000 in Rzhev to assist threatened Pskov. The princes Vasilii Ivanovich Shuiskii and Shestunov were stationed on the banks of the Oka to take defensive action in case of an invasion by the khan. Grand Prince Simeon of Tver, the Mstislavskiis and Kurlyatev were with the main force in Volok.

Thus the tsar had upwards of 300,000 troops in the field, an army that neither Russia nor Europe had seen since the Mongol invasion. Ivan finally left Aleksandrovskaya Sloboda and arrived in Staritsa with his entire court, his boyars and his guard detachment. It looked as if he would take personal command of his army, mobilizing its mass, on the example of the Hero of the Don, to meet this new Mamai. But Ivan was readying ruses and cajolery; he was not getting ready for combat.

On 18 August, the impatiently-awaited Jesuit Possevino arrived at Staritsa to see the sovereign. From Smolensk to this town he had everywhere been honored and received with splendor and kindness. The military guard units, gleaming with gold, stood at arms before the Jesuit; the officers dismounted, bowed low, and began their speeches. Never in Russia had such respect been shone to a royal or imperial emissary.

Two days later, after the travelers had been given time to rest, Antonio and four brothers of his order were presented to the sovereign. They were amazed by the splendor of the court, the great number of courtiers, the glittering of precious metals and gems, the discipline and the silence. Ivan and the heir-apparent stood up at the mention of Gregory XIII's name and paid close attention to his gifts: a cross depicting the sufferings of our Lord, a rosary with diamonds and a richly covered book about the Council of Florence.

Gregory had also written personally to the tsareviches and the tsaritsa (calling her Mariya *Anastasiya*); in his letter to Ivan, he called him his beloved son, while calling himself merely the deputy of Christ. He assured Russia of his sincere good wishes; he promised to persuade Batory towards peace – necessary for the common welfare of the Christian powers – and to the return of that which had been unjustly taken, in hopes that Ivan would bring peace to the Church through the union of ours with the Apostolic, recalling that the Greek empire had fallen because of its hostility to the provisions of the Council of Florence.

Antonio elucidated these words to the Duma councilors and the secretary Andrei Shchelkalov, declaring that he would fulfill the Pope's wishes, that he was prepared to give his life for the tsar and would persuade Batory not to demand money of us for his expenses in the war. He said that Stefan would be satisfied with just Livonia (but all of it), and that after concluding a peace with them and with the Swedish king (which the Pope desired), Ivan should join in a close alliance with Rome, the emperor, with the kings of Spain and France, with Venice and the other European powers against the Ottomans. The Pope would contribute 50,000 or more troops towards this Christian levy, in which the shah of Persia might also participate.

Finally, Antonio asked the sovereign to permit the Venetians to trade freely and to construct churches in Russia. He was answered kindly, but with a certain firmness. The tsar thanked the Pope for his love and good wishes and he praised his great plan to attack the Turks with the combined forces of Europe.

To please Gregory, he did not reject either the unification of the churches or peace with Sweden, but first he wanted peace with Batory. He expressed his faith in Possevino, telling him that he should travel once more to the king to complete the business he had started. Ivan said that Russia had ruled Livonia since the time of Yaroslav I; he would yield Stefan 66 towns and cities therein, as well as Velikie Luki, Zavoloche, Nevel, Velizh and Kholm while retaining only 35 Livonian towns and cities for himself: Derpt, Narva, etc., but could cede nothing further – it would be up to Stefan to cease hostilities on these conditions. After permitting Italian merchants to trade in Russia, to have Latin priests and to pray to God as pleased them, Ivan added,

"However, we have never had Roman churches and never will have them." During the course of these negotiations, the meek Jesuits dined with the sovereign on gold tableware, together with boyars and eminent men.

"I saw," writes Antonio, "not a menacing autocrat, but a cordial host amidst obliging guests; he was courteous and attentive, sending around viands and wine to all. Halfway through the dinner, Ivan leaned his elbows on the table and said to me,

'Antonio! Strengthen yourself with food and drink. You have made a long trip from Rome to Moscow, having been dispatched to us by the Holy Father, the head and pastor of the Roman Church, whom we respect sincerely.'"

Full of hopes of obliging the tsar by obtaining peace and thereby furthering the Pope's important goals in relation to Russia, Antonio rode to see Stefan and found him already in the midst of a bloodbath.

After they learned that Stefan was marching straight for Pskov, the local voivodes and troops, clergy and citizens circuited all the fortifications with crosses, wonder-working icons and the relics of the saint, Prince Vsevolod-Gavriil, and with mothers carrying their infants in their arms. They prayed that Olga's ancient city would be an unconquerable fastness to its enemies; that it would both save Russia and be saved by it. After the voivodes heard that Batory had taken Opochka, Krasnyi and Ostrov, and had defeated one of our light cavalry detachments on the banks of the Cherekha, our voivodes torched the outskirts on 18 August, mounted up and gave the order to ring the siege bell.

Soon they could see a dense cloud of smoke, which was being blown towards the city by a strong southern wind. Stefan's army also appeared: they were marching slowly and cautiously, in vast hordes. They occupied the Porkhovskaya Road and stationed themselves along the Velikaya River. The Russians made a spirited sally and ascertained the size of the enemy force; both sides took some prisoners.

Batory's multinational army consisted of Poles, Lithuanians, Mazovians, Hungarians, Germans from Braunschweig and Lübeck, Austrians, Prussians, Courlanders, Danes and Scots in numbers approaching 100,000 cavalry and infantry. They were in such good order and armed so beautifully that the Ottoman emissary who had arrived at the camp to see the king and saw his glittering army exclaimed in delight,

"If the sultan and Batory wanted to cooperate, they could conquer the world."

But this vast, beautiful army feared difficulties. They saw the citadel of the city, huge, filled with provisions, munitions and troops who had shown unusual valor in their very first battle.

Our turncoat, David Belskii, was still in Vilnius, advising the king not to move on Novgorod or Pskov, cities surrounded by bogs and rivers, with firm stone walls and Russian spirit, but rather to lay siege to Smolensk, less inaccessible and more familiar to Lithuanians.

The king rejected this prudent advice, nor did he heed his voivodes, who thought that Novgorod could be taken quickly. Iron-willed Batory was afraid to show fear or weakness; he preferred to trust in his good luck and his army's valor; he loved overcoming difficulties, and thus commenced the memorable siege of Pskov.

The enemy surrounded the city on 26 August beneath the thundering of all our gun emplacements, which were concealed from their volleys in the forest. To Stefan's amazement, he lost a considerable number of men: he did not want to believe that the Russian artillery could be so powerful or so accurate.

His forces were encamped along the Moscow highway near the Lyubatovsk Church of St. Nikolai, but they were obliged to escape the whistle of cannonballs flying overhead and removed to the banks of the Cherekha, beyond high ground and hills.

Five days passed quietly. The enemy fortified their camp on the Velikaya and kept an eye on the city. On 1 September, they began to dig trenches towards the Pokrovskie Gates, along the river. Working day and night, they rolled up gabions and built embankments. Pskov's voivodes saw this work, guessed the intent and built new outer fortifications with wooden walls and gun emplacements at this perilous and threatened location.

The best of the boyar cadets and musketeers, and a bold commander, Prince Andrei Khvorostinin, were chosen for its defense. They ordered hymns to be sung and holy water sprinkled on the ground to ready it for the blood of brave warriors. The Shuiskii princes and sovereign's secretaries were also ever-present to give them advice.

The Poles, after constructing emplacements, opened fire right at dawn on 7 September with 20 heavy cannons, pounding the wall between the Pokrovskie and Svinye gates. They broke it down in several places on the following day, and the king announced to his voivodes that the way into the city was open to heroes, that the Russians were terrified and that time was short. His voivodes, dining in the royal tent, said to Batory,

"Sovereign! We shall soon sup with you in Pskov's castle."

They hastened to the task, promising their troops all the riches of the city: loot and prisoners without limit. Hungarians, Germans and Poles unfurled their banners and charged at the breaks in the wall, shouting, to the sound of trumpets. The Russians were waiting for them. When the siege bell informed them of the assault, all the citizens bade farewell to their wives, blessed their children and stood together with the troops in the ruins of the stone wall and the gap in the unfinished newer wooden walls. Abbot Tikhon and the priests prayed at the main cathedral, and the Lord heard their prayers: 8 September stands in history as Pskov's most glorious day.

Ignoring the cruel fire from the city's gun emplacements, the enemy reached the fortress over the bodies of their own men, burst through the gaps and took the Pokrovskie and Svinye towers. They unfurled the king's banners atop them, to Batory's great delight: he had been observing the battle from the bell tower of St. Nikita the Martyr, half a verst from the city. The Poles fought with the citizens in the gaps in the wall and with the boyar cadets and musketeers. Bullets rained down on the weakening and sorely pressed Russians from the towers taken by the Hungarians and Germans.

Prince Shuiskii, covered in blood, now dismounted his wounded horse, restrained the retreating defenders and showed them the image of the Virgin and the relics of St. Vsevolod-Gavriil that the priests had brought from the main cathedral. Although they knew the Lithuanians were already in the towers and on the walls, they came with their sacred objects right into the smoke of battle to die or to save the city by the divine inspiration of their courage.

The Russians' hearts were fortified and they stood fast. At this crucial hour, the Svinye Tower, which we had undermined, blew up, taking the royal banners with it. The moat was filled with German, Hungarian and Polish corpses. New units sped towards our men from the distant, safer parts of the city; they linked up firmly and moved forward, shouting,

"We will not betray the Virgin and St. Vsevolod!"

The concerted strike crushed the bewildered enemy, forced them out through the breaches in the wall and cast them down from the gun platforms. Holed up in the Pokrovskaya tower, the Hungarians held out longer than the others, but they, too, were forced out by fire and sword. Blood flowed until evening, since Stefan reinforced the Poles with fresh troops.

The battle was now outside the fortress; inside there remained only the sick, the old, and children. When the women learned that the wall *had been cleansed of Lithuanian feet,* that the tsar's banners again waved over its gun emplacements, and that the enemy had abandoned a few light cannons in the gates, they came to the battle site: some with ropes to haul the captured artillery into the fortress, others with cold water to refresh the parched mouths of warriors faint from thirst. Many even came with spears to help their husbands and brothers in the battle. At last, all those who were not Russian had fled. The victors returned to the city with trophies: Lithuanian banners and trumpets, and a great number of prisoners. It was now dark; they praised God in the main cathedral, where the voivodes told the soldiers and citizens,

"Thus ends our first day of hardship, valor, weeping and rejoicing! Shall we finish what we have begun? Our powerful enemies have fallen, and we, the weak, stand with their armor before the altar of the Most High.

"A *proud giant has been deprived of his bread,* while we with Christian humility are nourished by Heavenly mercy. We shall fulfill the oath we gave without craftiness or cunning. We shall not betray our Church or our sovereign, neither through timidity or craven despair!" The soldiers and citizens replied, weeping tears of humility,

"We are ready to die for Christ's faith! As we have begun, so, with God, we shall finish, without any cunning!"

A courier was dispatched to Moscow with the joyful news; he safely got past the Lithuanian encampment. Money was taken from the state treasury to comfort and heal the wounded. These numbered 1,626, while 863 had been killed. Enemy fatalities were easily about 5,000, including more than 80 eminent officers, which number included Bekezy, a Hungarian commander whom Stefan particularly liked and respected. The king shut himself up in his tent and would not see his voivodes, who had promised to sup with him in the citadel of Pskov.

But, as if shamed by his heartfelt distress, Batory went out to his troops the following day with a placid expression. He summoned his council and told them that they must take Pskov or die, in fall or winter, despite any difficulties. He ordered mines to be dug and the fortress to be bombarded day and night in preparation for new assaults. He wrote to the Russian voivodes:

"Further bloodshed will be futile for you. You know how many cities I have conquered in two years! Surrender peaceably – we will be honorable and merciful, unlike the Muscovite tyrant. You will get civil privileges unknown in Russia and all the benefits of free trade, which once flourished in his land. Your customs, property and religion will be inviolable. My word is law. Insane obstinacy will doom you and your people!"

Chapter Ten

This message was shot into the city on an arrow (for the besieged did not want any sort of contact with their enemy). The voivodes used the same method to reply to the king:

"We are not Jews: we betray neither Christ, nor our tsar, nor our country. We pay no heed to blandishments; we are not afraid of threats. Come and fight – victory will depend on God."

They hastened to complete the wooden wall, covering the breach by digging a ditch across it and erecting a palisade of sharp oaken palings in it. They held services in the fortifications under fire from the Lithuanian gun emplacements and calmly awaited battle. Over the course of five or six weeks they gloriously repelled every assault.

The morale of the besieged kept improving, while the besiegers grew weaker in body and spirit. They endured misfortune and sometimes hunger as well. They grumbled, and not daring to blame their king, blamed the chief voivode, Zamoiskii, saying that he had learned everything in Italian academies except how to beat Russians. No doubt he would go to Warsaw with the king and wax eloquent at the Sejm, while his troops became victims of winter and the enemy's ferocity.

Batory ordered dugouts built and provisioned with powder and grain. He paid no attention to the grumbling, but put his hope in the effects of his mines. However, from a Lithuanian deserter, Shuiskii learned of these nine secret mines. He was able to intercept some of them; the rest collapsed on their own. All further attempts, ruses and efforts by Batory were in vain. Neither his fiery cannonballs, which had been so destructive at Velikie Luki and Sokol, nor his desperate audacity had the desired effect.

For example: on October 28th, accompanied by a terrific barrage from all the Lithuanian gun emplacements, the royal guards [*gaiduki*] charged from the Velikaya River directly at the city with picks and crowbars. Between the corner tower and the Pokrovskie Gate they began to break down the stone wall, while covering themselves with broad shields. They crawled through holes and tried to set fire to the inner wooden fortifications.

The Russians were dumbfounded, but destroyed Batory's bravos in just a few minutes by pouring flaming pitch on them, hurling jugs of liquid and setting fire to their shields. Some [of our troops] stabbed through the openings, others struck with stones, with bombards and flintlock muskets – few escaped.

The barrage continued for the next five days, then a breach appeared in the wall, and on 2 November Batory tried his luck for the last time with an assault from the Velikaya. Dense crowds of Lithuanians proceeded over the frozen river, at first bold and hearty, but suddenly they were showered with cannonballs from the fortress.

They stopped advancing and became disordered. Stefan's voivodes rode around on their mounts, futilely shouting, brandishing their sabers and even striking the timid. At the second powerful salvo from the city, both voivodes and troops turned and ran, with the king looking on.

He had fortitude, however, and needed it. To increase his vexation, Thedor Myasoedov, head of our musketeers, with a rather large unit of fresh Russian troops, opened a path through the chain of enemy legions and broke through into Pskov the Famous, to the unspeakable joy of its defenders, indefatigable in their valor, but reduced in numbers.

Stefan at last gave the order to abandon his fortifications, removing the cannons and gabions, and the active, fierce siege turned into a quiet blockade, the idea being to weaken the besieged with hunger. The Russians rejoiced on the walls as they saw the enemy, fleeing the fortress, withdrawing with their artillery.

But that was not all: to cheer up his exhausted army and keep his greedy mercenaries happy with some sort of small conquest, Batory tried to take the ancient Pecherskii Monastery, 56 versts from Pskov. It had been renovated in 1519 and decorated by the grand prince's secretary Munekhin; since that time it had been famous for miraculous healings of the devout and for its rich endowment and beautiful buildings.

Aside from the monks, there were 200 or 300 troops there for the defense of its stone walls and towers, commanded by the valiant Yurii Nechaev. They menaced Lithuanian transport with constant attacks.

Germans under the knight Georg Fahrensbach and Hungarians under the royal voivode Bornemiss arrived at the monastery and demanded its immediate surrender, but the good monks replied to them,

"Is it praiseworthy for knights to do battle with monks? If you want battle and glory, go to Pskov, where you will find worthy warriors. We will not surrender."

The monks did even better than they said: together with the soldiers and their wives and children, they repelled two assaults, capturing young Ketler, a duke's nephew, and two eminent Livonian officers. After this, the large enemy force did battle primarily with cold and hunger. Their troops froze on watch and became numb in their tents.

In Batory's camp, a chetvert of rye was selling for not less than 10 of today's silver rubles; a dry cow went for about 25. They had to send foragers, at great peril, nearly 150 versts. Horses, scantily nourished with hay and straw, perished. The treasury was exhausted and the troops were unpaid; 3,000 Germans left for home.

"The king intends to keep his word," the Lithuanian commanders wrote to their friends in Vilnius. "He will not take the city, but he may die in the snows of Pskov."

Death indeed seemed the probable consequence of Batory's stubbornness. If Prince Yurii Golitsyn had come from Novgorod, the Mstislavskiis from Volok and Shuiskii from Pskov to assault Batory, he would have seen that fate *had not yet handed him all of the Russian state.* But only Shuiskii acted, by harassing the enemy with his sallies. The famous fugitive Golitsyn sat tight within his stone walls.

When he heard that Lithuanian Cossacks had torched Rusa and almost reduced its entire trading quarter to ashes, he began to fear a siege. Grand Prince Simeon of Tver and the Mstislavskiis were immobile, guarding Moscow. The sovereign, frightened by news of new Swedish successes in Livonia and even more by the advent of Radziwill with one of Batory's light detachments in Rzhev itself, galloped out of Staritsa for Sloboda.

The bold raid of the Lithuanians on the banks of the Volga frightened Ivan, but did not furnish them with any other essential advantage. Radziwill fled when he encountered the superior forces of Moscow's voivodes; he tried to take Toropets, but was unable to do so, and returned to his king.

However, there were significant events in Livonia. Batory requested that the Swedes attack Russia's northern coast from the sea, wipe out the nest of our commerce with England and take the ports of St. Nikolai, Kholmogory and Belozersk, where the tsar's main treasury was kept. This plan, which was bold indeed, seemed audaciously reckless to the Swedes. They feared the distant, cold Russian wastes and to Batory's irritation sought nearer, surer and more lasting conquests in Livonia, nor would they consider yielding its districts to him without some sort of apportionment.

Making use of the protracted siege of Pskov and the inaction of Ivan's voivodes, over the course of two or three months they deprived us of Lode, Fikkel, Leal, Hapsal and Narva itself, where 7,000 Russians, both musketeers and residents, were killed in a bloody fray. For 20 years we had traded in this city with Europe: with Denmark, Germany and the Netherlands – a great amount of goods and wealth was to be found there.

> SWEDES TAKE NARVA

A few days later, the Swede's renowned voivode, the Frenchman De La Gardie, also set his foot on ancient Rus: he conquered Ivangorod, Yama and Koporye. He also captured the guards of the Muscovite courtiers. Among them was our dangerous traitor Athanasii Belskii, a worthy kinsman of Malyuta Skuratov and the fugitive David.

Belskii eagerly offered his services to the Swedes. After taking the stronghold of Wittenstein, the impressive De La Gardie celebrated his victory in Revel. It is written that he put such a fear into the Russians that church services were held so that Heaven might save them from this ferocious enemy.

Ivan was scared, at any rate. He did not see Russia's strength and advantage; he saw only the enemy's, and awaited salvation not from valor, not from victory, but only from the papist

Jesuit Antonio, who wrote to him from Batory's camp that this hero, a real Christian, was not tempted by glory, but was prepared, as before, to give peace to Russia on terms known to the tsar, rejecting any other, and to this end was expecting plenipotentiary officials from us. He wrote that the Lithuanian army was very large and in good spirits, and that further bloodshed would threaten us with great calamities.

This was satisfactory to Ivan. In council, he proposed to the tsarevich and the boyars,

"to yield to necessity and to Batory's and his ally Sweden's might, for he has marshaled the forces of many lands and peoples, and to cede to him *only as an ultimate necessity,* all of Russian Livonia, on condition that he return all his other conquests to us and exclude the Swedes from the agreement so that we might be free to check them."

PEACE TALKS

Ivan sent the court noble Prince Dmitrii Petrovich Eletskii and the keeper of the seal Roman Vasilievich Olferiev to Stefan to conclude a peace or a truce. The Roman emissary, the Jesuit Antonio Possevino, was waiting for them in the village of Beshkovichie, between Opoki and Porkhov. They arrived together on December 13th in the town of Kiverova Gora, 15 versts from Zapolskaya Yama, where Stefan's plenipotentiaries were to be found: the voivode Yanush Zbarazhskii, the marshalok Prince Albrycht Radziwill and the secretary of the Grand Principality of Lithuania, the renowned Mikhailo Garaburda.

In these places, laid waste and burned by the enemy, in the middle of a snowy wilderness, splendor and pomp made a sudden appearance: Ivan's officials and their men glittered in their finery, with their clothing and horses' accouterments gleaming with gold. Merchants brought in rich wares and laid them out in the tents, warmed by flaming bonfires.

They all stayed in smoky cabins, however, eating bad bread and drinking snow water. Some of our emissaries had meat provided to them in Novgorod and were able to entertain the Jesuit Antonio every day. Negotiations commenced at once, while Batory, having given all necessary instructions to his trusted representatives and to his chief voivode Zamoiskii, departed for Warsaw. His parting words were,

"I go, with my few tired guards to get strong, fresh troops."

This departure, a great risk for the king in these circumstances, was doubtless necessary in order to request a new grant from the Sejm. The exhausted troops manifested a mutinous spirit. They cursed the disastrous siege of Pskov, demanded peace and shouted that Stefan was fighting for Livonia so he could hand it over to his nephews. The presence of the king restrained the disgruntled – without him, a general rebellion might have flared up. But the king put as much trust in Zamoiskii as in himself, and was not disappointed. This nobleman commander, scorning cruel reproaches, caustic jibes and threats, pacified the rebels with severity and cheered the weak with hope.

"Moscow's emissaries," he said, "are watching us from Zapolskaya Yama. If you are brave and patient, they will yield up everything. If you display cowardice, they will take heart: we will be left with no peace or glory and will have lost the fruits of so many victories and such great effort!"

Yet Zamoiskii, with courageous resolve, was not ashamed to invent, or approve, a base ruse to get rid of Pskov's chief defender. A Russian prisoner showed up before our voivodes, released from the Lithuanian camp without any conditions, with a big coffer and the following letter for Shuiskii from the German, Moller:

"Sovereign Prince Ivan Petrovich! I long served the tsar with Georg Fahrensbach; I recall now his hospitality. I now wish to defect to your side and have sent my valuables on ahead. Unlock the drawer and take out the gold and dishes pending my arrival."

Fortunately, the voivodes had their doubts: they ordered a skilled master to open the drawer carefully and found inside some loaded arquebuses covered with gunpowder. If Shuiskii had incautiously raised the lid, he might have lost his life from the discharge or explosion of the arquebuses.

Saved by Heaven, he wrote to Zamoiskii that brave men fight their enemies only in battle and proposed an honorable one, single

CHAPTER TEN

combat, as Batory had proposed to Ivan. Our voivodes knew of the peace talks, but were heartened nonetheless. They did not rest, but day and night intimidated and struck at the weakening Lithuanians, who were finally left with only 26,000 men.

The men of the army did their job; the men of the Duma did likewise. If Prince Eletskii and Olferiev were unable to preserve the dignity and interests of Russia in carrying out Ivan's will precisely, it was not their fault. At a minimum they were able to observe the situation and inform the sovereign of the enemy's extremity. They were able to gain time and delay concessions, awaiting new orders or a happy change in spirit on the part of timid Ivan. They negotiated with the Lithuanian officials quietly, but courteously and did not abase themselves. They deprecated the Lithuanians vainglory, but not rudely.

"If we," said Pan Zbarazhskii, "came here for this business, and not for empty verbosity, then tell us that Livonia is ours, and heed the further conditions of the victor, who has now conquered a considerable portion of Russia and will take Pskov and Novgorod. He will give you three days for a definite reply." The Russian officials replied,

"Arrogance is not the same as loving peace. You want our sovereign to relinquish to you, without any requital, rich territory and deprive us of all our seaports, which are necessary for Russia's free communications with other powers. You have been besieging Pskov for four months now with praiseworthy courage, of course, but with success? Do you really hope to take it? And if you do not take it, does this not doom your army and all your conquests?"

Instead of the three days set by Batory, more than three weeks passed in meetings and debate with our side being [alternately] cool and hot with the Lithuanians. Ivan's emissaries offered to yield to the king 14 Livonian towns and cities that had been taken by Russian troops: Polotsk with all its suburbs, Ozerishche, Usvyat, Luki, Velizh, Nevel, Zavoloche and Kholm in order to retain just Derpt and 15 fortresses.

Stefan's nobles would not agree; they demanded both Livonia and money to defray the expenses of the war. They also wanted to include the Swedish king in the negotiations. In vain did Eletskii

431

and Olferiev request Possevino to use his good offices, but the Jesuit was sly, guessing the tsar's secret instructions. He praised the invincible Batory and insidiously regretted new, unavoidable miseries for Russia should our obstreperousness prolong the war. Genuine cooperation came only because of the voivodes of Pskov: on 4 January they launched a powerful attack by cavalry and infantry on Zamoiskii. They took a notable number of prisoners, killed many enemy officers and returned to their city with their trophies. This sally was the 46th and last: Zamoiskii gave notice to his emissaries that the troops' patience had been exhausted – it was necessary to sign the treaty or flee.

1582

The critical moment had arrived. Zbarazhskii announced that Stefan had ordered the negotiations to be concluded and this decisiveness won out over ours. Eletskii and Olferiev realized the Lithuanians' extremity, but they did not dare to return to Moscow without a peace; they did not dare to disobey their sovereign, and were obliged to accept the main conditions.

TRUCE CONCLUDED

In Ivan's name, they relinquished Livonia and ceded Polotsk and Velizh, while Batory agreed not to demand money from us and not to refer in the treaty document either to the Swedish king or the Estonian cities (Revel and Narva). He also agreed to return to us Velikie Luki, Zavoloche, Nevel, Kholm, Sebezh, Ostrov, Krasnyi, Izborsk, Gdov and all the other suburbs of Pskov they had occupied. Added to these conditions was a ten-year truce, beginning on 6 January 1582.

However, they still argued for several days over titles and wording, once with such heat that the mild Jesuit Antonio lost his temper: he tore the draft manuscript from Olferiev's hand, hurled it on the ground and grabbed him by the collar. Although Ivan had lost Livonia, he still wished to be titled in the document *Ruler and Tsar of Livonia* (*Tsar* having the sense of *Imperator*).

Neither Stefan's emissaries nor the Pope's would hear of this. The former, apparently in jest, demanded Smolensk, Velikie Luki, and all the Severskie towns in exchange for naming Ivan tsar of just Kazan and Astrakhan, in the same sense that Moldavian voivodes called themselves hospodars. Possevino, however, maintained

CHAPTER TEN

that only the Pope could grant new titles to crowned heads of state. Finally they agreed to give Ivan the title of *Tsar, Ruler of Smolensk and Livonia* only in the Russians' copy of the peace treaty, while in the king's it had simply *Sovereign,* and Stefan's title included *of Livonia.*

The treaty was affirmed by kissing the cross; the representatives of both powers embraced as friends and on 17 January informed Pskov's voivodes of the truce. The quiet, half dead Lithuanian camp came alive with noisy rejoicing; after completing their task honorably for Russia, the defenders of Pskov made offerings of thanks to Heaven with great emotion. Zamoiskii invited them to a feast. Prince Ivan Shuiskii sent some junior voivodes, but did not go himself: he was at peace, but did not feel like celebrating.

Thus concluded the three-year war, not so much bloody as unfortunate for Russia, and not as glorious for Batory as it was shameful for Ivan, who during its curious events had displayed all the weakness of a soul abased by tyranny. Through his indefatigable efforts he had enabled Lithuania to gloriously forestall [what would later be] Peter the Great's grand achievement – to have a sea and harbors for Russia's commercial and governmental relations with Europe.

Having fought incessantly for 24 years, advancing slowly, step by step towards his goal, having destroyed so many men and so much property, the tsar then ordered his nation's army, almost equal in strength to that of Xerxes, to suddenly hand over everything, both glory and advantage, to the exhausted remnants of Batory's mongrel host!

This was the first time we had concluded a peace so disadvantageous – almost dishonorable – with Lithuania. The honor must go to Pskov for retaining our ancient holdings and not giving away more. Like a sturdy bulwark, it had stopped the *invincible* Stefan. Had Batory taken it, he would not have been satisfied with Livonia; he would not have left Russia with either Smolensk or the Severskie lands.

Ivan was so *bewitched* by fear that it is possible Stefan might even have taken Novgorod – contemporaries indeed attribute our forces' amazing inaction to sorcery. They write that Ivan,

433

terrified by visions and marvels, expected only disaster in his war with Batory and disbelieved any favorable reports from his own voivodes. It was said that the appearance of a comet foretold misfortune for Russia and that in broad daylight in winter, on Christmas Day, a thunderbolt had set fire to Ivan's bedchamber at Aleksandrovskaya Sloboda.

They write that a terrible voice was heard near Moscow: *flee, Russians, flee!* A marble gravestone allegedly fell from the sky there, covered with secret, inscrutable inscriptions; the bewildered tsar saw it for himself and ordered his bodyguards to break it up. These are tales appropriate to an age of superstition, but the truth is that Pskov and Shuiskii saved Russia from the greatest peril, and the memory of this significant deed will not be expunged from our history so long as we have not lost our love for our country and its name.

On 4 February, Zamoiskii entered Livonia to receive its towns, cities and fortresses from us. His comrades-in-arms, beside themselves with joy, did not care to look at the walls and towers of Pskov, surrounded by the graves of their brothers. Only on this day were the gates of Olga's city opened at last. There the residents and troops, who had paid the debt of zeal to their country and had gloriously passed through peril, enjoyed the greatest satisfaction for man or citizen.

Not so for the Russians in Livonia, where they had long dwelt as if in their homeland, having families, homes, churches and a bishop in Derpt. In accordance with the treaty, they left for Novgorod and Pskov with their wives and children. They heard the Orthodox gospel there for the last time and prayed to the Lord in accordance with the rites of our Church. Subdued, exiled, they all wept bitterly, most of all over the graves of their loved ones.

Livonia had been a Russian possession for about 600 years; our country had ruled over its primitive inhabitants back in the time of St. Vladimir, built fortresses there in the age of Yaroslav the Great, and in the heyday of the Order, had collected tribute from the districts of Derpt. Russia had now formally renounced this land, dampened with our blood, and this would be for a long time – until the Hero of Poltava.* Meanwhile, the people, always peace-loving, blessed in Moscow and everywhere else the end of this destructive war. But did Ivan enjoy peace in his timid soul? God did not intend this, and chose this time for a terrible punishment of the tsar's heart, cruel, but not yet completely turned to stone – still fatherly, not yet dead.

With his elder, beloved son Ivan, the tsar was preparing a *second self* for Russia. Together they dealt with important matters, attended the Duma, traveled around the country; together they enjoyed voluptuousness and murder. It seemed the son was unashamed of his father and that Russia could expect nothing better from his succession. Without once being a widower, the young tsarevich now had a third wife, Elena Ivanovna of the Sheremetev line. The two previous, Saburova and Paraskeva Mikhailovna Solovaya, were now nuns. He changed wives on his own initiative, or to please his father, and also switched concubines, so as to resemble him in every way.

FILICIDE

But while he manifested a callous heart, frightening in one so young, and was unrestrained in his lusts, he showed intelligence in affairs of state and sensitivity for his country's glory, or lack thereof. During the peace negotiations, he felt for Russia and read sorrow in the boyars' faces, having perhaps heard of the general discontent. The tsarevich had become filled with a noble zeal, he had gone to his father and requested that he be sent with an army to expel the enemy, free Pskov and restore honor to Russia. In an outburst of wrath, his father screamed,

"Rebel! You and the boyars want to dethrone me!"

He raised his hand against his son; Boris Godunov tried to restrain it, and received several wounds from Ivan's sharp staff. The tsar then gave the tsarevich a powerful blow to the head with it. The unfortunate victim fell, bleeding. Ivan's fury vanished. Pale with horror, trembling, he cried out in a frenzy,

"I have killed my son!"

He leaned down to hug and kiss him and to stop the bleeding from his deep head wound. He wept, wailed and called for

---

* [Peter the Great, in 1709.]

doctors. He implored God for mercy, his son for forgiveness, but the judgment of Heaven had been pronounced. The son, kissing his father's hand, tenderly showed him love and sympathy, and tried to convince him not to despair, saying that he would die a loyal son and subject.

He lived four days and died on 19 November, in frightful Aleksandrovskaya Sloboda. There, where innocent blood had been spilled for so many years, Ivan, covered in his son's, sat numb and unmoving beside the corpse, without eating or sleeping for several days.

On 22 November, the nobles, boyars and princes, all dressed in black, took the body to Moscow. The tsar walked behind the bier all the way to the church of St. Michael the Archangel where a place was indicated to him among the memorials to his ancestors.

The funeral was lavish and touching. All mourned the fate of the young heir-apparent, who might have lived for fortune and virtue had not his father's hand, contrary to nature, plunged him into debauchery and the grave. Human nature triumphed, weeping even for Ivan himself. Devoid of any token of royal rank, in a chasuble of mourning, in the guise of a simple, despairing sinner, he beat against the coffin and the ground with piercing cries.

Thus does the justice of the Avenger on High occasionally punish in this world these monsters of inhumanity, more as an example than for their correction, for it seems there is a limit of evil beyond which there is no longer any real repentance, no voluntary, definitive return to virtue. There is only torment of hellish origin, with no hope of change of heart.

Ivan was now far beyond this fateful limit: the restitution of such a torturer might attract other weak people . . . For some time he suffered terribly and did not know peaceful sleep: at night, as if frightened by premonitions, he would jump up, fall out of bed, roll on the floor, moan and cry out; he would quiet down only when he was exhausted. He would sleep for a few moments on the floor, where a mattress and pillow had been placed for him. He awaited and feared the light of morning. He was afraid to see people and his face manifested the torment of filicide.

Chapter Ten

In this state of spiritual turmoil, Ivan summoned the country's eminent men and formally announced to them that since he had been so severely punished by God, he would spend the rest of his days in monastic seclusion. He said that his younger son Theodor was not fit to rule Russia and in any case would be unable to rule for long: the boyars should choose a worthy sovereign, to whom he would immediately entrust his power and turn over the state.

>   IVAN CONSIDERS
>   RENOUNCING
>   THE WORLD

Everyone was bewildered. Some believed Ivan's sincerity and were touched to the depths of their hearts, others feared trickery and believed that the sovereign only wanted to elicit their secret thoughts, and that neither they nor the one they might choose would avoid a cruel punishment. The unanimous response was,

"Do not leave us. We wish no tsar other than one God has given us – either you or your son!"

Seemingly reluctant, Ivan agreed to continue to bear the burden of rule, but he banished from his view all the accouterments of majesty, wealth and splendor; he cast aside his crown and scepter and dressed himself and his court in clothes of mourning. He performed a service for the dead, made confession, and sent 10,000 rubles to Constantinople, Antioch, Alexandria and Jerusalem, to the patriarchs there to pray for the peace of the tsarevich's soul, and at long last he was at peace himself.

However, it is written that he did not cease weeping for his beloved son, and even in *happy* conversations often recalled him with tears in his eyes, but then apparently would become happy once again. And once again, if we are to believe foreign historians, he raged and executed many military men who had supposedly surrendered fortresses to Batory out of cowardice, even though our enemies had been obliged to acknowledge the Russians' valor as redoubtable protectors of their own cities.

At the same time, and with the same guise of justice, Ivan devised an unusually cruel punishment for his wife's father. For a long time the tsar had not seen Godunov, who had been struck down and wounded trying to defend the tsarevich. He heard from Thedor Nagoi that his favorite was making himself scarce not

STROGANOV THE HEALER

because of indisposition, but from vexation and malice. Ivan wanted to learn the truth of this and went to see Godunov himself; he saw the wounds on him and the bandages, which had been applied by the merchant Stroganov, who was skilled at curing maladies. He embraced him, and as a token of his special favor, gave his healer the privilege of eminent men: to be named with the full patronymic, or "-vich," such as only the most distinguished royal officials used. He also ordered that Stroganov that same day should make very painful bandages for the sides and chest of the calumniator Thedor Nagoi! Slander is of course a significant crime, but does this ingenuity in means of torture actually reveal a heart moved and crushed by grief?

In any case, in affairs of state, we now see again Ivan's customary coolness, his circumspection and composure which could only proceed from an astonishing majesty of spirit, or else from a lack of sensitivity in circumstances so horrible for a father and a man. In Moscow on 28 November, he heard the report of his herald on the siege of Pskov, and during the negotiations was aware of everything and resolved the quandaries of our deputies, who returned to him in February with the peace agreement.

IVAN'S CONVERSATION WITH THE EMISSARY OF THE ROMAN CHURCH

The sly Jesuit Antonio soon appeared in Moscow to accept our gratitude, and he made use of it, i.e., he achieved the chief goal of his mission: fulfilling Rome's long-held idea of uniting the faith and power of all Christian states against the Ottomans. Ivan now displayed all his natural flexibility of mind, craftiness and prudence, which even the Jesuit had to respect. We describe here some of the interesting details.

"I found the tsar in deep despond," Possevino says in his memoirs. "His splendid court now seemed like a humble cloister of monks, the dark clothing expressing the darkness of Ivan's soul. But the ways of the Most High are inscrutable: the very sorrow of the tsar, at times so unrestrained, disposed him to moderation and patience while hearing my presentations."

CHAPTER TEN

Expressing the importance of the services he had rendered to the Russian state by achieving a successful peace treaty, Antonio first of all tried to persuade Ivan of the sincerity of Stefan's amity, repeating Batory's words:

"Tell the Muscovite sovereign that the enmity in my heart has been extinguished, that I have no secret plans of any kind for future conquests; I wish his sincere brotherhood, and good fortune for Russia. In all of our possessions the roads and ports shall be open for merchants and travelers of both countries, for their mutual benefit. Let Germans and Romans travel freely to him through Poland and Lithuania!

"Peace unto Christians but vengeance upon the Crimean brigands! I am marching against them; let the tsar do likewise! We shall put down these perfidious criminals, greedy for the gold and blood of our subjects. We shall agree on when and where to act. I shall not alter nor weaken in my efforts. Let Ivan give me witnesses from amongst his boyars and voivodes! I am not a Pole or a Lithuanian, but rather a newcomer to the throne: I wish to earn a good name forever in this world."

But Ivan, while grateful for Batory's amicable disposition, replied that we were no longer at war with the khan: our emissary, Prince Vasilii Mosalskii, after living for several years in the Taurid, had at last concluded a truce. Mahmet-Girei had need of a respite – he was exhausted by a protracted war with the Persians in which he was an unwilling ally of the Turks – this had saved Russia from his dangerous attacks for five years. Further on, Antonio arrived at the heart of the matter and asked for a special meeting with the tsar concerning the unification of the faiths.

"We are ready to talk with you," said Ivan, "but only in the presence of those closest to us, and without arguing, if possible, for each man praises his own religion and does not like to be contradicted. Disputes lead to more disputes and I wish for amity and tranquility."

On the designated day, February 21st, Antonio and three other Jesuits went from the chamber of councilors to the throne room, where Ivan was sitting with only his boyars, senior court nobles and service princes; the stewards and junior courtiers had been dismissed. Having shown the emissary kindness, the sovereign again tried to persuade him not to touch on religion, adding,

"Antonio! I am 51 years old and do not have much more time to live in this world. I was raised with the ordinances of our *Christian* Church, which has long been out of harmony with the *Latin*. Can I really change this before the end of my earthly existence? My day of judgment is approaching. It will reveal whose faith, yours or mine, is more true and holy. Speak if you wish, however." Antonio now did so with verve and fervor,

"Most radiant sovereign! Of all the kindnesses you have shown me heretofore, the greatest is your permission to speak with you on a subject so important for the salvation of Christian souls. Do not think, O sovereign, that the Holy Father has obliged you to abandon the Greek faith. No, he only wishes that you, who have a profound and well-educated mind, investigate the activities of the first Church councils; everything true and ancient has been established in your realm as immutable law. All the discrepancies between the Eastern and the Roman Churches will vanish; then we shall be as one in the body of Jesus Christ, to the joy of the sole true pastor of the Church, established by God.

"Sovereign! As you implore the Holy Father to bring peace to Europe and unity to all Christian monarchs so they may vanquish the infidel, will you not acknowledge him as the head of Christendom? Have you not shown especial respect for the apostolic Roman religion by allowing those who profess it to live freely in Russian territory and to pray to the Most High according to its holy rites?

"No one, great Tsar, is compelling you towards this triumphant truth, but are you not moved by the will of the King of Kings, without whom not even a tree leaf falls from its branch? How can this wished-for peace and alliance among monarchs have a solid foundation without a unitary faith?

"You know that this was approved by the Council of Florence, by the emperor and priesthood of the Greek empire and by the most eminent hierarch of your Church, Isidor. Read the proceedings presented to you of this Eighth Ecumenical Council, and if there are areas of doubt, then have me elucidate them.

Chapter Ten

"The truth is evident: once you acknowledge it, how can you fail to achieve glory and majesty in fraternal alliance with the most powerful monarchs of Europe? You will acquire not only Kiev, that ancient Russian possession, but also the whole Byzantine Empire, which God took from the Greeks for their schism and disobedience to Christ the Savior." Ivan replied calmly,

"We never wrote the Pope concerning religion. I would have preferred not to discuss it with you. Firstly, because I fear to wound your heart with harsh words; secondly, I occupy myself only with Russia's secular affairs of state. I do not interpret churchly teachings, which are the business of our intercessor, the metropolitan.

"You speak boldly since you are a priest and have come from Rome to deal with this matter. The Greeks are not gospel for us; we believe in Christ, not the Greeks. As far as the eastern empire is concerned, know that I am satisfied with what I have, nor do I wish for any further realms in this world. I only wish for God's grace in the future."

Ivan made no mention of the Council of Florence or a general Christian alliance against the sultan, but as a token of his friendship for the Pope, once again promised liberty and protection for all foreign merchants and priests of the Latin faith in Russia on condition they not discuss the Law with Russians.

But this ardent Jesuit desired further debate. He asserted that we were novices in Christendom, that Rome was its ancient capital. The tsar now began to get irritated.

"You boast of orthodoxy," he said, "But you shave your beards. Your Pope commands that he be borne on a throne and his shoes be kissed where there is a representation of the crucifixion. What arrogance for a humble Christian pastor! What a debasement of the things that are holy!"

"There is no debasement," Antonio responded. "Respect is given to the worthy. The Pope is the head of Christendom, the preceptor to all right-thinking monarchs, coregent with the apostle Peter and with Christ. We also honor you, as a successor to Monomakh, but the Holy Father..." here Ivan interrupted him, saying,

"The Christians have but one father, in Heaven! We secular rulers must honor worldly laws. Let the apostolic scholars be humble in their philosophizing. Our honor is a regal one, while the popes' and the patriarchs' is a priestly one. We esteem our metropolitan and ask his blessing, but he walks on the ground and does not exalt himself above the tsars.

"There indeed have been popes who have been apostolic scholars: Clement, Silvester, Agatho, Leo and Gregory, but someone who calls himself the regent of Christ and orders himself to be carried around on a sedan chair as if on a cloud, like the angels – he is not living in accord with Christian teachings; this Pope is the wolf, not the shepherd . . ." Antonio exclaimed in great indignation,

"If the Pope is a wolf, then there is nothing more to say." Ivan softened his voice and continued,

"This is why I did not wish to speak with you concerning religion! We cannot help irritating each other. Anyway, I am not calling Gregory XIII a wolf, but a pope who does not follow Christ's teachings. We shall part for now."

The sovereign tenderly placed his hand on Antonio and graciously dismissed him, and ordered his officials to take to him the best dishes from the tsar's table.

Two days later the Jesuit was again summoned to the palace. The tsar indicated seats for him opposite himself and spoke loudly, so all the boyars could hear,

"Antonio! I ask you to forget what I said, to your displeasure, about the popes. We are not in accord on some articles of faith, but I wish to live in friendship with all Christian sovereigns and will send one of my officials with you to Rome, and I also wish to express my gratitude for the services you have rendered to us."

The tsar ordered him to speak with the boyars, with whom Antonio once more made efforts to demonstrate the truth of the Roman confession, and in accordance with their desires (he assures us), wrote a whole book in three days concerning the alleged errors of the Greeks, based on the theological works of Gennadius, Patriarch of Constantinople, who had been installed as archprelate by Mehmet II! In the name of the Pope, he tried to convince

Chapter Ten

the tsar to send some literate young Russians to Rome so that they might find out about the true *dogmas of the ancient Greek Church* there, and to learn Italian or Latin and to teach the Italians our own language for more convenient correspondence with Moscow.

He also tried to persuade Ivan to expel the venomous Lutheran ministers, who reject the Virgin and the sanctity of Christ's saints, and to acknowledge only Latin priests. He was answered that the tsar would seek men skilled in learning, and *if* he found them, he would send them to Gregory; the Lutherans, just as people of other faiths, live freely in Russia, but do not dare to impart their errors to others. Antonio still wanted to reconcile Sweden and Russia, but insisted even more that we conclude an alliance with Europe to subdue the Turks.

"Let the Swedish king himself," said Ivan, "show me that he is indeed peace-loving, and then we shall see that he is sincere. I want to pacify the infidels, but the Pope, the emperor, the kings of Spain and France, and all the other monarchs must first, through a formal embassy, reach an agreement with me on how this Christian army is to be raised. I am quite unable to enter into this sort of obligation at present."

That is to say that Ivan, who now no longer feared Batory, clearly had cooled on the idea of expelling the Turks from Europe. The Jesuit perceived this change and complained that he was being crafty.

"The tsar does not expect anything further from the Holy Father to advance his policies," Antonio wrote. "He plans to use cunning to pacify superstitious Russians, and is unhappy with my forthright opinion concerning their creed. But what is to be done? He summoned me to his palace on the first Sunday of Lent and said,

'Antonio! I know you wish to see the rites of our Church. I have ordered you to be taken now to the Cathedral of the Dormition (where I will be also), where you may contemplate the beauty and majesty of a real mass. There we worship the things of Heaven, not of earth; we respect the metropolitan, but do not manually carry him around... nor did the faithful carry the apostle of St. Peter: he walked, and barefooted at that, while your Pope calls himself his vicar!' Astonished, I coolly replied to this latest rudeness,

'Sovereign! Every place where Christ is praised is holy. But as long as we disagree on certain dogmas, and as long as the Russian metropolitan has no relations with the Holy Father, I am unable to witness your services. I say to you once again, to honor the archpastor of the Church is a duty, not a sin. You do not carry your metropolitan, but you wash your eyes with the water with which he washes his hands.'

"After it was explained to me that this rite was established to commemorate the passion of our Lord and not to honor the metropolitan, Ivan gave a signal and the whole crowd of officials moved forward towards the doors, taking me with them, and from afar the tsar loudly told me,

'Antonio! See that no Lutherans follow you into the church.'

"But I did not want to go in. When the courtiers halted in front of the cathedral, I waited a few minutes, and then left quietly. Everyone thought that I would not escape disaster, but Ivan, astonished by my disobedience, thought a bit, wiped his forehead with his hand, and said,

'Let it be as he wishes!'

"What had been the tsar's intent? To show Russians the triumph of his faith: the emissary of Rome praying in their cathedral, kissing the hand of their metropolitan; to honor the Eastern Church and deprecate the Western, and thereby correct the people's error, which had resulted from the tsar's unusual signs of respect for the Pope."

It is likely that Possevino was not deceived in this surmise, but he *had* been deceived in his hopes of uniting the Roman Church with ours.

Nevertheless, right up to his departure, Ivan showed Possevino tokens of his favor. He was received and accompanied into the palace by eminent officials and usually taken past the glittering ranks of the tsar's huge guard: an honor which perhaps had never been accorded a Jesuit anywhere before. Possevino requested the release of 18 prisoners, Spaniards, who had entered Russia from Azov and had been sent to Vologda. He likewise interceded to ameliorate the conditions of Lithuanian and

German prisoners prior to their repatriation: they were released from prison and placed in citizen's homes. There were orders given to provide them with everything that was necessary.

However, the tsar once again rejected the Jesuit's strong solicitations concerning the construction of Latin churches in Russia. Antonio said that the Catholics would be willing to live amongst us without reproach or disgrace; that would be sufficient. In conversing with Duma councilors regarding our customs, which were strange to Europe, he referred to Herberstein's book about Russia, where it says that the tsar washed his hand with water right after the German emissaries kissed it, as if he had been defiled by the contact.

The boyars explained that Herberstein, who had twice been treated so kindly in Moscow, was an ungrateful slanderer who had fabricated tales of the Muscovite sovereigns. They were also surprised to hear from Possevino that Ivan's father, Grand Prince Vasilii, had supposedly promised the emperor Charles V 30,000 troops in return for permitting a large number of German artists and artisans to go to Russia. The boyars replied,

"Sovereigns provide other sovereigns with troops in accordance with a treaty, not in exchange for craftsmen."

Finally, on the day of his departure, Ivan formally thanked Possevino for his active participation in obtaining peace, and assured him of his personal respect. Ivan stood up, asked him to convey his greetings to Gregory and King Stefan, and gave him his hand. He also sent along some precious black sable pelts for the Pope and for Antonio himself.

The Jesuit at first did not want to accept this gift, praising the poverty of Christian scholars, but he did take it, and left Moscow on 15 March along with our herald, Yakov Molvyaninov, with whom Ivan had written a reply to the Pope's letter, assuring him that we were ready to participate in an alliance of Christian powers against the Ottomans, but not a word was said concerning the unification of the Churches.

Relations were interrupted between Rome and Moscow for a long time after this: they had been of no benefit to us or the Pope, for it had not been the Jesuit's intercession, but the valor of Pskov's voivodes that had inclined Batory to moderation. Stefan's glory was undiminished, nor did he lose his important acquisitions. For this result, the Polish hero was obliged more to the turmoil of Ivan's soul than his own valor.

CHAPTER XI

DEATH OF IVAN

1582-1584

War and truce with the Swedes. Lithuanian affairs. Mutiny of the Cheremis. Relations with various powers, especially with England. Ivan's intention to marry an Englishwoman. Description of the prospective fiancé. Embassy to London. Elizabeth's envoy. Ivan's illness and death. The Russians' love for autocracy. Ivan compared to other torturers. Uses of history. Mixture of good and evil in Ivan. Ivan as developer of the nation and as legislator. His ministries. His secretaries. His clerks. Duma nobles. Nobles of the peerage and junior nobles. Service princes. Stewards. Military organization. Laws. Value of the ruble. Church institutions. A memorable church ceremony. Building towns. Situation in Moscow. Luxury and splendor. Ivan's renown.

With Batory disarmed through our great sacrifices and the khan less frightening (but always dangerous), being satisfied by paltry gifts, Ivan was free to attack the Swedes, who had been abandoned by their ally. He wanted and hoped to subdue this audacious enemy and thereby enhance the honor of his arms in the eyes of Europe. Success seemed certain, and easy. Batory had not only betrayed the Swedish king to Ivan's vengeance, but was also threatening him with war over Estonia. In demanding this region, Stefan ordered the king to be told,

1582
WAR AND TRUCE WITH THE SWEDES

"You have profited from my successes and taken Narva and other German cities that belong to Poland for yourself." The king replied,

"What we have taken with our own blood is ours. I have been in the field and I still have not seen your banners. Remember that all Europe once trembled at the name of the Goths, from whom we inherited both strength and courage. We do not fear the swords of either Russia or Sedmigrad."

This hauteur, although courageous, would have fatal consequences for weak Sweden, still roiled by its crowned head's cruelty, his ardor for the Latin Church and his quarrel with his brother, Duke Karl. On the one side, the fiery Batory had said,

"I shall take what I have demanded," and prepared to march on the Swedes. On the other side, Ivan's voivodes, the princes Mikhailo Kotyrev-Rostovskii, Tyumenskii, Khvorostinin and Merkurii Shcherbatoi had set out from Novgorod, marched to Narva, Yama and across the Neva into Finland.

They engaged the enemy at the village of Lyalitsie in Botskaya Pyatina and soundly trounced them. Ivan sent the voivodes gold medals, singling out the person really responsible for this victory, Prince Dimitrii Khvorostinin, one of Pskov's heroes, who overran the Swedes with an assault by his vanguard.

A second affair, no less important and fortunate for us took place on the banks of the Neva. Following the advice of a defector, one Athanasii Belskii, General De La Gardie suddenly attacked Nöteburg, or Oreshek, intending to take it with a bold assault.

The voivodes Prince Vasilii Rostovskii, Sudakov and Khvostov were in charge there; they fought intrepidly, cutting up the Swedes and drowning them in the Neva, while Prince Andrei Shuiskii sped from Novgorod with a cavalry unit to save this important fortress. Proud De La Gardie fled.

However, fate assisted the Swedes. The hero Batory, strong in battle, had perceived his weakness at the Sejm, where the ungrateful and willful pans had rejected all his proposals even though they had been inspired by his true love for their country. They declared decisively,

"We do not want wars, with either the Crimea or with the Swedes. We will give you neither men nor money!"

Chapter Eleven

"You are king if you faithfully carry out the royal precepts," said one of them, Yakov Nemekovskii. "Otherwise you are just Batory, and I am just Nemekovskii."

But Ivan, to the joyful amazement of the Swedes, suddenly ceased all military movements by our forces and proposed peace to De La Gardie. Prince Lobanov and the court noble Tatishchev met with him in Shelonskaya Pyatina on the river Plyussa, and on 26 May 1583 concluded a two-month truce, and then a subsequent one for three years, leaving Yama, Ivan-gorod and Koporye in the hands of the Swedes! This unexpected tractability is explained by the following circumstances.

| 1583 |

First of all, the peace with Lithuania seemed somewhat shaky. Batory's emissaries, who were in Moscow to ratify the treaty, had announced new demands: they wanted Ivan's name not to be written with the title *of Livonia* and to acknowledge all of Estonia as Stefan's legitimate possession. The boyars only partially satisfied this request, giving them a written promise not to fight Estonia for the next 10 years. Ivan and Batory both swore to honorably fulfill all the conditions.

| LITHUANIAN AFFAIRS |

However, Lithuanian voivodes forcibly took places in the uezds of Toropets, Lutsk and Velizh, nor did they want to define a clear boundary between the two powers. They also insulted and dishonored our officials and hampered the promised exchange of prisoners: they accepted 20,000 gold pieces, or about 7,000 rubles, and 280 sable pelts for Thedor Sheremetev; 4,114 rubles for Prince Tatev; 3,228 for Prince Khvorostinin and 4,457 for Cheremisinov, but kept the rest in captivity.

Stefan, in his cordial relations with the tsar, sometimes found the latter's complaints justified, and promised to immediately curb the Lithuanian officials. At other times, he blamed the Russians and vindicated his own, and obliged Ivan to send, in September 1583, 2,000 boyar cadets and musketeers to the border to protect the residents there from further oppression by the Vitebsk voivode Pats, who had built a new fortress on Russian soil.

In brief, despite all Ivan's pusillanimous patience, enemy activity in this theater might easily be renewed.

MUTINY OF
THE CHEREMIS

In the second place, a general rebellion had broken out in the territory of the lowland Cheremis. It was so dangerous and ferocious that the Kazan voivodes were utterly unable to put it down. In October 1582, the anxious sovereign sent him troops under Prince Eletskii, but on learning that the rebellion had still not subsided, ordered his most distinguished commanders, the princes Ivan Mikhailovich Vorotynskii and valiant Dimitrii Khvorostinin, to proceed there from Murom.

Later news frightened Moscow still more: they learned that Khan Mahmet-Girei, despite the written peace treaty, was in communication with the Cheremis rebels and ready to move against Russia. Also, the Nogai, hitherto loyal, had been incited by him and the ruler of Siberia and were pillaging in the Kama region. It was necessary to act immediately with all our forces. An army was dispatched to the Kama and another under the command of the princes Thedor Mstislavskii, Kurlyatev and the Shuiskiis occupied the banks of the Oka. A third force was traveling by boat down the Volga to Sviyazhsk. The khan did not now dare to encroach on Russia, but the Cheremis rebellion continued with amazing frenzy until the end of Ivan's life.

Having neither the strength nor the skill for ordered battle in the field, these ferocious savages, perhaps embittered by the cruelty of the tsar's officials, fought the Muscovite troops fiercely on the ashes of their homes, in the forests and in their lairs, both in winter and in summer. They wanted independence or death. To constrain the rebels, the voivode Prince Turenin now built the fortress of Kozmodemyansk.

In this manner, after buying a truce with Lithuania at a high price in order to trample Sweden, Ivan, instead of gaining significant successes, had the shame of having to quietly yield Estonian towns and some very old Russian territory. He once again feared Batory and the khan. We are assured that Ivan displayed external calm on seeing the bloody rebellion in the eastern parts of his realm – at any rate, he did not lose his zest for dealing with national affairs, whether internal or external.

He now lived in Moscow, since he had abandoned ill-starred Aleksandrovskaya Sloboda, where in his imagination dwelt the bloody shade of the son he had murdered. He attended the Boyar Duma, entertained emissaries from the shah of Persia, the sultan, Bukhara and Khiva; he also found himself in close friendship with Tomas' successor, Godabend, as an enemy of the Ottoman Empire, which threatened us.

> RELATIONS WITH VARIOUS POWERS, ESPECIALLY ENGLAND

He was courteous to the sultan, but spoke not a word to him concerning war or peace. Ivan permitted his merchants to travel to Moscow and exchange Asiatic brocades for sable pelts. We likewise had only commercial relations with the rulers of the Caspian states. However, most curious of all were the relations between the Muscovite court and London.

Since 1572, trade with the English had flourished again in Russia. They once again boasted of the tsar's favor. They obtained justice, protection and assistance everywhere, to the irritation of Netherlanders and Germans, who in their intrigues and calumnies tried to turn Ivan against them. They were not stingy with their money in Moscow, bribing secretaries and royal courtiers.

Queen Elizabeth likewise paid no attention to representations by the northern powers that this commerce was injurious to a Europe threatened by the Russians' love of power. When she learned that the Danish king was demanding duties from English seafarers on the way to our borders in Lapland, she wrote of this to Ivan (in 1581). The tsar replied,

"I know that the perfidious Frederik of Denmark wants to sever Russia's relations with the European states. He is now encroaching on Kola and Pechenga, ancient possessions of my homeland. We shall frustrate his schemes. Clear the sea and the path to Dvina with your warships. I shall order my military units to occupy the harbors on the Northern Ocean to protect your merchants from Danish violence."

But King Frederik, after making his unjust demands, fell silent. He did not intend to fight Russia in the wild wastes of Lapland, and was afraid of aggravating the English, who by now had a powerful fleet.

Prompted by political wisdom, the sincere alliance of these two powers was also based on Ivan's personal friendship with the queen and nurtured in Moscow by English merchants' stories of her great qualities and deeds, of her beauty and graciousness, and of her kindly disposition and liking for the tsar. It was even written that he was thinking of marrying this 50-year old beauty.

Ivan's Intention to Marry an Englishwoman

This is a tale whose truth is not confirmed by historically contemporary witnesses, but Ivan, who had been married six or seven times, in the very first year of his current unfortunate marriage, *knowing that Mariya was already pregnant*, actively sought a distinguished bride in England so as to further strengthen friendly ties with Elizabeth! We present here the circumstances of this most curious affair in some detail.

After sending the royal physician Robert Jacob off to Moscow in 1581, the queen wrote to the tsar,

Embassy to London

"I am giving you my *blood brother*, a man most skilled in curing illnesses, not because I do not need him, but because you do. You may confidently entrust your health to him. For your pleasure, I am sending with him pharmacists and surgeons, even though we ourselves have an insufficiency of such people."

While conversing with Robert, Ivan asked him if in England there might be an eligible bride, widowed or not, for a monarch.

"I know of one," the doctor replied. "Mary Hastings, the 30-year old daughter of the *sovereign* Prince Huntingdon, nephew to the queen through his mother."

It is likely that Robert guessed Ivan's intention, which would benefit England, and captivated his imagination with a description of the unusual merits of the prospective bride. In any case, the tsar

Chapter Eleven

immediately dispatched the court noble Pisemskii to London with the following instructions:

"1) Get an agreement on a close alliance between England and Russia.

"2) Get alone with the queen and secretly divulge to her his sovereign's intention with regard to a marriage. Ascertain whether Mary Hastings has the requisite qualities for a tsar's bride and request a meeting with her as well as a painted portrait, on board or paper.

"3) Take note of her height, fertility, fairness and age.

"4) Determine her relation to the queen, and her father's rank. Does she have siblings? Find out everything about her that you can. If the queen asks if the sovereign has a wife, answer: *True, but she is not a tsarevna, not a sovereign princess; she is displeasing to him and would be replaced by the queen's niece.*

"5) State that Mary must accept the Greek faith, just like the people with her whom she wants to live at the court in Moscow. Further, the successor to the throne will be Tsarevich Theodor, but the sons of the English princess will be given their own local estates or appanages, as has anciently been the custom in Russia. These conditions are *absolute*, and in case the queen is not agreeable, you are ordered to request your leave."

Sailing from Kholmogory on 11 August 1582, Pisemskii disembarked on the English shore on 16 September coincident with an epidemic that was raging in London that had obliged Elizabeth to withdraw to Windsor to live in solitude. The emissary was taken from village to village, treated as a guest and became familiar with England, but was unable to suppress the complaint of boredom during his six or seven weeks of idleness.

Finally, on 4 November, he and his secretary Neudacha and the interpreter Beckman were presented to the queen at Windsor Castle amidst a great assembly of nobles, peers, court officials and merchants of the London Muscovy Company.

Elizabeth rose when she heard Ivan's name, took a few steps forward, received the gifts and the sovereign's letter, and said with a smile that she did not know Russian. She inquired about

453

the health of her friend and expressed sympathy over the death of the tsarevich. She was cheerful and cordial, and in reply to Pisemskii's words that Ivan was more fond of the queen than of any other European monarch, replied,

"I like him no less, and sincerely wish to some day see him with my own eyes."

She wanted to know if the emissary liked England and if things were tranquil in Russia. Pisemskii praised England as abundant and populous and assured her that all the rebellions had been quieted in Russia, that the perpetrators had shown repentance, and the sovereign, mercy. While pleased with his respectful and kindly reception, Pisemskii was not pleased with her lack of haste with regard to his business. He did not want to go for walks or amuse himself in hunts, as he had been invited to do, but said,

"We are here for business, not games; we are emissaries, not marksmen."

On 18 December, in the *village* of Greenwich, he had his first important opportunity to explain himself to the English ministers. He said that Batory was an ally of the Pope and the Kaiser, and an enemy of Russia; that Ivan had always been concerned for the English as much as for his own people.

He was intent on assuring Elizabeth's friendship with a formal treaty, to have the same friends and enemies as her, and to make war and peace together with her, and that the queen might act together with him, if not with arms, then with money. Russia had not forbidden England to have any of Russia's products, and requested of it gunpowder weapons, armor, sulfur, petroleum, copper, tin, lead and everything necessary for war.

"But is not the Livonian war really over?" Elizabeth's ministers inquired, "The Pope boasts of reconciling the tsar with Batory."

"The Pope may boast as he pleases," Ivan's official replied. "Our sovereign knows who his friends and enemies are."

The ministers announced that the queen had agreed to all of the tsar's proposals, and wrote down the chief articles of the treaty, calling Ivan Elizabeth's brother and *nephew* and used the expression:

Chapter Eleven

"The tsar *entreats* the queen."

They also added that no foreigners but the English would be permitted to trade in the [Northern] Dvina or Solovkie lands, nor on the rivers Ob, Pechora and Mezen. Pisemskii expressed some discontent:

"The tsar is Elizabeth's brother, not her *nephew*. When the tsar expresses his wishes, he requests or asks, he does not *entreat*, and he gives no one exclusive trading rights in Russia: our ports are open to all foreign navigators." The ministers crossed out the word *nephew*, explaining that it was affectionate, not demeaning; they also struck out *entreat*.

They argued that the English had found a route to northern Russia only through great dangers, efforts and expense: they might justifiably request the exclusive advantage of trade in the [Northern] Dvina area.

The English also complained about new duties, which were burdensome to their merchants. Pisemskii replied that these merchants had long been exempt from any duties and had been enriching themselves among us to an unheard of extent and so the sovereign had ordered merely a light *half* duty to be collected from them.

He had cruel wars going with Lithuania, with the khan and with other enemies, so in 1581 he had ordered the English merchants, like all other merchants, whether foreign or our own, to pay commensurate with their wealth into the Moscow treasury 1,000 rubles, and 500 in 1582 to defray military expenses. This concluded the governmental negotiations; now the matchmaking commenced.

On 18 January Elizabeth summoned the impatient Pisemskii and spoke alone with him. She asked about our sovereign's secret business, which was already known to her through the report of the physician Robert. She listened with great attention and expressed her gratitude for Ivan's desire to be related to her by marriage, but did not believe that Mary Hastings, who was distinguished only by exceptional moral qualities, would catch the fancy of one who was *a known lover of beauty*.

"In addition," Elizabeth continued, "she recently had smallpox. I would never on earth agree to let you see her, or a painter to depict her for Ivan, with a red face and deep pockmarks."

The emissary insisted, and the queen promised he could do so, but asked for time so that the prospective bride might completely recover her health. They spoke further on the conditions of the marriage. This daughter of Henry VIII, husband to six wives, was not surprised that the tsar, who already had a wife, was looking for another. However, in good time she wanted a formal agreement establishing the rights of the prospective tsaritsa and her children. With this, she dismissed the matchmaker, who waited for several months for the honor of seeing the prospective bride.

Meanwhile, in Moscow on 19 October, Ivan's wife gave birth to a son, Uar-Dimitrii, who, so unfortunately for himself and for Russia, was to be the innocent cause of protracted villainies and calamities. However, the joy of once again becoming a father did not touch Ivan's heart; he was all the more planning to banish Dimitrii's mother from his bed and marry Elizabeth's niece. He did not give Pisemskii any new orders, so that when this diligent official heard in London of the birth of a tsarevich, he did not care to believe it.

"Evil people," he told the English ministers, "have concocted this piece of news to prevent our sovereign's marriage, which would be a blessing for your country and mine. The queen should believe only the tsar's letter and myself, his emissary."

Finally, on 18 May, Pisemskii was ordered to appear at the garden of Chancellor Thomas Bromley, where the host and the bride's brother, Count Huntingdon, met him and entered into a pleasant conversation. Mary appeared after a few minutes with the chancellor's wife, the Countess Huntingdon, and many eminent Englishmen.

"Here she is," Bromley told the emissary. "Look at her and examine her at your leisure. The queen would be pleased if you were to see her, not in a dark place, not in chambers, but in the fresh air."

The prospective bride curtseyed and stood motionless in front of her appraiser, so daunting to feminine self-esteem. Trying to justify Ivan's great trust in him, he directed a curious, penetrating glance at this modest Englishwoman in order to see everything and forget nothing, to impress her image in his memory and transmit it correctly to his sovereign. Saying, "Very well," he strolled with her along the garden paths, separating from her and then meeting her again, always observing. In his report to the tsar, he wrote,

"Mary Hastings is tall, well-built, slim, and has a fair face. Her eyes are gray, hair blond; her nose is straight and her fingers are long."

He said not a word about beauty or attractiveness, but Elizabeth, who had seemed unwilling to put her niece on display, was now curious about Pisemskii's opinion. She said that he of course would not like Mary; that the portrait of her face that would be sent with him and no little embellished by the artist, would likewise no doubt fail to captivate the discriminating tsar. The matchmaker assured Elizabeth of the contrary and appeared to please her with his praises. Evidently she wanted this marriage, and it is written that Mary did as well. Mary soon changed her mind, however, frightened by stories of her monarch-groom's ferocity, and without difficulty persuaded the queen to free her from this honor.

> DESCRIPTION OF THE PROSPECTIVE FIANCÉE

After entertaining the emissary with a sumptuous dinner at Greenwich, Elizabeth gave him two letters for Ivan. In one she thanked him for proposing an alliance, in the other for *his intention to visit England* (for so she heard it), not in the event of some sort of peril, rebellion or calamity, but just to make the acquaintance of his tender sister, who was prepared to show him that her land would be a second Russia for him. She sent Pisemskii back to Moscow with an English emissary, Jerome Bowes, to decisively conclude all matters, both governmental and *secret*, as Elizabeth put it.

> ELIZABETH'S ENVOY

Ivan was pleased: on 24 October 1583 he very graciously received Bowes and questioned him with great interest about Elizabeth. He ordered the boyar Nikita Romanovich Yuriev, Bogdan Yakovlevich Belskii and the secretary Andrei Romanovich

Shchelkalov to work with him to get an alliance between England and Russia so that once the secret matter of a marriage proposal had been concluded, it could be immediately dealt with. Based on Pisemskii's reports, both of these issues now seemed easy and hardly in doubt.

But the tsar was mistaken and perhaps Elizabeth erred also in choosing Bowes to establish good will with Ivan: he was a stubborn and coarse man who in his first words decisively declared that it would be impossible to change a single word of the articles entrusted to our emissary in London by the English ministers. He said that Elizabeth was prepared to help reconcile the tsar with whomever he wished, but was not ready to fight our enemies, since she wanted to avoid shedding the blood of her people, who had been entrusted to her by God. She also said that England had friendly relations with Lithuania, Sweden and Denmark.

"If my principal enemies," asked Ivan, "are the queen's friends, how can I be her ally? Elizabeth should either persuade Batory to make a sincere peace with Russia (by compelling him to return Livonia and the Polotsk region to me) or else join me in an attack on Lithuania." Bowes heatedly replied,

"The queen would think me out of my mind were I to conclude such an agreement." He insisted that only Englishmen should enter our northern ports, as *before.*

The boyars replied that *previously* we had possessed the Baltic port of Narva for our general European trade – it had later been taken from us by Sweden – and that Germans, Netherlanders and the French were currently trading with Russia solely through our northern harbors and could not be expelled to please Elizabeth. The people's welfare is a sacred principle of the state and we found it embodied in free trade with all Europeans: we could not be subordinate to Englishmen, who were merchants, not sovereigns, in Russia.

We said that they were not ashamed to cheat in commercial dealings, were importing rotten cloth, and that some of them were in secret relations with the tsar's enemies: with the Swedish and Danish kings, whom they were making efforts to help, writing from Moscow to England defamatory things about our country, calling Russians ignorant and stupid. Further, that Ivan had ignored such matters only for the sake of the queen: doubtless she did not presume to give orders to a monarch whom neither emperors, nor sultans, nor eminent kings commanded.

The emissary retorted that there were no monarchs more distinguished than Elizabeth; that she was not inferior to the emperor whom her father hired to fight France, nor to a tsar, either. After these words, as Bowes writes, Ivan angrily dismissed him from the palace, but quickly had second thoughts, and praised the emissary for his ardor on behalf of his queen's honor, adding,

"May God grant I, too, would have such a loyal servitor!" As a token of his special indulgence the sovereign agreed to allow only the English into the harbors of Korela, Varguz, Mezen, Pechenga and Shuma, leaving Pudozhersk and Kola for the other merchants. Bowes was firm:

"We do not want rivals!" Believing that the tsar's nobles, especially the state secretary Andrei Shchelkalov, had been bribed by Netherlands merchants, he asked to deal personally with the tsar. Ivan received him repeatedly, but always dismissed him with displeasure as obstinate and inflexible.

Hoping at least to conclude the matter of a marriage with Bowes, the sovereign ordered him (on December 13) to see him *secretly, without sword or dagger*. All the court nobles left the chamber, leaving only the boyars, Prince Trubetskii, Nikita Romanovich Yuriev, Dimitrii Ivanovich Godunov, Belskii, and the Duma courtiers Tatishchev, Cheremisinov and Voeikov. They sat further away from the tsar, but the secretaries (Shchelkalov, Frolov and Streshnev) stood next to the stove.

After motioning with his hand for Bowes and his interpreter, and also Yuriev, Belskii and Andrei Shchelkalov to approach, Ivan related the whole history of the English matchmaking, including everything he had heard from the physician Robert and from Pisemskii.

He announced his good intention to marry Mary Hastings; he wanted to know if the queen wanted this marriage, and was she agreeable that the bride accept our faith. Bowes replied that

Christianity is as one everywhere, Mary would hardly decide to change her religion, and also, she was in poor health and of bad complexion. He added that the queen had other, closer relatives with attractive qualities, but that he would hardly dare name them without her knowledge, and that the tsar might marry for love . . .

"But what have you come with?" Ivan asked. "With a refusal? With empty words? With the immoderate demands to which my emissary already made reply to Elizabeth's ministers in London? With the proposal of a new, nameless and therefore impossible match?" He called him an uneducated and muddle-headed emissary, and said,

"I did not ask Elizabeth to be a judge between Batory and myself – I merely want England as an ally."

Ivan then ordered Bowes to get ready to depart. Regretting the poor progress of this matter, the emissary began to apologize for his ignorance of Russian customs. He tried to persuade the sovereign to explain himself to Elizabeth once again, assuring him that she was happy in the thought of a blood union with such a great tsar, and provided Ivan with depictions of 10 or more distinguished, charming and eligible young London ladies. He said she just *might*, notwithstanding her love of peace, positively assist us in our wars with men and money, if Ivan were to return to the English merchants *all* their former exclusive rights to the Dvina trade.

1584

Ivan was still captivated by the hope of being husband to an amiable Englishwoman and he also valued Elizabeth's friendship highly. Accordingly, he decided to send a new embassy to London. Although he was personally irritated with Bowes, when he learned of his grievance against some constables, he ordered them to be punished without even an investigation, so that this man, who was greedy and peevish, according to our ministerial papers, might not depart Russia with malice. However, Bowes did not manage to leave, nor did the sovereign designate an emissary for London!

Ivan's Illness and Death

We embark here on the description of a great and solemn hour. We have seen

Chapter Eleven

Ivan's life; now we shall see its end, equally amazing – desired by humanity but horrible to imagine – for the tyrant died as he lived, killing people, although according to contemporary tradition these were not his last victims. How is it possible to believe in immortality and not be horrified by such a death?

This terrible hour, long foretold for Ivan by his conscience and the innocent victims of his tortures, approached him quietly when he had not yet reached an advanced old age, while he was still hearty in spirit and ardent in the lusts of his heart. Strong of constitution, Ivan had hoped for a long life, but could such corporeal strength withstand the fierce agitation of the passions that gripped the dark life of this tyrant?

Constant trembling from rage or fear, the gnawing of a remorseless conscience, the vile delights of his abominable lusts, the torments of shame, impotent malice from his military setbacks, and finally, the hellish punishment of filicide had diminished Ivan's strength. He sometimes felt a sickly languor, the forerunner of a seizure and collapse, but fought against it and did not noticeably weaken until the winter of 1584. A comet appeared at this time along with cruciform heavenly portents between the churches of Ivan the Great and of the Annunciation. Curious, the tsar went out onto the Red Porch and watched it for a long time. His expression changed and he said to those around him,

"That is the portent of my death!"

Frightened by this thought, it is written that he sought out astrologers and supposed wizards in Russia and Lapland; he gathered up to 60 of them and brought them to a house in Moscow. Every day he would send his favorite, Belskii, to discuss the meaning of the comet with them. Soon he became dangerously ill. His whole interior began to decay and his body swelled up. We are assured that the astrologers foretold his inevitable death a few days hence, on 18 March, specifically, but that Ivan ordered them to remain silent, threatening to burn them all on a bonfire if they were indiscreet.

During the month of February he still tended to affairs, but on 10 March a Lithuanian emissary on the way to Moscow was ordered to stop *because of the sovereign's illness*. Ivan had given this order himself. He still hoped to recover, but he summoned his boyars and ordered his will to be written out.

He declared the tsarevich Theodor to be successor to the throne and monarch. For advisors and guardians of the state he selected eminent men: Prince Ivan Petrovich Shuiskii (renowned for the defense of Pskov), Ivan Thedorovich Mstislavskii (son of the niece of Grand Prince Vasilii), Nikita Romanovich Yuriev (brother of the first tsaritsa, the virtuous Anastasiya), Boris Godunov and Belskii. The intent was to lift the burden of administrative cares from young Theodor, who was weak in body and spirit.

He assigned as an appanage the town of Uglich to infant Dimitrii and his mother, and entrusted the boy's upbringing to Belskii alone. He expressed his gratitude to all his boyars and voivodes, calling them his friends and comrades in the conquest of infidel states, in the victories obtained over the Livonian Knights and over the khan and the sultan. He urged Theodor to rule piously, with love and charity. He counseled him and the five chief nobles to avoid wars with Christian powers and spoke of the unfortunate consequences of the Livonian and Swedish wars. He regretted Russia's exhaustion and prescribed a reduction in taxes and a freeing of all prisoners [of war], even Lithuanians and Germans. It seemed that, as he was preparing to depart the throne and his life, he wanted to be reconciled with his conscience, with humanity and with God.

It appeared that his soul, up till now intoxicated with evil, had sobered, and that he wished to save his young son from his fatal delusions. It was as if, on the threshold of the grave, the holy rays of truth were illuminating his cold, dark heart at last; that he was affected by remorse as the Angel of Death invisibly appeared before him with tidings of eternity.

But at this moment, while the court was silent in grief (for the court always grieves, be it sincerely or hypocritically, over a dying monarch), while Christian love moved the people's hearts, while the citizens of the capital, forgetting Ivan's ferocity, prayed in the cathedrals for the tsar's recovery, while even disgraced families and the widows and orphans of the slaughtered innocents prayed for him – at the brink of the grave, what was he doing?

Chapter Eleven

Rallying for a moment, he ordered himself to be carried to the palace, where lay his marvelous treasures, and looked upon his precious gems. On 15 March he delightedly showed them to the Englishman [Jerome] Horsey, and described the quality of his diamonds and rubies, using the words of a connoisseur! But is a more terrible tale to be believed than this? His daughter-in-law, Theodor's wife, came to the sick man with tender comforts, but fled in disgust from his shameless sensuality. Was this sinner repenting? Was he even thinking of the near and terrible judgment of the Most High?

Now his vitality was gone and his thoughts became clouded. After lying unconscious for a while on his deathbed, Ivan loudly summoned his murdered son, saw him in his imagination and talked tenderly with him. On 17 March, after a warm bath, he improved enough to order the Lithuanian emissary to ride immediately from Mozhaisk to the capital, and on the following day (if we are to believe Horsey), he told Belskii:

"Order the execution of the lying astrologers. According to their fables, I should now be dead, but I feel much better."

"But the day is not yet over," the astrologers replied to him. Another bath was prepared: he remained in it for about three hours, and then lay on his bed, got up and asked for a chess board. Sitting in his dressing gown, he set up the pieces himself; he wanted to play with Belskii. Suddenly he fell, and his eyes closed for the last time. The doctors rubbed him with astringent fluids as the metropolitan – carrying out, probably, Ivan's long-known wish – recited prayers to ordain the dying man as a monk, naming him Iona.

18 March

During these minutes a deep silence reigned in the palace and in the capital. People were waiting for what might happen, but dared not ask. Ivan already lay dead, but he was still fearsome to the courtiers standing about him; they could not believe their own eyes and for a long time did not announce his death.

But when the conclusive words *the sovereign is no more!* rang throughout the palace, the people began to howl loudly – either, it is written, because they knew of Theodor's weakness and feared its evil consequences for the nation, or because they were paying the Christian debt of regret for their deceased monarch, despite his cruelty.

A splendid funeral was held on the third day in the Cathedral of St. Michael the Archangel. Tears flowed down faces, expressing grief, and the earth quietly received Ivan's body into its bowels. Man's judgment was silent in the face of God's. For contemporaries, the curtain had fallen – for posterity, the memories and graves remained.

> THE RUSSIANS' LOVE FOR AUTOCRACY

Among the other severe trials of fate, in addition to the disastrous appanage system and the Mongol yoke, Russia had experienced the menace of an autocrat-torturer. It kept its love for autocracy, for it believed that plagues, earthquakes and tyrants were sent by God. It did not destroy the iron scepter in Ivan's hands, and for 24 years it had withstood the murderer, armed only with prayer and patience, so that in better times it might have Peter the Great and Catherine II (history does not like to mention the living [i.e., Aleksandr I]). His victims had died at the scaffold with humble courage, like the Greeks at Thermopylae, for their country, their faith and out of loyalty, with no thought of rebellion.

It is in vain that some foreign historians, excusing Ivan's cruelty, wrote of the plots he supposedly curtailed: according to all the testimony of our chronicles and our state papers these plots existed only in the tsar's confused mind. The priesthood, the boyars and eminent citizens would not have summoned the beast from that den of iniquity, Aleksandrovskaya Sloboda, if they were plotting revolt. That this is imputed to them is as absurd as sorcery. No, the tiger was drunk on the blood of the sheep, and his victims, expiring in their innocence, with their last look at their suffering land, demanded justice and the sympathetic remembrance of contemporaries and posterity.

> IVAN COMPARED TO OTHER TORTURERS

Despite all speculative suppositions, about the character of Ivan, who was a hero of virtue in his youth and insatiably bloodthirsty in his maturity and old age, it remains a puzzle

Chapter Eleven

for the mind, and we would doubt the veracity of our information concerning him if the chronicles of other peoples did not provide us with such amazing examples – if Caligula, *a model of a sovereign* and *a monster*, and that pupil of the wise Seneca, Nero – *an object of love, an object of loathing* – had not ruled in Rome.

They were pagans, but Louis XI was a Christian, who was hardly second to Ivan in cruelty and the external piety with which he attempted to efface his criminality. Both were devout out of fear and both were bloodthirsty voluptuaries, like the Asiatic and Roman torturers. These monsters without the law, without principles, without rationality, these terrible meteors, these fornicators with unbridled, fiery passions, illuminate for us over the ages the abyss of possible human depravity, so that we may see, and shudder.

> USES OF HISTORY

The life of a tyrant is a disaster for humanity, but his history is always of use to sovereigns and the people – to imbue a loathing for evil is to imbue a love for virtue. Glorious is the time in which the historian armed with the truth might under an autocratic system of government expose to shame such a ruler, in order that there would never be his like in the future. Graves are insensible, but the living fear the eternal condemnation of history, which while not reforming the criminals, sometimes prevents those crimes that are always possible – for wild passions forever rage within civilized society, commanding the mind to silence, or else to justify their excesses with servile voice.

And so Ivan, with an exceptional intellect that was no stranger to cultivation and knowledge, joined this with an unusual gift of speech to shamelessly indulge his vile passions.

> MIXTURE OF GOOD AND EVIL IN IVAN

He had an unusual memory; he knew the Bible by heart as well as the histories of Greece, Rome and our nation, but absurdly misinterpreted them to aid his tyranny.

He boasted of firmness and self-control and was able to laugh out loud at moments of fear or internal distress. He boasted of his charity and generosity, while enriching his favorites with the property of disgraced boyars and citizens. He boasted of his justice, punishing merit and criminality with equal enthusiasm. He boasted of his royal spirit and the upholding of his sovereign honor, ordering that an elephant that had been sent to Moscow from Persia be hacked to pieces because it would not kneel before him, and he cruelly punished miserable courtiers who were bold enough to play draughts or cards better than their ruler.

Finally, he boasted of his profound administrative sagacity, of [the merits of] his regime over the various periods of his reign, of his cool calculation in destroying eminent kinsmen who were supposedly a threat to his monarchical power and then raising new, base relatives to their ranks, touching even the distant future with his lethal hands. The cloud of informers, slanderers and oprichniki that he had developed, vanished like a cloud of hungry insects, but left evil seeds behind in the populace. If Baty's yoke had ever humbled the Russian soul, certainly it was never lifted by Ivan's reign.

But we shall grant justice even to a tyrant: Ivan even in the extremities of his evil appeared a phantasm of a great monarch – diligent, tireless and often perceptive in his administrative activities. Although he always loved to liken himself to Alexander of Macedonia in valor and although he did not have a shadow of courage in his soul, he remains a conqueror. In foreign policy, he steadfastly followed the great purposes of his grandfather.

He loved justice in the courts and he often tried cases himself: he would hear the charges, read all the documentation and then come to an immediate decision. He punished oppressors of the people, conscienceless officials and bribers both corporally and with shaming (he would array them in fine clothing, seat them in a chariot, and then order a knacker to take them from street to street). He did not tolerate foul drunkenness (only on Holy Week and Christmas were people permitted to celebrate in taverns; at all other times, drunks were thrown in jail). While Ivan did not like bold reproach, at times he was not fond of crude flattery, either.

We give an example: the voivodes and the princes Iosif Shcherbatyi and Yurii Boryatinskii, whom the tsar had ransomed from Lithuanian captivity, were awarded his favor, gifts and the honor of dining with him. He questioned them about Lithuania: Shcherbatyi told the truth, but Boryatinskii lied brazenly, asserting that the king had neither fortresses nor troops and trembled at Ivan's name.

"Poor king!" the tsar remarked quietly, nodding his head. "I am so sorry for you!" Then he suddenly grabbed his staff and broke it into small pieces over Boryatinskii, repeating again and again,

"That is for you, shameless one, for your base lies!"

Ivan was praised for his prudent religious toleration, which excluded only Jews, and allowed Lutherans and Calvinists to have churches in Moscow, but about five years later he ordered them burned down (did he fear subversion, or had he heard the people were displeased?). In any case, he did not interfere with these people gathering at the homes of their pastors for religious services.

He loved to argue with German scholars over religion, and tolerated contradiction: in 1570 he had a formal debate in the Kremlin palace with Rotsita, a Lutheran theologian, in which he accused him of heresy. Rotsita sat before him on a raised place covered with rich carpets. He spoke boldly, justifying the dogmas of the Augsburg Confession, and earned tokens of the tsar's good will, later writing a book about this curious conversation.

The German preacher Kaspar, wishing to ingratiate himself with Ivan, was baptized in Moscow according to the rites of our Church and joked with him about Luther. This irritated his compatriots, but none of them complained of mistreatment. They lived peacefully in Moscow in the new German Quarter on the banks of the Yauza and enriched themselves through crafts and artisanry. Ivan declared his esteem for the arts and sciences and favored well-educated foreigners.

He founded no academies, but facilitated public education by increasing the number of church schools, where laymen could learn literacy, religious principles and even history. This would prepare them in particular to be clerks, to the shame of the boyars, not all of whom could write at this time. Finally, Ivan is distinguished in history as a legislator and educator of the nation.

> IVAN AS DEVELOPER OF THE NATION AND AS LEGISLATOR

The Reign of Ivan the Terrible

His Ministries

There is no doubt that the truly great Ivan III, who gave us the Civil Code, also set up various government departments to improve the effectiveness of the autocracy. In addition to the ancient Boyar Duma, in the affairs of this era mention is also made of the treasury and ministries, but we know nothing further. We do have clear and reliable information about the many offices and law courts that existed in Moscow in the time of Ivan IV.

The main ministries were Emissaries, Ranks, Estates and "Kazan." The first dealt with foreign and diplomatic affairs in particular; the second, military; the third, with the lands distributed to officials and boyar cadets for their services; and the fourth dealt with Kazan, Astrakhan, Siberia and all the Volga towns.

In addition to the duties designated above, the first three also dealt with the administration of all the regional towns and cities – a strange mixture! Grievances, lawsuits and investigations all came to the ministries from the regions, where deputies judged and administered with their tiuns and elders, assisted by the centurions and decurions in the uezds.

From the ministries, then, where eminent state officials met, all important criminal and civil matters went up to the Boyar Duma, so that no one was executed or deprived of his property without the tsar's confirmation. Only the deputies of Smolensk, Pskov, Novgorod and Kazan, who were changed almost every year, could punish criminals, and then only in extraordinary circumstances. New laws, institutions and taxes were always promulgated through the ministries. The tsar's property, or votchina, which included many cities, had its own office.

In addition to this, there were other departments: guards, posts, palace, finance, brigandage, Moscow government, national revenue, armaments, provisions and the serf court, where suits concerning serfs were decided.

In these and also in regional administrations, the principal agents were secretary-clerks, who were employed in matters dealing with emissaries, the military and sieges and for correspondence and consultation – this aroused the envy and displeasure of the

His Secretaries
His Clerks

Chapter Eleven

military nobility. Knowing not only how to read and write better than others, but also having a firm knowledge of the law, traditions and ceremonies, the secretaries or clerks were a special kind of state servitor, lower in rank than the court nobles, but higher than the tenant boyar cadets and eminent merchants.

The *Duma* secretaries were second only to the state counselors. These were the boyars, okolnichie and new Duma nobles, established by Ivan in 1572 to bring into the Duma officials who were distinguished by intellect rather than by good pedigree. Despite all of Ivan's misuse of unbounded power, he occasionally respected the old customs. For example, he did not want to promote his favorite, Malyuta Skuratov, to boyar rank because he feared to demean this high rank by such a fast promotion of a man of low birth.

> DUMA NOBLES

After increasing the number of people in the ministries and giving them more importance in his administrative apparatus, Ivan, as a skillful ruler, formed yet another rank of distinction for nobles and princes. He divided the former into two types: *peer* and *junior*; the latter into *ordinary princes* and *service princes*. To the courtiers he added *stewards*, who served at the sovereign's table and also carried out military duties; they outranked the junior court nobles.

> NOBLES OF THE PEERAGE AND JUNIOR NOBLES

> SERVICE PRINCES

> STEWARDS

We have already written of the military establishments of this energetic reign. Even though he shamed our banners in the field through his cowardice, Ivan left Russia an army such as it had never had before. It was better organized and larger than previously. He destroyed his most renowned voivodes, but did not destroy the valor of the rank and file, who displayed it most of all in adversity, so that our immortal enemy Batory told Possevino with amazement how they did not consider their own lives in the defense of cities, but would coolly stand in places that had been broken down or blown up by mines and guard the gaps with their breasts; they would fight day and night, eating only bread; they would die of hunger, but not surrender, *so as not to betray their sovereign-tsar.*

> MILITARY ORGANIZATION

Even the women would display valor alongside of them – extinguishing fires or hurling timbers and stones at the enemy from the heights. In the field, these loyal patriots would distinguish themselves, if not by skill, then by their marvelous endurance, withstanding frosts, blizzards and foul weather under thin tents or in drafty huts. The oldest books of rank name only voivodes, but in this era they also name *heads*, or local administrators, who, along with the voivodes, were answerable to the tsar for all their dealings.

LAWS

As we have said, Ivan supplemented his grandfather's Civil Code [*Grazhdanskoe Ulozhenie*]: he added new laws, but did not change the general scheme or spirit of the old ones. His grandfather had ordered judges not to take bribes; the son set a heavy monetary fine for this and for *intentional* injustice, so that only unintentional cases went unpunished.

Crooked secretaries were imprisoned and lesser clerks got the knout. Those harmed by a deputy were obliged to continue to bring their complaints until he was replaced, but slanderers were subject to corporal punishment in addition to confiscation of funds following their disgrace.

VALUE OF THE RUBLE

Judicial and clerical fees were not increased, even though the value of money had decreased somewhat. (In 1557 a ruble was reckoned at 16 shillings, 8 pence; in 1582, about 3 old Polish gold pieces; one mark in the reign of Theodor Ivanovich; and at the beginning of the 17th century, 2 Reichsthalers and 10 dengas.)

Cases were decided, as before, by witnesses, oaths and single combat, but between foreigners and Russians, by *casting lots*: whoever won was declared vindicated. The secretary would record the case and the elders and court clerks would affix their signatures to the document. In the case of reconciliation, always desirable to the legislator, those being tried were exempted from any fees.

If someone were accused of robbery, then a mandatory inquiry would be made of the neighbors or a search would be made. A man known to be a miscreant would be tortured and permanently imprisoned if he did not confess to his crime, but a man cleared by the investigation would be tried according to the law.

Punishment was as before: knout for the first theft, death for the second. Death was the penalty for murderers, traitors, betrayers of the city and a theft from a church or an otherwise serious theft, as well as for arsonists, brigands, counterfeiters and even serious frauds and informers. Denials of theft were not to be believed without the testimony of 15 or 20 upright citizens. The deputy's men or officials could not seize anyone or place him in irons without informing the elder and the court clerks.

Here we see more caution, more respect for people than in the laws of Ivan III. The civil statutes are likewise more precise and complete. For example, inherited possessions are distinguished from those purchased: if the former are sold or pledged, the relatives can redeem the former within 40 years, but only if the deed of purchase or the pawn ticket has not been signed by witnesses. If it is shown that this property is not worth the money stated in the deed of purchase, they can recover only the actual value. Property legitimately acquired [i.e., purchased] cannot be recovered.

Loan documents are not valid without a boyar's seal and a secretary's signature, for which a fee will be collected. In monetary suits, the state records must always be consulted, where citizens' names, property and the amount they paid to the treasury are noted. One copy of this book is kept at the Moscow ministries, another at the district officials', with the elder and the court clerks. Demands exceeding the income of the respondent are charged to the plaintiff.

While respecting the rights of the lord in relation to his serfs, the legislator added to the old statutes that the children of an enslaved servant born prior to his enslavement are free people. Stewards and rural tiuns are not serfs unless there is a special, recorded deed of purchase. A father or mother who enters a monastery loses the right to commit his children to serfdom. Lenders cannot enslave debtors, who are obliged only to pay them interest.

If someone is taken into a household as a serf and leaves, even after stealing from his master, [and no respondent is available] there is no trial, nor satisfaction for the master. Boyar cadets and their descendants are forever exempted from serfdom. Affirming the power of a [written] discharge [from servitude], the sovereign ordered that it be sealed by a boyar or deputy in Moscow, Novgorod or Pskov only. It is invalid without the seal, even though signed by the lord.

In the law concerning free passage of peasants from one village to another, in addition to time spent in the household, they are also to pay the owner two altyns for *transfer*, and if there is grain remaining in the ground, after harvesting it he is to give his lord two altyns. He is always permitted to sell himself into serfdom to an owner.

In accordance with ancient custom, the tsar upheld ecclesiastical justice: he left the bishops the right to judge priests, deacons, monks and old widows who were fed by God's Church. He permitted the poor, but not tradesmen, to live in monasteries.

The statutes regarding purchases were supplemented with the following articles:

"1) nothing is to be bought from a market or shop without a guarantee;

"2) to avoid disputes any horse purchased must be branded the same day at the government branders and entered into their books, with a payment of two dengas to the treasury; violators of this statute are to be punished with a fine of no less than two rubles."

We also mention a new law bearing on [compensation for] dishonor: it is to be paid to boyar cadets commensurate with their income or salary; to palace secretaries as the sovereign directs; to traveling or distinguished merchants, 50 rubles; to tradesmen, people of the middle level and boyars' better servants, 5 rubles; to lower class people and peasants, one ruble. Women are always to receive twice that of a man, as a token of special respect for the honor of the weaker sex.

At the end of the Code document, it said that Ivan's [new] laws do not pertain to old cases and do not change previous decisions, even if not yet executed, and that new cases may be encountered in court which produce new statutes, and that these must be added to the Civil Code.

Chapter Eleven

From 1550 to 1580, Ivan issued many supplementary decrees that were significant in the circumstances of the nation at that time. In 1556 he eliminated judicial fees and decreed fixed salaries for deputies instead. He also imposed a general tax on towns, cities and volosts; he ordered criminal cases to be heard by select citizens and rural residents.

He forbade chiefs, elders and centurions from trial by combat in any case that might be decided by using witnesses or by kissing the cross. That is to say, he permanently eliminated this ancient custom dating from the days of knighthood and ignorance. Perjurers were to be punished by the knout and a heavy monetary fine.

Ivan also added the following statutes to the laws:

"1) If in a trial, people speak at odds, some for the plaintiff, some for the respondent, the majority is to be given credence – 50 or 60 of them. If the number of votes is the same on both sides, then a new trial is to be undertaken: people are to be summoned from other nearby settlements to ascertain the truth. The testimony of five or six people who are not well known is not sufficient for an indictment, but the word of a boyar, secretary or petty official is always to be considered reliable.

"If plaintiff and respondent call on the same person [to testify], then that person is to decide the case. If a boyar's or court noble's man commits perjury, his lord is subject to the tsar's wrath, but if that lord [previously] discloses the lie to the tsar, then he is guiltless. The chief duty of an elder is to prevent deception and collusion in giving civil evidence. In case of negligence, duplicity or partiality, these chosen officials are to be punished without mercy.

"2) If a lord seeks evidence against a free man who has served him without a deed of serfdom and has left him, or even secretly escaped from his home, the lord will not be given a judgment, since he might, in his irritation, slander an innocent servant whom he has held without papers, which is against the law, as well as imprudent.

"3) A freed serf may no longer serve his master, otherwise his papers are invalidated.

"4) If a lord takes a man into serfdom and this man proves that he is a free man, and he has been under guarantee, and he leaves, then the guarantor must pay the plaintiff four rubles, in addition to any other claims.

"5) Someone who draws up a false deed of servitude on someone else shall be punishable by death.

"6) A prisoner of war may become a serf, but the death of his master frees him. His children are always free if he has not married a serf or given himself into servitude. Baptized foreigners may enter into servitude, but only with the knowledge of the state treasury, and only if they are not in the tsar's service.

"7) For the recovery of a 100-ruble debt, one month is specified. From a servant, two months. After this, the insolvent debtor is to hand himself over to the plaintiff until repayment is made, but he is not permanently enserfed."

This recovery of debts was called *pravezh*, and was done in the following manner: a constable would take the debtor, shoeless, to the doors of the legal offices and flog him during the hours of business on his bare feet with a rod, sometimes just for appearance, sometimes to inflict pain, until such time as the judges went home. This was an Asiatic custom, halted by Peter the Great.

"8) The recovery of *old* debt from serving people over a five-year period (from 1558 to 1563) is to be without interest, but *new* debt is at half-interest, or 10 per 100 – the tsar has permanently eliminated burdensome interest (20 per 100).

"9) Recovery of debt with proper papers must be sure and exact for all, but without interest.

"10) In the case of someone who has not redeemed a pawned personal item, he must be notified that the term has expired and designate a new one for payment: a week or two. If the item is not subsequently redeemed, he is to take the item to the elder and his court clerks to sell honestly, with reliable witnesses, and then recover the debt with interest, but hand over the excess to the debtor. If the money from the sale is too little to repay the loan, the rest may be sought from the debtor.

"11) The plaintiff-lender need not have a written obligation if the respondent acknowledges himself as debtor in court.

"12) Many have pledged their patrimony, so that instead of interest, the lender can plow and sow grain therein. To lighten the burden on debtors, it is ordered that all such lands be returned to them, with the obligation not to sell them to anyone and to satisfy the lender over the course of five years, who, in the case of default, will again receive the patrimony."

In this decree, it speaks of books of patrimonies, serfs and pawned items, which are to be found at the secretaries'.

"13) If a wife, dying, designates in her will her husband as executor, this will is not to be given credence, since a wife is in her husband's power and writes whatever he tells her to write.

"14) Ecclesiastical punishment is imposed on Christians who have been imprisoned or detained against their will, have given their oath not to escape, but do so. This is because oath-breaking is a deadly sin, and it is better to die than break a holy promise.

"15) If both plaintiff and respondent are out-of-towners, they are tried in Moscow at the treasurer's offices if they are from different towns, but if they are from the same town, they are sent to the deputy of local affairs, but not in criminal cases, which are tried at the place of the crime.

"16) In the capital there are to be no executions or public punishments on the day of a great requiem for the dead, when the metropolitan dines with the sovereign."

After forbidding the priesthood from buying real property without the tsar's consent, in these supplements to the Code Ivan ordered that all state lands, villages and fisheries that had been unjustly acquired in the troubled time of the reign of the boyars be taken away from the bishops and the monasteries.

"Monks," he wrote to the Kazan prelate Gurii, "should cultivate not the land, but their hearts, sowing not grain, but the word of God and inheriting, not villages, but the Kingdom of Heaven. Many of our bishops think more of transitory gain than of the Church."

In thinking in this way, Ivan was bolder than his grandfather: he enriched the treasury with the property of the mute priesthood.

From this time up until the reign of Aleksei Mikhailovich,* the *New Code* was the common book of law for Russia. In addition, Ivan issued district administrators *letters statutory and gubnie***.

The former defined the revenues, rights and duties of deputies and others of the tsar's officials, and included the most important criminal statutes of the *Code*, along with some particular local regulations.

In one of these, given to the residents of Kholmogory in 1557, it said that the tsar freed them of the deputies' jurisdiction, conditional on them depositing 20 rubles per *sokh* into the treasury, i.e., from 64 homesteads, and that the Dvina chiefs must choose centurions and subordinate officers, who would be answerable for the safety and good order of their purviews, in order to eliminate robbery, brigandage, drunkenness and slander. If the chiefs or the people's magistrates should dare to misuse the trust of their fellow citizens for evil purposes, to oppress people or take bribes, the penalty would be death.

All other matters, investigative or judicial, were to be recorded at the local secretaries'. Dvina residents would be free to replace judges, but in such cases were obliged to send the new ones to Moscow to kiss the cross before the sovereign's secretaries, in observation of the law. In another regulation, the same Dvina letter also specified the dimensions of courts, cabins and ice-houses that the residents were obliged to construct for the deputies and tiuns.

In old German law, the word *guba**** designates a farmstead, but in ours, a volost or department. *Gubnie* letters were given to district magistrates, and contained only criminal laws. These letters prescribed that elders, gubnie court clerks and secretaries were to commence their duties with an investigation or session with the most eminent residents of their volost: princes, boyar cadets, archimandrites, abbots and trustees of each locality.

They were obliged to kiss the cross and declare all robbers and *bad people* known to them. This testimony was entered into a book,

---

*   [The second Romanov tsar. Reigned 1645-1676.]
** [This term will be explained in the next paragraph.]
*** [This is not the common Russian word for *lip*, but apparently comes from German *Hufe*, a hide of land, i.e., the amount of land needed to support a household.]

Chapter Eleven

the accused were brought to trial and tortured, and their property was distrained to satisfy the plaintiffs. Those who confessed were punished according to the Code. Those who were jailed but could not be convicted with reliable witnesses, and who presented a reliable guarantor, were released. Those not convicted, but strongly suspected, were imprisoned indefinitely. Someone who strongly supported a person convicted of a crime was to answer with his property and his life for that person's future crimes.

For the peace of mind of honest citizens, Ivan wished to be harsh rather than weak in trying to restrain criminals, contrary to the thinking of more recent Russian criminal legislation – that it is better 10 guilty men go free than one innocent man be punished.

Church Institutions

We now cross over from civil institutions to ecclesiastical ones, which are equally notable. We have already mentioned the Moscow Council of 1551: we note here its most significant and interesting articles. Following Ivan's instructions, the prelates determined:

"1) In Moscow and all the realm, there are to be eparchial elders and their assistants, chosen from the best priests to supervise church services, to perform all church rites precisely, and under the supervision of the priesthood, are obliged to instruct people by both word and deed.

"2) They are to strictly guard against errors in churchly books, and see that icons are copied [accurately] from the old Greek ones, or as Andrei Rublyov and other eminent artists painted them. This sacred task is only to be attended to by people acknowledged by the sovereign and the bishops to be worthy of it, not only by their skill, but also by their irreproachable lives. Their reward will be general respect!"

The following are the prescriptions for bells, church hymns, the liturgy, and morning and evening services:

"3) Let no prince, noble or other good Christian enter a church with his head covered, or with a Moslem's skullcap! Let not beer, or mead or bread be brought to the altar, except for communion bread! Let the absurd custom of laying an infant's caul on the altar be eliminated forever!

"4) Abuse of power and error are fatal to the morals of the priesthood. What do we see in the monasteries? People seek in them not the salvation of their souls, but corporal repose and enjoyment. Archimandrites and abbots do not know the fraternal table, but entertain lay guests in their cells. Monks have boys and youths, and shamelessly receive women and young girls, making merry and ruining monastery villages.

"Henceforth in the cloisters let there be but one table for all. Monks are to send away their young servants, and not admit women, nor keep wine (except for foreign wine) or strong mead, and they are not to travel to the villages or towns for amusement. Let criminals be ejected or excluded from all holy places. This law of moderation, restraint and chastity has been given to all the priesthood: to monks, deacons and junior deacons.

"5) Cloisters rich in land and income are not ashamed to request alms of the sovereign. Henceforth do not so annoy him!

"6) Prelates and monasteries are free to loan money to farmers and citizens, but without any interest.

"7) In many places Christian charity has established almshouses for the infirm and aged. Mismanagement has allowed in the young, as well as healthy spongers. Let the latter be expelled, but the former let in, consistent with charitable intent. Let good priests, townsmen and court clerks look after almshouses everywhere.

"8) Many monks, nuns and laymen boast of supernatural dreams and prophecy, wandering from place to place with holy monks and improperly and scandalously asking money to build churches, to the consternation of foreigners. The sovereign's commandments are to be announced in the marketplaces, that henceforth there shall be no such error. If these vagabonds do not cease, they are to be driven out, and their icons given to the church.

"9) Old cathedrals are deserted and new ones are being built, not out of ardor for the faith, but out of vainglory, and are likewise soon deserted for lack of priests, monks and books. We see yet another evil: idlers are leaving monasteries, building hermitages in the woods and pestering Christians for monetary assistance. The sovereign directs that bishops forbid either of these activities without special, strict supervision.

Chapter Eleven

"10) Parishioners select priests and deacons: the former must be at least 30, the latter, 25. They must lead a moral life and be literate; those who read and write poorly are to be sent to the schools that are now being established in all cities. Protegés are to pay only the set fee to the metropolitan and bishops: priests, one Moscow ruble and a *blessed* grivna; deacons, 50 kopecks.

"In accordance with the grand princes' statute, newlyweds pay Ivan Vasilievich and his son one altyn for the wedding, two for a second marriage, and four for a third. However baptism, confession, communion and burial are free of any charge. No churchman is to wear unusual clothing. Everyone is to have their own [proper dress]: the soldier and the officer, the merchant and the craftsman. Why should a servant of the Church adorn himself with gold and beads, braiding and embroidery, like a woman?

"Prelates are to be chosen from the abbots and archimandrites, the selection to be confirmed by the tsar. Widowered priests and deacons are once more forbidden to perform holy rites, and monks and nuns are barred from living in the same cloister, or in the village.

"11) Metropolitans and bishops are not to replace their boyars or majors-domo without the sovereign's knowledge; the replacement for a deceased one is to be from the same family line. The priesthood is obliged to eradicate pagan and all vile customs. For example, when a plaintiff and respondent are about to engage in trial by combat, sorcerers will appear who look at the stars, refer to something like the *Aristotelian Gates* or *Rafli*,* and foretell a happy victory; they thereby magnify the evil of bloodshed.

"The gullible possess Aristotelian books, books on astrology, the zodiac and almanacs filled with heretical learning. On [St.] John's Eve, people gather at night, sing, frolic and dance for a night and a day; they act just as crazily on Christmas Eve, the birthday of Vasilii the Great, and Epiphany. On Whitsuntide Saturday, they weep, howl and desecrate graveyards, jumping, clapping their hands and singing satanic hymns. On the morning of Maundy Thursday, they burn straw and call out the dead, while the priests on this day lay salt at the altar and treat the infirm with it.

---

* [These are both old books of divination.]

"False prophets race from village to village, naked and barefoot, with disheveled hair, trembling and falling on the ground, and fabulating about apparitions of St. Anastasii and St. Paraskevi. Throngs of minstrels and clowns, as many as a hundred, wander from town to town, eating and drinking off the farmers and even robbing travelers on the roads. Boyar cadets flock to taverns, play dice and are ruined. Men and women share the same bath, even monks and nuns, without shame.

"In the marketplace they sell hares, ducks and strangled grouse; people eat blood and sausage, contrary to the strictures of the Ecumenical Council. They follow Latin customs, shave off their beards and mustaches, wear foreign clothing, swear to lies in God's name and use bad language. Finally, most abominable of all and the reason God punishes Christians with war, famine and pestilence – they lapse into the sins of Sodom.

"Spiritual fathers! Halt this evil; admonish, threaten, punish with penance. Do not let the disobedient enter church! Teach Christians to fear God and be chaste, so that they may live peacefully in their neighborhood, without slandering, stealing, robbing, bearing false witness or perjuring. Let there be good morals everywhere in our beloved homeland, and let children respect their parents!"

This ecclesiastical legislation was more the tsar's doing than the priesthood's. He considered and advised: they only followed his directions. His style is surprisingly pure and clear.

We note an oddity: although he wanted to eliminate old customs contrary to the holy faith, in the *Stoglav* Ivan and the priesthood did not touch on the habit of giving non-Christian names in accordance with their moral qualities, not just to simple folk, but also to eminent officials.

While considering it a sin to name people after Ryurik and Oleg, even in government documents there are the names *Druzhina, Tishina, Istoma, Neudacha* and *Khozyain*, with only a Christian patronymic appended. The tsar considered this to be an innocent custom.

CHAPTER ELEVEN

In February 1581, on the death of the metropolitan Antonii, Abbot Dionisii of the Khutynskii Monastery was chosen to replace him. Ivan, the bishops and the boyars established a ritual of ordination to this lofty rank without including anything old, it seems, but sanctioning it with just this following council document:

"With regard to someone God wishes to be metropolitan, bishop, abbot or elder, he must be informed of this honor immediately. On the day of nomination and elevation, bells are rung and hymns sung. The prelates, after reciting the canon to the Virgin and to Pyotr the Wonderworker, send the two archimandrites of the Rozhestvenskii and Trinity Monasteries to fetch the nominee, who then goes with them to the sovereign. The tsar has the future metropolitan seated and makes a speech to him concerning prayer.

"After the nominee is nominated in the Cathedral of the Dormition, next to the holy icons and tombs, he goes with the bishops to the metropolitan's court in the White Palace, and there after sitting in his place, he awaits and meets the tsar and converses with him. Standing in the metropolitan's place, he hears the liturgy in the main church and dines in the White Palace with all the prelates. But after that, he receives no one until his ordination, eating in a cell with only a few close monks.

"Two days later, the *selection* is made and announced to him by the *blagovestniki*, who are the archimandrites of the Spasskii and Chudovskii monasteries. A place is prepared in the church and an eagle is painted above it.

"On the appointed day, when the church bells ring, the prelates put on their robes, and the future metropolitan with them if he is a bishop, but if he is not, he dresses in a side chapel. The sovereign enters the cathedral, surrounded by his boyars. After making the sign of the cross at the holy icons, he goes up to his prepared place and is seated, as are the prelates. The *chosen one* stands among eight candle-bearers and recites the confession of faith underneath the eagle. The mass begins.

"The archbishop of Novgorod or Kazan holds the icon lamp and the crozier. After they repeat *holy, holy* three times, the prelates install him in accordance with the ancient custom. He finishes the mass and the archbishop names him in a prayer after the line starting with *Izpryadna*. A candle-bearer, holding a candle and an icon lamp, bows to the metropolitan and takes his place before him at the altar, but when *With the fear of God* is intoned, the lamp and crozier are taken from the archbishop and the metropolitan's subdeacon stands by the tsar's doorway with the icon lamp and the crozier of the new archprelate.

"After the liturgy, the bishops elevate him to his seat next to the sovereign. They seat him three times, intoning *Ispollaeti Despota**. They remove his garments of office, place the portal icon on his chest, a cloak with texts on his shoulders, a black or white (as the sovereign directs) cylindrical hat on his head and lead him to the prelate's stone seat. The tsar approaches, makes a speech, and places the prelate's crozier in his right hand. Then the eminent churchmen, boyars and princes wish the new metropolitan long life. He blesses the tsar and makes a speech.

"Now the priests and the boyars wish long life to the tsar as well. On the porches, they likewise intone *many years*. They leave the church. The sovereign has a table [set] for all the eminent churchmen, nobles and officials. The metropolitan rides around Moscow on a donkey led by the boyars' and prelate's boyars. There are chalices [of wine] after the meal: Pyotr the Wonderworker's, the sovereign's and the metropolitan's."

> A MEMORABLE CHURCH CEREMONY

We also mention here a curious church ritual of this era that has now been long forgotten in Russia. On the week of Palm Sunday, before mass, all the people of Moscow gather in the Kremlin. A large tree is brought out of the Cathedral of the Dormition, hung with various fruits (apples, raisins, figs and dates). It is affixed to two runners and carried quietly. At the base of the tree, five youths in white garments sing hymns. Behind this sleigh come many youths with burning wax tapers and an enormous lantern, and behind them come two tall gonfalons, six thuribles and six icons.

Behind the icons come more than a hundred priests in splendid chasubles, covered with pearls, and behind them the boyars, and

---

* [Rather disconcertingly, for Americans at least, this is closely rendered by *Hail to the Chief*.]

finally, the sovereign and the metropolitan. The latter rides side-saddle on a donkey (or horse), dressed in white. In his left hand he holds in his lap the Gospels, bound in gold, and with his right hand, he blesses the people. A boyar leads the donkey. In one hand, the sovereign holds the long reins, in the other, a [sprig of] pussy willow. The metropolitan's route is covered with cloths. Still further to the rear come yet more boyars and officials and behind them an uncountable multitude of people. They proceed in this way around to the various Kremlin churches and return to the Church of the Dormition, where the metropolitan performs the liturgy.

Afterwards, he gives a meal for the tsar and the nobles. This church procession, commemorating Christ's reception in Jerusalem, probably originated in ancient times, but we have known about it only since Ivan's, from the descriptions of foreign observers.

Building Towns

Among the praiseworthy activities of this reign was the building of many new towns to pacify our borders. In addition to Laishev, Cheboksary, Kozmodemyansk, Bolkhov, Oryol and the other fortresses we have mentioned, Ivan also founded Donkov, Epifan, Venev, Chern, Kokshazhsk, Tetyushi, Alatyr and Arzamas.

Situation in Moscow

However, after building handsome strongholds in the forests and steppes, towards the end of his life, he was grieved to see ruins and empty lots in Moscow, which was burned by the khan in 1571. If we are to believe Possevino's estimate, around 1581 the city contained no more than 30,000 inhabitants – six-fold fewer than formerly, according to another foreign writer who heard this from old Moscow residents at the beginning of the 17th century.

The walls of these new fortresses were wooden, filled on the inside with earth and sand, or of strongly plaited brushwood. There were stone walls only at the capital, Aleksandrovskaya Sloboda, Tula, Kolomna, Zaraisk, Staritsa, Yaroslavl, Nizhnyi Novgorod, Belozersk, Porkhov, Novgorod and Pskov.

| TRADE | The proliferation of towns also promoted an extraordinary increase in commerce, which more and more enhanced the tsar's revenues (in 1588 this reached six million of today's silver rubles). There were duties not just on the importation of foreign wares, and on the export of our products, but even on edible goods brought into the cities. These were sometimes paid by the residents. In Novgorod, a local statute of 1571 states that from all goods imported by foreign merchants and appraised by officials, the treasury would take 7 dengas per ruble. Russian merchants would pay 4 and Novgorod ones 1 ½ dengas for meat, cattle, fish, caviar, mead, salt (German or overseas), onions, nuts and apples, in addition to a special assessment for carts, boats and sleighs. The duties on the import of precious metals were the same as the rest, but their export was considered a crime.

It is worth noting that not even government goods were exempt from duties. Smuggling was punished by a stiff monetary fine. At this time, Ryurik's ancient capital, although in ruins, was starting to be reinvigorated by commercial activity, benefiting from its proximity to Narva, where we traded with all of Europe. However, it soon sank into a deathly stillness when Russia, in the calamities of the Livonian and Swedish wars, lost this important harbor.

Our [Northern] Dvina trade flourished all the more. The English were now obliged to share its advantages with merchants from the Netherlands, Germany and France, importing their sugar, wine, salt, berries, tin, cloth and lace in exchange for our furs, hemp, flax, rope, wool, wax, mead, tallow, leather, iron and timber.

French merchants, who had brought a friendly letter to Ivan from Henry III, were permitted to trade in Kola, and the Spaniards and Netherlanders in Pudozherskii Ust. The most distinguished of these merchants was Ivan Devakh Beloborod [John de Wale in Hakluyt], who provided the tsar with precious stones and enjoyed his special favor, to the displeasure of the English.

In a discussion with Elizabeth's emissary Bowes, Ivan complained that the London merchants were not exporting anything good to us. He took off his signet ring, pointed to his emerald *cap* and boasted that Devakh had given him the former for 60 rubles and the latter for 1,000. This astonished Bowes, who appraised the ring at 300 rubles and the emerald at 40,000. We exported a notable amount of grain to Sweden and Denmark.

"This blessed land," writes Kobenzel of Russia, "abounds in everything necessary for human life and has no real need for foreign products." The conquest of Kazan and Astrakhan strengthened our trade with Asia.

> LUXURY AND SPLENDOR

Ivan enriched the treasury with imposts on commerce, cities and rural areas, and had likewise confiscated Church property in order to increase the size of his army. He established arsenals, where there were always no less than 2,000 siege guns and field pieces kept ready. He built fortresses, palaces and cathedrals – he also liked to spend his surplus revenue on luxury: we have told of the amazement of foreigners inspecting the Moscow treasury, where there were piles of pearls, and mountains of gold and silver in the palace. There were glittering gatherings and dinners, where in the course of five or six hours, 600 or 700 guests were surfeited not only with abundant, but expensive viands, fruits and wines from distant torrid climes.

Once, in addition to eminent guests, 2,000 Nogai allies on their way to the Livonian war dined with the tsar in the Kremlin palaces. The tsar's formal outings always presented an image of Asiatic splendor as well: the bodyguard units covered in gold, the richness of their weapons and the tack of their steeds.

For example, on 12 December, Ivan would usually ride out of town to see the artillery demonstration. In front of him there would be several hundred princes, voivodes and officials, three abreast, and in front of the officials there would be 5,000 crack musketeers, five abreast. In the middle of a vast snowy plain, on a tall platform at least 200 sazhens in length stood cannons and troopers, shooting at targets and destroying fortifications covered with icy earth.

In church ceremonies also, as we have seen, Ivan also would appear before the people in striking splendor, lending himself still more majesty through an air of artful humility, uniting a glittering worldliness with an appearance of Christian virtue. He entertained nobles and emissaries on secular holidays, and showered rich favors on the poor.

In conclusion, we may say that Ivan's good reputation outlived his bad *in people's memories:* the groaning quieted, the victims moldered away and the old tales were eclipsed by newer ones. Yet Ivan's name shines in the *Code,* and recalls the acquisition of three Tatar realms. The evidence of his terrible deeds lies in the archives, while the people over the course of centuries see Kazan, Astrakhan and Siberia as living monuments to this tsar-conqueror. They honor him as the celebrated source of our nation's strength and our civic development; they have spurned or forgotten the name of *torturer* given him by his contemporaries, and among the dark rumors of Ivan's cruelty, now only call him *formidable.** This is an appellation that does not distinguish the grandson from his grandfather, and in old Russia was used more in praise than in reproach. History is more unforgiving than the people!

---

* [*Groznyi*. This is a better translation than the traditional *terrible*.]

Glossary

Abattis: defensive obstacle made of felled trees.

Altyn: an altyn was a small coin worth six Moscow dengas (alty is Tatar for "six").

Ambo: an elevated platform in front of the iconostasis (which is the screen separating the nave from the sanctuary in an Orthodox church).

Appanage: an estate granted to male relatives of the sovereign.

Ataman: a Cossack chief.

Boyar: a member of the higher Russian nobility.

Boyar cadet: a junior boyar.

Centurion (sotnik): someone in charge of (nominally) 100 men.

Cossacks: semi-independent cavalrymen inhabiting southern European Russia.

Decurion (desyatnik): someone in charge of (nominally) 10 men.

Denga: a coin worth 1/2 a kopek, or 1/200th of a ruble.

Funt: a Russian pound: 409.5 grams, or about 14.5 avoirdupois ounces.

Gabion: wicker baskets filled with earth and stone; used to form portable fortifications.

Gonfalon: a banner suspended from a horizontal crosspiece.

Kalga: a Tatar official second in rank to the khan.

Kopeck: a hundredth part of a ruble.

Letter patent: a sovereign's published written order granting a privilege to a person or organization.

Little Russia: roughly the same territory as the present-day Ukraine.

Marshalok: a high official in Poland or Lithuania.

Mirza: a Tatar aristocratic title.

Oblast: see volost.

Okolnichii, -ie: a member of the nobility one rung down from boyar, *q.v.*

Oprichnina: Ivan the Terrible's system of secret police, as well as the system it operated under.

Oprichnik: one of Ivan's secret police.

Pan: a member of the Polish gentry.

Pyatina: an old territorial division in the Novgorod area.

Sazhen: 2.13 meters, or about 7 feet.

Schematic: The highest rank of Orthodox monasticism.

Seit: a distinguished official of the sultan's court; from Arabic *sayyid*, a male descendant of Mohammed.

Sejm: the Polish parliament.

Tiun: a low-level official.

Tsarevich: a son of a tsar; a crown prince.

Tsarevna: a daughter of a tsar.

Uezd: see volost.

Ulus: a Tatar encampment or settlement.

Voivode: a senior military officer, like a general. Sometimes a military governor as well.

Volost: a low-level administrative unit subordinate to an uezd, which in turn is subordinate to a district (oblast).

Gazetteer of Towns and Cities

Note: there is not enough room on the maps for all of these entries, but since the maps use a simple rectangular grid, the missing items may be readily located.

Åbo (**Turku**)	60.4°N	22.3°E	**Belozersk**	60.0°N	37.8°E
Akhtuba R.	48.7°N	44.5°E	Belyov	53.8°N	36.1°E
Aleksandrovskaya Sloboda			**Bolkhov**	56.9°N	35.9°E
	56.4°N	38.7°E	Borisov	54.2°N	28.5°E
Aleksin	54.5°N	37.1°E	**Borovsk**	55.2°N	36.5°E
Arkhangelsk	64.5°N	40.5°E	**Bratovshchina**	56.0°N	37.9°E
Arsk	56.1°N	49.9°E	Buigorod	56.1°N	36.0°E
Arzamas	55.4°N	43.8°E	Bukhara	39.8°N	64.4°E
Ascheraden (Aizkraukle)	56.6°N	25.3°E	Cheboksary	56.1°N	47.2°E
Astrakhan	46.3°N	48.0°E	**Cherek R.**	43.7°N	44.1°E
Azov	47.1°N	39.4°E	Chernigov	51.5°N	31.3°E
Aa	59.4°N	27.2°E	Dedilovo	54.0°N	37.9°E
Bakhchiserai	44.8°N	33.8°E	Derbent	42.1°N	48.3°E
Baku	40.4°N	49.9°E	Derpt (a.k.a. **Dorpat, Embach, Tartu, Yuriev**)		
Balakhna	56.5°N	43.6°E		58.4°N	26.7°E
Belgorod	50.6°N	36.6°E	**Dmitrov**	56.4°N	37.5°E
Beloozero	60.0°N	37.8°E	**Dmitrovsk**	52.5°N	35.1°E
			Dnieper	46.5°N	32.3°E
			Don R.	47.1°N	39.2°E
			Donets	47.6°N	40.9°E
			Donkov	53.2°N	39.2°E
			Dorogobuzh	54.9°N	33.3°E

Drissa	55.8°N	27.9°E	Kaluga	54.6°N 36.3°E
Drutsk	54.3°N	29.8°E	Kama R.	55.4°N 50.0°E
Dubrovno	54.6°N	30.7°E	Kamai	55.1°N 26.6°E
Elets	52.6°N	38.5°E	Kamenets	52.4°N 23.8°E
Embach (see Tartu)			Kanev	49.7°N 31.5°E
Ermistu	58.4°N	24.0°E	Kargopol	61.5°N 38.9°E
Fellin	58.4°N	25.6°E	Kashin	57.4°N 37.6°E
Galich	58.4°N	42.4°E	Kashira	54.8°N 38.2°E
Gdov	58.8°N	27.8°E	Kasimov	54.9°N 41.4°E
Gniezno	52.5°N	17.6°E	Kazan	55.8°N 49.2°E
Gomel	52.4°N	31.0°E	Kazanka R.	55.8°N 49.1°E
Gorodna	55.4°N	32.7°E	Kergedan (see Oryol)	
Gorokhovets	56.2°N	42.7°E	Kexholm (see Korela)	
Gripsholm	57.7°N	27.9°E	Kharkov	50.0°N 36.2°E
Grodno	53.7°N	23.8°E	Khiva	41.4°N 60.4°E
Hapsal	58.9°N	23.5°E	Kholm	57.2°N 31.2°E
Isker (Kashlyk)	58.1°N	68.5°E	Kholmogory	64.2°N 41.6°E
Islam-Kermen	46.8°N	33.5°E	Kiev	50.4°N 30.5°E
Ivan-gorod	59.4°N	28.2°E	Kineshma	57.4°N 42.2°E
Izborsk	57.7°N	27.9°E	Kitaigorod	55.8°N 37.6°E
Kadom	54.6°N	42.5°E	Klin	56.3°N 36.7°E
Kaffa	45.0°N	35.4°E	Kokenhusen	56.6°N 25.4°E

end notes

Koknese (see Kokenhusen)			L. Ilmen	58.3°N	31.3°E
Kola	68.9°N	33.0°E	L. Neshcherdo	55.9°N	29.1°E
Kolomenskoe	55.7°N	37.7°E	L. Peipus	58.7°N	27.5°E
Kolomna	55.1°N	38.8°E	Ladoga	60.0°N	32.3°E
Konda R.	60.7°N	69.7°E	Lais	58.8°N	26.5°E
Königsberg	54.7°N	20.5°E	Laishevo	55.4°N	49.6°E
Koporye	59.7°N	29.0°E	Leal	58.7°N	23.8°E
Kopys	54.3°N	30.3°E	Livny	52.4°N	37.6°E
Korela	61.0°N	30.1°E	Lopasnya R.	54.8°N	37.9°E
Kostroma	57.8°N	40.9°E	Lübeck	53.9°N	10.7°E
Kovel	51.2°N	24.7°E	Lutsk	50.8°N	25.3°E
Kozelsk	54.0°N	35.8°E	Lvov	49.8°N	24.0°E
Kozmodemyansk	56.3°N	46.6°E	Lyskovo	56.0°N	45.0°E
Krakow	50.1°N	20.0°E	Lyubech	51.7°N	30.7°E
Kremenchug	49.1°N	33.4°E	Lyublin (Lublin)	51.2°N	22.6°E
Krichev	53.7°N	31.7°E	Marienburg	54.0°N	19.0°E
Krivoi Rog	48.0°N	33.4°E	Mecklenberg	53.6°N	12.4°E
Kromy	52.7°N	35.8°E	**Medno**	51.9°N	23.7°E
Krutitsy	55.7°N	37.7°E	Medyn	55.0°N	35.9°E
Krym	45.0°N	35.1°E	Meshchovsk	54.3°N	35.3°E
Kursk	51.7°N	36.2°E	Meshchyora (region)	56.1°N	43.2°E
L. Baikal	53.2°N	107.8°E	Mezen R.	66.2°N	44.0°E

Mezen	65.8°N	44.2°E	Novgorod	58.6°N	31.3°E
Minsk	53.9°N	27.6°E	Novosil	53.0°N	37.0°E
Mogilyov	53.9°N	30.4°E	Nyslott	61.9°N	28.9°E
Mokshan	53.4°N	44.6°E	Oberpahlen	58.6°N	26.0°E
Molodechna	54.3°N	26.9°E	Ochakov	46.6°N	31.5°E
Molodi	55.3°N	37.5°E	Odoev	53.9°N	36.7°E
Mosalsk	54.5°N	35.0°E	Oka	56.3°N	44.0°E
MOSCOW	55.8°N	37.6°E	Opochka	56.7°N	28.6°E
Mozhaisk	55.5°N	36.0°E	Oreshek		
			(a.k.a. Nöteberg)		
Mozyr	52.0°N	29.2°E	Orsha	60.0°N	31.0°E
Mstislavl	53.3°N	36.6°E	Oryol	54.5°N	30.4°E
Münster	52.0°N	7.6°E	Ösel	53.0°N	36.1°E
Murmansk	69.0°N	33.1°E	Oskol	58.4°N	22.5°E
Murom	55.6°N	42.1°E	Ostrog	51.3°N	37.8°E
Narova R.	59.5°N	28.0°E	Ostyor	50.3°N	26.5°E
Narva	59.4°N	28.2°E	Otroch Monastery	51.0°N	30.9°E
Neuschloss (Vasknarva)	59.0°N	27.7°E	Paide (Weissenstein)	56.9°N	35.9°E
Neva R.	59.9°N	30.3°E	Pechenga	54.8°N	33.2°E
Nevel	56.0°N	29.9°E	Pecherskii Monastery	69.6°N	31.2°E
Nizhnyi Novgorod	56.3°N	44.0°E	Pechora	50.4°N	30.6°E
Nöteberg (see Oreshek)			Pelym	65.1°N	57.2°E
Novgorod Severskii	52.0°N	33.3°E		61.0°N	62.0°E

end notes

Perekop	46.1°N	33.7°E	Rezekne (see Rositten)		
Peremyshl	54.3°N	36.2°E	Rezitsa (see Rositten)		
Perevoz	55.6°N	44.6°E	Riga	57.0°N	24.1°E
Perm	58.0°N	56.3°E	**Ronneburg**	57.3°N	25.6°E
Pernau	58.4°N	24.5°E	**Rositten**	56.5°N	27.3°E
Pilten	57.2°N	21.7°E	Rostov	57.2°N	39.4°E
Plyussa R.	59.2°N	28.2°E	Rozhai R.	55.4°N	37.5°E
Polota R.	55.5°N	28.8°E	Rusa (see **Staraya Russa**)		
Polotsk	55.5°N	28.8°E	Ryazan	54.6°N	39.7°E
Poltava	49.6°N	34.6°E	Rylsk	51.6°N	34.7°E
Porkhov	57.8°N	29.6°E	Rzhev	56.2°N	34.3°E
Poznan	52.4°N	16.9°E	Samara	53.2°N	50.2°E
Priluki	49.6°N	34.6°E	**Samarkand**	39.7°N	67.0°E
Pronsk	54.1°N	40.0°E	**Sambor**	49.5°N	23.2°E
Pskov	57.8°N	28.3°E	Sandomir	50.7°N	21.8°E
Putivl	53.2°N	39.2°E	**Sarai**	48.7°N	45.3°E
Pyatigorsk	44.0°N	43.0°E	Saratov	51.5°N	46.0°E
Radogoshch	52.6°N	33.2°E	**Schwanenburg**	57.2°N	26.8°E
Radoml	54.0°N	31.0°E	Sebezh	56.3°N	28.5°E
Radul	51.8°N	30.7°E	**Sergiev Posad**	56.3°N	38.1°E
Revel (a.k.a. Revel, Tallinn			Serpukhov	54.9°N	37.4°E
	59.4°N	24.7°E	Sesswegen	57.0°N	26.3°E

Sestra R.	58.1°N	25.6°E	Tama	45.2°N 36.7°E
Sevsk	52.2°N	34.5°E	Tartu (see Derpt)	
Sheksna R.	59.1°N	37.9°E	Tarvastu	58.2°N 25.9°E
Shelon R.	58.2°N	30.9°E	Terek R.	43.6°N 47.6°E
Shklov	54.2°N	30.3°E	Tikhvin	59.6°N 33.5°E
Shuya	56.8°N	41.4°E	Tmutorokan	45.3°N 37.0°E
Sibir	58.2°N	68.5°E	Tobolsk	58.2°N 68.2°E
Simbirsk	54.3°N	48.4°E	Tomsk	56.5°N 85.0°E
Smolensk	54.8°N	32.0°E	Toropets	56.5°N 31.6°E
Solovetskii Monastery	65.0°N	35.7°E	Torzhok	57.0°N 35.0°E
Solovki	65.0°N	35.7°E	Trinity Sergiev Monastery	
Sosna R.	52.7°N	38.9°E	Trnovo	56.3°N 38.1°E
Staraya Russa	58.0°N	31.4°E	Trubchevsk	43.1°N 25.6°E
Staritsa	56.5°N	34.9°E	Tsaritsyn	52.5°N 33.8°E
Starodub	52.6°N	32.8°E	Tsna	48.7°N 44.5°E
Stockholm	59.3°N	18.1°E	Tsyvilsk	55.0°N 39.1°E
Sura R.	52.7°N	38.9°E	Tula	55.9°N 47.5°E
Suzdal	56.4°N	40.4°E	Turinsk	54.2°N 37.6°E
Sviyaga R.	55.7°N	48.6°E	Turku (see Åbo)	58.0°N 63.7°E
Sviyazhsk	55.8°N	48.7°E	Turov	52.1°N 27.7°E
Taininskoe	55.9°N	37.7°E	Tushino	55.8°N 37.4°E
Tallin	59.4°N	24.8°E		

end notes

Tver	56.9°N	35.9°E
Ufa	54.8°N	56.0°E
Uglich	57.5°N	38.3°E
Ugra R.	54.5°N	36.1°E
Ural R.	46.9°N	51.6°E
Urzhum	57.1°N	50.0°E
Ustyug	60.8°N	46.3°E
Usvyat	55.7°N	30.8°E
Vaga	62.1°N	42.9°E
Vardø	70.4°N	31.1°E
Vasilgorod	56.1°N	46.0°E
Velikie Luki	56.3°N	30.5°E
Velizh	55.6°N	31.2°E
Venyov	54.4°N	38.3°E
Vereya	55.4°N	36.2°E
Vilnius	54.7°N	25.3°E
Visby	57.6°N	18.3°E
Vitebsk	55.2°N	30.2°E
Vladimir	56.2°N	40.4°E
Volga R.	45.7°N	47.9°E
Volgograd	48.7°N	44.5°E
Volkhov R.	60.1°N	32.3°E
Vologda	59.2°N	39.9°E
Volok Lamskii (Volokolamsk)		
	56.0°N	36.0°E
Voronezh	51.7°N	39.2°E
Vorotynsk	54.5°N	36.0°E
Vozha R.	54.7°N	39.7°E
Vyatka	58.6°N	49.6°E
Vyazma	55.2°N	34.2°E
Vyborg	60.7°N	28.8°E
Vychegda R.	61.3°N	46.6°E
Vyshnyi Volochyok	57.6°N	34.6°E
Weissenstein (see Paide)		
Wenden	57.3°N	25.3°E
Werpol	52.4°N	23.2°E
Wesenberg	59.4°N	26.4°E
Wolmar	57.6°N	25.4°E
Yakhroma	56.3°N	37.5°E
Yarensk	62.2°N	49.1°E
Yaroslavets	55.0°N	36.5°E
Yaroslavl	57.6°N	39.8°E
Yauza R.	55.7°N	37.6°E
Yenisei R.	71.8°N	82.7°E

Yuriev (see Derpt)
Yurievets   57.3°N 43.1°E
Zaraisk   54.8°N 38.9°E
Zavolzhsk   57.5°N 42.1°E
Zvenigorod 55.7°N 36.8°E

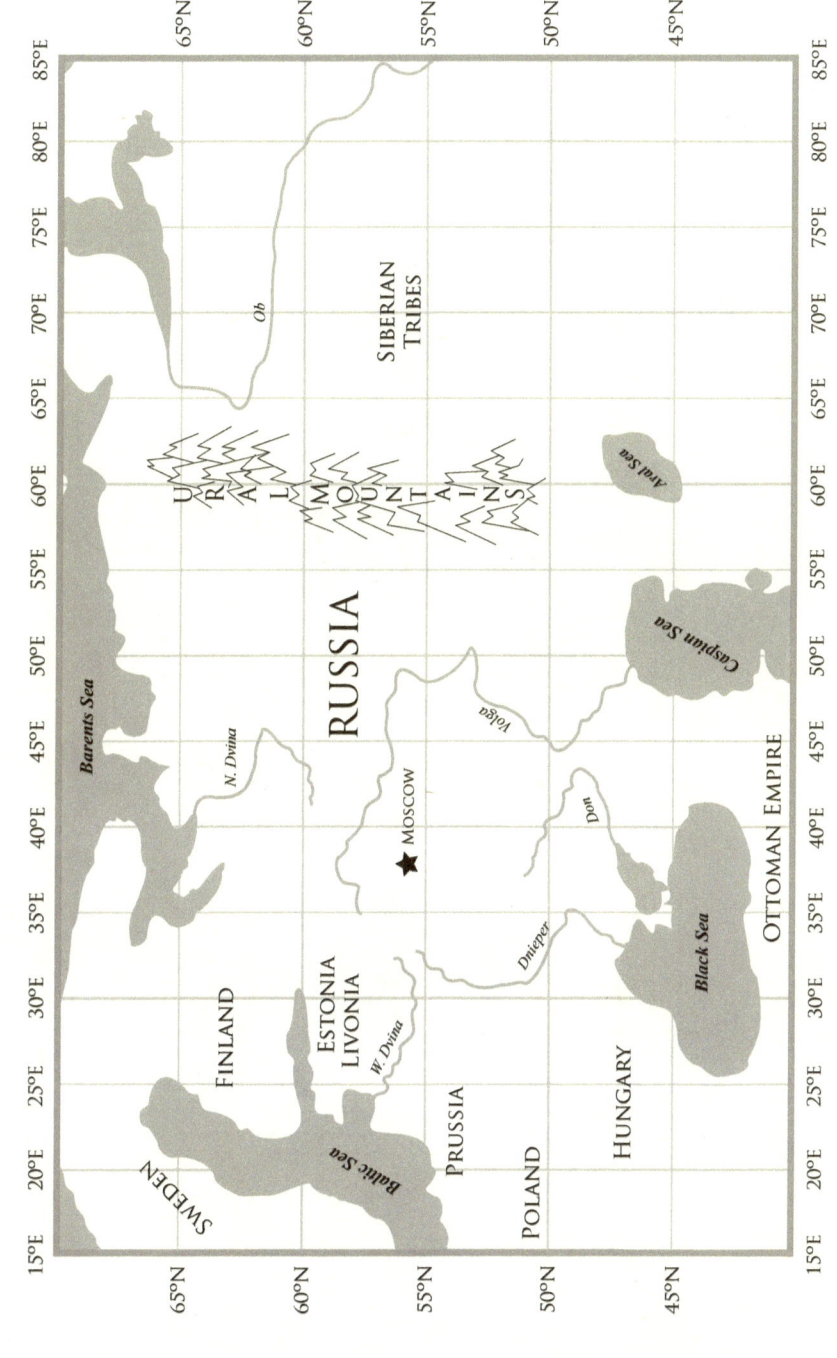

The Reign of Ivan the Terrible

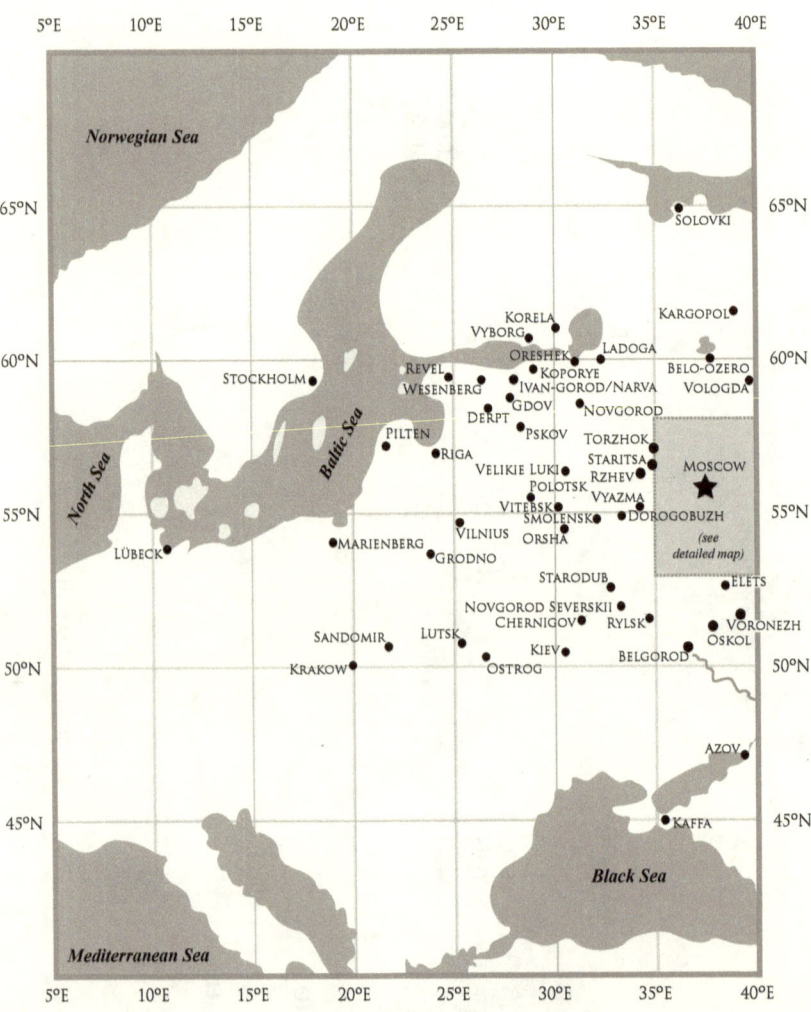

Moscow and West
circa 1550 CE

Moscow and Environs
circa 1550 CE

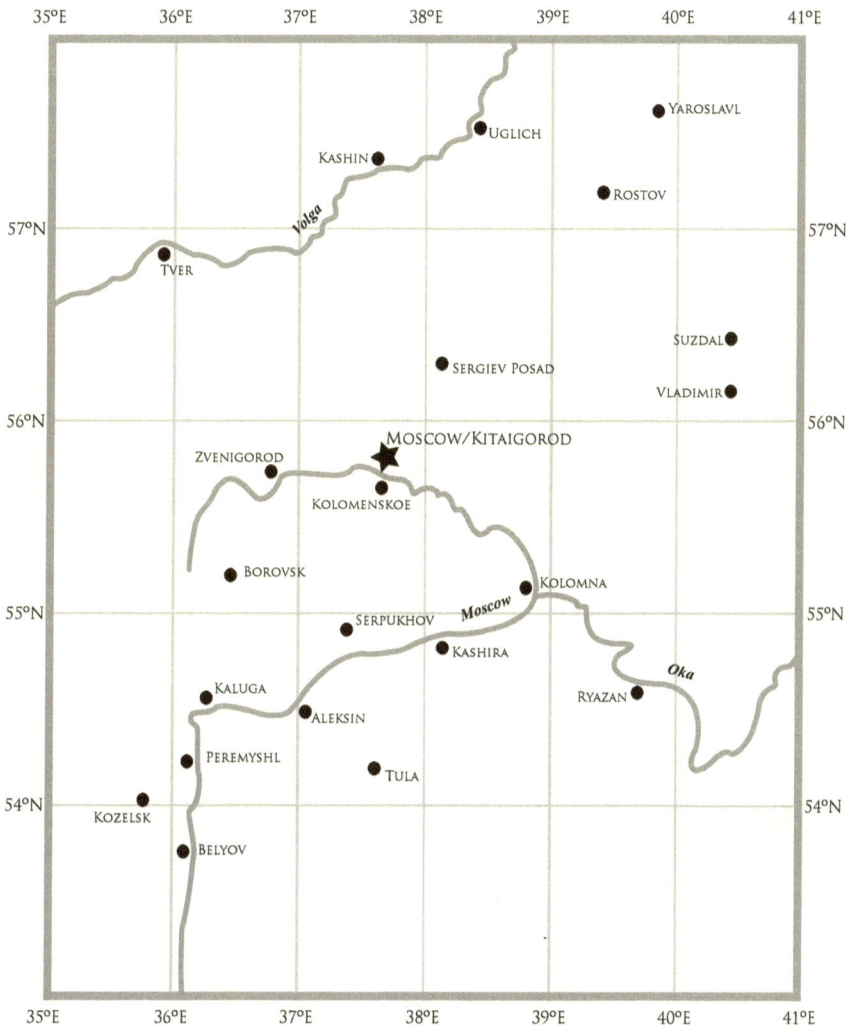

The Reign of Ivan the Terrible

Moscow and East
circa 1550 CE

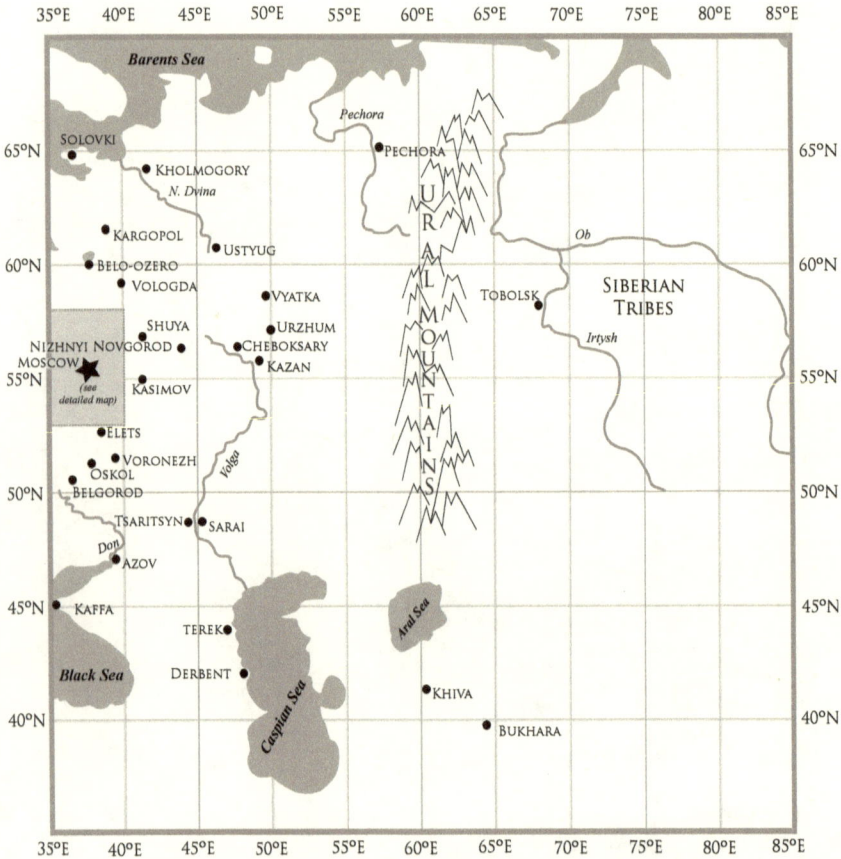

BATTLE OF KAZAN
1552

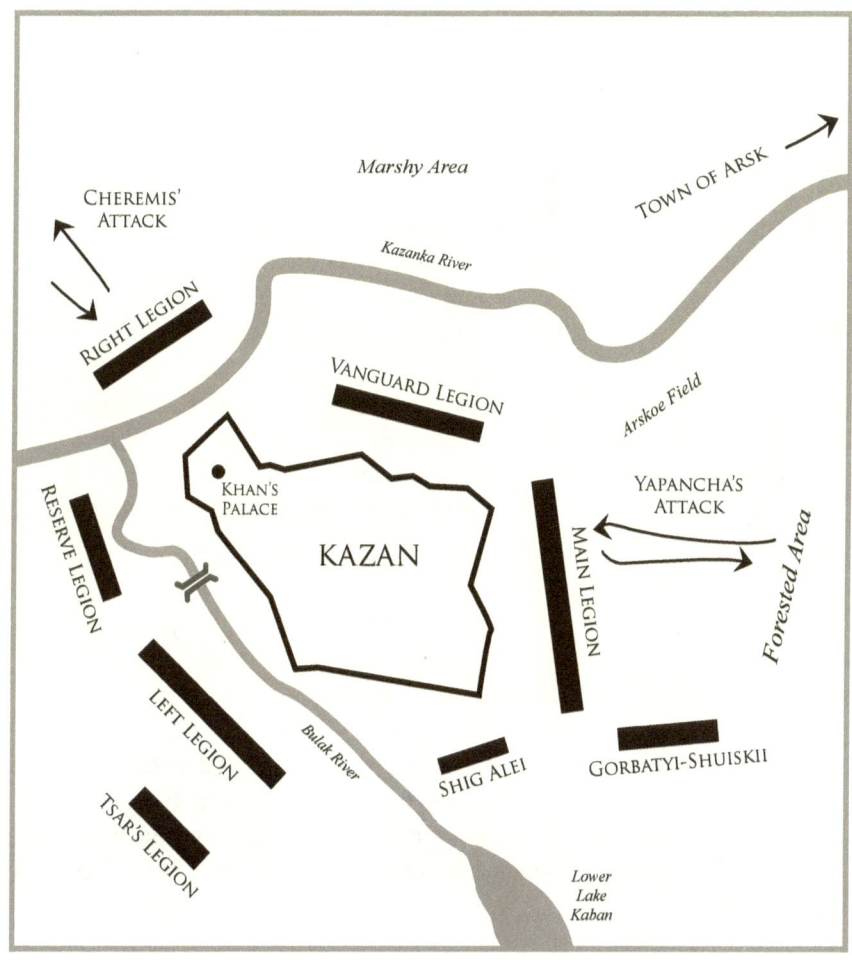

THE WALLED CITY WAS ABOUT 1.5 KM ACROSS AT ITS WIDEST.
BEYOND THE LEFT MARGIN WAS THE BROAD, GRASSY FLOODPLAIN OF THE VOLGA.

About the author

Nikolai Mikhailovich Karamzin was a major Russian literary figure – a writer, poet and critic. He was born in the province of Orenburg and when he was 14 he was sent to Moscow to an elite boarding school. In 1783, after brief military service, he began his literary efforts, which included some very popular, sentimental short stories. In 1803 he changed course and commenced work on his classic, monumental History, on which he labored until his death almost 23 years later.

About the translator

A retired systems software programmer, Geoff Baldwin is a graduate of the Army Language School and has worked as a translator for U.S. Intelligence agencies. He holds degrees in physics and mathematics from Reed College and San Francisco State.

Acknowledgments

I would like to express my appreciation to Kate Gladstone for copy editing, to Diane Moomey for consulting on publication, but last and most to Larissa Chiriaeva for her assistance on difficult Russian passages and her general encouragement over the years.

I should also note that Wikipedia (in both the English and Russian versions) has been an invaluable assistant, particularly with regard to annotation.

end notes

Index

The Index and Karamzin's Table of Contents are complementary means for looking things up. The Index here is primarily keyed on personal and place names. For more general or abstract topics, Karamzin's "Table of Contents" may be more useful. It served in lieu of an index and works in the following manner. It duplicates the chapter summaries, which then are duplicated once more on a phrase-by-phrase basis as sidebars next to the text. For instance, suppose you want to know about Ivan's first marriage. You need to know the approximate date (Wikipedia can be a help here). It occurred in 1547. Consult Karamzin's Table of Contents (on p. xxix) to find the right chapter and peruse the summary, where you will find the phrase "Marriage of the sovereign." Then page through the chapter until you find this phrase as a sidebar (on p. 61).

A
Åbo   *167, 288, 331*
Adashev, Aleksei   *35, 65, 68, 83, 86-88, 110, 112, 138, 140, 142-146, 148, 174, 180, 182, 185, 199, 211-219, 234, 245, 249, 266, 342, 379, 380*
Aleksandrovskaya Sloboda   *192, 239, 252, 255, 257, 260, 263, 270, 287, 297, 299, 301, 307, 332, 378, 411, 413, 418, 434, 436, 451, 464, 483*
Anastasiya, Ivan's first wife   *61, 62, 65, 70, 97, 129, 132, 133, 135, 144, 146, 207, 208, 211, 215, 217, 236, 260, 298, 328, 332, 419, 463*
Andreevich, Prince Vladimir of Staritsa   *36, 40, 56, 70, 78, 98, 104, 106, 107, 124, 129, 131, 133, 139-143, 146, 163, 208, 215, 230, 231, 236, 261, 298, 308, 318*
Antonii, metropolitan   *333, 463, 481*
Arbat   *63, 64, 207, 233, 259, 325*
Arsk   *106, 110, 111, 113-115, 126, 128, 131, 149*

Arskoe Field   75, 78, 82, 106-110, 113, 117
Astrakhan   9, 11, 35, 48, 77, 82, 94, 95, 150-155, 161, 162, 166, 169, 171,
    185, 233-235, 248, 279, 280, 289-293, 298, 310, 322, 323, 326, 327,
    334, 337-339, 344, 345, 365, 369, 388, 396, 432, 468, 485, 486
Athanasii, metropolitan   240, 254-257, 261, 265, 266
Augsburg Confession   190, 265, 319, 467
Augustus, Sigismund II   47, 54, 76, 92, 93, 147, 168-172
Austria   356, 358-360, 362, 364, 366, 385, 386
Azov   13, 39, 93, 94, 151, 153, 170, 198, 234, 279, 289-293, 345, 444

B

Balakhna   20, 26, 34, 129, 259
Baltic Sea   173, 198, 334, 369, 458
Basmanov, Aleksei   49, 119, 163, 164, 182, 217, 251, 252, 255, 261, 267,
    275, 276, 308, 309, 311, 380
Batory, Stefan, Polish king   363, 365-369, 371, 372, 374-376, 385, 387-391,
    393-422, 424-434, 437, 439, 443, 445-450, 454, 458, 460, 469
Baty, Mongol invader   34, 93, 151, 155, 162, 234, 246, 248, 279, 323, 341,
    466
Belo-ozero   19, 46, 147, 151, 220, 221, 237, 261, 311, 379
Belskii, Athanasii   428, 448
Belskii, Bogdan   373, 374, 412, 457, 459, 461-463
Belskii, David   413, 421
Belskii, Dimitrii   17, 31, 32, 38, 39, 41-43, 46, 48, 54, 75, 76, 78, 79, 380
Belskii, Ivan Dmitrievich   256, 258, 259, 268, 270, 271, 279, 292, 323-325
Belskii, Ivan Thedorovich   2, 5, 31, 32, 35-37, 44, 45, 47, 50, 51, 59
Belskii, Malyuta Skuratov   218, 261, 263, 264, 274, 299, 302, 303, 310, 311,
    330, 342, 346, 348, 380, 413, 428, 469
Belskii, Simeon   5, 13, 17, 22-24, 37, 39, 42
Bohemia   12, 364
Bomelius, Eliseus   295, 296, 328, 413
Bowes, Jerome, English emissary   457-460, 484
Bulak R.   78, 88, 106, 107, 109, 112, 119
Bulgakovs   69, 81, 85, 92, 93, 102, 113, 130, 272
Buturlins   2, 17, 37, 182, 183, 244, 253, 313, 372, 380, 412

C

Caesar Augustus   242, 249, 349, 356, 415
Caspian Sea   93, 154, 234, 289, 293, 371, 451
Catherine the Great   162, 402, 464
Chancellor, Richard   156-160
Charles V, Holy Roman emperor   12, 14, 188, 204, 445
Cheremis   20, 55, 81, 102, 103, 108, 113, 114, 118, 126, 128, 137, 148, 149,
    167, 179, 279, 350, 369, 450
Cheremisinov, Ivan   152, 153, 330, 410, 449, 459
Chernigov   13, 47, 241, 253, 380, 389
Chuvash   81, 103, 118, 128

end notes

Circassians *94, 150, 154, 162, 170, 172, 177, 179, 181, 193, 200, 229, 232, 233, 236, 279, 280, 291, 293, 332, 344, 371, 396*
Constantinople *10, 11, 22, 23, 35, 60, 64, 239, 244, 289, 291, 322, 345, 346, 349, 362, 382, 395, 437, 442*
Cossacks *11, 16, 24, 81, 92-95, 103, 106-109, 112, 113, 116, 119, 128, 137, 151, 152, 162, 169, 170, 172, 194, 198-200, 241, 244, 278, 279, 289, 345, 369, 388, 394, 396, 399, 400, 427*
Courland *194, 226, 242, 281, 282, 318, 321, 336, 357, 358, 372, 374, 383, 387, 389-391, 399, 409*
Crimea *11-13, 15, 17, 18, 23, 33, 38, 48, 53-55, 77, 78, 82-84, 92-95, 98, 100, 130, 150, 152, 153, 161-164, 170-172, 177, 197-200, 210, 220, 229, 233-235, 251, 252, 272, 279, 291, 292, 303, 313, 322, 323, 327, 336, 339, 343-345, 388, 393, 415, 439, 448*

D

Daniil, metropolitan *31, 32, 35, 36*
De La Gardie, Swedish general *428, 448, 449*
Denmark *164, 169, 187, 195-197, 200, 204, 205, 210, 225, 227, 235, 236, 278, 280, 286-288, 318, 319, 321, 330, 335, 348, 349, 351, 352, 363, 370, 371, 387, 390, 415, 428, 432, 447, 449-451, 458, 485*
Derbysh *106, 150-153*
Derpt (aka Dorpat, Tartu and Yuriev) *173-175, 180, 184-193, 197, 202-207, 216, 221, 226, 242-245, 253, 265, 281, 318, 320, 330, 336, 371, 372, 377, 378, 391, 392, 411, 415, 420, 431, 434*
Devlet-Girei, khan of the Crimea *94, 150, 152, 154, 161-163, 169-172, 197-199, 234, 235, 251, 252, 279, 280, 289-292, 323, 325-328, 337, 339, 343, 344, 350, 354, 369, 388*
Dmitrov *3, 4, 145, 298*
Dnieper R. *169-172, 198, 199, 244, 279, 345, 371, 388, 396*
Don R. *39, 43, 93, 94, 106, 169, 198, 234, 278, 289, 313, 337, 396*
Donskii, Dimitrii (Dmitrii Donskoi) *30, 101, 132, 139*
Dubrovno *14, 18, 230, 243, 412*
Dvina R. *156, 159, 161, 187, 194, 232, 252, 348, 357, 369, 390, 396-399, 451, 455, 460, 476, 484*

E

Ediger, ruler of Kazan *48, 95, 104-106, 121-125, 127, 136, 155*
Edward, king of England *156-158*
Elena Glinskaya, regent *1-9, 13, 14, 16, 20-28*
Elizabeth, Queen *293-295, 333-335, 386, 451-460, 484*
Enalei *12, 18, 19, 94*
England *156, 158-160, 164, 169, 294, 295, 333, 386, 428, 452-454, 457, 458, 460*
Erik, king of Sweden *286-288, 330, 331, 349*
Ernest, son of Emperor Maximilian *354, 359, 362-366*
Estonia *195-197, 200, 205, 225, 227, 236, 278, 280, 286-288, 318, 319, 321, 330, 348, 349, 352, 371, 387, 390, 415, 432, 447, 449, 450*

F

Fellin *184, 191, 192, 205, 207, 216, 221, 223, 224, 249, 336*
Ferdinand, emperor *12, 188, 195, 204, 254, 365*
Filipp, metropolitan *267-270, 273-277, 302*
Filothei, bishop, later archbishop, of Ryazan *147, 251, 256, 269, 342*
Finland *165, 166, 225, 330, 331, 352, 353, 370, 448*
France *356, 359, 364, 386, 416, 419, 443, 459, 484*
Frederik II, king of Denmark *195-197, 225, 227, 235, 335, 351, 387, 451, 452*
Fürstenberg, master of the Livonian Order *176, 179, 184, 187, 205-207, 221, 223, 224, 254, 317*

G

Garaburda, Mikhail, Lithuanian diplomat *239, 335, 336, 355, 357, 358, 429*
Germany *73, 74, 96, 173, 175, 177, 188, 190, 202, 238, 253, 295, 312, 317, 321, 386, 395, 398, 405, 428, 484*
Glinskii, Mikhailo Vasilievich, equerry *51, 59, 69, 92, 123, 148, 181, 319*
Glinskii, Mikhail *5, 6, 30*
Glinskiis *2, 51-53, 59, 62, 64, 65, 67, 69, 168, 179, 228, 380, 412*
Godunov, Boris *343, 383, 412, 413, 435, 437, 438, 462*
Golitsyns *31, 375, 391, 392, 397, 412, 418, 427*
Golovins *50, 52, 260, 284, 390, 395-397*
Gorbatyis *2-4, 10, 14, 17, 53, 55, 92, 95, 103, 111, 113, 128, 260*
Gorodishche *119, 290, 291, 303, 304*
Greece *59, 173, 217, 362, 465*
Gregory XIII, pope *416, 419, 442, 443, 445*
Gryaznoi, Vasilii *218, 274, 299, 344, 345*

H

Hansa *35, 74, 174, 293*
Hapsal *221, 225, 235, 353, 354, 387, 428*
Hastings, Mary, prospective bride for Ivan *452, 453, 455-457, 459*
Henri d'Anjou *359-361, 365, 367*
Herberstein, Baron *28, 445*
Horsey, Jerome *463*
Hungary *12, 228, 363, 364, 386, 387, 398, 405*

I

Ioasaf, metropolitan *32, 35, 37, 39, 44, 45, 47*
Islam, Crimean khan *15-17, 21, 23, 24*
Ismail, prince of the Nogai Tatars *150, 153-156, 235, 293*
Ivan-gorod *17, 180, 183, 449*

J

Jacob, Robert, English physician *452, 455, 459*
Jenkinson, Anthony *161, 294, 334, 335*

K

Kaffa *39, 93, 289, 290, 293*
Kama R. *55, 81, 82, 85, 92, 128, 148, 450*
Kasimov *38, 91, 97, 98, 102, 118, 280, 322, 329, 371*
Kazan *12, 18-20, 22, 24, 25, 31, 33-35, 38, 40, 42, 45, 46, 48, 54, 55, 75, 77-89, 91, 92, 94-102, 104-137, 144, 145, 148-153, 155, 161, 163, 168, 177, 178, 185, 198, 199, 205, 208, 217, 220, 224, 233, 234, 240, 245, 248, 260, 261, 278-280, 293, 310, 322, 323, 326-328, 337-339, 344, 365, 379, 380, 396, 403, 450, 468, 475, 485, 486*
Kazanka R. *19, 78, 84, 105, 106, 108, 110, 112, 114, 119, 123, 124*
Ketler, Gothard, master of the Livonian Order *184, 188, 193, 200-203, 205, 224-226, 427*
Khiva *127, 154, 288, 451*
Kholmogory *334, 428, 453, 476*
Khotkevich, Lithuanian hetman *270-272, 391*
Khvorostinins *391, 392, 412, 417, 422, 448-450*
Kiev *13, 14, 21, 22, 73, 242, 280, 322, 356-359, 363, 389, 441*
Kirill, metropolitan *277, 325, 332*
Kitaigorod *25, 26, 63, 309, 324, 325*
Kobenzel, Jan, Austrian emissary *362-364, 416, 485*
Kokenhusen *281, 372, 373, 408*
Kolomenskoe *97-99, 101, 152, 207, 255, 275, 325*
Kolomna *5, 17, 38, 39, 49, 53, 80, 92, 96, 98-100, 145, 161, 277, 323, 483*
Koshira *92, 96, 99, 100, 198, 323*
Kostroma *24, 26, 34, 40, 49, 75, 78, 224, 265, 299*
Krakow *21, 200, 366, 367, 393, 397, 407*
Krasnyi *193, 253, 283, 402, 420, 432*
Kremlin *25, 45, 51, 59, 61, 63-65, 67, 71, 80, 132, 136, 138, 154, 182, 207, 212, 236, 254, 259, 265, 298, 312, 324, 325, 364, 467, 482, 483, 485*
Kruse *265, 317-321, 335, 350, 373, 378*
Kurbskii, Andrei *66, 96, 99, 100, 102, 110, 114, 119, 122, 123, 145, 146, 148, 171, 179, 186, 188, 205, 206, 214, 216, 218, 222, 224, 230, 245-247, 250-254, 260, 273, 282, 285, 347, 376, 377, 379, 381, 382, 402-404, 413*

L

Lais *180, 192, 203, 312, 336*
Lithuania *2, 5, 9, 10, 12-15, 17, 18, 21-23, 25, 26, 35, 40, 47, 70, 76, 96, 147, 161, 162, 168-173, 194, 195, 201, 203-205, 210, 219, 227, 228, 230-232, 235, 238, 241, 242, 245, 251, 255, 261, 271, 279-286, 292, 301, 308, 312, 316, 330, 335, 341, 344, 348, 355-358, 360, 362-364, 367, 385, 388, 394-400, 405, 407, 409, 414, 415, 429, 433, 439, 449, 450, 455, 458, 466*
Livonia *9, 10, 74, 92, 161, 164, 173-176, 179-182, 185, 186, 188, 191-198, 201-207, 210, 213, 221-224, 226, 228-230, 235, 236, 242, 245, 248-251, 253, 279-284, 317-321, 323, 332, 335, 339, 341, 346, 348-354, 356-359, 362, 363, 365, 368, 369, 371-374, 377, 378, 385-387, 389,*

Livonia (cont.) *390, 392, 397-399, 404, 405, 407, 409-411, 413-415, 419, 420, 427-434, 449, 454, 458*
Livonian Order *9, 10, 222*
London *158-161, 293-295, 325, 334, 451, 453, 456, 458, 460*
London Muscovy Company (see Muscovy Company)
Lübeck *74, 238, 370, 421*
Lyatskii *5, 13, 14, 16, 22*

M

Magnus, Danish prince *225, 226, 318-321, 325, 330, 335, 348-351, 362, 370-375, 377, 378, 390, 391, 411*
Magnus, king of Sweden *9, 164*
Mahmet-Girei, Crimean khan *198, 280, 388, 439, 450*
Makarii, metropolitan *45-47, 49-51, 53, 57-60, 214, 215, 217, 229, 230, 232, 233, 237-239*
Maksim the Greek *144, 145*
Marienburg *180, 193, 205, 253*
Maximilian, Holy Roman emperor *169, 204, 321, 335, 354, 359, 360, 362, 364-368, 370, 383, 385, 386, 408*
Meshchera *20, 24, 26, 34, 75, 80, 81, 93, 97, 100, 322*
Mikulinskii, Simeon *75, 81, 85, 87, 88, 103, 113, 123, 148, 193*
Minsk *231, 232, 242, 284, 361, 389*
Moldavia *9, 10, 23, 33, 48, 244, 322, 386*
Mordvi *81, 102, 113, 128, 179, 244, 279, 371, 396*
Morozov, Mikhailo *2, 22, 47, 49, 76, 81, 105, 109, 110, 140, 193, 205, 235, 278, 287, 323, 324, 380, 391*
Mstislavskii, Ivan *17, 96, 102, 108-110, 118, 141, 148, 202, 205, 221, 224, 225, 256, 259, 270, 271, 279, 323, 324, 330, 332, 396, 411, 412, 418, 427, 462*
Mstislavskii, Theodor *368, 370, 371, 412, 418, 427, 450*
Murom *25, 34, 38, 78, 92, 96, 99-102, 116, 330, 350, 450*
Muscovy Company, the London *158, 160, 294, 453*

N

Nagois *70, 234, 251, 279, 282, 283, 290, 292, 327, 344, 412, 437, 438*
Narva *181-185, 226, 235, 293, 312, 334, 348, 390, 405, 415, 420, 428, 432, 447, 448, 458, 484*
Neglinnaya R. *6, 63, 64, 259, 324*
Netherlands *428, 459, 484*
Nevel *230, 244, 248, 278, 410, 420, 431, 432*
Nizhnyi-Novgorod *20, 34, 38, 75, 78, 79, 81, 92, 95, 97, 104, 127, 129, 265, 272, 290, 298, 299, 483*
Nogai Tatars *9, 11, 12, 19, 23, 24, 35, 39, 48, 55, 77, 80, 82, 86, 92-95, 106, 118, 150, 152-155, 162, 166, 171, 198, 200, 210, 233, 235, 279, 288, 290, 292, 293, 296, 322, 337, 338, 343, 344, 369, 371, 405, 450, 485*
Norway *197, 335, 387*

Novgorod 6, 8-10, 13, 14, 17, 22, 26, 30, 35, 36, 40, 45, 47, 56, 65, 73, 76, 137, 164-168, 175, 180, 196, 197, 202, 226-229, 235, 239-241, 278, 281, 283, 288, 301, 303-310, 314, 318, 329-332, 336, 337, 339, 348-355, 370, 371, 396, 397, 404, 406-409, 414, 418, 421, 427, 429, 431, 434, 448, 468, 472, 483, 484

O

Oberpahlen 192, 320, 321, 351, 378, 391
Obolenskiis 2, 5-9, 14, 18, 27, 33, 42, 76, 81, 84, 88, 103, 110, 118, 119, 140, 219, 242, 243, 252, 312
Oka R. 17, 34, 39-42, 96, 98, 99, 102, 163, 164, 251, 252, 279, 313, 323, 324, 336, 337, 354, 369, 396, 408, 418, 450
Oksa River 9
Oprichnina 258, 259, 261, 262, 266, 268-270, 285, 294, 342, 343, 380
Oreshek (Nöteberg) 165, 329, 330, 353, 448
Orsha 14, 18, 230, 242, 243, 281, 412
Ösel 225, 226, 235, 318, 321, 387
Ostrov 98, 420, 432
Ozerishche 244, 253, 278, 281, 355, 410, 431

P

Paletskii, Dimitrii 9, 22, 45, 49, 53, 54, 69, 81, 110, 113, 123, 124, 140, 142, 165, 166
Persia 127, 161, 292-294, 334, 419, 439, 451, 466
Pimen, archbishop 136, 256, 269, 277, 303, 305, 307, 308, 311
Pisemskii, emissary to England 414, 453-459
Plettenberg, Walter von 10, 174, 175
Poland 15, 23, 168, 173, 187, 201, 210, 226, 231, 235, 279, 280, 285, 286, 294, 316, 341, 351, 355-358, 360, 363, 364, 367, 377, 385, 387-389, 394, 396, 398, 405, 407, 414, 439, 447
Polotsk 14, 22, 231, 232, 239, 241-243, 251, 252, 278-280, 284, 333, 335, 348, 355, 357, 358, 368, 389, 397-404, 407, 409, 410, 414, 431, 432, 458
Possevino, Antonio, papal emissary 417-420, 429, 432, 438-445, 469, 483
Pronsk 26, 43, 49, 252, 273
Prussia 61, 164, 173, 194, 202, 242, 253, 271, 369
Pskov 14, 15, 17, 33, 36, 40, 56, 62, 72, 76, 136, 175, 180, 181, 183, 193, 205, 228, 241, 248, 253, 281, 301, 306, 308, 336, 371, 373, 378, 381, 396, 398, 399, 402, 405-409, 411, 414, 417, 420-422, 424, 426, 427, 430-435, 438, 446, 448, 462, 468, 472, 483

R

Radziwill, Nikolai 226, 228, 229, 231, 243, 252, 253, 427, 428
Radziwill, Yurii 17, 22
Revel (a.k.a Reval and Tallinn) 174, 180, 183, 184, 191, 192, 196, 202, 206, 225, 226, 236, 317-321, 330, 353, 370, 371, 377, 390, 405, 428, 432
Riga 174, 180, 185, 191, 193-195, 224, 226, 254, 281, 351, 362, 371, 376, 391, 398

Ringen *192, 193*
Rome *242, 265, 364, 408, 416, 419, 420, 438, 441-445, 465*
Rostov *145, 239, 325*
Rudolf, Holy Roman emperor *385, 386, 408, 416*
Ryazan *13, 17, 39, 48, 80, 93, 100, 147, 163, 198, 251, 256, 269, 323*
Ryurik *169, 238, 242, 480, 484*
Rzhev *21, 56, 65, 411, 418, 427*

S

Safa-Girei *19, 20, 22, 25, 38, 48, 54, 55, 75, 77, 78, 80, 84, 85, 97*
Saip-Girei *12, 13, 15-18, 21, 23-25, 34, 35, 37-39, 43, 44, 48, 77, 80*
Saltykovs *137, 255, 261, 304, 328, 375, 392, 393, 413*
Scotland *386*
Sejm *76, 181, 201, 202, 286, 354, 355, 358, 359, 361, 364, 365, 367, 393, 394, 396, 406, 410, 411, 425, 430, 448*
Selim, sultan *288-293, 310, 312, 321, 322, 341, 345, 356, 360, 365-367*
Serebryanyi-Obolenskii, Pyotr *42, 43, 81, 101, 103, 193, 228, 230, 284, 290, 291, 312, 397*
Serebryanyi-Obolenskii, Vasilii *96, 112, 119, 128, 186, 193, 194, 202, 205, 252, 261, 292*
Serebryanyis *41, 42, 81, 96, 101, 103, 112, 119, 128, 179, 186, 193, 194, 202, 205, 228, 230, 242, 252, 261, 284, 290-292, 312, 397*
Serpukhov *39, 45, 169, 323, 326, 337, 354, 408*
Shah of Persia *291, 292, 294, 419, 451*
Shchelkalov, Andrei, secretary *330, 335, 392, 404, 419, 458, 459*
Shchenyatev, Pyotr *45, 46, 96, 99, 100, 102, 110, 119, 140, 166, 252, 258, 272*
Shemyakin, Yurii *106-108, 110, 111, 119, 151, 152, 381*
Sheremetevs *89, 96, 119, 123, 140, 148, 162-165, 169, 179, 193, 198, 220, 234, 253, 323, 324, 330, 336, 370, 392, 397, 402, 435, 449*
Shig-Alei *19, 20, 39, 40, 54, 55, 75, 78-86, 88, 91, 94, 97, 98, 102, 104, 105, 118, 124, 171, 179, 181, 280*
Shuiskii, Aleksandr Borisovich *111, 113, 128, 260, 377*
Shuiskii, Andrei *2-4, 7, 31, 33, 36, 52*
Shuiskii, Ivan *7, 32, 35, 36, 38, 39, 42, 44-48*
Shuiskii, Ivan Mikhailovich *42, 44-46*
Shuiskii, Ivan Petrovich *238, 371, 417, 422, 427, 430, 433-435, 462*
Shuiskii, Pyotr *70, 92, 95, 103, 129, 150, 186, 189-192, 202, 204, 221, 232, 242, 243, 248, 253, 284*
Shuiskiis *34, 49-51, 53, 62, 79, 380, 396, 412, 413, 418, 422, 448, 450*
Shuiskii, Vasilii *16-19, 24, 25, 31, 32, 39*
Siberia *155, 161, 293, 450, 468, 486*
Sigismund, King of Poland-Lithuania *5, 10, 12-18, 21, 22, 35, 47, 54, 76, 172*
Silvestr, priest *65, 66, 68, 141, 144, 146, 211-217, 249, 267, 376*
Sitskiis *18, 330, 352, 371, 377, 383, 392, 407, 409-411, 413*
Skopin-Shuiskii, Thedor *42, 64, 67*

Skuratov, Malyuta *218, 261, 263, 264, 274, 299, 302, 303, 310, 311, 330, 342, 346, 348, 413, 428, 469*
Smolensk *14, 16, 18, 22, 76, 194, 228, 230, 243, 244, 249, 278, 280, 281, 283, 284, 319, 355, 358, 367-369, 389, 397, 402, 408-410, 412, 414, 418, 421, 432, 433, 468*
Spain *156, 169, 354, 363, 364, 386, 419, 443*
Staritsa *7, 8, 233, 237, 298, 418, 427, 483*
Starodub *13, 15, 17, 18, 21, 241, 402*
Stockholm *35, 165, 167, 227, 287, 288, 330, 332, 351, 352*
Sudebnik (law code) *70-72*
Suleiman the Magnificent *10, 11, 23, 48, 94, 162, 234, 288*
Suzdal *30, 78, 129, 239, 251, 256, 259, 260, 275, 369, 384*
Sviyaga R. *54, 55, 79-81, 84, 103*
Sviyazhsk *80-83, 85, 87-89, 91, 95, 99, 101-103, 108, 128, 129, 137, 450*
Sweden *9, 92, 161, 164, 167-169, 173, 177, 187, 210, 225-227, 235, 278, 280, 286-288, 292, 294, 317, 318, 331, 335, 339, 341, 346, 352, 363, 368, 370, 377, 385, 387, 405, 419, 429, 448, 450, 458, 485*
Syuyunbeka, Nogai princess *77, 82-84, 97, 150, 154*

T

Tarvastu *205, 224, 228, 229, 335*
Taube *265, 317-321, 335, 350, 372, 373, 378*
Taurid (Crimea) *10, 12, 15, 19, 24, 34, 37, 38, 77, 82, 94, 95, 154, 161, 162, 170-172, 198-200, 233, 244, 251, 278-280, 290, 325, 338, 345, 358, 367, 369, 388, 394, 439*
Telepnev, Ivan *2, 5-9, 14-16, 18, 19, 22, 24, 25, 27-31, 51*
Toropets *21, 147, 284, 409, 410, 428, 449*
Transylvania *366, 395, 396, 406*
Troekurov, Thedor *106-108, 110, 119, 185*
Tula *39, 98-100, 163, 164, 169, 198, 245, 248, 311, 483*
Turkey *11, 74, 290, 321, 322, 358, 359*
Tver *26, 46, 56, 144, 277, 302, 303, 371, 377, 411*

U

Ukraine *14, 18, 93, 98, 289*
Utemish-Girei, a ruler of Kazan *77, 83, 84, 136*

V

Vasa, Gustav *9, 10, 164-168, 195, 225, 227, 286, 353, 368*
Vasilii II Vasilievich, grand prince of Moscow *1-3, 5, 6, 9, 13, 16, 21, 25, 41, 42, 142, 144, 145, 445*
Vassian, former bishop *145, 146, 214, 403*
Velikie Luki *232, 252, 253, 278, 283, 284, 407, 409, 410, 413, 414, 420, 425, 431, 432*
Velizh *21, 284, 409, 420, 431, 432, 449*
Vienna *204, 361, 385, 416*
Vilnius *14, 16, 21, 172, 226, 227, 232, 242, 243, 364, 367, 397, 399, 404, 406, 407, 417, 421, 427*

Vishnevetskii, Dmitrii *170-172, 198-200*
Viskovatyi, Ivan Mikhailovich *308, 310, 311, 330*
Vitebsk *14, 21, 76, 230, 243, 244, 389, 401, 407, 449*
Vladimir (city) *26, 34, 38-40, 45, 46, 56, 73, 78, 100, 101, 129, 130, 265, 357, 402*
Volga R. *19, 20, 24, 38, 55, 75, 81, 84, 85, 88, 93, 96, 102-105, 129, 145, 148, 150, 177, 198, 234, 272, 289, 290, 292, 303, 350, 369, 396, 428, 450*
Volhynia *172, 242, 271, 280, 388, 398, 403*
Volkhov R. *304, 305, 330, 333, 337*
Vologda *26, 34, 37, 161, 259, 382, 444*
Vorontsovs *2, 6, 10, 17, 49, 51, 53, 287, 288, 312, 330, 331, 392*
Vorotynskii, Mikhailo Ivanovich *5, 43, 96, 99, 108, 109, 115-117, 119, 121, 124, 129, 138, 198, 220, 261, 270, 271, 323-325, 330, 336, 338, 339, 379, 380, 397*
Votyaks *128, 137, 149*
Vyatka *34, 54, 79, 81-83, 85, 92, 148, 149, 151*

W

Warsaw *243, 316, 347, 354, 356, 358-361, 364-366, 393, 396, 399, 406, 407, 410, 413, 425, 430*
Wenden *181, 187, 192, 194, 202-204, 224, 253, 254, 281, 372-375, 390-393, 397*
Willoughby, Hugh *156-158*
Wittenstein, *192, 206, 348, 371, 428*
Wolmar *205, 224, 245, 247, 250, 253, 276, 281, 372-374, 403*
Yamgurchei, ruler of Astrakhan *94, 150-153*

Y

Yapancha *106, 110-112*
Yaroslavl *26, 40, 46, 78, 104, 145, 247, 250, 324, 483*
Yauza R. *63, 64, 130, 467*
Yusuf, Nogai prince *19, 77, 80, 94, 150, 152, 154*

Z

Zamoiskii, Yan, Lithuanian hetman *366, 425, 430, 432-434*
Zavoloche *21, 22, 410, 420, 431, 432*

www.ingramcontent.com/pod-product-compliance
Lightning Source LLC
Chambersburg PA
CBHW030558230426
43661CB00053B/1769